Contents

KV-510-537

Further Information

Useful Indexes

A full list of indexes, including

How to use this guide

This official VisitEngland guide is packed with information from where to stay, to how to get there and what to see on arrival. In fact, this guide captures everything you need to know when exploring England.

Choose from a wide range of quality-assessed accommodation to suit all budgets and tastes. This guide contains a comprehensive listing of self-catering properties participating in the VisitEngland Quality Assessment Scheme, including boat accommodation and approved caravans.

Each property has been visited annually by professional assessors, who apply nationally agreed standards, so that you can book with confidence knowing your accommodation has been checked and rated for quality.

Check out the places to visit in each region, from towns and cities to spectacular coast and countryside, plus historic homes, castles and great family attractions! Maps show accommodation locations, selected destinations and some of the National Cycle Networks. For even more ideas go online at www.visitengland.com.

Regional tourism contacts and tourist information centres are listed in each of the regional sections of this guide. Before booking your stay, why not contact them to find out what's going on in the area? You'll also find events, travel information, maps and useful indexes that will help you plan your trip, throughout this guide.

OFFICIAL TOURIST BOARD GUIDE

New 40th Edition

Self Catering

England's star-rated holiday homes

2015

www.visitor-guides.co.uk

In 2014 ~~VisitEngland~~ celebrated 25 years of its Awards for Excellence programme. 25 years of honouring top quality English tourism! It has been a pleasure to see how our industry has grown and how the experience offered has evolved. We have invented words along the way like "glamping" (posh camping); "poshtels" (that's posh hostels for the uninitiated!) and "set-jetting" (holidays inspired by places seen as the back-drop to favourite films: think London, think Bond; think Alnwick Castle or Gloucester Cathedral, think Harry Potter). Our industry has embraced "staycationers" with packages and offers which help visitors make the most of their leisure time.

As we celebrate the 40th edition of the Official Tourist Board Guides, 2015 is a year jam-packed with opportunities to enjoy being in England. If sport floats your boat then follow the Rugby World Cup which is coming to England for six weeks in September, giving fans the perfect excuse to take a road-trip around the country. It doesn't get more English than a genteel game of cricket unfolding on a village lawn and the 40th Anniversary of the inaugural Cricket World Cup will take place this summer. Breaking with 183 years of history, the Women's Boat Race between Oxford and Cambridge will be combined with the more famous men's event, moving from its base in Henley to the traditional race location of the Tideway in south west London. A host of exhibitions are being held across the country to mark the 800th anniversary of the sealing of Magna Carta and its legacy in the world today. 2015 also sees the 50th anniversary of Churchill's death and the 125th anniversary of Agatha Christie's birth, with events being held to remember their contributions to England. It is 150 years since we were introduced to Alice in Wonderland and Lewis Carol's Oxford will be hosting tea parties galore. Dreamland returns to Margate this year, with one of the best-loved amusement parks in the country set to come back to life. Hampton Court Palace has teamed up with a Chelsea-winning gardener to create a new Magic Garden and Bristol, one of the UK's leading green cities, will be the 2015 Green European Capital.

So much to see and do! This book is packed full of information and ideas, ~~designed~~ designed to help you get the most from your stay. All the accommodation has been inspected to the official common quality standards, ensuring it has been thoroughly checked out so that you can check in with confidence.

Enjoy your stay in England and celebrate all it has to offer in 2015!

Penelope, Viscountess Cobham
Chairman of VisitEngland

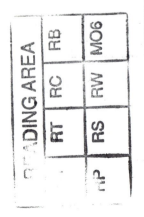

Accommodation entries explained

Each accommodation entry contains detailed information to help you decide if it is right for you. This has been provided by proprietors and our aim is to ensure that it is as objective and factual as possible.

① ② ③ ④ ⑤

NEWQUAY, Cornwall   Map ref 1B2

Units 60
Sleeps 2-12

PER UNIT PER WEEK
£425.00 - £3000.00

SPECIAL PROMOTIONS
Late availability discount of 20%

The Park

Contact: Reservations, Bookings Team, The Park, Mawgan Porth, Cornwall TR8 4BD
T: (01637) 860322 **E:** info@mawganporth.co.uk
W: www.mawganporth.co.uk **£ BOOK ONLINE**

Set within a rural location amidst 27 acres, yet only 400 metres from the beach. This unique venue offers all the luxury of a rural oasis whilst being close to all major roads and air links into the South West.

Facilities on site include heated indoor and outdoor swimming pools and award winning restaurant. Accommodation is an eclectic selection of eco-lodges, cottages and glamping.

Open: All year
Nearest Shop: Cornish Fresh supermarket
Nearest Pub: MerryMoor

Units: Units are from 1-6 bedrooms and some have hot-tubs and wood-burners.

Site: ✿ **P : Payment:** 💷 **Leisure:** 🚲 🎣 🛶 **Property:** 🐕 🖼 📶 🛋 **Children:** 🎠 🏓 🛝
Unit: 📺 📻 📷 🔧 🍳 📺 📀 🎵 BBQ 📞

---

① Listing sorted by town or village, including a map reference

② Rating (and/or) Award, where applicable

③ Prices per unit per week

④ Establishment name, address, telephone number and email address

⑤ Website information

⑥ Walkers, cyclists, pets and families welcome accolades, where applicable

⑦ Accessible rating, where applicable

⑧ Indicates when the property is open

⑨ Accommodation details

⑩ At-a-glance facility symbols

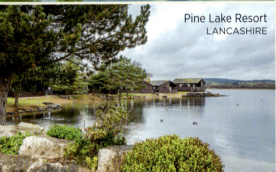

Key to symbols

Information about many of the accommodation services and facilities is given in the form of symbols.

Site Features

P Private parking
❀ Garden

Booking & Payment Details

€ Euros accepted
💳 Visa/Mastercard/Switch accepted

Leisure Facilities

🎾 Tennis court(s)
🏊 Swimming pool – outdoor
🏊 Swimming pool – indoor
🎱 Games room
U Riding/pony-trekking nearby
▶ Golf available (on site or nearby)
🎣 Fishing nearby
🚲 Cycles for hire

Children

🪑 High chairs available
🛏 Cots available
🐎 Children welcome

Property Facilities

🛏 Linen provided
🛏 Linen for hire
🧺 Laundry facilities
📶 Wi-Fi/Internet access
🐕 Dogs/pets accepted by arrangement
✂ Cleaning service

Unit Facilities

📞 Telephone
BBQ Barbecue
🔥 Real log/coal fires
📀 DVD player
📺 Satellite/cable/freeview TV
📺 Television
💇 Hairdryer
🧺 Washing machine
🍱 Microwave cooker
🍽 Dishwasher
🗄 Freezer

Visitor Attraction Quality Scheme Accolades

For top-scoring attractions where visitors can expect a really memorable visit.

For 'going the extra mile', ensuring that visitors are really well looked after.

For small, well-run attractions that deserve a special mention.

For particularly innovative and effective interpretation or tour, telling the story to capture visitors' imaginations.

For attractions with cafes and restaurants that consistently exceed expectations.

Pets Come Too - accommodation displaying this symbol offer a special welcome to pets. Please check for any restrictions before booking.

Businesses displaying this logo have undergone a rigorous verification process to ensure that they are sustainable (green). See page 22 for further information.

National Accessible Scheme
The National Accessible Scheme includes standards for hearing and visual impairment as well as mobility impairment – see pages 10-11 for further information.

Welcome Schemes
Walkers, cyclists, families and pet owners are warmly welcomed where you see these signs – see page 9 for further information.

Motorway Service Area Assessment Scheme
The star ratings cover over a wide range of aspects of each operation including cleanliness, the quality and range of catering and also the quality of the physical aspects, as well as the service provided. – See page 356 for further information.

A special welcome

To help make booking your accommodation easier, VisitEngland has four special Welcome schemes which accommodation in England can be assessed against. Owners participating in these schemes go the extra mile to welcome walkers, cyclists, families or pet owners to their accommodation and provide additional facilities and services to make your stay even more comfortable.

Families Welcome

If you are searching for the perfect family holiday, look out for the Families Welcome sign. The sign indicates that the proprietor offers additional facilities and services catering for a range of ages and family units. For families with young children, the accommodation will have special facilities such as cots and highchairs, storage for push-chairs and somewhere to heat baby food or milk. Where meals are provided, children's choices will be clearly indicated, with healthy options also available. They'll have information on local walks, attractions, activities or events suitable for children, as well as local child-friendly pubs and restaurants. However, not all accommodation is able to cater for all ages or combinations of family units, so do remember to check for any restrictions before confirming your booking.

Welcome Pets!

Do you want to travel with your faithful companion? To do so with ease make sure you look out for accommodation displaying the Welcome Pets! sign. Participants in this scheme go out of their way to meet the needs of guests bringing dogs, cats and/or small birds. In addition to providing water and food bowls, torches or nightlights, spare leads and pet washing facilities, they'll buy in pet food on request and offer toys, treats and bedding. They'll also have information on pet-friendly attractions, pubs, restaurants and recreation. Of course, not everyone is able to offer suitable facilities for every pet, so do check if there are any restrictions on the type, size and number of animals before you confirm your booking.

Walkers Welcome

If walking is your passion, seek out accommodation participating in the Walkers Welcome scheme. Facilities include a place for drying clothes and boots, maps and books for reference and a first-aid kit. Packed breakfasts and lunches are available on request in hotels and guesthouses, and you have the option to pre-order basic groceries in self-catering accommodation. On top of this, proprietors provide a wide range of information including public transport, weather forecasts, details of the nearest bank, all night chemists and local restaurants and nearby attractions.

Cyclists Welcome

Are you an explorer on two wheels? If so, seek out accommodation displaying the Cyclists Welcome symbol. Facilities at these properties include a lockable undercover area, a place to dry outdoor clothing and footwear, an evening meal if there are no eating facilities available within one mile and a packed breakfast or lunch on request. Information is also available on cycle hire, cycle repair shops, maps and books for reference, weather forecasts, details of the nearest bank, all night chemists and much much more.

National Accessible Scheme

Finding suitable accommodation is not always easy, especially if you have to seek out rooms with level entry or large print menus. Use the National Accessible Scheme to help you make your choice.

Proprietors of accommodation taking part in the National Accessible Scheme have gone out of their way to ensure a comfortable stay for guests with hearing, visual or mobility needs. These exceptional places are full of extra touches to make everyone's visit trouble-free, from handrails, ramps and step-free entrances (ideal for buggies too) to level-access showers and colour contrast in the bathrooms. Members of staff may have attended a disability awareness course and will know what assistance will really be appreciated.

Appropriate National Accessible Scheme symbols are included in the guide entries (shown opposite). If you have additional needs or specific requirements, we strongly recommend that you make sure these can be met by your chosen establishment before

you confirm your reservation. The index at the back of the guide gives a list of accommodation that has received a National Accessible Scheme rating.

'Holiday in the British Isles' is an annual guidebook produced by Disability Rights UK. It lists NAS rated accommodation and offers extensive practical advice to help you plan your trip.

£12.99 (inc. P&P),
www.disabilityrights.uk.org

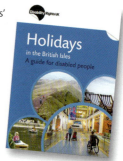

England

The criteria VisitEngland has adopted does not necessarily conform to British Standards or to Building Regulations. They reflect what the organisation understands to be acceptable to meet the practical needs of guests with mobility or sensory impairments and encourage the industry to increase access to all.

For more information on the NAS and tips and ideas on holiday travel in England go to:
www.visitengland.com/accessforall

Additional help and guidance on accessible tourism can be obtained from the national charity Tourism for All:

Tourism for All

Tourism for All UK
7A Pixel Mill
44 Appleby Road
Kendal
Cumbria LA9 6ES

Information helpline 0845 124 9971
(lines open 9-5 Mon-Fri)
E info@tourismforall.org.uk
W www.tourismforall.org.uk
    www.openbritain.net

Mobility Impairment Symbols

Older and less mobile guests
Typically suitable for a person with sufficient mobility to climb a flight of steps but who would benefit from fixtures and fittings to aid balance.

Part-time wheelchair users
Typically suitable for a person with restricted walking ability and for those who may need to use a wheelchair some of the time and can negotiate a maximum of three steps.

Independent wheelchair users
Typically suitable for a person who depends on the use of a wheelchair and transfers unaided to and from the wheelchair in a seated position. This person may be an independent traveller.

Assisted wheelchair users
Typically suitable for a person who depends on the use of a wheelchair and needs assistance when transferring to and from the wheelchair in a seated position.

Access Exceptional is awarded to establishments that meet the requirements of independent wheelchair users or assisted wheelchair users shown above and also fulfil more demanding requirements with reference to the British Standards BS8300.

Visual Impairment Symbols

Typically provides key additional services and facilities to meet the needs of visually impaired guests.

Typically provides a higher level of additional services and facilities to meet the needs of visually impaired guests.

Hearing Loss Symbols

Typically provides key additional services and facilities to meet the needs of guests with hearing loss.

Typically provides a higher level of additional services and facilities to meet the needs of guests with hearing loss.

Peace of Mind with Star Ratings

Many self-catering properties in England are star rated by VisitEngland. We annually check that our standards are comparable with other British tourist boards to ensure that wherever you visit you receive the same facilities and services at any star rated accommodation.

All the accommodation in this guide is annually checked by VisitEngland assessors and an on site assessment is made every year. This means that when you see the Quality Rose marque promoting the star rating of the property, you can be confident that we've checked it out.

The national standards used to assess accommodation are based on VisitEngland research of consumer expectations. The independent assessors work to strict criteria to check the available facilities and a quality score is awarded for every aspect of the layout and design, ease of use of all the appliances, comfort of the beds, range and quality of kitchen equipment and, most importantly, cleanliness. They also score the range and presentation of the visitor information on offer. For properties that exceed the already high expectations of assessors, a Gold Award may be awarded to recognise the accommodation's excellence.

The Quality Rose marque helps you decide where to stay, giving you peace of mind that the accommodation has been thoroughly checked out before you check in.

Accommodation in this Guide

Within this guide you'll find a wide range of self-catering accommodation, a requirement of this category is to be self-contained and have a kitchen so you will always have the option of eating in. NB: this requirement only applies to self-catering accommodation rated 4 star and above and therefore is not applicable to every property listed in this guide.

Holiday Cottages, Houses and Lodges – from cosy country cottages, smart town-centre apartments, seaside villas, grand country houses for large family gatherings, and even quirky windmills, railway carriages and lighthouse conversions. Most take bookings by the week, generally from Friday to Saturdays, but as short breaks are increasing in popularity, accommodation providers often take bookings for shorter periods, particularly outside of the main season.

Holiday Cottage Agencies – these range from small local organisations to large Britain-wide operators. Some agencies organise their own assessments, but the majority use national tourist board quality standards and are gradually bringing all their properties into the star-rating scheme. Many agencies have also been assessed and accredited by VisitEngland to ensure they are well-run and provide excellent customer care. For full details of Holiday Cottage Agencies, see pages 374 to 377.

Boat Accommodation – quality-assessed boats in small and large fleets across England's waterways also offer accommodation. Narrowboats are purpose-built, traditionally decorated boats on canals and rivers and can sleep up to 12 people; Cruisers operate mainly on the Norfolk Broads and the Thames and can range from practical affordable craft, to modern, stylish boats with accessories such as dishwashers, DVD players and flat-screen TV's.

Approved Caravan – approved caravan holiday homes are let as individual self-catering units and can be located on farms or holiday parks. All the facilities, including a bathroom and toilet, are contained within the caravan and all main services are provided. There are no star ratings for these caravans, however, they are assessed annually to check they meet the minimum quality standards.

All self-catering accommodation is awarded a rating from 1 to 5 stars (apart from Approved Caravans and Alternative Accommodation). All will meet the minimum standards shown below:

- Clear information prior to booking on all aspects of the accommodation including location, facilities, prices, deposit, policies on smoking, children, cancellation, etc.
- No shared facilities, with the exception of a laundry room in multi-unit sites.
- All appliances and furnishings will meet product safety standards for self-catering accommodation, particularly regarding fire safety.
- Clear information on emergency procedures, including who to contact.
- Contact details for the local doctor, dentist, chemist, etc.
- All statutory obligations will be met, including an annual gas safety check and public liability insurance.

The more stars, the higher the quality and the greater the range of facilities and services on offer. For example, a 3-star accommodation must offer bed linen (with or without additional charge) while at a 4-star, all advertised sleeping space will be in bedrooms (unless a studio) and beds will be made up on arrival.

Some self-catering establishments offer a choice of accommodation units that may have different star ratings. In this case, the entry in this guide indicates the star range available.

Gold Awards

How can you find those special places to stay? Those that, regardless of the range of facilities and services, achieve exceptional scores for quality (particularly the bedrooms and bathrooms, kitchen, public areas and most importantly the cleanliness). VisitEngland's Gold Awards highlight this excellence and are given to self-catering accommodation and caravan parks that offer the highest level of quality within their particular star rating.

High star ratings mean top quality in all areas and all the services expected of that classification. Lower star ratings with a Gold Award indicate limited facilities or services, delivered to a standard of high quality.

Gold Awards are given to individual units on sites with multiple lettings, therefore you should check with the owner before booking if you wish to stay in the unit which has been given the Gold Award.

An index to Gold Award winning self-catering accommodation and caravan parks featured in this guide is given on pages 380 to 381.

OFFICIAL TOURIST BOARD GUIDES

40th Anniversary Golden Ticket Giveaway!

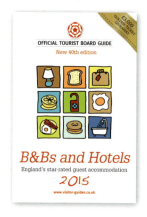

B&Bs and Hotels
England's star-rated guest accommodation
2015
www.visitor-guides.co.uk

Camping, Touring & Holiday Parks
Britain's star-rated holiday parks
2015

£3,000 GOLDEN TICKET
GIVEAWAY
★ ★ ★ ★ ★ see page 14 for details ★ ★ ★ ★ ★

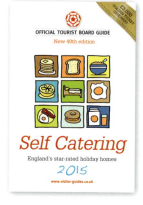

Self Catering
England's star-rated holiday homes
2015
www.visitor-guides.co.uk

Are you a winner in our Special 40th Anniversary golden ticket giveaway?

To celebrate the 40th anniversary edition of the Official Tourist Board Guides, we are giving away 6 x UK short breaks worth £500 each. We have randomly inserted 6 golden tickets in copies of the 2015 guides and if this guide contains one then you are a winner!

Check inside this copy of the guide and if you find a Golden Ticket call us on 01733 296910 quoting the reference number from your ticket to claim your prize. You will be asked to provide your ticket, together with the sales receipt for the guide in order to claim your prize.

www.visitor-guides.co.uk

AVAILABLE FROM ALL GOOD BOOKSHOPS AND ONLINE RETAILERS

Gold Awards

VisitEngland's unique Gold Awards are given in recognition of exceptional quality in self-catering accommodation.

VisitEngland professional assessors make recommendations for Gold Awards during assessments. They look for aspects of exceptional quality in all areas, in particular, housekeeping, hospitality, bedrooms and bathrooms.

While star ratings are based on a combination of quality, the range of facilities and the level of service offered, Gold Awards are based solely on quality.

Therefore a 2 star property with limited facilities but exceptional quality could still achieve the Gold Award status.

Self-catering establishments with a Gold Award are featured below. Detailed entries for these properties are also included in the regional pages and can be found using the property index on page 390.

Gold Award Self-catering Accommodation
with entries in the regional pages

Woodthorpe Hall Country Cottages
Alford, Lincolnshire

Cheriton Wood Studio
Alresford, Hampshire

Blythe Farmhouse
Alton, Staffordshire

Outchester & Ross Farm Cottages
Bamburgh, Northumberland

Hauxwell Grange Cottages (The Stone Byre & Curlew Cottage)
Barnard Castle, Co Durham

Greyfield Farm Cottages
Bath, Somerset

Nailey Cottages
Bath, Somerset

Heron Lakes
Beverley, East Yorkshire

Grange Farm Country Cottages
Bicester, Oxfordshire

Apartment 5, Burgh Island Causeway
Bigbury-on-Sea, Devon

The Pump House Apartment
Billericay, Essex

Oatfield Country Cottages
Blakeney, Gloucestershire

Rookery Farm Norfolk
Bodham, Norfolk

Bridge Cottage
Bradford-on-Avon, Wiltshire

Thornthwaite
Broughton-in-Furness, Cumbria

Tamar Valley Cottages
Bude, Cornwall

Whalesborough Cottages
Bude, Cornwall

Wooldown Holiday Cottages
Bude, Cornwall

Wychnor Park Country Club
Burton Upon Trent, Staffordshire

Lackford Lakes Barns
Bury St. Edmunds, Suffolk

Pyegreave Cottage
Buxton, Derbyshire

Brackenhill Tower & Jacobean Cottage
Carlisle, Cumbria

Riding House Farm Cottages
Castleton, Derbyshire

Church Court Cottages
Cheltenham, Gloucestershire

4* Gold Wharton Lock Canalside Balcony Apartment
Chester, Cheshire

Pottery Flat Chesterfield
Chesterfield, Derbyshire

Honer Cottage
Chichester, Sussex

Laneside
Chichester, Sussex

Heath Farm Holiday Cottages
Chipping Norton, Oxfordshire

The Stables
Cirencester, Gloucestershire

Craster Tower Penthouse Apartment
Craster, Northumberland

Cromer Country Club
Cromer, Norfolk

The Poplars Caravan & Chalet Park
Cromer, Norfolk

Hodges
Crowborough, Sussex

Wayside House
Cullompton, Devon

Abbey House
Easby, North Yorkshire

Medley Court - Hever Castle
Edenbridge, Kent

Log Cabin Holidays
Eye, Suffolk

2 Westgate Barns
Fakenham, Norfolk

Brazenhall Barn & Lodge
Fakenham, Norfolk

Hard Farm Barns
Field Dalling, Norfolk

Burgate Manor Farm Holidays
Fordingbridge, Hampshire

Caburn Cottages
Glynde, Sussex

Prestwick Self Catering
Godalming, Surrey

Owls roost
Gorran, Cornwall

Swallows' Nest
Grassington, North Yorkshire

Rhydd Barn
Guarlford, Worcestershire

Little Marshfoot
Hailsham, Sussex

Lizard Peninsula Holiday Cottages
Helston, Cornwall

Brinsop Court
Hereford, Herefordshire

Little Canwood House
Hereford, Herefordshire

Monkhall Cottages
Hereford, Herefordshire

Woodford Bridge Country Club
Holsworthy, Devon

Ingleby Manor
Ingleby Greenhow, North Yorkshire

Swallow Barn
Kendal, Cumbria

San Ging Keswick
Keswick, Cumbria

Rainbow Cottage
King's Lynn, Norfolk

White Heron Properties
Kington, Herefordshire

Cleveleymere 5* Luxury Lakeside Lodges
Lancaster, Lancashire

The Glassworks Apartments
Lancaster, Lancashire

Old Vicarage Cottages
Lincoln, Lincolnshire

Rivermead Farm
Liskeard, Cornwall

Church Cottage
Louth, Lincolnshire

Louth Barn
Louth, Lincolnshire

Ashford Farm Cottages
Ludlow, Shropshire

Castle House Lodgings
Ludlow, Shropshire

Glebe Barn
Ludlow, Shropshire

The Silver Pear Apartments
Ludlow, Shropshire

Home Farm Holiday Cottages
Malton, North Yorkshire

Walnut Garth
Malton, North Yorkshire

Holywell Suite
Malvern, Worcestershire

Foxton Locks Lodges
Market Harborough, Leicestershire

Anne's Place
Martock, Somerset

1 The Green
Melton Mowbray, Leicestershire

Holme House Barn
Mitcheldean, Gloucestershire

Headland Cottages
Newquay, Cornwall

The Park
Newquay, Cornwall

Link House Farm Holiday Cottages
Newton-by-the-Sea, Northumberland

Courtyard Barns
North Walsham, Norfolk

Woodview Cottages
Nottingham, Nottinghamshire

Blackthorn Gate
Nunthorpe, North Yorkshire

Peartree Cottage
Okehampton, Devon

Honeysuckle Cottage
Padstow, Cornwall

Sunday & School Cottages
Padstow, Cornwall

Yellow Sands Cottages
Padstow, Cornwall

Tirril Farm Cottages
Penrith, Cumbria

Hall Farm Kings Cliffe
Peterborough, Northamptonshire

Ashfield Cottages
Pickering, North Yorkshire

Kale Pot Cottage
Pickering, North Yorkshire

South Winchester Lodges
Pitt, Hampshire

Green Door Cottages Port Gaverne
Port Isaac, Cornwall

Rosehill Lodges
Porthtowan, Cornwall

Admiralty Apartments
Portsmouth and Southsea, Hampshire

Trengove Farm Cottages
Redruth, Cornwall

2 Nurse Cherry's Cottage
Reeth, North Yorkshire

Natural Retreats - Yorkshire Dales
Richmond, North Yorkshire

Upton Grange Holiday Cottages
Ringstead, Dorset

Buff's Old Barn
Saxmundham, Suffolk

The Sands Sea Front Apartments
Scarborough, North Yorkshire

Mount Brioni Holiday Apartments
Seaton, Cornwall

Drewstone Farm
South Molton, Devon

Dunmallard - Lower Flat
St Mary's, Isles Of Scilly

Natural Retreats - Trewhiddle
St. Austell, Cornwall

Cornish Holiday Lodges
St. Columb, Cornwall

The Apartment, Porthminster Beach
St. Ives, Cornwall

Broad Oak Cottages
Stow-on-the-Wold, Gloucestershire

4 Bancroft Place
Stratford-upon-Avon, Warwickshire

Heritage Mews
Stratford-upon-Avon, Warwickshire

Stretton Lakes
Stretton, Rutland

Barncastle
Stroud, Gloucestershire

Long Cover Cottage & The Coach House
Sutton, Worcestershire

Rochford Park Cottages
Tenbury Wells, Worcestershire

The Tythe House and Barn Complex
Tetbury, Gloucestershire

Lower Birks Farm
Todmorden, West Yorkshire

Aish Cross Holiday Cottages
Totnes, Devon

The Valley
Truro, Cornwall

Sunnymead Farm Cottages
Uckfield, Sussex

St Moritz Self Catering
Wadebridge, Cornwall

Lavender Lodge
Weasenham, Norfolk

Pear Tree Cottages
Wedmore, Somerset

The Cottage Beyond
Wellington, Somerset

Tone Dale House
Wellington, Somerset

Seascape
Westward Ho!, Devon

Long Barn Luxury Holiday Cottages
Whilborough, Devon

Forest Lodge Farm
Whitby, North Yorkshire

Lemon Cottage
Whitby, North Yorkshire

Nettlecombe Farm Holiday Cottages & Fishing Lakes
Whitwell, Isle of Wight

Church Farm Barns
Wickmere, Norfolk

Hop Pickers Rural Retreats
Worcester, Worcestershire

Mrs Bests Holiday Cottage
Yeovil, Somerset

Minster's Reach Apartments
York, North Yorkshire

Suite Stays
York, North Yorkshire

The Blue Rooms
York, North Yorkshire

The Dutch House
York, North Yorkshire

VisitEngland Awards for Excellence

In 2014 the annual VisitEngland Awards celebrated 25 years of excellence. Years during which the breadth of tourism experience offered to visitors in England has grown to suit every purse and preference whilst matching, and often exceeding, the quality and choice available on the international stage.

With a history stretching back over 25 years, the VisitEngland Awards for Excellence are firmly established as representing the highest accolade in English tourism. The Awards recognise businesses that incorporate best practice and demonstrate excellence in customer service throughout their operation and celebrate the very best in quality and innovation. The Awards are open to all tourism businesses and tourism support organisations which meet the published criteria for the award category or categories they are entering.

Competition to win one of the 15 categories is hotly contested with the majority of finalists having won their destination heats and truly out to show that they are the best of the best! A panel of expert judges review the entries and this year a total of 76 finalists, 15 gold, 16 silver, 15 bronze and 30 highly commended winners were selected from a total of 368 entries from areas spanning the length and breadth of England. You can find a complete list of winners online at:
www.visitenglandawards.org

The hunt for the Self-catering Provider of the Year shone the spotlight onto truly lovely establishments. The range of accommodation available is highlighted by the two Highly Commended experiences to be had at Staying Cool at the Rotunda in urban Birmingham and the Corner Cottage at Nettlecombe Farm Holidays, Whitwell on the Isle of Wight. The Bronze Awards went to the Dandelion Hideaway, Market Bosworth in Leicestershire for offering luxury glamping on a beautiful working farm; Silver went to East View Farm Holiday Cottages near Wroxham in Norfolk where self-catering holiday cottages have been created from traditional Norfolk barns, with great care taken to retain the oak-beamed character of the original buildings, while providing the very latest in comfort to create the perfect holiday escape. The 2014 Gold Winner, Trevase Cottages is a family run business providing two separate large luxury self-catering cottages set within the stunning Herefordshire countryside. The primary objective of the business is to create 'Total Guest Satisfaction' and the family's evident commitment to this, along with the passion they display for their job, ensure that this is guaranteed. The VisitEngland judging panel felt that the family's attention to detail and the facilities on offer are second to none, ensuring that visitors are provided with a memorable stay.

Self-catering Holiday of the Year 2014

GOLD WINNER

Trevase Cottages, Nr Hereford, Herefordshire	★ ★ ★ ★ ★

SILVER WINNER

East View Farm Holiday Cottages, Wroxham, Norfolk	★ ★ ★ ★ ★

BRONZE WINNERS

The Dandelion Hideaway, Market Bosworth, Leicestershire	**Accredited**

HIGHLY COMMENDED

Corner Cottage, Nettlecombe Farm Holidays Whitwell, Isle of Wight	★ ★ ★ ★
Staying Cool at the Rotunda, Birmingham, West Midlands	★ ★ ★ ★ - ★ ★ ★ ★ ★

Nettlecombe Farm Holidays

One of the Isle of Wight's best self-catering destinations was created out of a need to diversify once the farming industry became increasingly more challenging for the owners.

Nettlecombe Farm, nestled in a picturesque corner of the island and surrounded by beautiful South Wight countryside, is now popular with a wide range of visitors, who can participate in an impressive number of activities.

The farm, which has been in the Morris family for over a century, took its first steps in the tourism industry in the 1970s when the main farmhouse was converted into a six-bedroomed guesthouse offering bed and breakfast and evening meals.

Today, Nettlecombe Farm consists of nine converted self-catering premises benefiting from several delightful rustic play areas, three coarse fishing lakes, a light and airy function barn and a petting area that has a very wide selection of interesting animals, including alpaca, donkeys, poultry, goats, reindeer and an emu!

> *"We love Nettlecombe Farm. It has been our family home for over 100 years and we make our guests feel like it's their home during their stay."*
>
> Jose

During their stay visitors can join the morning feeding tours on the farm, experiencing a day in the life of a farmer. These tours take place from April until September (Monday to Friday). They also have full use of three fishing lakes and can take part in weekly yoga sessions.

The business also partners with local organisations such as beauty therapists, childcare providers, caterers and fitness coaches to help guests get more out of their holiday.

"We love Nettlecombe Farm," continues Jose. "It has been our family home for over 100 years and we make our guests feel like it's their home during their stay. One of our key objectives is to make guests want to come back, and we have evidence to suggest this is working. In 2013 over 50% of our customers were repeat bookings and we have generations of families who have been visiting for well over 30 years."

Nettlecombe Farm was Highly Commended in the VisitEngland Awards for Excellence 2014, Self-catering Holiday Provider of the Year category.

Contact Nettlecombe Farm, Whitwell, Isle of Wight PO38 2AF.
T 01983 730783.
E mail@nettlecombefarm.co.uk
W www.nettlecombefarm.co.uk

"For the past five years we have seen a year-on-year steady increase on very healthy occupancy rates," says owner Jose Morris. "We feel this consistent high rate is a testament to our ability to retain repeat customers as well as attract new ones. Word-of-mouth recommendations have helped us to remain popular and busy."

And there's no room for complacency at Nettlecombe Farm with 'continuous improvement' being at the heart of the business. "We always strive to do better and consistently aim to exceed expectations. We believe this philosophy is what keeps us firmly at the top of our league," adds Jose.

"We know that a holiday is a very special occasion that lives long in the memories of our guests and we do our best to leave them with an unforgettable and positive experience that makes them want to return year after year and tell all their friends.

We have a glorious setting with breath-taking views and provide a unique experience unrivalled by any of our competitors. This is backed up with excellent customer service and facilities."

OFFICIAL TOURIST BOARD POCKET GUIDE

Walkers & Cyclists Welcome

England's star-rated great places to stay and visit

The **OFFICIAL** and most comprehensive guide to England's independently inspected, star-rated guest accommodation specialising in Walkers and Cyclists.

Hotels • Bed & Breakfast • Self-catering • Camping, Touring & Holiday Parks

- Regional round ups, attractions, ideas and other tourist information
- National Accessible Scheme accommodation at a glance
- Web-friendly features for easy booking

www.visitor-guides.co.uk

Sustainable Tourism in England

More and more operators of accommodation, attractions and events in England are becoming aware of sustainable or "green" issues and are acting more responsibly in their businesses. But how can you be sure that businesses that 'say' they're green, really are?

Who certifies green businesses?

There are a number of green certification schemes that assess businesses for their green credentials. VisitEngland only promotes those that have been checked out to ensure they reach the high standards expected. The members of those schemes we have validated are truly sustainable (green) businesses and appear amongst the pages of this guide with our heart-flower logo
on their entry.

Businesses displaying this logo have undergone a rigorous verification process to ensure that they are sustainable (green) and that a qualified assessor has visited the premises.

The number of participating green certification scheme organisations applying to be recognised by us is growing all the time. At the moment we promote the largest green scheme in the world - Green Tourism Business Scheme (GTBS) - and the Peak District Environmental Quality Mark.

Peak District Environmental Quality Mark

This certification mark can only be achieved by businesses that actively support good environmental practices in the Peak District National Park. When you buy a product or service that has been awarded the Environmental Quality Mark, you can be confident that your purchase directly supports the high-quality management of the special environment of the Peak District National Park.

Green Tourism Business Scheme

GTBS recognises places to stay and attractions that are taking action to support the local area and the wider environment. With over 2000 members in the UK it's the largest sustainable (green) scheme to operate globally and assesses hundreds of fantastic places to stay and visit in Britain. From small bed and breakfasts to large visitor attractions and activity holiday providers.

Businesses that meet the standard for a GTBS award receive a Bronze, Silver, or Gold award based on their level of achievement. Businesses are assessed in areas that include Management and Marketing, Social Involvement and Communication, Energy, Water, Purchasing, Waste, Transport, Natural and Cultural Heritage and Innovation.

How are these businesses being green?

Any business that has been certified 'green' will have implemented initiatives that contribute to reducing their negative environmental and social impacts whilst trying to enhance the economic and community benefits to their local area.

Many of these things may be behind the scenes such as energy efficient boilers, insulated lofts or grey water recycling, but there are many fun activities that you can expect to find too. For example, your green business should be able to advise you about traditional activities nearby, the best places to sample local food and buy craft products, or even help you to enjoy a 'car-free' day out.

Natural Retreats

Natural Retreats, which promises its customers 'incredible places to stay in stunning locations', celebrated its 10th birthday in 2014, but the seed of this fast-growing company was planted many years before that. When founder and CEO Matthew Spence holidayed with his parents in America's Yellowstone Park, experiences of interacting with nature in such an idyllic and stunning place had a profound effect on him. So when the opportunity arose to grow that seed on his family farm in the heart of the picturesque Yorkshire Dales, Natural Retreats was born.

"We pride ourselves on being a unique leisure and travel company offering extraordinary experiences at a selection of stunning coastal, countryside and wilderness locations around the world," says Kayley Pearce, European Marketing Manager for Natural Retreats.

"We work and live by the principles that underpin the company, forever on a quest to help our guests and customers explore, dream and discover."

Natural Retreats operates at eight UK locations - three in Cornwall, three in Scotland, one in Wales and one in the Yorkshire Dales – as well as sites in Ireland, the Canary Islands and America.

The company is renowned for offering customers and guests high-quality tourism-based experiences in some of the most dramatic natural locations around the world. At some of the sites it offers luxury accommodation while at others it runs activity operations - for example, a Ski Resort at Cairngorm Mountain, Scotland, and a fly-fishing business in South Fork Lodge, Idaho.

"Natural Retreats appeals to anyone looking to escape to nature, as all of our locations have one common thread – they are all in areas of natural beauty. We are extremely family-friendly, yet also appeal to couples and experienced explorers," adds Kayley.

The company provides a holistic approach when designing and developing each location, to incorporate sustainable building practices that limit the impact on the surrounding environment. Guests can enjoy a sustainable rural holiday experience, while still supporting the local community and enjoying contemporary interiors.

"We will always strive where possible to buy locally, respect our environment, support our community and participate in the wellbeing of our surroundings," explains Kayley.

"Our founder developed the first Natural Retreats location on his family farm in the Yorkshire Dales close to the market town of Richmond. Sustainability and supporting the local community was an integral part of the vision for this site and where possible, local tradesmen and people were used to work there. This principle has been carried across to John O'Groats where the community was consulted right at the start of the planning process, and local tradesmen employed during the build phase and into the launch of operations."

Local knowledge also plays a big part in the operation of Natural Retreats. "Our locations may be utterly secluded but we live hand-in-hand with the local area," says Kayley. "So anything our guests need to know we'll know, and anywhere they want to go can be made possible by our skilled local guides.

"The way we look after our guests is by listening to what they need, not by following a corporate set of rules. Nothing is standardised at Natural Retreats, including how we make our guests happy.

We love what we do and where we are and we can't wait to share it."

"We work and live by the principles that underpin the company, forever on a quest to help our guests and customers explore, dream and discover."

Kayley Pearce

Contact Natural Retreats UK Ltd, 1st Floor, Whitecroft House, 51 Water Lane, Wilmslow SK9 5BQ.
www.naturalretreats.com/uk

Don't Miss...

Eden Project
St. Austell, Cornwall PL24 2SG
(01726) 811911
www.edenproject.com
Explore your relationship with nature at the world famous Eden Project, packed with projects and exhibits about climate and the environment, regeneration, conservation and sustainable living. Be inspired by cutting-edge buildings, stunning year round garden displays, world-class sculpture and art, as well as fabulous music and arts events. See all the sights and immerse yourself in nature with a walk among the the treetops on the Rainforest Canopy Walk or a ride on the land train.

Paignton Zoo
Paignton, Devon TQ4 7EU
(0844) 474 2222
www.paigntonzoo.org.uk
One of Britain's top wildilfe attractions, Paignton Zoo has all the usual suspects with an impressive collection of lions, tigers, gorillas, orangutans, rhinos and giraffes. It is also home to some of the planet's rarest creatures and plants too. For a day jam-packed with family fun and adventure there's Monkey Heights, the crocodile swamp, an amphibian ark and a miniature train, as well as the hands-on interactve Discovery Centre.

Roman Bath
Bath, Somerset BA1 1LZ
(01225) 477785
www.romanbaths.co.uk
Bathe in the naturally hot spa water at the magnificent baths built by the romans, indulge in a gourmet getaway, or enjoy a romantic weekend exploring the wealth of historic architecture. You can find all of this in the beautiful city of Bath and attractions such as Longleat Safari Park and Stonehenge are all within easy reach too.

Sherborne Castle & Gardens
Sherborne, Dorset DT9 5NR
(01935) 812072
www.sherbornecastle.com
Built by Sir Walter Raleigh in c1594, the castle reflects various styles from the Elizabethan hall to the Victorian solarium, with splendid collections of art, furniture and porcelain. The grounds around the 50-acre lake were landscaped by 'Capability' Brown and the 30 acres of tranquil lakeside gardens are the perfect place to escape.

Stonehenge
Amesbury, Wiltshire SP4 7DE
(0870) 333 1181
www.english-heritage.org.uk/stonehenge
The Neolithic site of Stonehenge in Wiltshire is one of the most famous megalithic monuments in the world, the purpose of which is still largely only guessed at. This imposing archaeological site is often ascribed mystical or spiritual associations and receives thousands of visitors from all over the world each year.

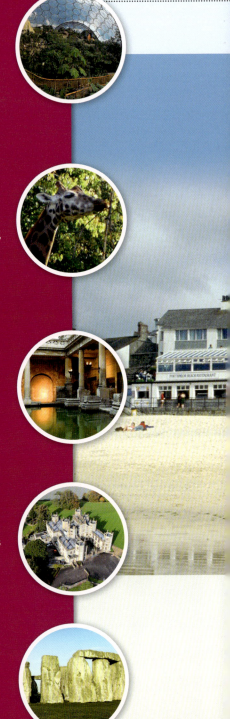

South West

Cornwall & Isles of Scilly, Devon, Dorset, Gloucestershire, Somerset, Wiltshire

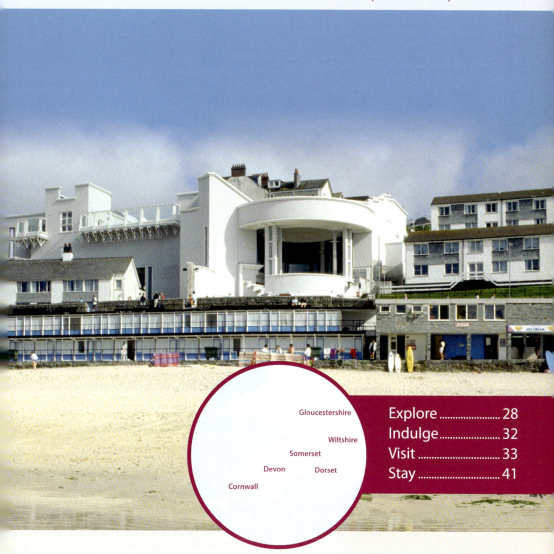

Gloucestershire

Wiltshire

Somerset

Devon   Dorset

Cornwall

A spectacular combination of ancient countryside and glorious coastline, Britain's South West is its most popular holiday area. It stretches from the soft stone and undulating hills of the Cotswolds in the north, through Wiltshire with its historic monuments, to the wild moors, turquoise waters, golden sands and pretty harbours of Dorset, Devon and Cornwall. The beauty of this region and all it has to offer never fails to delight.

Explore – South West

Cornwall

Spectacular turquoise seas and white sands dotted with fishing harbours, beautiful gardens and the remnants of Cornwall's fascinating industrial heritage draw visitors from far and wide. The pounding waves to be found along the coastline attract surfers from all over to the world famous beaches around Newquay and make Cornwall a mecca for watersports enthusiasts of all kinds.

Hotspot: Boardmasters, Europe's largest surf and music festival, takes place at Fistral Beach and Watergate Bay near Newquay in early August.
www.boardmasters.co.uk

The majestic and largely untouched wilderness of Bodmin Moor is only one example of the rich natural environment that can be found here, with miles of walking paths criss-crossing the impressive landscape and offering panoramic views.

The captivating landscape of West Cornwall continues to intrigue and inspire a vibrant art scene centred around St Ives, and Cornwall has a diverse history with prehistoric, Celtic and medieval roots. There are a huge number of heritage attractions, such as Tintagel Castle which overlooks the dramatic windswept Atlantic coast and the Grade I listed Port Eliot House & Gardens, a hidden gem nestling beside a secret estuary near Saltash.

Plymouth is famous for its seafaring heritage, with Plymouth Hoe as the backdrop for Sir Francis Drake's legendary game of bowls, as well as being one of the most beautiful natural harbours in the world. Climb Smeaton's Tower for the incredible views if you're feeling energetic, visit the world-famous Plymouth Gin Distillery at Sutton Harbour, or take the kids to the National Marine Aquarium for an afternoon of fishy fun.

Torquay, gateway to the English Riviera, boasts elegant Victorian villas, iconic palm trees, a sweeping sandy beach and a rich maritime history. Paignton offers great days out including its famous zoo, and the traditional fishing harbour of Brixham is awash with seafood restaurants, waterside pubs and cafés. This whole area is also home to a huge selection of beaches from small, romantic coves to larger, award-winning stretches. The Jurassic Coast is a UNESCO World Heritage Site which stretches for 95 miles along the Devon/Dorset coast, revealing 185 million years of geology and is a must for visitors to the South West.

Devon

Take a hike or a mountain bike and discover the rugged beauty of Exmoor, explore the drama of the craggy coastline, or catch a wave on some of the region's best surf beaches. North Devon is also rich in heritage with many stately homes and historic attractions including Hartland Abbey and the picturesque Clovelly village.

Stunningly beautiful, Dartmoor is perhaps the most famous of Devon's National Parks and offers miles of purple, heather-clad moorland, rushing rivers and stone tors. Walk the length and breadth of the moor or cycle the Drake's Trail, where you'll come across wild ponies and plenty of moorland pubs, perfect for a well earned rest. Head east and discover the imposing Blackdown Hills Area of Outstanding Natural Beauty, stopping off in one of the area's picture-postcard villages for a delicious Devon Cream Tea.

Hotspot: The Dartmouth Steam Railway runs from Paignton along the spectacular Torbay coast and through the wooded slopes bordering the Dart estuary. With stunning scenery and seascapes right across Lyme Bay to Portland Bill on clear days. www.dartmouthtrailriver.co.uk

Gloucestershire

Perfect for a relaxing break or as a base for touring the Cotswolds, Cheltenham is an elegant spa town where Regency town houses line the historic promenade and leafy squares. Relax in award-winning gardens or visit one of the impressive range of sporting and cultural events such as The Cheltenham Gold Cup or The Cheltenham Festival of music.

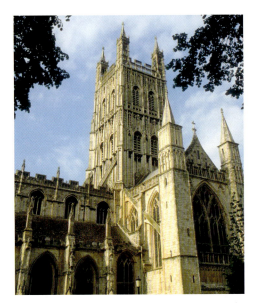

Dorset

Stretching from historic Lyme Regis in the west to Christchurch in the east, and including a number of designated heritage areas, the whole Dorset coastline is a treasure trove of geology. Interesting landforms are plentiful - Durdle Door, Lulworth Cove, the Isle of Portland with the famous Portland Bill lighthouse and the shingle bank of Chesil Beach to name but a few. Weymouth and Portland are two of the best sailing locations in Europe and offer water sports galore, as well as pretty harbours. For traditional English seaside resorts visit Victorian Swanage, or Bournemouth with its fine sandy beach, perfect for families.

Inland, enchanting market towns, quaint villages and rolling countryside play host to delightful shops, museums, family attractions, historic houses and beautiful gardens such as the Sub-Tropical Gardens at Abbotsbury. Explore Dorset's natural beauty on foot or by bicycle at Stoborough Heath and Hartland Moor nature reserves.

Hotspot: Step back in time at Lulworth Castle or the majestic ruins of Corfe Castle, perched above the Isle of Purbeck.

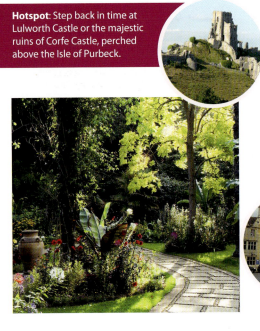

In the North of the Severn Vale, the ancient settlement of Tewkesbury, famous for its fine half-timbered buildings, network of alleyways and 12th Century Norman Abbey, is one of the best medieval townscapes in England. Enjoy a riverside stroll along the River Severn or a boat trip along the Avon. At the centre of the Severn Vale, Gloucester is a vibrant and multicultural city, combining historic architecture with numerous visitor attractions, shops and a collection of mouth watering tea shops, restaurants, bars and pubs. The city, with its impressive cathedral, is linked to Sharpness Docks via the historic 16 mile ship canal and the ancient woodlands of Forest of Dean are only a stone's throw away.

Hotspot: Stow-on-the-Wold is one of the best known Cotswold market towns. The large market square, with its ancient cross and stocks, is bordered with an elegant array of Cotswold stone town houses, antique shops, art galleries and gift shops.

Somerset & Bristol

The maritime city of Bristol is packed with historic attractions, exciting events and fabulous festivals. Cabot Circus offers first class shopping, while stylish restaurants and cafés on the Harbourside serve up locally produced food to tempt and delight. Out and about, Isambard Kingdom Brunel's Clifton Suspension Bridge and the Bristol Zoo Gardens are firm favourites.

Topped by the tower of the ruined 15th Century church, Glastonbury Tor is the stuff of myth and legend, rising high above the Somerset Levels near the delightful town of Glastonbury. Believed to be the site of a Saxon fortress, it has breathtaking views reaching to Wells, the Mendips and the Bristol Channel in the North, Shepton Mallet and Wiltshire in the East, South to the Polden Hills and to the Quantocks and Exmoor in the West.

Wiltshire

Surrounded by stunning scenery and home to a magnificent Cathedral, a wealth of heritage and cultural, dining and shopping venues, the medieval city of Salisbury is the jewel in the crown of South West England's rural heartland.

Further afield you can find an abundance of quintessential English market towns including Chippenham, Devizes, and the county town of Trowbridge. Marlborough, famed for its charming high street and independent shops, is stylish and sophisticated with a cosmopolitan café culture, while Wilton, the ancient capital of Wessex, is home to Wilton House and a beautiful Italianate Church.

Indulge – South West

Deli on the Quay serves fabulous fudge brownies, ideal with a coffee while the kids indulge in an ice cream. Dolphin Quays, The Quay, Poole. www.delionthequay.com

Enjoy delicious seafood at the fun and quirky **Rum & Crab Shack**, Wharf Road, St Ives, Cornwall www.rumandcrabshack.com

Relax with a sumptuous afternoon tea at **The Salty Monk**, Church Street, Sidford in Devon. T: 01395 513174

Indulge your sweet tooth with handmade luxury chocolates from **Cockington Chocolate Company** at Cockington Court in Devon. www.cockingtonchocolate.co.uk

Visit **Temple Quay Food Market** in Bristol for Jamaican patties, Thai curry, handmade falafel, home-made cakes, artisan breads and cheeses, hearty pies and much more!

Sample the delights and discover the history and heritage of Wadworth brewing at **Wadworth Visitor Centre**, Devizes, Wiltshire. T: (01380) 732277 www.wadworthvisitorcentre.co.uk

Attractions with this sign participate in the Visitor Attraction Quality Assurance Scheme.

Cornwall

Blue Reef Aquarium
Newquay, Cornwall TR7 1DU
(01637) 878134
www.bluereefaquarium.co.uk
A dazzling undersea safari through the oceans of the world.

Cornwall Film Festival
November, Cornwall
www.cornwallfilmfestival.com
A month long festival of fabulous films.

Cornwall's Crealy Great Adventure Park
Wadebridge, Cornwall PL27 7RA
(01841) 540276
www.crealy.co.uk/cornwall
Enter the magical land of Cornwall's Crealy and hold on tight for a thrilling ride.

Crantock Bale Push
September, Crantock, nr Newquay
www.balepush.co.uk
Over 100 teams pushing giant hay bales around the village.

Lost Gardens of Heligan
St. Austell, Cornwall PL26 6EN
(01726) 845100
www.heligan.com
An exploration through Victorian Productive Gardens & Pleasure Grounds, a sub-tropical Jungle, pioneering Wildlife Project and more.

Minack Theatre
Porthcurno, Cornwall TR19 6JU
(01736) 810181
www.minack.com
Cornwall's world famous Minack open-air theatre is carved into the granite cliff and set in glorious gardens with spectacular views.

National Maritime Museum Cornwall
Falmouth, Cornwall TR11 3QY
(01326) 313388
www.nmmc.co.uk
This multi award-winning museum delivers something for everyone.

National Seal Sanctuary
Helston, Cornwall TR12 6UG
(01326) 221361
www.sealsanctuary.co.uk
The National Seal Sanctuary rescues, rehabilitates and releases over 40 seal pups a year, providing a home for those that can't be released back to the wild.

Newquay Fish Festival
September, Newquay, Cornwall
www.newquayfishfestival.co.uk
Three days celebrating Newquay harbour and delightful fresh local produce.

Newquay Zoo
Newquay, Cornwall TR7 2LZ
(01637) 873342
www.newquayzoo.org.uk
Multi-award winning Newquay Zoo set in sub-tropical lakeside gardens and home to over 130 species of animals.

St Michaels Mount
Marazion, Cornwall TR17 0EF
(01736) 710265
www.stmichaelsmount.co.uk
Explore the amazing island world of St Michael's Mount and discover legend, myth and over a thousand years of incredible history.

Tate St Ives
St. Ives, Cornwall TR26 1TG
(01736) 796226
www.tate.org.uk
Tate St Ives offers an introduction to international Modern and contemporary art, including works from the Tate Collection.

Devon

Bournemouth Air Festival
August, Bournemouth, Devon
www.bournemouthair.co.uk
Free four-day seafront air show.

The Agatha Christie Festival
September, Torquay, Devon
www.agathachristiefestival.co.uk
*Celebrate the world's most
famous crime writer, Dame
Agatha Christie. A literary festival
with a murder mystery twist!*

Brixham Pirate Festival
May, Brixham, Devon
*www.brixhampiratefestival.co.uk
Brixham turns pirate with live music, games,
re-enactments, skirmishes on the Golden Hind.*

Clovelly Village
(01237) 431781
www.clovelly.co.uk
*Most visitors consider Clovelly to be unique.
Whatever your view, it is a world of difference not to
be missed.*

Dartmouth Castle
Dartmouth, Devon TQ6 0JN
(01803) 833588
www.english-heritage.org.uk/dartmouthcastle
*For over six hundred years Dartmouth Castle has
guarded the narrow entrance to the Dart Estuary and
the busy, vibrant port of Dartmouth.*

Escot Gardens, Maze & Forest Adventure
Ottery St. Mary, Devon EX11 1LU
(01404) 822188
www.escot-devon.co.uk
*Historical gardens and fantasy woodland
surrounding the ancestral home of the
Kennaway family.*

Fishstock
September, Brixham, Devon
www.fishstockbrixham.co.uk
*A one-day festival of seafood and entertainment
held in Brixham.*

Hartland Abbey & Gardens
(01237) 441496/234
www.hartlandabbey.com
*Hartland Abbey is a family home full of history in a
beautiful valley leading to a wild Atlantic cove.*

Ilfracombe Aquarium
Ilfracombe, Devon EX34 9EQ
(01271) 864533
www.ilfracombeaquarium.co.uk
*A fascinating journey of discovery into the aquatic life
of North Devon.*

Plymouth City Museum and Art Gallery
Devon PL4 8AJ
(01752) 304774
www.plymouth.gov.uk/museumpcmag.htm
*The museum presents a diverse range of
contemporary exhibitions, from photography to
textiles, modern art to natural history.*

Quay House Visitor Centre
Exeter, Devon EX2 4AN
(01392) 271611
www.exeter.gov.uk/quayhouse
*Discover the history of Exeter in 15 minutes
at the Quay House Visitor Centre on Exeter's
Historic Quayside.*

Dorset

Athelhampton House and Gardens
Athelhampton, Dorchester, Dorset DT2 7LG
(01305) 848363
www.athelhampton.co.uk
One of the finest 15th century Houses in England nestled in the heart of the picturesque Piddle Valley in the famous Hardy county of rural Dorset.

Christchurch Food and Wine Festival
May, Christchurch, Dorset BH23 1AS
www.christchurchfoodfest.co.uk
Celebrity chefs, over 100 trade stands, culinary treats, cookery theatres and some eminent food critics.

Corfe Castle Model Village and Gardens
Corfe Castle, Dorset BH20 5EZ
(01929) 481234
www.corfecastlemodelvillage.co.uk
Detailed 1/20th scale model of Corfe Castle and village before its destruction by Cromwell.

Dorset Knob Throwing Festival
May, Cattistock, nr Dorchester, Dorset
www.dorsetknobthrowing.com
World famous quirky festival.

Forde Abbey & Gardens
Chard, Dorset TA20 4LU
(01460) 221290
www.fordeabbey.co.uk
Founded 850 years ago, Forde Abbey was converted into a private house in c.1649 and welcomes visitors all year round.

Larmer Tree Festival
July, Cranborne Chase, North Dorset
www.larmertreefestival.co.uk
Boutique festival featuring over 70 diverse artists across six stages, a comedy club, 150 free workshops, street theatre, carnival procession, all in front of an intimate crowd of 4,000.

Lulworth Castle & Park
Wareham, Dorset BH20 5QS
0845 450 1054
www.lulworth.com
Walk in the footsteps of Kings & Queens as you enjoy wide open spaces, historic buildings & stunning landscapes. Enjoy the tranquillity of the nearby 18th century Chapel, wander through the park & woodland & bring a picnic.

Lyme Regis Fossil Festival
May, Lyme Regis, Dorset
www.fossilfestival.co.uk
A natural science and arts cultural extravaganza on the UNESCO World Heritage Jurassic Coast.

Portland Castle
Portland, Dorset DT5 1AZ
(01305) 820539
www.english-heritage.org.uk/portland
A well preserved coastal fort built by Henry VIII to defend Weymouth harbour against possible French and Spanish attack.

Sherborne Abbey Music Festival
May, Sherborne, Dorset
www.sherborneabbey.org
Five days of music performed by both nationally acclaimed artists and gifted young musicians.

Sturminster Newton Cheese Festival
September, Sturminster, Dorset
www.cheesefestival.co.uk
A celebration of the region's dairy heritage with quality local food and crafts.

Swanage Regatta
July - August, Swanage, Dorset
www.swanagecarnival.com
The South's premier carnival.

Bristol

At-Bristol
Bristol BS1 5DB
(0845) 345 1235
www.at-bristol.org.uk
21st century science and technology centre, with hands-on activities, interactive exhibits.

Avon Valley Railway

Bristol BS30 6HD
(0117) 932 5538
www.avonvalleyrailway.org
Railway that's much more than your average steam train ride, offering a whole new experience for some or a nostalgic memory for others.

City Sightseeing
The Bristol Tour
Central Bristol BS1 4AH
(03333) 210101
www.citysightseeingbristol.co.uk
Open-top bus tours, with guides and headphones, around the city of Bristol, a service that runs daily throughout the summer months.

Bristol Zoo Gardens
Bristol BS8 3HA
(0117) 974 7300
www.bristolzoo.org.uk
A visit to this city zoo is your passport for a day trip into an amazing world of animals, exhibits and other attractions.

Brunel's SS Great Britain
Bristol BS1 6TY
(0117) 926 0680
www.ssgreatbritain.org
Award-winning attraction showing the world's first great ocean liner and National Brunel Archive.

Gloucestershire

Chavenage
Chavenage, Tetbury, Gloucestershire GL8 8XP
(01666) 502329
www.chavenage.com
Elizabethan Manor Chavenage House, a TV/Film location is still a family home, offers unique experiences, with history, ghosts and more.

Corinium Museum
Cirencester, Gloucestershire GL7 2BX
(01285) 655611
www.coriniummuseum.org
Discover the treasures of the Cotswolds as you explore its history at this award winning museum.

Forest Food Showcase
October, Forest of Dean, Gloucestershire
www.forestshowcase.org
A celebration of the foods and fruits of the forest. Held annually at Speech House on the first Sunday in October. With many food stalls and demonstrations it's a great opportunity to try what the area has to offer.

Gloucester Cathedral
Gloucestershire GL1 2LR
(01452) 528095
www.gloucestercathedral.org.uk
A place of worship and an architectural gem with crypt, cloisters and Chapter House set in its precincts.

Gloucester Waterways Museum
Gloucester GL1 2EH
(01452) 318200
www.nwm.org.uk
Three floors of a Victorian warehouse house, interactive displays and galleries, which chart the story of Britain's waterways.

Hidcote Manor Garden
Chipping Campden, Gloucestershire GL55 6LR
(01386) 438333
www.nationaltrust.org.uk/hidcote
Famous for its rare trees and shrubs, outstanding herbaceous borders and unusual plants from all over the world.

Painswick Rococo Garden
Painswick, Gloucestershire GL6 6TH
(01452) 813204
www.rococogarden.org.uk
A unique Garden restoration, situated in a hidden valley.

Sudeley Castle Gardens and Exhibition
Winchcombe, Gloucestershire GL54 5JD
(01242) 602308
www.sudeleycastle.co.uk
Award-winning gardens surrounding Castle and medieval ruins.

Westonbirt, The National Arboretum
Tetbury, Gloucestershire GL8 8QS
(01666) 880220
www.forestry.gov.uk/westonbirt
600 acres with one of the finest collections of trees in the world.

Somerset

Glastonbury Abbey
Somerset BA6 9EL
(01458) 832267
www.glastonburyabbey.com
Glastonbury Abbey – Somewhere for all seasons ! From snowdrops and daffodils in the Spring, to family trails and quizzes during the school holidays and Autumn colour on hundreds of trees.

Glastonbury Festival
June, Pilton, Somerset
www.glastonburyfestivals.co.uk
Best known for its contemporary music, but also features dance, comedy, theatre, circus, cabaret and other arts.

Haynes International Motor Museum
Yeovil, Somerset BA22 7LH
(01963) 440804
www.haynesmotormuseum.co.uk
An excellent day out for everyone. With more than 400 vehicles displayed in stunning style, dating from 1886 to the present day, it is the largest international motor museum in Britain.

The Jane Austen Centre
Bath, Somerset BA1 2NT
(01225) 443000
www.janeausten.co.uk
Celebrating Bath's most famous resident.

Number One Royal Crescent
Bath, Somerset BA1 2LR
(01225) 428126
www.bath-preservation-trust.org.uk
The magnificently restored and authentically furnished town house creates a wonderful picture of fashionable life in 18th century Bath.

West Somerset Railway
Minehead, Somerset TA24 5BG
(01643) 704996
www.west-somerset-railway.co.uk
Longest independent steam railway in Britain at 20 miles in length.

Wiltshire

Castle Combe Museum
Castle Combe, Wiltshire SN14 7HU
(01249) 782250
www.castle-combe.com
Displays of life in Castle Combe over the years.

Longleat
Warminster, Wiltshire BA12 7NW
(01985) 844400
www.longleat.co.uk
Widely regarded as one of the best loved tourist destinations in the UK, Longleat has a wealth of exciting attractions and events to tantalise your palate.

Old Sarum
Salisbury, Wiltshire SP1 3SD
(01722) 335398
www.english-heritage.org.uk/oldsarum
Discover the story of the original Salisbury and take the family for a day out to Old Sarum, two miles north of where the city stands now. The mighty Iron Age hill fort was where the first cathedral once stood and the Romans, Normans and Saxons have all left their mark.

Salisbury Cathedral
Salisbury, Wiltshire SP1 2EJ
(01722) 555120
www.salisburycathedral.org.uk
Britain's finest 13th century cathedral with the tallest spire in Britain. Discover nearly 800 years of history, the world's best preserved Magna Carta (AD 1215) and Europe's oldest working clock (AD 1386).

Stourhead House and Garden
Warminster, Wiltshire BA12 6QD
(01747) 841152
www.nationaltrust.org.uk/stourhead
A breathtaking 18th century landscape garden with lakeside walks, grottoes and classical temples.

Wilton House
Wilton House, Wilton, Wiltshire SP2 0BJ
(01722) 746714
www.wiltonhouse.com
Wilton House has one of the finest art collections in Europe and is set in magnificent landscaped parkland featuring the Palladian Bridge.

Tourist Information Centres

When you arrive at your destination, visit the Tourist Information Centre for quality assured help with accommodation and information about local attractions and events, or email your request before you go.

Axminster	The Old Courthouse	01297 34386	touristinfo@axminsteronline.com
Barnstaple	Museum of North Devon	01271 375000 01271 346747	info@staynorthdevon.co.uk
Bath	Abbey Chambers	0906 711 2000	tourism@bathtourism.co.uk
Bideford	Burton Art Gallery	01237 477676	bidefordtic@torridge.gov.uk
Blandford Forum	Riverside House	01258 454770	blandfordtic@btconnect.com
Bodmin	Shire Hall	01208 76616	bodmintic@visit.org.uk
Bourton-on-the-Water	Victoria Street	01451 820211	bourtonvic@btconnect.com
Braunton	The Bakehouse Centre	01271 816688	brauntonmuseum@yahoo.co.uk
Bridport	Bridport Town Hall	01308 424901	bridport.tic@westdorset-weymouth.gov.uk
Bristol : Harbourside	E Shed	0906 711 2191	ticharbourside@destinationbristol.co.uk
Brixham	18-20 The Quay	01803 211 211	holiday@englishriviera.co.uk
Bude	Bude Visitor Centre	01288 354240	budetic@visitbude.info
Budleigh Salterton	Fore Street	01395 445275	info@visitbudleigh.com
Cartgate	South Somerset TIC	01935 829333	cartgate.tic@southsomerset.gov.uk
Chard	The Guildhall	01460 260051	chard.tic@chard.gov.uk
Cheltenham	Municipal Offices	01242 522878	info@cheltenham.gov.uk
Chippenham	High Street	01249 665970	info@chippenham.gov.uk
Chipping Campden	The Old Police Station	01386 841206	info@campdenonline.org
Christchurch	49 High Street	01202 471780	enquiries@christchurchtourism.info
Cirencester	Corinium Museum	01285 654180	cirencestervic@cotswold.gov.uk
Combe Martin	Seacot	01271 883319	mail@visitcombemartin.co.uk
Dartmouth	The Engine House	01803 834224	holidays@discoverdartmouth.com
Dawlish	The Lawn	01626 215665	dawtic@teignbridge.gov.uk
Dorchester	11 Antelope Walk	01305 267992	dorchester.tic@westdorset-weymouth.gov.uk
Exeter	Exeter Visitor Information Centre	01392 665700	tic@exeter.gov.uk
Exmouth	Travelworld	01395 222299	tic@travelworldexmouth.co.uk
Falriver	11 Market Strand	0905 325 4534	vic@falriver.co.uk
Fowey	5 South Street	01726 833616	info@fowey.co.uk
Frome	The Library	01373 465757	touristinfo@frome-tc.gov.uk

Glastonbury	The Tribunal	01458 832954	info@glastonburytic.co.uk
Gloucester	28 Southgate Street	01452 396572	tourism@gloucester.gov.uk
Honiton	Lace Walk Car Park	01404 43716	honitontic@btconnect.com
Ilfracombe	The Landmark	01271 863001	marie@visitilfracombe.co.uk
Ivybridge	The Watermark	01752 897035 01752 89222	info@ivybridgewatermark.co.uk
Launceston	The White Hart Arcade	01566 772321	info@launcestontic.co.uk
Looe	The Guildhall	01503 262072	looetic@btconnect.com
Lyme Regis	Guildhall Cottage	01297 442138	lymeregis.tic@westdorset-weymouth.gov.uk
Lynton and Lynmouth	Town Hall	01598 752225	info@lyntourism.co.uk
Malmesbury	Town Hall	01666 823748	tic@malmesbury.gov.uk
Minehead	19 The Avenue	01643 702624	minehead.visitor@hotmail.com
Modbury	5 Modbury Court,	01548 830159	modburytic@lineone.net
Moreton-in-Marsh	High Street	01608 650881	moreton@cotswold.gov.uk
Newquay	Municipal Offices	01637 854020	newquay.tic@cornwall.gov.uk
Newton Abbot	6 Bridge House	01626 215667	natic@teignbridge.gov.uk
Ottery St Mary	10a Broad Street	01404 813964	info@otterytourism.org.uk
Padstow	Red Brick Building	01841 533449	padstowtic@btconnect.com
Penzance	Station Approach	01736 335530	beth.rose@nationaltrust.org.uk
Plymouth: Mayflower	Plymouth Mayflower Centre	01752 306330	barbicantic@plymouth.gov.uk
Poole		0845 2345560	info@pooletourism.com
Salcombe	Market Street	01548 843927	info@salcombeinformation.co.uk
Salisbury	Fish Row	01722 342860	visitorinfo@salisburycitycouncil.gov.uk
Shepton Mallet	70 High Street	01749 345258	enquiries@visitsheptonmallet.co.uk
Sherborne	3 Tilton Court	01935 815341	sherborne.tic@westdorset-weymouth.gov.uk
Scilly, Isles Of	Hugh Street, Hugh Town	01720 424031	tic@scilly.gov.uk
Seaton	The Underfleet	01297 21660	visit@seaton.gov.uk
Shaftesbury	8a Bell Street	01747 853514	tourism@shaftesburydorset.com
Sidmouth	Ham Lane	01395 516441	ticinfo@sidmouth.gov.uk
Somerset Visitor Centre	Sedgemoor Services	01934 750833	somersetvisitorcentre@somerset.gov.uk
South Molton	1 East Street	01769 574122	visitsouthmolton@btconnect.com
St Austell	Southbourne Road	01726 879 500	staustelltic@gmail.com
St Ives	The Guildhall	01736 796297	ivtic@stivestic.co.uk
Street	Clarks Village	01458 447384	info@streettic.co.uk
Stroud	Subscription Rooms	01453 760960	tic@stroud.gov.uk
Swanage	The White House	01929 422885	mail@swanage.gov.uk
Swindon	Central Library	01793 466454	infocentre@swindon.gov.uk
Taunton	The Library	01823 336344	tauntontic@tauntondeane.gov.uk
Tavistock	The Den	01626 215666	teigntic@teignbridge.gov.uk
Tetbury	33 Church Street	01666 503552	tourism@tetbury.org
Tewkesbury	100 Church Street	01684 855040	tewkesburytic@tewkesbury.gov.uk
Tiverton	Museum of Mid Devon Life	01884 256295	tivertontic@tivertonmuseum.org.uk
Torquay	The Tourist Centre	01803 211 211	holiday@englishriviera.co.uk
Torrington	Castle Hill	01805 626140	info@great-torrington.com
Totnes	The Town Mill	01803 863168	enquire@totnesinformation.co.uk
Truro	Municipal Building	01872 274555	tic@truro.gov.uk
Wareham	Discover Purbeck	01929 552740	tic@purbeck-dc.gov.uk
Warminster	Central Car Park	01985 218548	visitwarminster@btconnect.com
Wellington	30 Fore Street	01823 663379	wellingtontic@tauntondeane.gov.uk
Wells	Wells Museum	01749 671770	visitwellsinfo@gmail.com
Weston-Super-Mare	The Winter Gardens	01934 417117	westontic@parkwood-leisure.co.uk
Weymouth	The Pavilion	01305 785747	tic@weymouth.gov.uk
Wimborne Minster	29 High Street	01202 886116	wimbornetic@eastdorset.gov.uk
Winchcombe	Town Hall	01242 602925	winchcombetic@tewkesbury.gov.uk
Woolacombe	The Esplanade	01271 870553	info@woolacombetourism.co.uk
Yeovil	Petters House	01935 462781	yeoviltic@southsomerset.gov.uk

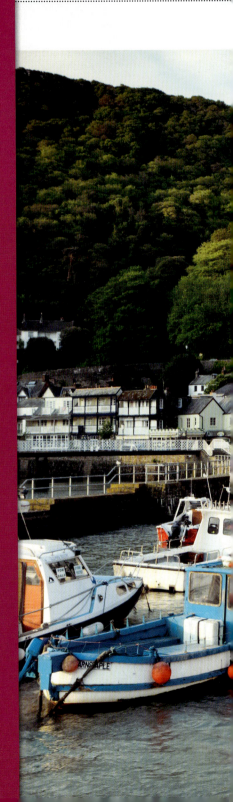

Regional Contacts and Information

For more information on accommodation, attractions, activities, events and holidays in South West England, contact one of the following regional or local tourism organisations. Their websites have a wealth of information and many produce free publications to help you get the most out of your visit.

www.visitsouthwest.co.uk
www.visitdevon.co.uk
www.visitcornwall.co.uk
www.visit-dorset.com
www.visitsomerset.co.uk
www.visitbristol.co.uk
www.visitbath.co.uk
www.southwestcoastpath.org.uk

Entries appear alphabetically by town name in each county. A key to symbols appears on page 7

BUDE, Cornwall Map ref 1C2

Units 1
Sleeps 5
PER UNIT PER WEEK
£200.00 - £600.00

Coombe View
Contact: Mrs Penny Kenyon, Owner, 1 The Coombe, Penstowe Park, Bude EX23 9QY
T: 07929 414914 **E:** penny@budeholidaylodge.co.uk
W: www.budeholidaylodge.co.uk

Located just North of Bude, this holiday lodge is situated in picturesque surroundings in North Cornwall. With a beautiful view across the valley and out to sea, this holiday lodge represents the ideal place to rest in tranquil surroundings. **Open:** 1st March - 1st November **Nearest Shop:** 0.5 miles **Nearest Pub:** 0.5 miles

Leisure: Property: Children: Unit:

BUDE, Cornwall Map ref 1C2

Units 1
Sleeps 4
PER UNIT PER WEEK
£360.00 - £710.00

Peace and Plenty Holidays
Contact: Peace and Plenty Cottage, Hartland, Bideford, Devon EX39 6EH
T: (01237) 440072 **E:** cottage@peaceandplentyholidays.co.uk
W: www.peaceandplentyholidays.co.uk

Pretty cottage set in rolling countryside with views of the Atlantic and Lundy. Central heating, wood burning stove, cosy and comfortable. A haven of tranquility set in rolling countryside with views of the Atlantic ocean and Lundy Island. **Open:** All year **Nearest Shop:** 3 miles **Nearest Pub:** 1.5 miles

Site: Property: Children: Unit: BBQ

BUDE, Cornwall Map ref 1C2

Units 4
Sleeps 4-8
PER UNIT PER WEEK
£375.00 - £1300.00

Tamar Valley Cottages
Contact: David Wright, North Tamerton House, North Tamerton, Cornwall EX22 6SA
T: (01409) 271284 / 07860 726957 **E:** bookings@tamarvalleycottages.co.uk
W: www.tamarvalleycottages.co.uk

Luxury family and dog friendly self-catering cottages at Tamar Valley Cottages offer peace and tranquillity whilst still being within a short drive of some of the West Country's most stunning unspoilt beaches, spectacular coastal paths and wild moors. With great access links to top attractions in both Devon & Cornwall it is easy to explore everything the West Country has to offer. **Open:** All year round **Nearest Shop:** 2.5 miles **Nearest Pub:** 0.5 miles

Site: Leisure: Property: Children: Unit: BBQ

BUDE, Cornwall Map ref 1C2

Units 11
Sleeps 2-10
PER UNIT PER WEEK
£385.00 - £2415.00

Treworgie Barton
Contact: St. Gennys, Bude, Cornwall EX23 0NL **T:** (03301) 230 374
E: enquiries@csmaclubretreats.co.uk
W: www.treworgie.co.uk

Set in 36 acres of peaceful farm and woodland, this North Devon accommodation boasts magnificent views over rolling countryside and sea beyond. Whether you are looking to relax, explore or just get away, Treworgie Barton Cottages offer the ideal break. Their beautifully preserved features of the past give each cottage a real feeling of character. **Open:** From 17th Jan throughout 2015 **Nearest Shop:** 2 miles **Nearest Pub:** 2 miles

Site: Payment: Leisure: Property: Children: Unit: BBQ

BUDE, Cornwall Map ref 1C2

Whalesborough Cottages

Contact: James & Sharran Proudfoot, Owners, Whalesborough Farm, Marhamchurch, Bude, Cornwall EX23 0JD **T:** (01288) 361215 / 07557 508641 **F:** 01288 361317
E: jproudfoot@whalesborough.plus.com **W:** www.whalesborough.co.uk **£ BOOK ONLINE**

Units   20
Sleeps   2-10

PER UNIT PER WEEK
£450.00 - £3750.00

SPECIAL PROMOTIONS
Short breaks between October and Easter. Late availability and offers on our website.

Whalesborough luxury self catering cottages, near Bude will appeal to visitors looking for contemporary, spacious holiday accommodation surrounded by the natural countryside of North Cornwall. Sixteen 5 star gold award winning cottages sleeping 2-10 people with indoor pool/spa, outdoor pool, tennis courts, indoor games barn and onsite cafe/bistro/shop. Walk/cycle from your cottage across the farm to the beach or down the Canal Towpath to Bude or use Whalesborough as a base to explore the rest of Cornwall and North Devon. Cottages all have private, enclosed gardens and are pet friendly too.

Open: All Year
Nearest Shop: 1 mile
Nearest Pub: 1 mile

Units: Most bedrooms have en suite facilities. 5 single storey cottages, all interiors professionally designed. Underfloor heating, woodburners. Enclosed gardens.

Site: ✿ P Payment: 🔲 Leisure: ♪ ⏃ ◥ ♦ ⚄ ⚄ Property: ∥ ⚘ 🖶 🔲 🔲 Children: 🛝 🏛 ⚲
Unit: 🔲 🔲 🔲 ⚄ 🔲 TV DVD 🌀 BBQ

BUDE, Cornwall Map ref 1C2

Woodland Lodge Holidays

Contact: Christopher Pym, Owner, Reservation Office, 10 Oak Tree Walk, Keynsham, Bristol BS31 2SA **T:** 07973 224287 **E:** info@woodlandlodgeholidays.co.uk
W: www.woodlandlodgeholidays.co.uk **£ BOOK ONLINE**

Units   1
Sleeps   4
PER UNIT PER WEEK
£167.00 - £639.00

Totally refurbished luxury lodge to modern standards. Sleeps 4 in double and twin bedrooms. Cozy lounge with flat-screen TV & DVD player. Open plan kitchen. Modern bathroom with bath & shower. Quiet location with patio overlooking woodland. 2 miles to unspoilt sandy beach; 4 miles from Bude. 10 minutes walk from local village. Pets welcome by prior arrangement. Ideal family holiday location.
Open: 1st March until 31st October **Nearest Shop:** 0.5 miles
Nearest Pub: 0.5 miles

Site: ✿ P Payment: 🔲 € Leisure: ♪ ⏃ ∪ ◥ ♦ ⚄ ⚄ Property: ⚘ 🔲 🔲 Children: 🛝 🏛 ⚲ Unit: 🔲 🔲
🔲 TV DVD

For **key to symbols** see page 7

BUDE, Cornwall Map ref 1C2

Units 15
Sleeps 2-8

PER UNIT PER WEEK
£220.00 - £1700.00

SPECIAL PROMOTIONS
All year short breaks from 1 night available with any day arrival/departure.

Wooldown Holiday Cottages

Contact: Mrs Susan Blewett, Wooldown Holiday Cottages, Sharlands Road, Marhamchurch, Bude, Cornwall EX23 0HP **T:** (01288) 361216 **E:** holidays@wooldown.com
W: www.wooldown.com **£ BOOK ONLINE**

Enjoy outstanding sea and countryside views in luxury, from cosy country cottages, to ultra-modern, apartment style romantic hideaways. Featuring underfloor heating, chunky super king size beds, spa baths and rainfall showers. Perfect for a romantic short break or a family holiday. Situated on the North Cornish coast on the outskirts of the picturesque village of Marhamchurch with pub/restaurant. Just two miles from the popular seaside town of Bude, with a variety of quality places to eat, walks and beaches.

Open: All year
Nearest Shop: 2 miles
Nearest Pub: 1.5 mile

Units: 12 luxury barn conversions just for two, 3 larger family properties (farmhouse and cottages).

Site: ✿ P **Payment:** 🔲 **Leisure:** ♿ ♪ ▶ ↺ **Property:** ⫽ 🖵 🔲 🔲 **Children:** 🚼 🛏 ⚲
Unit: 🗄 🗄 🖵 🗄 🖉 📺 📀 BBQ

EDMONTON, Cornwall Map ref 1B2

Units 2
Sleeps 1-4

PER UNIT PER WEEK
£200.00 - £600.00

SPECIAL PROMOTIONS
Weekend breaks £150 - £250. Please contact for details.

Quarrymans Cottages

Contact: Mr Huw Jenkins, Quarrymans Cottages 1 & 20, 17 Granville Terrace, Mountain Ash CF45 4AL **T:** 07866 386611 **E:** jenkins@choicecornishcottages.com
W: www.choicecornishcottages.com **£ BOOK ONLINE**

These tastefully decorated, cosy cottages are situated overlooking the Camel Estuary. Originally the homes of 19th century slate quarrymen, they are positioned around a stone-flagged courtyard and adjacent to a traditional Cornish inn. Fifteen-minute drive from Padstow's pretty harbour and sandy beaches.

Open: All year
Nearest Shop: 0.5 miles
Nearest Pub: 40 yards

Units: 2 bedrooms on 1st floor, 1 with double bed, 1 with twin beds.

Site: ✿ P **Leisure:** ♿ ♪ ↺ **Property:** 🖵 **Children:** 🚼 **Unit:** 🗄 🖵 📺 🖉

FALMOUTH, Cornwall   Map ref 1B3

Budock Vean Cottages

Contact: Budock Vean Cottages, Helford Passage, Nr Mawnan Smith, Falmouth, Cornwall TR11 5LG **T:** (01326) 250288 **F:** 01326 250892 **E:** management@budockvean.co.uk
W: www.budockvean.co.uk **£ BOOK ONLINE**

Units   4
Sleeps   4-8

PER UNIT PER WEEK
£470.00 - £2180.00

Situated just a stone's throw from the Budock Vean Hotel's front door are the four cottages and lodges. Owned and managed by the Barlow family, Budock Vean is set in 65 beautiful acres on the spectacular Cornish Coast with its own golf course, tennis courts, large indoor pool, health spa and award-winning restaurant. Completed to a four-star standard as rated by Quality in Tourism. Each has a small private garden, convenient parking, central heating and include full use of the hotel facilities including Wi-Fi, pool, golf course, sauna and outdoor hot tub. Includes electricity and heating.

Open: 25th Jan 2015 - 2nd Jan 2016
Nearest Shop: 1.5 miles
Nearest Pub: 1.5 miles

Units: Most rooms have a private bathroom or shower room and toilet. Beavers Lodge, Beavers Dam and Badgers Cottage are all on one level.

Site: ❀ P Payment: 💷 Leisure: ♿ ♪ ► ♨ 🎣 🎾 Property: ♫ 🐾 🖼 📦 🏠 🛏 Children: 🚼 🎠 🎢
Unit: 🖥 🔌 📺 📻 📡 📺 🎧 🎧 ✐ BBQ ☎

FALMOUTH, Cornwall   Map ref 1B3

Goodwinds Apartments

Contact: Mrs Jean Goodwin, 3 The Goodwinds, Penwerris Lane, Falmouth, Cornwall TR11 2PF **T:** (01326) 313200 / 07772 890999 **E:** goodwindsapartments@hotmail.co.uk
W: www.cgoodwin11.wix.com/goodwindsapartments

Units   4
Sleeps   2-5
PER UNIT PER WEEK
£285.00 - £525.00

Goodwinds Holiday Apartments are a modern development of four apartments all with their own balconies and central heating. All have marvellous views over Falmouth harbour, the Penryn River and the quaint fishing village of Flushing. Undercover private parking. **Open:** All Year **Nearest Shop:** 0.75 miles
Nearest Pub: 0.75 miles

Site: P Leisure: ► Property: 🐾 🏠 Children: 🚼 🎠 🎢 Unit: 📺 📡 📺

Book your accommodation online

Visit our websites for detailed information, up-to-date availability and to book your accommodation online. Includes over 20,000 places to stay, all of them star rated.

www.visitor-guides.co.uk

FALMOUTH, Cornwall   Map ref 1B3

Units   8
Sleeps   2-8

PER UNIT PER WEEK
£395.00 - £1370.00

SPECIAL PROMOTIONS
We offer short breaks
with a minimum stay
of three nights.
Regular promotions
are shown on our
website throughout
the year.

Mylor Harbourside Holidays

Contact: Mylor Yacht Harbour Hold Co., Mylor Yacht Harbour, Mylor Churchtown,
Falmouth TR11 5UF **T:** (01326) 372121 **E:** enquiries@mylor.com
W: www.mylorharbourside.com **£ BOOK ONLINE**

Our holiday accommodation can cater for a multitude of needs for the ideal getaway and offers a
mixture of 2 storey cottages and single storey apartments. All however, share one thing in common
- the stunning seafront location.

Nestled into the heart of a traditional working harbour in Mylor, Cornwall, these beautiful cottages
sit on the banks of the Fal River with views across the estuary and offer the ideal location for those
who like to get out and explore the coastline, countryside and not forgetting some of the best
sailing waters in the UK.

Open: All year
Nearest Shop: 2 miles
Nearest Pub: On site in the Harbour

Units: We have a range of 1 and 2 storey
properties all of which are fully furnished and
equipped with modern fitted kitchens, some
have en suite bathrooms.

Site: **P** Property: Children: Unit: **TV BBQ**

FOWEY, Cornwall   Map ref 1B3

Units   5
Sleeps   4-6

PER UNIT PER WEEK
£580.00 - £1450.00

SPECIAL PROMOTIONS
Long weekends, or
short breaks (Tuesday
to Friday) are available
from the end of
October until
beginning of March.
Please see website for
details.

South Torfrey Farm Ltd

Contact: Debbie Andrews, Owners, South Torfrey Farm, Golant, Fowey, Cornwall PL23 1LA
T: (01726) 833126 **E:** debbie.andrews@southtorfreyfarm.com
W: southtorfreyfarm.com **£ BOOK ONLINE**

At the heart of an organic farm, in a peaceful location above the Fowey estuary, our cottages offer
the perfect base from which to explore the delights of Cornwall. Great on-site facilities, including
indoor heated pool and sauna. Disability friendly. Family pets welcome. Short breaks available from
£300.

Open: All year
Nearest Shop: 2 miles
Nearest Pub: 0.25 miles

Units: Each cottage has at least on en suite
bath/shower. Honeypin is designed for easy
accessibility and has two shower wet-rooms.
Hoist available for pool.

Site: **P** Payment: Leisure: Property: Children:
Unit: **TV BBQ**

GORRAN, Cornwall   Map ref 1B3

Owls roost

Contact: Mrs Myra Welsh, Owner, Owls Roost, Gorran, Saint Austell PL26 6NY
T: (01726) 842295 **F:** 01726 842295 **E:** treveague@btconnect.com
W: www.treveaguefarm.co.uk

Units   1
Sleeps   2-4
PER UNIT PER WEEK
£480.00 - £950.00

Owls Roost is located on our organic farm with far reaching countryside and sea views. A secluded location offering peace and tranquillity, with walks to three local beaches and the chance to relax and swim in our new Swim Spa. Please refer to our website for more information. **Open:** All year including Christmas and New Year **Nearest Shop:** 0.5 miles **Nearest Pub:** 0.5 miles

Site: ✿ P **Payment:** 💳 € **Leisure:** 🚣 ⚓ 🎣 **Property:** 🐴 🚫 🖥 💻 **Children:** 🍼 🛏 👶 **Unit:** 📻 📺 📶 TV 📀 📀

HELFORD, Cornwall   Map ref 1B3

Mudgeon Vean Farm Holiday Cottages

Contact: Mrs Sarah Trewhella, Proprieter, Mudgeon Vean Farm Holiday Cottages, St Martin, Helston TR12 6DB **T:** (01326) 231341 **E:** mudgeonvean@aol.com
W: www.mudgeonvean.co.uk **£ BOOK ONLINE**

Units   4
Sleeps   1-6
PER UNIT PER WEEK
£300.00 - £870.00

3 & 4* Gold Award. Cosy cottages on small 18th century farm producing apple juice & cyder, near the Helford River. Play area and games room. Peaceful location. Area of Outstanding Natural Beauty. Please contact for individual facilities. **Open:** All year **Nearest Shop:** 2 miles **Nearest Pub:** 2 miles

Site: ✿ P **Payment:** 💳 **Leisure:** ⚓ ▸ ♻ ♞ **Property:** 🐴 🚫 🖥 💻 **Children:** 🍼 🛏 👶 **Unit:** 📻 📺 📶 TV 📀 📀 🔌 BBQ

HELSTON, Cornwall   Map ref 1B3

Lizard Peninsula Holiday Cottages

Contact: Mrs Alison McGregor, Proprietor, Hill Crest, School Hill, Coverack, Cornwall TR12 6SA **T:** (01326) 331 331 / 07867 551137 **E:** alison@lizardholidaycottages.co.uk
W: www.lizardholidaycottages.co.uk **£ BOOK ONLINE**

Units   6
Sleeps   2-6

PER UNIT PER WEEK
£348.00 - £1377.00

SPECIAL PROMOTIONS
Short breaks are available out of season (Nov - Feb) avoiding Christmas & New Year.

A collection of family owned and managed holiday cottages in Coverack and Helford on the beautiful Lizard Peninsula in SW Cornwall. All cottages have sea views and are close to local amenities, beaches & the SW Coastal Path. We take great pride in the presentation of our cottages & high level of customer service we offer our customers.

All prices include bed linen, bathrobes, towels & a Cornish cream tea on arrival. We also provide guests with a complimentary pasty voucher to be redeemed at Elizabeth's in Coverack. All guests receive a comprehensive holiday information pack prior to arrival.

Open: All year
Nearest Shop: 200 metres
Nearest Pub: 250 metres

Units: Five cottages in Coverack and one in Helford.

Site: ✿ **Property:** ♻ 🚫 🖥 💻 **Children:** 🍼 🛏 👶 **Unit:** 📻 📺 📶 TV 📀 📀 🔌 BBQ 📞

LISKEARD, Cornwall Map ref 1C2

Units   5
Sleeps   2-8
PER UNIT PER WEEK
£269.00 - £1249.00

Rivermead Farm

Contact: Twowatersfoot, Liskeard, Cornwall PL14 6HT **T:** (01208) 821464
E: enquiries@rivermeadfarmcottages.co.uk
W: www.farmcottagescornwall.co.uk **£ BOOK ONLINE**

The cottages at Rivermead Farm in Cornwall are set in 17 acres of beautiful countryside along half a mile of the idyllic River Fowey with a well stocked trout lake, making it a perfect destination for first class salmon and trout fishing, as well as relaxing family holidays and romantic breaks. From £269 - £549 (1 bedroom cottage) to £449 - £1249 (4 bedroom cottage). **Open:** Mid March - 3rd Jan **Nearest Shop:** 1.5 mile **Nearest Pub:** 0.5 mile

Site: ❄ P **Leisure:** ♪ **Property:** ⛺ ▭ ▣ **Unit:** ▭ ▤ ⚒ TV dvd

LOOE, Cornwall Map ref 1C2

Units   12
Sleeps   2-8
PER UNIT PER WEEK
£238.00 - £1144.00

f ✖

Tremaine Green Country Cottages

Contact: Justin & Penny Spreckley, Tremaine Green, Pelynt, Looe, Cornwall PL13 2LT
T: (01503) 220333 **F:** 01503 220633 **E:** vc@tremaine-green.co.uk
W: www.tremainegreen.co.uk **£ BOOK ONLINE**

Twelve beautiful traditional stone cottages, sleeping 2 - 8, centred around their own private hamlet green. Relax in the tranquil charm and splendour of the award winning grounds. Close to beaches and walks near Looe, Polperro, and Fowey. **Open:** All year
Nearest Shop: 1 mile **Nearest Pub:** 1.2 miles

 Site: ❄ P **Payment:** 💳 **Leisure:** ⚑ 🔍 ✎ **Property:** ⛺ ▭ ▣ ▣ **Children:** 🎠 🛏 🚶 **Unit:** ▯ ▤ ▭ ⚒ TV dvd ⌀ BBQ ☎

MARAZION, Cornwall Map ref 1B3

Units   16
Sleeps   1-5
PER UNIT PER WEEK
£220.00 - £925.00

f ✖

Trevarthian Holiday Homes

Contact: Mr Sean Cattran, Trevarthian Holiday Homes, West End, Marazion TR17 0EG
T: (01736) 710100 **F:** 01736 710111 **E:** info@trevarthian.co.uk
W: www.trevarthian.co.uk **£ BOOK ONLINE**

Trevarthian Holiday Homes is a family business focussing on quality self-catering accommodation in the beautiful town of Marazion, Cornwall. All our properties are located opposite the large sandy beach and St Michael's Mount, a must-see for any visit to the South West, and within a five minute walk of the children's playground, village pubs, restaurants, galleries, shops and bus-stops. Accommodation ranges in size from single bedroom apartments to a three-bedroom cottage with a private garden. **Open:** All year
Nearest Shop: 0.20 miles **Nearest Pub:** 0.20 miles

Site: ❄ P **Payment:** 💳 **Leisure:** ♿ ♪ ∪ **Property:** ▭ ▣ ▣ **Children:** 🎠 🛏 🚶 **Unit:** ▯ ▭ TV ◉ dvd ⌀

NEWQUAY, Cornwall Map ref 1B2

Units   1
Sleeps   2
PER UNIT PER WEEK
£290.00 - £420.00

Green Waters

Contact: Mrs R E Pullen, Owner, 19 Riverside Avenue, Pentire, Newquay TR7 1PN
T: (01637) 873551 **E:** bernruth.pullen@hotmail.co.uk
W: www.visitnewquay.org/stay-newquay/search_details.php?view=green-waters-p57753

A modern, comfortable, self-contained flat for two, in an elevated position with panoramic views of the winding River Gannel tidal estuary. Excellent position for walking and exploring the surrounding beautiful area. **Open:** All year **Nearest Shop:** 2k
Nearest Pub: 1k

Site: P **Property:** ∥ ▭ ▣ ▣ **Unit:** ▯ ▭ ▤ ⚒ TV dvd

NEWQUAY, Cornwall Map ref 1B2

Headland Cottages

Contact: Reception, Headland Road, Fistral Beach, Newquay, Cornwall TR7 1EW
T: (01637) 872211 **F:** 01637 872212 **E:** reception@headlandhotel.co.uk
W: www.headlandhotel.co.uk

Units   39
Sleeps   2-6

PER UNIT PER WEEK
£539.00

Truly outstanding position in arguably the best location in Cornwall. 39 traditionally constructed one, two and three bedroom slate and granite cottages and apartments, with warm, comfortable and stylish interiors. Your sanctuary by the sea. **Open:** All year
Nearest Shop: 1 mile **Nearest Pub:** 0 miles

Site: ✿ P **Payment:** 💳 **Leisure:** 🎵 ⚑ ⚒ ⚒ ⚒ **Property:** ∥ 🐕 🖥 📱 **Children:** 🍼 🛏 🚶 **Unit:** 📋 📺 📻 📺 📀 ☎

NEWQUAY, Cornwall Map ref 1B2

Natural Retreats - Fistral Beach

Contact: Natural Retreats Fistral Beach, Lighthouse, 4 Pentire Avenue, Newquay TR7 1FB
T: (01625) 416 430 **E:** info@naturalretreats.com
W: www.naturalretreats.com **£ BOOK ONLINE**

Units   7
Sleeps   2-8

PER UNIT PER WEEK
£483.00 - £2069.00

SPECIAL PROMOTIONS
Offers only available at www.naturalretreats.com

Fistral Beach is undoubtedly the best surf beach in the UK and ideally located to enjoy all the popular resort of Newquay has to offer. With excellent travel connections — the airport and train station are both within easy reach — Natural Retreats holiday residences are the perfect base for a holiday spent exploring this exciting, energetic area of Cornwall. Our two to four-bedroom spacious luxury apartments offer a high quality contemporary finish and are situated within a five minute walk from the beach.

Open: All Year
Nearest Shop: 0.1 miles
Nearest Pub: 0.3 miles

Units: Sea-view apartments, luxurious interiors, fully equipped, en suite and family bathrooms available.

Site: P **Payment:** 💳 **Leisure:** ⚑ **Property:** ∥ 🐕 🖥 📋 📱 📱 **Children:** 🍼 🛏 🚶
Unit: 📋 📋 📺 📺 📻 📷 📀

Looking for something else?

The official and most comprehensive guide to independently inspected, quality-assessed accommodation.

- **B&Bs and Hotels**
- **Self Catering**
- **Camping, Touring and Holiday Parks**

Now available in all good bookshops and online at

www.hudsons.co.uk/shop

NEWQUAY, Cornwall   Map ref 1B2

The Park

Contact: Reservations, Bookings Team, The Park, Mawgan Porth, Cornwall TR8 4BD
T: (01637) 860322 **E:** info@mawganporth.co.uk
W: www.mawganporth.co.uk **£ BOOK ONLINE**

Units	60
Sleeps	2-12

PER UNIT PER WEEK
£425.00 - £3000.00

SPECIAL PROMOTIONS
Late availability
discount of 20%

Set within a rural location amidst 27 acres, yet only 400 metres from the beach. This unique venue offers all the luxury of a rural oasis whilst being close to all major roads and air links into the South West.

Facilities on site include heated indoor and outdoor swimming pools and award winning restaurant. Accommodation is an eclectic selection of eco-lodges, cottages and glamping.

Open: All year
Nearest Shop: Cornish Fresh supermarket
Nearest Pub: MerryMoor

Units: Units are from 1-6 bedrooms and some have hot-tubs and wood-burners.

Site: ✿ P **Payment:** 💷 **Leisure:** 🚴 🎣 🏌 **Property:** 🐕 📺 📶 💻 **Children:** 🐴 🛏 🚼
Unit: 📻 📺 💻 📶 📶 📺 📀 🍳 BBQ 📞

PADSTOW, Cornwall   Map ref 1B2

Honeysuckle Cottage

Contact: Debbie Clarke, Owner, Manor Croft, Colebrooke, Crediton, Devon EX17 5DL
T: (01363) 84292 / 07773 421807 **F:** 01363 84559 **E:** debbie@cchaulage.com
W: www.honeysucklecottagepadstow.co.uk

Units	1
Sleeps	1-5

PER UNIT PER WEEK
£350.00 - £925.00

Built on the site of the old doctors surgery in the heart of old Padstow, yet quietly situated and only a one minute level walk from the Harbour. Fully equipped, well furnished cottage with small garden and allocated parking. Electric central heating. Washer/dryer, dishwasher, fridge, freezer, microwave, hob/oven. Sleeps 4/5 in two bedrooms. Free Wi-fi. 3 star Gold Award. Linen hire available.
Open: All year **Nearest Shop:** 200 metres **Nearest Pub:** 100 metres

Site: ✿ P **Payment:** 💷 **Property:** 📺 📶 💻 **Children:** 🐴 🛏 **Unit:** 📻 📺 💻 📶 📶 📺 📀

PADSTOW, Cornwall   Map ref 1B2

Sunday & School Cottages

Contact: Mrs Diane Hoe, Owner, Sunday Cottages, Lower Cottage, Preston-on-Stour, Stratford on Avon, Warwickshire CV37 8NG **T:** (01789) 450214 **E:** di@sundaycottage.co.uk
W: www.sundaycottage.co.uk

Units	2
Sleeps	2-6

PER UNIT PER WEEK
£525.00 - £1360.00

Two beautiful and comfortable cottages in old Padstow. Minutes from harbour, shops and restaurants, and walking distance of beaches, coastal path, and beautiful unspoilt coastline. School Cottage boasts a lovely walled garden and wood burner for winter visits.

Both cottages have off road parking and Wi-Fi. We accept children of 8yrs and over. No pets allowed. Availability can be checked on www.sundaycottage.co.uk

Open: All year except January
Nearest Shop: 0.10 miles
Nearest Pub: 0.10 miles

Units: Sunday Cottage sleeps 4 in 2 bedrooms. School Cottage sleeps up to 6 in 3 bedrooms.

Site: ✿ P **Property:** / ▦ ▯ ▯ **Unit:** ▯ ▯ ▭ ▯ ⌖ TV ⑧ ◿ BBQ ☎

PADSTOW, Cornwall   Map ref 1B2

Trevose Golf & Country Club

Contact: Reservations, Trevose Golf & Country Club, Constantine Bay, Padstow PL28 8JB
T: (01841) 520208 **F:** 01841 521057 **E:** info@trevose-gc.co.uk
W: www.trevose-gc.co.uk **£ BOOK ONLINE**

Units	31
Sleeps	2-6

PER UNIT PER WEEK
£390.00 - £1260.00

SPECIAL PROMOTIONS
Please see our website for speacial offers.

High quality accommodation which can accommodate up to 130 people. A beautiful golf resort situated on the north Cornwall coastline with stunning views of the Atlantic, over which the accommodation looks as does the clubhouse and restaurant. Facilities include: 3 golf courses, outdoor pool, tennis courts, beauty room, children's play area, bar & restaurant. For full details view www.trevose-gc.co.uk or follow us on Twitter @TrevoseGC.

Open: All year
Nearest Shop: 0.25 miles
Nearest Pub: 1.5 miles

Site: ✿ P **Payment:** 💷 **Leisure:** ⚴ ♪ ⏻ ◓ ⌖ ⚘ **Property:** ⼮ ▦ ▯ ▯ **Children:** ⛺ ▥ ⼊
Unit: ▯ ▯ ▭ ⌖ TV ④ ⑧

PADSTOW, Cornwall Map ref 1B2

3★ - 4★ SELF CATERING

Units 5
Sleeps 1-8

PER UNIT PER WEEK
£350.00 - £1745.00

Yellow Sands Apartments & House

Contact: Martin Dakin, Proprietor, Harlyn Bay, Padstow, Cornwall PL28 8SE
T: (01208) 895022 **E:** m.dakin338@btinternet.com
W: www.yellowsands.net

Come relax on a balcony and enjoy our stunning sea views during your stay in our 4 Star self-catering family accommodation, just 200 metres from superb sandy beach and coastal footpath at Harlyn Bay near Padstow. With private footpath to the beach. We have 1, 2 and 3 bedroom Apartments and a detached 4 bedroom House with private garden, play area and parking on site. Thoroughly cleaned by ourselves. **Open:** All year **Nearest Shop:** 1.5 km
Nearest Pub: 200 metres

Site: ✿ P **Property:** 🖥 📶 **Children:** 🚸 **Unit:** 🛏 🍴 📺 📻 TV 📀 📞

PADSTOW, Cornwall Map ref 1B2

3★ - 4★ SELF CATERING **Gold AWARD**

Units 6
Sleeps 1-7

PER UNIT PER WEEK
£320.00 - £1010.00

SPECIAL PROMOTIONS
We offer Short Breaks from October through to end of April.

From £70 per night for minimum of 3 nights.

We are happy to discuss any tariffs on enquiry.

Yellow Sands Cottages

Contact: Sharon Keast, Proprietor, Yellow Sands, Harlyn Bay, Padstow, Cornwall PL28 8SE
T: (01637) 881548 **E:** keast3@btinternet.com
W: www.yellowsands.co.uk

Yellow Sands Cottages are situated just 250 metres from one of North Cornwall's beautiful sandy beaches - Harlyn Bay - access to the shore is via a private pathway through the garden at Yellow Sands or just a short stroll down the road to the bridge, where there is level access, together with the Harlyn Inn, Harlyn Surf school and on a good day, Kelly's ice cream!

Padstow is also close by, just a short 5 minute drive from Harlyn or a public bus trip. Yellow Sands is in an idyllic location - and being local proprietors for over 40 years, we can be there if you need us. A base to visit the County.

Open: All Year
Nearest Shop: 1 mile
Nearest Pub: 250 metres

Units: Our holiday cottages are all ground level with parking adjacent, well kept gardens, high quality fixtures and fittings. Well maintained and serviced.

Site: ✿ P **Leisure:** ⚑ **Property:** 🐕 📶 🖥 📶 **Children:** 🚸 🍴 🧍 **Unit:** 🛏 🍴 📺 🔌 TV 📀 BBQ 📞

POLZEATH, Cornwall Map ref 1B2

★★★★ SELF CATERING

Units 1
Sleeps 6-8

PER UNIT PER WEEK
£450.00 - £1000.00

Trehenlie

Contact: Gary King, Owner, 16 Tinners Way, New Polzeath, Cornwall PL27 6UH
T: 07929 207518 **E:** bookings@trehenlie.com
W: www.trehenlie.com

A large, attractive, three double bedroomed detached bungalow. Only 5 minutes walk to the beautiful, sandy beaches of Polzeath that offer surfing, beach fun & glorious coastal walks. Trehenlie is furnished and equipped to Four Star VisitEngland quality standards. Full details and can be found on the website. A great location to relax in or use as a base to explore all the wonders of Cornwall. **Open:** All year **Nearest Shop:** 0.3 miles **Nearest Pub:** 0.5 miles

Site: ✿ P **Property:** ✎ 🐕 📶 🖥 📶 **Children:** 🚸 **Unit:** 🛏 🍴 📺 📻 TV ⊛ 📀

PORT ISAAC, Cornwall   Map ref 1B2

Green Door Cottages Port Gaverne

Contact: Port Gaverne, Port Isaac, Cornwall PL29 3SQ **T:** (01305) 789000
E: enquiries@greendoorcottages.co.uk
W: www.greendoorcottages.co.uk **£ BOOK ONLINE**

Units	10
Sleeps	2-8

PER UNIT PER WEEK
£309.00 - £1432.00

SPECIAL PROMOTIONS
Short Breaks available all year (except May half term, July & August. Please see website for current offers.

Nestling in the beautiful, secluded cove of Port Gaverne are the Green Door Cottages. All have achieved Visit England's 4* Gold rating. The tastefully restored 18th Century fishermen's cottages and Tregudda Apartments, sit a stone's throw from the beach which is owned by the National Trust; directly opposite is our local, the historic Port Gaverne Inn and the hustle and bustle of picturesque Port Isaac is only half a mile away.

The 8 cottages are situated around a private sheltered courtyard, perfect for barbeques or soaking up the sun. They all offer tasteful and comfortable décor, full self-catering facilities, Wi-Fi, flat screen TVs & iPod docks and we provide body boards and fishing nets for the kids – ideal for the ultimate day on the beach! Pets welcome.

Open: All Year
Nearest Shop: 1/2 mile
Nearest Pub: On site

Units: There are 8 Cottages: Venus, Marigold, Torca, Courtyard, Rose, Jasmine, Rashleigh and Thrift. Our two apartments are: Upper Trequdda & Lower Tregudda

Site: ✿ P **Payment:** 💷 **Leisure:** ♪ ▶ **Property:** ✎ 🐕 🛏 🗄 🖵 **Children:** 🚼 🛏 🎠
Unit: 🖥 🖥 🖵 🖥 🗄 📺 🖥 🖉 BBQ

PORTHTOWAN, Cornwall   Map ref 1B3

Rosehill Lodges

Contact: Mr John Barrow, Rosehill Lodges, Porthtowan, Cornwall TR4 8AR
T: (01209) 891920 **F:** 01209 891935 **E:** reception@rosehilllodges.com
W: www.rosehilllodges.com **£ BOOK ONLINE**

Units	10
Sleeps	1-6

PER UNIT PER WEEK
£508.00 - £1854.00

SPECIAL PROMOTIONS
Weekend and mid-week breaks available. Luxury upgrade package available for weddings, honeymoons and special occasions. See website for special offers and promotions.

Five star gold award, bespoke, self-catering lodges right on the Cornish coast. Situated in the coastal village of Porthtowan just five minutes walk to a sandy blue flag beach, bars and restaurants. Relax, leave your car behind. Each lodge is fully equipped and features super-king size beds, log burners, a hot tub spa and free Wi-Fi. Go green with our grass roofs and solar panels and dine al-fresco under glass covered decking whatever the weather. Each lodge has an external drench shower, ideal for washing down after a fun day on the beach. We look forward to giving you a warm welcome for your holiday.

Open: All year
Nearest Shop: 0.5 miles
Nearest Pub: 0.5 miles

Units: Bespoke timber eco lodges, built locally in our village, with materials from sustainable sources. Luxury and green better together.

Site: ✿ P **Payment:** 💷 **Leisure:** ♨ ♪ ▶ ↻ **Property:** 🛏 🗄 🖵 **Children:** 🚼 🛏 🎠
Unit: 🖥 🖥 🖵 🖥 🗄 📺 💿 🖥 🖉 BBQ 📞

For **key to symbols** see page 7

REDRUTH, Cornwall Map ref 1B3

Units   1
Sleeps   4
PER UNIT PER WEEK
£314.00 - £620.00

The Barn at Little Trefula

Contact: Ann & Bill Higgins, Owners, Little Trefula Farm, Trefula, Redruth, Cornwall
TR16 5ET **T:** (01209) 820572 / 07789 044602 **E:** barn@trefula.com
W: www.trefula.com/barn **£ BOOK ONLINE**

Situated in Cornwall's heritage mining area, yet surrounded by open fields, the Barn at Little Trefula's reverse level layout offers panoramic rural views. Trefula is near both coasts with harbours and swimming/surfing beaches and is well positioned for visiting the famous National Trust properties and attractions such as The Eden Project and St Ives Tate. **Nearest Shop:** 1km **Nearest Pub:** 300m

Site: ❀ P **Property:** ⫽ 🐕 🖵 🗐 🖳 **Children:** 🛝 🏭 ⚲ **Unit:** 🗐 📺 🗐 📶 📺 📀 BBQ

REDRUTH, Cornwall Map ref 1B3

Units   5
Sleeps   2-6
PER UNIT PER WEEK
£300.00 - £895.00

Trengove Farm Cottages

Contact: Lindsey Richards, Proprietor, Trengove Farm, Cot Road, Illogan, Redruth
TR16 4PU **T:** (01209) 843008 **E:** mail@trengovefarm.co.uk
W: www.trengovefarm.co.uk **£ BOOK ONLINE**

A traditional courtyard of charming well-equipped cottages, full of character, in the peace of the countryside, but close to the stunning coastline and golden sandy beaches. Beautiful walks, cycle trails and country park nearby. A convenient location for sightseeing. Shops, pubs and beach 1 mile. Central heating and free Wi-Fi. **Open:** All year **Nearest Shop:** 1 mile **Nearest Pub:** 1 mile

Site: ❀ P **Payment:** € **Leisure:** ▶ **Property:** 🖵 🗐 🖳 **Children:** 🏭 ⚲ **Unit:** 🗐 🖳 📺 🗐 📶 📺 📀 ⌀ BBQ

SEATON, Cornwall Map ref 1C2

Units   25
Sleeps   2-4
PER UNIT PER WEEK
£343.00 - £980.00

Mount Brioni Holiday Apartments

Contact: Roger & Cathy Stamp, Resident Owners, Mount Brioni, Looe Hill, Seaton, Nr Looe,
Cornwall PL11 3JN **T:** (01503) 250251 **E:** holidays@mountbrioni.co.uk
W: www.mountbrioni.co.uk **£ BOOK ONLINE**

Delightful cluster of 25 self catering apartments on quiet coastline of south Cornwall, near Looe. Luxury 3 & 4 star gold accommodation with free high speed broadband, superb sea views. Beach and ocean just yards away. Special offers always available. **Open:** All year **Nearest Shop:** 0.10 miles **Nearest Pub:** 0.10 miles

Site: ❀ P **Payment:** 💷 € **Leisure:** ♪ ▶ ∪ **Property:** 🐕 🖵 🗐 🖳 **Children:** 🛝 🏭 ⚲ **Unit:** 🗐 🖳 📺 🗐 📶 📺 📀 BBQ

Sign up for our newsletter

Visit our website to sign up for our e-newsletter and receive regular information on events, articles, exclusive competitions and new publications.
www.visitor-guides.co.uk

South West - Cornwall

ST. AUSTELL, Cornwall   Map ref 1B3

Units 34
Sleeps 2-8

PER UNIT PER WEEK
£473.00 - £2426.00

SPECIAL PROMOTIONS
Offers only available at
www.naturalretreats.
com

Natural Retreats - Trewhiddle
Contact: Natural Retreats, Trewhiddle Park, Pentewan Rd, St Austell, Cornwall PL26 7AD
T: (01625) 416 430 **E:** info@naturalretreats.com
W: www.naturalretreats.com **£ BOOK ONLINE**

Set in a peaceful countryside valley, these luxurious 2, 3 and 4 bedroom self-catering cottages and villas offer privacy and picturesque scenery, yet are ideally located. Trewhiddle is just two miles from Porthpean Beach and three miles from Pentewan Sands, a short drive from Eden Project and Lost Gardens of Heligan, and a stone's throw from the charming towns of Mevagissey and Charlestown. The villas boast spacious and modern interiors, rated Five Star by Visit England. Guests can also discover a private outdoor children's play area, farmland walks and cycling trails all on their doorstep.

Open: All year
Nearest Shop: 1.2 miles
Nearest Pub: 1.6 miles

Units: Spacious and modern villas and cottages. Pets welcome upon arrangement. Properties boast luxurious interiors, private outdoor space and parking.

ST. AUSTELL, Cornwall   Map ref 1B3

Units 1
Sleeps 1-6
PER UNIT PER WEEK
£245.00 - £790.00

The Old Inn, Pentewan
Contact: Mr & Mrs Robert Haskins, 19 Ullswater Drive, Wetherby LS22 6YF
T: (01937) 580217 / 07802 819409 **E:** rjhaskins@gmail.com
W: www.inncornwall.com

Stone cottage near beach in quiet location, in area of outstanding beauty. Close to Mevagissey (2 miles), the Lost Gardens of Heligan (2 miles) and The Eden Project (7 miles). Once an alehouse for visiting sailors, now a modern 3-star self-catering unit. It retains its character with low beams, pictures and open fireplace. Pentewan has a pub, Post Office stores and restaurant. Country walks. **Open:** All year **Nearest Shop:** 500 yards **Nearest Pub:** 200 yards

ST. COLUMB, Cornwall   Map ref 1B2

Units 2
Sleeps 1-8
PER UNIT PER WEEK
£520.00 - £1250.00

Cornish Holiday Lodges
Contact: Kelly Sharman, Cornish Holiday Lodges - Aspen and Enderley lodges, Retallack Resort & Spa, Winnards Perch, St Columb Major, Cornwall TR9 6DE
T: (01213) 084511 **E:** info@cornishholidaylodges.co.uk **W:** cornishholidaylodges.co.uk

Aspen and Enderley Holiday Lodges are purpose built luxury Scandinavian style self catering lodges in Cornwall. The interiors are exceptionally spacious, remarkably comfortable and beautifully decorated to ensure a relaxing holiday. Set in a rural retreat of the Retallack Resort and Spa a 5* family site with many facilities inc: pool, gym, spa, tennis, golf, bar and restaurant. **Open:** All year

ST. COLUMB, Cornwall Map ref 1B2

Meadow Rise

Contact: Mrs Helen Grimsey, Proprietor, Cornish Holiday, 24 Valley Mead, Anna Valley, Andover SP11 7SB **T:** (07881) 623483 **F:** 01264 335527 **E:** enquiries@cornishholiday.info
W: cornishholiday.info **£ BOOK ONLINE**

Cosy modern 2 bedroomed house in a quiet village location. An ideal base for all sightseeing and beach holidays. Padstow and Newquay less than 10 miles away. **Open:** All year **Nearest Shop:** 0.30 miles **Nearest Pub:** 0.5 miles

Units   1
Sleeps   1-4
PER UNIT PER WEEK
£220.00 - £525.00

Site: ✿ P Payment: 🖳 Leisure: ♿ 🎵 Property: 🔲 🔳 Children: 🔨 Unit: 🔲 🔳 🔲 🔳 🔲 TV 🔲 BBQ

ST. IVES, Cornwall Map ref 1B3

The Apartment, Porthminster Beach

Contact: Alan Hocking, Flat A, Primrose Court, Primrose Valley, St. Ives, Cornwall TR26 2ED
T: 07739 713876 **E:** info@theapartmentstives.com
W: www.homeaway.co.uk/p1005767 **£ BOOK ONLINE**

Luxury 2 bed, 2 bath apartment with sea views, parking and outside terrace. The Apartment is a calm beach retreat perched above Porthminster Beach. Enjoy the boutique style of a hotel with all the comfort and freedom of home. GOLD Award by Visit Britain Quality in Tourism. Master bedroom opens onto private terrace with sweeping sea views. SkyHD, cinema system, wireless broadband. **Open:** All year **Nearest Shop:** 300 metres **Nearest Pub:** 100 metres

Units   1
Sleeps   1-4
PER UNIT PER WEEK
£595.00 - £1680.00

Site: P Payment: 🖳 Leisure: ⛳ ✎ Property: ∥ 🖳 🔲 🔳 Children: 🔨 🎠 ⚟ Unit: 🔲 🔳 🔲 🔳 🔲 TV 🔲

ST. IVES, Cornwall Map ref 1B3

Cheriton Self Catering

Contact: Mr Alec Luke, Owner, Cheriton House, Market Place, St Ives TR26 1RZ
T: (01736) 795083 **E:** alec@cheritonselfcatering.com
W: www.cheritonselfcatering.com

In the centre of beautiful St Ives. Five nice flats and three traditional fisherman's cottages 25 yards from harbour & beach. Also one large flat on Porthminster Point with outstanding views and situated in beautiful gardens. All with parking. Clean and well equipped. Flats sleep two to four. Cottages up to five persons. Short breaks available 'off-season' Oct - May. **Open:** All Year **Nearest Shop:** 20 yards **Nearest Pub:** 20 yards

Units   8
Sleeps   1-5
PER UNIT PER WEEK
£295.00 - £750.00

Site: P Payment: € Property: 🔳 Children: 🔨 🎠 Unit: 🔲 🔲 🔳 TV 🔲

ST. IVES, Cornwall Map ref 1B3

St Nicholas Court, St Ives

Contact: Peter and Margaret Williams, Breentan Ltd, Timberline, Hookwood Lane, Ampfield, Romsey SO51 9BZ **T:** (023) 8026 7939 **E:** peter@stnicholascourt.plus.com
W: www.stnicholascourt.com

Five flats and penthouses in this superb block within great location near the beaches with spacious interior layout, superior internal furnishings and fittings. Each of the flats has one, two or three double bedrooms, kitchen, lounge and dining area. Colour TV, video, dishwasher, microwave and regular cookers. Covered garage space is provided for each flat. All beds have interior sprung mattresses. Bed linen is provided. No pets allowed. **Open:** All year **Nearest Shop:** 100 metres **Nearest Pub:** 300 metres

Units   5
Sleeps   2-8
PER UNIT PER WEEK
£465.00 - £2100.00

Site: P Property: 🖳 🔲 🔳 Children: 🔨 🎠 ⚟ Unit: 🔲 🔳 🔲 🔳 🔲 TV 🔲

ST. IVES, Cornwall   Map ref 1B3

SELF CATERING ★★★★

Units 4
Sleeps 2-6
PER UNIT PER WEEK
£240.00 - £810.00

Trevalgan Holiday Farm

Contact: Mrs Melanie Osborne, Trevalgan Holiday Farm, Little Trevalgan, Trevalgan Farm, St Ives, Cornwall TR26 3BJ **T:** (01736) 796529 / 07709 098167 **E:** holidays@trevalgan.co.uk **W:** www.trevalgan.co.uk **£ BOOK ONLINE**

Expect excellent accommodation, breathtaking scenery and a warm welcome on this family farm. Cottages are child-friendly, decorated, furnished and equipped to a very high standard. Why choose between a beach holiday and a countryside holiday when you can have both? With St Ives just a 5 minute drive our location is ideal for both families and couples to explore wonderful West Cornwall. **Open:** All year **Nearest Shop:** 1.5 miles **Nearest Pub:** 1.5 miles

Site: ❋ P Leisure: 🏊 ♨ ∪ ✎ Property: 🐕 🚲 📶 🖥 Children: 🐎 🏓 ☂ Unit: 🚪 📺 🍴 📺 📀 BBQ

TINTAGEL, Cornwall   Map ref 1B2

SELF CATERING ★★★

Units 4
Sleeps 2-5
PER UNIT PER WEEK
£272.00 - £872.00

Halgabron Mill Holiday Cottages

Contact: Robin Evans, Manager, The Keep, Halgabron Mill, St. Nectan's Glen, Tintagel, Cornwall PL34 0BB **T:** (01840) 779099 **E:** Robin@halgabronmill.co.uk **W:** www.halgabronmill.co.uk

Four well-equipped character stone cottages, with exposed beams and lead latticed windows, surround a former 18th century Water Mill. Situated in St. Nectan's Glen - a densely, wooded valley between Tintagel and Boscastle villages. Coastpath is 10 min walk. Closest Beaches are a 10 min walk or 5 min drive. **Open:** All Year (Millstream Cottage Easter-Oct). **Nearest Shop:** 1 mile **Nearest Pub:** 1 mile

Site: ❋ P Property: 🖥 Children: 🏓 ☂ Unit: 🚪 📶 📺 🍴 📺 ④ 🍴 ✎

TRURO, Cornwall   Map ref 1B3

SELF CATERING ★★★★★ **Gold AWARD**

Units 46
Sleeps 2-6
PER UNIT PER WEEK
£490.00 - £2195.00

The Valley

Contact: Meg, Resort Manager, Bissoe Road, Carnon Downs, Truro TR3 6LQ **T:** (01872) 862194 **F:** 01872 864343 **E:** info@the-valley.co.uk **W:** thevalleycornwall.co.uk **£ BOOK ONLINE**

The Valley...Cornwall at its best. Modern and tasteful self-catering accommodation with a personal service and great facilities. Pools, fitness suite, tennis, squash and stylish restaurant all situated in beautiful countryside. **Open:** All year **Nearest Shop:** 0.5 miles **Nearest Pub:** 0.5 miles

Site: ❋ P Payment: 💷 Leisure: 🏊 ▶ ✎ ⛷ ⚓ ✎ Property: ✂ 🐕 🚲 🖥 Children: 🐎 🏓 ☂ Unit: 🚪 🛁 📶 📺 🍴 📺 📀

Book your accommodation online

Visit our websites for detailed information, up-to-date availability and to book your accommodation online. Includes over 20,000 places to stay, all of them star rated.
www.visitor-guides.co.uk

WADEBRIDGE, *Cornwall* Map ref 1B2

St Moritz Self Catering

Contact: Reception, St Moritz, St Moritz Self Catering, Trebetherick, Wadebridge, Cornwall PL27 6SD **T:** (01208) 862242 **E:** reception@stmoritzhotel.co.uk
W: www.stmoritzhotel.co.uk **£ BOOK ONLINE**

Units 46
Sleeps 1-8

PER UNIT PER WEEK
£630.00 - £4900.00

The St Moritz Apartments and Garden Villas are situated near Rock, where the Camel Estuary meets the swell of the Atlantic Ocean. They are in the perfect setting whatever the season. Polzeath surfing beach is just down the coast path and Padstow is just a short ferry ride away.

With both indoor and outdoor pools, a gymnasium, an award winning restaurant, bar and a Cowshed Spa on site, the St Moritz has something to suit everyone.

Open: 24/7. 365 days
Nearest Shop: 200 metres
Nearest Pub: On site

Site: ✿ P **Payment:** 💳 **Leisure:** ➤ ⚓ ⟋ ⤳ ⚲ **Property:** ⫽ 🖥 🏢 🖼 **Children:** 🐎 🏠 🎣
Unit: 🗄 🗄 📺 🗄 🍴 TV 🔲 DVD BBQ 📞

WADEBRIDGE, *Cornwall* Map ref 1B2

Great Bodieve Farm Barns

Contact: Mrs Thelma Riddle, Bodieve, Wadebridge, Cornwall PL27 6EG **T:** (01208) 814916
E: enquiries@great-bodieve.co.uk
W: www.great-bodieve.co.uk

Units 4
Sleeps 2-8

PER UNIT PER WEEK
£200.00 - £1460.00

Relax in one of our luxury cottages in beautiful North Cornwall less than 1 mile from Wadebridge, on the B3314 towards Rock and Polzeath. 4 cottages in a rural setting with plenty of parking and free Wi-Fi. Spacious rooms. Well behaved dogs welcome. Close to the wonderful Camel Trail. 'The Mill House' Sleeps 8 plus cot. Spacious and stylish with four en suite bedrooms, two king-size and two twin. **Open:** All year **Nearest Shop:** 1 mile
Nearest Pub: 0.5 miles

Site: ✿ P **Leisure:** 🚲 ➤ **Property:** 🐾 🖥 🏢 🖼 **Children:** 🐎 🏠 🎣 **Unit:** 🗄 🗄 🗄 🍴 TV DVD 🧺 BBQ

WADEBRIDGE, *Cornwall* Map ref 1B2

Tregolls Farm Cottages

Contact: Mrs Marilyn Hawkey, Tregolls Farm Cottages, St Wenn, Bodmin PL30 5PG
T: (01208) 812154 **E:** tregollsfarm@btclick.com
W: www.tregollsfarm.co.uk. **£ BOOK ONLINE**

Units 4
Sleeps 2-8

PER UNIT PER WEEK
£325.00 - £980.00

Well-equipped holiday cottage, tastefully converted from redundant stone barns. Charming, mellow oak beams, slate window sills, log fires and wonderful views of the open countryside with fields of cows and sheep grazing and a stream meandering through the valley. Pets corner, games room, farm trail and barbeques. **Open:** All year **Nearest Shop:** 4 miles
Nearest Pub: 4 miles

Site: ✿ P **Payment:** 💳 **Leisure:** 🚲 🎵 ⚓ **Property:** 🖥 🖼 **Children:** 🐎 🏠 🎣 **Unit:** 🗄 🗄 📺 TV 🔲 DVD 🧺 BBQ

ST MARY'S, Isles of Scilly   Map ref 1A3

2★ - 3★ SELF CATERING

Units 2
Sleeps 1-7
PER UNIT PER WEEK
£450.00 - £1000.00

3 & 4 Well Cross

Contact: Ms Marlene Burton, Owner, Treboeth House, St Mary's, Isles of Scilly TR21 0HX
T: (01720) 422548 **E:** info@treboethguesthouse.vpweb.co.uk
W: www.treboethguesthouse.vpweb.co.uk

Situated close to shops and town centre, few hundred yards to the beach. Easy walking distance to harbour. Sky TV available.
Open: March - October **Nearest Shop:** 0.5 miles
Nearest Pub: Less than 0.5 miles

Site: ✿ P Leisure: 🏊 ♪ ⚲ ∪ ✎ Property: 🐕 🎱 🖥 Children: 🛏 🏠 ⚹ Unit: 🗄 💻 🎱 TV 🕕 DVD 🧺

ST MARY'S, Isles Of Scilly   Map ref 1A3

★★★ SELF CATERING

Gold AWARD

Units 1
Sleeps 2
PER UNIT PER WEEK
£340.00 - £465.00

Dunmallard - Lower Flat

Contact: Mr & Mrs Elliot, Owners, 2 Greenhill Mead, Pesters Lane, Somerton TA11 7AB
T: (01458) 272971

Comfortable, quiet ground floor near the seafront, harbour, shops and local amenities. Non-smoking. No pets. The flat has been owned by the the family for more than 25 years. This experience and our in-depth knowledge of Scilly has enabled us to provide everything that will help our visitors enjoy their holiday. Our 3* 'Gold Award' recognises that we offer fairly special accommodation. We like to have personal contact with our visitors and will be pleased to send you a brochure and booking form and answer any queries in a phone call. **Open:** Easter - October
Nearest Shop: 0.5 miles **Nearest Pub:** 0.5 miles

Property: 🖥 Children: 🛏 Unit: 🗄 💻 🎱 TV

ST MARY'S, Isles Of Scilly   Map ref 1A3

★★★ SELF CATERING

Units 1
Sleeps 2-4
PER UNIT PER WEEK
£415.00 - £825.00

No 9 Harbour Lights

Contact: A. Athawes, Manager, Homeview Cottages Ltd., Thorofare, St Mary's, Isles of Scilly, Cornwall TR21 0JN **T:** (01634) 290 210 **E:** aathawes@convar.co.uk
W: www.stayonscilly.co.uk

Attractive apartment refurbished 2009/10. Accommodates 4 people. Adjacent to the harbour beach, town centre amenities and island ferries and tours. **Open:** All year except Christmas and New Year **Nearest Shop:** 50 yards **Nearest Pub:** 50 yards

Property: ⁄ 📺 🎱 🖥 Unit: 💻 TV

ST MARY'S, Isles of Scilly   Map ref 1A3

★★★★ SELF CATERING

Units 1
Sleeps 4-8
PER UNIT PER WEEK
£1600.00 - £1800.00

Trevean Holidays

Contact: Mrs Rosemary Sharman, Owner, Trevean, Robinswood Farm, Bere Regis, Wareham, Dorset BH20 7JJ **T:** (01929) 471210 / (01929) 472181 **F:** 01929 472182
E: info@sharmanfencing.co.uk **W:** www.ownersdirect.co.uk/england/e622.htm

Trevean is a large, spacious granite town house, sleeps 8 with 4 double bedrooms each with vanity unit. Living accommodation on the top floor with views over the harbour. Central Heating and Sky+ TV. Utility room. Easy walking to shops, restaurants and off island boats. Ideal for all the extended family to get together for a holiday and enjoy the beautiful islands. Beaches two minutes from door.
Open: Easter - October and Christmas/New Year **Nearest Shop:** 2 mins **Nearest Pub:** 0.10 miles

Leisure: 🏊 ♪ ⚲ ∪ Property: 🎱 🖥 Children: 🛏 🏠 ⚹ Unit: 🗄 🖨 💻 🎱 🕕 TV 🕕 DVD

For **key to symbols** see page 7

BIGBURY-ON-SEA, Devon   Map ref 1C3

Apartment 5, Burgh Island Causeway

Contact: Mr John Smith, Apartment 5, Burgh Island Causeway, Mill Street, Chagford, Devon TQ13 8AW **T:** (01647) 433593 **F:** 01647 433694 **E:** help@helpfulholidays.com
W: www.burghislandcauseway.com **£ BOOK ONLINE**

Units 1
Sleeps 1-6

PER UNIT PER WEEK
£475.00 - £1750.00

SPECIAL PROMOTIONS
Bargain weekend and short-stay breaks available in autumn and winter months.

Luxury, modern, ground-floor apartment set into cliff with panoramic southerly views from large patio. Facilities include pool, gym, sauna, cafe/bar, grassy cliff-top grounds and direct access to beautiful large sandy beach and coastal path. Popular for surfing and near golf course and village shop/post office. View www.burghislandcauseway.com. Free Broadband.

Open: All year
Nearest Shop: 2 miles
Nearest Pub: 0.30 miles

Units: 1 double en suite bathroom, 1 twin en suite shower & sofa bed.

Site: ✿ P **Payment:** 💷 **Leisure:** 🏊 ⛳ 🎣 **Property:** 🐾 📺 📶 **Children:** 🐎 🛏 🧒
Unit: 📻 🍴 📺 🖥 ☎ 📺 💿 📀 BBQ 📞

BRIXHAM, Devon   Map ref 1D2

Harbour Reach

Contact: Jenny Pocock, Owner, 83 North View Road, Brixham TQ5 9TS **T:** (01142) 364761
E: enquiries@harbourreachholidays.co.uk
W: www.harbourreachholidays.co.uk

Units 2
Sleeps 1-11

PER UNIT PER WEEK
£230.00 - £590.00

The amazing views across the harbour, Torbay and out to sea, make this a perfect holiday home at any time of year. Harbour Reach is excellently furnished and equipped and divided into a maisonette and flat which are let separately or jointly thereby sleeping 1 to 11. We are within 10 minutes walk of the harbour side, town and South West costal footpath. Short breaks available from October to March. **Open:** All year including Christmas & New Year. **Nearest Shop:** 500 metres **Nearest Pub:** 200 metres

Site: P **Property:** 🐾 📺 📶 **Children:** 🐎 🛏 🧒 **Unit:** 📻 🍴 📺 🖥 📺 💿

COMBE MARTIN, Devon   Map ref 1C1

Wheel Farm Cottages

Contact: Berry Down, Combe Martin, North Devon EX34 0NT **T:** (03301) 230 374
E: enquiries@csmaclubretreats.co.uk
W: www.wheelfarmcottages.co.uk

Units 11
Sleeps 2-8

PER UNIT PER WEEK
£413.00 - £2891.00

A collection of beautiful stone built cottages, Wheel Farm is the perfect choice for a hideaway self-catering country cottage break. The cottages themselves are set in an 'Area of Outstanding Natural Beauty' only a few miles from some of the finest beaches and Exmoor's spectacular coastline. This hidden gem of a retreat also boasts a heated indoor pool with sauna and an outdoor tennis court. **Open:** From 17th Jan throughout 2015 **Nearest Shop:** 1.5 miles **Nearest Pub:** 1.5 miles

Site: ✿ P **Payment:** 💷 **Leisure:** 🎣 🎾 **Property:** 🚶 🐾 📺 📶 **Children:** 🐎 🛏 🧒 **Unit:** 📻 🍴 📺 🖥 📺 💿 BBQ 📞

The Official Tourist Board Guide to **Self Catering 2015**

CREDITON, Devon   Map ref 1D2

Units 1
Sleeps 1-2

PER UNIT PER WEEK
£200.00 - £500.00

SPECIAL PROMOTIONS
Short breaks available, bookings commence on Friday, other start days can be accommodated out of season and for short breaks.

Swallows at Falkedon

Contact: Helen Ford, Owner, Falkedon, Spreyton, Crediton, Devon EX17 5EF
T: (01647) 231526 / 07768 342 578   **E:** Helen@falkedon.net
W: www.falkedon.co.uk   **£ BOOK ONLINE**

Swallows holiday apartment, near Dartmoor, part of a Grade II listed property, situated three miles from the A30 and one mile from Spreyton. Close to the centre of Devon, it is in an ideal position to both relax and unwind and to be active walking or cycling.

Explore the North and South Devon coasts, a day trip to Cornwall and of course the beautiful Dartmoor National Park. The cathedral city of Exeter is half an hour drive to the east. Falkedon is set in a quiet position surrounded by the rolling Devon countryside. The apartment is approached via stone steps with its own entrance.

Open: All year
Nearest Shop: 0.8 miles
Nearest Pub: 1 mile

Units: All on one level, large separate bathroom and bedroom, super king bed, can be two singles, state at booking. Separate lounge, kitchen/diner.

Site: P Property: 🐾 ☕ 🖥 **Children:** 🏚 **Unit:** 🛁 ▥ 🍳 📺 📀 BBQ

CROYDE, Devon   Map ref 1C1

Units 1
Sleeps 2-6
PER UNIT PER WEEK
£750.00 - £1825.00

4 Out of the Blue

Contact: Mr David Royden, Owner, 4 Out of the blue, Moor Lane, Croyde, North Devon EX33 1FF **T:** 07711 026889 **E:** david@outoftheblue-croyde.co.uk
W: www.outoftheblue-croyde.co.uk **£ BOOK ONLINE**

The house is right on edge of stunning beach at Croyde Bay on North Devon Coast. It offers luxury five star accommodation in form of a large open plan kitchen/dining /living room, shower room and on first floor three bedrooms and two bathrooms.
However the main attraction is the wonderful south facing views. The sandy bay has something for everyone; surf, rock pools, lovely walks and great pubs **Open:** All Year

Site: ❀ **P Payment:** 💳 **Leisure:** ▶ **Property:** 🖥 ☕ 🖥 **Children:** 🏚 🏚 🎅 **Unit:** 🛁 🛁 ▥ 🍳 📺 📀 BBQ 📞

CULLOMPTON, Devon   Map ref 1D2

Units 1
Sleeps 13
PER UNIT PER WEEK
£1000.00 - £4500.00

Wayside House

Contact: Melanie Alford, Blackdown Luxury Lettings, Hackpen Hill, Blackbourgh, Cullompton, Devon EX15 2HX **T:** (01884) 849127 **E:** mel@blackdownluxurylettings.co.uk
W: www.blackdownluxurylettings.co.uk **£ BOOK ONLINE**

The Virginia creeper-covered traditional red-brick and slate roof exterior hides a stunningly contemporary interior to this beautiful modern farmhouse. Sleeping up to 13 people with large games room, outdoor play equipment and covered heated swimming pool, this property has it all. Set on its own with the most fantastic views across to the Blackdown Hills, its ideal for the perfect family holiday. **Open:** All year **Nearest Shop:** 1 mile **Nearest Pub:** 1 mile

Site: ❀ **P Payment:** 💳 **Leisure:** 🎵 ▶ ∪ ☂ **Property:** 🖥 ☕ 🖥 **Children:** 🏚 🏚 🎅 **Unit:** 🛁 🛁 ▥ 🍳 📺 📀 BBQ

DARTMOUTH, Devon   Map ref 1D3

Units   1
Sleeps   6

PER UNIT PER WEEK
£480.00 - £1018.00

Ferry View

Contact: Sarah Hammett, 31 Newcomen Road, Dartmouth, Devon TQ6 9BN
T: (01392) 461268 / 07870 655880 **E:** jarvishayes@btopenworld.com
W: www.ferryviewdartmouth.co.uk

Character town house with magnificent uninterrupted views over the estuary towards Kingswear and out to sea. Lovely position virtually on the level in the heart of Dartmouth. On road parking outside of house, but restricted April - Oct. All year round parking permit for the Mayor's Avenue Car park, 3 mins walk. Free Wi-Fi.
Open: All year **Nearest Shop:** 200 yards **Nearest Pub:** 100 yards

Property: 🔲 🗎 **Children:** 🐴 🛏 🚶 **Unit:** 🗎 🗎 📺 🗎 🗎 📺 📀

DARTMOUTH, Devon   Map ref 1D3

Units   4
Sleeps   2-6

PER UNIT PER WEEK
£345.00 - £775.00

The Old Bakehouse

Contact: Mrs Sylvia Ridalls, The Old Bakehouse, 7 Broadstone, Dartmouth TQ6 9NR
T: (01803) 834585 **F:** 01803 834585 **E:** oldbakehousecottages@yahoo.com
W: www.oldbakehousedartmouth.co.uk

Character cottages beams and old stone fireplaces. Two minutes from historic town centre and river. Beach 15 minutes drive. Free parking. Dogs free. Non smoking. Wi-Fi. Flat-screen TV/DVD with Freeview. Washing machines in all cottages and dishwashers in two. Spring, Autumn and Winter short breaks available. Reduced rates for OAPs Sept 1st - June 30th. Phone for Winter offers and more information. **Open:** All year
Nearest Shop: 0.10 miles **Nearest Pub:** 0.10 miles

Site: 🅿 **Payment:** 💳 **Leisure:** 🎵 🚶 **Property:** 🐴 🔲 🗎 🗎 **Children:** 🐴 🛏 🚶 **Unit:** 🗎 📺 🗎 📺 📀

DAWLISH, Devon   Map ref 1D2

Units   17
Sleeps   4-6

PER UNIT PER WEEK
£375.00 - £1060.00

SPECIAL PROMOTIONS
Special offers and short breaks are available early and late season. Free coarse fishing on site between November and February. Latest offers available via our website.

Cofton Country Holidays

Contact: Starcross, Nr Dawlish, Exeter, Devon EX6 8RP **T:** (01626) 890111 **F:** 01626 890160
E: info@coftonholidays.co.uk
W: www.coftonholidays.co.uk **£ BOOK ONLINE**

Twelve cottages and five luxury apartments, located either on our main holiday park or nearby on the Eastdon Estate. Cottages are converted from original farm buildings and apartments within the 18th century Georgian house. Enjoy views of the Exe Estuary and have acres of countryside to explore. Facilities on the park include swimming pools, indoor leisure complex, shop, takeaway, cafe & bar.

Open: All year
Nearest Shop: 0.10 miles
Nearest Pub: 0.10 miles

Units: Each cottage is individual and comprises of 2 or 3 bedrooms sleeping a maximum of 6 people. Units are fully equipped including bed linen & towels.

Site: ♻ 🅿 **Payment:** 💳 **Leisure:** 🏊 🎵 ⛱ 🎣 🚴 🏹 **Property:** 🔲 🗎 🗎 **Children:** 🐴 🛏 🚶
Unit: 🗎 🗎 📺 🗎 📺 📀

DAWLISH, Devon   Map ref 1D2

Units   1
Sleeps   2-6
PER UNIT PER WEEK
£345.00 - £605.00

Little Mermaid Cottage

Contact: 3 King Street, Dawlish, Devon EX7 9LG **T:** (01626) 863881
E: info@littlemermaidcottage.com
W: www.littlemermaidcottage.com

The Little Mermaid holiday cottage is over 200 years old and will accommodate 6 people comfortably. It is situated in the centre of town and it offers a spacious lounge with digital TV, dining room which has a double bed futon, galley kitchen which is fitted with washer/dryer, microwave, cooker and most of the necessities.
Open: All year **Nearest Shop:** 5 mins walk
Nearest Pub: 5 mins walk

Site: P   Unit: 🖼 🔲 📷

EXETER, Devon   Map ref 1D2

Units   3
Sleeps   1-4

PER UNIT PER WEEK
£270.00 - £576.00

SPECIAL PROMOTIONS
Short Breaks are available. Please ring to discuss.

Lower Southbrook Farm (LSF) Holiday

Contact: Angela Lang, Owner, Southbrook Lane, Whimple, Exeter, Devon EX5 2PG
T: (01404) 822989 **E:** lowersouthbrookfarm@btinternet.com
W: www.lowersouthbrookfarm.co.uk

We offer quality holiday accommodation set within the beautiful Devon countryside.

The cottages are an ideal base from which to explore the many attractions in and around the wonderful county of Devon. Alternatively if you are looking for somewhere to relax and unwind we are in a rural setting with the benefit of a heated outdoor swimming pool, a children's play area and 3 acres of private land.

Open: All Year   **Units:** All cottages are single storey.
Nearest Shop: 2 mile
Nearest Pub: 1 mile

Site: ❀ **P   Payment:** 💳 € **Leisure:** ⌇ **Property:** 🐾 🔲 💻 **Children:** 👶 🛏 🚼 **Unit:** 🔲 🖼 🔲 📺 📀

For **key to symbols** see page 7

HOLSWORTHY, Devon   Map ref 1C2

Units   103
Sleeps   1-6

PER UNIT PER WEEK
£270.00 - £1414.00

SPECIAL PROMOTIONS
Enjoy two nights or more with complimentary champagne and chocolates on arrival, please call for latest pricing.

Woodford Bridge Country Club

Contact: Milton Damerel, Nr Holsworthy, Devon EX22 7LL **T:** 0800 358 6991
E: EuHotels@diamondresorts.com
W: www.DiamondResortsandHotels.com **£ BOOK ONLINE**

A quiet haven in the heart of North Devon, this 15th-century former coaching inn is 33 miles from Tintagel Castle, the rumoured birthplace of King Arthur. It has a pool, a gym and free parking on site. Woodford Bridge Country Club is a charming thatched building, with a variety of elegant rooms. Each spacious apartment offers an en suite bathroom, a TV with Freeview, and tea and coffee making facilities.

Guests can enjoy a drink in the bar and breakfast, lunch and dinner in the restaurant. Woodford Bridge has a library where guests can relax with a book in the peaceful garden.

Open: All year
Nearest Shop: On Site
Nearest Pub: On Site

Units: A choice of Studio, one and two bedroom apartments available. All apartments boast a full kitchen, modern bathroom and Television with DVD player.

Site: ✿ P Payment: 🖃 Leisure: ♪ ▶ ☌ Property: ▭ ▱ Children: ⛟ 🛏 ♀ Unit: ▭ ⚒ TV dvd ☎

ILFRACOMBE, Devon   Map ref 1C1

Units   1
Sleeps   1-6

PER UNIT PER WEEK
£275.00 - £600.00

SPECIAL PROMOTIONS
Short breaks available. Also butchery, lambing and cider experiences out-of-season. Prices vary, based on the following percentages of the weekly rate; 3 nights 70%, 4 nights 80% and 5 nights 90%.

Mary's Cottage

Contact: Susan West, Indicknowle Farm, Long Lane, Combe Martin, Ilfracombe, North Devon EX34 0PA **T:** (01271) 883980 **E:** mark.sue@indicknowle.plus.com
W: www.indicknowle.co.uk

Adjoining a beautiful eighteenth century farmhouse, this delightful 4 star country cottage lies at the end of its own private lane. Indicknowle is a traditional family farm producing cider, lamb, pork and Ruby Red beef. Located in an area of outstanding natural beauty, close to Exmoor park, it has easy access to the popular North Devon beaches and the South West Coastal Path.
Mary's Cottage is the perfect base for a beach, walking or touring holiday, Christmas or Easter break. We offer peace, tranquility, relaxation and a taste of country life throughout the changing seasons of the farm year.

Open: All year
Nearest Shop: 3 miles
Nearest Pub: 3 miles

Units: Bedrooms en suite with shower & WC. Downstairs cloakroom. Cot/baby bath available on request. Fitted kitchen. Centrally heated with log burner & Wifi.

Site: ✿ P Property: ▭ ▱ ▱ Children: ⛟ 🛏 ♀ Unit: ▭ ▭ ▱ ⚒ TV dvd ⌁ BBQ

IVYBRIDGE, Devon Map ref 1C2

Units 4
Sleeps 2-6

PER UNIT PER WEEK
£260.00 - £720.00

SPECIAL PROMOTIONS
Short breaks are available from end September to May. Please contact for details.

Oldaport Farm Cottages

Contact: Miss CM Evans, Owner, Modbury, Ivybridge, Devon PL21 0TG **T:** (01548) 830842
F: 01548 830998 **E:** cathy@oldaport.com
W: www.oldaport.com

Four comfortable cottages converted from redundant stone barns sited on historic, working sheep farm in beautiful South Hams valley, it provides an ideal location for relaxing and absorbing the countryside in an area of outstanding natural beauty. There is an abundance of wildlife in the area, fascinating walks and attractions within easy reach. Dartmoor 8 miles, Plymouth 12 miles.

All cottages are furnished to the high standard of the English Tourism Council. The fitted kitchens are fully equipped with cooker, microwave, refrigerator, toaster, kettle and a comprehensive range of crockery, cutlery and cooking equipment. Heating in all rooms. Shaver points. Colour television. DVD player. Non-allergic duvet and pillows. Full bed linen will be provided. Adjacent is a laundry room with automatic washing machine, tumble dryer and ironing facilities.

Open: All Year
Nearest Shop: 2.2 Miles
Nearest Pub: 2.2 Miles

Site: P **Property:** **Children:** **Unit:** TV DVD BBQ

NEWTON ABBOT, Devon Map ref 1D2

Units 3
Sleeps 6-8

PER UNIT PER WEEK
£499.00 - £1799.00

Holwell Holiday Cottages

Contact: Sophia Newman, Cottage Manager, Widecombe In The Moor, Newton Abbot, Devon TQ13 7TT **T:** 07746 123878 **E:** info@holwelldartmoor.co.uk
W: www.holwelldartmoor.co.uk **£ BOOK ONLINE**

Holwell Holiday Cottages are ideally located for discovering Dartmoor and surrounding area. Stay in one of the three immaculate cottages that have been lovingly and tastefully converted from barns to luxury holiday cottages. Chinkwell Tor - 2 king, 1 double bedroom & two bathrooms, sleeps 6. Hound Tor - 1 king, 2 double bedrooms & 2 bathrooms, sleeps 6. Saddle Tor - 4 large bedrooms & 4 bathrooms. **Open:** All year
Nearest Shop: 5 miles **Nearest Pub:** 2.6 miles

Site: P **Payment:** **Leisure:** **Property:** **Children:** **Unit:** TV DVD BBQ

OKEHAMPTON, Devon Map ref 1C2

Units 1
Sleeps 4

PER UNIT PER WEEK
£350.00 - £935.00

Peartree Cottage

Contact: Mrs Jacqueline Ellis, Owner, Howards Gorhuish, Northlew, Okehampton, Devon EX20 3BT **T:** (01837) 658750 **E:** jackie.ann.ellis@btinternet.com
W: www.peartreecottage-devon.co.uk

Delightful Gold Award-winning Peartree Cottage stands in the 2 acre grounds of Howards Gorhuish and overlooks a wild flower meadow and small copse. The cottage adjoins the owner's country house standing in a quiet rural position and is well-located to explore the attractions and stunning landscape the south west has to offer, especially Dartmoor and the spectacular North Devon coast. **Open:** All year **Nearest Shop:** 2 miles **Nearest Pub:** 2 miles

Site: P **Property:** **Children:** **Unit:** TV DVD BBQ

OTTERY ST. MARY, Devon   Map ref 1D2

Units 1
Sleeps 6
PER UNIT PER WEEK
£475.00 - £965.00

The Hay House

Contact: Nick Broomfield, Blacklake Farm, East Hill, Ottery St. Mary, Devon EX11 1QA
T: (01404) 812122 / 07753 688283 **E:** nick@blacklakefarm.com
W: www.blacklakefarm.com

Privacy and tranquillity on a traditional organic Devon farm set amidst some of East Devon's most beautiful coast and countryside. The Hay House at Blacklake Farm has been carefully converted from original farm buildings forming part of the old Grade II listed farmyard. It offers spacious, homely accommodation for up to six persons. Being the only holiday house on the farm, the Hay House offers total peace and seclusion with only the ebb and flow of traditional farm life to punctuate the day. **Open:** All year **Nearest Shop:** 2 miles **Nearest Pub:** 2 miles

Site: ❀ P Leisure: ⚑ ♦ Property: 🐾 🖥 🗑 🖨 Children: 🐣 🛏 🚶 Unit: 🗄 🗄 📷 🗑 🔌 📺 📀 🧺 BBQ

PAIGNTON, Devon   Map ref 1D2

Units 5
Sleeps 2-20
PER UNIT PER WEEK
£170.00 - £450.00

Sandmoor Holiday Apartments

Contact: Mr & Mrs Rita & Brian Ellis, Owners, Sandmoor Holiday Apartments, 29 St Andrews Road, Paignton TQ4 6HA **T:** (01803) 525909 / 07941 660932
E: sandmoors@yahoo.co.uk **W:** www.sandmoorholidayapartments.co.uk

Sandmoor is ideally situated in a quiet area within easy walking distance of Paignton and Goodrington beaches, water park, harbour and town centre. Some apartments have sea views. High level of repeat bookings. **Open:** All year **Nearest Shop:** 0.25 miles **Nearest Pub:** 0.25 miles

Site: P Property: 🖨 🗑 Children: 🐣 🛏 🚶 Unit: 🗄 📷 🔌 📺

SEATON, Devon   Map ref 1D2

Units 1
Sleeps 1-4
PER UNIT PER WEEK
£225.00 - £595.00

West Ridge Bungalow

Contact: Mrs Hildegard Fox, West Ridge Bungalow, Harepath Hill, Seaton EX12 2TA
T: (01297) 22398 **E:** fox@foxwestridge.co.uk
W: www.cottagesdirect.co.uk/3031758-1/west-ridge-bungalow-devon.aspx
£ BOOK ONLINE

Comfortably furnished bungalow on elevated ground in 1.5 acres of gardens. Beautiful, panoramic views of Axe Estuary and sea. Nearby - Beer, Branscombe, Lyme Regis, Sidmouth. Excellent walking, sailing, fishing, golf. 10% reduction for 2 persons only, throughout booking period. **Open:** March to October **Nearest Shop:** 0.5 miles **Nearest Pub:** 1 mile

Site: ❀ P Leisure: ♪ ⚑ Property: 🐾 🗑 Children: 🐣 🛏 🚶 Unit: 🗄 📷 🔌 📺 📀 📀

SIDMOUTH, Devon   Map ref 1D2

Units 1
Sleeps 1-4
PER UNIT PER WEEK
£291.00 - £542.00

19 Anstis Court

Contact: Ms Louise Hayman, Milkbere Holiday Cottages, 3 Fore Street, Seaton, Devon EX12 2LE **T:** (01297) 20729 **E:** info@milkberehols.com
W: www.sidmouthholiday.com **£ BOOK ONLINE**

Bedroom with sumptuous kingsize bed and flatscreen TV/DVD, bathroom with bath & shower, kitchen with fridge/freezer, dishwasher, washerdryer, 4 ring gas hob & double electric oven, and lounge/dining room, 42" flat screen TV, cinema sound system/DVD player, Nintendo Wii, opulent chaise lounge sofabed. Changeover is Friday. **Open:** All year **Nearest Shop:** 0.01 miles **Nearest Pub:** 0.01 miles

Site: P Payment: 💷 Leisure: 🎣 ♪ ⚑ ♺ Property: 🖨 🗑 Children: 🐣⁶ Unit: 🗄 🗄 📷 🗑 🔌 📺 📀 📀

SOUTH MOLTON, Devon   Map ref 1C1

Drewstone Farm

Contact: Ruth Ley, Owner, Drewstone Farm, South Molton, Devon EX36 3EF
T: (01769) 572337 / 07540 293785 **E:** info@devonself-catering.co.uk
W: www.devonself-catering.co.uk **£ BOOK ONLINE**

| Units | 3 |
| Sleeps | 1-6 |

PER UNIT PER WEEK
£255.00 - £720.00

SPECIAL PROMOTIONS
Short breaks are
available out of season.
Please call or email for
details.

Drewstone is a traditional 300 acre family-run sheep/arable farm in an idyllic country setting in the foothills of Exmoor, full of unspoilt character and wildlife habitat with its own wildlife lake. We have 3 self-catering cottages, each of individual character and equipped to a high standard for holidays. Children are welcome.

Exmoor National Park with its heathered moorland, wooded valleys and winding rivers makes spectacular picnic spots. We are within easy reach of the area's fine beaches. The town of South Molton is nearby with a supermarket, shops, swimming pool, garages and pubs etc.

Open: All year
Nearest Shop: 2.5 miles
Nearest Pub: 2 miles

Units: Sleeping 4, 5 and 6 persons. Enclosed gardens, ample parking, central heating, woodburners, tasteful furnishings, Wi-Fi in 2 cottages and a children's play area.

Site: ❀ **P Property:** 🐾 🚌 🖥 🏊 **Children:** 🛝 🛏 🎯 **Unit:** 🛏 🖥 📺 🔥 📺 📀 🚿

SOUTH MOLTON, Devon   Map ref 1C1

Dunsley Mill Barn

Contact: Helen Sparrow, Owner, West Anstey, South Molton, North Devon EX36 3PF
T: (01398) 341374 **E:** helen@dunsleymill.co.uk
W: www.dunsleymill.co.uk

| Units | 1 |
| Sleeps | 1-6 |

PER UNIT PER WEEK
£400.00 - £700.00

Situated on the edge of the Exmoor National Park Dunsley Mill is surrounded by rolling Devon countryside and there are superb local walks accessible directly from the property. Lovingly restored the barn is brimming with character and charm with restored beams, rich heritage colours and a large wood burning stove that nestles in the corner of the spacious open plan living area.

Three charming double bedrooms on the first floor are each dressed in delicate country fabrics, the two front double bedrooms enjoying wonderful views of the valley. This is an amazing area for walking, riding, fishing, golfing and other amazing country pursuits.

Open: All year
Nearest Shop: 6 mile
Nearest Pub: 6 miles

Units: Detached, stone barn conversion, open-plan, ground floor with host of beams. Three bedrooms, 2 bathrooms. In beautiful secluded valley.

Site: ❀ **P Leisure:** 🎿 🎣 🏌 ⛳ **Property:** 🚌 🖥 🏊 **Children:** 🛝 **Unit:** 🛏 🖥 📺 🔥 📺 📀 🚿 BBQ

TORQUAY, *Devon* Map ref 1D2

SELF CATERING

Units	6
Sleeps	1-6

PER UNIT PER WEEK
£196.00 - £840.00

Belgravia Luxury Holiday Apartments

Contact: Mrs Nadine Green, Owner, Belgravia Luxury Holiday Apartments, 31 Belgrave Road, Torquay, Devon TQ2 5HX **T:** (01803) 293417 **E:** info@blha.co.uk **W:** blha.co.uk **£ BOOK ONLINE**

Belgravia Luxury Holiday Apartments are situated just 500m from the main seafront and promenade. The popular Riviera Leisure & Conference Centre is also only a 200m walk. **Open:** All year **Nearest Shop:** 0.01 miles **Nearest Pub:** 0.01 miles

Payment: **Leisure:** **Property:** **Children:** **Unit:**

TORQUAY, *Devon* Map ref 1D2

★★★★ SELF CATERING

Units	46
Sleeps	2-8

PER UNIT PER WEEK
£500.00 - £1055.00

SPECIAL PROMOTIONS
Last minute weekend & mid-week breaks available.

The Osborne Club

Contact: The Club Office, The Osborne Club, 5 Hesketh Crescent, Torquay TQ1 2LL **T:** (01803) 209600 **F:** 01803 200846 **E:** info@osborneclub.co.uk **W:** osborneclub.co.uk

Osborne Club apartments are set in a beautiful Regency style crescent on the English Riviera, with superb views over Torbay. Most of the individually designed apartments enjoy stunning sea views. Situated in a quiet area of Torquay, yet close to the coastal footpath and town centre. Guests have use of indoor and outdoor (seasonal) swimming pools & tennis court. 2 restaurants on site. Last minute weekend & mid-week breaks available with 3 night minimum stay.

Open: All year
Nearest Shop: 0.5 miles
Nearest Pub: 0.5 miles

Units: 1, 2 & 3 bed well equipped apartments. Sleeps 2-8.

Site: P **Payment:** **Leisure:** **Property:** **Children:** **Unit:**

TOTNES, *Devon* Map ref 1D2

★★★★★ SELF CATERING   Gold AWARD

Units	3
Sleeps	1-6

PER UNIT PER WEEK
£395.00 - £1390.00

Aish Cross Holiday Cottages

Contact: Mrs Angela Pavey, Aish Cross Holiday Cottages, Aish Cross House, Aish, Stoke Gabriel, Totnes, Devon TQ9 6PT **T:** (01803) 782022 / 07980 712586 **F:** 01803 782022 **E:** info@aishcross.co.uk **W:** www.aishcross.co.uk **£ BOOK ONLINE**

The cottages are adjoined to Aish Cross House a regency country house. The Coach House, The Stable & The Hayloft are three luxurious cottages which have been lovingly converted to very high standards, each individually styled and full of character. The perfect place to relax and unwind. Close to medieval town of Totnes, amenities of Torbay, South Hams coastline & Dartmoor. **Open:** All year **Nearest Shop:** 1.5 miles **Nearest Pub:** 1.5 miles

Site: P **Payment:** **Leisure:** **Property:** **Children:** **Unit:** BBQ

TOTNES, Devon   Map ref 1D2

Units 1
Sleeps 1-5
PER UNIT PER WEEK
£406.00 - £1195.00

Swift Cottage
Contact: Jacquie Quin, Cottage Owner, 42 Illingworth Way, Enfield, Middx EN1 2PA
T: 020 8245 0772 / 07505 136194 **E:** swiftcottage@yahoo.co.uk
W: www.swiftcottagedevon.co.uk

Swift Cottage is one of nine self catering cottages - that sleeps 4+1. Exposed beams, spiral staircase, wood burning log fire, Free Wi-Fi & 32" TV with Freeview & hard drive. Ground floor bedroom (twin bedded), first floor main bedroom, both with en suites & TVs. Free use of indoor heated swimming pool, games room & external play area - all located in the green pastures of South Devon near Totnes. **Open:** All year **Nearest Shop:** 1.5 miles **Nearest Pub:** 1.5 miles

Site: ✿ P **Payment:** 💷 **Leisure:** ➤ ✎ ☜ **Property:** ⁄ 🐕 ▭ 🖳 **Children:** ⚲ ♨ 🏃 **Unit:** 🖳 🖳 🖵 🖳 📺 📀 🖳 BBQ ☎

WESTWARD HO!, Devon   Map ref 1C1

Units 1
Sleeps 1-8
PER UNIT PER WEEK
£625.00 - £1190.00

Seascape
Contact: Mr Ian Gibson, 3 Wimborne Grove, Watford WD17 4JE **T:** 07801 916963
E: bookings@ace-holidayhomes.co.uk
W: www.devon-selfcatering-seascape.com £ BOOK ONLINE

Seascape is a luxurious 5 Star Gold Award, three-bedroom apartment in Westwood Ho! Waves at high - tide lap below the balcony. Sleeps six plus two plus travel cot. Beautiful views across Bideford Bay towards Lundy. Two-mile sandy beach. Rock pools. Fantastic walks in area. Golf at Royal North Devon Club included in price. **Open:** All year **Nearest Shop:** 0.10 miles **Nearest Pub:** 0.10 miles

Site: P **Leisure:** ⚓ ♪ ➤ ⛳ **Property:** ▭ 🖳 **Children:** ⚲ ♨ 🏃 **Unit:** 🖳 🖳 🖵 🖳 🖳 📺 📀 📀 ☎

WHILBOROUGH, Devon   Map ref 1D2

Units 4
Sleeps 2-29
PER UNIT PER WEEK
£400.00 - £3500.00

SPECIAL PROMOTIONS
Short breaks available Autumn, Winter and Spring, 3/4/5 nights, subject to availability. View website for prices and availability.

Long Barn Luxury Holiday Cottages
Contact: Michael & Sandra Lane, Owners, Long Barn Luxury Holiday Cottages, Long Barn, North Whilborough, Newton Abbot, Torbay TQ12 5LP **T:** (01803) 875044 / 07946 378137
E: stay@longbarncottages.co.uk **W:** www.longbarncottages.co.uk £ BOOK ONLINE

Four Luxury 4* Gold Award Holiday Cottages in the tranquil Devon countryside sleeping 2, 6, 8 and 13 plus cots. Family friendly, each with its own garden as well as the outdoor play area with swings, climbing frames, trampoline and plenty of space for ball games. The cottages share a bookable indoor heated pool and an indoor play area catering for all the family with pool, table tennis and toys.

Open: All year
Nearest Shop: 1.5 miles
Nearest Pub: 0.5 miles

Site: ✿ P **Payment:** 💷 **Leisure:** ➤ ⛳ ✎ ☜ **Property:** ▭ 🖳 🖳 **Children:** ⚲ ♨ 🏃
Unit: 🖳 🖳 🖵 🖳 🖳 📺 📀 📀 🖳 BBQ

WOOLACOMBE, Devon   *Map ref 1C1*

Units 6
Sleeps 3-8
PER UNIT PER WEEK
£250.00 - £1450.00

Trimstone Self-Catering Cottages

Contact: Reception, Trimstone Self-Catering Cottages, Trimstone, Nr Woolacombe, Ilfracombe, North Devon EX34 8NR **T:** (01271) 862841 **F:** (01271) 863808
E: info@trimstone.co.uk **W:** www.trimstone.co.uk **£ BOOK ONLINE**

The Cottages are set in 44 acres of landscaped gardens and beautiful North Devon countryside and provide the perfect location for those who want a peaceful and relaxing break. The fine sandy beaches and rolling surf of Croyde, Woolacombe and Saunton are a short drive away. **Open:** All year **Nearest Shop:** 2 miles **Nearest Pub:** 2 miles

Site: ❀ P **Payment:** 🎫 **Leisure:** ⚓ ♪ ▶ ♨ ♠ ⚓ ✎ **Property:** 🐾 🗄 🖳 **Children:** 🐕 🛏 🔥 **Unit:** 📺 🗄 🖏 📺 🔌 📀 BBQ 📞

BLANDFORD FORUM, Dorset   *Map ref 2B3*

Units 1
Sleeps 4
PER UNIT PER WEEK
£325.00

Dairy Cottage

Contact: Broadlea Farm, Sutton Waldron, Blandford Forum, Dorset DT11 8NS
T: (01747) 811330 **E:** j.s.asbury@btinternet.com

Fully-equipped cottage amidst lovely countryside, south of Shaftesbury. Two bedrooms, sitting/dining room, separate kitchen and bathroom. Good base for visiting tourist attractions. **Open:** All year **Nearest Shop:** 1.5 miles **Nearest Pub:** 1.5 miles

Site: ❀ P **Leisure:** ▶ **Property:** 🖥 🗄 🖳 🖏 **Children:** 🐕 🛏 🔥 **Unit:** 🗄 📺 🖏 🖏 📺 📀 📞

BLANDFORD FORUM, Dorset   *Map ref 2B3*

Units 4
Sleeps 2-19
PER UNIT PER WEEK
£235.00 - £1050.00

Newfield Holiday Cottages

Contact: Lucy Lucas-Rowe, Manager, Newfield Holiday Cottages, Newfield Farm, Pimperne, Blandford Forum, Dorset DT11 8BX **T:** (01258) 458623 / 07899 792106 **E:** bookings@newfieldholidays.co.uk
W: www.newfieldholidaysdorset.co.uk **£ BOOK ONLINE**

Barn conversion with games room in rural farm location. 4 joined cottages can be let together or individually sleeping between 2 and 19 people. Children's play area. Walking and cycling from the doorstep. Cottages are full of character, and are all finished to a high standard. **Open:** Open all year **Nearest Shop:** 1 mile **Nearest Pub:** 1mile

Site: ❀ **Leisure:** ♠ **Property:** 🖳 **Unit:** 🗄 🗄 📺 🖏 📺 🔌 📀 BBQ

BRIDPORT, Dorset   Map ref 2A3

RATING APPLIED FOR

Units   8
Sleeps   2-6

PER UNIT PER WEEK
£455.00 - £845.00

SPECIAL PROMOTIONS
Short Breaks Available

Chesil Beach Lodge

Contact: Linda Loveridge, Proprietor, Coast Road, Burton Bradstock, Bridport, Dorset
DT6 4RJ **T:** (01308) 897428 / 07814 666267 **E:** enquiries@chesilbeachlodge.co.uk
W: www.chesilbeachlodge.co.uk **£ BOOK ONLINE**

Chesil Beach Lodge is the most perfect coastal location on the beautiful World Heritage Jurassic
Coast, with stunning panoramic sea and coastal views from all the accommodation. With 4 Self-
Catering Apartments, 1 Self-Catering Studio Apartment and 3 Bed & Breakfast Rooms there is
something for everyone. Chesil Beach Lodge was voted one of the "50 BEST EUROPEAN BEACH
BREAKS" by the Independant, has TripAdvisor Certificates of Excellence for for 2011, 2012, 2013 and
2014 and is rated 4 Star Silver Award. Perfect for walkers and dog owners, we are a 2 minute walk
from the South West Coast Path.

Open: All year
Nearest Shop: 0.5 miles
Nearest Pub: 0.5 miles

Units: 4 Apartments (1 on the Ground Floor), 1
Studio Apartment, 3 Bed & Breakfast Rooms all
with panoramic sea views over 99 miles of
Jurassic Coastline

Property: 🖼 **Unit:** 🍳 🚫 ▣ 📺 ◉ 📀 ⬗

BRIDPORT, Dorset   Map ref 2A3

★★★ SELF CATERING

Units   1
Sleeps   6
PER UNIT PER WEEK
£330.00 - £650.00

Conway Cottage

Contact: Mrs M A Smith, Owner, Conway House, Bettiscombe, Bridport, Dorset DT6 5NT
T: (01308) 868313 **E:** h.smith976@btinternet.com
W: www.conway-cottage.co.uk

Comfortable semi-detached cottage set in beautiful countryside,
quiet location. Double bedroom en suite, twin ground floor
bedroom, wet room with power shower, toilet & hand basin, patio
& garden. Base for walking, sightseeing or relaxing. Short distance
from Dorset Jurassic Coast at Charmouth & Lyme Regis. Many
National Trust properties within easy reach. Short breaks please see
our website. **Open:** All year **Nearest Shop:** 1 mile
Nearest Pub: 2 miles

Site: ❀ **P Property:** ▭ 🖼 **Children:** 🍼1 🛏 **Unit:** 🍳 ▣ 🔌 📺 📀

BRIDPORT, Dorset   Map ref 2A3

Units   1
Sleeps   7
PER UNIT PER WEEK
£580.00 - £1480.00

The Guard House

Contact: Mrs Charlotte Wreaves, Seatown, Chideock, Bridport, Dorset DT6 6JU
T: 07801 289014 **E:** charlottewreaves@hotmail.com
W: www.guardhouse.co.uk

This 19th century cottage nestling in the hamlet of Seatown is
located just a stone's throw from the beach and the South Coastal
path and offers a perfect base to explore the local area or simply
relax and enjoy the sea air. Spectacular walks along the Jurassic
Coast. The house is deceptively spacious and offers plenty of living
space along with good sized bedrooms and two wash rooms (one
bathroom with shower over and one shower room). **Open:** All year
Nearest Shop: 100 metres **Nearest Pub:** 100 metres

Site: ❀ **P Property:** 🐕 ▭ 🍳 🖼 **Children:** 🍼 🛏 🔥 **Unit:** 🍳 🚫 ▣ 🗄 🔌 📺 ◉ 📀 ⬗ BBQ 📞

BRIDPORT, Dorset Map ref 2A3

Mead Cottage, 17 Bramble Drive

Contact: Mrs Chrissie Fielder, Owner, Erin Lodge, Jigs Lane South, Warfield, Berkshire RG42 3DR **T:** (01344) 303370 / 07974 809736 **E:** mead.cottage@hotmail.co.uk

Units 1
Sleeps 1-4

PER UNIT PER WEEK
£390.00 - £450.00

Situated within the heart of a World Heritage Conservation Area, offering some of best walking and coastal views in the country. Mead Cottage is a delightful, fully equipped modern mid terrace two bedroom cottage with secluded garden and private car parking. 7 minutes stroll to coastal walks/beach/harbour. It's an ideal touring base. **Open:** April-Mid October **Nearest Shop:** 0.25 miles **Nearest Pub:** 0.25 miles

Site: ✿ P **Leisure:** ♿ ✈ ▶ ∪ **Property:** 🖳 **Unit:** 🗇 ▣ 🗑 ⚲ 📺 🔊 📀

BURTON BRADSTOCK, Dorset Map ref 2A3

Cogden Cottages

Contact: Mrs Kim Connolly, Company Director, Cogden Cottages, Old Coastguard Holiday Park, Coast Road, Bridport DT6 4RL **T:** (01308) 897223 / 07530 051517 **E:** oldcoastguard@hotmail.com **W:** cogdencottages.co.uk **£ BOOK ONLINE**

Units 7
Sleeps 4-7

PER UNIT PER WEEK
£300.00 - £650.00

Cogden Cottages is a former Victorian coastguard station with seven 2/3 bedroom cottages. Outstanding coastal views. All cottages have individual decking or patios. Free wi-fi, dishwasher, towels and linen. **Open:** All year **Nearest Shop:** 0.80 miles **Nearest Pub:** 0.80 miles

Site: ✿ P **Payment:** 💳 **Leisure:** ♿ ✈ ▶ ∪ **Property:** 🐾 ▦ 🗑 🖳 **Children:** 🧸 🛏 ⚄ **Unit:** 🗇 ▣ 🗑 ▣ 🗑 📺 🔊 📀

DORCHESTER, Dorset Map ref 2B3

Luccombe Farm & Country Holidays

Contact: Murray & Amanda Kayll, Owners, Luccombe, Milton Abbas, Blandford, Dorset DT11 0BE **T:** (01258) 880558 **F:** 01258 881384 **E:** luccombeh@gmail.com **W:** www.luccombeholidays.co.uk **£ BOOK ONLINE**

Units 6
Sleeps 1-25

PER UNIT PER WEEK
£325.00 - £1950.00

SPECIAL PROMOTIONS
Flexible 2/3 night breaks. Many variations. Online availability, with a full pricing & booking facility on our web.

Six characterful converted Georgian cottages, maintained to high standards and set amongst beautiful landscaped gardens in a private and very peaceful hidden valley, within our family farm close to historic Milton Abbas. An excellent touring base for the Dorset Jurassic coast.

We offer extensive facilities including an indoor pool, sauna, gym, games/events room, riding centre, fishing, shooting, country walking, tennis, bike hire, children's play area and waterside BBQ. There is simply something for everyone here at Luccombe. Come and join us!

Open: All year
Nearest Shop: 2 miles
Nearest Pub: 2 miles

Units: Six comfortable cosy and quirky cottages, all graded 4 stars and with free Wi-Fi in the games room.

Site: ✿ P **Payment:** 💳 € **Leisure:** ♿ ✈ ▶ ∪ 🎣 🐎 ✎ **Property:** 🐾 ▦ 🗑 🖳 🖳 **Children:** 🧸 🛏 ⚄
Unit: 🗇 ▣ ▣ ⚲ 📺 🔊 📀 BBQ 📞

FOLKE, Dorset   *Map ref 2B3*

Units 4
Sleeps 4-8

PER UNIT PER WEEK
£350.00 - £1240.00

SPECIAL PROMOTIONS
Spring, Autumn and Winter Breaks. 3 nights minimum stay £210-£475 per cottage.

Folke Manor Farm Cottages
Contact: Mr & Mrs John & Carol Perrett, Folke Manor Farm Cottages, Folke Manor Farm, Folke, Sherborne DT9 5HP **T:** (01963) 210731 / 07929 139472
E: stay@folkemanorholidays.co.uk **W:** www.folkemanorholidays.co.uk **£ BOOK ONLINE**

Folke Manor Farm Cottages are spacious barn conversions in a quiet part of the Blackmore Vale area of North Dorset. We are off the beaten track and set within the peaceful grounds of the farm, which has two large ponds and over looks the stunning countryside. There is a heated indoor swimming pool open all year round.

Open: All year
Nearest Shop: 3 miles
Nearest Pub: 0.5 miles

Site: P Payment: Leisure: Property: Children: Unit: BBQ

LYME REGIS, Dorset   *Map ref 1D2*

Units 1
Sleeps 6
PER UNIT PER WEEK
£1300.00 - £1500.00

Cecilia's Cottage
Contact: Sammie Steepe, 11 Monmouth Street, Georges Square, Lyme Regis, Dorset DT7 3PX **T:** (01865) 318018 **E:** sammie@pennyandsinclair.co.uk
W: www.barkerevansproperties.com

Beautiful, boutique hideaway for romantic couples or small families. Open plan lounge/dining room area with wood burning stove and dining table to seat 6. Master bedroom with en suite bathroom. Further double bedroom and twin bedroom. Large master bathroom with free standing bath and separate shower enclosure. Illuminated decked patio area. Parking for one car with permit in local car park. **Open:** All year **Nearest Shop:** 0.2km **Nearest Pub:** 0.1km

Site: Payment: Property: Children: Unit:

LYME REGIS, Dorset   Map ref 1D2

Units   3
Sleeps   2-4

PER UNIT PER WEEK
£360.00 - £795.00

Sea Tree House

Contact: Mr David Parker, Sea Tree House, 18 Broad Street, Lyme Regis DT7 3QE
T: (01297) 442244 **F:** 01297 442244 **E:** info@seatreehouse.co.uk
W: www.seatreehouse.co.uk

Spacious, romantic, elegant apartments overlooking the sea and sandy beach just, five minutes walk away. Central yet quiet position giving easy access to restaurants, pubs and walks along Jurassic coast. Warm, friendly welcome from owners. **Open:** All year
Nearest Shop: 0.1 miles **Nearest Pub:** 0.1 miles

Site: ❀ P Leisure: ♪ ► ∪ Property: ⊨ 🖭 🗔 🗔 Children: ⛱ 🛏 ✦ Unit: 🗄 🗄 🖭 🗄 ⬚ 📺 ◉ 📀 ⊘

POOLE, Dorset   Map ref 2B3

Units   2
Sleeps   2-8

PER UNIT PER WEEK
£320.00 - £820.00

Harbour Holidays

Contact: RJ Saunders, Proprietor, Harbour Holidays, 1 Harbour Shallows,
15 Whitecliff Road, Poole BH14 8DU **T:** (01202) 741637 / 07720 842099
E: saunders.221@btinternet.com

Wychcott is a 3 bedroom bungalow, situated close to Poole Park with a delightful sheltered garden and parking for 3 cars. Bath/shower room and 2nd WC. Cable TV/Gas CH. Shops and restaurants in walking distance. Well-behaved pets welcome. Quay Cottage is situated in a quiet area near Poole Quay. 2-car parking. Cable TV/Gas CH. Small kitchen. 3-4 bedrooms. Views of Poole harbour. Good for families and well-behaved pets. **Open:** All year
Nearest Shop: 0.25 miles **Nearest Pub:** 0.25 miles

PETS! PETS! Site: ❀ P Payment: € Leisure: ♨ ♪ ► Property: ⊨ 🗔 🕮 Children: ⛱ 🛏 ✦ Unit: 🗄 🖭 🗄 📺 ◉
🗔 BBQ ☎

RINGSTEAD, Dorset   Map ref 2B3

Units   6
Sleeps   2-6

PER UNIT PER WEEK
£430.00 - £1300.00

SPECIAL PROMOTIONS
Short breaks available
from £175.00,
minimum 2 nights
stay.

Upton Grange Holiday Cottages

Contact: Mrs Kerrie Webster, Upton Farm, Ringstead, Dorchester, Dorset DT2 8NE
T: (01305) 853970 **E:** uptonfarmholiday@aol.com
W: www.uptongrangedorset.co.uk

Cosseted in the centre of the tiny unspoilt hamlet of Upton, where the World Heritage Jurassic Coastline rejoices in the simplicity of nearby Ringstead Bay, the Tithe barn of Upton Farm stands majestic as it has done, in part, since 1579.

Having been sympathetically converted into a small number of holiday cottages, furnished and equipped to the most exacting standards, these unique properties are guaranteed to incite feelings of nostalgia. We accept all major credit and debit cards.

Open: All year
Nearest Shop: 1 mile (approx)
Nearest Pub: 1 mile (approx)

Units: Some bedrooms feature 4 poster beds and log fires grace the lounges of the larger homes, our cottages can accommodate 2 - 6 persons.

Site: ❀ Payment: 💳 Leisure: ♨ ♪ ► ∪ Property: 🗔 🕮 Children: ⛱ 🛏 ✦
Unit: 🗄 🗄 🖭 🗄 ⬚ 📺 ◉ 📀 ⊘ BBQ

SHAFTESBURY, Dorset   Map ref 2B3

Units   1
Sleeps   4-5
PER UNIT PER WEEK
£250.00 - £650.00

Melbury Vale Cottages
Contact: 1 Melbury Vale Cottage, Redmans Lane, Shaftesbury, Dorset SP7 0DB
T: (01747) 850773 / 07834 871548 **E:** melburyvale@gmx.com
W: www.melburyvaleco.co.uk

Barn conversion in tranquil location with woods and vineyard. Less than 2 miles from Shaftesbury in River Stirkel Valley. Sleeps 4-5 people. Alpacas, horses, paintball, mountain biking track, archery and vineyard with working winery. **Open:** All year
Nearest Shop: 1 mile **Nearest Pub:** 0.75 miles

Site: ✿ P Leisure: ♪ ☂ Property: 🐴 ▦ ⬚ ⬚ Children: 🎠 ⊞ ⋏ Unit: ⬚ ⬚ ▣ ⬚ ⬚ TV ⬚ BBQ

SHERBORNE, Dorset   Map ref 2B3

Units   6
Sleeps   2-8
PER UNIT PER WEEK
£245.00 - £895.00

[f]

White Horse Farm
Contact: Mr & Mrs Stuart & Audrey Winterbottom, White Horse Farm, Middlemarsh, Sherborne DT9 5QN **T:** (01963) 210222 / 07798 617174 **F:** 01963 210621
E: enquiries@whitehorsefarm.co.uk **W:** www.whitehorsefarm.co.uk **£ BOOK ONLINE**

We offer a peaceful and relaxed self-catering holiday in beautiful rural Dorset. Four attractive barn conversion cottages, a charming farmhouse annexe and a three bedroomed 4 star lodge cabin.'Good Pub Guide' Inn just 150 yards away. Pets welcome.
Open: All year **Nearest Shop:** 2.5 miles **Nearest Pub:** 0.20 miles

Site: ✿ P Payment: 💷 Leisure: ⛷ ♪ 🎣 Property: ▦ ⬚ ⬚ Children: 🎠 ⊞ ⋏ Unit: ⬚ ⬚ ▣ ⬚ TV ⬚ ⬚ BBQ

SWANAGE, Dorset   Map ref 2B3

Units   1
Sleeps   4
PER UNIT PER WEEK
£225.00 - £340.00

Swanwic House
Contact: Mrs Carole Figg, Owner, Swanwic House, 41a Kings Road West, Swanage, Dorset BH19 1HF **T:** (01929) 423517

Small self-contained fully equipped ground floor flat. Part of the old Rectory next to the Parish Church. 2 single beds in bedroom area separated by folding doors to the living area with bed settee.
Open: April-October **Nearest Shop:** 0.5 miles
Nearest Pub: 0.2 miles

Site: ✿ Leisure: ⛷ Property: 🐴 ⬚ Children: 🎠 Unit: ⬚ ▣ TV ⬚

WEST BAY, Dorset   Map ref 2A3

Units   7
Sleeps   2-8
PER UNIT PER WEEK
£265.00 - £695.00

Westpoint Apartments
Contact: Mr & Mrs D P & B Slade, Westpoint Apartments, The Esplanade, West Bay, Bridport DT6 4HE **T:** (01308) 423636 **F:** 01308 458871 **E:** bea@westpointapartments.co.uk
W: www.westpointapartments.co.uk **£ BOOK ONLINE**

Quality self-catering apartments on seafront overlooking sea and harbour. Fishing, 18-hole golf course, beautiful cliff walks, Thomas Hardy Country. Three and four day breaks available. **Open:** All year
Nearest Shop: 0.25 miles **Nearest Pub:** 0.25 miles

Site: ✿ P Payment: 💷 Leisure: ♪ ▶ 🎣 Property: ⬚ ⬚ Children: 🎠⁵ Unit: ⬚ ▣ TV ⬚

BLAKENEY, Gloucestershire   Map ref 2B1

Oatfield Country Cottages

Contact: Alison Gray, Oatfield House Farm, Etloe, Blakeney, Gloucestershire GL15 4AY
T: (01594) 510372 **E:** cottages@oatfieldfarm.co.uk
W: www.oatfieldfarm.co.uk **£ BOOK ONLINE**

Units   5
Sleeps   2-18
PER UNIT PER WEEK
£375.00 - £1275.00

Oatfield Country Cottages offer magnificent character cottages set in an idyllic rural location. Five luxury, award winning cottages sleeping from 2 to 18 people and converted from listed 17th & 18th Century farm buildings. Lovely small farm with tennis court, games, farm animals, giving easy access to Forest of Dean, River Severn, Cotswolds and Wye valley **Open:** All year **Nearest Shop:** 1 mile **Nearest Pub:** 1 mile

Site: ✿ P Payment: 💷 Leisure: ⚲ ⚲ ⚲ Property: ⫽ 🐾 ☷ ▢ 🍴 Children: ⛹ ☷ ⚹ Unit: ▢
▢ ▦ ▣ 📺 💿 🍴 BBQ

CHELTENHAM, Gloucestershire   Map ref 2B1

Church Court Cottages

Contact: Mr Jan Tenvig, Managing Director, Tenvig (UK) Limited, Mill Street, Cheltenham, Gloucestershire GL52 3BG **T:** (01242) 573277 / 07712 106705
E: churchcourtcottages@tenvig.com **W:** www.churchcourtcottages.co.uk

Units   3
Sleeps   2-21
PER UNIT PER WEEK
£420.00 - £1785.00

At the foot of Cleeve Hill, the ancient village of Prestbury in Cheltenham is the setting for what must be one of the most attractive groups of cottages in the Cotswolds. A range of 19th century farm buildings, set around an attractive courtyard with its own meadow and converted with great skill and flair to provide outstandingly comfortable and well appointed accommodation. Rated Five Star Gold. **Open:** All year **Nearest Shop:** 0.25 miles **Nearest Pub:** 100 feet

Site: ✿ P Leisure: ↑ Property: ⫽ 🐾 ☷ ▢ 🍴 Children: ⛹ ☷ ⚹ Unit: ▢ ▣ ▦ ▣ 🍴 📺 💿 🍴 ☏

CHELTENHAM, Gloucestershire   Map ref 2B1

Cotswold Cottages

Contact: The Old Mill, Bourton On The Water, Cheltenham, Gloucestershire GL54 2BY
T: (03301) 230 374 **E:** enquiries@csmaclubretreats.co.uk
W: retreats.csmaclub.co.uk

Units   5
Sleeps   2-5
PER UNIT PER WEEK
£539.00 - £1141.00

Perfect for a romantic getaway or family escape, all four quaint cottage apartments are housed within an old mill building. The self-catering apartments all come with fully equipped kitchens and charming lounges and offer plenty of modern comforts for an unforgettable self-catering getaway. The larger semi-detached cottage 'Stepping Stones' is perfect for bigger groups and families. **Open:** From 3rd January throughout 2015 **Nearest Shop:** 0.1 Miles **Nearest Pub:** 0.1 Miles

Site: ✿ P Payment: 💷 Property: ⫽ 🐾 ☷ ▢ 🍴 Children: ⛹ Unit: ▢ ▣ 📺 💿 ☏

CHELTENHAM, Gloucestershire   Map ref 2B1

Ramblers Rest

Contact: Andrew & Nicole Sullivan, 81 New Barn Lane, Prestbury, Cheltenham, Gloucestershire GL52 3LF **T:** (01242) 231432 **E:** ramblersrest@tiscali.co.uk
W: www.cotswolds.info/webpage/ramblers-rest.htm

Units   1
Sleeps   6
PER UNIT PER WEEK
£350.00 - £800.00

Ramblers Rest is located in Prestbury, Cheltenham, just 5 minutes walk from the famous Cheltenham Racecourse. With three bedrooms, this bungalow is a perfect base for families and friends or colleagues sharing accommodation. The area is perfect for those wishing to explore nearby Cheltenham, and the surrounding Cotswold area. **Open:** All year **Nearest Shop:** 0.1 miles **Nearest Pub:** 1.5km

Site: ✿ P Property: ☷ 🍴 Children: ⛹ ☷ ⚹ Unit: ▢ ▣ ▦ ▣ 🍴 📺 💿

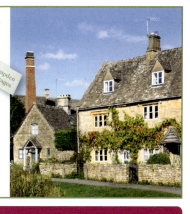
CIRENCESTER, Gloucestershire   Map ref 2B1

SELF CATERING ★★★★

Units 4
Sleeps 2-7
PER UNIT PER WEEK
£250.00 - £850.00

Old Mill Cottages
Contact: Mrs Alison Claxton, Old Mill Farm, Poole Keynes, Cirencester, Glos GL7 6ED
T: (01285) 771377 / 07760216070 **E:** oldmillcottages@outlook.com
W: oldmillcottages.co.uk **£ BOOK ONLINE**

Well-equipped, comfortable barn conversions, 4 miles from Cirencester. Quiet rural situation beside Thames. Adjacent Cotswold Water Park. Ideal touring centre for the Cotswolds. Ample parking. Dogs allowed. **Open:** All year **Nearest Shop:** 2 miles **Nearest Pub:** 1 mile

Site: ❀ P Payment: 🖪 Leisure: ► Property: 🐾 🖿 🖥 🖳 Children: 🏊 🛏 🖈 Unit: 🖥 🖨 🖵 🍴 📺 📀 BBQ

CIRENCESTER, Gloucestershire   Map ref 2B1

SELF CATERING ★★★★★ **Gold AWARD**

Units 1
Sleeps 1-8

PER UNIT PER WEEK
£595.00 - £1950.00

SPECIAL PROMOTIONS
Two, three and four night short breaks are available most of year except high season.

The Stables
Contact: Rowena Paul, Forge House, Limes Road, Kemble, Cirencester, Gloucestershire GL7 6FS **T:** (01285) 771157 / 07787 258758 **F:** 01285 771157
E: info@forgehousekemble.co.uk **W:** www.forgehousekemble.co.uk **£ BOOK ONLINE**

The Stables is a stunning newly converted barn conversion in a delightful courtyard across from the principal house. It has a 40ft beamed open plan living/dining room with contemporary log-burner perfect for celebrations or relaxing weekends away. It has a fully-equipped contemporary kitchen. Double patio doors open onto a seating area with teak garden furniture - the perfect place to relax in the day or evening. The bedrooms have every comfort for your stay: two doubles with en suites and two doubles which can be made up into twins with one an en suite and one with a private bathroom.

Open: All Year
Nearest Shop: Kemble Village Stores
Nearest Pub: The Wild Duck, Ewen

Units: 1 double with en suite bathroom; 1 double/twin with en suite shower room; 1 double/twin with private bathroom; 1 double with en suite shower room.

Site: ❀ P Payment: 🖪 Property: 🖿 🖳 Children: 🏊 🛏 🖈 Unit: 🖥 🖨 🖵 🖩 🍴 📺 📀 ⊘ BBQ

LYDNEY, Gloucestershire   Map ref 2A1

Units 1
Sleeps 6

PER UNIT PER WEEK
£400.00 - £850.00

2 Danby Cottages
Contact: Mr Gareth Lawes, 2 Danby Cottages, Yorkley, Lydney, Gloucestershire GL15 4SL
T: (0117) 9422301 **E:** glawes@talktalk.net
W: www.danbycottages.co.uk **£ BOOK ONLINE**

This tranquil forester's cottage is one of a pair, set deep in the woods but only half a mile from village amenities of shops, pubs, a health centre and bus stop. Sensitively restored and to meet the needs of those with limited mobility. **Open:** All year
Nearest Shop: 600 yards **Nearest Pub:** 500 yards

Site: ❀ P Property: 🐕 ... Children: ... Unit: ... BBQ

MITCHELDEAN, Gloucestershire   Map ref 2B1

Units 1
Sleeps 1-6

PER UNIT PER WEEK
£400.00 - £720.00

SPECIAL PROMOTIONS
Weekends and short midweek breaks available. Mimimum stay 2 nights.

Holme House Barn
Contact: Tim and Diana Bateman, Holme House, Jubilee Road, Mitcheldean, Gloucestershire GL17 0EE **T:** (01594) 543875 **E:** info@holmehousebarn.co.uk
W: www.holmehousebarn.co.uk **£ BOOK ONLINE**

Holme House Barn is a luxury holiday cottage nestling in rural farmland, surrounded by fields and woodland. It is located 300 metres from a country lane and is only visible from Holme House itself.

Open: All year except January
Nearest Shop: 1 mile
Nearest Pub: 1 mile

Units: Double, twin and bathroom on the ground floor. Open plan dinner with a sofa bed and easy chairs.

Site: ❀ P Leisure: 🎣 Property: 🐕 ... Children: ... Unit: ... BBQ ☎

STOW-ON-THE-WOLD, Gloucestershire   Map ref 2B1

Units 1
Sleeps 1-4
PER UNIT PER WEEK
£475.00 - £808.00

Broad Oak Cottages
Contact: Mrs Mary Wilson, Owner, Broad Oak Cottages, The Counting House, Stow-on-the-Wold GL54 1AL **T:** (01451) 830794 **F:** 01451 830794 **E:** mary@broadoakcottages.co.uk
W: broadoakcottages.co.uk **£ BOOK ONLINE**

May Cottage is a delightful, quiet 2 bedroom cottage all on one level and within a few minutes walk of Stow Square. It includes a Master Suite with luxury bathroom, a conservatory and enlarged sitting room opening onto a patio. Parking and private garden. **Open:** All year **Nearest Shop:** 0.10 miles **Nearest Pub:** 0.02 miles

Site: ❀ P Payment: € Leisure: ... Property: ... Children: ... Unit: ... BBQ ☎

STOW-ON-THE-WOLD, Gloucestershire   Map ref 2B1

Units 1
Sleeps 2-4
PER UNIT PER WEEK
£350.00 - £800.00

Traveller's Joy

Contact: Mrs S Doswell, Owner, Lower Swell, Near Stow-on-the-Wold, Gloucestershire
GL54 1LF **T:** (01451) 870807 / 07768 446321 **E:** graham@thedoswells.co.uk
W: www.travellersjoycottage.co.uk

Very well appointed and modernised listed terraced cottage with spacious accommodation and large garden. Property is over 200 years old and was once home to the village blacksmith. Ideal base for touring the Cotswolds and neighbouring Worcestershire. One mile from historic market town of Stow-on-the-Wold with easy access to nearby footpaths to Upper and Lower Slaughter. Free car parking opposite. **Open:** All year **Nearest Shop:** 1 mile **Nearest Pub:** 300 metres

Site: ❀ Property: 🖥 📶 📺 Unit: 📖 🍽 📷 📺 🕯 TV 🎧 DVD 🔥 BBQ

STROUD, Gloucestershire   Map ref 2B1

Units 1
Sleeps 4-10
PER UNIT PER WEEK
£1000.00 - £2750.00

Barncastle

Contact: Mrs Valerie King, Booking Enquiries, Barncastle, Wragg Castle Lane, Pitchcombe, Nr. Stroud, Gloucestershire GL6 6LU **T:** 07766 514114 **F:** 01452 814350
E: enquiries@barncastle.co.uk **W:** www.barncastle.co.uk

Beautiful 5 bedroom converted stone barn, nestled in the Painswick Valley and in the perfect location from which to explore the best of English countryside and numerous outdoor pursuits such as the Cotswolds Way, golf, equestrian, horse racing and rugby. Oak flooring is a main feature, with its two fireplaces and oak gallery together with modern conveniences as sky tv and broadband internet. **Open:** All year **Nearest Shop:** 2 miles **Nearest Pub:** 0.5 miles

Site: ❀ P Leisure: 🎵 ▶ ∪ Property: 🖥 📶 📺 Children: 🧸 🛏 ♟ Unit: 📖 🍽 📷 📺 🕯 TV 🎧 DVD 🔥 BBQ

TETBURY, Gloucestershire   Map ref 2B2

Units 16
Sleeps 1-16

The Tythe House and Barn Complex

Contact: Folly Farm, Tetbury, Gloucestershire GL8 8XA **T:** (01666) 502475
E: info@tythehouse.com
W: www.tythehouse.com

Elegant Cotswold Manor House circa 1700 and restored in 2009. The house consists of three spacious ground floor reception rooms, eight en suite double bedrooms, all completed in a contemporary and homely style. Also available within the complex are 10 self catering cottages and a 12 room bed lodge all beautifully appointed with modern facilities. Please contact for prices. **Open:** All year **Nearest Shop:** 0.5 Miles **Nearest Pub:** 0.5 Miles

Site: ❀ P Payment: 💷 € Leisure: ⛳ 🎵 ▶ ∪ Property: 🖥 📶 📺 Children: 🧸 🛏 ♟ Unit: 🍽 📷 🕯 TV 🎧 DVD 🔥 BBQ

TEWKESBURY, Gloucestershire   Map ref 2B1

Units 1
Sleeps 1-3
PER UNIT PER WEEK
£345.00 - £445.00

9 Mill Bank

Contact: Bill & Dawn Hunt, 7 Mill Bank, Tewkesbury, Gloucestershire GL20 5SD
T: (01684) 276190 **F:** 01684 276190 **E:** billhunt@9mb.co.uk
W: www.tewkesbury-cottage.co.uk

A bijou, 16th century, riverside cottage in a delightful medieval town, bordering the Cotswolds. Outstanding location with open views across to the Malvern Hills. Nightly/weekend bookings taken. "Peace, quiet and tranquility; it truly is a gem". Alistair Sawday approved. See us on TripAdvisor. Free Wi-Fi. The '2 Star' with a 5 Star Heart! **Open:** All year **Nearest Shop:** 0.1 miles **Nearest Pub:** 0.1 miles

Payment: € Leisure: ⛳ 🎵 ▶ ∪ Property: 🖥 📶 Children: 🧸 🛏 ♟ Unit: 📷 🕯 TV 🎧 DVD 🔥

WINCHCOMBE, Gloucestershire Map ref 2B1

The Old Stables

Contact: Miss Jane Eayrs, Proprietor, The Old Stables, Hill View, Farmcote, Winchcombe GL54 5AU **T:** (01242) 603860 **E:** janeaycote@tesco.net
W: www.cotswolds.info/webpage/the-old-stables.htm

Units 1
Sleeps 1-4

PER UNIT PER WEEK
£300.00 - £380.00

The Old Stables is a delightful conversion situated in an 'Area of Outstanding Natural Beauty' in the hamlet of Farmcote. Farmcote has some of the most beautiful views in Gloucestershire.
Open: All year **Nearest Shop:** 3.5 miles **Nearest Pub:** 2 miles

Site: ✿ P **Leisure:** ♪ ⏵ ∪ **Property:** ▣ **Children:** ⛺ **Unit:** ⬚ ▣ ▤ ⌇ TV ◉ ⊙ BBQ ☎

WINCHCOMBE, Gloucestershire Map ref 2B1

Sudeley Castle Country Cottages

Contact: Debbie Hillyard, Cottage Administrator, Sudeley Castle, Castle Street, Winchcombe, Gloucestershire GL54 5JA **T:** (01242) 609481 **F:** 01242 602959
E: debbie.hillyard@sudeley.org.uk **W:** www.sudeleycastle.co.uk **£ BOOK ONLINE**

Units 11
Sleeps 2-5

PER UNIT PER WEEK
£350.00 - £725.00

SPECIAL PROMOTIONS
For late availability offers, please refer to the website. Weekend is 75% of weekly price.

Sudeley Castle Country Cottages are located on the edge of the estate, midway between the Castle and the historic town of Winchcombe. This small attractive complex of Cotswold stone cottages is set around a central courtyard with landscaped gardens & ample parking. Guests enjoy complimentary admission to the Castle & gardens during the open season. The cottages each have individual charm. Most have been cleverly restored and converted from existing properties, retaining many original and unique features. Accommodation is carefully prepared for your arrival, with laundry & bedding supplied.

Open: All year
Nearest Shop: 0.5 miles
Nearest Pub: 0.3 miles

Units: Well equipped kitchens, shared gardens, 2 mins walk into Winchcombe.

Site: ✿ P **Leisure:** ⛷ ♪ ⏵ ∪ **Property:** ♞ ▦ ▣ ▣ **Children:** ⛺ ▥ ⚲ **Unit:** ▣ TV ⊙ ☎

WITHINGTON, Gloucestershire Map ref 2B1

Ballingers Farmhouse Cottages

Contact: Ian & Judith Pollard, Ballingers Farmhouse Cottages, Withington, Cheltenham GL54 4BB **T:** (01242) 890335 **F:** 01242 890150 **E:** pollardfam2005@btinternet.com
W: www.ballingersfarmhousecottages.co.uk **£ BOOK ONLINE**

Units 2
Sleeps 2

PER UNIT PER WEEK
£250.00 - £350.00

Delightful single storey cottages, converted from old farm buildings retaining many original features that tastefully combine old and new. Well furnished and equipped to ensure you enjoy your holiday. Set in a village location approximately 8 miles from Cheltenham and Cirencester. Ideal for exploring the Cotswolds and surrounding areas. **Open:** March - October **Nearest Shop:** 3 miles **Nearest Pub:** 0.06 miles

Site: ✿ P **Property:** ♞ ▣ **Children:** ⛺ ▥ **Unit:** ▣ ▤ ⌇ TV ◉ ⊙ ∅

WOOLSTONE, Gloucestershire   Map ref 2B1

SELF CATERING

Units   1
Sleeps   4

PER UNIT PER WEEK
£250.00 – £430.00

SPECIAL PROMOTIONS
Low season £250-300
pw, High season £350-
£430pw.

Hill Farm Cottages

Contact: Mrs Diane Andrews, Owner, Woolstone Hill Farm, Woolstone GL52 9RG
T: (01242) 672803 / 07747 758503 **E:** woolstonehillfarm@hotmail.co.uk
W: www.thehillfarmcottage.co.uk **£ BOOK ONLINE**

Delightful 3 bedroom house, set in an Area of Outstanding Natural Beauty. Visitors are welcome to walk in the fields surrounding the farm and many public footpaths run nearby. The cottage is situated 1 mile from the village of Gotherington which has a village shop, Post Office, and local pub. Ideally situated for exploring the Cotswolds and many picturesque towns and villages including Broadway, Chipping Campden, Stow-on-the-Wold and Moreton-in-Marsh. Cheltenham and its racecourse are just 4 miles away while Tewkesbury, Evesham, Stratford-upon-Avon are just a short drive away.

Open: All year
Nearest Shop: 1 mile
Nearest Pub: 1 mile

Units: Fully equipped kitchen/dining room, Lounge with leather sofas, large TV & DVD, log effect gas fire. Ground floor single bedroom with en suite. Upstairs has two bedrooms and a fully fitted shower room.

Site: ❋ P **Leisure:** ♪ ◡ **Property:** ▭ ▯ ▱ **Children:** ⛷5 **Unit:** ▯ ▯ ▭ ▯ ▯ 📺 ◉ ⊙ BBQ

ALLERFORD, Somerset   Map ref 1D1

SELF CATERING

Units   5
Sleeps   2-6
PER UNIT PER WEEK
£355.00 – £645.00

The Pack Horse

Contact: Mr & Mrs Brian & Linda Garner, Proprietors, The Pack Horse, Allerford, Nr Porlock, Exmoor, Somerset TA24 8HW **T:** (01643) 862475 **E:** holidays@thepackhorse.net
W: www.thepackhorse.net **£ BOOK ONLINE**

Located in the picturesque National Trust village of Allerford, alongside the shallow river and overlooking the ancient Packhorse bridge, you will find our quality 4* Self Catering riverside apartments and detached cottage. Well appointed with quality furnishings, flat-screen TVs / DVDs and bed linen, all situated around a pretty courtyard. Our location gives immediate access to Exmoor and its stunning countryside coast and moor.
Open: All year **Nearest Shop:** 0.1 miles **Nearest Pub:** 0.1 miles

Site: ❋ P **Payment:** 🆓 **Leisure:** ♿ ♪ ♪ ◡ **Property:** 🐾 ▭ ▯ ▱ **Children:** ⛷ ▥ ⚲ **Unit:** ▯ ▯ ▭ ▯ 📺 ◉ ⊙ BBQ

BATH, Somerset   Map ref 2B2

★★★ SELF CATERING

Units 3
Sleeps 2-5

PER UNIT PER WEEK
£475.00 - £530.00

SPECIAL PROMOTIONS
Please contact for
current offers.

68 Ashgrove

Contact: Sam Hopkins, Owner, 68 Ashgrove, Peasedown St John, Bath, Somerset BA2 8EF
T: (01761) 300005 / 07778 053838 **E:** cottage68uk@gmail.com
W: www.cottage68.co.uk **£ BOOK ONLINE**

Pretty cottage set in the rural Cam Valley just 5 miles from the World Heritage City of Bath. Public transport is a short, level walk away taking guests to local places of interest including Stonehenge and Laycock. The cottage has 1 double and 1 twin bedroom, plus a room fitted with a high level cabin bed for younger visitors.

There is a comfortable sitting room, separate dining room, kitchen and bathroom with shower. Baby equipment, linen and Wi-Fi are provided. Driveway parking, herb garden and attractive seating area. The ideal base for touring this beautiful part of South West England.

Open: All year
Nearest Shop: 300 metres
Nearest Pub: 500 metres

Units: 1 double bedroom, 1 twin bedroom, 1 cabin bedroom with baby equipment. Bathroom/shower, kitchen, sitting room, dining room, driveway parking.

Site: P Leisure: **Property:**   **Children:**   **Unit:**   BBQ

BATH, Somerset   Map ref 2B2

★★★★ - ★★★★★ SELF CATERING   Gold AWARD

Units 5
Sleeps 2-4
PER UNIT PER WEEK
£311.00 - £807.00

Greyfield Farm Cottages

Contact: Mrs June Merry, Greyfield Farm Cottages, Greyfield Farm, The Gug,
High Littleton, Somerset BS39 6YQ **T:** (01761) 471132 **E:** june@greyfieldfarm.com
W: www.greyfieldfarm.com **£ BOOK ONLINE**

Attractive stone cottages in peaceful, private, 3.5-acre setting overlooking the Mendips. The cottages are spacious, fully equipped, warm and very comfortable. Each enjoys its own garden/patio and adjacent safe parking. Free facilities include hot tub, sauna, mini-gym, information hut and barbecue hut/area.
Open: All year **Nearest Shop:** 0.5 miles **Nearest Pub:** 0.5 miles

 Site: ❀ **P Payment:** € **Leisure:**   **Property:**   **Children:**   **Unit:**   BBQ

BATH, Somerset   Map ref 2B2

★★★★ SELF CATERING   Gold AWARD

Units 3
Sleeps 2-15
PER UNIT PER WEEK
£455.00 - £985.00

Nailey Cottages

Contact: Mrs Brett Gardner, Owner, Nailey Farm, St Catherine's Valley, Bath BA1 8HD
T: (01225) 852989 **E:** cottages@naileyfarm.co.uk
W: www.naileyfarm.co.uk

A family-run livestock farm also offering exceptional self-catering holidays and short breaks in three beautifully converted, thoughtfully equipped and spacious holiday cottages. Magnificent views of Cotswold countryside, yet only a few miles from the vibrant cities of Bath and Bristol. An ideal location to explore the South West of England. 'A little piece of paradise on earth'.
Open: All year **Nearest Shop:** 2 miles **Nearest Pub:** 2 miles

Site: ❀ **P Payment:** € **Leisure:**   **Property:**   **Children:**   **Unit:**   BBQ

BINEGAR, Somerset   Map ref 2B2

Spindle Cottage

Contact: Mrs Angela Bunting, Owner, Spindle Cottage, Binegar, Nr Bath, Somerset BA3 4UE **T:** (01749) 840497 / 07837 782841 **E:** angela@spindlecottage.co.uk **W:** www.spindlecottage.co.uk **£ BOOK ONLINE**

Units   1
Sleeps   1-5
PER UNIT PER WEEK
£450.00 - £750.00

Fairytale 17th century cottage, quite magical, high on Mendip Hills. Garden, summerhouse, gazebo and conservatory. Full of charm and delight. Lovely sitting room, low ceiling and oak beams. Woodburning stove. Three bedrooms: double with en suite, twin, single. Full of charm. Wells, Glastonbury, Bath, Cheddar and Wookey Hole within easy reach. Holiday of your dreams. 3 unique playhouses for playtime. **Open:** All year **Nearest Shop:** 1 mile **Nearest Pub:** 0.5 miles

 FAMILIES ▦ FAMILIES ▦ **Site:** ✿ **P Leisure:** ♪ ▶ ♒ **Property:** ▭ 🗄 🖥 **Children:** 🦌 ▦ ⚲ **Unit:** 🛏 🗄 📺 🗄 🍴 TV ⓓ dvd ⌀ **BBQ**

BURNHAM-ON-SEA, Somerset   Map ref 1D1

Kings Lynn Holiday Flats

Contact: Mrs V Young, Kings Lynn Holiday Flat, 18 Oxford Street, Burnham-on-Sea TA8 1LQ **T:** (01278) 786666 **E:** mikevalyoung@btinternet.com

Units   2
Sleeps   2-4
PER UNIT PER WEEK
£220.00 - £435.00

Availability of either a two bedroom, ground floor flat sleeping 2 plus 2 (bunk beds) or a one bedroom, first floor flat sleeping 2 plus 2 (bed settee). Centrally located within sea side town of Burnham-on-Sea within easy walking distance of all amenities and sea front. Easy access to M5 motorway. **Open:** All year **Nearest Shop:** 0.25 miles **Nearest Pub:** 0.25 miles

Site: P Property: 🖥 **Children:** 🦌 **Unit:** 🛏 📺 🍴 TV dvd

BURNHAM-ON-SEA, Somerset   Map ref 1D1

Pear Tree Cottage

Contact: Susan Slocombe, Owner, Northwick Road, Mark, Nr Burnham-on-Sea, Somerset TA9 4PG **T:** (01278) 641228 **E:** S_slocombe@btinternet.com

Units   1
Sleeps   2-4
PER UNIT PER WEEK
£300.00 - £500.00

Pear tree cottage is a detached single storey barn conversion, situated on the Somerset Levels overlooking pleasant gardens and open farmland. Ideal base for exploring the many attractions of the surrounding area. Popular for cyclists, bird-watching and walkers. Only one mile from the village of Mark, offering village Post Office/store, church, pub and all within 3 miles of coast. **Open:** All year except Christmas/New Year. **Nearest Shop:** 1 mile **Nearest Pub:** 1 mile

Site: ✿ **P Payment:** 💳 **Leisure:** ♪ ▶ ⚓ ⛵ ⚲ **Property:** 🐾 ▭ 🗄 🖥 **Children:** 🦌 ▦ ⚲ **Unit:** 🛏 🗄 📺 🗄 🍴 TV ⓓ dvd ⌀ **BBQ** ☎

South West - Somerset

BURNHAM-ON-SEA, Somerset   Map ref 1D1

Stoddens Farm Cottages

Contact: Mrs Ruth Chambers, Owner, Stoddens Farm, 191 Stoddens Road,
Burnham on Sea, Somerset TA8 2DE **T:** 07896 886051 **E:** info@stoddensfarmcottages.com
W: www.stoddensfarmcottages.com **£ BOOK ONLINE**

Units   2
Sleeps   1-4
PER UNIT PER WEEK
£230.00 - £450.00

Located in a Grade II listed barn conversion with plenty of character. Spacious and comfortable accommodation for up to 4 people in each of the 2 cottages. Large private gardens and stunning views over Somerset Levels. **Open:** All year
Nearest Shop: 0.5 miles **Nearest Pub:** 0.5 miles

Site: ✿ P Property: 🖥 🖳 Children: 🍼 🍴 🕯 Unit: 📺 🖳 TV dvd BBQ

CHEDDAR, Somerset   Map ref 1D1

Sungate Holiday Apartments

Contact: Mrs M M Fieldhouse, Pyrenmount, Parsons Way, Winscombe, Somerset BS25 1BU
T: (01934) 842273 **E:** sunholaapartment@btinternet.com
W: www.sungateholidayapartments.co.uk

Units   4
Sleeps   2-4
PER UNIT PER WEEK
£200.00 - £260.00

The apartments are for 2 - 4 persons. They consist of a twin or double bedded room, lounge with sofa bed, bathroom and kitchen. Ground floor disabled friendly. Children and pets are welcome. Laundry facilities available. Please check our website or contact us for more details. **Open:** All year **Nearest Shop:** 1 mile
Nearest Pub: 1 mile

 Site: ✿ P Payment: € Property: 🐾 🖥 🖳 Children: 🍼 Unit: 📺 TV

CHURCHINFORD, Somerset   Map ref 1D2

South Cleeve Bungalow

Contact: Mr J Manning, South Cleeve Bungalow, Churchinford, Nr Taunton, Somerset
TA3 7PR **T:** (01823) 601378 / 07811 362740 **E:** enquiries@timbertopbungalows.co.uk
W: www.timbertopbungalows.co.uk

Units   2
Sleeps   2-6
PER UNIT PER WEEK
£150.00 - £630.00

SPECIAL PROMOTIONS
Late bookings available at discounted rate. Short breaks available upon request (2 nights minimum stay).

Set in a quiet, rural location in an Area of Outstanding Natural Beauty on the Devon/Somerset border. Within easy reach of attractions and amenities and north and south coastlines, this fully equipped bungalow set in its own large, secure lawned garden, that welcomes many wild and birdlife visitors, makes a superb holiday for all the family.

Wi-Fi installed.
Disabled friendly, wheelchair and ramp available.
One well behaved pet welcome.

Open: All year
Nearest Shop: 1 mile (Taunton 9 miles)
Nearest Pub: 1 mile

Units: Large, spacious bungalow set in a third of an acre of lawned garden, 2 double rooms (1 en suite) & 1 twin, lounge, kitchen/diner and conservatory.

Site: ✿ P Leisure: 🎵 🏌 ∪ 🎣 Property: 🐾 🖳 Children: 🍼 🍴 🕯 Unit: 🖥 🖳 📺 🖳 TV dvd BBQ

84 The Official Tourist Board Guide to **Self Catering 2015**

MARTOCK, Somerset Map ref 2A3

Anne's Place

Contact: Kathleen Mountjoy, Owner, 8 Water Street, Martock, Somerset TA12 6JN
T: (01935) 826440 **E:** gwmountjoy@aol.com
W: www.ownersdirect.co.uk

Units 1
Sleeps 2
PER UNIT PER WEEK
£285.00 - £370.00

Ground floor annexe, sleeps 2. Lounge, twin bedroom with en suite shower/toilet. Kitchen/dining area. Parking. Easy walking access. Full details www.ownersdirect.co.uk (property E7080). **Open:** All year except Christmas and New Year **Nearest Shop:** 800 yds **Nearest Pub:** 800 yds

Site: ✿ P Leisure: ▶ ◔ Property: ▭ ▣ Unit: ▯ ▭ ▤ ▧ TV ◉ DVD BBQ

MINEHEAD, Somerset Map ref 1D1

Woodcombe Lodges & Cottages

Contact: Mrs Nicola Hanson, Proprietor, Woodcombe Lodges, Bratton Lane, Minehead, Somerset TA24 8SQ **T:** (01643) 702789 / 07545 271536 **E:** nicola@woodcombelodge.co.uk
W: www.woodcombelodges.co.uk **£ BOOK ONLINE**

Units 8
Sleeps 2-10
PER UNIT PER WEEK
£255.00 - £1650.00

Six 4* Lodges and two cottages set in 3 acres of gardens with superb views over the slopes of the Exmoor National Park. Peaceful rural setting, ideal for walking or family holidays. Within a 5 minute drive of shops, restaurants, beach and sea front. Games room, putting green. Disabled Access, Wi-Fi. Dogs welcome. Open all year with short breaks from Oct to May. **Open:** All year **Nearest Shop:** 1 mile **Nearest Pub:** 1 mile

Site: ✿ P Payment: £ Leisure: 🎣 ▶ ◔ Property: 🐾 ▭ ▣ Children: 🚼 ▥ Unit: ▯ ▭ ▤ ▧ TV DVD ✆

PORLOCK, Somerset Map ref 1D1

Green Chantry

Contact: Mrs Margaret Payton, Owner, Green Chantry, Home Farm, Burrowbridge, Bridgwater TA7 0RF **T:** (01823) 698330 / 07860 135848 **E:** maggie_payton@hotmail.com

Units 1
Sleeps 1-4
PER UNIT PER WEEK
£198.00 - £395.00

A charming Victorian cottage in a tranquil setting yet close to High Street with its range of shops, pubs and cafes and good local bus services. Good walking from cottage. **Open:** All year **Nearest Shop:** 0.10 miles **Nearest Pub:** 0.10 miles

Site: ✿ Leisure: 🎣 ◔ Property: 🐾 ▣ Children: 🚼 Unit: ▯ ▭ ▤ ▧ TV DVD

Book your accommodation online

Visit our websites for detailed information, up-to-date availability and to book your accommodation online. Includes over 20,000 places to stay, all of them star rated.

www.visitor-guides.co.uk

SOMERTON, Somerset   Map ref 2A3

Sleepy Hollow Cottages

Contact: Mrs Catherine Lewis, Sleepy Hollow, Double Gates Drove, Mill Road, Barton St David, Somerton, Somerset TA11 6DF **T:** (01458) 850584
E: t.s.lewis@btinternet.com **W:** sleepyhollowcottages.co.uk

Units	3
Sleeps	1-8

PER UNIT PER WEEK
£250.00 - £450.00

SPECIAL PROMOTIONS
Late deal discounts available. Short breaks available all year. Up to 2 dogs by arrangement.

Deep in the heart of rural Somerset, 4* Sleepy Hollow offers comfortable cottages in perfect tranquility, with access to many varied local attractions, including Bath, Wells, Glastonbury, Dorset & Somerset coasts, Exmoor, Somerset Levels, National Trust properties & Cheddar Gorge. A wonderful place to relax and unwind. Excellent walking & cycling. Secure cycle storage and laundry facilities, Wi-Fi access in all cottages, ample parking, cot & high chair, table tennis available. Your Online food shopping can be delivered for your arrival.

Open: All year
Nearest Shop: 1 mile
Nearest Pub: 0.5 miles

Units: 2 single storey, 1 two storey all with modern kitchens and bathrooms with bath and over bath shower.

Site: ✿ **P Payment:** 💷 **Leisure:** 🎣 🎵 **Property:** 🐾 🚲 📺 💻 **Children:** 🪑 🛏
Unit: 🛏 🍳 📺 🔌 📺 📀 BBQ

SOUTH PETHERTON, Somerset   Map ref 1D2

Tanwyn

Contact: Mr & Mrs Rodney & Ann Tanswell, Planhigyn, Penylan Road, Saint Brides Major, Bridgend CF32 0SB **T:** (01656) 880524 / 07896 892448 **E:** rodney.tanswell@btinternet.com
W: www.tanwyncottage.com

Units	1
Sleeps	1-4

PER UNIT PER WEEK
£270.00 - £420.00

Tanwyn is a modernised hamstone cottage situated in a pleasant village with a pub and an award winning restaurant. Ideally located for South coast, Exmoor, Cheddar, Bath, Wells, National Trust gardens etc. Large garden and orchard. **Open:** All year except Christmas and New Year **Nearest Shop:** 1 mile
Nearest Pub: 0.25 miles

Site: ✿ **P Leisure:** 🎵 **Property:** 🚲 📺 💻 **Children:** 🪑10 **Unit:** 🛏 🍳 📺 🔌 📺 📀 📞

TAUNTON, Somerset   Map ref 1D1

The Garden Cottage

Contact: Alan Coles, Owner, Stoke Hill Barn, Stoke St Mary, Taunton, Somerset TA3 5BT
T: (01823) 443759 / 07434 812279 **E:** alancoles67@gmail.com
W: www.somerset-selfcatering.co.uk

Units	1
Sleeps	7

PER UNIT PER WEEK
£425.00 - £750.00

Architect's own spacious and elegantly styled garden hideaway. Only 10 minutes from Taunton but in the middle of nowhere with 6 acres of wildlife filled gardens, woods, ponds, meadow and wonderful views over a tranquil landscape. This is an ideal location for exploring the Jurassic coast around Lyme Bay, the Bristol channel coast, the Quantocks, Blackdowns, Brendons, Mendips and Exmoor. **Open:** All year **Nearest Shop:** Within 2 miles
Nearest Pub: Within 2 miles

Site: ✿ **P Payment:** € **Leisure:** 🎵 🏹 🎣 **Property:** 🚲 📺 💻 **Children:** 🪑 🛏 🔥 **Unit:** 🛏 📺 📺 🔌 BBQ

TAUNTON, Somerset   Map ref 1D1

Units 1
Sleeps 1-12
PER UNIT PER WEEK
£1000.00 - £4200.00

Millgrove House
Contact: Melanie Alford, Blackdown Luxury Lettings, Staplegrove Mills, Staplegrove, Taunton, Somerset TA2 6PX **T:** (01884) 849127 **E:** mel@blackdownluxurylettings.co.uk
W: www.blackdownluxurylettings.co.uk **£ BOOK ONLINE**

In a secluded setting with a pleasant countryside outlook. Millgrove offers luxury accommodation for the discerning holiday maker. Sleeping 10 people in five bedrooms as either double (kingsize) or twin single beds and a further 2 people on a double sofa bed. With its own covered heated swimming pool for all year round use, this property is perfect for family holidays or celebrations.
Open: End of February to Early January **Nearest Shop:** 0.2 miles
Nearest Pub: 0.2 miles

Site: ❈ P Payment: 💷 Leisure: 🎵 ▶ ♺ ♨ 🎣 Property: 📺 📷 🖥 Children: 🚼 🛏 🪑 Unit: 📟 📠 📺 📷 🗑
📺 💿 📀 BBQ

WEDMORE, Somerset   Map ref 1D1

Units 2
Sleeps 2-4

PER UNIT PER WEEK
£280.00 - £880.00

SPECIAL PROMOTIONS
Weekend breaks during low and mid season. 2 nights minimum stay.

Pear Tree Cottages
Contact: Mrs P Denbee, Pear Tree Farm, Stoughton Cross, Wedmore, Somerset BS28 4QR
T: (01934) 712243 **E:** info@peartree-cottages.co.uk
W: www.peartree-cottages.co.uk **£ BOOK ONLINE**

In the heart of the Somerset countryside are 2 luxury converted cottages with original features, on a working farm. A mecca for walkers, cyclists, nature lovers and golfers, they are also ideally situated for those who prefer exploring the villages, towns and cities of the area. Private south facing garden/patios.

Open: All year
Nearest Shop: 1.5 miles
Nearest Pub: 0.5 miles

Units: Cottages are furnished and equipped to luxury standard, with underfloor heating and woodburner and many kitchen and entertainment appliances.

Site: ❈ P Leisure: 🎵 ▶ ♺ Property: 📺 📷 🖥 Children: 🚼 🛏 🪑 Unit: 📟 📠 📺 📷 🗑 📺 📀 ⌀ BBQ

WELLINGTON, Somerset   Map ref 1D1

Units 1
Sleeps 1-16
PER UNIT PER WEEK
£2000.00 - £4800.00

The Cottage Beyond
Contact: Christine and Alan Ker, Owners, The Cottage Beyond, Kittisford Barton, Wellington, Somerset TA21 0RZ **T:** (01823) 672736 / 07843 529073
E: info@thecottagebeyond.co.uk **W:** www.thecottagebeyond.co.uk **£ BOOK ONLINE**

A unique, large family home that has been transformed from a modest 1930's farmworker's cottage into a fabulous architect-designed, contemporary residence brimming with "WOW" factor with its own swimming pool, sauna & hot tub for your exclusive use. The house is set in a secluded landscaped garden at the heart of the family's 260-acre organic farm. **Open:** All year
Nearest Shop: 2 miles **Nearest Pub:** 2 miles

Site: ❈ P Payment: 💷 Leisure: 🎵 ▶ 🎣 ♨ Property: 🐾 🐕 📺 📷 🖥 Children: 🚼 🛏 🪑 Unit: 📟 📠 📺 📷 🗑
📺 💿 📀 ⌀ BBQ 📞

WELLINGTON, Somerset   Map ref 1D1

Tone Dale House

Contact: Peter Insall, Owner, The Big House Company, Tone Dale House, Milverton Road, Wellington, Somerset TA21 0EZ **T:** (01823) 662673 **E:** peter@thebighouseco.com
W: www.thebighouseco.com

Impressive Georgian Palladian Villa set in 4 acres. Ideal for house parties, weddings and meetings. With over 18 years of experience in organising events for our guests we are pleased to help you make the most of your time at a Big House. We can organise excellent catering or if you prefer you can self cater. Activities can be arranged to take place either off site or in the grounds. **Open:** All year **Nearest Shop:** 200 yards **Nearest Pub:** 1 mile

| Units | 1 |
| Sleeps | 31 |

PER UNIT PER WEEK
£5500.00 - £8250.00

Site: ❀ P **Payment:** 💷 **Leisure:** 🏊 🎵 🏸 ⛳ 🎣 **Property:** 🚶 🐴 📺 📶 📖 **Children:** 🚼 🛏 🎑
Unit: 📱 🍴 📺 🔌 📶 TV DVD 🔥 BBQ ☎

WESTON-SUPER-MARE, Somerset   Map ref 1D1

Kyrenia Holiday Flats

Contact: Deanna & Sean Swords, Owners, 41 & 42 Beach Road, Weston-Super-Mare, Somerset BS23 1BQ **T:** (01934) 751056 **E:** info@go-south.co.uk
W: www.go-south.co.uk

Perfectly situated facing the beach with stunning seafront views. Close to the town centre and railway station. All apartments are immaculately presented for your arrival. All apartments have en suite bathrooms and fully equipped kitchens. Perfect for families, couples and business guests. On site parking, free Wi-Fi & a lovely relaxing garden. We are also cycle friendly. **Open:** All year **Nearest Shop:** 0.07 miles **Nearest Pub:** 0.05 miles

| Units | 6 |
| Sleeps | 1-5 |

PER UNIT PER WEEK
£395.00 - £495.00

Site: P **Payment:** 💷 **Property:** 📺 📶 📖 **Children:** 🚼 **Unit:** 📱 📺 TV

WESTON-SUPER-MARE, Somerset   Map ref 1D1

Martyndale Suites

Contact: Clive Sills, Owner, 7 Royal Crescent, Weston-super-Mare, Somerset BS23 2AX
T: (01458) 251399 / 07711893637 **E:** csills@whsmithnet.co.uk
W: www.martyndalesuites.com

Seven en suite apartments, with fitted kitchens. Situated in the heart of Weston's heritage area. 200 yards to the beach and promenade, bars and restaurants and the children's water park. Easy level walking to the High street, Playhouse theatre, and most attractions. Popular location and property for business people, many international ones included. Garden flat popular for those with infirmities. **Open:** All year **Nearest Shop:** 300 yards **Nearest Pub:** 100 yards

| Units | 7 |
| Sleeps | 1-6 |

PER UNIT PER WEEK
£160.00 - £520.00

Site: P **Payment:** 💷 **Property:** 📺 📶 📖 **Children:** 🚼 **Unit:** 📱 📺 🔌 TV ☎

WESTON-SUPER-MARE, Somerset   Map ref 1D1

Weston Sea-view apartments

Contact: Sean, Owner, Go South Ltd, 6-8 Victoria Square, Weston super Mare, Somerset BS23 1AW **T:** (01934) 751056 **E:** info@go-south.co.uk
W: www.go-south.co.uk

Salisbury Court & The Charlton Holiday Apartments in Weston Super Mare are situated on Weston's Seafront. Immaculately presented to the highest standards, our self-catering holiday apartments are stylish and contemporary throughout with modern bathrooms and fully fitted kitchens. Perfect for families, couples and business guests. **Open:** All Year **Nearest Shop:** 100 yards **Nearest Pub:** 100 yards

| Units | 8 |
| Sleeps | 1-6 |

PER UNIT PER WEEK
£395.00 - £595.00

Site: ❀ P **Leisure:** 🏊 🎵 🏸 ⛳ **Property:** 🚶 📺 📶 📖 **Children:** 🚼 🛏 🎑 **Unit:** 📱 🍴 📺 🔌 📶 TV 🎧 DVD

WINFORD, Somerset   Map ref 2A2

Regilbury Farm

Contact: Mrs. Jane Keedwell, Regilbury Farm, The Street, Regil, Winford BS40 8BB
T: (01275) 472369 **E:** stay@regilburyfarm.co.uk
W: www.regilburyfarm.co.uk **£ BOOK ONLINE**

Units 2
Sleeps 2-4
PER UNIT PER WEEK
£225.00 - £485.00

Working farm with cattle, sheep and chickens, set in a beautiful, quiet hamlet. Wonderful rambling, lots to see. Guided walks available. Cowshed - double, Parlour - double/twin. No pets. 3 nights 65% / 4 nights 75% / 5 nights 85% of weekly rate.
Open: All year **Nearest Shop:** 2 miles **Nearest Pub:** 1 mile

Site: ❀ P **Leisure:** ♪ **Property:** 🖥 🖵 **Children:** 🛏 🛏 🧍 **Unit:** 🖵 🖳 🗄 🖥 📺 🗂 BBQ

YEOVIL, Somerset   Map ref 2A3

Little Norton Mill

Contact: Peter & Julie Allard, Owner, Norton-sub-Hamdon, Yeovil, Somerset TA14 6TE
T: 01935881337 **E:** p.allard190@btinternet.com
W: www.littlenortonmill.co.uk **£ BOOK ONLINE**

Units 8
Sleeps 2-4
PER UNIT PER WEEK
£243.00 - £689.00

8 Self catering cottages and apartments set in beautiful spacious gardens next to a 18th century watermill. The 2 bedroom cottages overlooking the mill pond sleep 4. The 1 bedroom apartments are a cosy base for 2. Ideal for exploring the beautiful countryside of Somerset, numerous National Trust properties, cider mills and the World heritage coast of Dorset. **Open:** All year **Nearest Shop:** 950 metres **Nearest Pub:** 800 metres

Site: ❀ **Payment:** 💷 **Property:** 🖥 🗄 🖵 **Children:** 🛏 🛏 🧍 **Unit:** 🗄 🖳 🖥 🗂 📺 🗂 BBQ 📞

YEOVIL, Somerset   Map ref 2A3

Mrs Bests Holiday Cottage

Contact: Sarah Duncan, Owner, 16 Compton Pauncefoot, Yeovil, Somerset BA22 7EN
T: 07717 835262 **E:** sarahjaduncan@gmail.com
W: www.mrsbestsholidaycottage.com

Units 1
Sleeps 8
PER UNIT PER WEEK
£650.00 - £1500.00

Mrs Bests Holiday Cottage is a beautiful hamstone cottage located in a pretty South Somerset village. This luxury self-catering accommodation has the feel of a country house in a spacious cottage setting which sleeps up to eight people. The cottage consists of three good sized bedrooms and two family bathrooms upstairs together with a double bedroom and shower room on the ground floor. **Open:** All year **Nearest Shop:** 2 miles **Nearest Pub:** 0.5 miles

Site: ❀ P **Property:** 🐾 🖥 🗄 🖵 **Children:** 🛏 🛏 🧍 **Unit:** 🗄 🖳 🖥 🗄 🗂 📺 🗂 ⬗

BRADFORD-ON-AVON, Wiltshire   Map ref 2B2

Bridge Cottage

Contact: Lara Kent, Owner, 16A High Street, Rode BA11 6NZ **T:** (01373) 830996 / 07788 921110 **E:** lara.matthews@btinternet.com
W: www.visitbridgecottage.co.uk

Units 1
Sleeps 1-4
PER UNIT PER WEEK
£495.00 - £695.00

Delightful 2 bedroom cottage with 4* Gold Award, decorated with Cath Kidston fabrics, vintage furniture and luxury bed linen. A few minutes level walk from the centre of Bradford on Avon and 15 minutes train to Bath. Bright and sunny south facing accommodation recently refurbished to a high standard.
Open: All year **Nearest Shop:** 50m **Nearest Pub:** 50m

Leisure: 🚲 **Property:** ✀ 🖥 🗄 🖵 **Children:** 🛏 🛏 🧍 **Unit:** 🗄 🖳 🖥 🗄 🗂 📺 🗂 ⬗

HANGING LANGFORD, Wiltshire   Map ref 2B2

Units 1
Sleeps 1-6

PER UNIT PER WEEK
£450.00 – £700.00

Kingfisher Lodge
Contact: Mrs Georgina Helyer, Lottmead Farm, Hanging Langford, Salisbury SP3 4PA
T: (01722) 790396 / 07970 153550 **E:** helyerlottmead@aol.com
W: kingfisherlangford.co.uk

Kingfisher Lodge is purpose built, all on one easy level accommodation. Sleeps 5/6. Hanging Langford, 10 miles Salisbury. Disabled friendly. Plenty of parking close to the front door. Short breaks availaible for 3 nights from £275. **Open:** All year
Nearest Shop: 3 miles **Nearest Pub:** 1 mile

Site: ❀ **P Leisure:** ♪ **Property:** 🖥 📱 💻 **Children:** 🐎 🎠 🚶 **Unit:** 📺 📀 BBQ

MARLBOROUGH, Wiltshire   Map ref 2B2

Units 3
Sleeps 1-8

SPECIAL PROMOTIONS
Please contact us for prices.

Dairy Cottage, Cherry & Walnut Lodge
Contact: Mr & Mrs Mark & Hazel Crockford, Dairy Cottage, Cherry & Walnut Lodge, Browns Farm, Marlborough SN8 4ND **T:** (01672) 515129 / 07931 311985
E: crockford@farming.co.uk **W:** marlboroughhoilidaycottages.com **£ BOOK ONLINE**

Dairy Cottage is situated on Browns Farm which is a working beef/arable farm set on the edge of Savernake Forest overlooking open farmland. The cottage offers peace and tranquillity for a true North Wiltshire holiday. A modern, spacious, well-equipped bungalow with open fire awaits your arrival.

Open: All year
Nearest Shop: 2 miles
Nearest Pub: 2 miles

Site: ❀ **P Payment:** 💳 **Leisure:** ♪ ♂ ♀ **Property:** 🐾 🖥 📱 💻 **Children:** 🐎 🎠 🚶 **Unit:** 📺 📀 BBQ

Welcome Pets!

Want to travel with your faithful companion? Look out for accommodation displaying the **Welcome Pets!** sign. Participants in this scheme go out of their way to meet the needs of guests bringing dogs, cats and/or small birds. In addition to providing water and food bowls, torches or nightlights, spare leads and pet washing facilities, they'll buy in food on request, and offer toys, treats and bedding. They'll also have information on pet-friendly attractions, pubs, restaurants and recreation. Of course, not everyone is able to offer suitable facilities for every pet, so do check if there are any restrictions on type, size and number of animals when you book.

Look out for the following symbol in the entry.

Don't Miss...

Beaulieu National Motor Museum, House and Garden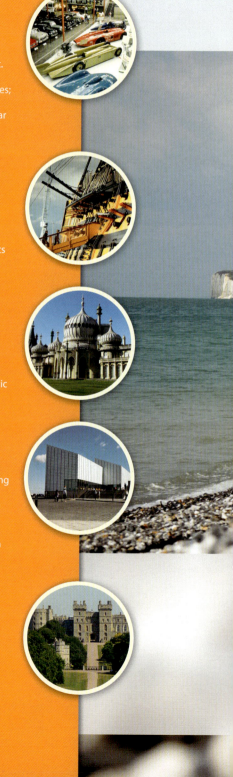
Beaulieu, Hampshire SO42 7ZN
(01590) 612345
www.beaulieu.co.uk
In the New Forest, Beaulieu is one of England's top family days out. There's lots to enjoy including the world famous National Motor Museum, home to a stunning and historic collection of automobiles; Palace House, home of the Montagu family; historic Beaulieu Abbey founded in 1204 by Cistercian Monks, and World of Top Gear features vehicles from some of the most ambitious challenges.

Portsmouth Historic Dockyard
Portsmouth, Hampshire PO1 3LJ
(023) 9283 9766
www.historicdockyard.co.uk
Portsmouth Historic Dockyard offers a great day out for all the family and spans over 800 years of British Naval history. The state-of-the-art Mary Rose Museum is home to the remains of Henry VIII's flagship and an astounding collection of 400 year old artefacts recovered from the sea.

The Royal Pavilion Brighton
Brighton, East Sussex BN1 1EE
03000 290900
www.brighton-hove-rpml.org.uk/RoyalPavilion
This spectacularly extravagant seaside palace was built for the Prince Regent, later King George IV, between 1787 and 1823. Housing furniture, works of art and a splendid balconied tearoom overlooking the gardens, it is one the most extraordinary and exotic oriental buildings in the country.

Turner Contemporary Art Gallery
Margate, Kent, CT19 1HG
(01843) 233000
www.turnercontemporary.org
Situated on Margate's seafront, Turner Contemporary is a welcoming space that offers world-class exhibitions of contemporary and historical art, events and activities. Taking inspiration from Britain's best-known painter JMW Turner and designed by internationally acclaimed David Chipperfield Architects, this gleaming structure hovering over the town is the largest exhibtiion space in the South East outside of London and admission to the gallery is free.

Windsor Castle
Windsor, Berkshire SL4 1NJ
(020) 7766 7304
www.royalcollection.org.uk
Built by Edward III in the 14th century and restored by later monarchs, Windsor Castle is the largest and oldest occupied castle in the world and has been the family home of British kings and queens for almost 1,000 years. It is an official residence of Her Majesty the Queen and encapsulates more than 900 years of English history. St George's Chapel within the Castle Precincts is the spiritual home of the Order of the Garter, the oldest order of chivalry in the world.

South East

Berkshire, Buckinghamshire, Hampshire,
Isle of Wight, Kent, Oxfordshire, Surrey, Sussex

Oxfordshire

Buckinghamshire

Berkshire

Surrey   Kent

Hampshire

Sussex

Isle of Wight

The Thames sweeps eastwards in broad graceful curves, cutting through the beeches of the Chiltern Hills. Miles of glorious countryside and historic cities offer heritage sites, gardens, parks and impressive architecture for you to visit. In the far south, fun-filled resorts and interesting harbours are dotted along 257 miles of delightful coastline and the Isle of Wight is a only a short ferry ride away. The South East of England is an area of great beauty that will entice you to return again and again.

Explore – South East

Berkshire

Renowned for its royal connections, the romantic county of Berkshire counts Windsor Castle as its most famous building. Cliveden House, former seat of the Astor family and now a famous hotel, is nearby. Highclere Castle, the setting for Downton Abbey, as well as Eton College and Ascot Racecourse can be found here too.

Hotspot: LEGOLAND® Windsor
Berkshire SL4 4AY (0871) 222 2001
www.legoland.co.uk
With over 55 interactive rides and attractions, there's just too much to experience in one day!

Buckinghamshire

Buckinghamshire, to the north east of the region, is home to the most National Trust properties in the country as well as the magnificent 'Capability Brown' landscape at Stowe, now a famous public school.

The city of Milton Keynes has its infamous concrete cows and the delights of its vast shopping centre but there's plenty more to see and do in the county. Experience a hands-on history lesson at the fascinating Chiltern Open Air Museum or get your adrenalin pumping and test your head for heights with a zip wire adventure at Go Ape Wendover Woods. For a gentler pace, enjoy a tranquil bike ride through beautiful countryside along the meandering Thames.

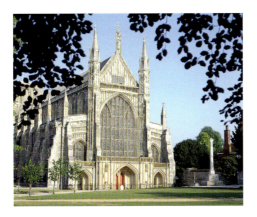

Hampshire & Isle Of Wight

Historic Winchester is a must-visit for its charming medieval streets, imposing Cathedral, vibrant galleries and stylish, independent shops. The ancient heaths and woodlands of the New Forest National Park were once a royal hunting ground for William the Conqueror and deer, ponies and cattle continue to roam free. Cycle, walk or go horseriding in this tranquil, car-free environment or visit attractions such as the National Motor Museum at Beaulieu and Exbury Gardens & Steam Railway for a great day out.

Coastal Hampshire, with the Solent, Southampton Water and the Isle of Wight, is one of the sailing playgrounds of England. Nearby Portsmouth Harbour has Nelson's Victory, the Mary Rose and the ironclad HMS Warrior. Stroll gently around the picturesque village of Lymington or explore the cliffs along the coast. The Isle of Wight can be reached by ferry and is a great destination for amazing beaches, exciting events such as Bestival, or a step back in time, counting Osborne House and Carisbrooke Castle among its historic gems.

Kent

The Garden of England is a diverse county full of romantic villages and unmissable heritage. The opulent Leeds Castle, surrounded by its shimmering lake and set in 500 acres of spectacular parkland and gardens, has attractions and events aplenty. Take a tour of Kent's rural past with a scenic cruise along the River Medway to Kent Life, a museum and working farm with animals galore and a real sense of nostalgia for bygone days. At the northeast tip of the county, where stunning sea- and sky-scapes famously inspired JMW Turner, Margate is home to the brilliant Turner Contemporary art gallery and the Shell Grotto, a subterranean wonder lined with 4.6 million shells. Broadstairs hosts an acclaimed annual folk festival and Ramsgate is a firm favourite, with its sophisticated café culture, marina and award-winning sandy beach.

Hotspot: Hever Castle in Kent is a romantic 13th century moated castle with magnificently furnished interiors, award winning gardens, miniature Model House Exhibition, Yew Maze and a unique Splashing Water Maze. www.hevercastle.co.uk

Oxfordshire

Oxford's dreaming spires, echoing quads and cloistered college lawns have a timeless beauty. The Ashmolean Museum, Britain's oldest public museum, opened in 1683 and contains gold and jewellery believed to have belonged to King Alfred, the lantern carried by Guy Fawkes and riches from ancient Egypt and Greece. The Bodleian Library, founded in 1596, contains over one million volumes, including a copy of every book published in the UK since 1900. Just north of Oxford at Woodstock sits magnificent Blenheim Palace, the birthplace of Sir Winston Churchill. Oxfordshire's quiet paths and roads are perfect for cycling, and charming picture postcard villages like Great Tew make excellent rest points.

Surrey

Ashdown Forest, now more of a heath, covers 6400 acres of upland, with a large deer, badger and rare bird population. The heights of Box Hill and Leith Hill rise above the North Downs to overlook large tracts of richly wooded countryside, containing a string of well protected villages. The Devil's Punchbowl, near Hindhead, is a two mile long sandstone valley, overlooked by the 900-ft Gibbet Hill. Farnham, in the west of the country, has Tudor and Georgian houses flanking the 12th century castle. Nearby Aldershot is the home of the British Army and county town Guildford is a contemporary business and shopping centre with a modern cathedral and university. The north of the county borders Greater London and includes the 2400 acre Richmond Park, Hampton Court Palace and Kew Gardens.

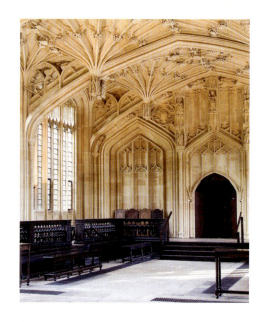

Sussex

Sussex is a popular county for those wanting a short break from the hustle and bustle of London. Cosmopolitan Brighton, surely the capital of East Sussex, oozes culture, boutique hotels, marina, shops and 'buzz'. The eccentric Royal Pavilion testifies to its history as the Regency summer capital of Britain.

Hotspot: The Brighton Festival in May is a sensational programme of art, theatre, dance, music, literature and family shows starting with a Children's Parade winding its way through the city. www.brightonfestival.org

To the west is the impressive Arundel Castle, with its famous drama festival, nearby popular marinas and Wittering sands. Bognor Regis is a traditional seaside resort with a blue flag beach and the usual attractions. To the east the impressive Beachy Head and Seven Sisters cliffs provide a dramatic backdrop for Eastbourne. The Sussex section of the South Downs National Park stretches from Beachy Head to Harting Down with miles of open chalk grassland, lush river valleys and ancient forests to explore.

If heritage is your thing then Sussex has a plethora of historic houses and gardens and three of the historic cinque ports. Rye in particular, with its cobbled streets, transports the visitor back three centuries. The 1066 Story is told at Battle, near Hastings and Groombridge Place, Great Dixter and Borde Hill all feature stunningly beautiful heritage gardens.

The world famous **Blackbird Tea Rooms** in Brighton is a treat to be savoured, evoking the charm of a bygone era with delicious breakfasts and home-made cakes served on original vintage china in an elegant pre-war setting.
www.blackbirdtearooms.com

For retro-style sweet treats in Kent, **Morelli's ice** cream parlour on Victoria Parade in Broadstairs can't be beaten.

The Grapes in George Street, Oxford is the sole surviving Victorian pub in the city centre and is a fabulous example of a traditional pub with a contemporary approach.

Take a tour of the **Chiltern Brewery**, the oldest independent brewery in the Chiltern Hills and Buckinghamshire, and test its award-winning range of bottle conditioned and draught ales.
www.chilternbrewery.co.uk

For sheer luxury, book a visit to the Elizabethan **Ockenden Manor Hotel & Spa** in Cuckfield near Haywards Heath and enjoy full use of the spa facilities and dinner in the Michelin starred restaurant. Tel (01444) 416111
www.hshotels.co.uk/ockenden-manor-hotel-and-spa

Barefoot Books in Oxford is the perfect place to browse and experience live storytelling, educational games, music, arts, crafts and more.
www.barefootbooks.com

Visit – South East

 Attractions with this sign participate in the Visitor Attraction Quality Assurance Scheme.

Berkshire

French Brothers Ltd
Windsor, Berkshire SL4 5JH
(01753) 851900
www.boat-trips.co.uk
Large range of public trips on weather-proof vessels from Windsor, Runnymede and Maidenhead.

Go Ape! Bracknell, Swinley Forest
Berkshire RG12 7QW
(0845) 643 9215
www.goape.co.uk
Go Ape! and tackle a high-wire forest adventure course of rope bridges, Tarzan swings and zip slides up to 35 feet above the forest floor.

Ascot CAMRA Beer Festival
Ascot Racecourse, October
An action packed day of flat racing and an array of over 240 real ales, ciders and perries at the Ascot CAMRA Beer Festival.

Highclere Castle and Gardens
Newbury, Berkshire RG20 9RN
(01635) 253210
www.highclerecastle.co.uk
Visit the spectacular Victorian Castle which is currently the setting for Downton Abbey. Splendid State Rooms, Library and Egyptian Exhibition in the Castle Cellars, plus gardens inspired by Capability Brown.

The Look Out Discovery Centre
Bracknell, Berkshire RG12 7QW
(01344) 354400
www.bracknell-forest.gov.uk
A hands-on, interactive science exhibition with over 80 exhibits, set in 1,000 hectares of Crown woodland.

Reading Festival
August, Reading, Berkshire
www.readingfestival.com
The Reading and Leeds Festivals are a pair of annual music festivals that take place simultaneously.

REME Museum of Technology

Reading, Berkshire RG2 9NJ
(0118) 976 3375
www.rememuseum.org.uk
The museum shows the developing technology used by the Royal Electrical and Mechanical Engineers in maintaining and repairing the army's equipment since 1942.

Buckinghamshire

Aerial Extreme Milton Keynes

Milton Keynes, Buckinghamshire MK15 0DS
0845 652 1736
www.aerialextreme.co.uk/courses/willen-lake
Amaze yourself as you take each of the challenges head on.

Bekonscot Model Village and Railway

Beaconsfield, Buckinghamshire HP9 2PL
(01494) 672919
www.bekonscot.co.uk
Use your imagination in this unique world of make-believe that has delighted generations of visitors.

Gulliver's Land

Milton Keynes, Buckinghamshire MK15 0DT
(01908) 609001
www.gulliversfun.co.uk
Family theme park with 40 rides aimed at children between 2 and 12 years.

Kop Hill Climb

September, Princes Risborough, Buckinghamshire
www.kophillclimb.org.uk
In the 1900s Kop Hill Climb was one of the most popular hill climbs in the country for cars and motorcycles. Now the spirit of the climb is revived.

Marlow Regatta

June, Eton Dorney, Buckinghamshire
www.themarlowregatta.com
Marlow Regatta is one of the multi-lane regattas in the British Rowing calendar.

National Trust Stowe

Buckinghamshire MK18 5DQ
(01280) 817156
www.nationaltrust.org.uk/stowe
Over 40 temples and monuments, laid out against an inspiring backdrop of lakes and valleys.

Reading Real Ale and Jazz Festival

June, Reading, Buckinghamshire
www.readingrealalejazzfest.co.uk
This year's festival is going to be the biggest and best yet, featuring some of the best jazz acts on the circuit.

Roald Dahl Festival

July, Aylesbury Town Centre, Buckinghamshire
www.aylesburyvaledc.gov.uk/dahl
An annual celebration of the famous author, including a 500-strong parade of pupils, teachers and musicians with puppets and artwork based on the Roald Dahl stories.

Roald Dahl Museum and Story Centre

Great Missenden, Buckinghamshire HP16 0AL
(01494) 892192
www.roalddahl.com/museum
Where Roald Dahl (1916-1990) lived and wrote many of his well-loved books.

Waddesdon Manor

Aylesbury, Buckinghamshire HP18 0JH
(01296) 653226
www.waddesdon.org.uk
This National Trust property houses the Rothschild Collection of art treasures and wine cellars. It also features spectacular grounds with an aviary, parterre and woodland playground, licensed restaurants, gift and wine shops.

Xscape

Milton Keynes, Buckinghamshire MK9 3XS
01908 397007
www.xscape.co.uk
Xscape, Milton Keynes offers a unique combination of extreme sports and leisure activities for all ages.

Hampshire & Isle Of Wight

Alton Summer Beer Festival
May, Alton, Hampshire
www.altonbeerfestival.co.uk
Celebrating the cultural heritage of Alton as a traditional area for brewing, based on the clear waters rising from the source of the River Wey, and locally grown hops.

Blackgang Chine
Chale, Isle of Wight PO38 2HN
(01983) 730330
www.blackgangchine.com
Great family fun in over 40 acres of spectacular cliff-top gardens.

Cowes Week
August, Cowes, Isle of Wight
www.aamcowesweek.co.uk
Cowes Week is one of the longest-running regular regattas in the world.

Dinosaur Isle
Sandown, Isle of Wight PO36 8QA
(01983) 404344
www.dinosaurisle.com
In a spectacular pterosaur shaped building on Sandown's blue flag beach walk back through fossilised time and meet life sized replica dinosaurs.

Exbury Gardens and Steam Railway
Beaulieu, Hampshire SO45 1AZ
(023) 8089 1203
www.exbury.co.uk
World famous woodland garden, home to the Rothschild Collection of rhododendrons, azaleas, camellias, rare trees and shrubs, with its own steam railway.

Isle of Wight Festival
June, Newport, Isle of Wight
www.isleofwightfestival.com
Annual music festival featuring some of the UK's top acts and bands.

Isle of Wight Walking Festival
May, Isle of Wight
www.isleofwightwalkingfestival.co.uk
The festival boasts 16 days of unbeatable, informative and healthy walks.

Marwell Zoo
Winchester, Hampshire SO21 1JH
(01962) 777407
www.marwell.org.uk
A chance to get close to the wonders of the natural world – and play a big part in helping to save them.

New Forest and Hampshire Show
July, New Park, Brockenhurst, Hampshire
www.newforestshow.co.uk
The show attracts, on average, 95,000 visitors every year and brings together a celebration of traditional country pursuits, crafts, produce and entertainment.

Osborne House
East Cowes, Isle of Wight PO32 6JX
(01983) 200022
www.english-heritage.org.uk/daysout/properties/osborne-house
Step into Queen Victoria's favourite country home and experience a world unchanged since the country's longest reigning monarch died here just over 100 years ago.

Paultons Family Theme Park
Romsey, Hampshire SO51 6AL
(023) 8081 4442
www.paultonspark.co.uk
A great family day out with over 60 different attractions and rides included in the price!

Shanklin Chine
Shanklin, Isle of Wight PO37 6BW
(01983) 866432
www.shanklinchine.co.uk
Historic gorge with dramatic waterfalls and nature trail.

Southampton Boat Show
September, Southampton, Hampshire
www.southamptonboatshow.com
See the best boats and marine brands gathered together in one fantastic water-based show.

Ventnor Botanic Gardens
St. Lawrence, Isle of Wight PO38 1UL
(01983) 855397
www.botanic.co.uk
The Botanic Garden on the Isle of Wight is a place where the pleasure of plants can be enjoyed to the fullest.

Winchester Hat Fair
July, Winchester, Hampshire
www.hatfair.co.uk
Named after the tradition of throwing donations into performer's hats, it's Britain's longest running festival of street theatre and outdoor arts.

Kent

Bedgebury National Pinetum & Forest
Cranbrook, Kent TN17 2SL
(01580) 879820
www.forestry.gov.uk/bedgebury
Visit the world's finest conifer collection at Bedgebury National Pinetum.

Deal Festival of Music and the Arts
June/July, Deal, Kent
(01304) 370220
www.dealfestival.co.uk
Experience great classical and contemporary music from some of the world's finest music-makers, as well as theatre, opera, cinema and dance – in the beautiful and historic surroundings of Deal and Dover on England's south coast.

The Historic Dockyard Chatham
Kent ME4 4TZ
(01634) 823807
www.thedockyard.co.uk
A unique, award-winning maritime heritage destination with a fantastic range of attractions, iconic buildings and historic ships to explore, plus a fabulous programme of touring exhibitions.

Kent & East Sussex Railway
Tenterden, Kent TN30 6HE
(01580) 765155
www.kesr.org.uk
England's finest rural light railway enables visitors to experience travel and service from a bygone age aboard beautifully restored Victorian coaches and locomotives.

Rochester Castle
Kent ME1 1SW
(01634) 335882
www.visitmedway.org/site/attractions/rochester-castle-p44583
One of the finest keeps in England. Also the tallest, partly built on the Roman city wall. Good views from the battlements over the River Medway.

Oxfordshire

Blenheim Palace
Woodstock, Oxfordshire OX20 1PX
(0800) 849 6500
www.blenheimpalace.com
Birthplace of Sir Winston Churchill and home to the Duke of Marlborough, Blenheim Palace, one of the finest baroque houses in England, is set in over 2,000 acres of landscaped gardens.

Didcot Railway Centre
Oxfordshire OX11 7NJ
(01235) 817200
www.didcotrailwaycentre.org.uk
Living museum recreating the golden age of the Great Western Railway. Steam locomotives and trains, Brunel's broad gauge railway, engine shed and small relics museum.

Henley Royal Regatta
July, Henley, Oxfordshire
www.hrr.co.uk
Attracting thousands of visitors over a five-day period and spectators will be thrilled by over 200 races of international standard.

Oxford Official Guided Walking Tour
owtours@visitoxfordshire.org
The Official Guided Walking Tours are a fascinating and entertaining way to explore and learn about this unique city, its history, University, famous people and odd traditions. Covering a wide range of topics from an introduction to the city and its University to Inspector Morse, Harry Potter, J.R.R. Tolkien and more.

Surrey

British Wildlife Centre

Lingfield, Surrey RH7 6LF
(01342) 834658
www.britishwildlifecentre.co.uk
The best place to see and learn about Britain's own wonderful wildlife, with over 40 different species including deer, foxes, otters, badgers, pine martens and red squirrels.

Guildford Cathedral
Surrey GU2 7UP
(01483) 547860
www.guildford-cathedral.org
New Anglican Cathedral, the foundation stone of which was laid in 1936. Notable sandstone interior and marble floors. Restaurant and shops.

Investec Derby
June, Epsom Racecourse, Surrey
www.epsomderby.co.uk
The biggest horse race in the flat-racing calendar.

Loseley Park
Guildford, Surrey GU3 1HS
(01483) 405120
www.loseleypark.co.uk
A beautiful Elizabethan mansion, set in stunning gardens and parkland. Built in 1562 it has a fascinating history and contains a wealth of treasures.

RHS Garden Wisley
Woking, Surrey GU23 6QB
(0845) 260 9000
www.rhs.org.uk/wisley
Stretching over 240 acres of glorious garden.

RHS Hampton Court Palace Flower Show
July, Hampton Court, Surrey
www.rhs.org.uk
One of the biggest events in the horticulture calendar.

Thorpe Park
Chertsey, Surrey KT16 8PN
(0871) 663 1673
www.thorpepark.com
Thorpe Park Resort is an island like no other, with over 30 thrilling rides, attractions and live events.

Wings & Wheels
August, Dunsfold Aerodrome, Surrey
www.wingsandwheels.net
Outstanding variety of dynamic aviation, motoring displays and iconic cars.

Sussex

1066 Battle Abbey and Battlefield
East Sussex TN33 0AD
(01424) 775705
www.english-heritage.org.uk
An abbey founded by William the Conqueror on the site of the Battle of Hastings.

Arundel Festival
August, Arundel, Sussex
www.arundelfestival.co.uk
Ten days of the best music, theatre, art and comedy.

Arundel Wetland Centre
West Sussex BN18 9PB
(01903) 883355
www.wwt.org.uk/visit/arundel
WWT Arundel Wetland Centre is a 65-acre reserve in an idyllic setting, nestled at the base of the South Downs National Park.

Brighton Digital Festival
September, Brighton, Sussex
www.brightondigitalfestival.co.uk
With a month of exhibitions, performances, workshops and outdoor events, Brighton & Hove is certainly a leading digital destination. There will be workshops, interactive demonstrations and displays throughout the city.

Brighton Fringe
May, Brighton, Sussex
www.brightonfestivalfringe.org.uk
One of the largest fringe festivals in the world, offering cabaret, comedy, classical concerts, club nights, theatre and exhibitions, as well as street performances.

Brighton Marathon
April, Brighton, Sussex
www.brightonmarathon.co.uk
Having grown enormously in just two years, the Brighton Marathon is now one of the top 12 running events in the UK.

Chichester Cathedral

West Sussex PO19 1RP
(01243) 782595
www.chichestercathedral.org.uk
A magnificent Cathedral with treasures ranging from medieval stone carvings to world famous 20th century artworks.

Denmans Garden

Fontwell, West Sussex BN18 0SU
(01243) 542808
www.denmans-garden.co.uk
Beautiful 4 acre garden designed for year round interest through use of form, colour and texture. Beautiful plant centre, award-winning and fully licensed Garden Café.

Eastbourne Beer Festival

October, Winter Gardens, Eastbourne, Sussex
www.visiteastbourne.com/beer-festival
Eastbourne's annual beer festival features over 120 cask ales, plus wines, international bottled beers, ciders and perries. Each session features live music.

Eastbourne Festival

July, Eastbourne, Sussex
www.eastbournefestival.co.uk
Eastbourne Festival is an Open Access Arts Festival which takes place annually for three weeks. It has become recognised as an annual showcase for local professional and amateur talent.

England's Medieval Festival

August, Herstmonceux Castle, Sussex
www.englandsmedievalfestival.com
A celebration of the Middle Ages.

Fishers Adventure Farm Park

Billingshurst, West Sussex RH14 0EG
(01403) 700063
www.fishersfarmpark.co.uk
Award-winning Adventure Farm Park and open all year. Ideally suited for ages 2-11 years. Huge variety of animals, rides and attractions from the skating rink, to pony rides, toboggan run, bumper boats, theatre shows and more!

Glorious Goodwood

July, Chichester, Sussex
www.goodwood.com
Bursting with fabulous fashions, succulent strawberries, chilled Champagne and top horse racing stars, as well as music and dancing.

Glyndebourne Festival

May - August, Lewes, Sussex
www.glyndebourne.com
An English opera festival held at Glyndebourne, an English country house near Lewes.

Great Dixter House and Gardens

Rye, East Sussex TN31 6PH
(01797) 252878
www.greatdixter.co.uk
An example of a 15th century manor house with antique furniture and needlework. The house is restored and the gardens were designed by Lutyens.

London to Brighton Bike Ride

June, Ends on Madeira Drive, Brighton, Sussex
www.bhf.org.uk/london-brighton
The annual bike ride from the capital to the coast in aid of the British Heart Foundation. The UK's largest charity bike ride with 27,000 riders.

Pashley Manor Gardens
Wadhurst, East Sussex TN5 7HE
(01580) 200888
www.pashleymanorgardens.com
Pashley Manor Gardens offer a blend of romantic landscaping, imaginative plantings, fine old trees, fountains, springs and large ponds plus exciting special events.

Petworth House and Park

West Sussex GU28 0AE
(01798) 342207
www.nationaltrust.org.uk/petworth
Discover the National Trust's finest art collection displayed in a magnificent 17th century mansion within a beautiful 700-acre park. Petworth House contains works by artists such as Van Dyck, Reynolds and Turner.

RSPB Pulborough Brooks

West Sussex RH20 2EL
(01798) 875851
www.rspb.org.uk
Set in the scenic Arun Valley with views to the South Downs, the two mile circular nature trail leads around this beautiful reserve.

Tourist Information Centres

When you arrive at your destination, visit the Tourist Information Centre for quality assured help with accommodation and information about local attractions and events, or email your request before you go.

Aldershot	Prince's Hall	01252 320968	aldershotvic@rushmoor.gov.uk
Ashford	Ashford Gateway Plus	01233 330316	tourism@ashford.gov.uk
Aylesbury	The Kings Head, Kings Head Passage	01296 330559	tic@aylesburyvaledc.gov.uk
Banbury	Within Castle Quay Shopping Centre	01295 753752	banbury.tic@cherwell-dc.gov.uk
Battle	Yesterdays World	01797 229049	battletic@rother.gov.uk
Bexley (Hall Place)	Central Library	0208 3037777	touristinfo@bexleyheritagetrust.org.uk
Bicester	Unit 86a Bicester Village	01869 369055	bicestervisitorcentre@valueretail.com
Bracknell	The Look Out Discovery Centre	01344 354409	thelookout@bracknell-forest.gov.uk
Brighton	Brighton Centre Box Office	01273 290337	visitor.info@visitbrighton.com
Buckingham	The Old Gaol Museum	01280 823020	buckinghamtic@touismse.com
Burford	33a High Street	01993 823558	burford.vic@westoxon.gov.uk
Burgess Hill	Burgess Hill Town Council	01444 238202	touristinformation@burgesshill.gov.uk
Canterbury	The Beaney House	01227 378100	canterburyinformation@canterbury.gov.uk
Chichester	The Novium	01243 775888	chitic@chichester.gov.uk
Deal	The Landmark Centre	01304 369576	info@deal.gov.uk
Dover	Dover Museum and VIC	01304 201066	tic@doveruk.com

Eastbourne	Cornfield Road	0871 663 0031	tic@eastbourne.gov.uk
Fareham	Westbury Manor	01329 221342	farehamtic@tourismse.com
Faringdon	The Corn Exchange	01367 242191	tic@faringdontowncouncil.gov.uk
Faversham	Fleur de Lis Heritage Centre	01795 534542	ticfaversham@btconnect.com
Folkestone	20 Bouverier Place Shopping Centre	01303 258594	chris.kirkham@visitkent.co.uk
Fordingbridge	Kings Yard	01425 654560	fordingbridgetic@tourismse.com
Gosportq	Gosport TIC, Bus Station Complex	023 9252 2944	tourism@gosport.gov.uk
Gravesend	Towncentric	01474 337600	info@towncentric.co.uk
Guildford	155 High Street	01483 444333	tic@guildford.gov.uk
Hastings	Queens Square	01424 451111	hic@hastings.gov.uk
Hayling Island	Central Beachlands	023 9246 7111	tourism@havant.gov.uk
Henley-On-Thames	Town Hall,	01491 578034	vic@henleytowncouncil.gov.uk
High Wycombe	High Wycombe Library	01494 421892	tourism_enquiries@wycombe.gov.uk
Horsham	9 The Causeway	01403 211661	visitor.information@horsham.gov.uk
Lewes	187 High Street	01273 483448	lewes.tic@lewes.gov.uk
Littlehampton	The Look & Sea Centre	01903 721866	jo-lhvic@hotmail.co.uk
Lymington	St Barbe Museum	01590 676969	office@stbarbe-museum.org.uk
Lyndhurst & New Forest	New Forest Visitor Centre	023 8028 2269/ 023 8028 5492	info@thenewforest.co.uk
Maidenhead	Maidenhead Library	01628 796502	maidenhead.tic@rbwm.gov.uk
Maidstone	Maidstone Museum	01622 602169	tourism@maidstone.gov.uk
Marlow	55a High Street	01628 483597	tourism_enquiries@wycombe.gov.uk
Midhurst	North Street	01730 812251	midtic@chichester.gov.uk
Newbury	The Wharf	01635 30267	tourism@westberks.gov.uk
Oxford	Oxford Information Centre	01865 252200	info@visitoxfordshire.org
Petersfield	County Library	01730 268829	petersfieldinfo@btconnect.com
Portsmouth	D-Day Museum	023 9282 6722	vis@portsmouthcc.gov.uk
Princes Risborough	Tower Court	01844 274795	risborough_office@wycombe.gov.uk
Ringwood	Ringwood Gateway	01425 473883	town.council@ringwood.gov.uk
Rochester	95 High Street	01634 338141	visitor.centre@medway.gov.uk
Romsey	Museum & TIC	01794 512987	romseytic@testvalley.gov.uk
Royal Tunbridge Wells	Unit 2 The Corn Exchange	01892 515675	touristinformationcentre@ tunbridgewells.gov.uk
Rye	4/5 Lion Street	01797 229049	ryetic@tourismse.com
Sandwich	The Guildhall	01304 613565/ 617197	tourism@sandwichtowncouncil.gov.uk
Seaford	37 Church Street	01323 897426	seaford.tic@lewes.gov.uk
Sevenoaks	Stag Community Arts Centre	01732 450305	tic@sevenoakstown.gov.uk
Swanley	Swanley Library	01322 614660	touristinfo@swanley.org.uk
Tenterden	Tenterden Gateway	08458 247 202	
Thame	Town Hall	01844 212833	oss@thametowncouncil.gov.uk
Thanet	The Droit House	01843 577577	visitorinformation@thanet.gov.uk
Tonbridge	Tonbridge Castle	01732 770929	tonbridge.castle@tmbc.gov.uk
Winchester	Guildhall	01962 840500	tourism@winchester.gov.uk
Windsor	Old Booking Hall	01753 743900	windsor.tic@rbwm.gov.uk
Witney	Welsh Way	01993 775802/ 861780	witney.vic@westoxon.gov.uk
Worthing	The Dome	01903 239868	tic@adur-worthing.gov.uk

Regional Contacts and Information

For more information on accommodation, attractions, activities, events and holidays in South East England, contact one of the following regional or local tourism organisations. Their websites have a wealth of information and many produce free publications to help you get the most out of your visit.

www.visitsoutheastengland.com
email enquiries@tourismse.com or
call (023) 8062 5400.

www.visitnewbury.org.uk
www.visitbuckinghamshire.org
www.visit-hampshire.co.uk
www.visitisleofwight.co.uk
www.visitkent.co.uk
www.visitoxfordandoxfordshire.com
www.visitsurrey.com
www.visitbrighton.com

Entries appear alphabetically by town name in each county. A key to symbols appears on page 7

BUCKINGHAM, *Buckinghamshire* Map ref 2C1

Huntsmill Farm Holidays

Contact: Huntsmill Farm Holidays, Shalstone, Buckingham MK18 5ND **T:** (01280) 704852 / 07970 871104 **E:** fiona@huntsmill.com
W: www.huntsmill.com

Units   6
Sleeps   1-9

PER UNIT PER WEEK
£295.00 - £750.00

SPECIAL PROMOTIONS
Additional rooms may be added from B&B on special room-only rate.

Converted traditional stone, timber and slate barns in quiet location on working farm. Exposed beams, quality furnishings and views over open countryside. Large gardens, easy access to footpaths. Close to Silverstone and National Trust properties. Ideal touring base.

Open: All year
Nearest Shop: 2 miles
Nearest Pub: 2 miles

Site: ✿ P Payment: £€ Leisure: ♪ ∪ ✎ Property: ▢▣ Children: ⊶ ⊨ ✶ Unit: ▢▣▣ ◥ TV DVD

CHALFONT ST. GILES, *Buckinghamshire* Map ref 2D2

Hilborough

Contact: Mr Peter Bentall, Owner, Hilborough, Mill Lane, Chalfont St. Giles, Buckinghamshire HP8 4NX **T:** (01494) 872536 **E:** pbentall@btopenworld.com

Units   1
Sleeps   1

PER UNIT PER WEEK
£160.00

Self-catering annexe attached to house. Sleeps 1-2. Kitchenette with belling stove, microwave and fridge. Shower room with wash basin and toilet. Patio area with access to garden. All linen is provided. Electricity and central heating are inclusive.
Open: All year **Nearest Shop:** 0.5 miles **Nearest Pub:** 0.5 miles

Site: ✿ P Property: ▭▢▣ Unit: ▢▣▣ ◥ TV DVD

GREAT MISSENDEN, Buckinghamshire   Map ref 2C1

Lower Bassibones Farm

Contact: Anthea and Geoff Hartley, Owners, Lower Bassibones Farm, Ballinger Road, Great Missenden, Buckinghamshire HP16 9LA **T:** (01494) 837798 **F:** 01494 837778 **E:** lowerbassibones@yahoo.co.uk **W:** www.discover-real-england.com

Units   2
Sleeps   1-5

PER UNIT PER WEEK
£345.00 - £695.00

Lower Bassibones Farm is situated in a rural position in the Chiltern Hills, in an officially designated Area of Outstanding Natural Beauty, but within easy reach of London (40mins) and Heathrow & Luton Airports (50mins). The farm comprises two, completely separate, self-contained, properties.

The Barn: A beautifully restored period barn with a large private garden and parking. Sleeps 4/5 guests. Inglenook Cottage: Situated across the lane from the farm, a cosy period cottage with private garden. Sleeps 4 guests. Both properties have free Wi-Fi access, a TV & DVD player. Both are non-smoking.

Open: All year
Nearest Shop: 0.5 miles
Nearest Pub: 0.75 miles

Units: Both properties furnished to a high standard.

Site: ❀ **P Payment:** ▦ € **Leisure:** ▶ **Property:** 🐾 ▭ ▣ ▨ **Children:** ⚘ ▥ ⚲
Unit: ▯ ▢ ▤ ▨ ⚲ TV ⊙ BBQ 📞

ALRESFORD, Hampshire   Map ref 2C2

Cheriton Wood Studio

Contact: Kate Flesher, Bishops Sutton, Alresford, Hampshire SO24 0HR **T:** (01962) 734840 **E:** cheriton.123@btinternet.com
W: www.cheritonwoodstudio.com

Units   1
Sleeps   2
PER UNIT PER WEEK
£325.00 - £450.00

Homely, rural, detached property, beautifully situated along a quiet country lane on the site of the Battle of Cheriton, surrounded by tranquil countryside; ideal for a relaxing holiday or romantic short break. Only 15 minutes from Winchester, The Studio - with delightful private walled garden, is very thoughtfully furnished and equipped, with particular attention paid to cleanliness and comfort. Short breaks available. **Open:** All year **Nearest Shop:** 1.78 miles **Nearest Pub:** 1.26 miles

Site: ❀ **P Property:** ▦ ▣ ▨ **Unit:** ▯ ▭ ⚲ TV ⊙ BBQ

FAREHAM, Hampshire   Map ref 2C3

Cowes View Coastguard Cottage

Contact: Mel Vennis, Hill Head, Fareham, Hampshire PO14 3JJ **T:** (01329) 664236 / 07712 650805 **E:** enquiries@cowesview.co.uk
W: www.cowesview.co.uk

Units   1
Sleeps   1-5
PER UNIT PER WEEK
£405.00 - £795.00

Welcome to Cowes View, your seaside home from home, a place where smugglers were stopped bringing whisky and tobacco ashore and later where coastguards aided seafaring folk. Now you can soak up the history, the whisky, the sea and fantastic panoramic ever changing views across The Solent. Lay in bed and listen to the sea lapping against the shore, beautiful sunsets, smell the sea, enjoy the air and relax. **Open:** All year **Nearest Shop:** 1 mile **Nearest Pub:** 100m

  Site: ❀ **Leisure:** 🎣 **Property:** ▦ ▣ ▨ **Children:** ⚘ ▥ ⚲ **Unit:** ▯ ▢ ▭ ▨ ⚲ TV ◉ ⊙ BBQ

New Forest and Dorset Holidays
Perfect locations by Forest and Coast

Choose from luxury caravans and lodges (some with hot tubs). We also welcome pets in selected units. There are great leisure facilities including 'Go Active' with fun entertainment for everyone. Pamper yourself in our 'Reflections' Elemis Day Spa, explore the New Forest and the Jurassic Coast, or relax on Bournemouth's sandy beaches. NEW - 'Wisteria House' which sleeps up to 12 guests in luxury accommodation.

Ref VESC

SHOREFIELD
HOLIDAYS LIMITED

Tel 01590 648 331

holidays@shorefield.co.uk
www.shorefield.co.uk
follow us on 🐦📘 @shorefieldparks

HAMPSHIRE
Shorefield Country Park, SO41 0LH
Oakdene Forest Park, BH24 2RZ (tents only)
Forest Edge Holiday Park, BH24 2SD

DORSET
Swanage Coastal Park, BH19 2RS
Merley Court Touring Park, BH21 3AA

FORDINGBRIDGE, *Hampshire*   Map ref 2B3

Burgate Manor Farm Holidays

Contact: Mrs Bridget Stallard, Burgate Manor Farm Holidays, Burgate Manor Farm, Burgate, Fordingbridge SP6 1LX **T:** (01425) 653908 **F:** 01425 653908
E: info@newforestcottages.com **W:** www.newforestcottages.com

Units   8
Sleeps   2-18

PER UNIT PER WEEK
£376.00 - £3460.00

SPECIAL PROMOTIONS
Short breaks available.

New Forest/Avon Valley. Small and medium-sized farm cottages and large, recently converted, galleried, beamed barn. Short walk pub/restaurant. Games barn. Fishing. Grazing. Beach 15 miles. The Granary has 8 bedrooms with 6 bathrooms so is ideal for large families and gatherings of friends.

The Granary can be taken on its own or with one or more of our smaller cottages. Everyone can get together in The Granary, the dining tables can seat any number up to 36. Small groups can take Swan, Heron, Teal or Kingfisher which sleep 4/6, or Grebe which sleeps 4. Mallard and Appletrees sleep 6/8.

Open: All year   **Units:** 8 cottages, sleeping 2-18 people.
Nearest Shop: 1 mile
Nearest Pub: 0.30 miles

Site: ❀ P **Leisure:** 🎵 🏹 ↻ 🎣 **Property:** 🐴 🖼 📷 🍴 **Children:** 🚸 🛏 🏃 **Unit:** 📟 📠 📺 📻 📺 🔲 🖥 ♨ BBQ

MILFORD ON SEA, Hampshire   Map ref 2C3

Units   1
Sleeps   1-5

PER UNIT PER WEEK
£275.00 - £620.00

Windmill Cottage

Contact: Mrs S Perham, Proprietor, 14 Kivernell Road, Milford-on-Sea, Lymington, Hampshire SO41 0PQ **T:** (01590) 643516 **F:** 01590 641255
E: michaelperham@btinternet.com **W:** www.windmillcottage.info **£ BOOK ONLINE**

Georgian style cottage/town house in quiet residential area and located in private traffic free close. Tastefully furnished and recently refurbished kitchen & bathroom. There is a small, enclosed south west facing garden. Garage and easy parking. Five minutes walk to village centre and beach areas are three minutes by car - plenty of parking.
Sleeps five.

Open: All year
Nearest Shop: 0.25 miles
Nearest Pub: 0.25 miles

Units: Fitted carpets, fully automatic gas central heating. Comfortable & fully furnished Sitting room / dining room with colour TV & DVD, electric fire & French doors to patio & garden. Modern, well fitted kitchen. 1 double, 1 twin & 1 single bedroom. Bathroom & WC.

Site: ❀ P **Leisure:** ⚓ 🏌 ⚲ ⛵ **Property:** 🐾 🗄 ▨ **Children:** 🛝 🏕 ✴ **Unit:** ▢ 🗄 ▭ 🗄 TV ⊙

PITT, Hampshire   Map ref 2C3

Units   14
Sleeps   1-6
PER UNIT PER WEEK
£575.00 - £1150.00

South Winchester Lodges

Contact: Lesley Ross, South Winchester Golf Club, Romsey Road, Winchester, Hampshire SO22 5SW **T:** (01962) 820490 **E:** info@southwinchesterlodges.co.uk
W: www.southwinchesterlodges.co.uk **£ BOOK ONLINE**

Award winning, two and three bedroom, five star lodges, some with hot tubs, beautifully set on South Winchester Golf Course just 3 miles from the city centre of Winchester. Short breaks available from £380.00 **Open:** All year **Nearest Shop:** 0.10 miles **Nearest Pub:** 0.10 miles

Site: ❀ P **Payment:** 💷 **Leisure:** ⚓ 🏌 ⚲ ⛵ **Property:** 🐾 🚃 🗄 ▨ **Children:** 🛝 🏕 ✴ **Unit:** ▢ 🗄 ▭ 🗄 ⊙
TV ⊙ DVD BBQ

PORTSMOUTH AND SOUTHSEA, Hampshire   Map ref 2C3

Admiralty Apartments

Contact: Booking Enquiries, Portsmouth Naval Base Property Trust, 19 College Road, HM Naval Base, Portsmouth PO1 3LJ **T:** (023) 9282 0921 **F:** (023) 9286 2437
E: admiraltyquarter@pnbpt.co.uk **W:** www.pnbpropertytrust.org

| Units | 4 |
| Sleeps | 2-6 |

PER UNIT PER WEEK
£870.00 - £1400.00

Admiralty Quarter is ideally located within easy walking distance of the City's historic attractions, overlooking Portsmouth Harbour and the Historic Dockyard. The contemporary apartments are furnished to an exceptionally high standard, offering fast broadband connection, secure parking and most enjoying spectacular views towards the Solent and the Isle of Wight.

Open: All year
Nearest Shop: 0.01 miles
Nearest Pub: 0.01 miles

Site: P Payment: ⊞ Property: ▭ ▯ Children: ☇ ▥ ⚲ Unit: ▯ ▤ ▭ ▨ ⚲ TV ◉ ▭

WINCHESTER, Hampshire   Map ref 2C3

Mallard Cottage

Contact: Mr David Simpkin, Owner, 64 Chesil Street, Winchester, Hampshire SO23 0HX
T: (01962) 853002 **E:** bookings@mallardcottage.co.uk
W: www.mallardcottage.co.uk

| Units | 1 |
| Sleeps | 1-4 |

PER UNIT PER WEEK
£500.00 - £650.00

Attractive Grade II listed building, two bedroom, two shower room cottage annexe, accommodating up to 4 people plus travel cot. Based within a five minute walk of the historic heart of the city of Winchester. Peaceful riverside garden with summerhouse. The cottage and garden are both non-smoking throughout. We regret that we cannot accommodate pets. **Open:** All year
Nearest Shop: 400 yards **Nearest Pub:** 200 yards

Site: ✿ P Payment: ⊞ Leisure: ♪ ► ∪ Property: ▭ ▯ ▯ Children: ☇ ▥ ⚲ Unit: ▯ ▤ ▭ ▨ ⚲ TV ◉ ▭ BBQ

WINCHESTER, Hampshire   Map ref 2C3

Riverside Cottage

Contact: Clare Dryden, Owner, Riverside Lifestyle, Bransbury, Barton Stacey, Winchester, Hampshire SO21 3QJ **T:** 07973 215 407 **E:** csdryden.clark@btinternet.com
W: www.riversidelifestyle.co.uk

| Units | 1 |
| Sleeps | 10 |

PER UNIT PER WEEK
£2300.00

Riverside Cottage is a detached, thatched period property beautifully positioned in 5 acres. Both modern and old. It sits in a quiet lane on the bank of the River Dever. There is a large lawned garden overlooking fields, a swimming pool, play climbing frame for children and a quiet terrace. Lovely walks, village and city culture all close by. Sleeps 8 with guest sofa bed. Weekend Rate from £1200. Dogs welcome at a premium. **Open:** All year
Nearest Shop: 1 mile **Nearest Pub:** 1 mile

Site: ✿ P Payment: ⊞ € Leisure: ♪ ⚘ Property: ⚲ ⌂ ▭ ▯ ▯ Children: ☇ ▥ ⚲ Unit: ▯ ▤ ▭ ▨ ⚲ TV ◉ ▭ BBQ ☎

Island Cottage Holidays
Isle of Wight & Dorset Cottages
01983 403377
www.islandcottageholidays.com

NEWPORT, Isle of Wight   Map ref 2C3

SELF CATERING

Newbarn Country Cottages

Contact: Steve Harvey, Newbarn Farm, Newbarn Lane, Gatcombe, Newport, Isle of Wight PO30 3EQ **T:** (01983) 721202 / 07739 868201 **E:** newbarncountrycottages@gmail.com **W:** www.newbarncountrycottages.co.uk **£ BOOK ONLINE**

Units   3
Sleeps   2-6
PER UNIT PER WEEK
£250.00 - £800.00

Three beautiful barn conversions in a secluded downland valley in the centre of the Isle of Wight, Parlour Cottage sleeping up to 6 (4 adults and 2 children) and Stable and Dairy Cottages sleeping 4 people. Being centrally located all of the islands attractions are within easy reach and the rural location is ideal for walkers or mountain bikers. **Open:** All year **Nearest Shop:** 2 miles **Nearest Pub:** 3 miles

Site: P Leisure: ⚡ ▸ ∪ **Property:** ∥ 🖥 📺 🖳 **Children:** 🐎1 🏛 ⚡ **Unit:** 🖥 📺 🖳 ⚡ 📺 🎧 📀

RYDE, Isle of Wight   Map ref 2C3

SELF CATERING

Claverton House Self Catering

Contact: Mr Harry Metz, Manager, Claverton House Self Catering, Claverton House, 12 The Strand, Ryde PO33 1JE **T:** (01983) 613015 **F:** 01983 613015 **E:** clavertonhouse@aol.com

Units   2
Sleeps   2-3
PER UNIT PER WEEK
£200.00 - £350.00

Beautiful holiday residence is situated in the idyllic seaside town of Ryde on the seafront. Five minutes walk to town centre and passenger ferries, ten minutes drive to car ferry. **Open:** All year except Christmas and New Year **Nearest Shop:** 0.20 miles **Nearest Pub:** 0.20 miles

Site: ✿ **P Payment:** € **Leisure:** ⚡ **Property:** 🖥 📺 🖳 **Children:** 🐎 🏛 **Unit:** 🖥 📺 ⚡ 📺 📀

SHANKLIN, Isle of Wight   Map ref 2C3

SELF CATERING

Luccombe Villa Holiday Apartments

Contact: Mr & Mrs Miles & Fiona Seymour, Luccombe Villa, 9 Popham Road, Shanklin, Isle of Wight PO37 6RF **T:** (01983) 862825 / 07774 784116 **E:** info@luccombevilla.co.uk **W:** www.luccombevilla.co.uk **£ BOOK ONLINE**

Units   9
Sleeps   1-6
PER UNIT PER WEEK
£350.00 - £1210.00

Nine apartments in Shanklin Old Village. Wonderful location, close to the town, beach and beautiful walks. Comfortably furnished with well equipped kitchens, digital TV, DVD and free Wi-Fi. Guests' garden with outdoor swimming pool. Plenty of parking. Pets welcome. Tariff includes ferry. **Open:** All year **Nearest Shop:** 0.10 miles **Nearest Pub:** 0.10 miles

FAMILIES WELCOME / PETS **Site:** ✿ **P Payment:** 💳 **Leisure:** ⚡ ♪ ▸ ∪ ⚡ **Property:** 🐕 🖥 📺 🖳 **Children:** 🐎 🏛 ⚡ **Unit:** 🖥 📺 ⚡ 📺 🎧 📀 **BBQ**

ST. HELENS, Isle of Wight   Map ref 2C3

Units 2
Sleeps 1-7
PER UNIT PER WEEK
£320.00 - £780.00

The Castle

Contact: Mr Jonathan Bacon, Duver Road, St Helens PO33 1XY **T:** (01983) 875993 / 07973 872150 **E:** enquiries@sthelenscastle.co.uk
W: www.sthelenscastle.co.uk

The Castle offers two comfortable and characterful Victorian holiday lets sleeping up to seven persons (including two children). Situated in the picturesque village of St Helens, close to local facilities and areas of stunning natural beauty, both properties have been recently upgraded and have extensive facilities including grounds for guests' use. The Castle is also a short walk from the beach **Open:** All year **Nearest Shop:** 0.20 miles **Nearest Pub:** 0.20 miles

Site: ✿ P **Payment:** 🆔 € **Leisure:** ♪ ► ∪ **Property:** 🖥 📀 🔲 **Children:** 🍼 🛏 ⚲ **Unit:** 🗔 🗲 🔲 🗄 🔌 TV 📀

VENTNOR, Isle Of Wight   Map ref 2C3

Units 2
Sleeps 2-5
PER UNIT PER WEEK
£220.00 - £390.00

Garfield Holiday Flats

Contact: Mrs S Stead, Proprietor, 13 Spring Gardens, Ventor, Isle of Wight PO38 1QX
T: (01983) 854084 / 07779 075612 **E:** info@islandbreaks.co.uk
W: www.garfieldflats.co.uk

For a really carefree relaxing break we offer self-catering holidays in Ventnor, the Isle of Wight's most southerly resort. Our flats are well-equipped with wonderful sea views. Situated in a quiet private road and only a short walk to town and beach, perfect for exploring our beautiful island. 3 night breaks from £90 - low season only.
Open: All Year **Nearest Shop:** 3 minutes **Nearest Pub:** 5 minutes

Property: 🐾 🖥 📀 🔲 **Children:** 🍼 **Unit:** 🔲 🔌 TV 📀

WHITWELL, Isle of Wight   Map ref 2C3

Units 1
Sleeps 2-6
PER UNIT PER WEEK
£340.00 - £860.00

Maytime Cottage

Contact: Mr Jonathan McCulloch, Maytime Cottage, c/o 5 King Edward Road, Christs Hospital, Horsham RH13 0ND **T:** (01403) 211052 / 07711 807137
E: jonty@bpmd.co.uk **W:** www.maytimecottage.co.uk **£ BOOK ONLINE**

Exceptionally spacious well equipped stone cottage for up to six people in rural South Wight. Large kitchen-diner, garden room, living room with woodburning stove, 3 bedrooms, 1 bathroom plus 1 downstairs shower room, enclosed private gardens, great views. Superb downland and coastal walks straight from the door. Many superb beaches plus a wide variety of attractions and activities nearby. **Open:** All year **Nearest Shop:** 2 miles **Nearest Pub:** 1 mile

Site: ✿ P **Payment:** € **Leisure:** 🚲 ♪ ► ∪ **Property:** 🐾 🔲 **Children:** 🍼 🛏 ⚲ **Unit:** 🗔 🔲 🗄 🔌 TV 📀 📀 ⬚ BBQ

WHITWELL, Isle of Wight   Map ref 2C3

Units 9
Sleeps 3-10
PER UNIT PER WEEK
£310.00 - £1810.00

Nettlecombe Farm Holiday Cottages & Fishing Lakes

Contact: Jose Morris, Proprietor, Nettlecombe Farm Holiday Cottages & Fishing Lakes, Nettlecombe Lane, Whitwell, Nr Ventnor, Isle of Wight PO38 2AF **T:** (01983) 730783
E: enquiries@nettlecombefarm.co.uk **W:** www.nettlecombefarm.co.uk **£ BOOK ONLINE**

Nettlecombe Farm is nestled in the heart of the rolling South Wight countryside offering luxurious self-catering accommodation in 9 high quality self-contained properties that sleep between 3-10 situated in the main farmhouse. **Open:** All year **Nearest Shop:** 2 miles **Nearest Pub:** 0.5 miles

Site: ✿ P **Payment:** 🆔 **Leisure:** 🚲 ♪ ► ∪ **Property:** ✎ 🐾 🖥 📀 🔲 **Children:** 🍼 🛏 ⚲ **Unit:** 🗔 🗄 🔲 🗲
🔌 TV 📀 📀 BBQ

ASHFORD, Kent Map ref 3B4

Shaws Farm Cottage

Contact: Mrs Susan Hayden, Owner, Shaws Farm Cottage, Stowting Common, Ashford, Kent TN25 6BH **T:** (01233) 750426 **E:** shaws.farm@gmail.com
W: www.shawsfarmcottage.co.uk

A quiet rural location, but only 20 minutes away from Canterbury, Folkestone or Hythe. Easy access to the Channel Tunnel or Dover ferry for a day trip to France. Off road parking for 1 car. Ideal location for walking, cycling or relaxing. **Open:** All year **Nearest Shop:** 8 miles **Nearest Pub:** 3 miles

Units 1
Sleeps 3
PER UNIT PER WEEK
£330.00 - £415.00

Site: ✿ **P Property:** 🖥 📶 **Children:** 🐕 🛏 ⚱ **Unit:** 🍴 📺 📼 ⚲ 📀 💿

ASHFORD, Kent Map ref 3B4

The Stable at Staple Farm

Contact: Mr & Mrs Martindale, Owners, Staple Farm, Hastingleigh, Kent TN25 5HF
T: (01233) 750248 **E:** stable_kent@btinternet.com

Compact cottage, adjacent to owner's farmhouse, displaying beams and original features and offering modern facilities. Open plan sitting room with dining and kitchen areas. One double with en suite bathroom. **Open:** All year **Nearest Shop:** 2.5 miles **Nearest Pub:** 0.5 miles

Units 1
Sleeps 2
PER UNIT PER WEEK
£350.00

Site: ✿ **P Property:** 📶 **Unit:** 🍴 📺 📼 ⚲ 📺 💿

BIRCHINGTON, Kent Map ref 3C3

Raleigh Cottage

Contact: Mrs Jill Edwards, Raleigh Cottage, Band Box, 79 Station Road, Birchington CT7 9RE **T:** (01843) 841764 - Evening / (01843) 841101 - Day
E: lou@landway99.freeserve.co.uk **W:** www.birchingtonholidays.co.uk

Units 1
Sleeps 1-6
PER UNIT PER WEEK
£300.00 - £550.00

SPECIAL PROMOTIONS
Off-season short breaks available.

Birchington is a delightful seaside town in beautiful Kent, "The Garden of England". Situated on the North Kent coast and within easy reach of London, picturesque Canterbury and the seaside towns of Margate, Broadstairs and Ramsgate, you will find plenty of opportunity to relax, go sightseeing, breathe in some unpolluted sea air and enjoy a break away from it all.

Raleigh Cottage is a comfortable detached house with pleasant enclosed garden. One twin and two double bedrooms. Two large reception rooms, one opening onto a sunny conservatory. Desirable location close to unspoilt sandy beaches, two minutes to sea, shops, station. Linen provided. Off-street parking.

Open: All year
Nearest Shop: 0.25 miles
Nearest Pub: 0.25 miles

Site: ✿ **P Leisure:** ♿ ⚲ ∪ **Property:** 🐕 📶 **Children:** 🐕 🛏 ⚱ **Unit:** 🍴 📺 📼 ⚲ 📺 💿 📞

Broome Park Golf and Country Club

Contact: Barham, Canterbury, Kent CT4 6QX **T:** (0800) 358 6991
E: EuHotels@diamondresorts.com
W: www.DiamondResortsandHotels.com **£ BOOK ONLINE**

Units   14
Sleeps   1-6

PER UNIT PER WEEK
£420.00 - £1393.00

SPECIAL PROMOTIONS
Enjoy two nights or more with complimentary champagne and chocolates on arrival, please call for latest pricing.

This huge private estate has a historical building at its centre. Broome Park is a relaxing resort with modern log cabins, fine dining, indoor swimming and golf. The 17th-century main house has the restaurant and bar. The accommodation is spread throughout the grounds, in well-equipped woodland cabins. The cabins feature a TV in each bedroom, 2 bathrooms, and a fully-fitted kitchen.

The Broome Park grounds feature a full championship golf course, where there are discounts for hotel guests. The Jacobean Restaurant has an antique crystal chandelier and beautiful countryside views.

Open: All year
Nearest Shop: 2 miles
Nearest Pub: 2 miles

Units: 2 Bedroom Lodges with 1 Double room, 1 twin room and full kitchen unit. Each unit also boasts 2 complete bathroom units.

Site: ✿ P **Payment:** 💳 **Leisure:** ▶ ⚲ ⚓ ⚲ **Property:** 🖥 📠 **Children:** 🍼 🛏 ⚲
Unit: 🗄 🖥 📺 🛏 🍳 📺 📀 📞

Monckton Cottages

Contact: Helen Kirwan, Owner, Heron Manor, Chilham, Canterbury, Kent CT4 8DG
T: 07789 431760 **E:** helen@rwkirwan.plus.com
W: www.moncktoncottages.com

Units   3
Sleeps   2-5

PER UNIT PER WEEK
£320.00 - £730.00

SPECIAL PROMOTIONS
Short breaks available by arrangement; please ask for prices.

Three charming self-contained cottages in historic 15C manor, listed Grade II by English Heritage set in c. four acres. Stunning rural location, with lovely gardens overlooking Chilham Castle Parkland in an Area of Outstanding Natural Beauty, on the ancient Pilgrims' Way/ North Downs Way to Canterbury. Immaculate; log fire/woodburning stove, free Wi-Fi, very well equipped, full details on cottages website. Haven of tranquility, numerous footpaths, ideal for walking. Two cottages have large private gardens for guests' exclusive use. Many guests return every year and recommend us to others.

Open: All year
Nearest Shop: 0.25 miles
Nearest Pub: 0.25 miles

Units: Mistletoe and Heron cottage have dishwashers, (Lavender does not), Lavender and Mistletoe cottages have large private gardens, (but Heron does not) All cottages have washing machines and private parking.

Site: ✿ P **Payment:** € **Leisure:** ⚲ **Property:** 🖥 📠 📠 **Children:** 🍼10 🛏 ⚲
Unit: 🗄 🖥 📺 🛏 🍳 📺 📀 🚿 BBQ

CRANBROOK, Kent   Map ref 3B4

Units 1
Sleeps 2

PER UNIT PER WEEK
£300.00 - £350.00

Bakersbarn Annexe

Contact: Mrs Hooper, Owner, Golford Road, Cranbrook, Kent County TN17 3NW
T: (01580) 713344   **E:** hooper.jm@btinternet.com

Bakersbarn is a non-smoking accommodation in a quiet rural situation, within seven minutes walk from the town centre of Cranbrook. All rooms overlook the garden and grazing land and are well equipped. The bedroom has optional zipped twin beds and all linen and electricity is included. The bathroom has a bath with overhead shower, toilet and hand basin. Fully furnished kitchen.
Open: All year **Nearest Shop:** 0.25 miles **Nearest Pub:** 0.25 miles

Site: ✿ **P** **Property:** 🗔 🖳 **Unit:** 🗔 📺

EDENBRIDGE, Kent   Map ref 2D2

Units 1
Sleeps 2-7

PER UNIT PER WEEK
£1785.00 - £3400.00

SPECIAL PROMOTIONS
Short breaks available throughout the year, contact Hever Castle for further information.

Medley Court - Hever Castle

Contact: Miss Kate Rowbottom, Sales Manager, Medley Court at Hever Castle, Hever Castle, Hever, Edenbridge TN8 7NG   **T:** (01732) 861744   **F:** 01732 867860
E: krowbottom@hevercastle.co.uk
W: www.hevercastle.co.uk/stay/medley-court/   **£ BOOK ONLINE**

Medley Court is a luxurious four bedroom property forming part of the Astor Wing, William Waldorf Astor's magnificent addition to Hever Castle in 1903. The double moated Castle provides a stunning backdrop to Medley Court and creates a truly historical setting.

Open: All year
Nearest Shop: 5 miles
Nearest Pub: 0.5 miles

Site: ✿ **P** **Payment:** 💳 **Leisure:** 🎣 ▶ ♻ ⚲ **Property:** 🖥 🗔 🖳 **Children:** 🐎 🎰 🍼
Unit: 🗔 🗄 📺 🍳 📺 🎧 📀 ⁄

FAVERSHAM, Kent   Map ref 3B3

Units 1
Sleeps 2
PER UNIT PER WEEK
£300.00 - £420.00

The Loft at Acorns

Contact: Beryl Chipperton, Acorns, Butlers Hill, Dargate, Faversham ME13 9HG
T: (01227) 752 912   **E:** beryl@chipperton.plus.com
W: www.loftatacorns.com

Peacefully situated apartment for 2 people in an Area of Outstanding Natural Beauty adjoining the Blean. Just 15mins from Canterbury and the historic towns of Faversham & Whitstable and 30mins from the Turner Centre in Margate and Dover Port.
Open: All Year **Nearest Shop:** 1 mile **Nearest Pub:** 200 yards

Site: ✿ **P** **Leisure:** 🎣 ▶ ♻ ⚘ **Property:** 🖥 🗔 🖳 **Unit:** 🗔 🗄 📺 🍳 📺 🎧 ⁄ **BBQ**

FOLKESTONE, Kent   Map ref 3B4

3★ - 4★
SELF CATERING

Units   19
Sleeps   2-10

PER UNIT PER WEEK
£95.00 - £475.00

SPECIAL PROMOTIONS
Short breaks, Mon-Fri or Fri-Mon: low season - min £65, max £195; high season - min £100, max £315.

The Grand

Contact: Mr Robert Richardson, The Grand, The Leas, Folkestone CT20 2XL
T: (01303) 222222 **F:** 01303 220220 **E:** info@grand-uk.com
W: www.grand-uk.com **£ BOOK ONLINE**

The Grand, Folkestone is a Grade 2 listed Edwardian building in an unrivalled position on the South Coast with stunning views of the English Channel.

The Grand's suites of accommodation are self-catering, which include kitchens, living rooms and bathrooms. The Palm Court Restaurant offers fine dining with its stunning views. Live Pianist on selected nights.

For something more informal, try a pint of "The Grand Ale" in Keppels Bar and Bistro and finally, why not visit the Salon De Thé and try our homemade Scones or a Tea-Pigs tea.

Open: All year
Nearest Shop: 0.5 miles
Nearest Pub: 0.01 miles

Site: ❀ P **Payment:** 💷 € **Leisure:** 🚲 ♪ ► ∪ **Property:** ⁄⁄ 🖥 🔒 ▣ **Children:** 🛝 🏠 🎯
Unit: ▯ 🗄 📷 🔌 📺 ◉ ☏

HYTHE, Kent   Map ref 3B4

★★★★
SELF CATERING

Units   1
Sleeps   1-4

PER UNIT PER WEEK
£550.00 - £700.00

SPECIAL PROMOTIONS
£550 per week 1st Oct-30th April or £100 per night minimum 3 nights. £700 per week 1st May-30th Sept or £125 per night minimum 3 nights.

8 The Terrace Apartments

Contact: Mrs Joanna Porter, 8 The Terrace Apartments, 27 Castle Road, Hythe CT2 15EZ
T: (01303) 239334 **E:** joanna@liquidlighthealing.com

Luxury 2 bedroom 2nd floor apartment on seafront in Hythe. South facing balcony with lovely views of Hythe bay. Superb accommodation for 4 people. Fully equipped kitchen. Parking for 2 cars. Lift. Easy walking distance to shops, pubs, restaurants and local amenities. Newly furnished and decorated. Utility room, washing machine.

Open: All year
Nearest Shop: 500 metres
Nearest Pub: 500 metres

Units: Master bedroom with en suite shower, plus family bathroom.

Site: P **Leisure:** 🚲 ♪ ► ∪ **Property:** 🖥 🔒 ▣ **Children:** 🛝 **Unit:** ▯ 🗄 📷 🔌 📺 ◉ 📀 ☏

MAIDSTONE, Kent   Map ref 3B3

Units   1
Sleeps   1-4
PER UNIT PER WEEK
£300.00 - £410.00

Lime Tree Cottages

Contact: Peter & Stella Hasler, Owners, 4 Lime Tree Cottages, Faversham Road, Lenham, Kent ME17 2EY **T:** (01622) 851310 / 07777 661716 **E:** pvhasler@gmail.com
W: www.kentcottage.com

A 100+ year old cottage on the historic Pilgrims Way (AONB) is an ideal base to explore Kent - easy access to London and Europe. Only 5 minutes drive from Leeds Castle and 30 minutes to Canterbury or Rochester. A warm welcome awaits you.
Open: All year **Nearest Shop:** 0.5 miles **Nearest Pub:** 0.5 miles

Site: ✿ P **Property:** ⌾ 🖾 🗄 🖵 **Children:** ⎈ 🛏 ⭑ **Unit:** 🖳 🖾 🖳 ⎃ TV DVD ⌀ BBQ ✆

ROYAL TUNBRIDGE WELLS, Kent   Map ref 2D2

Units   2
Sleeps   2-4
PER UNIT PER WEEK
£375.00 - £400.00

Ford Cottage

Contact: Mrs Wendy Cusdin, Ford Cottage, Linden Park Road, Tunbridge Wells, Kent TN2 5QL **T:** (01892) 531419 **E:** fordcottage@gmail.com
W: fordcottage.co.uk

Picturesque Victorian cottage three minutes walk from the Pantiles. Self-contained studio flats with own front doors, fully fitted kitchens, en suites and showers. Free Wi-Fi available and off-street parking. Ideal for visiting many local gardens, castles and historic houses. Special quotations available on request for longer or shorter stay periods. Prices per week based on 2 people sharing. £455pw for a family of 4. **Open:** All year **Nearest Shop:** 0.15 miles **Nearest Pub:** 0.15 miles

Site: ✿ P **Payment:** 💷 **Leisure:** 🏊 ♪ ♪ ♪ U **Property:** 🖾 🗄 🖵 **Children:** ⎈ 🛏 **Unit:** 🗄 🖳 🖾 ⎃ TV ⏻ ✆

ROYAL TUNBRIDGE WELLS, Kent   Map ref 2D2

Units   6
Sleeps   2-4

PER UNIT PER WEEK
£310.00 - £486.00

Plaisance

Contact: Mrs Angela Worsell, Office Manager, Itaris Properties, 12 Mount Ephraim, Royal Tunbridge Wells, Kent TN4 8AS **T:** (01892) 511065 **E:** enquiries@itaris.co.uk
W: www.itaris.co.uk

Royal Tunbridge Wells is surrounded by beautiful and unspoilt countryside and is the ideal location for a short break or relaxing holiday. Our self-contained and fully equipped holiday apartments are situated in the very heart of Tunbridge Wells within walking distance of its many amenities.

Open: All year
Nearest Shop: 0.5 miles
Nearest Pub: 0.10 miles

Site: P **Payment:** 💷 **Leisure:** 🏊 ♪ ♪ **Property:** 🖾 🗄 🕮 🖵 **Children:** ⎈ 🛏 ⭑ **Unit:** 🗄 🖳 ⎃ TV ⏻ DVD

SNODLAND, Kent   Map ref 3B3

Units   1
Sleeps   1-4

PER UNIT PER WEEK
£425.00 - £550.00

Sandhole Barn

Contact: Mrs Elaine Scutt, c/o South Cottage, 235 Sandy Lane, Sandhole, Snodland
ME6 5LG **T:** (01634) 241988 **E:** info@sandholebarnkent.co.uk
W: www.sandholebarnkent.co.uk

Comfortable, well-equipped ground floor accommodation with 1 double, 1 twin-bed room. Good accessibility for those with limited mobility. Wi-Fi access. Pretty private garden, off-road parking. Quiet rural location nr Leybourne Lakes, good for walkers/cyclists. 5 mins junc 4 M20. Excellent touring base: Rochester (7 miles), Brands Hatch, NT properties. Hi-speed rail link to London (Strood 6 miles). **Open:** May-end Sept plus Oct Half term, Xmas/NY
Nearest Shop: 0.1 miles **Nearest Pub:** 0.1 miles

Site: ✿ **P** **Leisure:** ♪ ▶ **Property:** 🖥 🖨 **Children:** 🐎 🏠 **Unit:** 🗄 📺 🔌 🍳 📺 🔊 💿 BBQ

ABINGDON-ON-THAMES, Oxfordshire   Map ref 2C1

Units   6

SPECIAL PROMOTIONS
Please contact us for prices and details of special offers and short breaks.

Kingfisher Barn Holiday Cottages

Contact: Rye Farm, Abingdon, Oxon OX14 3NN **T:** (01235) 537538
E: info@kingfisherbarn.com
W: www.kingfisherbarn.com

All cottages are spacious and fully furnished, set in the Oxfordshire countryside, we offer beautiful views, the river Thames is a short walk away, as well as the historical town of Abingdon.

All self-catering guests will have exclusive use of our private indoor heated pool, time slots can be pre booked or taken as and when during your stay. If you don't feel like cooking we can arrange for a full English or Continental breakfast to be delivered to your cottage or can enjoy breakfast in our new log cabin breakfast area.

Nearest Shop: Nearby
Nearest Pub: Nearby

Units: The self catering cottages and lodges at Kingfisher Barn vary in size from our one bedroom loft apartment to a four bedroom / three bathroom lodge.

Site: ✿ **P** **Leisure:** 🏊 **Property:** 🐾 🖥 🖨 **Unit:** 🗄 📺 🔌 🍳 📺 BBQ

ADDERBURY, Oxfordshire   Map ref 2C1

Units   1
Sleeps   2

PER UNIT PER WEEK
£385.00 - £420.00

Hannah's Cottage at Fletcher's

Contact: Mrs Charlotte Holmes, Owner, Fletchers, High Street, Adderbury, nr Banbury,
Oxfordshire OX17 3LS **T:** (01295) 810308 **E:** charlotteaholmes@hotmail.com
W: www.holiday-rentals.com

The cottage is designed and equipped for 2, with a double bedroom at the top of a good flight of stairs. This bedroom has a toilet and washbasin adjoining it. Also on this floor is the large lounge with good views. Downstairs is a well equipped kitchen and dining area. Situated in quiet location in beautiful old village, within walking distance of 4 pubs and village shop. **Open:** All year
Nearest Shop: 50 yards **Nearest Pub:** 50 yards

Site: ✿ **P** **Property:** 🖥 🖨 **Unit:** 🗄 📺 🔌 🍳 📺 💿 BBQ

BICESTER, Oxfordshire   Map ref 2C1

Grange Farm Country Cottages

Contact: Mrs Penelope Oakey, Grange Farm Country Cottages, Grange Farm Estates, Godington, Bicester, Oxfordshire OX27 9AF **T:** (01869) 278778 / 07919 002132
E: penelope@grangefarmcottages.co.uk **W:** www.grangefarmcottages.co.uk

Units   5
Sleeps   1-8

PER UNIT PER WEEK
£295.00 - £895.00

SPECIAL PROMOTIONS
Late breaks sometimes available. Please just call or email for details.

A warm welcome from the Oakey family awaits you at Grange Farm. A working farm, this lovely location offers all the delights of the English countryside. Converted from Victorian barns, our Gold Award cottages are equipped to the highest standards. Their style reflects beautiful country charm combined with outstanding levels of comfort. Easy access and a perfect base for exploring the many delights of North Oxfordshire and the Cotswolds. Wi-Fi, private fishing lake, guests gardens and lovely walks in peaceful surroundings. See our gorgeous alpacas and ponies! Visiting horses and dogs welcome.

Open: All year
Nearest Shop: 3 miles
Nearest Pub: 2 miles

Units: Cottages of various sizes featuring private bathrooms, ground and first floor bedrooms, lovely outdoor seating area with guests gardens and barbecues.

Site: ✿ P **Payment:** £ € **Leisure:** ✿ ♪ ▶ ♡ ✎ **Property:** ✿ ▦ ▣ ▣ **Children:** ✿ ▦ ✿
Unit: ▯ ▯ ▣ ✎ TV ◉ DVD BBQ

CHARLBURY, Oxfordshire   Map ref 2C1

The Stable

Contact: Mrs Christina Pratley, Owner, The Stable, Reeves Barn, Pound Hill, Charlbury, Oxfordshire OX7 3QN **T:** (01608) 810077 / 07903 978798
E: christinapratley@homecall.co.uk **W:** cottagesatthecotswolds.co.uk

Units   1
Sleeps   1-2
PER UNIT PER WEEK
£370.00 - £410.00

Situated on the outskirts of the Cotswold town of Charlbury. The Stable is the ideal base for touring the Cotswolds, Stratford-upon-Avon and Warwick. Easy access to Oxford and London. Mainline Train Station only 15 minutes walking distance. Comfortable and cosy. Beautiful countryside in area of outstanding natural beauty. Off road parking. Inns, supermarket and shops within walking distance. **Open:** All year **Nearest Shop:** 500 metres **Nearest Pub:** 500 metres

Site: P **Payment:** £ **Property:** ▯ ▣ **Unit:** ▣ ▣ ✎ TV ◉ DVD

CHIPPING NORTON, Oxfordshire   Map ref 2C1

Heath Farm Holiday Cottages

Contact: Nena and David Barbour, Heath Farm, Swerford, Chipping Norton, Oxfordshire OX7 4BN **T:** (01608) 683270 **F:** 01608 683222 **E:** barbours@heathfarm.com
W: www.heathfarm.com **£ BOOK ONLINE**

Units   5
Sleeps   2-4
PER UNIT PER WEEK
£400.00 - £1200.00

Five beautiful, award-winning, quality handcrafted stone cottages. Exquisite interiors, wonderful views. Natural materials, scrupulously clean. Stunning paved courtyard and water garden. Croquet lawn, woodlands and wildflower meadows. Green Tourism Gold. Log fires, free firewood. Ideal base for Cotswolds, Oxford, Stratford, Bicester village. Excellent pubs, farmers markets. No pets. No Smoking. Flexible short/long breaks. **Open:** All year
Nearest Shop: 3 miles **Nearest Pub:** 1 mile

Site: ✿ P **Payment:** £ **Leisure:** ✿ ▶ ✎ **Property:** ▦ ▣ ▣ **Children:** ✿ ▦ ✿ **Unit:** ▯ ▯ ▣ ▣ ✎ TV DVD ♨ BBQ ✆

OXFORD, Oxfordshire   Map ref 2C1

SELF CATERING

Units   4
Sleeps   2-24

PER UNIT PER WEEK
£475.00 - £840.00

SPECIAL PROMOTIONS
Short break 75% of weekly rate. B&B not offered. Wedding parties catered for. Also on the farm we have an Honesty Shop, Master Butcher offering Oxfordshire's finest meats and a Micro-brewery

Oxford Country Cottages
Contact: James & Felicity Dolleymore, Lower Farm, Noke, Oxford OX3 9TX
T: 07830 165830 **E:** james@oxfordcountrycottages.co.uk
W: www.oxfordcountrycottages.co.uk **£ BOOK ONLINE**

Oxford Country Cottages on Lower Farm in Noke are just 5 miles from the centre of Oxford. Four 4* self-catering cottages sleeping up to 24 in total. Made up of 1, 2 & 3 bedroom cottages all within 50 yards of each other, the cottages are available for short lets year-round. The cottages are beautifully converted single storey barns and have just undergone extensive modernisation, combining farmhouse furniture with discrete essentials (1000Mbps broadband WiFi & Smart TVs), set in a stunning courtyard garden, a peaceful & secluded country retreat with RSPB Otmoor as our neighbour

Open: All Year
Nearest Shop: 0 miles
Nearest Pub: 2 miles

Units: Single storey converted barns with exposed beams - 1, 2 & 3 bedroom cottages. Free WiFi - Ultrafast broadband at 1000Mbps!

Site: ❀ P **Payment:** 💷 **Leisure:** ▶ ∪ ♦ **Property:** ∥ 🐾 ▦ 🖥 🖳 **Children:** 🚼 🎠 🏃
Unit: 🍴 🍽 📺 🔌 📺 🎬 📀 🚿 BBQ 📞

ESHER, Surrey   Map ref 2D2

SELF CATERING

Units   1
Sleeps   1-2

PER UNIT PER WEEK
£300.00

Lynwood Studio
Contact: Ms Becky Hughes, Owners, Lynwood Studio, Greenways, Hinchley Wood, Esher, Surrey KT10 0QJ **T:** 020 8339 3739 / 07758 958651 **E:** hughesbex@sky.com

Self contained studio with access via owners side entrance. Fully equipped with all bed linen and towels provided. Washing machine, fridge, electric oven, microwave, sky tv and Wi-Fi. Double bed with a separate shower room/toilet. Easy access to London.
Open: All year **Nearest Shop:** 500 metres **Nearest Pub:** 500 metres

Site: ❀ P **Property:** 🖳 **Unit:** 📺 📺

Sign up for our newsletter

Visit our website to sign up for our e-newsletter and receive regular information on events, articles, exclusive competitions and new publications.
www.visitor-guides.co.uk

FARNHAM, Surrey Map ref 2C2

Bentley Green Farm

Contact: Mrs Glenda Powell, Bentley Green Farm, The Drift, Bentley, Farnham GU10 5JX
T: (01420) 23246 / 07711 981614 **E:** enquiries@bentleygreenfarm.co.uk
W: www.bentleygreenfarm.co.uk

Units 1
Sleeps 1-5

PER UNIT PER WEEK
£350.00 - £560.00

Luxury self-contained accommodation in purpose-built annexe of listed 16th century farmhouse. Set in 40 acres with outdoor swimming pool, tennis court, and fishing rights. Fully fitted and very spacious. Ideally located between Alton and Farnham with ample parking. Public transport is nearby and London is 55 minutes away by train. Heathrow, Gatwick, Bournemouth and Southampton airports are all an hour away by car. Full details available on website.

Open: All year
Nearest Shop: 0.5 miles
Nearest Pub: 0.5 miles

Units: Beautifully decorated and spacious King sized bedroom. Extra luxury folding beds are available and there is space for an extra bed or cot if needed.

Site: P **Payment:** € **Leisure:** ♪ ▶ ♒ **Property:** **Children:** **Unit:** BBQ

FARNHAM, Surrey Map ref 2C2

Kilnside Farm

Contact: Mr Bob Milton, Booking Enquiries, Kilnside Farm, Moor Park Lane, Farnham GU10 1NS **T:** (01252) 710325 / 07860 718464 **E:** bobmilton@kilnsidefarm.fsnet.co.uk

Units 1
Sleeps 2-4
PER UNIT PER WEEK
£250.00 - £350.00

Self-catering cottage with two single beds and a small fold up upstairs and a 4'6" sofa bed downstairs. Open plan kitchen / dining area. Wi-Fi available. Situated on a sheep / horse farm, 1m east of Farnham. North Downs Way starts only ½ a mile away and runs through the farm. Access from Rock House Lane Runfold.
Open: All year **Nearest Shop:** 0.5 miles **Nearest Pub:** 0.5 miles

Site: P **Payment:** € **Leisure:** ♪ **Property:** **Children:** **Unit:** BBQ

GODALMING, Surrey Map ref 2D2

Prestwick Self Catering

Contact: Paul Mills, Proprietor, Prestwick Lane, Chiddingfold, Godalming, Surrey GU8 4XP
T: (01428) 654695 / 07966 452256 **E:** prestwick.farm@btconnect.com
W: www.prestwickfarm.co.uk

Units 1
Sleeps 5-6
PER UNIT PER WEEK
£450.00 - £520.00

Prestwick is a working sheep farm, with 500 Ewes set in the picturesque 'Surrey Hills' between Chiddingfold and Haslemere. The bungalow style converted building in 'Area of outstanding Natural Beauty' is ideally located for walkers and provides a comfortable base. Midway between London and the South Coast you really do have access to most of the attractions that the South East has to offer. **Open:** All year **Nearest Shop:** 1.5 miles
Nearest Pub: 1 mile

Site: P **Payment:** **Leisure:** ▶ **Property:** **Children:** **Unit:** BBQ

GUILDFORD, Surrey Map ref 2D2

Lavender

Contact: Mr & Mrs Elizabeth Liew, Lavender, 8-10 Martyr Road, Guildford GU1 4LF
T: (01483) 506819 / 07504 574252 **F:** 01483 506819 **E:** successbee@hotmail.co.uk

Well-presented, fully furnished, comfortable house, conveniently situated in town centre, close to high street shops, river, theatre, leisure facilities and railway station. Airports 40 minutes.
Open: All year

Units   1
Sleeps   5-6
PER UNIT PER WEEK
£600.00

Site: ✿ P Payment: € Property: 🖵 Children: 🎠 🛏 🧍 Unit: 🗄 📺 📻 🔌 TV

GUILDFORD, Surrey Map ref 2D2

Rydes Hill Cottage

Contact: Penny Wilson-Smith, Owner, 176 Aldershot Road, Guildford, Surrey GU2 8BL
T: (01483) 535841 **E:** pjws@btinternet.com
W: www.guildfordapartment.com

Comfortable and up-to-date, newly renovated two bedroom apartment. Ideally located and convenient both for business and leisure visitors. Includes living room, dining area, kitchen and bathroom with bath & power shower. Within easy reach of Guildford town centre and with quick access to Woking, Pirbright, Aldershot, Farnham and the Surrey countryside. Please contact for prices. **Open:** All Year **Nearest Shop:** 0.2 miles
Nearest Pub: 0.2 miles

Units   1
Sleeps   4

Site: P Property: 🍽 📻 🖵 Children: 🎠 🛏 🧍 Unit: 📺 📻 🔌 TV 📀 📞

BARNHAM, Sussex Map ref 2D3

Orchard Cottage Holidays

Contact: Mrs Lorraine Holden, Owner, Orchard Cottage Holidays, High Ground Orchards, High Ground Lane, Barnham, Nr Bognor Regis, West Sussex PO22 0BT **T:** (01243) 558536 / 07966 223614 **F:** 01243 554568 **E:** lorraine.holden@solufeed.com
W: orchardcottageholidays.org.uk **£ BOOK ONLINE**

Units   4
Sleeps   2-4

PER UNIT PER WEEK
£400.00 - £900.00

SPECIAL PROMOTIONS
Short breaks by negotiation.

Two-bedroom flint cottages, newly-built to highest specification. Near to well supplied, popular village close to downs and sea. Perfect base to explore Chichester, Arundel and West Sussex area. Rural outlook, ample parking and easy level access. Both bedrooms en suite (one downstairs). Own sunny conservatory. Private, secure individual gardens with patio.

Open: All year
Nearest Shop: 0.5 miles
Nearest Pub: 0.5 miles

Site: ✿ P Leisure: ♿ 🎣 ▶ ∪ Property: 🍽 📻 📺 🖵 Children: 🎠 🛏 🧍 Unit: 🗄 🗄 📺 📻 🔌 TV 📀 📀 📞

CHICHESTER, Sussex Map ref 2C3

Honer Cottage

Contact: Mrs Sarah Green, Honer House, Honer Lane, South Mundham, Chichester, W. Sussex PO20 1LZ **T:** (01243) 262299 **E:** info@paghamharbourcottage.co.uk
W: www.paghamharbourcottage.co.uk **£ BOOK ONLINE**

Units   1
Sleeps   2-4

PER UNIT PER WEEK
£375.00 - £700.00

Detached single storey two bedroom cottage. Open plan modern kitchen/living area. Very rural. Good walking and birdwatching. 5 miles from Chichester. Sleeps 4. **Open:** All year **Nearest Shop:** 3 miles **Nearest Pub:** 3 miles

Site: ❀ **P Payment:** € **Leisure:** 🎵 ▶ 🔍 **Property:** 🖥 🗐 **Children:** 🛏 ⛺ 🚶 **Unit:** 📱 🖫 📺 🖾 🖙 📺 🎧 📀 🎧 **BBQ**

CHICHESTER, Sussex Map ref 2C3

Laneside

Contact: Mrs Clare Sherlock, General Manager, Millstream Hotel, Bosham Lane, Bosham, Chichester, West Sussex PO18 8HL **T:** (01243) 573234 **F:** 01243 573459
E: info@millstreamhotel.com **W:** www.millstreamhotel.com

Units   3
Sleeps   2-10

PER UNIT PER WEEK
£350.00 - £750.00

SPECIAL PROMOTIONS
Please contact us for prices.

Three apartments, which are located just 200 metres from the shores of Chichester Harbour. Laneside is owned and managed by the Millstream Hotel - in whose AA 2 Rosette Restaurant dinner can be taken. Sleeps 10 in three units.

Open: All Year
Nearest Shop: Co-op 0.6 miles
Nearest Pub: Berkeley Arms 0.3 miles

Units: Three individual apartments, 2 x two bedroom apartments and 1 x one bedroom apartment with the bedroom on the ground floor. All with seperate bathroom.

Site: ❀ **Property:** 🖥 **Unit:** 📺 🎧 📀 **BBQ**

CHICHESTER, Sussex Map ref 2C3

Quay Quarters

Contact: Mrs Lorraine Sawday, Booking Enquiries, Apuldram Manor Farm, Appledram Lane South, Dell Quay, Chichester PO20 7EF **T:** (01243) 839900
E: cottages@quayquarters.co.uk **W:** www.quayquarters.co.uk **£ BOOK ONLINE**

Units   5
Sleeps   2-6

PER UNIT PER WEEK
£380.00 - £1300.00

SPECIAL PROMOTIONS
Short breaks available
Oct - Easter.

Five award winning, five star holiday cottages located at Apuldram Manor Farm, a 650 acre arable and dairy farm, just 2 miles south of Chichester. They sleep between 2-6 people.

They are all extremely well equipped, stylish and comfortable throughout the year, (whatever the weather), due to underfloor heating and electric wood burning stoves. Four of them are single storey for easy accessibility. Ample private parking.

Come and enjoy our beautiful and fragrant rose garden or the picturesque walks that begin right from your door. Guests return again and again, come and discover why...

Open: All year
Nearest Shop: 2 miles
Nearest Pub: 1 mile

Units: Quay and Stable Cottages sleep 2, Apuldram Cottage sleeps 4, Dairy and Rose Cottages sleep 6.

Site: ❀ **P** **Property:** ⚓ 🖥 🖨 **Children:** 🛏 ⊞ ⚲ **Unit:** 🗄 🗄 🖵 🗄 🗄 **TV** **DVD** BBQ

CROWBOROUGH, Sussex Map ref 2D3

Hodges

Contact: Mrs Hazel Colliver, Hodges, Eridge Road, Steel Cross TN6 2SS **T:** (01892) 652386 / 07887 505718 **E:** hazel.colliver@hodges.uk.com
W: www.hodges.uk.com

Units   1
Sleeps   1-3
PER UNIT PER WEEK
£325.00 - £395.00

Ground floor luxury accommodation. Kitchen. Large double bed. Superking bed/en suite. Sitting/dining room, triple aspect adjoining small sunny conservatory. Owners plantaholic garden for guest use. Perfect for NT and South Gardens. Sleeps 3.
Open: All year **Nearest Shop:** 1 mile **Nearest Pub:** 1mile

Leisure: ♪ ⚲ ⚲

FELPHAM, Sussex Map ref 2C3

The Beach Hut

Contact: Mr & Mrs Jackie and Clive Jourdain, Yew Tree Cottage, Church Lane, Rowledge, Farnham GU10 4EN **T:** (01252) 794171 / 07880 731082 **E:** Jackie@thebeachhut.plus.com
W: www.thebeachhut.org.uk **£ BOOK ONLINE**

Units   1
Sleeps   4
PER UNIT PER WEEK
£400.00 - £450.00

Cosy bungalow with wood-burning stove. On a quiet private estate. 1 min from sea. Visit our website thebeachhut.org.uk. Within easy reach Goodwood, Chichester and Arundel. **Open:** All year
Nearest Shop: 0.42 miles **Nearest Pub:** 0.25 miles

Site: ❀ **P** **Payment:** € **Leisure:** ♪ ▶ ⚲ **Property:** 🖥 🖨 **Children:** 🛏10 **Unit:** 🗄 🗄 🖵 🗄 🗄 **TV** **DVD** ⊘ BBQ

GLYNDE, Sussex   Map ref 2D3

Caburn Cottages

Contact: Rosemary Norris, Caburn Cottages, Ranscombe Farm, Ranscombe Lane, Glynde, Lewes BN8 6AA   **T:** (01273) 858062   **E:** enquiries@caburncottages.co.uk
W: caburncottages.co.uk

Units	9
Sleeps	2-6

PER UNIT PER WEEK
£300.00 - £560.00

Lovely flint and brick cottages on working farm. Very comfortable. Non-smoking. Downland walks. Close to Glyndebourne, Lewes and Brighton. Friendly welcome. **Open:** All year **Nearest Shop:** 1.5 miles **Nearest Pub:** 1.5 miles

Site: ✿ **P** **Payment:** € **Property:** 🐾 ▭ ▣ ▢ **Children:** ⛏ ▥ ⚘ **Unit:** ▯ ▭ 📺 ☎

HAILSHAM, Sussex   Map ref 2D3

Little Marshfoot

Contact: Kathryn Dewhurst, Owner, Mill Road, Hailsham, East Sussex BN27 2SJ
T: (01323) 844690   **E:** kew@littlemarshfoot.biz
W: www.littlemarshfoot.biz   **£ BOOK ONLINE**

Units	1
Sleeps	4

PER UNIT PER WEEK
£450.00 - £575.00

SPECIAL PROMOTIONS
Short breaks pro rata, special offers available on request.

Light and airy self contained single storey apartment equipped to a high standard, sleeping four in two en suite rooms, located in the grounds of a former farmhouse, overlooking the Pevensey Levels with restful views from the wide windows, opening onto the loggia and terraced garden.

Full central heating, with free Wi-Fi, garden games and extensive wildlife. Only six miles from the sea and the South Downs National Park, this secluded and peaceful venue is well located for touring Sussex, Kent and the Home Counties, including Eastbourne, Hastings, Lewes, Tunbridge Wells, Battle, Rye and Brighton.

Open: All year
Nearest Shop: 0.75 miles
Nearest Pub: 0.5 miles

Units: Both bedrooms on ground floor, each with en suite shower room.

Site: ✿ **P** **Payment:** 💳 € **Leisure:** ♪ ▶ ∪ **Property:** ▭ ▣ ▢ **Children:** ⛏ ▥ ⚘
Unit: ▯ ▤ ▭ ▣ ✎ 📺 📀 BBQ

HORSHAM, Sussex   Map ref 2D3

Ghyll Cottage

Contact: High Street, Rusper, Horsham, West Sussex RH12 4PX   **T:** (03301) 230 371
E: enquiries@ghyllmanor.co.uk
W: www.ghyllmanor.co.uk

Units	1
Sleeps	4-6

PER UNIT PER WEEK
£595.00 - £700.00

The gorgeous authentic Tudor beamed, two bedroom self-catering cottage is set across two floors. With its own private driveway and garden, galley style kitchen, spacious lounge and dining area and family bathroom you'll be delighted by the utterly irresistible mix of original features and modern comforts. Dinner, bed and breakfast options (and even room service) are also available. **Open:** All Year **Nearest Shop:** 0.1 miles **Nearest Pub:** 0.1 miles

Site: ✿ **P** **Payment:** 💳 **Property:** ⚊ ▭ ▢ **Children:** ⛏ **Unit:** ▯ ▭ 📺 ☎

LEWES, Sussex   Map ref 2D3

White Lion Farm Cottages

Contact: Mrs Diana Green, Owner, White Lion Farm, Shortgate, East Sussex BN8 6PJ
T: (01825) 840288 **E:** dgreen384@btinternet.com
W: www.whitelionfarmcottages.co.uk

Units   2
Sleeps   2-4
PER UNIT PER WEEK
£170.00 - £300.00

Two converted holiday cottages, tastefully decorated throughout and provide comfortable accommodation for up to four people in each. Each cottage is completely separate with its own entrance, private patio and small garden with wonderful rural views and parking area. Each cottage has a spacious double bedroom, a good sized bathroom with a shower and large living room with a sofa-bed and a well equipped kitchen area with amenities.
Open: All year **Nearest Shop:** 3 miles **Nearest Pub:** 3 miles

Site: ✿ P Leisure: ✦ ▶ ↻ Property: 🖥 📶 Children: 🐾 🛏 Unit: 🍴 📺 🛁 📺 BBQ

LITTLEHAMPTON, Sussex   Map ref 2D3

Angmering Court

Contact: Mrs Angela Gilmour, Angmering Court, Sea Lane, East Preston BN16 1NF
T: 07549 522338 **E:** angelagilmour181@btinternet.com
W: www.selfcateringsussexbythesea.co.uk / www.holidaylettings.co.uk/221336

Units   1
Sleeps   1-4
PER UNIT PER WEEK
£375.00 - £450.00

Angmering Court is situated close to the beach and the vibrant village centre of East Preston which is a "Haven for watersports" and has good public transport links, shops, bars and restaurants. The 1st floor apartment offers deceptively large modern, light, well-equipped accommodation with 2 bedrooms, 2 bathrooms, a kitchen/dining room, sitting room and communal gardens.
Open: All year **Nearest Shop:** 300 yards **Nearest Pub:** 300 yards

Site: ✿ P Payment: € Leisure: ✦ ▶ ⚲ Property: 🖥 🖥 📶 Children: 🐾 🛏 ⚘ Unit: 🍴 🖥 📺 🛁 🔔 📺 🕐 📀

RYE, Sussex   Map ref 3B4

Brandy's Cottage Cadborough

Contact: Jane Apperly, Proprietor, Cadborough Farm cottages, Udimore Road, Rye, East Sussex TN31 6AA **T:** (01797) 225426 / 07714 455634 **E:** apperly@cadborough.co.uk
W: www.cadborough.co.uk

Units   1
Sleeps   2
PER UNIT PER WEEK
£360.00 - £495.00

Brandy's Cottage offers luxury accommodation for 2. Gas fired central heating, Wi Fi, en suite large bathroom, vaulted living area, and all linen and towels provided Situated 1 mile outside Rye in peaceful location with direct access to 1066 walks. Parking away from road and next to cottage. Small private secure garden with BBQ. One small well behaved dog welcome. **Open:** Open all year
Nearest Shop: 1 mile Rye **Nearest Pub:** 1 mile

Site: ✿ P Property: 🐾 🖥 🖥 📶 Unit: 🍴 🖥 📺 🛁 🔔 📺 📀 BBQ

RYE, Sussex Map ref 3B4

Units 1
Sleeps 1-4

PER UNIT PER WEEK
£245.00 - £570.00

The Quarter House

Contact: Ms Sally Bayly, Rye Cottages, The Mint, Rye TN31 7EN **T:** (01797) 222498 / 07956 280257 **E:** info@ryecottages.net
W: www.ryecottages.net

Enchanting Grade II listed, 17th century, 2 storey apartment in the heart of Medieval Rye. Original beams and floorboards, open fireplace and jacuzzi bath. Wander Rye's cobbled streets and Church Square, visit its historic pubs, restaurants, art galleries, antique and boutique shops.

Kent and Sussex walks and bike paths on the doorstep, beautiful beaches, wind and kite surfing, dinghy sailing and kayaking 10 mins away. Dungeness and Rye Harbour Nature Reserves, Bird Sanctuaries and Sailing Club also close by. Historic towns of Battle, Hastings, Canterbury, Bodiam and Leeds and Dover Castles an easy drive away.

Open: All year
Nearest Shop: 0.10 miles
Nearest Pub: 0.10 miles

Leisure: ⚡ ▶ ∪ Property: ▭ ▢ ▣ Children: ⛵ ▥ Unit: ▭ ▯ ⚲ TV Ⓒ dvd ∂

UCKFIELD, Sussex Map ref 2D3

Units 2
Sleeps 1-2

PER UNIT PER WEEK
£295.00 - £520.00

Sunnymead Farm Cottages

Contact: Joan Cooper, Sunnymead Farm, Perrymans Lane, High Hurstwood, Uckfield, East Sussex TN22 4AG **T:** (01825) 733618 **E:** sunnymeadcottages@hotmail.co.uk
W: www.sunnymeadcottages.co.uk **£ BOOK ONLINE**

In a designated AONB situated in a High Weald village are two adjoining cottages. They are at the end of a 200m drive set amid 12 acres of gardens, fields and orchard, a haven for wildlife and birds. Excellent walking, near Ashdown Forest. **Open:** All year **Nearest Shop:** 2 miles **Nearest Pub:** 400 metres

Site: ❄ P Property: ▭ ▢ ▣ Children: ▥ ♿ Unit: ▯ ▭ ▯ ⚲ TV dvd BBQ

Sign up for our newsletter

Visit our website to sign up for our e-newsletter and receive regular information on events, articles, exclusive competitions and new publications.
www.visitor-guides.co.uk

Don't Miss...

Buckingham Palace

London, SW1A 1AA
(020) 7766 7300
www.royalcollection.org.uk
Buckingham Palace is the office and London residence of Her Majesty The Queen. It is one of the few working royal palaces remaining in the world today. The State Rooms are used extensively by The Queen and Members of the Royal Family and during August and September, when The Queen makes her annual visit to Scotland, the Palace's nineteen state rooms are open to visitors.

Houses of Parliament

Westminster, London SW1A 0AA
020 7219 4565
www.parliament.uk/visiting
Tours of the Houses of Parliament offer a unique combination of one thousand years of history, modern day politics, and stunning art and architecture. Visit the Queen's Robing Room, the Royal Gallery and the Commons Chamber, scene of many lively debates.

National Gallery

Westminster WC2N 5DN
(020) 7747 2888
www.nationalgallery.org.uk
The National Gallery houses one of the greatest collections of Western European painting in the world. Discover inspiring art by Botticelli, Caravaggio, Leonardo da Vinci, Monet, Raphael, Rembrandt, Titian, Vermeer and Van Gogh.

Natural History Museum

Kensington and Chelsea SW7 5BD
(020) 7942 5000
www.nhm.ac.uk
The Natural History Museum reveals how the jigsaw of life fits together. Animal, vegetable or mineral, the best of our planet's most amazing treasures are here for you to see - for free.

Madame Tussauds

Marylebone Road, London, NW1 5LR
(0871) 894 3000
www.madametussauds.com/London/
Experience the legendary history, glitz and glamour of Madame Tussauds London. Visit the 14 exciting, interactive zones and the amazing Marvel Super Heroes 4D movie experience. Strike a pose with your favourite movie star, enjoy an audience with the Queen or plant a cheeky kiss on Prince Harry's cheek.

London

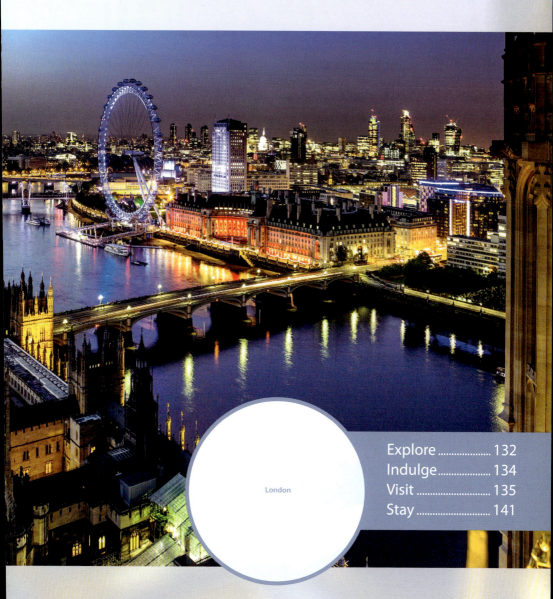

London

Grand landmarks, gorgeous gardens, spectacular shopping, exciting attractions, museums, galleries, theatres, sporting venues and all the buzz and history of the capital - London's treasures are beyond measure. A single trip is never enough and you'll find yourself returning time and again to take in the many unforgettable sights and experiences on offer.

Explore – London

In the Central/West End area the most visited sights are the now public rooms of Buckingham Palace, the National Gallery in Trafalgar Square, Tate Britain on Millbank, Westminster Abbey, Houses of Parliament and Cabinet War Rooms.

Hotspot: Watch the Changing the Guard ceremony at Buckingham Palace for an impressive display of British pomp and ceremony at 11.30am every day.

Westminster Abbey, nearly a thousand years old, has tombs of many English kings, queens, statesmen and writers. The British Museum in Bloomsbury houses one of the world's largest selections of antiquities, including the Magna Carta, the Elgin Marbles and the first edition of Alice in Wonderland. This entire area can be well viewed from The London Eye on the South Bank.

No visit to London is complete without a spot of shopping. Head for bustling Oxford Street and the stylish shops on Regent Street and Bond Street, or check out the trendy boutiques around Carnaby Street.

For entertainment, enjoy a wide range of theatre, bars, restaurants and culture in Covent Garden and don't forget to take in a musical or an off-beat play and the amazing nightime atmosphere around Leicester Square. Madame Tussauds features all your favourite celebrities and super heroes, or if you fancy an historical fright, visit the London Dungeon near Tower Bridge or explore the streets of old London on a Jack the Ripper tour.

London's parks are its lungs. St James, the oldest, was founded by Henry VIII in 1532. Hyde Park, bordering Kensington, Mayfair and Marylebone, is the largest at 630 acres and one of the greatest city parks in the world. You can enjoy any number of outdoor activities, visit the Serpentine Galleries for contemporary art or Speakers' Corner, the most famous location for free speech in the world. Regents Park, with its zoo, lies north of Oxford Circus and was given to the nation by the Prince Regent.

Heading East, St Pauls Cathedral in the city of London was redesigned by Sir Christopher Wren and the nearby the Tower of London, a medieval fortress dominated by the White Tower and dating from 1097, houses The Crown Jewels, guarded by the famous Beefeaters. Even further East, the Queen Elizabeth Olympic Park is the exciting legacy of the 2012 Olympic Games and is situated at the heart of a new, vibrant East London. The main stadium re-opens in October 2015 for the Rugby World Cup, before being permanently transformed into the national centre for athletics in the UK and the new home of West Ham United Football Club.

To the South East of the capital, Canary Wharf is one of Londons main financial centres and on the south bank, opposite Docklands, attractions include the National Maritime Museum incorporating the Royal Greenwich Observatory, the Cutty Sark and The O2, one of London's premier entertainment venues.

Hotspot: Come face to face with some of the hairiest, scariest, tallest and smallest animals on the planet - right in the heart of the capital at the ZSL London Zoo.
T: (020) 7722 3333
www.zsl.org/zsl-london-zoo

On Saturday 14th November 2015, the 800th Lord Mayors Show will feature a parade of over 6,000 people, military marching bands, acrobats, a procession of decorated floats, a gilded State Coach that the Lord Mayor travels and starts with an RAF flypast. After the procession London's City Guides will be on hand to lead free guided tours of the City's more strange and wonderful corners, and in the evening fireworks will light up the sky over the river. Visit their website for more information. www.lordmayorsshow.org.

In the North of the capital, trendy Camden is an eclectic mix of intriguing and unique experiences. Locals and visitors alike hunt for vintage treasures in the open air markets at Camden Lock and far-out attire in the alternative shops that line the high street, or spend time celebrity spotting or strolling along Regent's Canal. There's a different kind of food at every turn, from street vendors to swanky sushi restaurants, and Camden is also home to an extraordinary array of bars, live music and arts venues including the Roundhouse.

Hotspot: The Globe Theatre, Globe Exhibition & Tour and Globe Education seek to further the experience and international understanding of Shakespeare in performance.
www.shakespearesglobe.com

Indulge – London

Relax and take in the breathtaking views of London while you enjoy a glass of chilled champagne on the **London Eye** with a Champagne Experience, perfect for couples and celebrations. www.londoneye.com

Head to the stunning open-air Vista bar on the rooftop of **The Trafalgar Hotel** for cheeky cocktails. Relax and enjoy the view as you sip on something delicious. 2 Spring Gardens, Trafalgar Square SW1A 2TS www.thetrafalgar.com.

For a well earned pampering, head to the opulent **St Pancras Spa** in the basement of the beautifully renovated St Pancras Renaissance hotel. This subterranean haven has a stunning pool area bedecked in Victorian tiles, steam room, sauna and luxurious treatment rooms offering exotic sounding treatments like Balinese massage and a Creme de Rassoul Moroccan body wrap. www.stpancrasspa.co.uk

Porters has served mouth watering food in the heart Covent Garden since 1979. World renowned for traditional dinners like Steak and Kidney Pudding and Fisherman's Pie, not to mention the heavenly steamed syrup sponge pudding and homemade ice creams, this is a treat not to be missed. www.porters.co.uk T: 020 7836 6466

Since its foundation in 1707, **Fortnum & Mason** has been supplying Londoners and visitors with the very finest goods and services. Enjoy a thoroughly delightful English tradition in elegant surroundings with afternoon tea in the Diamond Jubilee Tea Salon. www.fortnumandmason.com

Attractions with this sign participate in the Visitor Attraction Quality Assurance Scheme.

Apsley House
Westminster W1J 7NT
(020) 7499 5676
www.english-heritage.org.uk/daysout/properties/apsley-house/
This great 18th century town house pays homage to the Duke's dazzling military career, which culminated in his victory at Waterloo in 1815.

Bateaux London Restaurant Cruisers
Westminster WC2N 6NU
(020) 7695 1800
www.bateauxlondon.com
Bateaux London offers lunch and dinner cruises, combining luxury dining, world-class live entertainment and five-star customer care.

The Boat Race
April, Putney Bridge
www.theboatrace.org
Boat crews from the universities of Oxford and Cambridge battle it out on the Thames.

British Museum
Camden WC1B 3DG
(020) 7323 8299
www.britishmuseum.org.uk
Founded in 1753, the British Museum's remarkable collections span over two million years of human history and culture, all under one roof.

Chessington World of Adventures
Kingston upon Thames KT9 2NE
0870 444 7777
www.chessington.com
Explore Chessington - it's a whole world of adventures! Soar on the Vampire rollercoaster, discover the mystery of Tomb Blaster or visit the park's own SEA LIFE Centre.

Chinese New Year
February, Various venues
www.visitlondon.com
London's Chinese New Year celebrations are the largest outside Asia, with parades, performances and fireworks.

Chiswick House
Hounslow W4 2RP
(020) 8995 0508
www.english-heritage.org.uk/daysout/properties/
chiswick-house/
*The celebrated villa of Lord Burlington with impressive
grounds featuring Italianate garden with statues,
temples, obelisks and urns.*

Churchill Museum and Cabinet War Rooms
Westminster SW1A 2AQ
(020) 7930 6961
www.iwm.org.uk
*Learn more about the man who inspired Britain's finest
hour at the highly interactive and innovative Churchill
Museum, the world's first major museum dedicated
to life of the 'greatest Briton'. Step back in time and
discover the secret.*

City of London Festival
June-July, Various venues
www.visitlondon.com
*The City of London Festival is an annual extravaganza
of music, dance, art, film, poetry, family and
participation events that takes place in the city's
Square Mile.*

Eltham Palace
Greenwich SE9 5QE
(020) 8294 2548
www.elthampalace.org.uk
*A spectacular fusion of 1930s Art Deco villa and
magnificent 15th century Great Hall. Surrounded
by period gardens.*

Greenwich Heritage Centre
Greenwich SE18 4DX
(020) 8854 2452
www.royalgreenwich.gov.uk
*Local history museum with displays of archaeology,
natural history and geology. Also temporary exhibitions,
schools service, sales point and Saturday club.*

Hampton Court Palace
Richmond upon Thames KT8 9AU
(0870) 752 7777
www.hrp.org.uk
*This magnificent palace set in delightful gardens was
famously one of Henry VIII's favourite palaces.*

HMS Belfast
Southwark SE1 2JH
(020) 7940 6300
www.iwm.org.uk
*HMS Belfast, launched 1938, served throughout WWII,
playing a leading part in the destruction of the German
battle cruiser Scharnhorst and in the Normandy Landings.*

Imperial War Museum
Southwark SE1 6HZ
(020) 7416 5000
www.iwm.org.uk
*This award-winning museum tells the story of
conflict involving Britain and the Commonwealth
since 1914. See thousands of imaginatively displayed
exhibits, from art to aircraft, utility clothes to U-boats.*

Kensington Palace State Apartments
Kensington and Chelsea W8 4PX
(0844) 482 7777
www.hrp.org.uk
*Home to the Royal Ceremonial Dress Collection, which
includes some of Queen Elizabeth II's dresses worn
throughout her reign, as well as 14 of Diana, Princess of
Wales' evening dresses.*

Kenwood House
Camden NW3 7JR
(020) 8348 1286
www.english-heritage.org.uk/daysout/properties/
kenwood-house/
*Beautiful 18th century villa with fine interiors, and
a world class collection of paintings. Also fabulous
landscaped gardens and an award-winning restaurant.*

London Eye River Cruise Experience
Lambeth E1 7PB
0870 500 0600
www.londoneye.com
See London from a different perspective and enjoy a unique 40 minute circular sightseeing cruise on the river Thames.

London Festival of Architecture
June - July
www.londonfestivalofarchitecture.org
See London's buildings in a new light during the Festival of Architecture.

London Film Festival
October, Various venues
www.bfi.org.uk/lff
A two-week showcase of the world's best new films, the BFI London Film Festival is one of the most anticipated events in London's cultural calendar.

London Transport Museum
Westminster WC2E 7BB
(020) 7379 6344
www.ltmuseum.co.uk
The history of transport for everyone, from spectacular vehicles, special exhibitions, actors and guided tours to film shows, gallery talks and children's craft workshops

London Wetland Centre
Richmond upon Thames SW13 9WT
(020) 8409 4400
www.wwt.org.uk
The London Wetland Centre is a unique wildlife visitor attraction just 25 minutes from central London. Run by the Wildfowl and Wetlands Trust (WWT), it is acclaimed as the best urban site in Europe to watch wildlife.

Lord's Tour
Westminster NW8 8QN
(020) 7616 8595
www.lords.org/history/tours-of-lords/
Guided tour of Lord's Cricket Ground including the Long Room, MCC Museum, Real Tennis Court, Mound Stand and Indoor School.

Museums At Night
May, Various venues
www.visitlondon.com
Explore arts and heritage after dark at museums across London. Packed with special events, from treasure trails to pyjama parties, Museums at Night is a great opportunity to explore culture in a new light.

Museum of London
City of London EC2Y 5HN
(020) 7001 9844
www.museumoflondon.org.uk
Step inside Museum of London for an unforgettable journey through the capital's turbulent past.

National Maritime Museum
Greenwich SE10 9NF
(020) 8858 4422
www.nmm.ac.uk
Britain's seafaring history housed in an impressive modern museum. Themes include exploration, Nelson, trade and empire, passenger shipping, luxury liners, maritime London, costume, art and the sea, the future and environmental issues.

National Portrait Gallery
Westminster WC2H 0HE
(020) 7306 0055
www.npg.org.uk
The National Portrait Gallery houses the world's largest collection of portraits. Visitors come face to face with the people who have shaped British history from Elizabeth I to David Beckham. Entrance is free.

Notting Hill Carnival
August, Various venues
www.thenottinghillcarnival.com
The streets of West London come alive every August Bank Holiday weekend as London celebrates Europe's biggest street festival.

RHS Chelsea Flower Show
May, Royal Hospital Chelsea
www.rhs.org.uk/Chelsea-Flower-Show
Experience the greatest flower show in the world at London's Royal Hospital Chelsea.

Royal Air Force Museum Hendon
Barnet NW9 5LL
(020) 8205 2266
www.rafmuseum.org
Take off to the Royal Air Force Museum and flypast the history of aviation with an exciting display of suspended aircraft, touch screen technology, simulator rides, hands-on section, film shows, licensed restaurant.

Royal Observatory Greenwich
Greenwich SE10 9NF
(020) 8858 4422
www.rmg.co.uk
Stand on the Greenwich Meridian Line, Longitude Zero, which divides East and West. Watch the time-ball fall at 1 o'clock. Giant refracting telescope.

Science Museum
Kensington and Chelsea SW7 2DD
0870 870 4868
www.sciencemuseum.org.uk
The Science Museum is world-renowned for its historic collections, awe-inspiring galleries, family activities and exhibitions - and it's free!

Somerset House
Westminster WC2R 1LA
(020) 7845 4670
www.somersethouse.org.uk
This magnificent 18th century building houses the celebrated collections of the Courtauld Institute of Art Gallery, Gilbert Collection and Hermitage Rooms.

Southbank Centre
Lambeth SE1 8XX
(020) 7960 4200
www.southbankcentre.co.uk
A unique arts centre with 21 acres of creative space, including the Royal Festival Hall, Queen Elizabeth Hall and The Hayward.

Southwark Cathedral
Southwark SE1 9DA
(020) 7367 6700
http://cathedral.southwark.anglican.org
Oldest Gothic church in London (c.1220) with interesting memorials connected with the Elizabethan theatres of Bankside.

Tate Britain
Westminster SW1P 4RG
(020) 7887 8888
www.tate.org.uk
Tate Britain presents the world's greatest collection of British art in a dynamic series of new displays and exhibitions.

Tate Modern
Southwark SE1 9TG
(020) 7887 8888
www.tate.org.uk/modern
The national gallery of international modern art and is one of London's top free attractions. Packed with challenging modern art and housed within a disused power station on the south bank of the River Thames.

Tower Bridge Exhibition
Southwark SE1 2UP
(020) 7403 3761
www.towerbridge.org.uk
Inside Tower Bridge Exhibition you will travel up to the high-level walkways, located 140 feet above the Thames and witness stunning panoramic views of London before visiting the Victorian Engine Rooms.

Tower of London
Tower Hamlets EC3N 4AB
0844 482 7777
www.hrp.org.uk
The Tower of London spans over 900 years of British history. Fortress, palace, prison, arsenal and garrison, it is one of the most famous fortified buildings in the world, and houses the Crown Jewels, armouries, Yeoman Warders and ravens.

Victoria and Albert Museum
Kensington and Chelsea SW7 2RL
(020) 7942 2000
www.vam.ac.uk
The V&A is the world's greatest museum of art and design, with collections unrivalled in their scope and diversity.

Virgin London Marathon
April, Various venues
www.virginlondonmarathon.com
Whether you run, walk or cheer from the sidelines, this is a London sporting institution you won't want to miss.

Vodafone London Fashion Weekend
www.londonfashionweekend.co.uk
London's largest and most exclusive designer shopping event.

Wembley Stadium Tours

Brent HA9 0WS
0844 847 2478
www.wembleystadium.com
Until your dream comes true, there's only one way to experience what it's like winning at Wembley - take the tour.

William Morris Gallery
Lloyd Park, Forest Road, Walthamstow E17 4PP
(020) 8496 4390
www.wmgallery.org.uk
The William Morris Gallery is devoted to the life and legacy of one of Britain's most remarkable designers and is housed in the grade II listed Georgian house that was his family home in north-east London from 1848 to 1856.*

Wimbledon Lawn Tennis Championships
June - July, Wimbledon
www.wimbledon.com
The world of tennis descends on Wimbledon in South West London every summer for two weeks of tennis, strawberries and cream, and good-natured queuing.

Wimbledon Lawn Tennis Museum

Merton SW19 5AG
(020) 8944 1066
www.wimbledon.com
A fantastic collection of memorabilia dating from 1555, including Championship Trophies, Art Gallery, and special exhibitions, reflecting the game and championships of today.

Tourist Information Centres

When you arrive at your destination, visit a Tourist Information Centre for quality assured help with accommodation and information about local attractions and events, or email your request before you go.

City of London
St Paul's Churchyard
(020) 7606 3030
stpauls.informationcentre@cityoflondon.gov.uk

Greenwich
2 Cutty Sark Gardens
(0870) 608 2000
tic@greenwich.gov.uk

Harrow
Gayton Library
(0208) 427 6012
gayton.library@harrow.gov.uk

Regional Contacts and Information

For more information on accommodation, attractions, activities, events and holidays in London, contact Visit London.

Go to visitlondon.com for all you need to know about London. Look for inspirational itineraries with great ideas for weekends and short breaks.

Or call 0870 1 LONDON (0870 1 566 366) for:

• A London visitor information pack
• Visitor information on London
• Accommodation reservations

Speak to an expert for information and advice on museums, galleries, attractions, riverboat trips, sightseeing tours, theatre, shopping, eating out and much more!

Entries appear alphabetically by town name in each county. A key to symbols appears on page 7

LONDON E1, Inner London   Map ref 2D2

Hamlet

Contact: Renata, General Manager, Hamlet, 47 Willian Way, Letchworth SG6 2HJ
T: (01462) 678037 **F:** 01462 679639 **E:** hamlet_uk@globalnet.co.uk
W: www.hamletuk.com

Units   4
Sleeps   4-6

PER UNIT PER WEEK
£675.00 - £929.00

SPECIAL PROMOTIONS
Discounted last-minute and long-term lets.

Hamlet was established in 1990 and offers a handful of affordable, excellent value self-catering holiday apartments in a unique and quiet location: St. Katharine Marina is a hidden treasure adjacent to Tower Bridge and the Tower of London on the north bank of the river Thames.

Open: All year
Nearest Shop: 0.10 miles
Nearest Pub: 0.10 miles

Units: One and two bedroom apartments, some overlooking the yachts in St. Katharine Marina.

Site: ✿ P Payment: 💳 Property: 📺 📻 📶 Children: 🐴 🛏 🏃 Unit: 🚪 📺 📷 🍳 📺 🎧 📀 📞

LONDON SE9, Inner London   Map ref 2D2

Beechhill House

Contact: Mrs Bethan Farrar, Proprietor, Beechhill House, 50 Beechhill Road, Eltham, London SE9 1HH **T:** 020 8850 4863 / 07538 787594 **E:** cass@stayinselondon.co.uk
W: stayinselondon.co.uk

Units   1
Sleeps   4-12
PER UNIT PER WEEK
£1100.00 - £1400.00

5 bedrooms, 3 en suite, large Edwardian house. Sleeps 10/12. Two lounges, modern kitchen and dining room/conservatory. Large garden and patio. Off street parking. Greenwich 4 miles. 5 min walk to Eltham train station, Central London 20mins. **Open:** All year **Nearest Shop:** 0.20 miles **Nearest Pub:** 0.20 miles

Site: ✿ P Property: 📺 📻 📶 Children: 🐴 🛏 🏃 Unit: 🚪 📺 📷 🍳 📺 🎧 BBQ

LONDON SW3, Inner London   Map ref 2D2

The Apartments - Chelsea & Marylebone

Contact: Kasia Tymoczko, General Manager, 36 Draycott Place, London SW3 2SA
T: 020 7589 3271 **F:** 020 7589 3274 **E:** sales@theapartments.co.uk
W: www.theapartments.co.uk **£ BOOK ONLINE**

Units   40
Sleeps   2-6
PER UNIT PER WEEK
£1092.00 - £2982.00

The Apartments is a family run serviced apartment business with over 15 years experience, offering an elegant selection of studios, one and two-bedroom apartments, in two of London's premier locations. Housed in prestigious Victorian buildings, each apartment is individually designed with fitted kitchens & bathrooms, with a full range of modern amenities including complimentary Wi-Fi. **Open:** All year **Nearest Shop:** 0.10 miles
Nearest Pub: 0.10 miles

Payment: 💳 Property: ⫽ 📺 📻 📶 Children: 🐴 🛏 🏃 Unit: 🚪 📺 📷 🍳 📺 🎧 📞

LONDON SW20, Inner London   Map ref 2D2

Thalia Holiday Home

Contact: Mr Peter & Mrs Ann Briscoe-Smith, 150 Westway, Raynes Park, Wimbledon, London SW20 9LS **T:** 020 8542 0505 **E:** info@thaliaholidayhome.co.uk
W: www.thaliaholidayhome.co.uk

Thalia is a three-bedroomed house in the residential suburban area of West Wimbledon. Home from home, with easy access to central London. Wi-Fi/LAN broadband. Special offers: £50 discount on complete 2nd & subsequent weeks of same booking. Bookings can start and end on any day of the week. **Open:** All year **Nearest Shop:** 0.2 miles **Nearest Pub:** 0.5 miles

Units 1
Sleeps 5-6
PER UNIT PER WEEK
£800.00

LONDON W14, Inner London   Map ref 2D2

Castletown House

Contact: Mr Mark Poppleton, Manager, Castletown House, 11 Castletown Road, London W14 9HE **T:** 020 7386 9423 / 07887 863266 **F:** 020 7386 0015
E: info@castletownhouse.co.uk **W:** www.castletownhouse.co.uk **£ BOOK ONLINE**

Castletown House offer a small collection of Victorian, modernised self catering apartments. Ranging from studios to one, two & three bedroom apartments conveniently located a few minutes away from West Kensington and Barons Court Tube Station. Our area is renowned for the annual AEGON Queen's Tennis Championship and we are perfectly located in between Earls Court and Olympia Exhibition Centre's **Open:** All year **Nearest Shop:** 0.25 miles **Nearest Pub:** 0.25 miles

Units 13
Sleeps 1-6
PER UNIT PER WEEK
£600.00 - £2000.00

BECKENHAM, Outer London   Map ref 2D2

Oakfield Apartments

Contact: Mr John Deane, Flat 1, 107 South Eden Park Road, Beckenham, Kent BR3 3AX
T: 020 8658 4441 **F:** 020 8658 9198 **E:** enquiry@oakfield.co.uk
W: www.oakfield.co.uk **£ BOOK ONLINE**

Victorian mansion with a large garden in a semi-rural setting, three minutes walk to Eden Park rail station, 25 minutes by rail or nine miles by road to central London. Mr and Mrs Deane live on the premises and welcome children but not pets. **Open:** All year **Nearest Shop:** 0.10 miles **Nearest Pub:** 0.10 miles

Units 10
Sleeps 2-6
PER UNIT PER WEEK
£300.00 - £750.00

Book your accommodation online

Visit our websites for detailed information, up-to-date availability and to book your accommodation online. Includes over 20,000 places to stay, all of them star rated.

www.visitor-guides.co.uk

Don't Miss

Audley End House & Gardens
Saffron Walden, Essex CB11 4JF
www.english-heritage.org.uk
At Audley End near Saffron Walden, you can discover one of
England's grandest stately homes. Explore the impressive mansion
house, uncover the story behind the Braybrooke's unique natural
history collection, visit an exhibition where you can find out about
the workers who lived on the estate in the 1800s and even try
dressing the part with dressing up clothes provided.

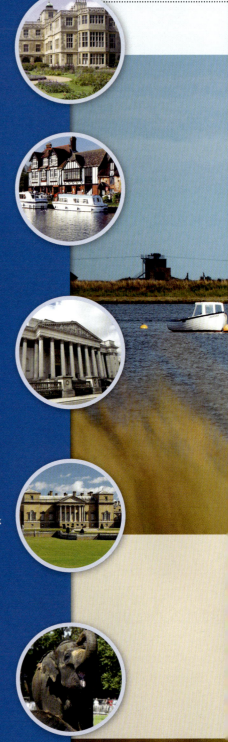

The Broads
Norfolk
www.broads-authority.gov.uk
The Norfolk Broads with its scenic waterways, rare wildlife and rich
history has National Park status. This ancient mosaic of lakes, land
and rivers covering 303 square kilometres in the east of England, is
the UK's largest protected wetland and boasts a variety of habitats
including fen, carr woodland and grazing marshes, as well as
pretty villages and no less than 11,000 species of wildlife. Walking,
cycling, fishing, boating, wildlife spotting, the list of things to do
here is endless and there is something for all ages to enjoy.

The Fitzwilliam Museum
Trumpington Street, Cambridge CB2 1RB
(01223) 332900
http://www.fitzmuseum.cam.ac.uk/
A short walk away from the colleges and the River Cam in the
heart of Cambridge, the Fitzwilliam Museum with its imposing
neo-classical facade and columns is one of the city's most iconic
buildings. Founded in 1816 when the 7th Viscount Fitzwilliam
of Merrion left his vast collections of books, art and music to the
University of Cambridge, it now has over half a million artworks
and artefacts dating back as far as 2500BC in its collection.

Holkham Hall
Wells-next- the-Sea, Norfolk, NR23 1AB
(01328) 710227
www.holkham.co.uk
Steeped in history, magnificent Holkham Hall on the North Norfolk
Coast, is a stunning Palladian mansion with its own nature reserve.
It is home to many rare species of flora and fauna, a deer park and
one of the most beautiful, unspoilt beaches in the country. Step
back in time in the Bygones Museum or explore the 18th Century
walled gardens which are being restored, while the children have
fun in the woodland adventure play area.

ZSL Whipsnade Zoo
Dunstable, Bedfordshire LU6 2LF
(020) 7449 6200
www.zsl.org/zsl-whipsnade-zoo
Set on 600 acres in the rolling Chiltern Hills, Whipsnade is home
to more than 2500 species and you can get close to some of the
world's hairiest, scariest, tallest and smallest animals here. Meet
the animals, take a steam train ride, visit the Hullabazoo Farm or
even be a keeper for the day.

East of England

Bedfordshire, Cambridgeshire, Essex, Hertfordshire, Norfolk, Suffolk

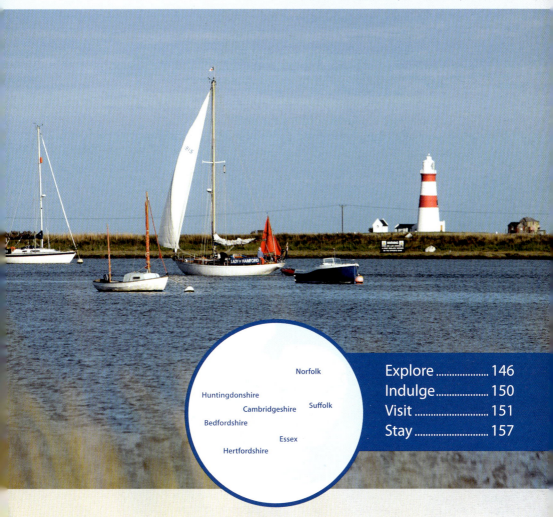

Norfolk

Huntingdonshire

Cambridgeshire   Suffolk

Bedfordshire

Essex

Hertfordshire

Loved for its unspoiled character, rural landscape, architecture and traditions, the East of England is full of beautiful countryside, idyllic seaside, historic cities and vibrant towns. The Norfolk Broads and Suffolk Coast have always been popular with yachtsmen and the North Norfolk Coast has become a fashionable getaway in recent years. Cambridge is steeped in history and oozes sophistication, while Bedfordshire, Hertfordshire and Essex each have their own charms, with pockets of beauty and fascinating heritage. This is a diverse region where you'll find plenty to keep you busy.

Bedfordshire & Hertfordshire

History, the arts, family entertainment and relaxing, unspoilt countryside - this area has it all. Bedfordshire has plenty of attractions, from exotic animals at Whipsnade Zoo to vintage aeroplanes at The Shuttleworth Collection and notable historic houses. Woburn Abbey, the still inhabited home of the Dukes of Bedford, stands in a 3000-acre park and is part of one of Europe's largest drive-through game reserves. The 18th century mansion's 14 state apartments are open to the public and contain an impressive art collection. Luton Hoo is a fine Robert Adam designed house in a 1200-acre Capability Brown designed park.

Hertfordshire also has its fair share of stately homes, with Hatfield House, built from 1707 by Robert Cecil, first Earl of Salisbury, leading the way. Nearby Knebworth House is the venue for popular summer concerts and events.

Roman walls, mosaic floors and part of an amphitheatre are still visible at Verulanium, St Albans and Much Hadham, where the Bishops of London used to have their country seat, is a showpiece village. Welwyn Garden City, one of Britain's first 20th century new towns retains a certain art deco charm.

Hotspot:
Dunstable Downs Kite Festival
July, Dunstable, Bedfordshire
www.dunstablekitefestival.co.uk
Kite enthusiasts from around the
UK converge on Dunstable.

Cambridgeshire & Essex

Cambridge is a city of winding streets lined with old houses, world-famous colleges and churches, while the gently flowing Cam provides a serene backdrop to the architectural wonders. Kings College Chapel, started by Henry VI in 1446 should not be missed and the Fitzwilliam Museum is one of Europe's treasure houses, with antiquities from Greece and Rome. First-class shopping can be found in the quirky stores and exquisite boutiques tucked away along cobbled streets, and there's a vast choice of places to eat and drink.

Further afield, Cambridgeshire is a land of lazy waterways, rolling countryside, bustling market towns and quaint villages. Climb grand sweeping staircases in the stately homes of the aristocracy or relax as you chug along in a leisure boat, watching the wildlife in one of the wonderful nature reserves. Peterborough has a fine Norman cathedral with three soaring arches, whilst Ely has had an abbey on its cathedral site since AD 670.

Western Essex is dotted with pretty historic market towns and villages like Thaxted and Saffron Walden and plenty of historic sites. County town Colchester was founded by the Romans and its massive castle keep, built in 1067 on the site of the Roman Temple of Claudius, houses a collection of Roman antiquities. Explore the beautiful gardens and 110ft Norman Keep at Hedingham Castle, which also holds jousting and theatre performances.

Some of the region's loveliest countryside lies to the north, on the Suffolk Border around Dedham Vale where Constable and Turner painted, while further east you can find family seaside resorts such as Walton on the Naze and Clacton-on-Sea. Following the coast south, the Blackwater and Crouch estuaries provide havens for yachts and pleasure craft. Inland, Layer Marney Tower is a Tudor palace with buildings, gardens and parkland dating from 1520 in a beautiful, rural Essex setting. The county city of Chelmsford has a historic 15th century cathedral and Hylands House is a beautiful Grade II* listed neo-classical villa, set in over 500 acres of Hylands Park.

Hotspot: The Essex Way walking route weaves through rural Essex all the way from Epping to Harwich via picturesque Constable Country. Taking in open farmland, ancient woodlands, tranquil river valleys, charming villages and historic sites, it has plenty of country pubs worth a stop along the route.

The county town of Norfolk and unofficial capital of East Anglia is Norwich, a fine city whose cathedral walls are decorated with biblical scenes dating from 1046. There are 30 medieval churches in central Norwich and many other interesting historic sites, but modern Norwich is a stylish contemporary city with first rate shopping and cultural facilities. Sandringham, near Kings Lynn in the north west of the county, is the royal palace bought by Queen Victoria for the then Prince of Wales and where the present Queen spends many a family holiday.

The North Norfolk coast has become known as 'Chelsea-on-Sea' in recent years and many parts of the region have developed a reputation for fine dining. From Hunstanton in the west to Cromer in the east, this stretch of coastline is home to nature reserves, windswept beaches and quaint coastal villages. Wells-next-the-Sea, with its long sweeping beach bordered by pine woodland has a pretty harbour with small fishing boats where children fish for crabs.

Norfolk

Norfolk is not as flat as Noel Coward would have you believe, as any cyclist will tell you, but cycling or walking is still a great way to see the county. In the west Thetford Forest is said to be the oldest in England while in the east, the county is crisscrossed by waterways and lakes known as The Broads - apparently the remains of medieval man's peat diggings!

Hotspot: It's hard to beat Bressingham Steam and Gardens, where world renowned gardener and horticulturist Alan Bloom combined his passion for plants and gardens with his love of steam to create a truly unique experience for all the family.
www.bressingham.co.uk

Suffolk

Suffolk is famous for its winding lanes and pastel painted, thatched cottages. The county town of Ipswich has undergone considerable regeneration in recent years, and now boasts a vibrant waterfront and growing arts scene. For history lovers, Framlingham Castle has stood intact since the 13th century and magnificent churches at Lavenham, Sudbury and Long Melford are well worth a visit.

The Suffolk Coast & Heaths Area of Outstanding Natural Beauty has 155 square miles of unspoilt wildlife-rich wetlands, ancient heaths, windswept shingle beaches and historic towns and villages for you to explore. Its inlets and estuaries are extremely popular with yachtsmen. Gems such as Southwold, with its brightly coloured beach huts, and Aldeburgh are home to some excellent restaurants. Snape Maltings near Aldeburgh offers an eclectic programme of events including the world famous Aldeburgh Festival of music.

The historic market town of Woodbridge on the River Deben, has a working tide mill, a fabulous riverside walk with an impressive view across the river to Sutton Hoo and an abundance of delightful pubs and restaurants.

In the south of the county, the hills and valleys on the Suffolk-Essex border open up to stunning skies, captured in paintings by Constable, Turner and Gainsborough. At the heart of beautiful Constable Country, Nayland and Dedham Vale Area of Outstanding Natural Beauty are idyllic places for a stroll or leisurely picnic.

Hotspot: The Anglo-Saxon burial site at Sutton Hoo is set on a stunning 255 acre estate with breathtaking views over the River Deben and is home to one of the greatest archaeological discoveries of all time. www.nationaltrust.org.uk

Indulge – East of England

Punting is quintessentially Cambridge and a great way to see The Backs of seven of the colleges and their beautiful bridges. Relax and enjoy a glass of Champagne on a leisurely chauffered punt tour or hire your own for an afternoon of delightful DIY sightseeing. (01223) 359750 or visit www.scudamores.com

Moored among the pleasure and fishing boats in the harbour at Wells-next-the-Sea, **The Albatros** is a restored Dutch clipper built in 1899. It now serves up delicious sweet and savoury pancakes, real ale and live music, providing an interesting pit stop on the north Norfolk coast. www.albatroswells.co.uk

Pay a visit to **Adnams Brewery** in Southwold where you can explore behind the scenes of one of the most modern breweries in the UK, discover how their award-winning beers and spirits are made, or get creative and make your very own gin! www.adnams.co.uk

Aldeburgh Fish and Chip Shop has been serving up freshly caught, East coast fish since 1967. A tantalisingly tasty treat whether you are enjoying a day at the beach in the height of summer or a brisk walk on a stormy winter day, and especially when you eat them sitting on the sea wall. www.aldeburghfishandchips.co.uk

Indulge every little boy's fantasy with a trip to the **Shuttleworth Collection**, a vast collection of vintage aeroplanes, cars, motorcycles and bicycles at Old Warden Aerodrome, Nr. Biggleswade in Bedfordshire. www.shuttleworth.org

Visit – East of England

 Attractions with this sign participate in the Visitor Attraction Quality Assurance Scheme.

Bedfordshire

Bedfordshire County Show
July, Biggleswade, Bedfordshire
www.bedfordshirecountyshow.co.uk
*Held in the beautiful grounds of Shuttleworth the
Bedfordshire County Show is a showcase of town
meets country.*

Luton International Carnival
May, Luton, Bedfordshire
www.luton.gov.uk
*The highlight is the spectacular carnival parade – an
eye-catching, breathtaking procession through the
town centre, superbly reflecting the diverse mix of
cultures in Luton.*

Woburn Safari Park
Bedfordshire MK17 9QN
(01525) 290407
www.woburnsafari.co.uk
*Drive through the safari park with 30 species of
animals in natural groups just a windscreen's width
away, or even closer!*

Wrest Park
Silsoe, Luton, Bedfordshire, MK45 4HR
0870 333 1181
www.english-heritage.org.uk
*Enjoy a great day out exploring one of Britain's
most spectacular French style mansions and 'secret'
gardens. With hidden gems including a thatched-
roof Bath house, ornate marble fountain, Chinese
Temple and bridge and over 40 statues, as well as
a kids audio trail and play area, it's popular with
families and garden lovers alike.*

Cambridgeshire

Cambridge Folk Festival
July/August, Cherry Hinton, Cambridgeshire
www.cambridgefolkfestival.co.uk
Top acts make this a must-visit event for folk fans.

Duxford Air Show
September, Duxford, nr Cambridge, Cambridgeshire
www.iwm.org.uk/duxford
*Set within the spacious grounds of the famous former
First and Second World War airfield, the Duxford Air
Show features an amazing array of aerial displays.*

Imperial War Museum Duxford
Cambridge CB22 4QR
(01223) 835000
www.iwm.org.uk/duxford
*With its air shows, unique history and atmosphere,
nowhere else combines the sights, sounds and
power of aircraft quite like Duxford.*

Kings College Chapel

Cambridge CB2 1ST
(01223) 331212
www.kings.cam.ac.uk
It's part of one of the oldest Cambridge colleges sharing a wonderful sense of history and tradition with the rest of the University.

The National Stud

Newmarket, Cambridgeshire CB8 0XE
(01638) 663464
www.nationalstud.co.uk
The beautiful grounds & facilities are a renowned tourist attraction in the eastern region.

Oliver Cromwell's House

Ely, Cambridgeshire CB7 4HF
(01353) 662062
www.olivercromwellshouse.co.uk
Visit the former Lord Protector's family's home and experience an exhibition on 17th Century life.

Peterborough Dragon Boat Festival

June, Peterborough Rowing Lake,
Thorpe Meadows, Cambridgeshire
www.peterboroughdragonboatfestival.com
Teams of up to 11 people, dragon boats and all equipment provided, no previous experience required. Family entertainment and catering stalls.

The Raptor Foundation

Huntingdon, Cambridgeshire PE28 3BT
(01487) 741140
www.raptorfoundation.org.uk
Bird of prey centre, offering 3 daily flying displays with audience participation, gift shop, Silent Wings tearoom, Raptor crafts shop.

Essex

Adventure Island

Southend-on-Sea, Essex SS1 1EE
(01702) 443400
www.adventureisland.co.uk
One of the best value 'theme parks' in the South East with over 60 great rides and attractions for all ages. No admission charge, you only 'pay if you play'.

Central Museum and Planetarium

Southend-on-Sea, Essex SS2 6ES
(01702) 434449
www.southendmuseums.co.uk
An Edwardian building housing displays of archaeology, natural history, social and local history.

Clacton Airshow

August, Clacton Seafront, Essex
www.clactonairshow.com
Impressive aerobatic displays take to the skies while a whole host of exhibition, trade stands, food court and on-site entertainment are available at ground level.

Colchester Medieval Festival

June, Lower Castle Park, Colchester, Essex
www.oysterfayre.co.uk
This medieval style fair remembers a time when folk from the countryside and neighbouring villages would travel to the 'Big Fair' in the town.

Colchester Zoo

Essex CO3 0SL
(01206) 331292
www.colchester-zoo.com
Enjoy daily displays, feed elephants and giraffes and see over 260 species in over 60 acres of parkland!

Maldon Mud Race

April, Maldon, Essex
www.maldonmudrace.com
The annual Maldon Mud Race is a wacky fun competition in which participants race to become the first to finish a 400m dash over the bed of the River Blackwater.

RHS Garden Hyde Hall

Chelmsford, Essex CM3 8AT
(01245) 400256
www.rhs.org.uk/hydehall
A garden of inspirational beauty with an eclectic range of horticultural styles from traditional to modern providing year round interest.

Royal Gunpowder Mills

Waltham Abbey, Essex EN9 1JY
(01992) 707370
www.royalgunpowdermills.com
A spectacular 170-acre location for a day of family fun. Special events including Spitfire flypast, award winning Secret History exhibition, tranquil wildlife walks, guided land train tours and rocket science gallery.

Sea-Life Adventure

Southend-on-Sea, Essex SS1 2ER
(01702) 442200
www.sealifeadventure.co.uk
With more than 30 display tanks and tunnels to explore, there are loads of fishy residents to discover at Sea-Life Adventure.

Southend Carnival

August, Southend-on-Sea, Essex
www.southend-on-seacarnival.org.uk
A wide range of events held over eight days.

Hertfordshire

Cathedral and Abbey Church of St Alban

St. Albans, Hertfordshire AL1 1BY
(01727) 860780
www.stalbanscathedral.org
St Alban is Britain's first Christian martyr and the Cathedral, with its shrine, is its oldest place of continuous worship.

Chilli Festival
August, Benington Lordship Gardens, Stevenage, Hertfordshire
www.beningtonlordship.co.uk
A popular family event attracting thousands of visitors over two days, offering a chance to buy Chilli plants, products and sample foods from around the world.

Hertfordshire County Show

May, Redbourn, Hertfordshire
www.hertsshow.com
County show with all the usual attractions.

Knebworth House

Hertfordshire SG1 2AX
(01438) 812661
www.knebworthhouse.com
Historic house, home to the Lytton family since 1490. Knebworth House offers a great day out for all the family with lots to do for all ages.

Norfolk

Banham Zoo
Norwich, Norfolk NR16 2HE
(01953) 887771
www.banhamzoo.co.uk
Wildlife spectacular which will take you on a journey to experience tigers, leopards and zebra plus some of the world's most exotic, rare and endangered animals.

Blickling Hall, Gardens and Park
Norwich, Norfolk NR11 6NF
(01263) 738030
www.nationaltrust.org.uk/blickling-estate
A Jacobean redbrick mansion with a garden, orangery, parkland and lake. Spectacular long gallery, plasterwork ceilings and fine collections of furniture, pictures and books. Walks.

Cromer Pier
Cromer, Norfolk NR27 9HE
www.cromer-pier.com
Cromer Pier is a Grade II listed seaside pier on the north coast of Norfolk. The pier is the home of the Cromer Lifeboat Station and the Pavilion Theatre

Fritton Lake Country World
Great Yarmouth, Norfolk NR31 9HA
(01493) 488288
A woodland and lakeside haven with a children's assault course, putting, an adventure playground, golf, fishing, boating, wildfowl, heavy horses, cart rides, falconry and flying displays.

Great Yarmouth Maritime Festival
September, Great Yarmouth, Norfolk
www.great-yarmouth.co.uk/maritime-festival
A mix of traditional and modern maritime vessels will be moored on South Quay for visitors to admire and go aboard.

King's Lynn May Garland Procession
May, King's Lynn, Norfolk
www.thekingsmorris.co.uk
The King's Morris dancers carry the May Garland around the town.

Norwich Castle Museum and Art Gallery
Norfolk NR1 3JU
(01603) 493649
www.museums.norfolk.gov.uk
Ancient Norman keep of Norwich Castle dominates the city and is one of the most important buildings of its kind in Europe.

Royal Norfolk Show
July, Norwich, Norfolk
www.royalnorfolkshow.co.uk
The Royal Norfolk Show celebrates everything that's Norfolk. It offers 10 hours of entertainment each day from spectacular grand ring displays, traditional livestock and equine classes, to a live music stage, celebrity guests and over 650 stands.

Sainsbury Centre for Visual Arts
UEA, Norwich, Norfolk NR4 7TJ
(01603) 593199
www.scva.ac.uk
Containing a collection of world art, it was one of the first major public buildings to be designed by the architect Norman Foster.

Sandringham
King's Lynn, Norfolk PE35 6EN
(01485) 545400
www.sandringhamestate.co.uk
H.M. The Queen. A fascinating house, an intriguing museum and the best of the Royal gardens.

Suffolk

Aldeburgh Music Festival
June, Snape Maltings, Suffolk IP17 1SP
www.aldeburgh.co.uk
The Aldeburgh Festival of Music and the Arts offers an eclectic mix of concerts, operas, masterclasses, films and open air performances at different venues in the Aldeburgh/Snape area in Suffolk.

Gainsborough's House
Sudbury, Suffolk CO10 2EU
(01787) 372958
www.gainsborough.org
Gainsborough's House is the only museum situated in the birthplace of a great British artist. The permanent collection is built around the works of Thomas Gainsborough.

Go Ape! High Wire Forest Adventure - Thetford, Suffolk
IP27 0AF (0845) 643 9215
www.goape.co.uk
Experience an exhilarating course of rope bridges, tarzan swings and zip slides... all set high in the trees above the forest floor.

Ickworth House, Park and Gardens
Bury St. Edmunds, Suffolk IP29 5QE
(01284) 735270
www.nationaltrust.org.uk/ickworth
Fine paintings, a beautiful collection of Georgian silver, an Italianate garden and stunning parkland.

Latitude Festival
July, Southwold, Suffolk
www.latitudefestival.com
Primarily a music festival but also has a full spectrum of art including film, comedy, theatre, cabaret, dance and poetry.

National Horseracing Museum and Tours
Newmarket, Suffolk CB8 8JH
(01638) 667333
www.nhrm.co.uk
Discover the stories of racing from its early origins at Newmarket to its modern-day heroes

RSPB Minsmere Nature Reserve
Saxmundham, Suffolk IP17 3BY
(01728) 648281
www.rspb.org.uk/minsmere
One of the UK's premier nature reserves, offering excellent facilities for people of all ages and abilities.

Somerleyton Hall and Gardens
Lowestoft, Suffolk NR32 5QQ
(01502) 734901
www.somerleyton.co.uk
12 acres of landscaped gardens to explore including our famous 1864 Yew hedge maze. Guided tours of the Hall.

Suffolk Show
May, Ipswich, Suffolk
www.suffolkshow.co.uk
Animals, food and drink, shopping…there's lots to see and do at this popular county show.

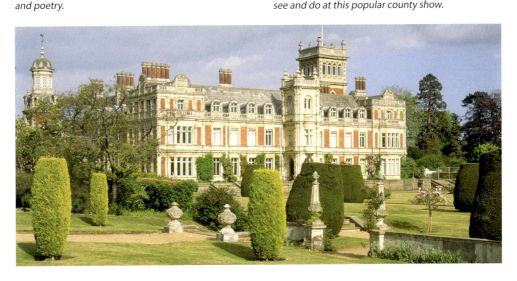

Tourist Information Centres

When you arrive at your destination, visit the Tourist Information Centre for quality assured help with accommodation and information about local attractions and events, or email your request before you go.

Aldeburgh	48 High Street	01728 453637	atic@suffolkcoastal.gov.uk
Aylsham	Bure Valley Railway Station	01263 733903	aylsham.tic@broadland.gov.uk
Beccles	The Quay	01502 713196	admin@beccles.info
Bedford	St Pauls Square	01234 718112	touristinfo@bedford.gov.uk
Bishop's Stortford	2 Market Square	01279 655831	tic@bishopsstortford.org
Brentwood	Town Hall	01277 312500	
Burnham Deepdale	Deepdale Information	01485 210256	info@deepdalefarm.co.uk
Bury St Edmunds	6 Angel Hill	01284 764667	tic@stedsbc.gov.uk
Cambridge	Peas Hill	0871 226 8006	info@visitcambridge.org
Clacton-On-Sea	Town Hall	01255 686633	clactontic@tendringdc.gov.uk
Colchester	1 Queen Street	01206 282920	vic@colchester.gov.uk
Cromer	Louden Road	0871 200 3071	cromerinfo@north-norfolk.gov.uk
Diss	Meres Mouth	01379 650523	dtic@s-norfolk.gov.uk
Dunstable	Priory House	01582 891420	tic@dunstable.gov.uk
Ely	Oliver Cromwell's House	01353 662062	tic@eastcambs.gov.uk
Felixstowe	91 Undercliff Road West	01394 276770	ftic@suffolkcoastal.gov.uk
Great Yarmouth	25 Marine Parade	01493 846346	gab@great-yarmouth.gov.uk
Hertford	10 Market Place	01992 584322	tic@hertford.gov.uk
Holt	3 Pound House	0871 200 3071/ 01263 713100	holtinfo@north-norfolk.gov.uk
Hoveton	Station Road	01603 782281	hovetontic@broads-authority.gov.uk
Hunstanton	Town Hall	01485 532610	info@visithunstanton.info
Ipswich	St Stephens Church	01473 258070	tourist@ipswich.gov.uk
King's Lynn	The Custom House	01553 763044	kings-lynn.tic@west-norfolk.gov.uk
Lavenham	Lady Street	01787 248207	lavenhamtic@babergh.gov.uk
Letchworth Garden City	33-35 Station Road	01462 487868	tic@letchworth.com
Lowestoft	East Point Pavilion	01502 533600	touristinfo@waveney.gov.uk
Luton	Luton Central Library	01582 401579	tourist.information@lutonculture.com
Maldon	Wenlock Way	01621 856503	tic@maldon.gov.uk
Newmarket	63 The Guineas	01638 719749	tic.newmarket@forest-heath.gov.uk
Norwich	The Forum	01603 213999	tourism@norwich.gov.uk
Peterborough	9 Bridge Street	01733 452336	tic@peterborough.gov.uk
Saffron Walden	1 Market Place	01799 524002	tourism@saffronwalden.gov.uk
Sandy	Rear of 10 Cambridge Road	01767 682 728	tourism@sandytowncouncil.gov.uk
Sheringham	Station Approach	01263 824329	sheringhaminfo@north-norfolk.gov.uk
Skegness	Embassy Theatre	0845 6740505	skegnessinfo@e-lindsey.gov.uk
Southend-On-Sea	Pier Entrance	01702 215620	vic@southend.gov.uk
Southwold	69 High Street	01502 724729	southwold.tic@waveney.gov.uk
St Albans	Old Town Hall	01727 864511	tic@stalbans.gov.uk
Stowmarket	The Museum of East Anglian Life	01449 676800	tic@midsuffolk.gov.uk
Sudbury	Sudbury Library	01787 881320/ 372331	sudburytic@sudburytowncouncil.co.uk
Swaffham	The Shambles	01760 722255	swaffham@eetb.info
Waltham Abbey	6 Highbridge Street	01992 660336	tic@walthamabbey-tc.gov.uk
Wells-Next-The-Sea	Staithe Street	0871 200 3071/ 01328 710885	wellsinfo@north-norfolk.gov.uk
Whitlingham	Whitlingham Country Park	01603 756094	whitlinghamtic@broads-authority.gov.uk
Wisbech	2-3 Bridge Street	01945 583263	tourism@fenland.gov.uk
Witham	61 Newland Street	01376 502674	tic@witham.gov.uk
Woodbridge	Woodbridge Library	01394 446510/ 276770	felixstowetic@suffolkcoastal.gov.uk
Wymondham	Market Cross	01953 604721	wymondhamtic@btconnect.com

Regional Contacts and Information

For more information on accommodation, attractions, activities, events and holidays in the East of England, contact the following regional tourism organisation. Their website has a wealth of information.

East of England Tourism (01284) 727470 info@eet.org.uk www.visiteastofengland.com

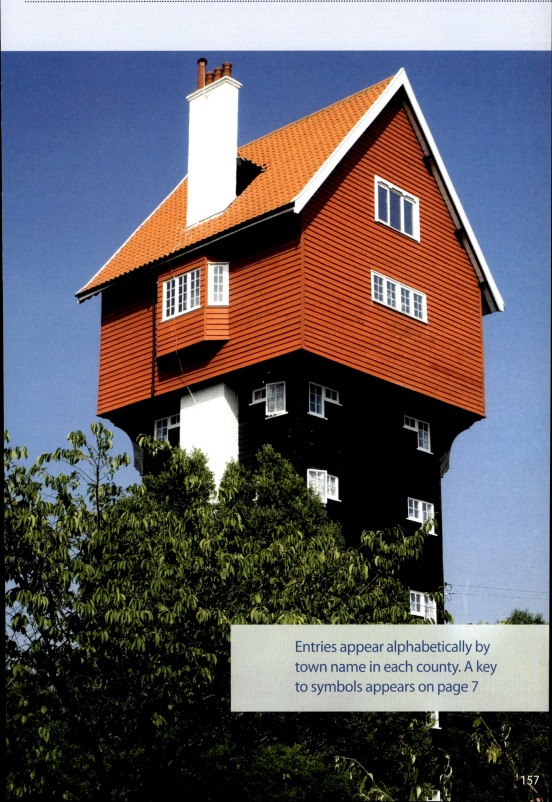

Entries appear alphabetically by town name in each county. A key to symbols appears on page 7

BEDFORD, Bedfordshire   Map ref 2D1

SELF CATERING

Dovecote Self-Catering

Contact: Ros and Ian Northern, Owners, Priory Farm, Lavendon Road, Harrold, Bedford
MK43 7EE **T:** (01234) 720293 **E:** info@dovecoteselfcatering.co.uk
W: www.dovecoteselfcatering.co.uk

Units   3
Sleeps   1-11
PER UNIT PER WEEK
£385.00 - £600.00

Three comfortable self-catering cottages in the picturesque village of Harrold. The Dovecote is a range of traditional stone and brick built buildings set around a sunny courtyard. Each cottage has an individual character but they all have modern facilities. The countryside is on your doorstep, but we are near good pubs and shopping. We welcome families young and old as well as business people. **Open:** All year **Nearest Shop:** 350 metres
Nearest Pub: 250 metres

Site: ❀ P Payment: 💷 Property: 📺 📷 💻 Children: 🍴 🎠 🚶 Unit: 🛏 🍳 📺 📼 📺 📀

CAMBRIDGE, Cambridgeshire   Map ref 2D1

SELF CATERING

Glebe Cottage

Contact: Mrs Fiona Key, Owner, 44 Main Street, Hardwick, Cambridge, Cambridgeshire
CB3 7QS **T:** (01954) 212895 **E:** info@camcottage.co.uk
W: www.camcottage.co.uk **£ BOOK ONLINE**

Units   1
Sleeps   2
PER UNIT PER WEEK
£400.00 - £450.00

Recently refurbished, the soft furnishings of velvet drapes and blinds bring a warm cosy feel. New kitchen with dishwasher. Upstairs brand new en suite bathroom to double bedroom. Views of over two acres of established garden with furniture and BBQ. A little bit of paradise and a quiet spot but close enough to the city and transport links. **Open:** All year except Christmas - New Year
Nearest Shop: 0.5 miles **Nearest Pub:** 300 yards

Site: ❀ P Leisure: 🚴 🎵 🏹 ⛳ Property: 📺 💻 📷 Children: 🍴 Unit: 🛏 🍳 📺 📼 📺 📀 BBQ

HUNTINGDON, Cambridgeshire   Map ref 3A2

SELF CATERING

The Old Post Office

Contact: Hilton Hall, High Street, Hilton, Huntingdon, Cambridgeshire PE28 9NE
T: (01480) 831721 **E:** ann.goodridge@gmail.com
W: www.hiltonoldpo.co.uk

Units   1
Sleeps   2
PER UNIT PER WEEK
£490.00 - £560.00

What our guests say: true gem - fantastic, great décor, good equipment, lovely feel, comfortable, everything thought of – in stunning village, peaceful spot – warm friendly welcome: wouldn't hesitate to recommend. **Nearest Shop:** 0.5 miles
Nearest Pub: 0.5 miles

Site: ❀ Property: 📺 Unit: 📺 📼 📀 🎵

Units 1
Sleeps 1-6

PER UNIT PER WEEK
£640.00 - £1490.00

SPECIAL PROMOTIONS
Price depends on number of bedrooms reserved. 5% discount for stays of 4 weeks or more against 2-3 bedroom options.

The Pump House Apartment
Contact: Mr John Bayliss, The Pump House Apartment, 132 Church Street, Great Burstead, Billericay, Essex CM11 2TR **T:** (01277) 656579 **F:** 01277 631160
E: enquiries@thepumphouseapartment.co.uk
W: thepumphouseapartment.co.uk **£ BOOK ONLINE**

The apartment is on two floors and luxuriously furnished, with air-conditioning. The accommodation comprises two living rooms, fitted kitchen/diner and the option of one, two or three bedrooms all with bath/shower rooms. Guests have use of heated pool (May to September), hot tub, gazebo and gardens, free Wi-Fi.

Open: All year
Nearest Shop: 0.5 miles
Nearest Pub: 0.5 miles

Site: **P** **Payment:** € **Leisure:** **Property:** **Children:**
Unit: TV BBQ

For **key to symbols** see page 7

COLCHESTER, Essex   Map ref 3B2

Birds Farm

Contact: Gill & Steve Beadle, School Lane, Elmstead, Colchester, Essex CO7 7EY
T: (01206) 823838 **E:** birdsfarm@btconnect.com
W: www.birds-farm.co.uk

Units   5
Sleeps   2-6

PER UNIT PER WEEK
£265.00 - £580.00

Birds Farm is in a semi rural location to the east of Colchester and within 2 miles of the University of Essex. Converted from farm buildings, the cottages are equipped to provide guests with a comfortable stay, nearly all of them are on ground level. A seasonal outdoor pool, gardens, games room and Wi-Fi are among the facilities available. **Open:** All Year **Nearest Shop:** 200 yards **Nearest Pub:** 1.5 miles

Site: ✿ P **Payment:** 💷 **Leisure:** 🔍 🎣 **Property:** 🐾 🖥 ▣ 🖧 **Children:** 🎠 🛏 🚼 **Unit:** ▯ 🖥 🔌 TV 📀 BBQ ☎

COLCHESTER, Essex   Map ref 3B2

Stoke by Nayland Country Lodges

Contact: Keepers Lane, Leavenheath, Colchester, Essex CO6 4PZ **T:** (01206) 265835
E: sales@stokebynayland.com
W: www.stokebynaylandlodges.com **£ BOOK ONLINE**

Units   10
Sleeps   2-12

PER UNIT PER WEEK
£595.00 - £2050.00

SPECIAL PROMOTIONS
Short breaks: Minimum stay 2 nights. Rate from £310 per unit for 2 nights for up to 4 guests. For current special offers please see our website or contact us by phone.

Ideal for a short break or a longer holiday, the fabulous new luxury Stoke by Nayland Country Lodges are set amidst stunning countryside with 2 championship golf courses, luxurious spa facilities and award winning cuisine. There is a 24 hour porter service & free shuttle provided to the Stoke by Nayland Hotel, Golf & Spa as well as the option of private dining with personal chef in your lodge.

Location: Situated north of Colchester on the Essex/Suffolk border just off the A134, only an hour from London via the A12.

Open: All year
Nearest Shop: On Site
Nearest Pub: 1 mile

Units: Exquisite open plan interiors with floor to ceiling glazing and contemporary furnishings with views across stunning countryside. Free hi-speed Wi-Fi.

Site: P **Payment:** 💷 **Leisure:** 🎵 ⚑ 🎣 **Property:** ⫻ 🖥 🖧 **Children:** 🎠 🛏 🚼
Unit: ▯ 🖥 🔌 TV 📀 BBQ ☎

SAFFRON WALDEN, Essex   Map ref 2D1

Stable Cottage

Contact: Kate Muskett, Owner, Little Henham Hall Farm, Little Henham, Saffron Walden, Essex CB11 3XR **T:** (01279) 850228 **E:** kgmletting@mac.com

Units   1
Sleeps   2-3

PER UNIT PER WEEK
£310.00

This property is situated in a rural area, halfway between London and Cambridge with easy access to rail and motorway routes. Sleeps 2-3 and a third person can be accommodated on a sofa bed. Euros are accepted by prior arrangement. Fully equipped with comfortable furniture and all necessary kitchen amenities. Excellent parking available and lovely garden area with gazebo and furniture. Per Unit per week from £310 for two persons. **Open:** All year **Nearest Shop:** 1.5 miles **Nearest Pub:** 1 mile

Site: ✿ P **Payment:** € **Property:** ▣ 🖧 **Children:** 🎠 **Unit:** ▯ 🖥 ▣ 🔌 TV 📀

STANSTED MOUNTFITCHET, Essex   Map ref 2D1

Walpole Farmhouse

Contact: Mrs Jill Walton, Proprietor, Walpole Farmhouse, Cambridge Road, Stansted Mountfitchet CM24 8TA **T:** (01279) 812265 **E:** info@walpolefarmhouse.com
W: www.walpolefarmhouse.com **£ BOOK ONLINE**

Units   2
Sleeps   1-5

PER UNIT PER WEEK
£250.00 - £450.00

Charmingly converted single storey building with its own spacious private garden. Both the Cottage and Studio are tastefully decorated with all modern facilities, including Wi-Fi & ample parking. Ideal for both foreign and UK visitors. Close to Stansted Airport, the UK motorway network, and with easy access to London & Cambridge by train or car. The local train station is a 15 minute walk away. Frequent buses pass-by to Saffron Walden, a picturesque medieval town and to Bishop's Stortford for great shopping, the cinema, and accessing the main commuter railway station.

Open: All year (please call or email for booking)
Nearest Shop: 0.25 miles (& more in village)
Nearest Pub: 0.5 miles (Pubs in Village)

Units: Please see our detailed floor maps & descriptions on www.walpolefarmhouse.com

Site: ✿ P Payment: 💷 Leisure: ➤ Property: 🛏 🖼 📖 Children: 🚼 🍴 Unit: 🚪 🗄 📺 📻 🖥 🛜 📺 🛜

BUNTINGFORD, Hertfordshire   Map ref 2D1

The Old Swan Tea Shop

Contact: Lynda Sullivan, Owner, Hare Street, Buntingford, Hertfordshire SG9 0DZ
T: (01763) 289265 **E:** sullivan@oldswanteashop.co.uk
W: www.oldswanteashop.co.uk

Units   2
Sleeps   4
PER UNIT PER WEEK
£410.00 - £550.00

A picturesque 15th Century Hall House set in two acres of garden and orchard, situated on the B1368, the old London to Cambridge coach road, where you will always find a warm and friendly welcome from your hosts Lynda and Bill. Ideally located in the East Hertfordshire countryside to offer easy access to Cambridge, Saffron Walden and other local attractions. Double unit for B&B at £75/night or £55 for a single person also available.
Open: All year **Nearest Shop:** 2 miles

Site: ✿ P Leisure: ➤ Property: 〽 🛏 🖼 📖 Children: 🚼 🍴 ♿ Unit: 🚪 🗄 📺 📻 🛜 📺

SOUTH MIMMS, Hertfordshire   Map ref 2D1

Black Swan

Contact: Mr William Marsterson, Black Swan, 64 Blanche Lane, South Mimms, Potters Bar EN6 3PD **T:** (01707) 644180 / 07932 181441 **F:** 01707 642344
E: wmarsterson@yahoo.co.uk

Units   3
Sleeps   2-6
PER UNIT PER WEEK
£250.00 - £330.00

Cottage and self-contained flats, 16th century listed building. Rail connections at Potters Bar and London Underground at Barnet allow travel to London within 45 minutes.
Open: All year **Nearest Shop:** 0.25 miles **Nearest Pub:** 0.25 miles

Site: ✿ P Property: 🛏 🖼 📖 Children: 🚼 🍴 Unit: 🚪 📺 📻 🛜 📺 🎧 ☎

WARE, Hertfordshire Map ref 2D1

Emerald Cottages

Contact: 1 Levens Green, Ware, Hertfordshire SG11 1HD **T:** (01920) 438372
E: veritygarner@hotmail.com
W: www.emerald-cottages.com

Units 5
Sleeps 2-4
PER UNIT PER WEEK
£420.00 – £575.00

Five self-contained cottages in rural courtyard setting, a mile from A10. Situated in ideal area to visit London, Cambridge or local attractions. The Cottages are made up of three one bedroomed cottages with separate living and kitchen area, all with en suite wet rooms. The two bedroomed cottages are both large and decorated in a rustic/modern feel, with their own patio areas. Private parking. No public transport available. Pepe Cottage suitable for wheelchair access. **Open:** All year **Nearest Shop:** 1 mile **Nearest Pub:** 1 mile

BACTON, Norfolk Map ref 3C1

Primrose Cottage

Contact: Paul and Claire Medd, Primrose Cottage, Cable Gap Holiday Park, Coast Road, Bacton, Norfolk NR12 0EW **T:** (01692) 650667 **E:** holiday@cablegap.co.uk
W: www.cablegap.co.uk **£ BOOK ONLINE**

Units 1
Sleeps 2-6
PER UNIT PER WEEK
£425.00 – £710.00

Primrose Cottage is a spacious 2 bedroom bungalow designed to accommodate older and less mobile guests and part-time wheelchair users. It is 3 star self-catering accommodation and benefits from central heating, fully fitted kitchen, large level wet-room bathroom, with its own parking and direct access ramp. **Open:** Mid March to Mid November **Nearest Shop:** 0.1 miles **Nearest Pub:** 0.1 mile

BODHAM, Norfolk Map ref 3B1

Rookery Farm Norfolk

Contact: Mrs Emma McNeil Wilson, Booking Enquiries, Rookery Farm Norfolk, Rookery Farm, West Beckham, Holt, Norfolk NR25 6NX **T:** (01263) 821232 **F:** 01263 822242
E: holiday@rookeryfarmnorfolk.com **W:** www.rookeryfarmnorfolk.com **£ BOOK ONLINE**

Units 7
Sleeps 2-32
PER UNIT PER WEEK
£367.00 – £3633.00

SPECIAL PROMOTIONS
Please refer to website for details.

The perfect holiday retreat, Rookery Farm offers comfortable, contemporary self-catering accommodation in a tranquil coastal location. We aim to combine luxury, character and everything you could possibly need for a stress free break.

Rookery Farm is tucked away but perfectly placed for all that's good about beautiful north Norfolk with its unspoilt beaches, rolling countryside and charming towns and villages. The barns are set round a garden courtyard, each with its own private patio, lawn and herb garden. There is a small play area for younger children.

Open: All year
Nearest Shop: 0.5 miles
Nearest Pub: 0.5 miles

BRANCASTER STAITHE, *Norfolk* Map ref 3B1

Units   2
Sleeps   2-6
PER UNIT PER WEEK
£400.00 - £875.00

Vista & Carpenters Cottage

Contact: Mrs Gloria Smith, Dale View, Main Road, Brancaster Staithe, King's Lynn, Norfolk PE31 8BY **T:** (01485) 210497 **F:** 01485 210497

These lovely cottages have amazing views along the Norfolk coast. From the gardens you meet the saltmarsh and coastal path. Open fires and central heating. Close to amenities. Pets welcome. **Open:** All year **Nearest Shop:** 0.25 miles **Nearest Pub:** 0.25 miles

Site: ✿ P Leisure: ♿ ⚑ Property: 🐴 🔲 Children: 🛝 🛏 ☂ Unit: 🔲 🔳 📺 📻 🎧 BBQ

CROMER, *Norfolk* Map ref 3C1

Units   5
Sleeps   3-4
PER UNIT PER WEEK
£134.00 - £478.00

Beverley House Holiday Apartments

Contact: Robert & Susan Collins, Beverley House Holiday Apartments, 17 Alfred Road, Cromer NR27 9AN **T:** 07960 796309 **F:** 01263 512787 **E:** sue@beverley-house.co.uk

Very comfortable Victorian property. Six well-furnished, warm, cosy apartments, some with sea view. Retains many original period features. Shops, pubs, station all within ten minutes walk. Street parking. **Open:** All year **Nearest Shop:** 0.25 miles **Nearest Pub:** 0.25 miles

Site: P Leisure: ♿ ♪ ⚑ Property: 🐴 🚲 🔲 Children: 🛝 🛏 ☂ Unit: 🔲 🔳 📺 📻 🎧

CROMER, Norfolk   Map ref 3C1

Cliff Hollow

Contact: Ms L Willins, Booking Enquiries, Cliff Haven, 35 Overstrand Road, Cromer NR27 0AL **T:** (01263) 512447 **F:** 01263 512447 **E:** l.willins@btinternet.com

Cottage in a quiet loop road, 3-5 minutes from the beach, cliffs and town. Secluded garden with garden furniture. Bird watching, walking, golf, cycling all available. **Open:** April - October, Christmas & New Year, February half term **Nearest Shop:** 1 mile **Nearest Pub:** 1 mile

Units 1
Sleeps 1-6
PER UNIT PER WEEK
£280.00

Site: ❖ P Leisure: ... Property: ... Children: ... Unit: ...

CROMER, Norfolk   Map ref 3C1

Cromer Country Club

Contact: 127 Overstrand Road, Cromer, Norfolk NR27 0DJ **T:** (0800) 358 6991
E: EuHotels@diamondresorts.com
W: www.DiamondResortsandHotels.com **£ BOOK ONLINE**

Units 85
Sleeps 1-6

PER UNIT PER WEEK
£300.00 - £1414.00

SPECIAL PROMOTIONS
Enjoy two nights or more with complimentary champagne and chocolates on arrival, please call for latest pricing.

With views of the picturesque Norfolk coastline, Cromer Country Club is ideally placed for a delightful break in a pleasant Victorian seaside town. Apartments are equipped with practical and modern conveniences and are furnished to a very comfortable standard.

The extensive leisure facilities make the resort a lively family destination. There is a swimming pool, steam room, a pool-side whirlpool and spa area. The Amber Bar and Restaurant offers an extensive menu in pleasant surroundings. Daily specials are created using the best locally sourced ingredients.

Open: All year
Nearest Shop: 1 mile
Nearest Pub: On Site

Units: A choice of Studio, one and two bedroom apartments available. All apartments boast a full kitchen, modern bathroom and Television with DVD player.

Site: ❖ P Payment: Leisure: Property: Children: Unit: ...

CROMER, Norfolk   Map ref 3C1

The Poplars Caravan & Chalet Park

Contact: Kevin and Dena Parfitt, Brick Lane, East Runton, Cromer, Norfolk NR27 9PL
T: (01263) 512892 **F:** 01263 512892 **E:** info@poplarscaravanandchaletpark.co.uk
W: www.poplarscaravanandchaletpark.co.uk

Set in an idyllic rural location on the edge of the fishing village of East Runton, yet just a few minutes stroll from the beach. Could not be better placed for exploring the beauty of North Norfolk. Relax in privacy and enjoy the views. **Open:** March - November **Nearest Shop:** 0.5 miles **Nearest Pub:** 0.5 miles

Units 9
Sleeps 2-6
PER UNIT PER WEEK
£246.00 - £685.00

Site: ❖ P Payment: € Leisure: ... Property: ... Children: ... Unit: ... BBQ

FAKENHAM, Norfolk   Map ref 3B1

2 Westgate Barns

Contact: Bettina Gresham, Wareham Road, Binham, Norfolk NR21 0DQ **T:** (01483) 473653
E: enquiries@westgatebarn.co.uk
W: www.westgatebarn.co.uk

Units   1
Sleeps   2-8
PER UNIT PER WEEK
£761.00 - £1380.00

Luxury self-catering accommodation sleeping up to eight people, situated close to the North Norfolk coast in the beautiful village of Binham. **Open:** All year **Nearest Shop:** 0.5 miles
Nearest Pub: 0.5 miles

Site: ✿ P **Property:** 🖥 📶 🖧 **Children:** 👶 🛏 ⚲ **Unit:** 🍳 🍽 📺 📻 📶 ⊘ BBQ

FAKENHAM, Norfolk   Map ref 3B1

Brazenhall Barn & Lodge

Contact: Peter Allingham, 67 Beryl Road, Hammersmith, London W6 8JS
T: (08432) 892501 **E:** brazenhall@ancient.co.uk
W: www.brazenhall.com **£ BOOK ONLINE**

Units   2
Sleeps   2-22
PER UNIT PER WEEK
£700.00 - £2900.00

A five star, Gold Award winning barn conversion comprising The Barn (sleeping 14) and The Lodge (sleeping 6+2) which can be hired together or separately. The Barn has dining facilities, inside and out, for 22. Located just 9 miles from the coast, Brazenhall Barns have a lovely rural setting, nestling under the church of St Peter, in a quiet valley. The barns are surrounded on three sides by lovely summer meadows, which are yours to use and enjoy.
Open: All year **Nearest Shop:** 2 miles **Nearest Pub:** 2 miles

Site: ✿ P **Payment:** 💳 **Leisure:** ♨ ♪ ⚲ ♿ **Property:** 🐾 🖥 🖧 **Children:** 👶 🛏 ⚲ **Unit:** 🍳 🍽 📺 📻 📶 ⊘ BBQ ☎

FAKENHAM, Norfolk   Map ref 3B1

Moor Farm Stable Cottages

Contact: Paul Davis, Owner, Moor Farm, The Street, Foxley, Dereham NR20 4QP
T: (01362) 688523 **F:** 01362 688523 **E:** mail@moorfarmstablecottages.co.uk
W: www.moorfarmstablecottages.co.uk

Units   16
Sleeps   3-10
PER UNIT PER WEEK
£280.00 - £1060.00

Situated on a working farm a courtyard of 2/3/4 bedroomed converted stables and barns. Central for North Norfolk coast, Sandringham, Broads and Norwich. Fishing in owner's lakes. Indoor heated swimming pool and spa. **Open:** All Year including Christmas/New Year **Nearest Shop:** 1 mile **Nearest Pub:** 1 mile

Site: ✿ P **Leisure:** ♪ ⚲ **Property:** 🐾 🖥 🖧 **Children:** 👶 🛏 ⚲ **Unit:** 🍳 🍽 📺 📻 📶 ⊘ BBQ ☎

FAKENHAM, Norfolk   Map ref 3B1

Pollywiggle Cottage

Contact: Mrs Marilyn Farnham-Smith, Owner, 79 Earlham Road, Norwich NR2 3RE
T: (01603) 471990 / 07974 804039 **F:** 01603 612221 **E:** marilyn@pollywigglecottage.co.uk
W: www.pollywigglecottage.co.uk **£ BOOK ONLINE**

Units   1
Sleeps   1-7

PER UNIT PER WEEK
£340.00 - £990.00

SPECIAL PROMOTIONS
Short breaks available out of peak times and reductions for a couple sharing one bedroom.

This well equipped 4 bedroomed comfortable retreat is situated on the edge of a small village but close to many attractions. The mature gardens to the front and rear are laid to lawns with pretty flower beds and a small pond. There are attractive rural views and a stunning coast nearby.

There are two bathrooms, both with showers over, one upstairs and one downstairs. The cottage is ideally situated for families or a romantic twosome! There is parking for 4 cars & two cycle shelters. Small-party reductions out of season and short breaks are available - min 3 nights off peak.

Open: All year
Nearest Shop: 4 miles
Nearest Pub: 3 miles

Units: This is a 1700s cottage with some low ceilings and narrow stairs.

Site: ✿ P **Payment:** ▣ **Leisure:** ♨ ♪ **Property:** ▦ ▯ ▯ **Children:** ⚊ ▦ ⚹
Unit: ▯ ▯ ▣ ▯ ▯ ▯ TV ◉ ▯ ∅ BBQ ☎

FIELD DALLING, Norfolk   Map ref 3B1

Hard Farm Barns

Contact: Mrs Angela Harcourt, Hard Farm Barns, Hard Farm House, Little Marsh Lane, Field Dalling, Holt, Norfolk NR25 7LL **T:** (01328) 830655 / 07790 631760
E: harcog@farming.co.uk **W:** www.hardfarm.co.uk **£ BOOK ONLINE**

Units   3
Sleeps   1-2

PER UNIT PER WEEK
£245.00 - £405.00

SPECIAL PROMOTIONS
Weekend breaks from £175, low season or last minute.

Spacious 4* Gold Award barn conversions sleeping 2, beautifully furnished and equipped with pretty gardens. The ancient flint barns retain their character with original beams and offer warmth and comfort all year round with full central heating. Oak Barn is ground floor, Beech and Ash are over 2 floors. They offer twin or super king beds, all have spacious bathrooms. Hard Farm is the ideal peaceful location for Holt, Blakeney and North Norfolk Coast with its abundance of bird-watching and walking opportunities. A pet is welcome in Ash Barn only. WiFi. Personally supervised and a warm welcome.

Open: All year
Nearest Shop: 1.5 miles
Nearest Pub: 1.5 miles

Units: 3 Barns each sleeping 2 people, one ground floor.

Site: ✿ P **Leisure:** ♨ **Property:** ⚊ ▦ ▯ **Unit:** ▯ ▯ ▣ ▯ ▯ TV ◉ ▯

GREAT YARMOUTH, *Norfolk* Map ref 3C1

Clippesby Hall Holiday Park

Contact: Chris Haycock, Park manager, Clippesby Hall, Clippesby, Norfolk NR29 3BL
T: (01493) 367800 **F:** 01493 367809 **E:** holidays@clippesby.com
W: www.clippesby.com **£ BOOK ONLINE**

Units 15
Sleeps 1-8

PER UNIT PER WEEK
£375.00 - £1535.00

SPECIAL PROMOTIONS
Short breaks of 3
nights available during
Spring, Autumn and
Winter, charged at 65%
of weekly price.

The self-catering accommodation at Clippesby Hall is located in the heart of the Norfolk Broads, at an award-winning, independent, family holiday park, suitable for all ages. There is a wide range of accommodation available, from one-bedroom apartments, two-bedroom cottages, and three-bedroom Pine Lodges, to four-bedroom houses. Fully fitted kitchens, bathrooms and all heating are included, together with bed linen. The holiday park has its own bar, restaurant, cafe, outdoor pool, tennis, mini-golf, cycle hire, bike trails, and childrens play areas. Great scenery and beaches.

Open: All year (cafe, bar, resturant and pool Apr-Oct)
Nearest Shop: 3 miles
Nearest Pub: 2 miles

Units: 1-4 bedroom apartments, cottages and lodges set in 34 acre holiday park.

Site: ✿ **P Payment:** 🖃 **Leisure:** 🏊 ⚲ ⚘ ⚴ **Property:** 🐕 ☷ 🗄 🗄 **Children:** 🐎 🛏 🎎
Unit: 🖥 🖿 🗄 ⚷ 📺 📀 BBQ 📞

HOLT, *Norfolk* Map ref 3B1

★★★
SELF CATERING

6 Carpenters Cottages

Contact: Sally Beament, Owner, Norwich Road, Holt, Norfolk NR25 6SD
T: (02476) 545577 / 07787 992209 **E:** sallybeament@hotmail.com
W: www.6carpenterscottagesholt.co.uk

Units 1
Sleeps 3
PER UNIT PER WEEK
£220.00 - £430.00

Pretty flint and pantiled terraced cottage on the edge of the lovely Georgian market town of Holt. All mod cons. Enclosed, flower filled, gravelled yard in front of cottage and dedicated parking behind. Coast is 3 miles away, excellent walks close by. **Open:** All year
Nearest Shop: 100 yards **Nearest Pub:** 100 yards

Site: ✿ **P Property:** ⫽ **Unit:** 🖿 ⚷ 📺 📀

HOLT, *Norfolk* Map ref 3B1

★★★★
SELF CATERING

Garden Cottage

Contact: Rosemary Kimmins, Owner, Chequers, Bale Road, Sharrington, Norfolk NR24 2PG
T: (01263) 860308 / 07779 267330 **E:** rosemary@kimmins1.wanadoo.co.uk

Units 1
Sleeps 2-4
PER UNIT PER WEEK
£320.00 - £550.00

This high quality conversion of an 18th century building overlooks a large garden in a quiet village convenient to Holt, Blakeney and the whole North Norfolk coast. Fitted and furnished to the highest standard with one double and one twin bedroom, bathroom with over bath shower, downstairs cloakroom, fully fitted kitchen. comfortable sitting room with digital TV, DVD and free Wi-Fi.
Open: All year except Christmas and New Year
Nearest Shop: 1 mile **Nearest Pub:** 1.5 miles

Site: ✿ **P Leisure:** 🎣 **Property:** ⫽ ☷ 🗄 🗄 **Unit:** 🖥 🖿 🗄 ⚷ 📺 📀

HUNSTANTON, *Norfolk* Map ref 3B1

★★★★ SELF CATERING

Units 1
Sleeps 1-6

PER UNIT PER WEEK
£525.00 - £1150.00

SPECIAL PROMOTIONS
Short breaks (min 3 nights) available during school term time. Change over day is Saturday. Other days may be available out of season. Towels available. Contact owner to discuss your requirements.

Chilvers

Contact: Harriet Huntsman, Owner, Stockpot, 27 Hall Orchard Lane, Welbourn, Lincoln LN5 0NG **T:** (01400) 273474 / 07778 002858 **E:** hhuntsman@btinternet.com
W: www.chilverscosycottage.co.uk **£ BOOK ONLINE**

A charming Victorian cottage, modernised and well equipped with spectacular views and direct access onto the salt marsh. Downstairs comprises a sitting room with open fire, flatscreen TV and DVD player, a dining room and kitchen with hob, oven, microwave, fridge-freezer, dishwasher and washing machine. The twin, double and superking/twin bedrooms and bathroom are upstairs. Heated by electric oil filled wall mounted radiators. Outside is a BBQ and garden furniture. Ideally situated for sailing, walking, tennis, golf, bird watching, the Coast Hopper bus, excellent hostelries and dining out.

Open: All Year
Nearest Shop: 168 metres
Nearest Pub: 100 metres

Units: The double and superking/twin bedrooms plus the bathroom are on the first floor and the twin room is on the second floor.

Site: ✿ P **Property:** ▯ ▣ ▤ **Children:** ⚓ ⛱ ☆ **Unit:** ▯ ▯ ▭ ▯ ☌ TV ⊙ ✎ BBQ

HUNSTANTON, *Norfolk* Map ref 3B1

★★★★ SELF CATERING

Units 1
Sleeps 1-4
PER UNIT PER WEEK
£280.00 - £550.00

Forget Me Not Cottage

Contact: Forget Me Not Cottage, 56 Old Hunstanton Road, Hunstanton, Norfolk PE36 6HX
T: 07957 351250 / 02033 550080 **F:** 08704 909308 **E:** streetsaheadlondon@gmail.com
W: www.holidayhomesnorfolk.co.uk **£ BOOK ONLINE**

Beautiful 2 bedroom cottage. In the picturesque village of Old Hunstanton. One small dog welcome. Private parking. With a lovely enclosed cottage garden. Only 5 minutes walk to the wide sandy beaches of Old Hunstanton, and close to the golf course, behind the sand dunes. **Open:** All year **Nearest Shop:** 0.10 miles
Nearest Pub: 0.10 miles

Site: ✿ P **Leisure:** 🚲 🎣 ▸ **Property:** 🐾 ▣ **Children:** ☆ **Unit:** ▯ ▭ ▯ TV ⊙ ⊙

KING'S LYNN, *Norfolk* Map ref 3B1

★★★★ SELF CATERING

Units 1
Sleeps 4-6
PER UNIT PER WEEK
£350.00 - £600.00

Butlers Barn

Contact: Ian & Angie Nicholson, Owners, East Wing, Butlers Barn, Meadow Road, Narborough, Kings Lynn, Norfolk PE32 1JR **T:** (01760) 338991 / 07871 284035
E: Ian.i.nicholson@btinternet.com **W:** www.norfolkcottagehire.co.uk

Large converted wing of beamed barn set in 10 acres, consisting of two large bedrooms one en suite bath with shower over. The other has its own bathroom double shower and corner bath. Separate large kitchen/diner, all facilities provided. Also a very comfortable sitting room, Wi-Fi and televisions in most rooms. All tastefully decorated and furnished, in rural location. Pets welcome. Owners on premises. **Open:** All year **Nearest Shop:** 2 miles
Nearest Pub: 1.5 miles

Site: ✿ P **Leisure:** 🎣 ▸ ∪ **Property:** 🛏 ▣ ▯ ▤ **Children:** ☆ ⛱ ☆ **Unit:** ▯ ▭ ▯ ☌ TV ⊙

KING'S LYNN, *Norfolk* Map ref 3B1

Rainbow Cottage

Contact: Jacquie Sindle, Owner, Church View, 13 Goodminns, Sedgeford, Norfolk PE36 5NB **T:** (01485) 572402 / 07944 576 767 **E:** sindle965@btinternet.com

Units 1
Sleeps 1-5

PER UNIT PER WEEK
£320.00 - £485.00

SPECIAL PROMOTIONS
Please contact the owner for short break prices and any special deals.

Rainbow Cottage is an appealing little cottage, with a charming enclosed rear patio garden, ideal for sitting out with garden furniture and BBQ. Parking is close by. The cottage has recently been refurbished, keeping several little interesting features. Offers modern accommodation and is very comfortably furnished to a high standard throughout. Suitable for breaks at any time of year, the cottage walls are very thick thus retaining heat in the cold months and keeping cool in hotter weather, although there are Rointe electric heaters in most rooms. Double bed, double sofa bed and cot.

Open: All year
Nearest Shop: 3 miles
Nearest Pub: 0.5 miles

Units: Double bedroom with double sofa bed in sitting room, both of which are upstairs. Enclosed garden. Well equipped kitchen. Bath with shower overhead.

Site: ✿ Payment: 💷 Property: 🐾 🖙 🖵 Children: 🥢 🛏 🎠 Unit: 🚪 🍴 📺 🖵 🔌 📺 📀 BBQ

KING'S LYNN, *Norfolk* Map ref 3B1

Thompson Brancaster Farms

Contact: Sussex Farm, Burnham Market, King's Lynn, Norfolk PE31 8JY **T:** (01485) 210000
E: jet@brancasterhall.co.uk
W: www.tbfholidayhomes.co.uk

Units 7
Sleeps 4-10
PER UNIT PER WEEK
£260.00 - £1495.00

Tastefully restored flint and brick farm cottages near Brancaster and Burnham Market, in an area of outstanding natural beauty.
Open: All year **Nearest Shop:** Walking distance
Nearest Pub: Walking distance

Site: ✿ P Payment: 💷 Leisure: ↑ ∪ Property: 🐾 🖙 🖵 Children: 🥢 Unit: 🍴 📺

Book your accommodation online

Visit our websites for detailed information, up-to-date availability and to book your accommodation online. Includes over 20,000 places to stay, all of them star rated.

www.visitor-guides.co.uk

For **key to symbols** see page 7

MUNDESLEY, *Norfolk* Map ref 3C1

Units 1
Sleeps 1-4

PER UNIT PER WEEK
£369.00 - £526.00

SPECIAL PROMOTIONS
3 nights from £278.00.

Seaescape Cottage

Contact: Valerie Daniels, Mill Farmhouse, Weybread, Diss IP21 5RS **T:** (01379) 586395
E: valerie@seaescapecottage.com
W: www.norfolkcottages.co.uk/cottage-details/1366 **£ BOOK ONLINE**

A newly refurbished, Victorian two storey end terrace cottage overlooking Gold Park in the centre of Mundesley, with two bedrooms sleeping up to four people. Kitchen, lounge, dining area, first floor bathroom with shower over bath. Patio doors from the kitchen leading to a small garden.

Open: All year
Nearest Shop: 0.25 miles
Nearest Pub: 0.25 miles

Site: ✿ P **Leisure:** 🏊 **Property:** 🖥 **Children:** 👶 **Unit:** 🛏 📺 🍴 🔧 TV dvd BBQ

NORTH WALSHAM, *Norfolk* Map ref 3C1

Units 2
Sleeps 1-9

PER UNIT PER WEEK
£300.00 - £700.00

SPECIAL PROMOTIONS
Short breaks available all year on request. Barns can be booked together to sleep up to 9 guests.

Courtyard Barns

Contact: Susan Millett, Owner, Courtyard Barns 1 & 2, Church Road, Skeyton, Norfolk NR10 5AX **T:** (01692) 538446 / 07769 257361 **E:** info@courtyardbarn.co.uk
W: www.courtyardbarn.co.uk

Courtyard Barns are set in a peaceful, rural location. A good touring location, close to the Norfolk Broads, the coast, Norwich and Holt. Market towns of Aylsham/North Walsham close by. Also close by are the pretty Broadland villages of Coltishall, Horning and Wroxham.

The properties are both single storey and are easily accessible. Each has a south facing courtyard area which is secure for children and pets. Garden furniture is provided. There is a large gravel parking area and the properties are accessed via a wide ramp. There is a sofa bed in Courtyard Barn 1. Friday start for Courtyard Barn 1, Saturday start for Courtyard Barn 2.

Open: All year inc Christmas and New Year.
Nearest Shop: 2 miles in Felmingham
Nearest Pub: 1 mile in Skeyton - The Goat

Units: Double bedrooms are en suite on ground floor. Two steps up to Courtyard Barn 2 double room. CourtyardBarn 1 has a sofa bed for child/ teenager. Sleeps 5.

Site: ✿ P **Property:** 🐕 🚗 📺 🖥 **Children:** 👶 🎠 🚼 **Unit:** 📺 🔧 TV 🍴 dvd

NORWICH, Norfolk   Map ref 3C1

Poolside Lodges

Contact: Pippa & Steve Nurse, South Lodges, Salhouse Road, Rackheath, Norwich, Norfolk NR13 6LD **T:** (01603) 720000 / 07554 088058 **E:** pippanurse@gmail.com
W: www.poolsidelodgeselfcatering.co.uk

Units   3
Sleeps   1-12

PER UNIT PER WEEK
£250.00 - £850.00

SPECIAL PROMOTIONS
Discounts available for multiple lodge bookings.

A small family run site perfectly suited for families, groups and couples alike. Adults can relax around the outdoor pool or unwind in the hot tub, whilst the children splash about and play in the games room. Our site can accommodate up to 12 people over 3 lodges. Lodges can be booked individually or hired together. We offer short breaks and weekly bookings.

Located on the outskirts of Norwich and the Norfolk Broads (5 miles) meaning we have the best of both worlds on our doorstep; the beautiful medieval city of Norwich to the peaceful Norfolk Broads.

Open: All Year
Nearest Shop: 0.8 miles
Nearest Pub: 0.6 miles

Units: Poolside: 1 twin room & 1 double room. Studio: 1 double bedroom. Woodside: 1 twin & 1 double room. Living areas are open plan.

Site: **P** **Leisure:** **Property:** **Children:** **Unit:** BBQ

SHERINGHAM, Norfolk   Map ref 3B1

3 The Promenade

Contact: Jasmine Jefferies, Owner, 3 The Promenade, Sheringham, Norfolk NR26 8BH
T: (01603) 304315 / 07836 758323 **E:** jgjefferies@gmail.com

Units   1
Sleeps   2

PER UNIT PER WEEK
£335.00 - £495.00

Stunning seaviews. Ground floor one bedroomed apartment. Fully equipped and serviced. Recently refurbished. Private entrance and patio. Space for travel cot (available upon request). Sleeps 2. Part weeks early & late season. Out of season short lets available from £60 per night. **Open:** All Year **Nearest Shop:** 200 yards **Nearest Pub:** 100 yards

Property: **Unit:** TV

SHERINGHAM, Norfolk   Map ref 3B1

Glendalough

Contact: Janet Teather, Proprietor, 8 Cromer Road, Sheringham, Norfolk NR26 8RR
T: (01263) 825032 / 07876 583475 **E:** janetteather@hotmail.com
W: www.glendaloughsheringham.co.uk

Units   1
Sleeps   2-8

PER UNIT PER WEEK
£350.00 - £700.00

Comfortable family house, twin room and family bedroom on 1st floor, single bedroom & all other rooms on ground floor. Modern kitchen, lounge & dining room, secluded paved garden. Private off road parking. Convenient for beach, shops, leisure centre and all amenities. Concessions for couples, seniors and members of North Norfolk Railway (excluding school holidays). Off peak short breaks available. **Open:** All year **Nearest Shop:** 100m **Nearest Pub:** 0.25 miles

Site: **P** **Leisure:** **Property:** **Children:** **Unit:** BBQ

SPIXWORTH, Norfolk   Map ref 3C1

Units   8
Sleeps   3-12

PER UNIT PER WEEK
£295.00 - £1300.00

Spixworth Hall Cottages

Contact: Mrs Sheelah Cook, Booking Enquiries, Spixworth Hall Cottages, Grange farm, Buxton Rd, Norwich NR10 3PR **T:** (01603) 898190 **F:** 01603 897176
E: hallcottages@btinternet.com **W:** www.hallcottages.co.uk

These cottages are ideal for exploring Norwich (4 miles), the Norfolk Broads and Coast. Wonderful period buildings have original features, yet have been adapted to 21st century standards with central heating and log fires. Farm walks, play barn, swimming, fishing and tennis. Stables Cottage (2 bedrooms) has level access for people with mobility problems and Gaffer's Cottage (5 bedrooms) has a ground floor bedroom & shower room. A warm welcome always and space to relax and unwind.

Open: All year
Nearest Shop: 0.80 miles
Nearest Pub: 0.30 miles

Site: ✿ **P** **Payment:** 💷 € **Leisure:** ♿ 🎵 🏌 ♺ 🎣 🏹 ⚲ **Property:** 💻 📻 📠 **Children:** 🐾 🛏 🧸
Unit: 🔌 🖥 📶 📺 📀 ⌀ **BBQ** 📞

STALHAM, Norfolk   Map ref 3C1

Units   325
Sleeps   2-12

PER UNIT PER WEEK
£280.00 - £2300.00

Richardsons Boating Holidays

Contact: The Staithe, Stalham, Norfolk NR12 9BX **T:** (01692) 582277
E: boating@richardsonsgroup.net
W: www.richardsonsboatingholidays.co.uk **£ BOOK ONLINE**

Self-catering boating holidays on the Norfolk broads, boats available to sleep 2-12. Pets welcome on certain boats. Weekly hire or short breaks. Richardson's has over 300 boats making it the largest operator on the Norfolk Broads. The Norfolk Broads are Britain's finest and best loved holiday boating location. A Richardson's boating holiday provides holidaymakers with unique scenery, fantastic pubs and restaurants and great fun family days out. No experience necessary - full trial run given. On board facilities include toilets, showers, equipped kitchen and sleeping quarters and TV.

Open: March-November

Units: Equipped kitchens and sleeping quarters plus toilet and shower. Buoyancy aids provided.

Site: P Payment: 💷 **Property:** 🐾 📻 📠 **Children:** 🐾 **Unit:** 🖥 📺 📀

THURSFORD, Norfolk Map ref 3B1

Station Farm Barn

Contact: Les Walton, Station Farm Barn, 32 Hall Street, Soham, Cambridgeshire CB7 5BW
T: (01353) 720419 / 07801 050267 **E:** enquiries@norfolk-barn-holidays.co.uk
W: www.norfolk-barn-holidays.co.uk **£ BOOK ONLINE**

Units 3
Sleeps 5-6
PER UNIT PER WEEK
£240.00 - £600.00

Barn conversion providing one three-bedroomed and two two-bedroomed cottages. Fully equipped for self-catering family holidays. Well situated for exploring the whole of North Norfolk. 3 day weekend breaks available in off-peak periods at 65% of the weekly rate. Also available during peak on late availability basis.
Open: All year **Nearest Shop:** 5 miles **Nearest Pub:** 0.10 miles

Site: P Payment: € Property: Children: Unit: BBQ

WALSINGHAM, Norfolk Map ref 3B1

Waterside Barn

Contact: Mrs Liz Harris, 10 High Barns, Blakeney Road, Near Binham, Norfolk NR21 0BU
T: (01400) 250023 / 07808 333600 **E:** enquiries@watersidebarn.co.uk
W: www.watersidebarn.co.uk

Units 1
Sleeps 6
PER UNIT PER WEEK
£725.00 - £1335.00

Waterside Barn is a comfortable, contemporary barn conversion that sleeps 6 in 3 bedrooms. Furnished to high standards and set in grounds of an acre, its south-facing patio overlooks a large wildlife pond. Located a short drive from many of North Norfolk's beautiful beaches, it is a tranquil home from home whatever the season. Most of the accommodation is on ground level making access easy.
Open: All year **Nearest Shop:** 1.2 miles **Nearest Pub:** 1.2 miles

Site: P Property: Children: Unit:

WEASENHAM, Norfolk Map ref 3B1

Lavender Lodge

Contact: Mrs. V.A. Varley, Windwhistle Cottage, 49/50, Massingham Road, Weasenham, King's Lynn, Norfolk PE32 2ST **T:** (01328) 838711
W: www.lavender-lodge.co.uk

Units 1
Sleeps 4
PER UNIT PER WEEK
£239.00 - £522.00

This single storey Cottage is nestled on the edge of the village of Weasenham All Saints in Norfolk, surrounded by open countryside, offering peace and tranquillity. From the doorstep you can enjoy walking and cycling. The natural Norfolk coastline is approx. 15 miles away and many historical visitor sites are nearby, including Sandringham House, Castle Acre Priory, Walsingham Abbey, Holkham Hall, and many more.
Open: Start of April - End of October **Nearest Pub:** 0.5 miles

Site: P Property: Unit:

Looking for something else?

The official and most comprehensive guide to independently inspected, quality-assessed accommodation.

- **B&Bs and Hotels**
- **Self Catering**
- **Camping, Touring and Holiday Parks**

Now available in all good bookshops and online at

www.hudsons.co.uk/shop

For **key to symbols** see page 7

WELLS-NEXT-THE-SEA, Norfolk *Map ref 3B1*

enjoyEngland.com ★★★★ SELF CATERING

Units 1
Sleeps 1-6

PER UNIT PER WEEK
£525.00 - £850.00

SPECIAL PROMOTIONS
Short breaks, of 3 or more nights, are possible in out-of-season months.

Bexwell

Contact: John Stannard, Mill Lodge, Polka Road, Wells-next-the-Sea NR23 1ED
T: (01328) 710752 **E:** info@bexwellcottage.co.uk
W: bexwellcottage.co.uk

Bexwell is a charming, spacious detached house, with ample, on-site parking space, surrounded by private gardens, including a large south-facing lawn. The house is easily accessible to wheelchair users. On the ground floor, the accommodation consists of a large kitchen/dining room, sitting room, garden room, conservatory/utility room and a single bedroom, with adjacent WC and shower room. On the first floor, there are two bedrooms, both en suite, one with a large double bed and the other with twin beds.

Bexwell is very conveniently situated close to all of the town's amenities, as well as to the quay, and well placed for the many beautiful beaches and dramatic salt marshes, in Wells and the surrounding coastal area.

Open: All year
Nearest Shop: 150 metres
Nearest Pub: 150 metres

Units: All bedrooms, along with the sitting room have TVs. Wifi is among the many facilities in the very well-equipped house.

Site: P **Leisure:** **Property:** **Children:** **Unit:**

WELLS-NEXT-THE-SEA, Norfolk *Map ref 3B1*

enjoyEngland.com ★★★★ SELF CATERING

Units 1
Sleeps 1-4
PER UNIT PER WEEK
£250.00 - £575.00

Harbour View Cottage

Contact: Mrs Louise Evans-Evans, Harbour View Cottage, 48 Wingate Drive, Ampthill, Bedfordshire MK45 2XF **T:** (01525) 405494 **E:** cottageinwells@live.co.uk
W: www.cottageinwells.tripod.com **£ BOOK ONLINE**

Refurbished in 2008, this warm and inviting cottage with Harbour views retains many original features and sleeps four. Modern bathroom and bespoke kitchen including washer and dishwasher, south facing garden. We will consider 3 or 4 night breaks depending on availability, please contact us for details.
Open: All year **Nearest Shop:** 0.30 miles **Nearest Pub:** 0.30 miles

Site: P **Payment:** € **Leisure:** **Property:** **Children:** 2 **Unit:**

WICKMERE, Norfolk   Map ref 3B1

Church Farm Barns

Contact: Mr & Mrs Dom & Gill Boddington, Church Farm Barns, Regent Street, Wickmere, Norfolk NR11 7NB **T:** (01263) 577300 **E:** dom@churchfarmbarnsnorfolk.co.uk
W: www.churchfarmbarnsnorfolk.co.uk **£ BOOK ONLINE**

| Units | 3 |
| Sleeps | 2-9 |

PER UNIT PER WEEK
£280.00 - £1090.00

SPECIAL PROMOTIONS
Please contact for short breaks or last minute bookings.

Weekend break for two from £196.00.

Discounts may be available for booking all 3 barns sleeping up to 17.

Lost in rural North Norfolk, barns converted to a luxurious standard, offering peaceful retreats for bird watchers, wildlife enthusiasts, dog owners, walkers and cyclists. Blickling (NT), Felbrigg (NT), Wolterton and Mannington all within walking distance. Close to attractions: Broads National Park and North Norfolk coast. Ideal for family parties/reunions. Friendly owners on site.

Open: All year
Nearest Shop: 1.25 miles
Nearest Pub: 0.75 miles

Site: ✿ P **Leisure:** 🚲 ⌨ ⏸ ∪ 🔍 **Property:** 🐕 🚗 📺 🖥 **Children:** 🎠 🛏 🧸
Unit: ▯ ▤ ▣ 🍳 📺 ◉ 📀 🖊 BBQ

ALDEBURGH, Suffolk   Map ref 3C2

Aldeburgh Bay Holidays

Contact: Reception Office -Thorpeness Hotel, Aldeburgh Bay Holidays, Thorpeness Hotel, Nr Aldeburgh, Suffolk IP16 4NH **T:** (01728) 451031 **E:** info@thorpeness.co.uk
W: www.aldeburghbayholidays.co.uk

| Units | 34 |
| Sleeps | 2-14 |

PER UNIT PER WEEK
£335.00 - £3100.00

SPECIAL PROMOTIONS
Short breaks, max 4 nights (incl Christmas and New Year, excl high season).

Self-catering properties available in Aldeburgh and Thorpeness. Apartments, cottages and larger houses are available in beach side, town and rural locations. Guests benefit from discounts on dining at 5 local hotels, golf and tennis in Thorpeness. The location is ideal for family holidays, visitors to the famous Aldeburgh Music, Poetry or Literary Festivals and those who enjoy coastal walks, cycling and bird watching.

Open: All year
Nearest Shop: 0.20 miles
Nearest Pub: 0.20 miles

Units: All have well equiped kitchen, living areas, some have gardens. Linen and services included in the price.

Site: ✿ P **Payment:** 💳 **Leisure:** 🚲 ⌨ ⏸ ∪ 🔍 **Property:** 🖥 **Children:** 🎠 🛏 🧸 **Unit:** ▯ ▤ ▣ 🍳 📺

ALDEBURGH, *Suffolk*   Map ref 3C2

SELF CATERING ★★★★

Units   1
Sleeps   1-3

PER UNIT PER WEEK
£220.00 - £450.00

Cragside

Contact: Mrs Lesley Valentine, Rookery Farm, Cratfield, Halesworth IP19 0QE
T: (01986) 798609 **E:** j.r.valentine@btinternet.com
W: aldeburgh-cragside.co.uk **£ BOOK ONLINE**

Deceptively spacious ground floor flat of character. 2 bedrooms, sleeps 3. Well equipped winter/summer. Inglenook fireplaces. TV's in sitting room and bedroom. Good lights for reading in bed. Electric blankets, down duvets. 20 yards from the sea and marshes just down the road. Gas C/H. Comfortable beds. TV and Wi-Fi.
Open: All year **Nearest Shop:** Less than 0.5 miles
Nearest Pub: Less than 0.5 miles

Site: P Leisure: ⚓ ⚓ ▶ ♻ Property: 🖥 🗑 🗑 Unit: 🛏 🗑 📺 📻 📶 📺 📀 ☎

ALDEBURGH, *Suffolk*   Map ref 3C2

SELF CATERING ★★

Units   1
Sleeps   1-5

PER UNIT PER WEEK
£300.00 - £450.00

Dial Flat

Contact: Mrs Pamela Harrison, Booking Enquiries, Dial Flat, 5 Dial Lane, Aldeburgh IP15 5AG **T:** (01728) 453212 **E:** p.harrison212@btinternet.com

Comfortably furnished top floor flat with wonderful sea views overlooking Moot Green. 2 double bedrooms plus Z-bed. Living room with a colour TV with integral DVD player, kitchenette, bathroom with bath and walk in shower. Near to shops, restaurants, cinema and Jubilee Hall. Ideal for Snape, birdwatching, walking etc. Wi-Fi, electricity and garage parking included in rent. **Open:** All year
Nearest Shop: 2 mins **Nearest Pub:** 2 mins

 Site: P Leisure: ▶ Property: 🖥 🗑 Unit: 🛏 📺 📺 📀 📀

ALDEBURGH, *Suffolk*   Map ref 3C2

SELF CATERING ★★★

Units   1
Sleeps   14

PER UNIT PER WEEK
£700.00 - £2900.00

SPECIAL PROMOTIONS
Weekend and midweek bookings welcome. Ideal for a family weekend at the seaside. Perfect to celebrate those special family occasions.

Orlando

Contact: Mr Peter Hatcher, Martlesham Hall, Church Lane, Martlesham IP12 4PQ
T: (01394) 382126 / 07860 567913 **F:** 01394 278600 **E:** peter@hatcher.co.uk
W: www.holidayhomealdeburgh.co.uk

Orlando is a spacious, well-equipped six bedroom house adjacent to beach with magnificent, panoramic sea views. Friendly open kitchen with Aga. Ideal for three families or groups for that perfect seaside getaway. Free Wi-Fi broadband.

Open: All year
Nearest Shop: 0.01 miles
Nearest Pub: 0.01 miles

Site: P Payment: € Leisure: ⚓ ▶ ♻ Property: 🖥 🗑 🗑 Children: 🚼 🛏 🖊
Unit: 🛏 🗑 📺 📻 📶 📺 📀 📀 🍳 ☎

The Official Tourist Board Guide to **Self Catering 2015**

BURY ST. EDMUNDS, *Suffolk* Map ref 3B2

Culford Farm Cottages

Contact: Mr Steve Flack, Culford Farm Cottages, Home Farm, Culford, Bury St Edmunds, Suffolk IP28 6DS **T:** (01284) 728334 / 07725 201086 **E:** enquiries@homefarmculford.co.uk
W: www.culfordfarmcottages.co.uk **£ BOOK ONLINE**

Units	3
Sleeps	2-6

PER UNIT PER WEEK
£355.00 - £804.00

Unique, well-equipped farm cottages offering an indoor pool available all year, private hot tubs, and riverside walks on our peacefully located working farm with easy access to Bury St Edmunds and beyond. **Open:** All year **Nearest Shop:** 2 miles **Nearest Pub:** 2 miles

Site: ✿ P **Leisure:** ▶ ⌇ **Property:** ☈ ⌨ ⊡ ◫ **Children:** ⌂ ▥ ⚲ **Unit:** ⊡ ⊟ ▣ ▦ ⚲ TV DVD BBQ

BURY ST. EDMUNDS, *Suffolk* Map ref 3B2

Lackford Lakes Barns

Contact: Owner, Lackford Hall, Lackford, Nr Bury St Edmunds, Suffolk IP28 6HX
T: (01284) 728041 **E:** emmaramsay22@gmail.com
W: www.lackfordlakesbarns.co.uk **£ BOOK ONLINE**

Units	4
Sleeps	4-23

PER UNIT PER WEEK
£350.00 - £1200.00

SPECIAL PROMOTIONS
Weekly and short breaks of 3 or 4 nights with a flexible start date.

Situated within the picturesque and tranquil Lackford Lakes Nature Reserve, our charming accommodation is set in the heart of the beautiful Suffolk countryside, only 5 miles from historic and vibrant Bury St Edmunds, offering 4 self catering holiday cottages sleeping up to 23 guests.

Our grade 2 listed renovated barns are The Cart Lodge (sleeps 7), Holm Oak (sleeps 6), Lark Lodge (sleeps 6) and curlew Cottage (sleeps 4).

Open: All year round
Nearest Shop: 4 miles
Nearest Pub: 2 miles

Units: Grade 2 listed, converted barns of brick, flint and timber, insulated, double glazed, underfloor heating, comfortably furnished with modern bathrooms

Site: ✿ P **Payment:** ▦ **Leisure:** ♪ ▶ ∪ ✎ **Property:** ∥ ⌨ ⊡ ◫ **Children:** ⌂ ▥ ⚲
Unit: ⊡ ⊟ ▣ ▦ ⚲ TV DVD ⌀ BBQ

BURY ST. EDMUNDS, *Suffolk* Map ref 3B2

Rede Hall Farm Park

Contact: Mrs Christine Oakley, Partner, Rede Hall Farm Park, Rede Hall Farm, Chedburgh IP29 4UG **T:** (01284) 850695 **F:** 01284 850345 **E:** chris@redehallfarmpark.co.uk
W: www.redehallfarmpark.co.uk

Units	2
Sleeps	2-6

PER UNIT PER WEEK
£300.00 - £665.00

Country retreat in old-fashioned farmyard. Jenny Wren has two ground floor double bedrooms and galleried twin room. Nuthatch has two ground floor double en suite bedrooms and sofa bed. Also supplied is a shared Hot Spa Tub. We also have a Shepherds Hut that sleeps two in a private field with its own Hot Spa Tub. This is only available from March to end of September. Patio, BBQ, wood burner etc. **Open:** All year **Nearest Shop:** 2 miles **Nearest Pub:** 2 miles

Site: ✿ P **Leisure:** ♪ **Property:** ☈ ⌨ ◫ **Children:** ⌂ ▥ ⚲ **Unit:** ⊡ ⊟ ▣ ▦ ⚲ TV ⓒ DVD BBQ

DUNWICH, Suffolk   Map ref 3C2

Tower Bungalow

Contact: Eleanor Barnes, Greyfriars Wood, Dunwich, Suffolk IP17 3DF **T:** (01787) 269916
E: evb@harper-morris.co.uk
W: www.towerbungalow.co.uk

Units   1
Sleeps   6

PER UNIT PER WEEK
£350.00 - £700.00

Peaceful wooded setting in Dunwich, close to Minsmere Bird Reserve and Dunwich Heath. Sleeps six in three bedrooms with one bathroom , and one shower room. Cosy in Winter with central heating and wood burner, light and airy in Summer. All mod cons. Parking, patio and enclosed garden. **Open:** All year round
Nearest Shop: 2 miles **Nearest Pub:** 1 mile

Site: ✿ P Property: ∥ ⌖ 🖥 🖥 🖥 Children: 🚼 Unit: 🖥 🖥 📺 🖥 ⚲ 📺 DVD ⌀ ☎

EYE, Suffolk   Map ref 3B2

Log Cabin Holidays

Contact: Peter Havers, Owner, Athelington Hall, Horham, Eye, Suffolk IP21 5EJ
T: (01728) 628233 **E:** info@logcabinholidays.co.uk
W: www.logcabinholidays.co.uk

Units   11
Sleeps   2-6

PER UNIT PER WEEK
£319.00 - £729.00

Enjoy 4* Log cabins in an idyllic location in the beautiful North Suffolk countryside. The perfect reason to escape the pressures of urban life and embrace a well earned mini break in well appointed lodges, double glazed and central heated for year round comfort with outdoor hot tubs. **Open:** All year **Nearest Shop:** 1 mile
Nearest Pub: 3 miles

Site: ✿ P Payment: 💷 Leisure: 🏊 🎣 ⛳ ♨ 🔍 Property: ⌖ 🖥 🖥 🖥 Children: 🚼 🛏 🔥 Unit: 🖥 🖥 📺 🖥
🖥 📺 💿 DVD BBQ

KERSEY, Suffolk   Map ref 3B2

Wheelwrights Cottage

Contact: Doreen Gowan, The Forge, Kersey Upland, Kersey, Ipswich, Suffolk IP7 6EN
T: (01473) 829311 / 07785 572878 **E:** peter@pjgowan.net
W: www.wheelwrightscottage.co.uk

Units   1
Sleeps   2

PER UNIT PER WEEK
£360.00

SPECIAL PROMOTIONS
£60 per night - minimum of three nights.

Two nights are available at £180.

Wheelwrights is a cottage recently converted from an 18th century wheelwrights barn situated in the wilds of Suffolk, close to the picturesque village of Kersey. Wonderful countryside for walking or cycling. It consists of one bedroom with a 6ft bed, en suite bathroom with bath and shower, fully equipped kitchen and a large lounge with wood-burning stove.

Wheelwrights is situated in the grounds of a 16th century thatched cottage - 'The Forge' in Kersey Upland where the owners live. The villages of Hadleigh, Lavenham, Long Melford and Dedham are a short drive away and Felixstowe beach is only 40 mins.

Open: All year
Nearest Shop: 2.5 miles
Nearest Pub: 1 mile

Units: Large lounge with wood-burning stove. Fully fitted kitchen. Bedroom with king size bed and en suite bathroom.

Site: P Leisure: ⌁ Property: 🖥 🖥 🖥 Unit: 🖥 🖥 📺 🖥 🖥 📺 DVD ⌀

KESSINGLAND, *Suffolk*   Map ref 3C2

Kew Cottage

Contact: Mrs Joan Gill, 46 St Georges Avenue, Northampton NN2 6JA **T:** (01604) 717301
F: 01604 791424 **E:** b.s.g@btinternet.com

Units	1
Sleeps	4-5

PER UNIT PER WEEK
£190.00 - £270.00

Modernised, two-bedroomed, semi-detached cottage in the middle of village, ten minutes walk from the sea. Large back garden with patio and seating area. Norfolk Broads three miles, Lowestoft three miles, Southwold five miles, Norwich 30 miles. Prices per Unit Per Week: April £190, May £205, June £210, July & August £270, September £215, October £200.

Open: April - October
Nearest Shop: 0.5 miles
Nearest Pub: 0.5 miles

Units: Bedrooms are upstairs, one double bed and one with 2 single beds. Each has its own wash hand basin. Separate dining room & sitting room.

Site: ❋ **P Property:** 🖼 **Children:** 👶 **Unit:** 🛏 📺 📻 🍳 📺 📀 BBQ 📞

LAVENHAM, *Suffolk*   Map ref 3B2

Staddles

Contact: Helen Burgess, Owner, The White Horse, 57-58 Water Street, Lavenham, Suffolk CO10 9RW **T:** (07827) 911539 **E:** helen424@btinternet.com
W: www.staddlescottage-lavenham.co.uk **£ BOOK ONLINE**

Units	1
Sleeps	2

PER UNIT PER WEEK
£245.00 - £575.00

Lavenham is a historic medieval village boasting over 340 listed buildings. Lavenham has a long and colourful history, featuring at different times: Edward de Vere, 17th Earl of Oxford, one of those proposed as the real Shakespeare and Louis Napoleon in the 19th century. **Open:** All year **Nearest Shop:** 0.10 miles
Nearest Pub: 0.10 miles

Site: ❋ **P Leisure:** 🚴 ▶ 🎣 **Property:** 🐴 🖼 🖼 **Unit:** 🛏 📺 🍳 📺 📀 BBQ

LOWESTOFT, *Suffolk*   Map ref 3C1

23 Alandale Drive

Contact: Karen Foster, Owner, Kessingland, Lowestoft, Suffolk NR33 7SD
T: (01223) 576874 / 07952 779046 **E:** karenfoster251@yahoo.co.uk

Units	1
Sleeps	4

PER UNIT PER WEEK
£198.00 - £360.00

Holiday Bungalow in quiet village location, a very quick walk away from the beach. In Kessingland near Lowestoft, Southwold and Broads. Short breaks available. Guide dogs accepted, no pets. Great for walkers, cyclists and bird watchers, the property is located alongside the Suffolk Coastal Path. Buses run regularly to Southworld, Lowesoft and Great Yarmouth. 2 bedrooms, one double bed and an adult bunk bed. **Open:** 1st March - 4th January
Nearest Shop: 1.5 miles **Nearest Pub:** 0.5 miles

Site: ❋ **P Payment:** € **Leisure:** 🚴 🎵 ▶ ⛳ **Property:** 🖼 **Children:** 👶 **Unit:** 🛏 📺 📺 📀

MIDDLETON, Suffolk   Map ref 3C2

The Cottage at Red Lodge Barn

Contact: Mrs Patricia Dowding, Owner, Red Lodge Barn, Middleton Moor, Saxmundham IP17 3LN **T:** (01728) 668100 / 07977 196156 **E:** pat_roy16@hotmail.com
W: www.redlodgebarnsuffolk.co.uk **£ BOOK ONLINE**

Units   1
Sleeps   2-4

PER UNIT PER WEEK
£360.00 - £530.00

SPECIAL PROMOTIONS
W/E & weekday short breaks (excl school holidays) min 3 nights.

Spacious, well-equipped accommodation, in acre of grounds. Large, freshwater pond frequented by many birds. Sleeps 4. This delightful cottage has a good-sized kitchen, large lounge/diner, one double bedroom and one twin room. Bathroom has separate shower as well as bath & bidet. Full central heating and wood-burning stove.

There are many places of interest nearby including RSPB Minsmere, Aldeburgh, Walberswick, Dunwich, Southwold, Framlingham. Five miles from Heritage Coast. Many walks close by to enjoy the countryside, heaths and forests.

Open: All year except Christmas
Nearest Shop: 1 mile
Nearest Pub: 1 mile

Units: Part of a barn conversion, the cottage is on two floors. Both bedrooms upstairs together with the bathroom.

Site: ❀ **P Payment:** € **Leisure:** 🐾 🥾 ▶ ∪ **Property:** ▣ 🖥 **Children:** 🐥5 🛏 🏃
Unit: 🗂 🍽 📺 🎍 📺 🎧 🎧 ⬛

PIN MILL, Suffolk   Map ref 3C2

Alma Cottage

Contact: Mr John Pugh, Alma Cottage, Culver End, Amberley, Stroud GL5 5AG
T: (01453) 872551 **E:** john.pugh@talk21.com

Units   1
Sleeps   1-4
PER UNIT PER WEEK
£260.00 - £450.00

In centre of Pin Mill, 25m from high water, views over Orwell Estuary. A traditional sailing village, free public access to water, ideal for families, walkers, birdwatchers and painters. **Open:** All year
Nearest Shop: 0.75 miles **Nearest Pub:** 0.10 miles

Site: ❀ **P Payment:** € **Leisure:** 🥾 **Property:** 🐕 🖥 ▣ 🖥 **Children:** 🐥 🏃 **Unit:** 🗂 📺 🍽 🎍 📺 🎧 ⬛
🎧 📞

SAXMUNDHAM, Suffolk   Map ref 3C2

Buff's Old Barn

Contact: Jeannie Wright, Owner / Managing Director, Woodside Barn Cottages, Buffs Old Barn, Woodside Farm, Church Road, Friston, Saxmundham, Suffolk IP17 1PU
T: (08452) 680785 / 07899 891498 **E:** jeannie@woodsidebarncottages.co.uk
W: www.woodsidebarncottages.co.uk **£ BOOK ONLINE**

Units   1
Sleeps   6
PER UNIT PER WEEK
£523.00 - £1181.00

This converted barn's design makes it great for families to enjoy a relaxing holiday close to the Suffolk Coast. A delightful location on the owner's 32-acre working farm. Own enclosed private garden area, direct access to public footpaths. Located in the pretty village of Friston, a short drive from the coastal delights of Aldeburgh & Southwold. **Open:** All year including Christmas & New Year.
Nearest Shop: 3 Miles **Nearest Pub:** 3 Miles

Site: ❀ **P Payment:** 🖃 **Leisure:** ▶ **Property:** 🐕 🖥 ▣ 🖥 **Children:** 🐥1 🛏 🏃 **Unit:** 🗂 🍽 📺 🍽 🎍 📺 🎧 ⬛

SAXMUNDHAM, Suffolk   Map ref 3C2

Saxmundham Cottages

Contact: Bookings, All Seasons Cottage Breaks, North Road, Brentwood, Essex CM14 4UZ
T: (01277) 210551 / 07860 887653 **E:** info@allseasonscottagebreaks.com
W: www.allseasonscottagebreaks.com

Units   2
Sleeps   1-8

PER UNIT PER WEEK
£365.00 - £675.00

SPECIAL PROMOTIONS
Mid-Week Breaks offer: 4-nights Mid-Week for the same price as 3-nights at Weekends. Ring or visit our website for prices, current seasonal offers/promotions. Gift Vouchers available.

Charming period holiday cottages in historic market-town close to Aldeburgh, on the unspoilt Suffolk Heritage coast. Both cottages are single-storey and fully equipped for an enjoyable stay - a real 'Home from Home' on holiday! Ideal touring base to explore all that Suffolk has to offer - there's so much to see and do. Most popular attractions within 30 mins drive, incl: Southwold, Woodbridge, Orford, Thorpeness, Snape, etc. Ideal for walkers, birdwatching, or just a relaxing break to enjoy the peaceful location and excellent local food. Just as popular for winter breaks - lovely log-fires!

Open: All year - including Christmas & New Year
Nearest Shop: 0.10 miles
Nearest Pub: 0.10 miles

Units: Ground floor bedrooms & bathrooms. Baths with showers, Central Heating, log-burners. Parking outside/adjacent (on-street).

Site: **Payment:** **Leisure:** **Property:** **Children:**
Unit:

Sign up for our newsletter

Visit our website to sign up for our e-newsletter and receive regular information on events, exclusive competitions and new publications.

www.visitor-guides.co.uk

SOMERTON, *Suffolk* *Map ref 3B2*

Cartlodge & Granary

Contact: Mrs Sarah Worboys, Cartlodge & Granary, Worboys Farm Partners, Francis Farm, Upper Somerton, Nr. Bury St Edmunds, Suffolk IP29 4BF **T:** (01284) 789241
F: 01284 789241 **E:** enquiries@francisfarmcottages.co.uk **W:** francisfarmcottages.co.uk

Units   2
Sleeps   2-4

PER UNIT PER WEEK
£240.00 - £480.00

SPECIAL PROMOTIONS
We also have 3 and 4 night breaks throughout the year, subject to availability. Please phone for prices.

Taking the name of, and built on, land once owned by French Benedictine Monks as far back as 1198, these sympathetically restored farm buildings offer accommodation with a great deal of character. Set amidst rolling countryside, it is a working farm producing cereals. Cottages sleep 2/4. (If using Sat Nav put in IP29 4ND and carry on down our lane.)

Open: All year
Nearest Shop: 5 miles
Nearest Pub: 2 miles

Units: An original Granary and Cartlodge converted to a high 4* standard. The Cartlodge and Granary are powered by Solar Panels to help the environment.

Site: ✿ P Payment: 💷 Property: 📶 Unit: 📺 ▣ ▤ ◵ TV DVD

SOUTHWOLD, *Suffolk* *Map ref 3C2*

Field View

Contact: Bernie & Paula Burns, Owners, Norfolk Road, Wangford, Suffolk NR34 8RE
T: (01788) 536446 **E:** paula@alexburns.co.uk
W: www.cottageguide.co.uk/fieldview

Units   1
Sleeps   4-5
PER UNIT PER WEEK
£335.00 - £540.00

Cosy centrally heated bungalow in quiet village of Wangford - 3.5 miles from Southwold . Two double bedrooms - Sleeps 4/5. Beds made up ready for guests and towels provided. Kitchen has washing machine, cooker and microwave oven. Off road enclosed parking. Sunny patio and enclosed grass garden overlooking fields and Reydon Woods. Unlimited free Wi-Fi. Village store and pubs close by. **Open:** All year **Nearest Shop:** 1 mile **Nearest Pub:** 1 mile

Site: ✿ P Property: 📶 ▣ 📶 Children: 🚼 Unit: ▣ ▤ TV DVD

SOUTHWOLD, Suffolk   Map ref 3C2

Units   1
Sleeps   2-4

PER UNIT PER WEEK
£360.00 - £590.00

SPECIAL PROMOTIONS
3 night weekend breaks and 4 night weekday breaks available. Discount of 5% offered for party of 2 people only, using one bedroom only, if booking a full week.

Highsteppers at Blythview

Contact: Patricia Dowding, Owner, Highsteppers Holidays, Red Lodge Barn, Middleton Moor, Saxmundham, Suffolk IP17 3LN **T:** (01728) 668100 / 07977 196156
E: pat_roy16@hotmail.com **W:** www.highsteppers-suffolk.co.uk **£ BOOK ONLINE**

Highsteppers is a 2 storey apartment on the 1st and 2nd floors situated within a converted Georgian Grade II listed building. Once a Workhouse but now an established and an ongoing development. It also has the benefit of a shared indoor swimming pool, games room and mini-gym. Fully equipped kitchen, good sized lounge and diner on first floor. Two double bedrooms, one en suite and one separate bathroom.

Less than 10 miles from RSPB Minsmere as featured on Springwatch. Stunning views over the Blyth Valley and only 5 miles from Southwold.

Open: All year
Nearest Shop: 1 mile
Nearest Pub: 1 mile

Units: A beautifully appointed apartment with stunning views over the Blyth Valley. There are 2 double bedrooms, one with shower room and en suite.

Site: P Leisure: 🏊 ♪ ▶ ∪ ♣ ☂ Property: 🖥 Children: 🐾 🛏 🚶 Unit: 🍳 🍽 📺 📷 💷

THORPENESS, Suffolk   Map ref 3C2

Units   1
Sleeps   12
PER UNIT PER WEEK
£2165.00 - £3235.00

House In The Clouds

Contact: Mrs Sylvia Le Comber, House In The Clouds, 4 Hinde House, 14 Hinde Street, London W1U 3BG **T:** 020 7224 3615 **F:** 020 7224 3615
E: houseintheclouds@btopenworld.com **W:** houseintheclouds.co.uk **£ BOOK ONLINE**

Wonderfully-eccentric 'fantasy unmatched in England'. Five bedrooms, three bathrooms, unrivalled views from 'Room at the Top'. Billiards, snooker, table tennis, tennis, boules, bird watching. Sea, golf, Meare, music and walks. **Open:** All year
Nearest Shop: 0.30 miles **Nearest Pub:** 0.30 miles

Site: ❀ P Leisure: 🏊 ♪ ▶ ∪ ♣ ☂ Property: 🐕 🖥 Children: 🐾 🛏 🚶 Unit: 🍳 🍽 📺 📷 💷 BBQ ☎

WICKHAM MARKET, Suffolk   Map ref 3C2

Sleeps   2-4
PER UNIT PER WEEK
£250.00 - £385.00

Sampsons Mill

Contact: Miss Jo Turner, Booking Enquiries, Sampson's Mill, c/o Mill House, 21 Mill Lane, Wickham Market, Suffolk IP13 0SF **T:** (01728) 885138 **E:** enquires@sampsonsmill.co.uk

Close to heritage coast, cosy unique property, personally maintained by the owner. Down quiet country lane with views over surrounding countryside. Short walk to village shops/church. Ideal place to relax. **Open:** All year **Nearest Shop:** 0.5 miles
Nearest Pub: 1.5 miles

Site: ❀ P Property: 🖥 Unit: 📺 📷 BBQ

WOODBRIDGE, Suffolk   Map ref 3C2

Units   5
Sleeps   2-5

PER UNIT PER WEEK
£285.00 - £665.00

Ore Valley Holiday Cottages

Contact: Justine Howe, Booking administrator, Sink Farm, Little Glemham, Woodbridge, Suffolk IP13 0BJ **T:** (01728) 602783 / 07796 148220 **E:** cottages@fridaystfarm.co.uk
W: www.orevalleyholidaycottages.co.uk **£ BOOK ONLINE**

The Ore Valley Holiday Cottages are set amidst the rural Suffolk countryside. Just a short drive away from Suffolk's Heritage Coast, these five converted farm stables offer a 4 star self-catering stay for the keen explorer. All of the cottages give you the chance to take in a piece of the breathtaking views that make Suffolk the perfect getaway. **Open:** All year **Nearest Shop:** 3 miles
Nearest Pub: 1 mile

Site: ✿ P **Payment:** 💳 **Leisure:** 🎣 **Property:** ✓ 🐴 ⬛ 📖 🖥 **Children:** 🐴 🛏 🎠 **Unit:** 🗄 📧 📺 🖥 🌾 📺 📀 BBQ

WORTHAM, Suffolk   Map ref 3B2

Units   3
Sleeps   4-11

PER UNIT PER WEEK
£360.00 - £1985.00

SPECIAL PROMOTIONS
Short breaks available: please contact for details.

Ivy House Farm

Contact: Mr Paul Bradley, Owner, Ivy House Farm Cottages, Long Green, Wortham, Diss, Norfolk IP22 1RD **T:** (01379) 898395 **E:** prjsbrad@aol.com
W: www.ivyhousefarmcottages.co.uk **£ BOOK ONLINE**

This peaceful complex standing in spacious gardens is surrounded by common land in the heart of East Anglia. Consists of a 17th century farmhouse and two purpose-built cottages, one has facilities for the disabled. Indoor heated swimming pool, cosy barn with table tennis, pool table & piano. Snooker room and library. Bicycles to loan. Horse riding available. Masseurs onsite. No smoking. Owners on site.

Open: All year
Nearest Shop: 0.5 miles
Nearest Pub: 0.5 miles

Units: Farm house - sleeps 11, Owl Cottage (Mobility 2) - sleeps 7, Suffolk Punch - sleeps 4.

Site: ✿ P **Payment:** 💳 € **Leisure:** ♿ 🎵 ▶ ∪ 🎣 🎿 **Property:** 🐴 ⬛ 📖 🖥 **Children:** 🐴 🛏 🎠
Unit: 🗄 📧 📺 🖥 🌾 📺 📀 🍴 BBQ

YOXFORD, Suffolk   Map ref 3C2

Units   1
Sleeps   4

PER UNIT PER WEEK
£360.00 - £460.00

Rookery Park

Contact: Gemma Minter, Rookery Park LLC, Yoxford, Saxmundham, Suffolk IP17 3LQ
T: (01728) 668310 / 07984 864694 **E:** gemma@rookerypark.org
W: www.rookerypark.org

Attractively converted building. Ground floor open plan, downstairs bathroom, a twin and double bedroom upstairs. Stands alone, situated on a country estate. Convenient for the exploration of the beautiful Suffolk and Norfolk coast, as well as Yoxford itself offering a variety of restaurants/pubs and shops. **Open:** All year
Nearest Shop: 0.5 miles **Nearest Pub:** 0.5 miles

Site: ✿ P **Leisure:** ▶ **Property:** ⬛ 🖥 **Children:** 🐴 **Unit:** 🗄 📧 📺 🖥 🌾 📺 🔊 📀

So much to see, so little time – how do you choose?

Make the most of your leisure time; look for attractions with the Quality Marque.

VisitEngland operates the Visitor Attraction Quality Assurance Scheme.

Annual assessments by trained impartial assessors test all aspects of the customer experience so you can visit with confidence.

For ideas and inspiration go to www.visitengland.com

Don't Miss...

Burghley House

Stamford, Lincolnshire PE9 3JY
(01780) 752451
www.burghley.co.uk

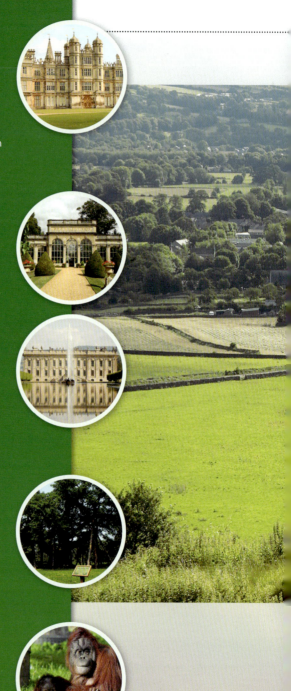

Used in films Pride and Prejudice and The Da Vinci Code, the house boasts eighteen magnificent State Rooms and a huge collection of works and art, including one of the most important private collections of 17th century Italian paintings, the earliest inventoried collection of Japanese ceramics in the West and wood carvings by Grinling Gibbons and his followers.

Castle Ashby Gardens

Northamptonshire NN7 1LQ
(01604) 695200
www.castleashbygardens.co.uk

A haven of tranquility and beauty in the heart of Northamptonshire. Take your time to explore these beautiful gardens and enjoy fascinating attractions, from the rare breed farmyard to the historic orangery.

Chatsworth

Bakewell, Derbyshire DE45 1PP
(01246) 565300
www.chatsworth.org

Chatsworth is a spectacular historic house set in the heart of the Peak District in Derbyshire, on the banks of the river Derwent. There are over 30 rooms to explore, including the magnificent Painted Hall and Sculpture Gallery. In the garden, discover water features, giant sculptures and beautiful flowers set in one of Britain's most well-known historic landscapes.

Sherwood Forest

Sherwood Forest Visitor Centre,
Edwinstowe, Nottinghamshire NG21 9HN
www.nottinghamshire.gov.uk

Once part of a royal hunting forest and legendary home of Robin Hood, Sherwood Forest National Nature Reserve covers 450 acres of ancient woodlands where veteran oaks over 500 years old grow, as well as being home to a wide variety of flora and fauna.

Twycross Zoo

Hinckley, Leicestershire CV9 3PX
(01827) 880250
http://twycrosszoo.org

Set in more than 80 acres and renowned as a World Primate Centre, Twycross Zoo has around 500 animals of almost 150 species, including many endangered animals and native species in the Zoo's Nature Reserve. Pay a visit to meet the famous orangutans, gorillas and chimpanzees plus many other mammals, birds and reptiles.

East Midlands

Derbyshire, Leicestershire, Lincolnshire, Northamptonshire, Nottinghamshire, Rutland

Derbyshire
Lincolnshire
Nottinghamshire
Rutland
Leicestershire
Northamptonshire

The East Midlands is a region of historic castles and cathedrals, lavish houses, underground caves, a rich industrial heritage and spectacular countryside including the Peak District and the Lincolnshire Wolds. Climb to enchanting hilltop castles for breathtaking views. Explore medieval ruins and battlefields. Discover hidden walks in ancient forests, cycle across hills and wolds, or visit one of the regions many events and attractions.

Explore – East Midlands

Derbyshire

'There is no finer county in England than Derbyshire. To sit in the shade on a fine day and look upon verdure is the most perfect refreshment' according to Jane Austen. Derbyshire is the home of the UK's first National Park, the Peak District, which has been popular with holidaymakers for centuries. It forms the beginning of the Pennine Chain and its reservoirs and hills are second to none in beauty. This is excellent walking, riding and cycling country and contains plenty of visitor attractions and historic sites such as Gullivers Theme Park at Matlock Bath and the 17th century Palladian Chatsworth, seat of the Duke of Devonshire.

Hotspot: Speedwell Cavern and Peak District Cavern offer the chance for amazing adventures in the heart of the Peak District, with unusual rock formations, the largest natural cave entrance in the British Isles and an incredible underground boat trip. www.speedwellcavern.co.uk

Hotspot: There's plenty to keep everyone entertained at Rutland Water, with a huge range of watersports, fantastic fishing, an outdoor adventure centre and nature reserves teeming with wildlife. www.rutlandwater.org.uk

Leicestershire & Rutland

Leicester is a cathedral city with a 2000-year history, now host to a modern university and the county's pastures fuel one of its main exports: cheese. Foxton Locks is the largest flight of staircase locks on the English canal system with two 'staircases' of five locks bustling with narrowboats. Belvoir Castle in the east dominates its vale. Rockingham Castle at Market Harborough was built by William the Conqueror and stands on the edge of an escarpment giving dramatic views over five counties and the Welland Valley below. Quietly nestling in the English countryside, England's smallest county of Rutland is an idyllic rural destination with an array of unspoilt villages and two charming market towns, packed with rich history and character.

Lincolnshire

Lincolnshire is said to produce one eighth of Britain's food and its wide open meadows are testament to this. Gothic triple-towered Lincoln Cathedral is visible from the Fens for miles around, while Burghley House hosts the famous annual Horse Trials and is a top tourist attraction. The Lincolnshire Wolds, a range of hills designated an Area of Outstanding Natural Beauty and the highest area of land in eastern England between Yorkshire and Kent, is idyllic walking and cycling country

Northamptonshire

County town Northampton is famous for its shoe making, celebrated in the Central Museum and Art Gallery, and the county also has its share of stately homes and historic battlefields. Silverstone in the south is home to the British Grand Prix. Althorp was the birthplace and is now the resting place of the late Diana Princess of Wales.

Nottinghamshire

Nottingham's castle dates from 1674 and its Lace Centre illustrates the source of much of the city's wealth, alongside other fine examples of Nottinghamshire's architectural heritage such as Papplewick Hall & Gardens. Legendary tales of Robin Hood, Sherwood Forest and historic battles may be what the county is best known for, but it also hosts world class sporting events, live performances and cutting edge art, and there's plenty of shopping and fine dining on offer too. To the north, the remains of Sherwood Forest provide a welcome breathing space and there are plenty of country parks and nature reserves, including the beautiful lakes and landscape of the National Trust's Clumber Park.

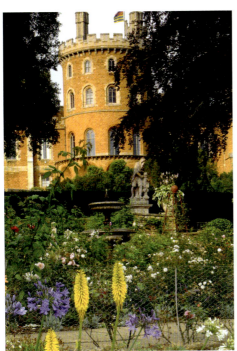

Dine in style with a four-course lunch aboard one of the **Great Central Railway**'s First Class Restaurant Cars as a steam locomotive takes you on a leisurely journey through the Charnwood's glorious countryside. A pause on Swithland viaduct takes in the magnificent view across the reservoir to Charnwood Forest. www.gcrailway.co.uk

Enjoy a Champagne Sunset hot air balloon flight over the Peak District and the Derbyshire Dales with **Ladybird Balloons**, based in the Vale of Belvoir near Belvoir Castle and Langar Hall. (01949) 877566 or visit www.ladybirdballoons.co.uk

Indulge in lunch or a sumptuous afternoon tea at **The Dining Room at 78 Derngate** in Northampton, the beautifully restored house remodelled by the world-famous designer and architect, Charles Rennie Mackintosh in his iconic Modernist style. www.78derngate.org.uk / www.thediningroom.org

Stamford Cheese Cellar has a mouth-watering range of artisan cheeses, chutneys, jams, crackers, pâtés and sundries to tantalise your taste buds. Treat yourself to a couple of chunks of something delicious for lunch, or even a luxury hamper and a nice bottle from their selection of specialist drinks upstairs at 17 St Mary's Street, Stamford. www.stamfordcheese.com

A stone's throw from Nottingham railway station, cool and quirky **Hopkinson** is three eclectic floors of art, antiques, vintage clothes, and collectibles with a café and tea bar offering a staggering twenty-one varieties of tea. A paradise for treasure seekers, vintage lovers and curators of beautiful home aesthetics, it is housed in a restored historic building that is also home to local artists, designers and makers. www.hopkinson21.co.uk

Attractions with this sign participate in the Visitor Attraction Quality Assurance Scheme.

Derbyshire

Buxton Festival
July, Buxton, Derbyshire
www.buxtonfestival.co.uk
A summer celebration of the best opera, music and literature, at the heart of the beautiful Peak District.

Creswell Crags
Chesterfield, Derbyshire S80 3LH
(01909) 720378
www.creswell-crags.org.uk
A world famous archaeological site, home to Britain's only known Ice Age cave art.

Derby Museum and Art Gallery
Derby DE1 1BS
(01332) 716659
www.derbymuseums.org
Derby Museum and Art Gallery holds collections and displays relating to the history, culture and natural environment of Derby and its region.

Derbyshire Food & Drink Festival
May, Derby, Derbyshire
www.derbyshirefoodfestival.co.uk
Over 150 stalls will showcase the best local produce from Derbyshire and the Peak District region, as well as unique and exotic foods from further afield.

Gulliver's Kingdom Theme Park
Matlock Bath, Derbyshire DE4 3PG
(01629) 580540
www.gulliversfun.co.uk
With more than 40 rides & attractions, Gulliver's provides the complete family entertainment experience. Fun & adventure with Gully Mouse, Dora the explorer, Diego and "The Lost World".

Haddon Hall
Bakewell, Derbyshire DE45 1LA
(01629) 812855
www.haddonhall.co.uk
Haddon Hall is a stunning English Tudor and country house on the River Wye at Bakewell in Derbyshire, Haddon Hall is one of England's finest examples of a medieval manor.

Hardwick Hall
Chesterfield, Derbyshire S44 5QJ
(01246) 850430
www.nationaltrust.org.uk/hardwick
Owned by the National Trust, Hardwick Hall is one of Britain's greatest Elizabethan houses. The water-powered Stainsby Mill is fully functioning and the Park has a fishing lake and circular walks.

Renishaw Hall and Gardens
Dronfield, Derbyshire S21 3WB
(01246) 432310
www.renishaw-hall.co.uk
The Gardens are Italian in design and were laid out over 100 years ago by Sir George Sitwell. The garden is divided into 'rooms' with yew hedges, flanked with classical statues.

Kedleston Hall
Derby DE22 5JH
(01332) 842191
www.nationaltrust.org.uk/main/w-kedlestonhall
A fine example of a neo-classical mansion built between 1759-65 by the architect Robert Adam and set in over 800 acres of parkland and landscaped pleasure grounds. Administered by The National Trust.

The Silk Mill - Museum of Industry and History
Derby DE1 3AF
(01332) 255308
www.derbymuseums.org
The Silk Mill was completed around 1723 and the re-built Mill now contains displays on local history and industry.

Sudbury Hall
Ashbourne, Derbyshire DE6 5HT
(01283) 585305
www.nationaltrust.org.uk/sudburyhall/
Explore the grand 17th Century hall with its richly decorated interior and see life below stairs.

Leicestershire & Rutland

Artisan Cheese Fair
May, Melton Mowbray, Leicestershire
www.artisancheesefair.co.uk
A chance to taste the huge range of cheeses that are made locally and further afield.

Ashby-de-la-Zouch Castle
Leicestershire LE65 1BR
(01530) 413343
www.english-heritage.org.uk/daysout/properties/
ashby-de-la-zouch-castle
Visit Ashby-de-la-Zouch Castle where you will see the ruins of this historical castle, the original setting for many of the scenes of Sir Walter Scott's classic tale 'Ivanhoe'.

Bosworth Battlefield Heritage Centre
Market Bosworth, Leicestershire CV13 0AD
(01455) 290429
www.bosworthbattlefield.com
Delve into Leicestershire's fascinating history at Bosworth Battlefield Country Park - the site of the 1485 Battle of Bosworth.

Conkers Discovery Centre
Ashby-de-la-Zouch, Leicestershire DE12 6GA
(01283) 216633
www.visitconkers.com/thingstodo/discoverycentre
Enjoy the great outdoors and explore over 120 acres of the award winning parkland.

Easter Vintage Festival
April, Great Central Railway, Leicestershire
www.gcrailway.co.uk
A real treat for all this Easter with traction engines, classic cars and buses, fairground rides, trade stands, a beer tent as well as lots of action on the double track.

Great Central Railway
Leicester LE11 1RW
(01509) 230726
www.gcrailway.co.uk
The Great Central Railway is Britain's only double track main line steam railway. Enjoy an exciting calendar of events, a footplate ride or dine in style on board one of the steam trains.

National Space Centre

Leicester LE4 5NS
(0845) 605 2001
www.spacecentre.co.uk
The award winning National Space Centre is the UK's largest attraction dedicated to space. From the moment you catch sight of the Space Centre's futuristic Rocket Tower, you'll be treated to hours of breathtaking discovery & interactive fun.

Twinlakes Theme Park
Melton Mowbray, Leicestershire LE14 4SB
(01664) 567777
www.twinlakespark.co.uk
Twinlakes Theme Park - packed with variety, fun and endless adventures for every member of your family.

Lincolnshire

Ayscoughfee Hall Museum and Gardens
Spalding, Lincolnshire PE11 2RA
(01775) 764555
www.ayscoughfee.org
Ayscoughfee Hall Museum is housed in a beautiful wool merchant's house built in 1451 on the banks of the River Welland.

Belton House
Belton, Lincolnshire NG32 2LS
(01476) 566116
www.nationaltrust.org.uk/main/w-beltonhouse
Belton, is a perfect example of an English Country House.

Burghley Horse Trials
September, Burghley House, Lincolnshire
www.burghley-horse.co.uk
*One of the most popular events in the British
equestrian calendar.*

Doddington Hall
Lincoln LN6 4RU
(01522) 694308
www.doddingtonhall.com
*A superb Elizabethan mansion by the renowned
architect Robert Smythson. The hall stands today as
it was completed in 1600 with walled courtyards,
turrets and gatehouse.*

Hardys Animal Farm
Ingoldmells, Lincolnshire PE25 1LZ
(01754) 872267
www.hardysanimalfarm.co.uk
*An enjoyable way to learn about the countryside and
how a farm works. There are animals for the children
to enjoy as well as learning about the history and
traditions of the countryside.*

Lincolnshire Show
June, Lincolnshire Showground
www.lincolnshireshow.co.uk
*Agriculture remains at the
heart of the Lincolnshire Show
with livestock and equine
competitions, machinery displays
and the opportunity to find out
where your food comes from and to
taste it too!*

Lincolnshire Wolds Walking Festival
May, Louth, Lincolnshire
www.woldswalkingfestival.co.uk
*Over 90 walks, taking place in an Area of Outstanding
Natural Beauty and surrounding countryside.*

Normanby Hall Museum and Country Park
Scunthorpe, Lincolnshire DN15 9HU
(01724) 720588
www.normanbyhall.co.uk
*Normanby Hall is a classic English mansion set in
300 acres of gardens, parkland, deer park, woods,
ornamental and wild birds, with a well-stocked
gift shop.*

RAF Waddington Air Show
July, Waddington, Lincoln, Lincolnshire
www.waddingtonairshow.co.uk
*The largest of all RAF air shows, regularly attended by
over 150,000 visitors.*

Tattershall Castle
Lincolnshire LN4 4LR
(01526) 342543
www.nationaltrust.org.uk/tattershall-castle
*Tattershall Castle was built in the 15th Century to
impress and dominate by Ralph Cromwell, one of
the most powerful men in England. The castle is a
dramatic red brick tower.*

Northamptonshire

Althorp
Northampton NN7 4HQ
(01604) 770107
www.althorp.com
Come and visit one of England's finest country houses, home of the Spencer family for over 500 years and ancestral home of Diana, Princess of Wales.

British Grand Prix
July, Silverstone, Northamptonshire
www.silverstone.co.uk
The only place in the UK to see the world's best Formula One drivers in action.

Lamport Hall and Gardens
Northamptonshire NN6 9HD
(01604) 686272
www.lamporthall.co.uk
Grade 1 listed building that was home to the Isham family and their collections for over four centuries.

National Waterways Museum - Stoke Bruerne
Towcester, Northamptonshire NN12 7SE
(01604) 862229
www.stokebruernecanalmuseum.org.uk
Stoke Bruerne is an ideal place to explore the story of our waterways.

Northampton Museum & Art Gallery
Northampton NN1 1DP
(01604) 838111
www.northampton.gov.uk/museums
Displays include footwear and related items, paintings, ceramics and glass and the history of Northampton.

Prebendal Manor Medieval Centre
Nassington, Northamptonshire PE8 6QG
(01780) 782575
www.prebendal-manor.co.uk
Visit a unique medieval manor and enjoy the largest recreated medieval gardens in Europe.

Rockingham Castle
Market Harborough, Northamptonshire LE16 8TH
(01536) 770240
www.rockinghamcastle.com
Rockingham Castle stands on the edge of an escarpment giving dramatic views over five counties and the Welland Valley below.

Salcey Forest
Hartwell, Northamptonshire NN17 3BB
(01780) 444920
www.forestry.gov.uk/salceyforest
Get a birds eye view of this wonderful woodland on the tremendous Tree Top Way.

Sulgrave Manor
Northamptonshire OX17 2SD
(01295) 760205
www.sulgravemanor.org.uk
A Tudor manor house and garden, the ancestral home of George Washington's family with authentic furniture shown by friendly guides

Wicksteed Park
Kettering, Northamptonshire NN15 6NJ
(01536) 512475
www.wicksteedpark.co.uk
Wicksteed Park remains Northamptonshire's most popular attraction and entertainment venue.

Nottinghamshire

Armed Forces Weekend
June, Wollaton Park, Nottingham, Nottinghamshire
www.experiencenottinghamshire.com
Nottingham welcomes the annual national event celebrating our Armed Forces past and present.

Festival of Words
Nottingham, Nottinghamshire
www. nottwords.org.uk
Celebrating Nottingham's love of words, this dazzling line up of events and diverse range of host venues pay a fitting tribute to Nottinghamshire's rich literary heritage.

Galleries of Justice Museum
Nottingham NG1 1HN
(0115) 952 0555
www.galleriesofjustice.org.uk
You will be delving in to the dark and disturbing past of crime and punishment.

GameCity
October, Nottingham, Nottinghamshire
www.gamecity.org
GameCity is the largest festival dedicated to the videogame culture in Europe.

Holme Pierrepont Country Park
Newark, Nottinghamshire NG24 1BG
(01636) 655765
www.newark-sherwood.gov.uk
Set in 270 acres of beautiful parkland and home to the National Watersports Centre. With excellent water sports facilities, Family Fun Park, Life Fitness Gym and marvellous nature trails for cycling and walking,

Newark Castle
Holme Pierrepont, Nottinghamshire NG12 2LU
(0115) 982 1212
www.nwscnotts.com
At the heart of the town for many centuries the castle has played an important role in historical events.

Newark Air Museum
Nottinghamshire NG24 2NY
(01636) 707170
www.newarkairmuseum.org
The museum is open to the public every day except December 24th, 25th, 26th and January 1st.

Nottingham Castle
Nottingham NG1 6EL
(0115) 915 3700
www.nottinghamcity.gov.uk/museums
Situated on a high rock, Nottingham Castle commands spectacular views over the city and once rivalled the great castles of Windsor and the Tower of London.

Nottinghamshire County Show
May, Newark Showground, Nottinghamshire
www.newarkshowground.com
A fantastic traditional county show promoting farming, food, rural life and heritage in Nottinghamshire and beyond.

Papplewick Hall & Gardens
Nottinghamshire NG15 8FE
(0115) 963 3491
www.papplewickhall.co.uk
A fine Adam house, built in 1787 and Grade I listed building with a park and woodland garden.

Robin Hood Beer Festival
October, Nottingham Castle, Nottinghamshire
www.beerfestival.nottinghamcamra.org
Set in the stunning grounds of Nottingham Castle, the Robin Hood Beer Festival offers the world's largest selection of real ales and ciders.

Robin Hood Festival
August, Sherwood Forest, Nottinghamshire
www.nottinghamshire.gov.uk/robinhoodfestival
Celebrate our most legendary outlaw in Sherwood Forest's medieval village.

Sherwood Forest Country Park
Nottinghamshire NG21 9HN
(01623) 823202
www.nottinghamshire.gov.uk/sherwoodforestcp
Sherwood Forest Country Park covers 450 acres and incorporates some truly ancient areas of native woodland.

Sherwood Forest Farm Park
Nottinghamshire NG21 9HL
(01623) 823558
www.sherwoodforestfarmpark.co.uk
Meet over 30 different rare farm breeds, plus other unusual species!

Sherwood Pines Forest Park
Edwinstowe, Nottinghamshire NG21 9JL
(01623) 822447
www.forestry.gov.uk/sherwoodpines
The largest forest open to the public in the East Midlands and centre for a wide variety of outdoor activities.

Tourist Information Centres

When you arrive at your destination, visit the Tourist Information Centre for quality assured help with accommodation and information about local attractions and events, or email your request before you go.

Ashbourne	13 Market Place	01335 343666	ashbourneinfo@derbyshiredales.gov.uk
Ashby-de-la-Zouch	North Street	01530 411767	ashby.tic@nwleicestershire.gov.uk
Bakewell	Old Market Hall	01629 813227	bakewell@peakdistrict.gov.uk
Boston	Boston Guildhall	01205 356656/ 720006	ticboston@boston.gov.uk
Buxton	The Pavilion Gardens	01298 25106	tourism@highpeak.gov.uk
Castleton	Buxton Road	01433 620679	castleton@peakdistrict.gov.uk
Chesterfield	Rykneld Square	01246 345777	tourism@chesterfield.gov.uk
Derby	Assembly Rooms	01332 643411	tourism@derby.gov.uk
Glossop	Glossop One Stop Shop	0845 1297777	
Grantham	The Guildhall Centre, Council Offices	01476 406166	granthamtic@southkesteven.gov.uk
Horncastle	Wharf Road	01507 601111	horncastle.info@cpbs.com
Kettering	Municipal Offices	01536 315115	tic@kettering.gov.uk
Leicester	51 Gallowtree Gate	0844 888 5181	info@goleicestershire.com
Lincoln Castle Hill	9 Castle Hill	01522 545458	visitorinformation@lincolnbig.co.uk
Loughborough	Loughborough Town Hall	01509 231914	loughborough@goleicestershire.com
Louth	Cannon Street	01507 601111	louth.info@cpbs.com
Mablethorpe	Louth Hotel, Unit 5	01507 474939	mablethorpeinfo@e-lindsey.gov.uk
Melton Mowbray	The Library, Wilton Road	0116 305 3646	
Newark	Keepers Cottage, Riverside Park	01636 655765	newarktic@nsdc.info
Northampton	Sessions House, County Hall	01604 367997/8	tic@northamptonshire.gov.uk
Nottingham City	1-4 Smithy Row	08444 775 678	tourist.information@nottinghamcity.gov.uk
Retford	40 Grove Street	01777 860780	retford.tourist@bassetlaw.gov.uk
Rutland Water	Sykes Lane	01780 686800	tic@anglianwater.co.uk
Sherwood	Sherwood Heath	01623 824545	sherwoodtic@nsdc.info
Silverstone	Silverstone Circuit	0844 3728 200	Elicia.Bonamy@silverstone.co.uk
Spalding	South Holland Centre	01775 725468/ 764777	touristinformationcentre@sholland.gov.uk
Stamford	Stamford Tourist Information	01780 755611	stamfordtic@southkesteven.gov.uk
Swadlincote	Sharpe's Pottery Museum	01283 222848	gail.archer@sharpespotterymusuem.org.uk
Woodhall Spa	The Cottage Museum	01526 353775	woodhall.spainfo@cpbs.com

Regional Contacts and Information

For more information on accommodation, attractions, activities, events and holidays in the East Midlands, contact one of the following regional or local tourism organisations. Their websites have a wealth of information and many produce free publications to help you get the most out of your visit.

East Midlands Tourism
www.eastmidlandstourism.com

Experience Nottinghamshire
www.experiencenottinghamshire.com

Peak District and Derbyshire
www.visitpeakdistrict.com

Discover Rutland
(01572) 722577
www.discover-rutland.co.uk

Lincolnshire
(01522) 545458
www.visitlincolnshire.com

VisitNorthamptonshire
www.visitnorthamptonshire.co.uk

Leicestershire
0844 888 5181
www.goleicestershire.com

Stay - East Midlands

Entries appear alphabetically by town name in each county. A key to symbols appears on page 7

ASHBOURNE, Derbyshire   Map ref 4B2

Paddock House Farm Holiday Cottages

Contact: Mark Redfern, Paddock House Farm Holiday Cottages, Paddock House Farm, Alstonefield, Ashbourne, Derbyshire DE6 2FT **T:** (01335) 310282 / 07977 569618
E: info@paddockhousefarm.co.uk **W:** www.paddockhousefarm.co.uk **£ BOOK ONLINE**

Units	6
Sleeps	2-40

PER UNIT PER WEEK
£125.00 - £881.00

Luxury Derbyshire holiday cottages in the Peak District National Park. Wonderful views of the open countryside in a very peaceful location. 1, 2 and 3 bedroom available. Many excellent local attractions, near Alton Towers, Chatsworth House, Dovedale, Tissington Trail. Twitter @paddockcottages, www.facebook.com/paddockhousefarm. **Open:** All year **Nearest Shop:** 1.5 miles **Nearest Pub:** 1.5 miles

Site: ✿ P **Payment:** ▦ **Leisure:** ⚴ ♪ ► ♻ ♖ **Property:** ⌖ ▭ ▣ ▨ **Children:** ⛺ ⊞ ⚘ **Unit:** ⊡ ▤ ▭ ▨ ◔ TV ⊙ ⏿ ⌁ BBQ

BUXTON, Derbyshire   Map ref 4B2

Pyegreave Cottage

Contact: Mr & Mrs N C Pollard, Pyegreave Cottage, Pyegreave Farm, Combs, High Peak SK23 9UX **T:** (01298) 813444 **F:** 01298 815381 **E:** rita.pollard@allenpollard.co.uk
W: www.pyegreavecottage.com **£ BOOK ONLINE**

Units	1
Sleeps	1-2

PER UNIT PER WEEK
£290.00 - £400.00

Character stone cottage maintained to a high standard, situated within the Peak District National Park. Spectacular views. Ideal for walking, golf, theatre, fishing, cycling and climbing. Idyllic and tranquil hideaway. **Open:** All year **Nearest Shop:** 3 miles **Nearest Pub:** 1 mile

 Site: ✿ P **Payment:** ▦ € **Leisure:** ⚴ ♪ ► ♻ **Property:** ▨ **Children:** ⛺ **Unit:** ⊡ ▤ ▭ ▨ ⌁ TV ⊙ ⏿ ☎ BBQ ☎

CASTLETON, Derbyshire   Map ref 4B2

Riding House Farm Cottages

Contact: Mrs Denise Matthews, Owner, Riding House Farm, Castleton, Hope Valley, Derbyshire S33 8WB **T:** (01433) 620257 **E:** denise@riding-house-cottages.co.uk
W: www.riding-house-cottages.co.uk **£ BOOK ONLINE**

Units	2
Sleeps	2-4

PER UNIT PER WEEK
£340.00 - £580.00

Newly converted farm cottages in the heart of the Peak District National Park. Both cottages are equipped to a very high standard, with charm, character and in a stunning location. Castleton caves and castle, Chatsworth House and Haddon Hall all nearby. **Open:** All year **Nearest Shop:** 1 mile **Nearest Pub:** 1 mile

 Site: ✿ P **Leisure:** ⚴ ♪ ► ♻ **Property:** ⌖ ▣ ▨ **Children:** ⛺ ⊞ ⚘ **Unit:** ⊡ ▤ ▭ ▨ ⌁ TV ⊙ ⏿ BBQ

CHESTERFIELD, Derbyshire   Map ref 4B2

Pottery Flat Chesterfield

Contact: Janine Mannion-Jones, Potter and Landlady, JMJ Pottery, 140 Chatsworth Road, Brampton, Chesterfield S40 2AR **T:** (01246) 555461 / 07790 949583
E: orders@jmjpottery.com **W:** thepotteryflatchesterfield.co.uk **£ BOOK ONLINE**

Units	3
Sleeps	2-5

PER UNIT PER WEEK
£400.00 - £600.00

Contemporary spacious self catering apartment, with single, double & twin bedrooms. Living/dining room, fully fitted and equipped kitchen, shower room/separate toilet. Private parking. Within walking distance of town centre on the road into the Peak District. Graded 3 star gold. **Open:** All year **Nearest Shop:** 0.20 miles **Nearest Pub:** 0.01 miles

 Site: ✿ P **Payment:** ▦ **Property:** ⌖ ▭ ▣ ▨ **Children:** ⛺ ⊞ **Unit:** ⊡ ▤ ▭ ▨ ⌁ TV ⊙

CRESSBROOK, Derbyshire   Map ref 4B2

Cressbrook Hall Self Catering Cottages

Contact: Mrs Bobby Hull-Bailey, Cressbrook Hall Self Catering Cottages, Cressbrook Hall, Cressbrook, Buxton, Derbyshire SK17 8SY **T:** (01298) 871289 **F:** 01298 871845
E: stay@cressbrookhall.co.uk **W:** www.cressbrookhall.co.uk **£ BOOK ONLINE**

Accommodation with a difference! Self-catering or B&B in magnificent surroundings. Nine en suite bedrooms, underfloor heating, spectacular views. Special catering services and leisure facilities ensure a carefree holiday. Colour brochure. **Open:** All year **Nearest Shop:** 2 miles **Nearest Pub:** 1 mile

Units   3
Sleeps   1-18
PER UNIT PER WEEK
£395.00 - £925.00

Site: ❀ P Payment: 💷 Property: 🐕 📷 💻 Children: 🪑 🛏 🚶 Unit: 📷 💻 📺

HARTINGTON, Derbyshire   Map ref 4B2

1 Staley Cottage

Contact: Mr Joseph Oliver, Carr Head Farm, Penistone, Sheffield S36 7GT
T: (01226) 762387

Spacious, well maintained, 3 bedrooms, double facilities, dining room, lounge, laundry room, large garden and parking. Owner maintained for 30 years to a high standard. Log fire, summer house and garden room. **Open:** All year **Nearest Shop:** 200 yards **Nearest Pub:** 200 yards

Units   2
Sleeps   6-8
PER UNIT PER WEEK
£365.00 - £590.00

Site: ❀ P Leisure: ⛏ Property: 📷 💻 Children: 🛏 🚶 Unit: 📷 📟 💻 📺 📀 🍴 BBQ 📞

HARTINGTON, Derbyshire   Map ref 4B2

Ash Tree Cottage

Contact: Mrs Clare Morson, Ash Tree Cottage, Nettletor Farm, Mill Lane, Hartington, NR Buxton SK17 0AN **T:** (01298) 84247 / 07517 220972 **E:** nettletorfarm@btconnect.com
W: www.nettletorfarm.co.uk

Single storey cottage, sleeps four and private parking for two cars. Own contained patio and garden area. Ideally located for Hartington village and picturesque walks into the dales. **Open:** All year **Nearest Shop:** 5 min walk **Nearest Pub:** 5 min walk

Units   1
Sleeps   4
PER UNIT PER WEEK
£300.00 - £500.00

Site: ❀ P Leisure: 🚴 🏌 ⛳ Property: 💻 Children: 🪑 🛏 🚶 Unit: 📷 💻 📺 🎮 📀 BBQ

HARTINGTON, Derbyshire   Map ref 4B2

Old House Farm Cottages

Contact: Sue Flower, Manager, Old House Farm Cottages, Old House Farm, Newhaven, Hartington, Derbyshire SK17 0DY **T:** (01629) 636268 / 07751 056476
E: s.flower1@virgin.net **W:** www.oldhousefarm.com **£ BOOK ONLINE**

Peak District Cottages - 4* working Dairy Farm. Piggery Place - sleeps 4, welcomes all, including those in Wheelchairs with wet floor shower room & wheel in shower chair. Shires Rest - sleeps 2. Cosy rural retreat. Beautifully renovated to blend original character with quality modern comforts. Cycle/walking track (former rail line) High Peak trail leads from the farm through stunning scenery. **Open:** All year **Nearest Shop:** 0.3 mile **Nearest Pub:** 0.3 mile

Units   2
Sleeps   2-4
PER UNIT PER WEEK
£230.00 - £495.00

Site: ❀ P Property: 🐕 🚲 📷 💻 Children: 🪑 🛏 🚶 Unit: 📷 📟 💻 📷 🍴 📺 🎮 📀

East Midlands - Derbyshire

HATHERSAGE, Derbyshire Map ref 4B2

Pat's Cottage
Contact: John & Bobbie Drakeford, 110 Townhead Road, Dore S17 3GB
T: (01142) 366014 / 07850 200711 **E:** johnmdrakeford@hotmail.com
W: www.patscottage.co.uk **£ BOOK ONLINE**

Units 1
Sleeps 4-6
PER UNIT PER WEEK
£285.00 - £455.00

An attractive 18th century stone cottage, sympathetically refurbished, retaining original features including black beams. Use of owners swimming pool included in season. On the edge of the Peak District, close to Hathersage and the city of Sheffield.
Open: All year **Nearest Shop:** 0.30 miles **Nearest Pub:** 0.30 miles

Site: ❖ P Leisure: ↑ ∪ ⚡ Property: 🐾 🖥 📺 Children: 🚼 🏠 Unit: 📷 🗑 ⚡ 📺 ◎ 📀 BBQ

MATLOCK, Derbyshire Map ref 4B2

Eagle Cottage and Swallows Nest
Contact: Mrs Mary Prince, Owner, Eagle Cottage and Swallows Nest, Haresfield House, Keeling Lane, Birchover, Nr Matlock, Derbyshire DE4 2BS **T:** (01629) 650634
E: maryprince@msn.com **W:** www.bakewellselfcatering.co.uk

Units 2
Sleeps 1-5
PER UNIT PER WEEK
£260.00 - £380.00

SPECIAL PROMOTIONS
Min. 3 days £180, £60 each extra day November to April.

Quiet end cottage in the centre of a Peak District village with two pubs. Surrounded by a network of public footpaths, stunning scenery and attractions including Chatsworth House and Haddon Hall nearby.

Cosy sitting room with log burning stove, dining kitchen, two double bedded rooms and folding bed. Telephone and Wi-Fi. Five miles from the market town of Bakewell and seven miles from Matlock, both with supermarkets. Nearest village shop two miles away. See also Swallows Nest.

Open: All year
Nearest Shop: 2 miles
Nearest Pub: 200 Yards

Units: Bathroom with shower over bath. Electric storage radiators throughout. Electricity free. Parking for one car.

Site: ❖ P Leisure: ♿ ♪ ↑ ∪ Property: 🖥 📺 Children: 🚼 Unit: 📷 🗑 📺 ⚡ 📺 ◎ 📀 📞

NETHERSEAL, Derbyshire Map ref 4B3

Sealbrook Farm
Contact: Jane Kirkland, Sealbrook Farm, Grangewood, Swadlincote DE12 8BH
T: (01827) 373236 **E:** info@sealbrookfarmcottages.co.uk
W: www.sealbrookfarmcottages.co.uk **£ BOOK ONLINE**

Units 2
Sleeps 1-12
PER UNIT PER WEEK
£309.00 - £992.00

Located in quiet hamlet. Local shops, pubs, attractions and walks. In the heart of the National Forest. Easy reach of motorway networks and airports. Private off-road parking, large lockable storage available. Wi-Fi.
Open: All year **Nearest Shop:** 2 miles **Nearest Pub:** 1.5 miles

Site: ❖ P Leisure: ♿ ♪ Property: 🖥 📺 Children: 🚼 🏠 ♿ Unit: 📷 🗑 📺 ⚡ 📺 ◎ BBQ

ASHBY-DE-LA-ZOUCH, Leicestershire   Map ref 4B3

Units 1
Sleeps 4

PER UNIT PER WEEK
£120.00 - £600.00

Forest Lodge

Contact: Janice Pearson, Owner, The Rowans, Packington, Ashby de la Zouch, Leicestershire LE65 1WU **T:** (01530) 411984 **E:** hillfarmpackington@hotmail.co.uk

Luxury rural retreat located on the outskirts of a village in The National Forest. Near historic Ashby de la Zouch, major tourist attractions, off road cycle centre and country walks. Relaxing hot tub overlooks beautiful countryside. Rare breed animals and farm shop on site selling home produce. Clay Pigeon Shooting, Champneys Health Spa resort nearby (2 miles). Golf Courses within 5 miles, 2 leisure centres within 5 miles. Pony trekking / horse riding - we can accommodate your own horse on our livery yard. Children welcome from any age. The log cabin is furnished to a high standard and includes TV and DVD player, a music centre, washing machine and dishwasher, and a fully equipped kitchen. The cabin has 2 kingsize bedrooms, 1 of which can be spilt into single beds. There are 2 bathrooms, 1 of which is en suite. Linen and towels are provided.

Open: All year
Nearest Shop: 1 mile
Nearest Pub: 1 mile

Units: 1 unit, sleeps 4. Hot Tub and horse riding on site, kitchen has all mod cons. Parking available.

Site: ❀ **P** **Leisure:** ⅍ ▶ ∪ **Property:** ⫽ ⊶ ▣ 🖳 **Children:** ⅍ **Unit:** 🗋 🗖 ▣ 🖳 🖳 📺 📀

ASHBY-DE-LA-ZOUCH, Leicestershire   Map ref 4B3

Units 1
Sleeps 2-5

PER UNIT PER WEEK
£360.00 - £550.00

Normans Barn

Contact: Mrs Isabel Stanley, Proprietor, F Stanley & Son, Ingles Hill Farm, Burton Road, Ashby-de-la-Zouch LE65 2TE **T:** (01530) 412224 **E:** isabel_stanley@hotmail.com
W: www.normansbarn.co.uk

Luxuriously appointed barn conversion incorporating minstrels' gallery. Both double bedrooms (one twin) en suite. On working farm including 130 acres of woodland walks. Easy access to M42, NEC, Calke Abbey and Castle Donington Park/Airport, Nottingham, Leicester and Derby. 1 mile from Ashby-de-la-Zouch. **Open:** All year plus Christmas and New Year **Nearest Shop:** 0.5 miles **Nearest Pub:** 0.5 miles

Site: ❀ **P** **Leisure:** ⅍ ♪ ▶ ∪ **Property:** ⊶ ▣ 🖳 **Children:** ⅍ **Unit:** 🗋 🗖 ▣ 🖳 🖳 📺 📀 📀

BARROW UPON SOAR, Leicestershire   Map ref 4C3

Units 1
Sleeps 4-6

PER UNIT PER WEEK
£400.00 - £600.00

Kingfisher Cottage

Contact: Mr David Petty, 8072 Little Britton Road, Yonges Island, South Carolina, U.S.A 29449 **T:** +1-843-889-1299 **F:** +1-843-889-1299 **E:** dvdpetty1@gmail.com

Semi-detached roadside cottage comprising two reception rooms, two bedrooms, two bathrooms and rear garden to canal. Quiet part of village, convenient for shops and transport. Friendly pub nearby. **Open:** All year **Nearest Shop:** 0.25 miles **Nearest Pub:** 0.10 miles

Site: ❀ **P** **Leisure:** ♪ ∪ **Property:** 🖳 **Children:** ⅍³ **Unit:** 🗋 🗖 ▣ 🖳 🖳 📺 📀 📀 ⌀ BBQ ☎

MARKET HARBOROUGH, Leicestershire   Map ref 4C3

4★ - 5★ SELF CATERING

Gold AWARD

Units   3
Sleeps   2-12

PER UNIT PER WEEK
£430.00 - £900.00

SPECIAL PROMOTIONS
Short breaks from
Monday to Friday or
Friday to Monday.

Foxton Locks Lodges

Contact: Laura, Director, Westleigh Farm, North Lane, Foxton, Market Harborough
LE16 7RF **T:** 07859 924395 **E:** info@foxtonlockslodges.com
W: www.foxtonlockslodges.com **£ BOOK ONLINE**

Foxton Locks Lodges comprises three log cabins located in the heart of the Midlands, each cabin is
finished to the highest of standards with each cabin having its own private hot tub. There are
uninterrupted views of the beautiful surrounding countryside from the private decking area.

The cabins have all the mod cons needed to relax and unwind with comfy beds and large en suite
bathrooms boasting standalone baths and walk in showers. The log cabins are available to rent all
year round and are the perfect alternative to holiday cottages with luxury, comfort and tranquillity
in mind.

Open: All year
Nearest Shop: 200 metres
Nearest Pub: 500 metres

Units: All on one floor, en suite bathrooms,
central heating, TV, DVD, iPod Docking, SMEG
fridge/freezer, Oven, microwave, boardgames,
maps and books.

Site: ✿ P **Payment:** 🖃 **Leisure:** ♿ **Property:** 🐕 🖳 **Children:** 🐾 🛏 **Unit:** 🗔 🗄 🖳 🖳 📶 TV dvd BBQ

MELTON MOWBRAY, Leicestershire   Map ref 4C3

★★★ SELF CATERING

Gold AWARD

Units   1
Sleeps   6

PER UNIT PER WEEK
£360.00 - £635.00

1 The Green

Contact: Lynn Lawton, Owner, 1 The Green, Muston, Nottinghamshire NG13 0FQ
T: (01483) 892940 **E:** lynnlawton@mac.com
W: www.onethegreen.co.uk

4 bedroom detached cottage with front garden and patio. Off
street parking. In quiet village in the Vale of Belvoir. Log fire, 2
single and 2 double bedrooms, bathroom, shower, downstairs
toilet, Gas Central Heating and a lockable outside store for bikes.
Open: All year **Nearest Shop:** 2 miles **Nearest Pub:** 0.6 miles

Site: ✿ P **Leisure:** ♪ ⚲ ∪ **Property:** 🐕 🖳 🗔 🖳 **Children:** 🐾 🛏 🎋 **Unit:** 🗔 🖳 🗄 TV dvd ⌇ BBQ 📞

ALFORD, Lincolnshire   Map ref 4D2

★★★★ SELF CATERING

Gold AWARD

Units   4
Sleeps   2-6

PER UNIT PER WEEK
£205.00 - £560.00

Woodthorpe Hall Country Cottages

Contact: Alford, Lincolnshire LN13 0DD **T:** (01507) 450294
E: enquiries@woodthorpehallleisure.co.uk
W: www.woodthorpehallleisure.co.uk

Cottages overlooking golf course, quiet location with all the
modern amenities. One cottage has its own sauna, wet room and
hot tub. There is fishing, golf, hairdresser/holistic salon and a
restaurant and bar with garden and aquatic centres close by.
Open: All year **Nearest Shop:** 0.20 miles **Nearest Pub:** 0.20 miles

Site: ✿ P **Payment:** 🖃 **Leisure:** ♪ ⚲ 🔍 **Property:** 🐕 🖳 🗔 🖳 **Children:** 🐾 **Unit:** 🗔 🖳 🗄 ⌇ ◉ dvd

BOSTON, Lincolnshire   Map ref 3A1

SELF CATERING ★★★★
enjoyEngland.com

Units   2
Sleeps   2-5

The Forge and The Smithy

Contact: Johanne Roberts, Chapel Road, Tumby Woodside, Boston, Lincolnshire PE22 7SP
T: (01526) 342943 **F:** 01526 345729 **E:** jbr@ageltd.co.uk
W: www.the4ge.co.uk

The Forge (sleeps 5) and the Smithy (sleeps 2) are detached self catering cottages located in rural Lincolnshire and situated within their own enclosed garden. Four Star Visit England plus awarded Highly Commended by Tastes of Lincolnshire. Both cottages are fully equipped and include bedding and towels. Please see www.the4ge.co.uk for price list. **Open:** All year
Nearest Shop: 4 miles **Nearest Pub:** 3 miles

Site: ✿ P Leisure: ♪ Property: ⊞ ⊡ Children: ⊰ ⊞ ⚶ Unit: ⊡ ⊟ ▭ ⊟ ⊗ TV DVD

BRATTLEBY, Lincolnshire   Map ref 4C2

SELF CATERING ★★★★
enjoyEngland.com

Units   1
Sleeps   2-4
PER UNIT PER WEEK
£275.00 - £475.00

The Stable

Contact: Jerry Scott, The Stable Cottage, Sunnyside, East Lane, Brattleby, Lincoln LN1 2SQ
T: (01522) 730561 **E:** jerry@lincolncottages.co.uk
W: lincolncottages.co.uk

200 year old stone and pantile cottage of character. Conservation village six miles from the historic cathedral city of Lincoln. Tastefully furnished and decorated. Cottage garden, views over open fields.
Open: All year **Nearest Shop:** 1.5 miles **Nearest Pub:** 1 mile

Site: ✿ P Payment: € Property: ⊰ ⊞ ⊡ Children: ⊰ ⊞ Unit: ⊡ ▭ ⊗ TV DVD

Need more information?

Visit our websites for detailed information, up-to-date availability and to book your accommodation online. Includes over 20,000 places to stay, all of them star rated.

www.visitor-guides.co.uk

GREAT CARLTON, *Lincolnshire*   Map ref 4D2

Willow Farm

Contact: Jim Clark, Willow Farm, Lordship Road, Great Carlton LN11 8JT
T: (01507) 338540 / 07876 482738 **E:** willowfarmfishing@gmail.com
W: www.willowfarmfishing.co.uk

Units   1
Sleeps   1-5

PER UNIT PER WEEK
£200.00 - £400.00

SPECIAL PROMOTIONS
Short breaks in low season, ring for details

A cosy bungalow set in a peaceful, rural location on the outskirts of the market town of Louth. High standard of accommodation (refurbished in 2010) comprising of 3 bedrooms, sleeping 5. Paved patio area overlooking the beautiful countryside. Fly and coarse fishing available onsite. Within easy reach of coastal resorts, golf courses, Cadwell Park, Donna Nook and Louth market town.

Open: All year
Nearest Shop: 2 miles
Nearest Pub: 2 miles

Units: Two twin rooms, one single room, lounge, kitchen/diner, shower, electric heating, washing machine/dryer, electric cooker, microwave, TV, two toilets.

Site: ✿ P Leisure: ♪ Property: ⌂ 🖼 Children: ⚲ Unit: 📺 📻 TV

HOGSTHORPE, *Lincolnshire*   Map ref 4D2

Helsey House Holiday Cottages

Contact: Elizabeth Elvidge, Joint Owner, Helsey House Holiday Cottages, Helsey House, Helsey, Hogsthorpe, Skegness PE24 5PE **T:** (01754) 872927 **E:** info@helseycottages.co.uk
W: www.helseycottages.co.uk **£ BOOK ONLINE**

Units   2
Sleeps   1-5
PER UNIT PER WEEK
£375.00 - £520.00

Situated in the private grounds of Helsey House. Each award winning cottage converted from original cattle stalls. Furnished to the highest standard. Single storey cottages with no steps. Rural location but close to quiet sandy beaches. Ample parking within the grounds. Large play area and heated outdoor pool (summer only). Special needs families, less mobile guests and pets are all welcome! **Open:** All year **Nearest Shop:** 3 miles
Nearest Pub: 3 miles

⚠ Site: ✿ P Leisure: ♪ ▶ ∪ ⚲ Property: ⌂ 🖼 📻 🖼 Children: ⚲ 🏏 ⚓ Unit: 📻 📺 🍴 TV ⓐ 📀 BBQ

INGOLDMELLS, *Lincolnshire*   Map ref 4D2

Skegness Water Leisure Park - Bungalows

Contact: Reception, Skegness Water Leisure Park, Walls Lane, Skegness PE25 1JF
T: (01754) 899400 **F:** 01754 897867 **E:** enquiries@skegnesswaterleisurepark.co.uk
W: www.skegnesswaterleisurepark.co.uk

Units   3
Sleeps   5
PER UNIT PER WEEK
£325.00 - £525.00

Recently refurbished luxury holiday bungalows just ¼ mile from award winning beaches. Sited on award winning family friendly holiday park, just 10 minutes walk from golden beaches. **Open:** 1st March - 30th November each year **Nearest Shop:** 0.10 miles
Nearest Pub: 0.10 miles

Site: ✿ P Payment: 💷 Leisure: ♪ ▶ ∪ Property: ⌂ 📻 🖼 🖼 Children: ⚲ 🏏 ⚓ Unit: 📻 📺 🍴 TV BBQ

LINCOLN, Lincolnshire Map ref 4C2

Old Vicarage Cottages

Contact: Susan Downs, Bluestone, 15 Crescent Close, Nettleham, Lincoln LN2 2SP
T: (01522) 750819 **F:** 01522 750819 **E:** susan@oldvic.net
W: www.oldvic.net

| Units | 2 |
| Sleeps | 2-4 |

PER UNIT PER WEEK
£285.00 - £440.00

Delightful stone cottages offering spacious, well equipped accommodation, free Wi-Fi. Both properties have private gardens and off road parking/garage. Located within two minutes walking distance of the centre of this attractive award winning village with shops, library, pubs which serve both lunch and evening meals, Village Green and picturesque Beckside. **Open:** All year
Nearest Shop: 0.20 miles **Nearest Pub:** 0.10 miles

Site: ✿ P Payment: 💷 Property: 📺 📷 📠 Children: 🚼 Unit: 🛁 🍳 📺 📟 🔌 📺 📀

LOUTH, Lincolnshire Map ref 4D2

Church Cottage

Contact: Pam Wallis, Biscathorpe Park, Biscathorpe, Louth, Lincolnshire LN11 9RA
T: (01507) 313203 / 07788 281419 **E:** info@churchcottagebiscathorpe.co.uk
W: www.churchcottagebiscathorpe.co.uk **£ BOOK ONLINE**

| Units | 1 |
| Sleeps | 2-6 |

PER UNIT PER WEEK
£400.00 - £750.00

Self catering luxury holiday accommodation, recently refurbished, open plan ground floor with under floor heating and sleeps 6, all bedrooms are en suite. Situated in the beautiful Lincolnshire Wolds Area of Outstanding Natural Beauty. The cottage was awarded Finalist Status at 2014 LABC Building Excellence Awards.
Open: All year **Nearest Shop:** 1 mile **Nearest Pub:** 1 mile

WALKERS FAMILIES CYCLISTS PETS Site: ✿ P Leisure: ∪ Property: 🐾 📺 📷 📠 Children: 🚼 🎮 🎿 Unit: 🛁 🍳 📺 📟 🔌 📺 📀 ⊘ BBQ

LOUTH, Lincolnshire Map ref 4D2

Louth Barn

Contact: Ronnie & Louise Millar, Louth Barn, Grosvenor House, 74 Keddington Road, Louth, Lincolnshire LN11 0BA **T:** (01507) 609381 / 07986 524395
E: enquiries@louthbarn.com **W:** www.louthbarn.com **£ BOOK ONLINE**

| Units | 1 |
| Sleeps | 2-4 |

PER UNIT PER WEEK
£331.00 - £444.00

Situated on the edge of Louth our converted Victorian barn is adjacent to the main house. Relaxing, comfortable, well-equipped, super-king size bed, internet, shared mature garden, summerhouse, playhouse, swings, own patio, covered parking. Extensive DVD Library, Lego and Brio available, also outdoor table football, pool table and table tennis available. **Open:** All year **Nearest Shop:** 0.20 miles **Nearest Pub:** 0.20 miles

WALKERS FAMILIES CYCLISTS Site: ✿ P Property: 📺 📷 Children: 🚼 🎮 🎿 Unit: 🛁 🍳 📺 📟 🔌 📺 📀 BBQ

LOUTH, Lincolnshire Map ref 4D2

Mill Lodge

Contact: Mrs Pamela M Cade, Owner, Mill Lodge, Benniworth, House Farm, Donington-on-Bain, Louth, Lincolnshire. LN11 9RD **T:** (01507) 343265 **E:** pamela.cade@btconnect.com
W: www.lincs-wildlife-cottage.co.uk

enjoyEngland.com ★★★ SELF CATERING

Units 1
Sleeps 1-4

PER UNIT PER WEEK
£150.00 - £350.00

SPECIAL PROMOTIONS
Special rates available for 2 person stays.

Mill Lodge is a comfortable, detached cottage, with garden and conservatory in an Area Of Outstanding Natural Beauty. The land is managed as Countryside Stewardship, with open access to grassland which supports a wealth of wildlife including rare species.

Old airfields and places of historic interest are within easy travelling distance. Ezra, Pam and Bryn offer you a warm welcome to our lovely farm.

Open: All year
Nearest Shop: 0.80 miles
Nearest Pub: 1 mile

Units: Mill Lodge has an open fire, energy efficient electric heaters and environmentally approved insulation.

Site: P **Leisure:** **Property:** **Children:** **Unit:** TV

MABLETHORPE, Lincolnshire Map ref 4D2

Dunes Cottage

Contact: Sheila Morrison, Bank House, Brickyard Lane, Theddlethorpe St Helen LN12 1NR
T: (01507) 338342 **E:** sheila.a.morrison@btopenworld.com
W: www.dunesholidaycottage.co.uk

enjoyEngland.com ★★★ SELF CATERING

Units 1
Sleeps 1-6

PER UNIT PER WEEK
£300.00 - £475.00

Charming 19th century cottage nestling on the edge of a National Nature Reserve. Next to the dunes with sandy beach and wonderful views of the dunes to the wolds and out to sea. Offers visitors peace and tranquillity, a place to get away from stresses and strains of modern life.

Open: All year
Nearest Shop: 4 miles
Nearest Pub: 2 miles

Units: Two bedrooms, sitting room with sofa bed, dining room and large breakfast kitchen.

Site: P **Property:** **Children:** **Unit:** TV DVD BBQ

MARKET RASEN, Lincolnshire   Map ref 4C2

Masondale Cottage

Contact: Mr Neil Cooper, Otby House Farm, Walesby, Lincolnshire LN8 3UU
T: (01673) 838530 / 07768 714281 **E:** n.cooper@otby-lake.co.uk
W: www.otby-lake.co.uk **£ BOOK ONLINE**

Units 1
Sleeps 6
PER UNIT PER WEEK
£400.00 - £575.00

Spacious peaceful farm cottage converted to high quality 4 star self catering accommodation. Perfect base for outdoor activities or a totally relaxing break. Panoramic views. Livery. Quite exceptional trout fishing. Masondale Cottage sits at the edge of the Lincolnshire Wolds with unrivalled panoramic views of the Vale of Ancholme looking across to Lincoln Cathedral prominent on the horizon. **Open:** All year **Nearest Shop:** 4 miles **Nearest Pub:** 4 miles

Site: ❀ P Payment: 💷 Leisure: ♪ ▶ ↻ ✎ Property: 📶 📺 🗄 📶 Children: 🎠 🛏 ⚲ Unit: 📱 🗄 📺 📶 📺 📀 BBQ 📞

SLEAFORD, Lincolnshire   Map ref 3A1

The Old Stable

Contact: Nigel Redmond, The Old Vicarage, 9 Church Street, Great Hale, Sleaford, Lincolnshire NG34 9LF **T:** (01529) 460307 **E:** caroline@theoldstable-greathale.co.uk
W: www.theoldstable-greathale.co.uk

Units 1
Sleeps 2
PER UNIT PER WEEK
£275.00

Delightful self-catering accommodation set in centre of a quiet village. Extremely well equipped and furnished. Ideal for visiting market towns of Boston, Sleaford, Grantham, Spalding, Bourne and Lincoln. Perfect for a relaxing break. **Open:** All year
Nearest Shop: 1 mile **Nearest Pub:** 1 mile

Site: P Leisure: ♪ ▶ Property: 📶 🐾 🗄 📶 Children: 🎠 Unit: 📱 📺 📶 🗄 📺 📀

SPILSBY, Lincolnshire   Map ref 4D2

Hope Cottages

Contact: Steve Taylor, Owner, Dukes Head Lane, Old Bolingbroke, Spilsby, Lincolnshire PE23 4EX **T:** (01673) 861412 / 07710 714060 **E:** hopecottages@aol.com
W: www.hopecottages.co.uk **£ BOOK ONLINE**

Units 2
Sleeps 1-3
PER UNIT PER WEEK
£225.00 - £420.00

[f] [t]

Hope Cottages are well appointed 4 Star retreats in a rural village and undiscovered county. They are in an excellent location for exploring the Lincolnshire Wolds, sea resorts and the historic City of Lincoln. The cottages have their own gardens and car parking and each sleeps 3 people in a double and single bedroom. Well behaved pets are accepted in cottage No2. **Open:** All year - Short breaks available. **Nearest Shop:** In Spilsby **Nearest Pub:** 500 yards

Site: ❀ P Payment: 💷 Property: 🐾 📺 🗄 📶 Children: 🎠 Unit: 📱 🗄 📺 📶 📺 📀 BBQ

WEST BARKWITH, Lincolnshire   Map ref 4D2

Glebe Farm Apartments

Contact: Stephen Campion, Glebe Farm Apartments, The Barn, Glebe Farm, West Barkwith LN8 5LF **T:** (01673) 858919 **E:** enquiries@glebeapart.co.uk
W: www.glebeapart.co.uk **£ BOOK ONLINE**

Units 4
Sleeps 2-4
PER UNIT PER WEEK
£200.00 - £280.00

Converted farm buildings into cosy apartments in rural countryside. Large grounds to enjoy, including free fishing in well-stocked lake. Online booking. **Open:** All year **Nearest Shop:** 1 mile
Nearest Pub: 1 mile

Site: ❀ P Leisure: ♪ Property: 🐾 🗄 📶 Children: 🎠 🛏 ⚲ Unit: 📱 📺 📶 📺 📀 BBQ

WITHERN, Lincolnshire   Map ref 4D2

Park Farm Holidays

Contact: Mrs Elsie Burkitt, Park Farm Holidays, Aby Road, Withern, Alford, Lincolnshire LN13 0DF **T:** (01507) 450331 **E:** info@parkfarmholidayswithern.com
W: www.parkfarmholidayswithern.com **£ BOOK ONLINE**

Units   6
Sleeps   4-6

PER UNIT PER WEEK
£250.00 - £520.00

SPECIAL PROMOTIONS
Short breaks low season - please enquire for details.

Situated just off the Wolds and seven miles from the sea. On the private lane that leads up to Park Farm. Two cottages at the side of the lane, four log cabins in woodland nearby. One mile from the village. Very peaceful. Good walking and cycling country. Seven miles from Mablethorpe, ten from Louth and six from Alford. Wi-Fi Tablets do not always work as well as laptops.

Open: All year
Nearest Shop: 2 miles
Nearest Pub: 2 mile

Units: Two cottages, with one double room and two singles. Two log cabins with one double room and one with two beds. Two cabins with one double and two twin.

Site: ❀ P Leisure: ♪ ↑ Property: ⊓ ⊑ ▤ ⊡ Children: ⊱ Unit: ▣ ▤ ⚲ TV ▣ BBQ ☏

CRANFORD, Northamptonshire   Map ref 3A2

No. 4 The Green

Contact: Mrs Emma Robinson, 36 Duck End House, Cranford, Kettering, Northamptonshire NN14 4AD **T:** (01536) 330608 **E:** no4thegreen@btinternet.com

Units   1
Sleeps   2-6
PER UNIT PER WEEK
£325.00 - £450.00

Charming 3 bed thatched cottage in the heart of the village. Fully modernised with all the home from home facilities you need. Close to major roads and train station. Pets welcome by arrangement. **Open:** All year **Nearest Shop:** 3 miles **Nearest Pub:** 0.10 miles

Site: ❀ P Property: ⊓ ⊑ ▤ ⊡ ▣ Children: ⊱ ⊞ ⚹ Unit: ▤ ▤ ▣ ▤ ⚲ TV ⊙ ▣

GREAT DODDINGTON, Northamptonshire   Map ref 3A2

The Old Watermill

Contact: Mrs. Anne Newman, Hardwater Mill, Hardwater Road, Great Doddington, Wellingborough NN29 7TD **T:** (01933) 276870 / 07702 512022 **F:** 01933 276870
E: sales@watermillholidays.co.uk **W:** www.watermillholidays.co.uk **£ BOOK ONLINE**

Units   1
Sleeps   2-4
PER UNIT PER WEEK
£360.00 - £600.00

A charming and historic former watermill, Grade II listed. The well equipped accommodation is on three floors. One four-poster double and one twin bedroom. Central heating Double glazed. Plenty of old elm beams and oak floors. Pets welcome, garden plus riverside walks. Special Christmas and New Year breaks available. **Open:** All year **Nearest Shop:** 1 mile **Nearest Pub:** 1.5 miles

Site: ❀ P Leisure: ♪ ↑ Property: ⊓ ▤ ⊡ Children: ⊱10 Unit: ▤ ▤ ▣ ▤ ⚲ TV ⊙ ▣ ⌀

PETERBOROUGH, *Northamptonshire* Map ref 3A1

Hall Farm Kings Cliffe

Contact: Ms Sarah Winfrey, Hall Farm Kings Cliffe - SC & GA, Hall Farm, Hall Yard, Kings Cliffe PE8 6XQ **T:** (01780) 470796 / 07906 502494 **E:** info@hallfarmkingscliffe.co.uk
W: www.hallfarmkingscliffe.co.uk **£ BOOK ONLINE**

Units 2
Sleeps 1-2

PER UNIT PER WEEK
£315.00 - £450.00

SPECIAL PROMOTIONS
Please contact us for prices.

Hall Farm Kings Cliffe is in a quiet village location within easy reach of Stamford, Oundle, Rutland Water and Peterborough and offers two types of self-catering accommodation each with its own private entrance and furnished to a high standard.

The Stables Cottage is on two floors in a 17th century stable block and faces into a courtyard. It provides stylish comfortable living with old oak beams and ancient stone.

The Archway Apartment is recently refurbished with windows overlooking the church and an old stone courtyard. With old oak beams and high ceilings it has a fresh modern style.

Open: All year except Christmas and New Year
Nearest Shop: 0.10 miles
Nearest Pub: 0.10 miles

Units: Both the Cottage and Apartment have a super-king size bed that can be separated to make two single beds if required.

Site: P Leisure: ♪ Property: 🖾 🖳 Children: 🐾12 🎱 Unit: 🗄 🔲 🗄 🗄 📺 🔌 📀

NEWARK, *Nottinghamshire* Map ref 4C2

Rose and Sweet Briar Cottages

Contact: Mrs Janet Hind, Owner, Rose and Sweet Briar Cottages, Hill Farm, Kersall, Newark, Nottinghamshire NG22 0BJ **T:** (01636) 636274 **E:** hind-hillfarm@hotmail.co.uk
W: www.roseandsweetbriar.co.uk

Units 2
Sleeps 2-4
PER UNIT PER WEEK
£130.00 - £285.00

Single storey cottages set in 1½ acre of private grounds of Hill farm in the hamlet of Kersall, Nr Newark (no longer working farm). Quiet location, beautiful views, large garden, off road parking. Close to Newark, Southwell, Ollerton, Edwinstowe and within easy travelling distance of Lincoln and Nottingham. Ideal location for exploring Sherwood Forest / Robin Hood country. Sorry no pets/no smoking.
Open: All year
Nearest Shop: 5 miles **Nearest Pub:** 1 mile

Site: ❀ P Leisure: 🐎 ♪ ┣ ∪ Property: 🖳 Children: 🎱 Unit: 🗄 🔲 🗄 🗄 📺 📀

NOTTINGHAM, *Nottinghamshire* Map ref 4C2

Woodview Cottages

Contact: Jane Morley, Woodview Cottages, Newfields Farm, Owthorpe NG12 3SG
T: (01949) 81985 / 07949 973470 **F:** 01949 81985 **E:** enquiries@woodviewcottages.co.uk
W: www.woodviewcottages.co.uk

Units 2
Sleeps 1-4
PER UNIT PER WEEK
£400.00 - £575.00

Woodview Holiday Cottages, Owthorpe, Nottinghamshire, are two delightful stone properties surrounded by beautiful gardens and stunning views. The cottages nestle in the centre of a working arable farm, on the edge of the Vale of Belvoir that is complete with trout and course fishing lakes and set amongst a beautiful patchwork of fields and woodlands. **Open:** All year
Nearest Shop: 3 miles **Nearest Pub:** 3 miles

Site: ❀ P Payment: 💳 Leisure: ♪ Property: 🖾 🗄 🖳 Children: 🎱 Unit: 🗄 🗄 🔲 🗄 🗄 📺 🔌 📀

BROOKE, Rutland Map ref 4C3

Units 1
Sleeps 2-9

PER UNIT PER WEEK
£500.00 - £700.00

SPECIAL PROMOTIONS
Weekend breaks off-season or as late availability: 2 nights £375; 3 nights £405; 2 nights late departure Sunday (6pm) £399.

America Lodge
Contact: Mrs Lesley MacCartney, Proprietor, The Office, America Lodge, Brooke LE15 8DF
T: (01572) 723944 / 07850 937653 **F:** 01572 759399 **E:** americalodge@btconnect.com
W: www.americalodge.co.uk

A lovely secluded farmhouse close to Rutland Water, just south of Oakham, the County Town of Rutland. Views over classic rolling English Countryside. Graded high 3 star. Private garden and grounds, large well appointed kitchen. Very central in UK. Will sleep 9 plus a cot. Refurbished December 2013 www.americalodge.co.uk.

Open: All year
Nearest Shop: 3 miles
Nearest Pub: 2 miles

Units: Farmhouse accommodation.

Site: ❀ P Leisure: 🚲 ♪ ⚲ ∪ Property: 🐕 ▣ 🖥 Children: 🦴 ▦ ⚲ Unit: ▯ 🗄 📺 🎬 📺 💿 🍴 BBQ

STRETTON, Rutland Map ref 3A1

Units 6
Sleeps 2-4
PER UNIT PER WEEK
£430.00 - £925.00

Stretton Lakes
Contact: Mrs Rachel Needham, Owner, Stretton Lakes, Clipsham Road, Stretton, Oakham, Rutland LE15 7QS **T:** (01780) 410507 **E:** info@strettonlakes.co.uk
W: www.strettonlakes.co.uk **£ BOOK ONLINE**

Enjoy England Silver Award for Self Catering holiday of the year 2011. Six luxury log cabins overlooking fishing lakes surrounded by woodland, all with Hot Tubs, our 5* lodges also have a Sauna. Mini breaks available 3 or 4 nights prices start from £310 low season.
Open: All year **Nearest Shop:** 3 miles **Nearest Pub:** 1 mile

Site: ❀ P Payment: 💷 Leisure: 🚲 ♪ ⚲ ∪ Property: ▣ 🖥 Children: 🦴 ▦ ⚲ Unit: ▯ 🗄 📺 💿 TV 🎬 💿 BBQ

The Official Tourist Board Guide to **Self Catering 2015**

Trevalsa Court Country House Hotel & Restaurant, Cornwall

Don't Miss...

Alton Towers

Alton, Staffordshire, ST10 4DB
0871 222 3330
www.altontowers.com
Alton Towers Resort is an exciting destination, with tons of terrific rides, blockbusting attractions, amazing live shows, weird and wonderful costume characters and much more. There's something for the whole family to enjoy!

Dudley Zoological Gardens

Dudley, West Midlands DY1 4QB
(01384) 215313
www.dudleyzoo.org.uk
From lions and tigers to snakes and spiders there's something for all ages. Animal feeding, encounters, face painting, land train and fair rides.

Iron Bridge and Toll House

Telford, Shropshire TF8 7DG
(01952) 433424
www.ironbridge.org.uk
The Ironbridge Gorge is a remarkable and beautiful insight into the region's industrial heritage. Ten award-winning Museums spread along the valley beside the wild River Severn - still spanned by the world's first Iron Bridge, where you can peer through the railings and conjure a vision of sailing vessels heading towards Bristol and the trading markets of the world.

Shakespeare's Birthplace Trust

Stratford-upon-Avon, Warwickshire CV37 6QW
www.shakespeare.org.uk
A unique Shakespeare experience with outstanding archive and library collections, inspiring educational and literary event programmes and five wonderful houses all directly relating to Shakespeare. Shakespeare's Birthplace itself is a fascinating house that offers a tantalising glimpse into Shakespeare's early world.

Warwick Castle

Warwickshire CV34 4QU
0871 265 2000
www.warwick-castle.co.uk
Battlements, towers, turrets, History, magic, myth and adventure - Warwick Castle is a Scheduled Ancient Monument and Grade 1 listed building packed with things to do, inside and out.

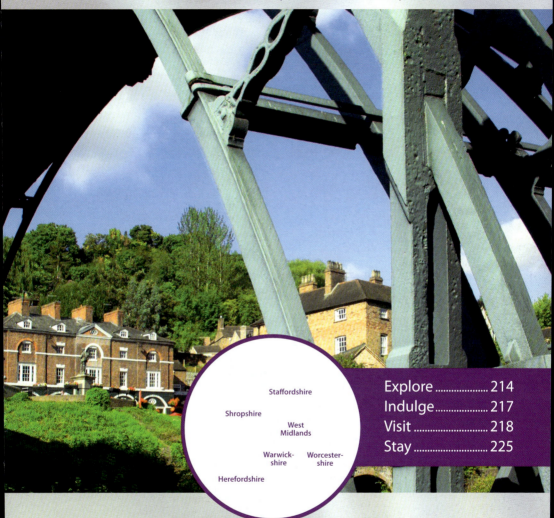

Heart of England

Herefordshire, Shropshire, Staffordshire, Warwickshire, West Midlands, Worcestershire

Staffordshire

Shropshire

West
Midlands

Warwick-
shire
Worcester-
shire

Herefordshire

The Heart of England: a name that defines this lovely part of the country so much better than its geographical name: The Midlands. Like a heart it has many arteries and compartments, from the March counties of Shropshire and Herefordshire, through Birmingham and the West Midlands, birthplace of the Industrial revolution. It is a region rich in history and character and you'll find pretty villages, grand castles and plenty of canals and waterways to explore.

Explore – Heart of England

Coventry & Warwickshire

From castles and cathedrals to art galleries, museums and exciting events, this region captivates visitors from all over the world.

A beautifully preserved Tudor town on the banks of the Avon and Warwickshire's most visited, Stratford-upon-Avon is the bard's birthplace with numerous theatres playing Shakespeare and other dramatists' work. The city of Warwick is dominated by its 14th century castle and its museums, and plenty of family activities are staged throughout the year. Historic Coventry has over 400 listed buildings and is most famous for its cathedrals, with the modern Church of St Michael sitting majestically next to the 'blitzed' ruins of its 14th century predecessor.

Herefordshire

Herefordshire's ruined castles in the border country and Iron Age and Roman hill-forts recall a turbulent battle-scarred past. Offa's Dyke, constructed by King Offa of Mercia in the 8th century marks the border with Wales but today the landscape is peaceful, with delightful small towns and villages and Hereford cattle grazing in pastures beside apple orchards and hop gardens.

Hereford has an 11th century cathedral and the Mappa Mundi while in the west, the Wye meanders through meadows and valleys. Hay-on-Wye is now best known for its annual Book Festival and plethora of second hand bookshops.

Staffordshire

Staffordshire, squeezed between the Black Country to the south and Manchester to the north, is home to the Potteries, a union of six towns made famous by Wedgwood, Spode and other ceramic designers. Lichfield has a magnificent three-spired 13th century cathedral and was birthplace of Samuel Johnson.

The unspoilt ancient heathland of Cannock Chase, leafy woodlands of the National Forest and secluded byways of South Staffordshire all offer the chance to enjoy the great outdoors.

Shropshire

Tucked away on the England/Wales border, Shropshire is another March county that saw much conflict between English and Welsh, hostilities between warring tribes and invading Romans.

The Wrekin and Stretton Hills were created by volcanoes and in the south the Long Mynd rises to 1700 ft with panoramic views of much of the Severn plain. Ironbridge, near the present day Telford, is said to be where the Industrial Revolution started in Britain. County town Shrewsbury was an historic fortress town built in a loop of the river Severn and these days joins Ludlow, with its 11th century castle, as one of the gastronomic high spots of Britain.

Hotspot: The British Ironwork Centre at Oswestry is a treasure trove of magnificent animal sculptures and decorations, including of a 13ft-high gorilla made from an incredible 40,000+ spoons donated by people from all over the world.
www.britishironworkcentre.co.uk

West Midlands

The Industrial revolution of the 19th century led to the growth of Birmingham into Britain's second city - the city of a thousand trades. Its prosperity was based on factories, hundreds of small workshops and a network of canals, all of which helped in the production of everything from needles and chocolate to steam engines and bridges. Nowadays the city has one of the best concert halls in Europe, excellent shopping and a regenerated waterside café culture.

The West Midlands is an urban area, criss-crossed by motorways, and still represents the powerhouse of Central Britain. Wolverhampton has been called Capital of the Black Country, made famous through its ironwork and Walsall, birthplace of Jerome K Jerome, has three museums.

Hotspot: Visit the 15 acres of ornamental gardens and glasshouses at Birmingham Botanical Gardens and Glasshouses in Edgbaston. www.birminghambotanicalgardens.org.uk

Affluent Sutton Coldfield and Solihull have proud civic traditions and a number of pretty parks including Sutton Park and Brueton Park. Many of Solihull's rural villages sit along the Stratford-upon-Avon canal and offer plenty of picturesque pubs along the tow path from which to watch the gentle meander of passing narrow boats.

Worcestershire

The beautiful county of Worcestershire has a fantastic selection of historic houses and gardens to discover and Worcester itself has a famous cathedral, cricket ground, and 15th century Commandery, now a Civil war museum.

Hotspot: Ride the Severn Valley Railway for a 16 mile long, steam powered journey through the breathtaking landscape of the Severn Valley from Kidderminister all the way to Bridgnorth in Shropshire. www.svr.co.uk

Great Malvern, still a Spa town, is famous as the birthplace of Sir Edward Elgar, who drew much of his inspiration from this countryside and who is celebrated at the annual Malvern Festival. The old riverside market town of Evesham is the centre of the Vale of Evesham fruit and vegetable growing area which, with the tranquil banks of the river Avon and the undulating hills and peaceful wooded slopes of the Cotswolds, offers some of the prettiest landscapes in the country.

Droitwich, known in Roman times as Salinae, still has briny water in its spa baths and can trace the origins of salt extraction in the area back to prehistoric times, it even holds an annual Salt Festival to celebrate this unique heritage.

Indulge – Heart of England

Enjoy a romantic cruise along the **River Avon** at Stratford-upon-Avon on a traditional Edwardian passenger launch. Cruise downstream from the Bancroft gardens past the Royal Shakespeare Theatre and Holy Trinity Church (the site of Shakespeare's tomb) before turning around and passing under the 15th Century Clopton Bridge to discover quiet riverbanks and meadows. www.avon-boating.co.uk

Dine in style at **Harry's Restaurant** at The Chase Hotel, a magnificent georgian country house hotel set in 11 acres of award-winning parkland on the outskirts of Ross-on-Wye. (01989) 768330, www.chasehotel.co.uk

In the quaint, sleepy town of Church Stretton lies one of the best delicatessens in Britain. **Van Doesburg's** deli serves gourmet treats all made on the premises and the desserts are incredible. 3 High Street, Church Stretton, Shropshire. www.vandoesburgs.co.uk

Cadbury World, at the historic Bourneville village near Birmingham, tells the mouth-watering story of Cadbury's chocolate and includes chocolate-making demonstrations with free samples, attractions for all ages, free parking, shop and restaurant. Phone to check availability and book admission. 0845 450 3599 www.cadburyworld.co.uk

Arts and crafts lovers can indulge in a spot of shopping for unusual gifts and artworks at the delightful **Jinney Ring Craft Centre** in Hanbury near Redditch. A range of craftspeople work on site and there's a quirky gift shop and gallery, as well as a daytime restaurant in a rustic old barn, and all set in lovely gardens with duck ponds and stunning views across to the Malvern Hills. www.jinneyring.co.uk

Visit – Heart of England

Coventry & Warwickshire

Coventry Cathedral - St Michael's
West Midlands CV1 5AB
(024) 7652 1257
www.coventrycathedral.org.uk
Glorious 20th century Cathedral, with stunning 1950's art & architecture, rising above the stark ruins of the medieval Cathedral destroyed by German air raids in 1940.

Compton Verney
Stratford-upon-Avon CV35 9HZ
(01926) 645500
www.comptonverney.org.uk
Award-winning art gallery housed in a grade I listed Robert Adam mansion.

Festival of Motoring
August, Stoneleigh, Warwickshire
www.festival-of-motoring.co.uk
This major event takes place at Stoneleigh Park in Warwickshire. In addition to hundreds of fantastic cars to look at, there will be the traditional historic vehicle 'run' through delightful Warwickshire countryside, car gymkhanas and auto tests.

Godiva Festival
July, Coventry, Warwickshire
www.godivafestival.com
The Godiva Festival is the UK's biggest free family festival held over a weekend in the War Memorial Park, Coventry. The event showcases some of the finest local, national and International artists, live comedy, family entertainment, Godiva Carnival, and lots more.

Heart Park
Fillongley, Warwickshire CV7 8DX
(01676) 540333
www.heartpark.co.uk
"We believe that the heart of our Park is the beach and lake. But for those of you who'd like to try out a few 'different' activities - we've got a great assortment for you to try."

Heritage Open Days
September, Coventry, Warwickshire
www.coventry.gov.uk/hod
Heritage Open Days celebrate England's architecture and culture by allowing visitors free access to interesting properties that are either not usually open or would normally charge an entrance fee. Heritage Open Days also include tours, events and activities that focus on local architecture and culture.

Kenilworth Castle and Elizabethan Garden
Warwickshire CV8 1NE
(01926) 852078
www.english-heritage.org.uk/kenilworth
One of the most spectacular castle ruins in England.

Packwood House
Solihull, Warwickshire B94 6AT
0844 800 1895
www.nationaltrust.org.uk/main/w-packwoodhouse
Restored tudor house, park and garden with notable topiary.

Ragley Hall
Stratford-upon-Avon, Warwickshire B49 5NJ
(01789) 762090
www.ragley.co.uk
Ragley Hall is set in 27 acres of beautiful formal gardens.

Ryton Pools Country Parks
Coventry, Warwickshire CV8 3BH
(024) 7630 5592
www.warwickshire.gov.uk/parks
The 100 acres of Ryton Pools Country Park are just waiting to be explored. The many different habitats are home to a wide range of birds and other wildlife.

Stratford River Festival
July, Stratford, Warwickshire
www.stratfordriverfestival.co.uk
The highly successful Stratford-upon-Avon River Festival brings the waterways of Stratford alive, with boatloads of family fun, on the first weekend of July.

Three Counties Show
June, Malvern, Warwickshire
www.threecounties.co.uk
Three jam-packed days of family entertainment and fun, all in celebration of the great British farming world and countryside.

Herefordshire

Eastnor Castle
Ledbury, Herefordshire HR8 1RL
(01531) 633160
www.eastnorcastle.com
Fairytale Georgian Castle dramatically situated in the Malvern Hills.

Goodrich Castle
Ross-on-Wye, Herefordshire HR9 6HY
(01600) 890538
www.english-heritage.org.uk/goodrich
Come and relive the turbulent history of Goodrich Castle with our free audio and then climb to the battlements for breathtaking views over the Wye Valley.

The Hay Festival
May, Hay-on-Wye, Herefordshire
www.hayfestival.com
Some five hundred events see writers, politicians, poets, scientists, comedians, philosophers and musicians come together on a greenfield site for a ten day fesitval of ideas and stories at the Hay Festival.

Hereford Cathedral
Herefordshire HR1 2NG
(01432) 374202
www.herefordcathedral.org
Some of the finest examples of architecture from Norman times to the present day.

Hereford Museum and Art Gallery
Herefordshire HR4 9AU
(01432) 260692
www.herefordshire.gov.uk/leisure/museums_galleries/2869.asp
In the museum, aspects of Herefordshire history and life - in the Gallery, regularly changing exhibitions of paintings, photography and crafts.

Hergest Croft Gardens

Kington, Herefordshire HR5 3EG
(01544) 230160
www.hergest.co.uk
The gardens extend over 50 acres, with more than 4000 rare shrubs and trees. With over 60 champion trees and shrubs it is one of the finest collections in the British Isles.

Ledbury Heritage Centre
Herefordshire, HR8 1DN
(01432) 260692
www.herefordshire.gov.uk/leisure
The story of Ledbury's past displayed in a timber-framed building in the picturesque lane leading to the church.

Shropshire

Darby Houses (Ironbridge)
Telford, Shropshire TF8 7EW
(01952) 433424
www.ironbridge.org.uk
In the Darby houses, Dale House and Rosehill House, you can delve in to the everyday life of Quaker families.

Enginuity
Telford, Shropshire TF8 7DG
(01952) 433424
www.ironbridge.org.uk
At Enginuity you can turn the wheels of your imagination, test your horse power and discover how good ideas are turned in to real things.

English Haydn Festival
June, Bridgnorth, Shropshire
www.englishhaydn.com
An array of the music of Joseph Haydn and his contemporaries, performed in St. Leonards Church, Bridgnorth.

Ludlow Food Festival
September, Ludlow, Shropshire
www.foodfestival.co.uk
More than 160 top quality independent food and drink producers inside Ludlow Castle.

Much Wenlock Priory
Shropshire TF13 6HS
(01952) 727466
www.english-heritage.org.uk/wenlockpriory
Wenlock Priory, with its stunning clipped topiary, has a pastoral setting on the edge of lovely Much Wenlock

RAF Cosford Air Show
June, Shifnal, Shropshire
www.cosfordairshow.co.uk
This RAF-organised show usually features all the airshow favourites, classic and current British and foreign aircraft, exhibits and trade stalls all on this classic RAF airbase.

Royal Air Force Museum Cosford
Shifnal, Shropshire TF11 8UP
(01902) 376200
www.rafmuseum.org
FREE Admission. The award winning museum houses one of the largest aviation collections in the United Kingdom.

Shrewsbury Folk Festival
August, Shrewsbury, Shropshire
www.shrewsburyfolkfestival.co.uk
Shrewsbury Folk Festival has a reputation for delivering the very finest acts from the UK and around the world.

Stokesay Castle
Craven Arms, Shropshire SY7 9AH
(01588) 672544
www.english-heritage.org.uk/stokesaycastle
Stokesay Castle, nestles in peaceful South Shropshire countryside near the Welsh Border. It is one of more than a dozen English Heritage properties in the county.

V Festival
August, Weston Park, Shropshire
www.vfestival.com
Legendary rock and pop festival.

Wenlock Olympian Games
July, Much Wenlock, Shropshire
www.wenlock-olympian-society.org.uk
The games that inspired the modern Olympic Movement.

Wroxeter Roman City
Shrewsbury, Shropshire SY5 6PH
(01743) 761330
www.english-heritage.org.uk/wroxeter
Wroxeter Roman City, or Viroconium, to give it its Roman title, is thought to have been one of the largest Roman cities in the UK with over 200 acres of land, 2 miles of walls and a population of approximately 5,000.

Staffordshire

Abbots Bromley Horn Dance
September, Abbots Bromley, Staffordshire
www.abbotsbromley.com
Ancient ritual dating back to 1226. Six deer-men, a fool, hobby horse, bowman and Maid Marian perform to music provided by a melodian player.

Aerial Extreme Trentham

Staffordshire ST4 8AX
0845 652 1736
www.aerialextreme.co.uk/index.php/courses/trentham-estate
Our tree based adventure ropes course, set within the tranquil grounds of Trentham Estate is a truly spectacular journey.

Etruria Industrial Museum
Staffordshire ST4 7AF
(07900) 267711
www.stokemuseums.org.uk
Discover how they put the 'bone' in bone china at the last working steam-powered potters mill in Britain. Includes a Bone and Flint Mill and family-friendly interactive exhibition.

Lichfield Cathedral
Staffordshire WS13 7LD
(01543) 306100
www.lichfield-cathedral.org
A medieval Cathedral with 3 spires in the heart of an historic City set in its own serene Close.

Midlands Grand National
March, Uttoxeter Racecourse, Staffordshire
www.uttoxeter-racecourse.co.uk
Biggest fixture in Uttoxeter's calendar.

National Memorial Arboretum
Lichfield, Staffordshire DE13 7AR
(01283) 792333
www.thenma.org.uk
150 acres of trees and memorials, planted as a living tribute to those who have served, died or suffered in the service of their Country.

The Roaches
Upper Hulme, Leek, Staffordshire ST13 8UB
www.staffsmoorlands.gov.uk
The Roaches (or Roches) is a wind-carved outcrop of gritstone rocks that rises above the waters or Tittesworth reservoir, between Leek in Staffordshire and Buxton in Derbyshire. It's impressive gritstone edges and craggy rocks are loved by walkers and climbers alike.

Stone Food & Drink Festival
October, Stone, Staffordshire
www.stonefooddrink.org.uk
Staffordshire's biggest celebration of all things gastronomic.

Tamworth Castle
Staffordshire B79 7NA
(01827) 709629
www.tamworthcastle.co.uk
The number one Heritage attraction located in the town. Explore over 900 years of history in the magnificent Motte and Bailey Castle.

Wedgwood Visitor Centre
Stoke-on-Trent, Staffordshire ST12 9ER
(01782) 282986
www.wedgwoodvisitorcentre.com
Enjoy the past, buy the present and treasure the experience. The Wedgwood Visitor Centre offers a unique chance to immerse yourself in the heritage of Britain's greatest ceramics company.

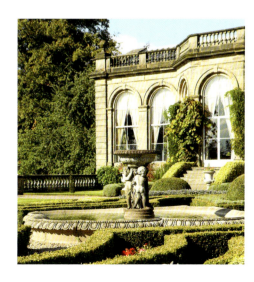

West Midlands

Artsfest
September, Birmingham, West Midlands
www.visitbirmingham.com
Artsfest is one of the UK's biggest free arts festival and showcases work across the performing arts, visual arts and digital arts genres to promote emerging and established talent.

Barber Institute of Fine Arts
Edgbaston, West Midlands B15 2TS
(0121) 414 7333
www.barber.org.uk
British and European paintings, drawings and sculpture from the 13th century to mid 20th century.

Birmingham Literature Festival
October, Birmingham, West Midlands
www.visitbirmingham.com
Celebrating the city's literature scene, the Birmingham Literature Festival takes places every year with its trademark mix of literature events, talks and workshops.

Birmingham International Jazz and Blues Festival
July, Birmingham, West Midlands
www.visitbirmingham.com
Musicians and fans come to the city from every corner of the UK as well as from further afield and significantly, almost all of the events are free to the public.

Black Country Living Museum
Dudley, West Midlands DY1 4SQ
(0121) 557 9643
www.bclm.co.uk
Britain's friendliest open-air museum - visit original shops and houses, ride on fair attractions, take a look down the underground coalmine.

Frankfurt Christmas Market & Craft Fair
November-December, Birmingham, West Midlands
www.visitbirmingham.com
The largest authentic German market outside Germany and Austria and the centrepiece of the city's festive event calendar.

Moseley Folk Festival
September, Birmingham, West Midlands
www.visitbirmingham.com
Offering an inner city Shangri-la bringing together people from all ages and backgrounds to witness folk legends playing alongside their contemporaries.

Thinktank-Birmingham Science Museum
West Midlands B4 7XG
(0121) 202 2222
www.thinktank.ac
Thinktank is Birmingham's science museum where the emphasis is firmly on hands on exhibits and interactive fun.

Worcestershire

The Almonry Museum & Heritage Centre
Evesham, Worcestershire WR11 4BG
(01386) 446944
www.almonryevesham.org
The 14th century house has 12 rooms of exhibits from 2000 years of Evesham history and pleasant gardens to the rear.

Hanbury Hall
Droitwich Spa, Worcestershire WR9 7EA
(01527) 821214
www.nationaltrust.org.uk/hanburyhall
Early 18th century house, garden & park owned by the Vernon family for nearly 300 years.

Worcester Cathedral
Worcestershire WR1 2LA
(01905) 732900
www.worcestercathedral.co.uk
Worcester Cathedral is one of England's most magnificent and inspiring buildings, a place of prayer and worship for 14 centuries.

West Midland Safari and Leisure Park Bewdley, Worcestershire DY12 1LF (01299) 402114 www.wmsp.co.uk
Are you ready to SAFARI and come face to face with some of the fastest, tallest, largest and cutest animals around?

Worcester City Art Gallery & Museum
Worcestershire WR1 1DT
(01905) 25371
www.worcestercitymuseums.org.uk
The art gallery & museum runs a programme of exhibitions/events for all the family. Explore the fascinating displays, exhibitions, café, shop and Worcestershire Soldier Galleries.

Tourist Information Centres

When you arrive at your destination, visit the Tourist Information Centre for quality assured help with accommodation and information about local attractions and events, or email your request before you go.

Bewdley	Load Street	0845 6077819	bewdleytic@wyreforestdc.gov.uk
Birmingham Library	Centenary Square	0844 888 3883	visit@marketingbirmingham.com
Bridgnorth	The Library	01746 763257	bridgnorth.tourism@shropshire.gov.uk
Bromyard	The Bromyard Centre	01885 488133	enquiries@bromyard-live.org.uk
Church Stretton	Church Street	01694 723133	churchstretton.scf@shropshire.gov.uk
Droitwich Spa	St Richard's House	01905 774312	heritage@droitwichspa.gov.uk
Ellesmere, Shropshire	The Boathouse Visitor Centre	01691 622981	ellesmere.tourism@shropshire.gov.uk
Evesham	The Almonry	01386 446944	tic@almonry.ndo.co.uk
Hereford	1 King Street	01432 268430	reception@visitherefordshire.co.uk
Ironbridge	Museum of The Gorge	01952 433424/ 01952 435900	tic@ironbridge.org.uk
Kenilworth	Kenilworth Library	0300 5558171	kenilworthlibrary@warwickshire.gov.uk
Ledbury	38 The Homend	0844 5678650	info@vistledbury.info
Leek	1 Market Place	01538 483741	tourism.services@staffsmoorlands.gov.uk
Leominster	1 Corn Square	01568 616460	leominstertic@herefordshire.gov.uk
Lichfield	Lichfield Garrick	01543 412112	info@visitlichfield.com
Ludlow	Castle Street	01584 875053	ludlow.tourism@shropshire.gov.uk
Malvern	21 Church Street	01684 892289	info@visitthemalverns.org
Market Drayton	49 Cheshire Street	01630 653114	marketdrayton.scf@shropshire-cc.gov.uk
Much Wenlock	The Museum - VIC	01952 727679/ 01743 258891	muchwenlock.tourism@shropshire.gov.uk
Newcastle-Under-Lyme	Newcastle Library	01782 297313	tic.newcastle@staffordshire.gov.uk
Nuneaton	Nuneaton Library	0300 5558171	nuneatonlibrary@warwickshire.gov.uk
Oswestry (Mile End)	Mile End	01691 662488	oswestrytourism@shropshire.gov.uk
Oswestry Town	The Heritage Centre	01691 662753	ot@oswestry-welshborders.org.uk
Redditch	Palace Theatre	01527 60806	info.centre@bromsgroveandredditch.gov.uk
Ross-On-Wye	Market House	01989 562768/ 01432 260675	visitorcentreross@herefordshire.gov.uk
Royal leamington spa	Royal Pump Rooms	01926 742762	vic@warwickdc.gov.uk
Rugby	Rugby Art Gallery Museum	01788 533217	visitor.centre@rugby.gov.uk
Shrewsbury	Barker Street	01743 281200	visitorinformation@shropshire.gov.uk
Solihull	Central Library	0121 704 6130	artscomplex@solihull.gov.uk
Stafford	Stafford Gatehouse Theatre	01785 619619	tic@staffordbc.gov.uk
Stoke-On-Trent	Victoria Hall, Bagnall Street	01782 236000	stoke.tic@stoke.gov.uk
Stratford-Upon-Avon	Bridge Foot	01789 264293	tic@discover-stratford.com
Tamworth	Philip Dix Centre	01827 709581	tic@tamworth.gov.uk
Telford	The Telford Shopping Centre	01952 238008	tourist-info@telfordshopping.co.uk
Upton Upon Severn	The Heritage Centre	01684 594200	upton.tic@malvernhills.gov.uk
Warwick	Visit Warwick	01926 492212	info@visitwarwick.co.uk
Whitchurch (Shropshire)	Whitchurch Heritage Centre	01948 664577	heritage@whitchurch-shropshire-tc.gov.uk
Worcester	The Guildhall	01905 726311/ 722561	touristinfo@visitworcester.com
Coventry	St Michael's Tower, Coventry Cathedral Ruins	024 7622 5616	tic@coventry.gov.uk

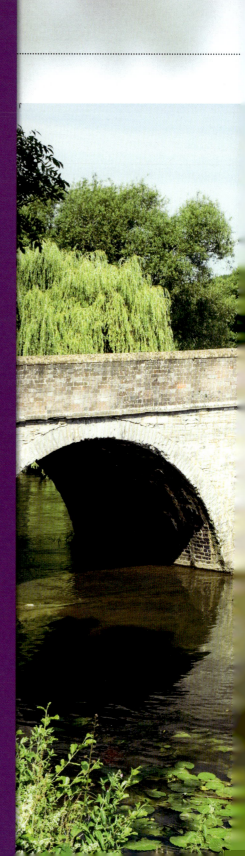

Regional Contacts and Information

For more information on accommodation, attractions, activities, events and holidays in the Heart of England, contact one of the following regional or local tourism organisations. Their websites have a wealth of information and many produce free publications to help you get the most out of your visit.

Marketing Birmingham
(0844) 888 3883
www.visitbirmingham.com

Visit Coventry & Warwickshire
(024) 7622 5616
www.visitcoventryandwarwickshire.co.uk

Visit Herefordshire
(01432) 268430
www.visitherefordshire.co.uk

Shakespeare Country
(0871) 978 0800
www.shakespeare-country.co.uk

Shropshire Tourism
(01743) 261919
www.shropshiretourism.co.uk

Destination Staffordshire
(01785) 277397
www.enjoystaffordshire.com

Stoke-on-Trent
(01782) 236000
www.visitstoke.co.uk

Destination Worcestershire
(0845) 641 1540
www.visitworcestershire.org

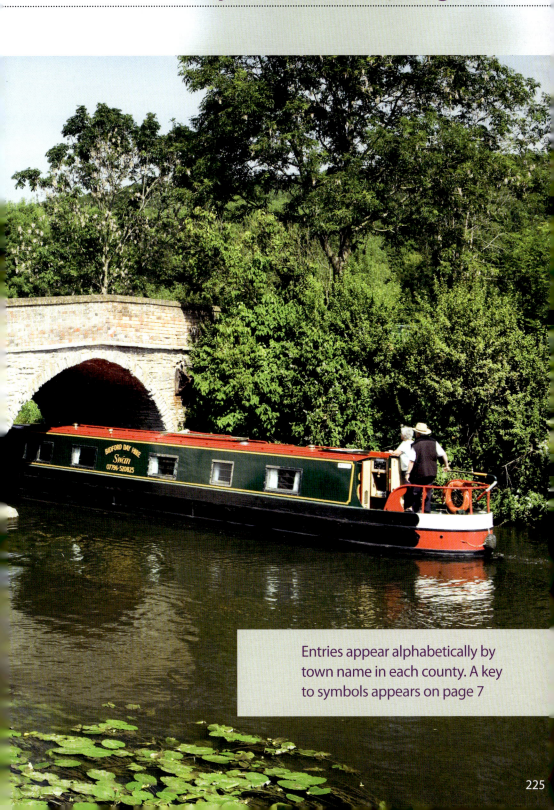

Entries appear alphabetically by
town name in each county. A key
to symbols appears on page 7

BROMYARD, Herefordshire   Map ref 2B1

Units   1
Sleeps   2-8

PER UNIT PER WEEK
£450.00 - £950.00

SPECIAL PROMOTIONS
Short breaks available.

Elcocks Cottage
Contact: Mr Mike Hogg, 61 Pereira Road, Harborne, Birmingham B17 9JB
T: (01214) 271395 **E:** mike@elcocks.net
W: www.elcocks.net

A beautifully restored detached 17th century cottage set in 3 acres of fields. Features include exposed beams, wood burning stove, period style furnishings, cider mill and press. The garden and cottage face south towards the Malvern Hills.

Situated 6 miles from Bromyard, 1.5 miles from Whitbourne. Very rural and secluded with magnificent views.

Sleeps up to 8 in 4 bedrooms, two double rooms and two twin bedded rooms, one twin bedroom and bathroom are on the ground floor. Pets welcome. Free Wi-Fi available.

Open: All year
Nearest Shop: 1.5 miles
Nearest Pub: 1.5 miles

Units: Detached cottage with parking on site for 5 cars.

Site: ✿ P Leisure: ✎ Property: 🐕 🚐 📷 🖥 Children: 🐴 🛏 🛝 Unit: 🖥 🗄 📺 📟 🔌 📺 📻 📀 📼 🍳 BBQ 📞

HEREFORD, Herefordshire   Map ref 2A1

Units   1
Sleeps   22-34

PER UNIT PER WEEK
£6500.00 - £7200.00

SPECIAL PROMOTIONS
Two nights available from £2,670 mid week.

Brinsop Court
Contact: Lorina Walden, Office Manager, Brinsop Court, The Office, Dansey House, Brinsop Court Estate, Brinsop, Hereford, Herefordshire HR4 7AX **T:** (01432) 509925
E: enquiries@brinsopcourt.com **W:** www.brinsopcourt.com **£ BOOK ONLINE**

Fabulous moated medieval manor house in rural Herefordshire, only 6 miles from Hereford city. 4 star plus rating: beautifully refurbished with a comfortable mix of antique and contemporary furniture. Large kitchens with Agas, games room, 800 acres to enjoy, open fires and woodburners, hot tub, fishing, tennis court, croquet lawn, gardens and lots of walks and trails.

From the medieval carp pools to the exposed beams and leaded windows, this historic house is ideal for family reunions, rural retreats or unforgettable parties. Once home to the Hollywood star Madeleine Carroll. William Wordsworth was a frequent visitor and St George slayed the dragon in a neighbouring field.

Open: All Year
Nearest Shop: 2 Miles
Nearest Pub: 1.5 Miles

Units: 15 bedrooms, 11 bath or shower rooms, two en suites on the ground floor with disabled access.

Site: ✿ P Payment: 💳 € Leisure: ⛳ 🎵 ▶ ✎ 🎣 Property: 〃 🐕 🚐 🖥 🖥 Children: 🐴 🛏 🛝
Unit: 🖥 🗄 📺 📟 🔌 📺 📻 🍳 BBQ 📞

HEREFORD, Herefordshire   Map ref 2A1

SELF CATERING

Units   1
Sleeps   1-6

PER UNIT PER WEEK
£425.00 - £895.00

Castle Cliffe East

Contact: Mr Phil Wilson, Owner, Castle Cliffe West, 14 Quay Street, Hereford HR1 2NH
T: (01432) 272096 / 07786 605123 **E:** info@castlecliffe.co.uk
W: www.castlecliffe.co.uk

Relax & unwind in luxury accommodation, surrounded by parkland, on the banks of the River Wye. Open fires, four-poster bed, period furniture & lovely views. Walking distance to the Cathedral & Mappa Mundi Exhibition, shops, pubs, restaurants, theatre & cinema. Easy access to beautiful countryside - Ludlow, Hay-on-Wye, Tintern, Malvern, the Brecon Beacons & Black Mountains. Short breaks available. **Open:** All year **Nearest Shop:** 0.5 miles
Nearest Pub: 0.5 miles

Site: ✿ **P** **Leisure:** 🏊 ♪ ▸ ♺ **Property:** 🐴 🚐 🖥 🖩 **Children:** 🐎 🛏 🎎 **Unit:** 📱 🗄 📺 🗄 🍳 📺 ⓒ 📀 🧺 **BBQ**

HEREFORD, Herefordshire   Map ref 2A1

SELF CATERING   **Gold AWARD**

Units   1
Sleeps   2-8

PER UNIT PER WEEK
£850.00 - £1850.00

SPECIAL PROMOTIONS
Recieve 5% off Short breaks and 10% off weekly bookings in November!

Little Canwood House

Contact: Charmaine Brooks, Little Canwood, Checkley HR1 4NF **T:** 07887 714973
E: info@littlecanwoodhouse.co.uk
W: www.littlecanwoodhouse.co.uk

Little Canwood House is situated in heart of rolling countryside offering beautiful views over Herefordshire's rural farmland. The house has been sympathetically restored to create a traditional yet modern feel, offering 5 Star Tourist Board rated, self catering accommodation suitable for families and groups - sleeps 8. There are 4 bedrooms.

Bedroom 1: 5ft bed, T.V. and En Suite with power shower. Bedroom 2: 5ft bed. Bedroom 3: 4ft.6" bed. Bedroom 4: Single bed with another bed underneath to accommodate 1 more person. All Bedrooms are upstairs.

Open: All year
Nearest Shop: 4 miles
Nearest Pub: 1.4 miles

Units: There is 1 en suite bathroom with power shower and 1 family bathroom with bath and shower over located upstairs. There is a toilet downstairs.

Site: ✿ **P** **Leisure:** ▸ **Property:** 🐴 🚐 🖥 🖩 **Children:** 🐎 🛏 🎎 **Unit:** 📱 🗄 📺 🗄 🍳 📺 ⓒ 📀 🧺 **BBQ** ☎

HEREFORD, Herefordshire   *Map ref 2A1*

Monkhall Cottages

Contact: Sally Price, PFP, Monkhall Court, Callow, Hereford, Herefordshire HR2 8DA
T: (01432) 352900 **E:** stay@monkhallcottages.co.uk
W: www.monkhallcottages.co.uk **£ BOOK ONLINE**

| Units | 2 |
| Sleeps | 4-7 |

PER UNIT PER WEEK
£560.00 - £1050.00

SPECIAL PROMOTIONS
Friday and Monday are our changeover days. Short breaks can be arranged for weekends or mid-weeks almost all year round (only usually excluding half term and Christmas).

Our two luxury five star cottages combine the building's classic Granary features with beautifully crafted fittings (oak doors, windows and staircases), bespoke hand-painted kitchens, renewably heated limestone flooring (biomass energy from the farm), and modern technological comforts (3D TV, WiFi and sound system) in a beautiful countryside setting.
Outside, enjoy the company of the local wildlife from a private seating area with barbecue and parasol, set within the main lawn overlooking the duck pond. The Stables has a hot tub while The Granary features a heated outdoor dining area.

Open: All Year
Nearest Shop: 4 miles
Nearest Pub: 5 miles

Units: The Stables (7): 2 double en suite, 1 twin, 1 single. The Granary (4): 1 king size with en suite, 1 double with bathroom and private dressing room.

Site: ❀ P **Property:** 🚃 📱 🏠 **Children:** 🛏 🎠 ⚡ **Unit:** 📱 🍽 📺 📀 BBQ

KINGTON, Herefordshire   *Map ref 2A1*

White Heron Properties

Contact: Jo Hilditch, Managing Director, Whittern Farms Ltd., Lyonshall, Kington HR5 3JA
T: (01544) 340241 **F:** 01544 340253 **E:** info@whiteheronproperties.com
W: www.whiteheronproperties.com **£ BOOK ONLINE**

| Units | 5 |
| Sleeps | 2-32 |

PER UNIT PER WEEK
£500.00 - £640.00

SPECIAL PROMOTIONS
We offer Friday to Sunday, Friday to Monday and Monday to Friday as standard stays.

We have five lovely properties in rolling Herefordshire countryside. They vary from pet friendly small cottages to large contemporary accommodation for house parties, all with en suite bedrooms. The largest has a swimming pool, sauna, hot tub, table tennis, cinema, Wii, Xbox and even a squash court.

We can host small conferences, weddings, hen parties or just provide luxurious accommodation for a romantic weekend away in the country. With great service from a friendly team we can offer full catering, or leave it all to you - the choice is yours, whichever you choose you will not be disappointed! Prices shown are based on a small unit. Please contact for larger unit rates.

Open: All year
Nearest Shop: 3 miles
Nearest Pub: 2 miles

Units: At White Heron properties we have a total of 23 bedrooms in 5 properties, some en suite.

Site: ❀ P **Payment:** 💷 **Leisure:** ♪ ▶ ∪ ✎ ⚡ **Property:** ∥ 🚃 📱 🏠 **Children:** 🛏 🎠 ⚡
Unit: 📱 📺 📀 🚲 BBQ ☎

LEDBURY, Herefordshire   Map ref 2B1

Old Kennels Farm

Contact: Mr Brian Wilce, Owner, Old Kennels Farm, Bromyard Road, Ledbury HR8 1LG
T: (01531) 635024 / 07779 728209 **E:** info@oldkennelsfarm.co.uk
W: oldkennelsfarm.co.uk

Units   6
Sleeps   2-6
PER UNIT PER WEEK
£270.00 - £720.00

Six comfortable cottages sleeping 2-6 people situated on the edge of Ledbury on a small, friendly, family-run farm. **Open:** All year **Nearest Shop:** 0.5 miles **Nearest Pub:** 0.60 miles

Site: ❀ P **Leisure:** **Property:** **Children:** **Unit:**

LEOMINSTER, Herefordshire   Map ref 2A1

Bellwood Lodges

Contact: Mrs Linda Stokes, Owner, Shobdon, Leominster, Herefordshire HR6 9NJ
T: (01568) 708642 **E:** info@bellwoodlodges.co.uk
W: www.bellwoodlodges.co.uk **£ BOOK ONLINE**

Units   2
Sleeps   1-12
PER UNIT PER WEEK
£420.00 - £490.00

Holiday chalets set in the beautiful Herefordshire countryside. Well equipped, including one which is fully wheelchair accessible throughout. All linen and towels included. We also have a play area and plenty of space for children to enjoy. One chalet has been graded by the AA as 4 star accommodation whilst the other received a 3 star grading. Walkers are welcome. **Open:** All year except November **Nearest Shop:** 1.5 miles **Nearest Pub:** 1.5 miles

Site: ❀ P **Property:** **Children:** **Unit:** BBQ

ROSS-ON-WYE, Herefordshire   Map ref 2A1

Bramley Cottage

Contact: Lucy Snell, c/o Bramley House, Pencoyd, Harewood End, Hereford HR2 8JY
T: (01989) 730416 / 07747 041026 **E:** lucy@bramleyholidaycottage.co.uk
W: www.bramleyholidaycottage.co.uk

Units   1
Sleeps   1-4
PER UNIT PER WEEK
£310.00 - £520.00

Bramley Cottages lies in the heart of the Wye Valley. 5 miles from Ross on Wye and near the cathedral town of Hereford. It provides the perfect location from which to explore the stunning countryside, whether on foot along the banks of the Wye to Symonds Yat or on bikes in the Forest of Dean, or just canoeing gently down the river. **Open:** All year **Nearest Shop:** 2 miles **Nearest Pub:** 1.25 miles

Site: ❀ P **Property:** **Children:** **Unit:** BBQ

ROSS-ON-WYE, Herefordshire   Map ref 2A1

Flanesford Priory

Contact: Kath Taylor-Jessup, General Manager, Flanesford Priory, Goodrich, Ross-on-Wye, Herefordshire HR9 6HZ **T:** (01600) 890 506 **F:** 01600 891019
E: info@flanesfordpriory.co.uk **W:** www.flanesfordpriory.co.uk **£ BOOK ONLINE**

Units   10
Sleeps   2-42
PER UNIT PER WEEK
£240.00 - £1200.00

Ten beautifully appointed self catering apartments and cottages, situated in the picturesque village of Goodrich in the Wye Valley; on the doorstep of the Forest of Dean. Ranging from 2 to 8 persons there is accommodation to suit every taste and budget, including the luxury and award winning 5 star Cider Mill. Fishing, cycling, canoeing and much more available locally. **Open:** All year **Nearest Shop:** 0.5 miles **Nearest Pub:** 0.5 miles

Site: ❀ P **Payment:** **Leisure:** **Property:** **Children:** **Unit:** BBQ

ROSS-ON-WYE, Herefordshire   Map ref 2A1

Units   2
Sleeps   2-4
PER UNIT PER WEEK
£285.00 - £520.00

Game Larders & Old Bakehouse
Contact: Miss Anthea McIntyre, Game Larders & Old Bakehouse, Wythall Estate, Walford, Ross-on-Wye HR9 5SD **T:** (01989) 562688 **F:** 01989 566531
E: bookings@wythallestate.co.uk **W:** www.wythallestate.co.uk

Wythall is a 16th century half-timbered manor house in a secluded setting, with garden, duck pond and wooded grounds. You will enjoy peace and quiet here and see an abundance of wildlife. The cottages are self-contained and set in the west wing of the house. They are well equipped, warm and comfortable and have digital television with freeview channels and DVD player and free Wi-Fi access. **Open:** All year **Nearest Shop:** 2 miles **Nearest Pub:** 1 mile

BRIDGNORTH, Shropshire   Map ref 4A3

Units   1
Sleeps   2-4
PER UNIT PER WEEK
£180.00 - £220.00

The Granary
Contact: Mrs Sarah Allen, The Granary, The Old Vicarage, Ditton Priors, Bridgnorth WV16 6SP **T:** (01746) 712272 **E:** sixteenridges@gmail.com

Farm granary in unspoilt South Shropshire countryside. Bridgnorth within easy reach, Ludlow 16 miles. Studio sitting room, bedroom, kitchen, bathroom. Excellent walking. **Open:** All year **Nearest Shop:** 0.5 miles **Nearest Pub:** 0.5 miles

CHAPEL LAWN, Shropshire   Map ref 4A3

Units   2
Sleeps   1-6

The Squire Farm Holiday Cottages
Contact: Mrs Becky Whitton, The Squire Farm, Chapel Lawn, Bucknell, Shropshire SY7 0BW **T:** (01547) 530530 **E:** becky@squirefarm.co.uk
W: www.squirefarm.co.uk **£ BOOK ONLINE**

The Squire Farm has two unusual and interesting cottages. With beautiful views and peaceful surroundings, you can enjoy walks right from your door and explore the historical Shropshire countryside. Please contact us for prices. **Open:** All year **Nearest Shop:** 3 miles **Nearest Pub:** 3 miles

Need more information?
Visit our websites for detailed information, up-to-date availability and to book your accommodation online. Includes over 20,000 places to stay, all of them star rated.
www.visitor-guides.co.uk

IRONBRIDGE, Shropshire   Map ref 4A3

★★★★
SELF CATERING

Units   2
Sleeps   4-6

PER UNIT PER WEEK
£495.00 - £1025.00

SPECIAL PROMOTIONS
Weekend and short breaks are available all year round. Check out the latest special offers online at www.coalportstation.com/special-offers

Coalport Station Holidays

Contact: Stephen Rawlings, Joint Owner, Coalport Station Holidays, Station House, Coalport, Telford, Shropshire TF8 7JF **T:** (01952) 885674 **E:** info@coalportstation.com
W: www.coalportstation.com **£ BOOK ONLINE**

Set in the scenic beauty of the UNESCO World Heritage Site of the Ironbridge Gorge, Coalport Station is one of England's most unique holiday destinations. Today it hosts two fabulous railway carriages offering award-winning accommodation.

The renovated carriages still wear traditional GWR livery with pride, but on the inside they offer everything for the modern luxury self-catering experience. This tranquil setting is also within walking distance of excellent quality food and traditional ales. The surrounding Ironbridge Gorge has plenty of activities to enjoy and fantastic places to explore.

Open: February - December
Nearest Shop: 2 miles

Nearest Pub: 100 yards

Units: Both Carriages have deceptively spacious Kitchen/lounge/diners C1: Sleeps 6 - 1 en suite double, 2 twin bedrooms. C2: Sleeps 4 - 2 en suite doubles.

Site: ✿ **P** **Payment:** 💷 € **Leisure:** ▸ **Property:** 🖥 📶 📺 **Children:** 🐾 🛏 🏸
Unit: 🗑 🍴 📺 📻 🍳 📺 📀 **BBQ**

LUDLOW, Shropshire   Map ref 4A3

4★ - 5★
SELF CATERING   *Gold* AWARD

Units   5
Sleeps   4-6
PER UNIT PER WEEK
£540.00 - £1050.00

Ashford Farm Cottages

Contact: Norman or Lynda Tudge, Owners, Ashford Farm, Ashford Carbonel, Ludlow, Shropshire SY8 4DB **T:** (01584) 831243 **E:** cottages@ashfordfarms.co.uk
W: www.ashfordfarms.co.uk

 Five lovely cottages just 3 miles from historic Ludlow, the perfect base from which to explore the Welsh Marches. All master bedrooms en suite. Well behaved dogs welcome free of charge. Individual secure garden with each cottage. Freshly prepared meals delivered on request. Cul-de-sac village location, no through traffic. Owners on site, available to help. All inclusive, no hidden charges.
Open: All year. **Nearest Shop:** 3 miles **Nearest Pub:** 3 miles

 Site: ✿ **P** **Leisure:** ▸ **Property:** 🐕 🖥 📶 📺 **Children:** 🐾 🛏 🏸 **Unit:** 🗑 🍴 📺 📻 🍳 📺 📀 BBQ ☎

LUDLOW, Shropshire   Map ref 4A3

★★★
SELF CATERING

Units   1
Sleeps   3-4
PER UNIT PER WEEK
£220.00 - £400.00

The Balcony Flat

Contact: Greenwich House, 2 Mill Street SY8 1AZ **T:** (01584) 841225
E: suewalsh@tesco.net
W: www.virtual-shropshire.co.uk/greenwich

 Superb apartment in centre of "gourmet" Ludlow. Sleeps 3-4. Stunning balcony views over fascinating Ludlow. Private garden. Short breaks available. **Open:** All year **Nearest Shop:** Next door **Nearest Pub:** Opposite flat

Site: ✿ **Leisure:** 🎵 ▸ ♾ **Property:** 🚭 🐕 🖥 📶 📺 **Children:** 🐾 🛏 🏸 **Unit:** 🗑 🍴 📺 📻 🍳 📺 📀 📀 BBQ

LUDLOW, Shropshire Map ref 4A3

Castle House Lodgings

Contact: Castle House Lodgings, Ludlow Castle, Castle Square, Ludlow SY8 1AY
T: (01584) 874465 **E:** info@ludlowcastle.com
W: www.castle-accommodation.com **£ BOOK ONLINE**

Units 3
Sleeps 1-4

PER UNIT PER WEEK
£895.00 - £1230.00

SPECIAL PROMOTIONS
Three night weekend break
(Friday to Sunday)

Four night break
(Monday to Thursday)

Seven night break
(Friday to Thursday).

Castle House Lodgings comprise of three 4-5* self catering apartments, full of character features and finished to the highest of standards, set within the walls of Ludlow Castle. Each apartment provides a sitting room/dining room, fully equipped kitchen, two twin bedrooms and two bathrooms and a car parking space.

Open: All year
Nearest Shop: 0.10 miles
Nearest Pub: 0.10 miles

Site: P Payment: 🔢 **Leisure:** 🎣 🎵 ⛳ **Property:** 🐾 🛏 📶 🖥 **Children:** 🐴 🛏 🚶
Unit: 🍴 🍽 📺 🖥 🍳 📺 📀 📀 📞

LUDLOW, Shropshire Map ref 4A3

Glebe Barn

Contact: Mr & Mrs Jones, Glebe Barn, Caynham, Ludlow, Shropshire SY8 3BN
T: (01584) 705027 **E:** info@glebebarnludlow.co.uk
W: www.glebebarnludlow.co.uk **£ BOOK ONLINE**

Units 1
Sleeps 7

PER UNIT PER WEEK
£339.00 - £798.00

SPECIAL PROMOTIONS
Why not enjoy a relaxing weekend break! Available during off season & winter weekends Fri-Mon.

A delightful detached barn conversion in the picturesque rural village of Caynham, 3 miles from Ludlow. Superbly renovated to perfectly blend original character and contemporary fixtures and fittings, this lovely property boasts a wealth of exposed oak beams, trusses and doors, creating a lovely welcoming atmosphere.

Open: All year
Nearest Shop: 2.30 miles
Nearest Pub: 2.30 miles

Site: P Leisure: 🎣 🎵 🚶 ⛳ **Property:** 🛏 🖥 **Children:** 🐴 🛏 🚶 **Unit:** 🍴 🍽 📺 🖥 🍳 📺 📀 📀 🖊 BBQ

LUDLOW, Shropshire   Map ref 4A3

★★★ SELF CATERING

Units   1
Sleeps   1-4
PER UNIT PER WEEK
£230.00 - £370.00

Posthorn Cottage

Contact: Ms Helen Davis, Proprietor, Posthorn Cottage, 32 Leamington Drive, Chilwell, Nottingham NG9 5LJ **T:** (01159) 222 383 / 07794 669810 **E:** helendavis233@outlook.com
W: www.posthorncottage.co.uk

Charming two-storey cottage in historic town-centre building with exposed beams. Small, private patio. In quiet courtyard off Broad Street. Conveniently situated for town centre amenities and places of interest. **Open:** All year **Nearest Shop:** 0.10 miles
Nearest Pub: 0.10 miles

Site: ✿ Property: 🖥 🖴 Children: ⛟ Unit: 📺 🗗 📺 📷 📀 ✐

LUDLOW, Shropshire   Map ref 4A3

★★★★ SELF CATERING

Gold AWARD

Units   2
Sleeps   2-6

The Silver Pear Apartments

Contact: Mr Christopher Tuffley, Director, Silver Pear Apartments, 68-69 Broad Street, Ludlow SY8 1NH **T:** (01584) 879096 **F:** 01584 879124 **E:** sales@silverpear.co.uk
W: www.silverpearapartments.co.uk

Our apartments have been restored to the highest specification, utilising all the original features of such an important building, and much of the original oak features have been saved. **Open:** All year
Nearest Shop: 0.01 miles **Nearest Pub:** 0.02 miles

WALKERS FAMILIES CYCLISTS   Payment: 💷 Leisure: 🚲 🎣 ▶ ♻ Property: 📺 🖴 Children: ⛟ 🛏 ⚲ Unit: 🗄 🗗 📺 🗗 📺 📷 📀

LUDLOW, Shropshire   Map ref 4A3

3★ - 4★ SELF CATERING

Units   6
Sleeps   2-6
PER UNIT PER WEEK
£245.00 - £560.00

Sutton Court Farm Cottages

Contact: Mrs Jane Cronin, Sutton Court Farm, Little Sutton, Ludlow, Shropshire SY8 2AJ
T: (01584) 861305 **E:** enquiries@suttoncourtfarm.co.uk
W: www.suttoncourtfarm.co.uk

6 comfortable cottages surrounding a peaceful, sunny courtyard, 5 miles from historic Ludlow in an Area of Outstanding Natural Beauty. Ironbridge, Shrewsbury, Hereford and the Welsh borders within easy reach. Breakfast packs, cream teas and evening meals available to order. Short breaks (min. 2 nights) all year round. Special offer from Nov to Mar (excl holidays), 3 nights for 2, 4 nights for 3. **Open:** All year **Nearest Shop:** 6 miles **Nearest Pub:** 3 miles

WALKERS CYCLISTS   Site: ✿ P Payment: € Leisure: 🚲 🎣 ▶ ♻ Property: 🐾 📺 🗗 🖴 Children: ⛟ 🛏 ⚲ Unit: 🗄 📺 🗗 📺 📀 ✐ BBQ ☎

ALTON, Staffordshire   Map ref 4B2

★★★ SELF CATERING

Gold AWARD

Units   1
Sleeps   2-6
PER UNIT PER WEEK
£525.00

Blythe Farmhouse

Contact: Mrs Irene Bullock, Booking Enquiries, Blythe Farmhouse, Riverside Road, Tean ST10 4JW **T:** (01538) 724061 / 07969 443869 **E:** irene@blythefarmhouse.co.uk
W: www.blythefarmhouse.co.uk **£ BOOK ONLINE**

Blythe Farmhouse is a grade II listed building. It has been extensively renovated retaining many of the original features. Fantastic views over the Staffordshire countryside. Accommodation equipped with quality fittings. **Open:** All year **Nearest Shop:** 1.5 miles **Nearest Pub:** 1.5 miles

Site: ✿ P Leisure: 🚲 🎣 ♻ Property: 📺 🗗 🖴 Children: ⛟ 🛏 ⚲ Unit: 📺 🗗 📺 📷 📀 ✐ BBQ

ALTON TOWERS AREA, *Staffordshire* Map ref 4B2

The Wolery

Contact: Mrs Michelle McGinn, Owner, Green Stile, Clerk's Bank, Ipstones, Staffordshire Moorlands ST10 2LQ **T:** (01538) 266797 **E:** TheWolery21314@gmail.com

Units	1
Sleeps	2

PER UNIT PER WEEK
£210.00 - £325.00

SPECIAL PROMOTIONS
Short Breaks Available: Friday - Monday or Monday-Friday. Please contact for Short Break rates.

The Wolery is a restored 17th Century stone barn, styled and converted to a high standard of design to offer comfort. There is a good sized, enclosed garden to take advantage of the sun, shade and views. As dog lovers ourselves, we welcome pets and there are many easily accessible walks and some from the front door.

The Wolery is situated on the outskirts of the Moorlands village of Ipstones, set in the undiscovered gem that is the Staffordshire Moorlands. Only a short drive to The Potteries, Alton Towers and the Peak District and ten minutes from the market town of Leek, it is the perfect base for a wonderful holiday. There are no hidden charges, we provide bed linen, towels and tea towels.

Open: All year
Nearest Shop: 0.5 Miles
Nearest Pub: 0.5 Miles

Units: Double bedroom with plenty of storage. Well equipped Kitchen/dining room. Bathroom with shower over bath, laundry provisions. Lounge with TV/DVD & small music system. Plenty of parking.

Site: ✿ P Leisure: ⚓ ♪ ▶ ♌ Property: 🐾 🛢 🖳 Unit: 🗄 🖥 📺 DVD BBQ

BIDDULPH, *Staffordshire* Map ref 4B2

Heritage Wharf Bungalow

Contact: Mike Dowse, Heritage Narrow Boats, The Marina, Scholar Green ST7 3JZ
T: (01782) 785700 **E:** email@heritagenarrowboats.co.uk
W: www.heritagenarrowboats.co.uk

Units	1
Sleeps	14

PER UNIT PER WEEK
£578.00 - £1113.00

Large accommodation comprised of five bedrooms, three bathrooms (two en suite), fully equipped kitchen with electric 'range style' cooker, tall fridge/freezer, dishwasher and utility room with washing machine and dryers. The spacious lounge area has three large sofas and an armchair, a large open fireplace and a TV and DVD. Other features include large patio with picnic table and barbecue, overlooking a private marina to the front with a large secluded side garden for sunbathing in privacy. **Open:** All year **Nearest Shop:** 0.5 miles **Nearest Pub:** 0.25 miles

Site: ✿ P Property: 🖳 🛢 🖳 Children: 🧒 Unit: 🗄 🖥 📺 DVD BBQ

BURTON UPON TRENT, *Staffordshire*   *Map ref 4B3*

3★ - 4★ SELF CATERING
Gold AWARD

Units 44
Sleeps 1-6

PER UNIT PER WEEK
£490.00 - £1267.00

SPECIAL PROMOTIONS
Enjoy two nights or more with complimentary champagne and chocolates on arrival, please call for latest pricing.

Wychnor Park Country Club

Contact: Wychnor Hall, Nr Barton-Under-Needwood, Staffordshire DE13 8BU
T: (0800) 358 6991 **E:** EuHotels@diamondresorts.com
W: www.DiamondResortsandHotels.com **£ BOOK ONLINE**

Set in a private, peaceful estate, this country club has landscaped gardens and combines the best of old and new for a relaxing environment.

All beautiful accommodation at Wychnor Park Country Club offers a high standard of luxury. Guests may be allocated rooms in the historic main building, the coach house and courtyard buildings or spacious log cabins in the grounds. The superb gardens provide a host of sporting activities. Above all, Wychnor Park Country Club is an peaceful country retreat.

Open: All year
Nearest Shop: 3 miles
Nearest Pub: On Site

Units: A choice of one and two bedroom apartments available. All apartments boast a full kitchen, modern bathroom and Television with DVD player.

Site: ✿ P **Payment:** 💳 **Leisure:** ▶ ⚲ ⚲ **Property:** 🛏 🔲 🔳 **Children:** 🐾 🛏 🏓
Unit: 🔲 🔲 🔲 🔳 🔳 📺 💿 📞

DILHORNE, *Staffordshire*   *Map ref 4B2*

★★★★ SELF CATERING

Units 2
Sleeps 1-5
PER UNIT PER WEEK
£200.00 - £500.00

Little Summerhill Cottages

Contact: Mrs Beth Plant, Little Summerhill Farm, Tickhill Lane, Dilhorne ST10 2PL
T: (01782) 550967 / 07976 068560 **F:** (01782) 550967
E: info@holidaycottagesstaffordshire.com **W:** holidaycottagesstaffordshire.com

Newly converted, one and two bedroomed cottages in Staffordshire Moorlands. Convenient for Peak District, Potteries and Alton Towers, yet a cosy, well equipped retreat with scenic views, on working smallholding. **Open:** All year **Nearest Shop:** 3 miles **Nearest Pub:** 2 miles

Site: ✿ P **Payment:** € **Property:** 🔳 **Unit:** 🔲 🔳 🔳 📺 💿 📀 BBQ

ENDON, *Staffordshire*   *Map ref 4B2*

★★★★ SELF CATERING

Units 1
Sleeps 1-2
PER UNIT PER WEEK
£420.00

Middle Cottage

Contact: Mike & Alison Benson, Brook Cottage, The Village, Stoke-on-Trent, Endon ST9 9EY **T:** (01782) 505089 / 07817 712296 **E:** alison@middlecottageholidays.co.uk
W: middlecottageholidays.co.uk

Quaint country cottage. 1 double bedroom, log fire, full central heating. Old village location. Cottage garden, Ideal for Peak District or Potteries. Perfect for walkers, antique hunters or a place for relaxing. **Open:** All year **Nearest Shop:** 1 mile **Nearest Pub:** 0.12 miles

Site: ✿ P **Leisure:** ♉ **Property:** 🔳 **Children:** 🐾 🛏 **Unit:** 🔲 🔲 🔳 🔳 📺 💿 📀 ✎

LEEK, Staffordshire   Map ref 4B2

Units 1
Sleeps 6

PER UNIT PER WEEK
£250.00 - £395.00

Rosewood Cottage

Contact: Lower Berkhamsytch Farm, Bottomhouse, Nr Leek, Staffordshire ST13 7QP
T: (01538) 308213 **E:** a.e.mycock@gmail.com
W: www.rosewoodcottage.co.uk

Set in picturesque Staffordshire Moorlands, bordering Peak District. Attractive three bedroomed cottage including four poster bed. Central to Alton Towers, Potteries and Peak District. Field available for pet walking and ball games. **Open:** All year **Nearest Shop:** 2 miles **Nearest Pub:** 2 miles

Site: ✿ P **Leisure:** 🚴 ▶ **Property:** 🐾 📺 🖳 **Children:** 🍼 🛏 🏃 **Unit:** 🖥 📷 📺 🔌 📺 🎛 📹

STONE, Staffordshire   Map ref 4B2

Units 15
Sleeps 2-8

PER UNIT PER WEEK
£481.00 - £1699.00

SPECIAL PROMOTIONS
Please our website for our special offers.

Canal Cruising Company Ltd

Contact: Mrs Karen Wyatt, Booking Enquiries, Canal Cruising Company Ltd, Crown Street, Stone ST15 8QN **T:** (01785) 813982 **F:** 01785 819041 **E:** mail@canalcruising.co.uk
W: www.canalcruising.co.uk **£ BOOK ONLINE**

Situated in the Heart of England, Stone is the ideal starting point for a different type of Holiday. Canal Boating in the slow lane, an adventure, seeing England from a different view point. We have several choices of routes including Four Counties Ring, The Caldon, The Cheshire Ring and Llangollen.

We Offer Day Hire, Shortbreak, Weekly and longer. A week or more from Stone, you have several choices of routes, for an energetic week you can do the Four Counties Ring visiting Shropshire, Staffordshire, Cheshire and the Midlands. Alternately, for an easier week for example - The Caldon. Gift Vouchers are available.

Open: Mid March to End October
Nearest Shop: 0.5 miles
Nearest Pub: 0.5 miles

Site: P **Payment:** 💳 € **Leisure:** 🎵 **Property:** 🐾 🖳 **Children:** 🍼 🛏 **Unit:** 🔌 📺

WATERHOUSES, Staffordshire   Map ref 4B2

Units 2
Sleeps 1-6

PER UNIT PER WEEK
£215.00 - £495.00

Greenside Cottages

Contact: Mr & Mrs Terry & Sue Riley, Owner, Greenside Cottages, Brown End Farm, Waterhouses, Staffordshire ST10 3JR **T:** (01538) 308313 / 07779 320975 **F:** 01538 308053
E: sriley01@gmail.com **W:** www.greenside-cottages.co.uk

2 delightful converted stone cottages in Peak District. Well equipped, very welcoming and comfortable. Ideal base for walking and cycling from doorstep. Historic houses and visitor attractions are within easy reach. Alton Towers is only 15 minutes away. Day's cycling for guests. **Open:** All year **Nearest Shop:** 0.40 miles **Nearest Pub:** 0.40 miles

Site: ✿ P **Leisure:** 🚴 🎵 ⛳ **Property:** 🖳 **Children:** 🍼 🛏 🏃 **Unit:** 🖥 🍽 📷 🔌 📺 🎛 📹 🍴 BBQ

ATHERSTONE, *Warwickshire*   *Map ref 4B3*

Units   8
Sleeps   2-6
PER UNIT PER WEEK
£350.00 - £800.00

Hipsley Farm Cottages

Contact: Hipsley Lane, Hurley, Atherstone, Warwickshire CV9 2LR **T:** (01827) 872437
E: ann@hipsley.co.uk
W: www.hipsley.co.uk

Eight comfortable, attractive cottages sleeping 2-7, converted from old farm barns. Beautiful countryside, putting green, and farm walks. Each cottage furnished to the highest standards with full central heating, TV/DVD & CD player, Wi-Fi. **Open:** All year **Nearest Shop:** 1.75 miles **Nearest Pub:** 1.75 miles

  Site: ✿ **P Payment:** 🔲 **Leisure:** 🚣 🎣 ⛳ ∪ **Property:** ⫽ 🐾 🖥 📺 🖼 **Children:** 🛝 🛏 🪑
Unit: 📟 📠 💻 🔌 📺 📀 BBQ ☎

DUNCHURCH, *Warwickshire*   *Map ref 4C3*

Units   1
Sleeps   4-6
PER UNIT PER WEEK
£450.00 - £600.00

Toft Manor Cottage

Contact: Mrs Shirley Bettinson, Toft Manor Cottage, Toft Manor, Toft Lane, Dunchurch CV22 6NR **T:** (01788) 810626 / 07970 626245 **F:** 01788 522347
E: shirley@toft-alpacas.co.uk **W:** www.toft-alpacas.co.uk **£ BOOK ONLINE**

A two, double-bedroomed stable conversion set in the grounds of Toft Manor amongst a prize-winning herd of Toft Alpacas. Offers outstanding views across Draycote Water, and beautiful walks amongst the alpacas. **Open:** All year **Nearest Shop:** 0.5 miles **Nearest Pub:** 0.5 miles

Site: ✿ **P Payment:** 🔲 € **Leisure:** 🚣 🎣 ⛳ ∪ **Property:** 🖥 📺 🖼 **Children:** 🛝 **Unit:** 📟 📠 💻 🔌 📺 📀

HENLEY-IN-ARDEN, *Warwickshire*   *Map ref 4B3*

Units   1
Sleeps   8
PER UNIT PER WEEK
£600.00 - £950.00

SPECIAL PROMOTIONS
Short stay 3 nights and 4 nights.

The Cottage Kyte Green

Contact: Kirstie Lodder, Owner, The Cottage, Kyte Green, Henley-in-Arden, Warwickshire B95 5DU **T:** (01564) 793981 / 07887 752506 **E:** kirstie@thecottage-kytegreen.co.uk
W: www.thecottage-kytegreen.co.uk **£ BOOK ONLINE**

Secluded country cottage in the heart of the Warwickshire countryside. Sleeps 8 with 4 double bedrooms, one with en suite bathroom. Large kitchen and 2 sitting rooms, one with a sofa bed. Central heating and 2 open fires. The perfect place for a relaxing or adventure filled holiday for the family or group of friends with everything included. Pets welcome with a large garden with immediate access to the farm fields and footpaths. Ample private parking. Wifi available. Information (pubs, shops, activities) and maps are provided of the local area.

Open: All year
Nearest Shop: 1 mile
Nearest Pub: 1 mile

Units: 4 double bedrooms, one en suite, bathroom, 1 WC on ground floor.

  Site: ✿ **P Property:** 🐾 🖥 📺 🖼 **Children:** 🛏 🪑 **Unit:** 📟 📠 📺 📀 📀 ∅ BBQ ☎

LEAMINGTON SPA, Warwickshire   Map ref 4B3

Furzen Hill Farm Cottages

Contact: Mrs Christine Whitfield, Owner, Furzen Hill Farm Cottages, Coventry Road, Cubbington Heath, Leamington Spa, Warwickshire CV32 7UJ **T:** (01926) 424791
F: 01926 424791 **E:** christine.whitfield1@btopenworld.com
W: furzenhillfarmcottages.co.uk

Units   4
Sleeps   1-6
PER UNIT PER WEEK
£290.00 - £500.00

Cottages at Cubbington, ideally situated for Warwick, Stratford-upon-Avon and NEC. Large shared garden. Use of hard tennis court and swimming pool. Families especially welcome on our working arable farm. **Open:** All year **Nearest Shop:** 1.25 miles
Nearest Pub: 1.25 miles

Site: ✿ P Leisure: ♪ ↟ ⚲ ⚲ Property: ⌖ ▭ ◫ ▣ Children: ⚞ ▦ Unit: ▯ ▤ ▭ ▣ ⚲ TV dvd

SHIPSTON-ON-STOUR, Warwickshire   Map ref 2B1

Burmington View

Contact: Vanessa Barney, Burmington Grange Cottage, Cherington, Shipston on Stour, Warwickshire CV36 5HZ **T:** (01608) 686526 **E:** vanessa@burmington-view.co.uk
W: www.burmington-view.co.uk

Units   1
Sleeps   1-2
PER UNIT PER WEEK
£330.00 - £440.00

Situated in a lovely rural location, Burmington View is two miles from the historic Shipston-on-Stour. Bright and comfortable, fully equipped, one bedroom loft conversion with views over open countryside. **Open:** All year **Nearest Shop:** 2 miles
Nearest Pub: 2 miles

Site: ✿ P Leisure: ♪ ⚲ Property: ∥ ▭ ◫ ▣ Unit: ▯ ▤ ▭ ▣ TV dvd BBQ

STRATFORD-UPON-AVON, Warwickshire   Map ref 2B1

4 Bancroft Place

Contact: Mrs Carolann Barnett, Stratford-upon-Avon, Warwickshire CV37 6YZ
T: (01920) 871849 **E:** carolannbarnett@yahoo.co.uk
W: www.4bancroftplace.com

Units   1
Sleeps   2

PER UNIT PER WEEK
£350.00 - £395.00

SPECIAL PROMOTIONS
Flexible start days. Short breaks (3-night weekend, 4-night midweek) available.

10% discount available for returning guests.

Town centre, canalside, light and airy, first floor studio apartment for two adults. Living area overlooks the canal and cleverly converts into a bedroom with fully sprung 4'6" sofabed. Very well equipped kitchen, shower room and hallway dressing area. Within walking distance of everything Stratford offers. Off-road dedicated parking for one vehicle. All linen and towels and electricity costs are included.

Open: All year
Nearest Shop: 300 yards
Nearest Pub: 100 yards

Units: Guests met on arrival and shown round the fully-serviced apartment. Public Wi-Fi hotspot accessible from apartment.

Site: ✿ P Property: ∥ ▣ Unit: ▯ ▭ ⚲ TV dvd

STRATFORD-UPON-AVON, *Warwickshire*   Map ref 2B1

3★ - 4★
SELF CATERING

Units   2
Sleeps   1-3
PER UNIT PER WEEK
£320.00 - £430.00

As You Like It

Contact: Mr & Mrs Ian & Janet Reid, c/o Inwood House, New Road, Stratford-upon-Avon CV37 8PE **T:** (01789) 450266 / 07956 692015 **E:** ian@alderminster99.freeserve.co.uk
W: www.asyoulikeitcottage.co.uk / no1collegemews.co.uk **£ BOOK ONLINE**

'As You Like It' is a character cottage in central Stratford and No.1 College Mews is an apartment, within easy walking distance of the theatres and the town's many attractions. **Open:** All year **Nearest Shop:** 0.25 miles **Nearest Pub:** 0.25 miles

Site: P Property: 🐾 🚗 🖥 **Unit:** 🖥 📖 ⚲ 📺 ◐ ☎

STRATFORD-UPON-AVON, *Warwickshire*   Map ref 2B1

★★★★★
SELF CATERING

Gold
AWARD

Units   1
Sleeps   3
PER UNIT PER WEEK
£525.00 - £785.00

Heritage Mews

Contact: Val and Simon Broke-Smith, Owners, 15 Bullivents Close, Solihull B93 9BT
T: (01564) 778649 / 07946 200740 **E:** info@heritagemews.co.uk
W: www.heritagemews.co.uk

Delightful two bedroom cottage in an excellent, peaceful location in Stratford-upon-Avon's Old Town. Within 10 minutes stroll of the historic town centre, Shakespeare Houses, theatres and many excellent restaurants and pubs. Close to the River Avon, with beautiful riverside walks. Attractive private courtyard garden. Wi-Fi. Private off-road parking. Ideal base for exploring the Cotswolds. **Open:** All Year **Nearest Shop:** 250 metres **Nearest Pub:** 250 metres

Site: ❀ **P Property:** 🖥 📖 🖥 **Children:** 👶 🛏 🚶 **Unit:** 🖥 🍴 🖥 📖 ⚲ 📺 📀 ☎

BEWDLEY, *Worcestershire*   Map ref 4A3

★★★★
SELF CATERING

Units   1
Sleeps   1-4
PER UNIT PER WEEK
£395.00 - £485.00

Fern Cottage

Contact: Jenny, Bewdley, Worcestershire DY12 2ER **T:** 07899 797535
E: bookings@ferncottagebewdley.co.uk
W: www.ferncottagebewdley.co.uk **£ BOOK ONLINE**

A rebuilt cosy cottage. Conveniently situated, an easy walk from Bewdley's pubs, shops, restaurants, the River Severn and beautiful countryside. Sleeps 4 in two en suite bedrooms. Wi-Fi availiable. Courtyard garden. Parking. Available for short lets. **Open:** All year **Nearest Shop:** 0.10 miles **Nearest Pub:** 0.20 miles

  Site: ❀ **P Leisure:** 🎵 🚶 **Property:** 🖥 🖥 **Children:** 👶 🚶 **Unit:** 🖥 🍴 🖥 📖 ⚲ 📺 📀 ☎

BEWDLEY, *Worcestershire*   Map ref 4A3

★★★★
SELF CATERING

Units   1
Sleeps   2-6
PER UNIT PER WEEK
£480.00 - £645.00

Fern View

Contact: Jenny, Bewdley, Worcestershire DY12 2ER **T:** 07899 797535
E: bookings@fernviewbewdley.co.uk
W: www.fernviewbewdley.co.uk **£ BOOK ONLINE**

Situated a short walk from Georgian Bewdley, this refurbished bungalow sleeps 6 in three bedrooms, two en suite. Ideal for families and the less mobile. Wireless broadband. Private garden. Parking. Available for short lets. **Open:** All year **Nearest Shop:** 0.10 miles **Nearest Pub:** 0.10 miles

Site: ❀ **P Leisure:** 🎵 🚶 ⛳ **Property:** 🖥 🖥 🖥 **Children:** 👶 🛏 🚶 **Unit:** 🖥 🍴 🖥 📖 ⚲ 📺 📀 ☎

DROITWICH, *Worcestershire* *Map ref 2B1*

The Hayloft

Contact: Gill Lumsdon, Owner, Mayhouse Farm, Hadley, Nr Droitwich Spa, Worcestershire WR9 0AS **T:** (01905) 620126 / 07770 883091 **E:** g.lumsdon@btinternet.com
W: www.mayhousefarm.com

Units   1
Sleeps   1-3
PER UNIT PER WEEK
£420.00 - £525.00

The Hayloft is a beautifully appointed two-bedroom apartment on the upper floor of a newly reconstructed Cart House adjoining Mayhouse farmhouse. Situated at the end of a long private drive, The Hayloft is in a quiet and peaceful location but it is easily accessible being only a few miles from junctions 5 and 6 of the M5 motorway. **Open:** All year **Nearest Shop:** 3 miles
Nearest Pub: 1 mile

Site: ❀ **P** **Leisure:** ▶ **Property:** ∥ ▭ ◫ ▣ **Children:** ⛀ ⛺ ♠ **Unit:** ▯ ▯ ▬ ▤ ⚲ TV ◉ ⊙ BBQ ☎

GUARLFORD, *Worcestershire* *Map ref 2B1*

Rhydd Barn

Contact: Miss Rosemary Boaz, Under Ley, Doverhay, Porlock, Somerset TA24 8LL
T: (01643) 862359 **E:** info@rhyddbarn.co.uk
W: www.rhyddbarn.co.uk

Units   1
Sleeps   1-2
PER UNIT PER WEEK
£320.00 - £440.00

Outstanding barn conversion with spacious accommodation on three floors and wonderful views of the Malvern Hills. Tiled and wooden floors, white walls interspersed with pine beams and black iron work. Commended finalist for the Best Self Catering Award - Visit Worcestershire Awards for Excellence 2013. **Open:** All year
Nearest Shop: 2 miles **Nearest Pub:** 0.25 miles

 Site: ❀ **P** **Property:** ▣ **Unit:** ▯ ▯ ▬ ▤ ⚲ TV ⊙

MALVERN, *Worcestershire* *Map ref 2B1*

Apartment 3 Highlea

Contact: Mr Gareth Richards, 43 Addicott Road, Weston super Mare BS23 3PY
T: 07799 691929 **E:** garethrichards77@yahoo.com

Units   1
Sleeps   1-4
PER UNIT PER WEEK
£420.00 - £490.00

SPECIAL PROMOTIONS
Available any number of nights, minimum stay 2 nights.

A beautiful, comfortable, well equipped, modern, light and airy apartment with designated parking within the grounds of this elegant Edwardian building. Quiet and relaxing yet close to amenities (e.g. theatre, restaurants, priory, hills).

Free Wi-Fi. Price includes linen, towels and electricty. Visitor guidebook gives 100% complimentary comments.

Open: All year
Nearest Shop: 0.01 miles
Nearest Pub: 0.03 miles

Units: One double bed (pocket sprung with memory foam) with en suite. One comfortable double sofa bed in lounge. High quality linen and towels. Please note the property is accessed by five front door steps.

 Site: **P** **Leisure:** ♿ ♪ ▶ ∪ **Property:** ⌖ ▭ ◫ ▣ **Children:** ⛀ **Unit:** ▯ ▯ ▬ ▤ ⚲ TV ◉ ⊙

MALVERN, *Worcestershire*   *Map ref 2B1*

Beesoni Lodge

Contact: Laura Smith, Beesoni, Hill End, Castlemorton, Malvern WR13 6BL
T: 07788 492648 / (01684) 830016 **E:** info@beesonilodge.co.uk
W: www.beesonilodge.co.uk

Units   1
Sleeps   10
PER UNIT PER WEEK
£597.00 - £1416.00

Fabulous spacious four star detached barn conversion, exceptional standard, exposed beams. Sleeps ten, four bedrooms (one four-poster), three bathrooms (one with spa bath). Large fully equiped kitchen. Own private grounds. Stunning views of Malverns and Cotswolds. Within easy reach of Malvern, Upton upon Severn, Cheltenham and Worcester. **Open:** All year **Nearest Shop:** 3 miles **Nearest Pub:** 2.5 miles

Site: ✿ P Property: ⫽ 🐕 🖥 📷 ▣ Children: 👶 🛏 🚶 Unit: 🍴 🧺 📺 🔌 📻 📺 📀 🎧 BBQ

MALVERN, *Worcestershire*   *Map ref 2B1*

Holywell Suite

Contact: Andrea, Holywell Suite, Wells House, Holywell Road, Malvern, Worcestershire WR14 4LH **T:** 07905 827082 **E:** bookings@holywellsuite.co.uk
W: www.holywellsuite.co.uk **£ BOOK ONLINE**

Units   1
Sleeps   1-4
PER UNIT PER WEEK
£350.00 - £550.00

Holywell Suite has an enviable, 4 Star Gold rated, specification throughout. Serviced by lift access, the third floor, award-winning apartment provides a private retreat with awesome, uninterrupted views across the Worcestershire countryside. The Malvern Hills are right on your doorstep. **Open:** All year **Nearest Shop:** 0.3 miles **Nearest Pub:** 0.1 miles

Site: ✿ P Payment: 💳 € Leisure: 🏊 🏌 ⚲ ⛳ Property: ⫽ 🖥 📷 ▣ Unit: 🍴 🧺 📺 🔌 📻 📺 📀

PERSHORE, *Worcestershire*   *Map ref 2B1*

Garth Cottage

Contact: Mrs Margaret Smith, 8 Pensham Hill, Pershore, Worcestershire WR10 3HA
T: (01386) 561213 / 07759 655717 **F:** 01386 561213 **E:** stephen.smith@homecall.co.uk
W: garthcottage.co.uk

Units   1
Sleeps   1-3
PER UNIT PER WEEK
£305.00 - £420.00

Delightful detached cottage in peaceful location, 10 minutes leisurely walk from Pershore. Large airy bedroom, double bed settee in lounge. Use of owners outdoor swimming pool (seasonal May to October weather dependent), by arrangement. Short breaks from £135. Special rates for Bank Holidays, Xmas, & New Year. **Open:** All year **Nearest Shop:** 1 mile **Nearest Pub:** 0.75 miles

 Site: ✿ P Leisure: 🏌 ⚲ ⛳ 🚲 Property: 🐕 🖥 📷 ▣ Children: 👶 🛏 🚶 Unit: 📺 🔌 📻 📺 📀 🎧 BBQ

SEDGEBERROW, *Worcestershire*   *Map ref 2B1*

Hall Farm Cottages

Contact: Rebecca Barclay, Manager, Hall Farm, Main Street, Sedgeberrow, Evesham WR11 7UF **T:** (01386) 881243 **E:** rebecca@hallfarmcottages.co.uk
W: www.hallfarmcottages.co.uk

Units   4
Sleeps   2-18
PER UNIT PER WEEK
£270.00 - £980.00

A delightful range of 18th Century barns have been sympathetically converted into self-catering cottages and modernised to meet extremely high standards, but retain a wealth of old beams and original features. An ideal place from which to explore the Cotswolds and surrounding areas or merely relax in the garden, swim in the pool, or try a spot of fishing along the riverbank! **Open:** Easter to November **Nearest Shop:** 0.10 miles **Nearest Pub:** 0.10 miles

Site: ✿ P Payment: 💳 Leisure: 🏌 ⚲ ⛳ 🚲 Property: 🖥 📷 ▣ Children: 👶 🛏 🚶 Unit: 🍴 🧺 📺 📺 🔌 📺 📀 🎧

For **key to symbols** see page 7

SUTTON, *Worcestershire*   *Map ref 4A3*

Units 2
Sleeps 2-8

PER UNIT PER WEEK
£700.00 - £900.00

Long Cover Cottage & The Coach House

Contact: Mrs Eleanor Van Straaten, Holiday Cottage, Fishpool Cottage, Kyre, Tenbury Wells WR15 8RL **T:** (01885) 410208 / 07725 972486
E: ellie_vanstraaten@yahoo.co.uk **W:** www.a-country-break.co.uk

Long Cover Cottage: A retreat from the outside world with magnificent views in all directions over the Teme and Kyre Valleys. Exposed beams, oak/elm staircase, Aga, woodburning stove. Coach House: Retire to your own private viewpoint with its picture-postcard views across open pastures to the Teme and Kyre valleys.

Open: All year
Nearest Shop: 3 miles
Nearest Pub: 3 miles

Site: ❀ Leisure: ♪ ▶ ∪ ⚲ Property: ☎ ▦ ▣ ▣ Children: ⛱ ▦ ⚓ Unit: ▯ ▤ ▣ ⚲ TV ▣ ▣ ∅ BBQ

Book your accommodation online

Visit our websites for detailed information, up-to-date availability and to book your accommodation online. Includes over 20,000 places to stay, all of them star rated.

www.visitor-guides.co.uk

The Official Tourist Board Guide to **Self Catering 2015**

TENBURY WELLS, Worcestershire   Map ref 4A3

Rochford Park Cottages

Contact: Mrs Jarka Robinson, Rochford Park, Nr Tenbury Wells, Worcestershire WR15 8SP
T: (01584) 781392 **F:** 01584 781392 **E:** cottages@rochfordpark.co.uk
W: www.rochfordpark.co.uk

| Units | 3 |
| Sleeps | 3-8 |

PER UNIT PER WEEK
£193.00 - £740.00

Former farm outbuildings, now stylish, comfortable cottages suitable for couples, families or groups of friends, situated in beautiful Teme valley. Restful places, full of character. Woodlands, lakes nearby. **Open:** All year **Nearest Shop:** 3 miles
Nearest Pub: 1.5 miles

Site: ✿ P **Leisure:** 🚴 🏊 🏇 ♺ 🎣 **Property:** 🛅 🖥 **Children:** 🎠 🛏 🧸 **Unit:** 🛅 🍳 🖳 🖥 📺 📀 🍴 BBQ

WORCESTER, Worcestershire   Map ref 2B1

Hop Pickers Rural Retreats

Contact: Mrs Louise Wild, Owner, Pigeon House Farm, Dingle Road, Leigh, Worcestershire WR6 5JX **T:** (01886) 833668 / 07834 652132 **E:** enquiries@hoppickersbarn.co.uk
W: www.hoppickersbarn.co.uk

| Units | 2 |
| Sleeps | 4-5 |

PER UNIT PER WEEK
£395.00 - £780.00

SPECIAL PROMOTIONS
Short breaks available.
Please call for details.

Hop Pickers Rural Retreats comprise of the 17th century Barn which comfortably sleeps 5 and the new luxury log Cabin which sleeps 4. The location is in an idyllic rural location at the end of a No through road with fabulous walks from the doorstep leading up to the Malvern Hills. If you are looking for peace and relaxation this is the place for you. You are welcome to wander through the 9 acre smallholding, pick seasonal fruit and take the woodland walk leading up to a small wildlife hide overlooking the original oast ponds where you can spot badgers, bats and butterflies. During the summer months the heated outdoor swimming pool is available plus the tennis court and year round games room with table tennis, darts and scalextric. Proud winners of 2014 Destination Worcestershire Self catering property of the year.

Open: All Year
Nearest Shop: 2 miles
Nearest Pub: 2.3 miles

Units: Comfortable beds and spacious open plan living either under the original trusses in the Barn or in the Cabin which is nestled in the corner of the old orchard.

Site: ✿ P **Leisure:** 🚴 🏊 🏇 🎣 ♺ 🎾 **Property:** 🐾 🖥 🛅 🖳 **Children:** 🎠 🛏 🧸
Unit: 🛅 🍳 🖳 🖥 📺 📀 BBQ

WORCESTER, Worcestershire   Map ref 2B1

Roseland Holiday Bungalow

Contact: Guy and Mary Laurent, Partners, Roseland Bungalow, Clifton, Severn Stoke, Nr. Worcester, Worcestershire WR8 9JF **T:** (01905) 371463
E: guy@roselandworcs.demon.co.uk **W:** www.roselandworcs.demon.co.uk

| Units | 1 |
| Sleeps | 3 |

PER UNIT PER WEEK
£250.00 - £350.00

Self contained bungalow with 1 double and 1 single bedroom, bathroom, utility, kitchen/dining room, sitting room, double bed settee, conservatory. Dogs welcome. **Open:** Summer lets weekly, Winter lets monthly **Nearest Shop:** 1.5 miles **Nearest Pub:** 1 mile

Site: ✿ P **Leisure:** 🏊 🏇 **Property:** 🐾 🖥 🛅 🖳 **Children:** 🎠 🛏 🧸 **Unit:** 🛅 🍳 🖳 🖥 📺 📀

Don't Miss...

Castle Howard

Malton, North Yorkshire YO60 7DA
(01653) 648444
www.castlehoward.co.uk
A magnificent 18th century house situated in breathtaking parkland, dotted with temples, lakes statues and fountains; plus formal gardens, woodland garden and ornamental vegetable garden. Inside the House guides share stories of the house, family and collections, while outdoor-guided tours reveal the secrets of the architecture and landscape.

National Media Museum

Bradford, West Yorkshire BD1 1NQ
0870 701 0200
www.nationalmediamuseum.org.uk
The Museum is home to over 3.5 million items of historical significance including the National Photography, National Cinematography, National Television and National New Media Collections. Admission to the National Media Museum is free (charges apply for cinemas/IMAX).

National Railway Museum

York, North Yorkshire YO26 4XJ
0844 815 3139
www.nrm.org.uk
Awesome trains, interactive fun – and the world's largest railway museum make for a great day out.

The Deep

Hull, East Riding of Yorkshire HU1 4DP
(01482) 381000
www.thedeep.co.uk
Full with over 3500 fish and more than 40 sharks, The Deep tells the amazing story of the world's oceans through stunning marine life, interactives and audio-visual presentations making it a fun-filled family day out for all ages.

Yorkshire Wildlife Park

Doncaster, South Yorkshire DN3 3NH
(01302) 535057
www.yorkshirewildlifepark.co.uk2
A fabulous fun day and animal experience. Walk through 'Lemur Woods' and meet these mischievous primates, or come face to face with the wallabies in Wallaby Walk.

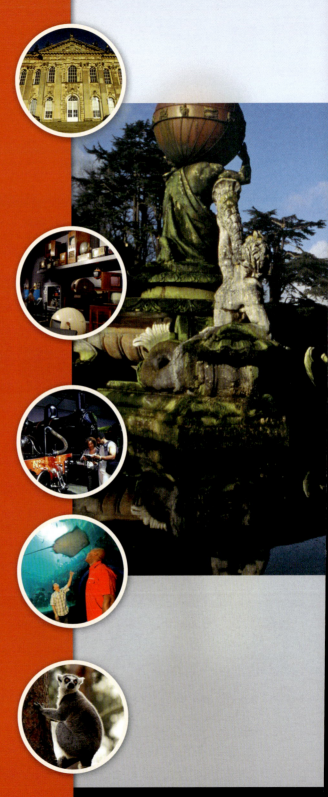

Yorkshire

Yorkshire

Yorkshire, the largest county in England, is one of the most popular and boasts award-winning culture, heritage and scenery. There's cosmopolitan Leeds, stylish Harrogate and rural market towns full of charm and character. The wild moors and deserted dales of the Yorkshire Dales and North York Moors National Parks are majestic in their beauty and the county has a spectacular coastline of rugged cliffs and sandy beaches. The region also has a wealth of historic houses, ruined castles, abbeys and fortresses for visitors to discover.

Explore – Yorkshire

North Yorkshire

Steeped in history, North Yorkshire boasts some of the country's most splendid scenery. Wherever you go in The Dales, you'll be faced with breathtaking views and constant reminders of a historic and changing past. In medieval days, solid fortresses like Richmond and Middleham were built to protect the area from marauding Scots. Ripley and Skipton also had their massive strongholds, while Bolton Castle in Wensleydale once imprisoned Mary, Queen of Scots. The pattern of history continues with the great abbeys, like Jervaulx Abbey, near Masham, where the monks first made Wensleydale cheese and the majestic ruins of Fountains Abbey in the grounds of Studley Royal. Between the Dales and the North York Moors, Herriot Country is named for one of the world's best loved writers, James Herriot, who made the area his home for more than 50 years and whose books have enthralled readers with tales of Yorkshire life.

Hotspot: The Forbidden Corner is a unique labyrinth of tunnels, chambers, follies and surprises in the heart of the beautiful Yorkshire Dales. www.theforbiddencorner.co.uk

Hotspot: Take a classic steam train from Pickering to Grosmont on the famous North Yorkshire Moors Railway for breathaking scenery. www.nymr.co.uk

Escape to the wild, deserted North York Moors National Park with its 500 square miles of hills, dales, forests and open moorland, neatly edged by a spectacular coastline. Walking, cycling and pony trekking are ideal ways to savour the scenery and there are plenty of greystone towns and villages dotted throughout the Moors that provide ideal bases from which to explore. From Helmsley, visit the ruins of Rievaulx Abbey, founded by Cistercian monks in the 12th century or discover moorland life in the Ryedale Folk Museum at Hutton-le-Hole. The Beck Isle Museum in Pickering provides an insight into the life of a country market town and just a few miles down the road you'll find Malton, once a Roman fortress, and nearby Castle Howard, the setting for Brideshead Revisited.

Leeds & West Yorkshire

For centuries cloth has been spun from the wool of the sheep grazing in the Pennine uplands and the fascinating story of this industrial heritage can be seen in the numerous craft centres and folk museums throughout West Yorkshire. To enjoy the countryside, take a trip on the steam hauled Keighley and Worth Valley Railway. Not far from Haworth is Bingley, where the Leeds & Liverpool canal makes its famous uphill journey, a route for the coal barges in days gone by, nowadays replaced by holidaymakers in gaily painted boats. Leeds itself is a vibrant city with its Victorian shopping arcades, Royal Armouries Museum and lively arts scene.

Hotspot: Stop off at **Haworth**, home of the Bronte sisters, to visit The Bronte Parsonage museum and experience the rugged atmosphere of Wuthering Heights. www.bronte.org.uk

York

Wherever you turn within the city's medieval walls, you will find glimpses of the past. The splendours of the 600-year old Minster, the grim stronghold of Clifford's Tower, the National Railway Museum, the medieval timbers of the Merchant Adventurers' Hall and the fascinating Jorvik Viking Centre all offer an insight into the history of this charming city. Throughout the city, statues and monuments remind the visitor that this was where Constantine was proclaimed Holy Roman Emperor, Guy Fawkes was born and Dick Turpin met his end.

Modern York is has excellent shopping, a relaxed cafe culture, first class restaurants and bars, museums, tours and attractions. Whether you visit for a romantic weekend or a fun-filled family holiday, there really is something for everyone.

Yorkshire Coastline

The Yorkshire coastline is one of the UK's most naturally beautiful and rugged, where pretty fishing villages cling to rocky cliffs, in turn towering over spectacular beaches and family-friendly seaside destinations.

At the northern end of the coastline, Saltburn is a sand and shingle beach popular with surfers and visitors can ride the Victorian tram from the cliff to the promenade during the summer. Whitby is full of quaint streets and bestowed with a certain Gothic charm. At Scarborough, one of Britain's oldest seaside resorts, the award-winning North Bay and South Bay sand beaches are broken by the rocky headland, home to the historic Scarborough Castle. Filey, with its endless sands, has spectacular views and a 40-mile stretch of perfect sandy beach sweeps south from the dramatic 400 ft high cliffs at Flamborough Head. Along this coastline you can find the boisterous holiday destination of Bridlington, or a gentler pace at pretty Hornsea and Withernsea.

Hotspot: With its 3,000 year history, stunning location and panoramic views over the dramatic Yorkshire coastline, Scarborough Castle is one of the finest tourist attractions in Yorkshire.
www.english-heritage.org.uk

East Yorkshire

From cosmopolitan Hull to the hills and valleys of the Yorkshire Wolds, East Yorkshire is wonderfully diverse. A landscape of swirling grasslands, medieval towns, manor houses and Bronze Age ruins contrasting with the vibrant energy and heritage of the Humber. The Wolds are only a stones throw from some great seaside resorts and Beverley, with its magnificent 13th century minster and lattice of medieval streets, is just one of the many jewels of architectural heritage to be found here. Hull is a modern city rebuilt since the war, linked to Lincolnshire via the impressive 1452 yd Humber Bridge.

Hotspot: The St Leger at Doncaster Racecourse is the oldest classic horse race in the world, and the town celebrates in style with a whole festival of events. www.visitdoncaster.co.uk

South Yorkshire

The historic market town of Doncaster was founded by the Romans and has a rich horseracing and railway heritage. The area around Sheffield - the steel city - was once dominated by the iron and steel industries and was the first city in England to pioneer free public transport. The Industrial Museum and City Museum display a wide range of Sheffield cutlery and oplate. Today, Meadowhall shopping centre, with 270 stores under one roof, is a must-visit for shopaholics.

Indulge in a spot of retail therapy with a trip to **Leeds**. The Grand Arcade is one of the oldest shopping arcades in Leeds City Centre and is well worth a visit for its independent retailers. The stunning architecture of the Victoria Quarter's Grade II* arcades are a spectacular setting for a shopping spree, while VQ is home to over 75 of the world's leading fashion and lifestyle brands, including Vivienne Westwood, Paul Smith, Louis Vuitton, Mulberry and Illamasqua.

Tantalise your taste buds with traditional fish & chips from **The Quayside**, the UK's Fish and Chip Shop of the year 2014. Find them at 7 Pier Road, Whitby. (01947) 825346 or visit www.whitbyfishandchips.com

The bustling **Lewis & Cooper** store in Northallerton has been a multi award-winning independent gourmet food store since 1899 and is packed with flavoursome foodie treats, fine wines, delicious gift baskets and sumptuous food hampers. Treat yourself to a mouth watering picnic spread and head out into the surrounding countryside. www.lewisandcooper.co.uk

Enjoy an elegant afternoon tea at the famous **Bettys Cafe Tea Rooms**, Harrogate. Speciality teas, dainty sandwiches, handmade cakes and scones, and splendid surroundings make this a truly indulgent occasion and you can even buy your favourites from the bakery to take home. (01423) 814070 or visit www.bettys.co.uk

Feel relaxed, exhilarated and cleansed after a visit to the **Turkish Baths** in Harrogate. The unique Royal Baths building first opened in 1896 and today you can enjoy a contemporary spa experience in magnificent surroundings. Treatments, refreshments and a spot of lunch are all available. (01423) 556746 or visit www.turkishbathsharrogate.co.uk

Visit – Yorkshire

🌹 **Attractions with this sign participate in the Visitor Attraction Quality Assurance Scheme.**

North Yorkshire

Flamingo Land Theme Park and Zoo
Malton, North Yorkshire YO17 6UX
0871 911 8000
www.flamingoland.co.uk
One-price family funpark with over 100 attractions, 5 shows and Europe's largest privately-owned zoo.

Grassington Festival
June, Grassington, North Yorkshire
www.grassington-festival.org.uk
15 days of music and arts in the Yorkshire Dales.

Malton Food Lovers Festival
May, Malton, North Yorkshire
www.maltonyorkshire.co.uk
Fill up on glorious food and discover why Malton is considered 'Yorkshire's Food Town' with mountains of fresh produce.

Ripon International Festival
September, Ripon, North Yorkshire
www.riponinternationalfestival.com
A festival packed with music events, solo dramas, intriguing theatre, magic, fantastic puppetry, literary celebrities, historical walks - and more!

Scarborough Jazz Festival
September, Scarborough, North Yorkshire
www.jazz.scarboroughspa.co.uk
Offering a variety and range of jazz acts with a balanced programme of predominantly British musicians, with the addition of a few international stars.

Scarborough Seafest
July, Scarborough, North Yorkshire
www.discoveryorkshirecoast.com
Seafest celebrates Scarborough's maritime heritage and brings together seafood kitchen cooking demonstrations, exhibitor displays and musical performances.

Swaledale Festival
May - June, Various locations, North Yorkshire
www.swaledale-festival.org.uk
Varied programme of top-quality events, individually ticketed, realistically priced, and spread over two glorious weeks.

The Walled Garden at Scampston

Malton, North Yorkshire YO17 8NG
(01944) 759111
www.scampston.co.uk
An exciting 4 acre contemporary garden, created by Piet Oudolf, with striking perennial meadow planting as well as traditional spring/autumn borders.

York

York Early Music Festival
July, York, North Yorkshire
www.ncem.co.uk
The 2015 festival takes as its starting point the 600th anniversary of the Battle of Agincourt and features cross-currents between France and England from the Middle Ages through to the Baroque.

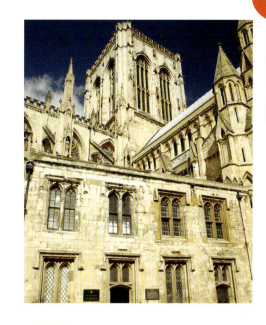

JORVIK Viking Centre
York, North Yorkshire YO1 9WT
(01904) 615505
www.jorvik-viking-centre.co.uk
Travel back 1000 years on board your time machine through the backyards and houses to the bustling streets of Jorvik.

York Boat Guided River Trips
North Yorkshire YO1 7DP
(01904) 628324
www.yorkboat.co.uk
Sit back, relax and enjoy a drink from the bar as the sights of York city and country sail by onboard a 1 hour Guided River Trip with entertaining live commentary.

York Minster
York, North Yorkshire YO1 7JN
(0)1904 557200
www.yorkminster.org
Regularly voted one of the most popular things to do in York, the Minster is not only an architecturally stunning building but is a place to discover the history of York over the centuries, its artefacts and treasures.

Yorkshire Air Museum
York, North Yorkshire YO41 4AU
(01904) 608595
www.yorkshireairmuseum.org
The Yorkshire Air Museum is based on a unique WWII Bomber Command Station with fascinating exhibits and attractive award-winning Memorial Gardens.

Leeds & West Yorkshire

Eureka! The National Children's Museum
Halifax, West Yorkshire HX1 2NE
(01422) 330069
www.eureka.org.uk
Eureka! The National Children's Museum is a magical place where children play to learn and grown-ups learn to play.

Harewood House
Leeds, West Yorkshire LS17 9LG
(0113) 218 1010
www.harewood.org
Harewood House, Bird Garden, Grounds and Adventure Playground - The Ideal day out for all the family.

Haworth 1940's Weekend
May, Haworth, West Yorkshire
www.haworth1940sweekend.co.uk
A fabulous weekend celebrating and comemorating the 1940s.

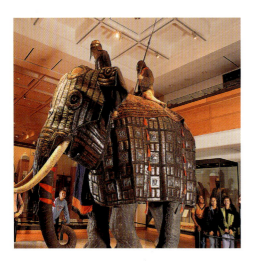

Leeds Festival
August, Wetherby, Leeds
www.leedsfestival.com
From punk and metal, through rock, alternative and indie to dance, Leeds offers music fans a chance to see hot new acts, local bands, huge stars and exclusive performances.

Lotherton Hall & Gardens
Leeds, West Yorkshire LS25 3EB
(0113) 264 5535
www.leeds.gov.uk/lothertonhall
Lotherton is an Edwardian country house set in beautiful grounds with a bird garden, red deer park and formal gardens.

National Coal Mining Museum for England
Wakefield, West Yorkshire WF4 4RH
(01924) 848806
www.ncm.org.uk
The National Coal Mining Museum offers an exciting and enjoyable insight into the working lives of miners through the ages.

Pontefract Liquorice Festival
July, Wakefield, West Yorkshire
www.yorkshire.com
The festival celebrates this unusual plant, the many wonderful products created from it and its historic association with the town.

Royal Armouries Museum
Leeds, West Yorkshire LS10 1LT
0870 034 4344
www.royalarmouries.org
Over 8,000 objects displayed in five galleries - War, Tournament, Oriental, Self Defence and Hunting. Among the treasures are Henry VIII's tournament armour and the world record breaking elephant armour. Regular jousting and horse shows.

Xscape Castleford
Castleford, West Yorkshire WF10 4TA
(01977) 5230 2324
www.xscape.co.uk
The ultimate family entertainment awaits! Dine, bowl, snow, skate, climb, movies, shop, dance on ice.

Yorkshire Sculpture Park
West Bretton,
West Yorkshire WF4 4LG
(01924) 832631
www.ysp.co.uk
YSP is an extraordinary place that sets out to challenge, inspire, inform and delight.

East Yorkshire

East Riding Rural Life Museum
Beverley, East Yorkshire HU16 5TF
(01482) 392777
www.museums.eastriding.gov.uk
Working early 19th century four-sailed Skidby Windmill, plus Museum of East Riding Rural Life.

Ferens Art Gallery
Hull, East Riding of Yorkshire HU1 3RA
(01482) 613902
www.hullcc.gov.uk/museums
Combines internationally renowned permanent collections with a thriving programme of temporary exhibitions.

RSPB Bempton Cliffs Reserve
Bridlington, East Riding of Yorkshire YO15 1JF
(01262) 851179
www.rspb.org.uk
A family favourite, and easily the best place in England to see, hear and smell seabirds! More than 200,000 birds (from April to August) make the towering chalk cliffs seem alive.

Skipsea Castle
Hornsea, East Riding of Yorkshire
0870 333 1181
www.english-heritage.org.uk/daysout/properties/skipsea-castle/
The remaining earthworks of a motte-and-bailey castle dating from the Norman era.

Treasure House and Art Gallery
Beverley, East Riding of Yorkshire HU17 8HE
(01482) 392790
www.museums.eastriding.gov.uk/treasure-house-and-beverley-art-gallery
Enthusiasts for East Riding history can access archive, library, art gallery and museum material. Exhibitions.

Wilberforce House
Hull, East Riding of Yorkshire HU11NQ
(01482) 300300
www.hullcc.gov.uk/museums
Slavery exhibits, period rooms and furniture, Hull silver, costume, Wilberforce and abolition.

South Yorkshire

RSPB Old Moor Nature Reserve
Barnsley, South Yorkshire S73 0YF
(01226) 751593
www.rspb.org.uk
Whether you're feeling energetic or just fancy some time out visit Old Moor to get closer to the wildlife.

Brodsworth Hall and Gardens
Doncaster, South Yorkshire DN5 7XJ
(01302) 722598
www.english-heritage.org.uk/daysout/properties/brodsworth-hall-and-gardens
One of England's most complete surviving Victorian houses. Inside many of the original fixtures & fittings are still in place, although faded with time. Outside the 15 acres of woodland & gardens have been restored to their 1860's heyday.

Magna Science Adventure Centre
Rotherham, South Yorkshire S60 1DX
(01709) 720002
www.visitmagna.co.uk
Magna is the UK's 1st Science Adventure Centre set in the vast Templeborough steelworks in Rotherham. Fun is unavoidable here with giant interactives.

Sheffield Botanical Gardens
South Yorkshire S10 2LN
(0114) 268 6001
www.sbg.org.uk
Extensive gardens with over 5,500 species of plants, Grade II Listed garden pavillion.

Sheffield: Millennium Gallery
South Yorkshire S1 2PP
(0114) 278 2600
www.museums-sheffield.org.uk
One of modern Sheffield's landmark public spaces. Whether you're in town or just passing through, the Gallery always has something new to offer.

Tourist Information Centres

When you arrive at your destination, visit the Tourist Information Centre for quality assured help with accommodation and information about local attractions and events, or email your request before you go.

Aysgarth Falls	Aysgarth Falls National Park Centre	01969 662910	aysgarth@yorkshiredales.org.uk
Beverley	34 Butcher Row	01482 391672	beverley.tic@eastriding.gov.uk
Bradford	Brittainia House	01274 433678	bradford.vic@bradford.gov.uk
Bridlington	25 Prince Street	01262 673474/ 01482 391634	bridlington.tic@eastriding.gov.uk
Brigg	The Buttercross	01652 657053	brigg.tic@northlincs.gov.uk
Danby	The Moors National Park Centre	01439 772737	moorscentre@northyorkmoors.org.uk
Doncaster	Blue Building	01302 734309	tourist.information@doncaster.gov.uk
Filey	The Evron Centre	01723 383637	fileytic2@scarborough.gov.uk
Grassington	National Park Centre	01756 751690	grassington@yorkshiredales.gov.uk
Halifax	The Piece Hall	01422 368725	halifax@ytbtic.co.uk
Harrogate	Royal Baths	01423 537300	tic@harrogate.gov.uk
Hawes	Dales Countryside Museum	01969 666210	hawes@yorkshiredales.org.uk
Haworth	2/4 West Lane	01535 642329	haworth.vic@bradford.gov.uk
Hebden Bridge	New Road	01422 843831	hebdenbridge@ytbtic.co.uk
Holmfirth	49-51 Huddersfield Road	01484 222444	holmfirth.tic@kirklees.gov.uk
Hornsea	Hornsea Museum	01964 536404	hornsea.tic@eastriding.gov.uk

Horton-In-Ribblesdale	Pen-y-ghent Cafe	01729 860333	mail@pen-y-ghentcafe.co.uk
Huddersfield	Huddersfield Library	01484 223200	huddersfield.information@kirklees.gov.uk
Hull	1 Paragon Street	01482 223559	tourist.information@hullcc.gov.uk
Humber Bridge	North Bank Viewing Area	01482 640852	humberbridge.tic@eastriding.gov.uk
Ilkley	Town Hall	01943 602319	ilkley.vic@bradford.gov.uk
Ingleton	The Community Centre Car Park	015242 41049	ingleton@ytbtic.co.uk
Knaresborough	9 Castle Courtyard	01423 866886	kntic@harrogate.gov.uk
Leeds	The Arcade	0113 242 5242	tourinfo@leedsandpartners.com
Leeming Bar	The Yorkshire Maid, 88 Bedale Road	01677 424262	thelodgeatleemingbar@btconnect.com
Leyburn	The Dales Haven	01969 622317	
Malham	National Park Centre	01969 652380	malham@ytbtic.co.uk
Otley	Otley Library & Tourist Information	01943 462485	otleytic@leedslearning.net
Pateley Bridge	18 High Street	0845 389 0177	pbtic@harrogate.gov.uk
Pickering	Ropery House	01751 473791	pickeringtic@btconnect.com
Reeth	Hudson House, The Green	01748 884059	reeth@ytbtic.co.uk
Richmond	Friary Gardens	01748 828742	hilda@richmondtouristinformation.co.uk
Ripon	Minster Road	01765 604625	ripontic@harrogate.gov.uk
Rotherham	40 Bridgegate	01709 835904	tic@rotherham.gov.uk
Scarborough	Brunswick Shopping Centre	01723 383636	scarborough2@scarborough.gov.uk
Scarborough (Harbourside)	Harbourside TIC	01723 383636	scarborough2@scarborough.gov.uk
Selby	Selby Library	0845 034 9540	selby@ytbtic.co.uk
Settle	Town Hall	01729 825192	settle@ytbtic.co.uk
Sheffield	Unit 1 Winter Gardens	0114 2211900	visitor@marketingsheffield.org
Skipton	Town Hall	01756 792809	skipton@ytbtic.co.uk
Sutton Bank	Sutton Bank Visitor Centre	01845 597426	suttonbank@northyorkmoors.org.uk
Todmorden	15 Burnley Road	01706 818181	todmorden@ytbtic.co.uk
Wakefield	9 The Bull Ring	0845 601 8353	tic@wakefield.gov.uk
Wetherby	Wetherby Library & Tourist Centre	01937 582151	wetherbytic@leedslearning.net
Whitby	Langborne Road	01723 383637	whitbytic@scarborough.gov.uk
Withernsea	Withernsea Lighthouse Museum	01964 615683/ 01482 486566	withernsea.tic@eastriding.gov.uk
York	1 Museum Street	01904 550099	info@visityork.org

Regional Contacts and Information

For more information on accommodation, attractions, activities, events and holidays in Yorkshire, contact one of the following regional or local tourism organisations.

Welcome to Yorkshire
www.yorkshire.com
(0113) 322 3500

Entries appear alphabetically by town name in each county. A key to symbols appears on page 7

BEVERLEY, East Yorkshire   Map ref 4C1

Heron Lakes

Contact: Mrs Lynne Lakin, Reception, Fdbird & Sons Ltd, Heron Lakes, Main Road, Routh, Beverley HU17 9SL **T:** (01964) 545968 / 07966 805593 **E:** lynne@heron-lakes.co.uk
W: heron-lakes.co.uk

Units   5
Sleeps   4

PER UNIT PER WEEK
£430.00 - £850.00

SPECIAL PROMOTIONS
Please contact us for prices or view our website.

Peaceful and tranquil are some of the words that can only describe the wonderful lodge breaks here at Heron Lakes set in 75 acres of beautiful landscaped lakes and woodland. Heron lakes has been sympathetically designed to encourage wildlife and we are very proud of the fact that we have been given a Silver Award for Conservation from Professor David Bellamy and the Puffin Award from the Yorkshire Wildlife Trust.

Open: All year
Nearest Shop: 2 miles
Nearest Pub: 0.5 Miles

Units: All units have a twin room and a double with en suite, fully fitted kitchens and large decking areas.

Site: ✿ **P Payment:** 💷 **Leisure:** 🎵 ⚓ ☋ **Property:** 🐾 ▦ 🗐 🗐 **Children:** 🛝
Unit: 🗐 🗐 🖥 🗐 📶 📺 📀

BRIDLINGTON, East Yorkshire   Map ref 5D3

Breil Newk and Sandpiper Cottage, Flamborough

Contact: John & Val English, Owners, 56 Woodhall Way, Beverley, East Yorkshire HU17 7BJ
T: (01482) 862268 / 07711 363277 **F:** 01482 887474 **E:** surveyors@johnenglish.co.uk
W: www.flamboroughcottages.co.uk

Units   2
Sleeps   1-4

PER UNIT PER WEEK
£200.00 - £600.00

Character 2 bedroom barn conversions on the edge of Flamborough Village, a renowned beauty spot on the East Yorkshire coast. Cosy and well equipped, yet retaining exposed beams and original features. Tiled floors with underfloor heating. Sandpiper Cottage has easy access (all ground floor). Breil Newk with 2 bathrooms is ideal for 2 couples. Ideal location for walkers, birdwatchers and families. **Open:** All year **Nearest Shop:** 0.25 miles **Nearest Pub:** 0.25 miles

Site: ✿ **P Property:** ▦ 🗐 **Children:** 🛝 🪑 🚶 **Unit:** 🗐 🗐 🖥 🗐 📶 📺 📀 **BBQ**

BRIDLINGTON, East Yorkshire Map ref 5D3

★★★★
SELF CATERING

Units   6
Sleeps   1-4

PER UNIT PER WEEK
£311.00 - £640.00

SPECIAL PROMOTIONS
Discounts available for stays over 3 days - please enquire

Carlton Apartments

Contact: Andrew Bell, Owner, Carlton Apartments, 6 The Crescent, Bridlington YO15 2NX
T: 01262 672807 **E:** info@carltonapartments.co.uk
W: www.carltonapartments.co.uk

Remarkable East Yorkshire Tourism Award Finalist 2010, 2013, 2014. Winner 2011.

Less than 100 yards from Bridlington's seafront and just around the corner from the town centre. Each apartment has a king-size bed, en suite, dishwasher, fridge, cooker, kettle, toaster etc and a dining area, hair dryer, iron, sofa/arm chairs, TV and except for the Lower Ground Floor all have sea views.

A welcome pack containing loo roll, toiletries, tea, coffee, sugar, milk, washing up liquid and dishwasher tablets to get you started is included in each apartment. The ideal alternative to a hotel.

Open: All year
Nearest Shop: 50 yds
Nearest Pub: 100 yds

Units: 6 apartments ranging from Studio (sleeps 2), 1 bedroom (sleeps 2), 2 bedroom (sleeps 2 adults + 2 children) and our Penthouse (sleeps 2)

Payment: 🔲 **Leisure:** 🎵 ▶ **Property:** 🔲 🔲 **Children:** 🔲¹⁴ 🔲 🔲 **Unit:** 🔲 🔲 🔲 📺 📀

NORTH DALTON, East Yorkshire Map ref 4C1

★★★
SELF CATERING

Units   1
Sleeps   1-4

PER UNIT PER WEEK
£250.00 - £440.00

SPECIAL PROMOTIONS
Short breaks available, 2 nights (excluding Christmas, New Year, Easter and Bank Holidays - 4 days min).

Old Cobbler's Cottage

Contact: Ms Chris Wade, Waterfront Cottages, 2 Mere Cottages, Star Row, North Dalton, Driffield, East Yorkshire YO25 9UX **T:** (01377) 219901 / 07801 124264 **F:** 01377 217754
E: chris.wade@adastra-music.co.uk **W:** www.waterfrontcottages.co.uk **£ BOOK ONLINE**

19th century, mid-terraced, oak-beamed cottage on the edge of a picturesque pond in a peaceful and friendly farming village, between York and Yorkshire's Heritage Coast. The cottage has a small garden for sitting in with BBQ facilities. Dining area and main bedroom look directly over the pond - where the local ducks can be watched from! Open fire. Ideally located for walking, visiting the coast, historic houses, races at York and Beverley and Hockney country. Excellent pub serving meals adjacent, which welcomes dogs and children. Up to 2 pets welcome, free of charge. Parking at the cottage.

Open: All year
Nearest Shop: 3 miles
Nearest Pub: 0.10 miles

Units: Double bedroom and single bedroom (with opportunity for a Z Bed), Shower room and toilet on ground floor. Drying area in entrance.

Site: ❀ P **Payment:** 🔲 **Leisure:** ▶ **Property:** 🐾 🔲 🔲 🔲 **Children:** 🔲 🔲 🔲
Unit: 🔲 🔲 🔲 📺 🔲 📀 🔲 BBQ 📞

ALLERSTON, North Yorkshire   Map ref 5D3

The Old Station

Contact: Carol Benson, Proprietor, The Old Station, Main Street, Allerston, Pickering YO18 7PG **T:** (01723) 859024 **E:** mcrbenson@aol.com
W: www.theoldstationallerston.co.uk

Units   3
Sleeps   1-6
PER UNIT PER WEEK
£360.00 - £630.00

Three railway carriage conversions at former village station. Modern conveniences, countryside views, proprietors on hand in station house. This unique accommodation provides an excellent base from which to explore North Yorkshire's countryside, coast and attractions. Allerston is situated on the edge of the North York Moors National Park and Dalby Forest, just 12 miles from the coast. **Open:** All year **Nearest Shop:** 3 miles **Nearest Pub:** 1 mile

Site: ✿ P **Leisure:** ↟ **Property:** ▯ ▭ **Children:** ⛶ ⛺ ⚓ **Unit:** ▯ ▭ ▤ ⚑ TV ⊙ BBQ

DANBY, North Yorkshire   Map ref 5C3

Clitherbecks Farm

Contact: Catherine Harland, Proprietor, Clitherbecks Farm, Danby, Whitby, North Yorkshire YO21 2NT **T:** (01287) 660321 **E:** enquiries@clitherbecks.co.uk
W: www.clitherbecks.co.uk

Sleeps   1-7
PER UNIT PER WEEK
£220.00 - £370.00

Dwelling mentioned in Doomsday Book. Present building built in 1780. Self-contained accommodation with separate entrance. Two bedrooms that can comfortably sleep 7 people. Shared bathroom.
Downstairs is one living room with central heating and coal fire adjoining a kitchen with electric cooker, microwave, and a fridge-freezer.
Towels and bedding are provided. Heating and electric are included in the price with the exception of coal and wood for which there will be an additional charge. You have your own entrance through a fenced in garden.

Open: All year
Nearest Shop: 1 mile (supermarket 3 miles)
Nearest Pub: 1 mile

Site: ✿ P **Property:** ⚓ ▯ ▭ **Children:** ⛶ **Unit:** ▯ ▭ ⌀ BBQ

EASBY, North Yorkshire   Map ref 5C3

Abbey House

Contact: Mr John Martin, Proprietor, Abbey House, The Old Stables, Easby DL10 7EU
T: (01748) 825298 **F:** 01748 825311 **E:** easbycottage@hotmail.co.uk

Units   1
Sleeps   1-6
PER UNIT PER WEEK
£545.00 - £1000.00

13th century cottage providing high quality accommodation. Three en suite doubles, large comfortable lounge, cloakroom, fully equipped kitchen/diner, large enclosed courtyard. BT Vision includng BT Sport. Fishing from garden. A truly peaceful, idyllic retreat. **Open:** All year **Nearest Shop:** 1 mile **Nearest Pub:** 1 mile

Site: ✿ P **Payment:** € **Leisure:** ♪ ↟ ♺ **Property:** ▭ ▭ **Children:** ⛶ ⛺ ⚓ **Unit:** ▯ ▯ ▭ ▤ ⚑ TV ⊙ BBQ

FADMOOR, *North Yorkshire*   Map ref 5C3

Units   1
Sleeps   1-2
PER UNIT PER WEEK
£200.00 - £265.00

Boonhill Holidays

Contact: Mrs Madeline Johnson, Boonhill Holidays, Boon Hill House, Boonhill Road, Fadmoor, York YO62 7HA **T:** (01751) 431171 / 07974 726291
E: boonhillhouse@gmail.com **W:** www.fadmoorholiday.co.uk **£ BOOK ONLINE**

Self contained accommodation forms part of the farmhouse but is completely self-contained & accessed via wooden staircase leading onto verandah & private entrance. Located on the edge of the North Yorkshire moors offering stunning views, affording privacy peace & quiet. Flexible dates, minimum of two nights stay £45 weekday or £50 weekend per night. Facilities for caravan & camping members. **Open:** All year **Nearest Shop:** 2 miles
Nearest Pub: 1 mile

Site: ✿ P **Leisure:** ⚓ ♪ ▶ ∪ **Property:** 🖥 🔲 🗑 **Unit:** 🔳 ✎ 📺 🎧 📀 BBQ

FILEY, *North Yorkshire*   Map ref 5D3

Units   1
Sleeps   1-8
PER UNIT PER WEEK
£275.00 - £800.00

Kev's Cottage

Contact: Mrs Sophie Revell, Kev's Cottage NG33 4PP **T:** (01780) 410364 / 07885 021027
E: kevscottagefiley@yahoo.co.uk
W: www.kevscottagefiley.org.uk **£ BOOK ONLINE**

Kev's Cottage is a fully modernised, cosy cottage five minutes from the beach and town in the most historical part of the traditional seaside resort, Filey. The cottage has two double bedrooms, 1 bunk bedroom, one single room, a fully equipped kitchen, courtyard and central heating for year round comfort. **Open:** All year
Nearest Shop: 0.10 miles

Site: ✿ P **Payment:** € **Leisure:** ♪ ▶ ∪ ♞ **Property:** ∥ 🖥 🔲 🗑 **Children:** 🔆 🛏 **Unit:** 🔲 🔳 🖥 🎧 ✎ 📺 🎧 📀 ☎

GIGGLESWICK, *North Yorkshire*   Map ref 5B3

Units   1
Sleeps   6

PER UNIT PER WEEK
£295.00 - £550.00

SPECIAL PROMOTIONS
Short Breaks and Special Offers by arrangement.

Ivy Cottage (Giggleswick) Limited

Contact: David & Betty Hattersley, 22 Malvern Drive, Woodford Green IG8 0JW
T: (020) 8504 8263 **F:** (020) 8559 0227 **E:** info@ivycottagegiggleswick.co.uk
W: www.ivycottagegiggleswick.co.uk **£ BOOK ONLINE**

A bright and well maintained stone cottage in the centre of Giggleswick village, sleeping 6 in two doubles and one twin-bedded room. The upstairs bathroom is by Villeroy & Bosch with a separate shower unit, whilst downstairs there is a second WC and a clothes drying area. There is also central heating, an open fire, private parking and a cycle store.

For your leisure there is a flat screen TV in both kitchen and lounge, Wi-Fi, an iPod dock and a library of local books and maps.

The ancient church and two inns with restaurants are close by and a walk into Settle takes around ten minutes.

Open: All year
Nearest Shop: 0.80 miles
Nearest Pub: 0.05 miles

Units: Ivy Cottage (Giggleswick) Limited is a family owned business established in 1987.

Site: ✿ P **Payment:** € **Leisure:** ⚓ ▶ **Property:** 🖥 🗑 **Children:** 🔆⁵ **Unit:** 🔲 🔳 🖥 🎧 ✎ 📺 🎧 📀 🛁 ☎

GIGGLESWICK, North Yorkshire Map ref 5B3

Pendle View Holiday Apartment

Contact: Mrs Chris Chandler, Owner, Pendle View Holiday Apartment, 2 Pendle View, Giggleswick, Settle BD24 0AZ **T:** (01729) 822147 / 0787 9643878
E: pendleview@hotmail.com **W:** www.settleholiday.co.uk

Units	1
Sleeps	2-3

PER UNIT PER WEEK
£280.00 - £340.00

Pendle View is a spacious, self-contained, garden flat with a kitchen, living room, bedroom and shower room. It is the lower ground floor of a grade II listed early Victorian semi-detached house, stone-built in the local style. It has car parking and patio. **Open:** All year except Christmas and New Year **Nearest Shop:** 1 mile
Nearest Pub: 0.01 miles

Site: ✿ P **Property:** 📶 📠 **Children:** 🐎 ♨ ♦ **Unit:** 📋 📺 🖥 🚿 📺 📀

GRASSINGTON, North Yorkshire Map ref 5B3

Garrs House Apartment

Contact: Ann & Malcolm Wadsworth, Owners, 25 Watson Road, Blackpool FY4 1EG
T: (01253) 404726 / 07801 450624 **E:** garrshouse@gmail.com
W: www.garrshouse.co.uk

Units	1
Sleeps	2-4

PER UNIT PER WEEK
£195.00 - £275.00

Self contained Holiday Apartment, situated above The Corner House cafe, at the top of and overlooking Grassington Square. Accommodates 4 people in 1 double and 1 twin bed en suite bedrooms. All bedding & towels are provided. There is a large comfortable Lounge/Diner & separate well equipped kitchen. Gas & Electricity are inclusive.

Visit Bolton Abbey, Burnsall, Linton, Haworth or Skipton, travel on the spectacular Settle-Carlisle railway or a narrowboat on the Leeds-Liverpool Canal. There are Stately Homes, Castles, Caverns and the area is full of attractions for all ages.

Open: All year
Nearest Shop: 0.1 miles
Nearest Pub: 0.01 miles

Units: 1st floor apartment, accomodates up to 4 people. 1 double & 1 twin bedroom, both en suite. Large lounge/diner separate kitchen.

Property: 🐾 📠 **Children:** 🐎 **Unit:** 📺 🚿 📺 📀

GRASSINGTON, North Yorkshire Map ref 5B3

Swallows' Nest

Contact: Bob and Suzanne Evans, 1 Chapel Lane, Hebden, Grassington, North Yorkshire BD23 5DT **T:** (01535) 273758 / 07789 895949 **E:** bob@swallowsnesthebden.co.uk
W: www.swallowsnesthebden.co.uk **£ BOOK ONLINE**

Units	1
Sleeps	1-5

PER UNIT PER WEEK
£460.00 - £650.00

Swallows Nest is a luxurious cottage in the heart of the Yorkshire Dales with spectacular views. It sleeps 5 adults and is an ideal base for walking and touring the Yorkshire Dales. Swallows Nest is a surprisingly spacious extended 19th Century former lead miner's cottage, enjoying a very peaceful location on the edge of the village, with on-site parking and a great pub nearby. **Open:** All year
Nearest Shop: 300 metres **Nearest Pub:** 300 metres

Site: P **Property:** 📶 📠 **Unit:** 📋 📺 🖥 🚿 📺 📀 ⌀ 📞

HARROGATE, *North Yorkshire*   *Map ref 4B1*

Units 14
Sleeps 2-4
PER UNIT PER WEEK
£371.00 - £658.00

Ashness Apartments

Contact: Hazel Spinlove, Ashness Apartments, 15 St Marys Avenue, Harrogate HG2 0LP
T: (01423) 526894 **F:** 01423 700038 **E:** office@ashness.com
W: www.ashness.com **£ BOOK ONLINE**

High quality apartments, superbly situated in a nice, quiet road of fine Victorian townhouses very near the town centre of Harrogate. Well equipped with high speed wired and wireless internet throughout. Excellent shops, restaurants and cafes are a short walk away through Montpellier Gardens with the Stray, Valley Gardens, Royal Hall and Conference Centre just around the corner. **Open:** All year **Nearest Shop:** 0.10 miles **Nearest Pub:** 0.10 miles

Site: P Payment: Property: Children: Unit:

HARROGATE, *North Yorkshire*   *Map ref 4B1*

Units 1
Sleeps 1-5
PER UNIT PER WEEK
£395.00 - £470.00

Ashrigg

Contact: Mr & Mrs Peter & Angela Holt, Ashrigg, 39 Spring Lane, Pannal HG3 1NP
T: (01423) 871177 **E:** pholt@westrigg.freeserve.co.uk
W: www.ashrigg.co.uk

Fully furnished/equipped first-floor apartment. One double, one twin and one single. Full central heating, fully fitted kitchen. Garden for guests use. Off-road parking. **Open:** All year **Nearest Shop:** 0.25 miles **Nearest Pub:** 0.50 miles

Site: P Property: Children: Unit:

HARROGATE, *North Yorkshire*   *Map ref 4B1*

Units 14
Sleeps 2-7
PER UNIT PER WEEK
£340.00 - £1169.00

Rudding Holiday Park

Contact: Follifoot, Harrogate HG3 1JH **T:** (01423) 870439
E: holiday-park@ruddingpark.com
W: www.ruddingholidaypark.co.uk

The 5 star luxury lodges and 4 star cottages are set in the beautiful Rudding Park grounds, whilst the 3 star chalet lodges are in delightful woodland clearings, many surrounding a small lake. **Open:** All year **Nearest Shop:** Onsite **Nearest Pub:** Onsite

Site: P Payment: Leisure: Property: Children: Unit:

HELMSLEY, *North Yorkshire*   *Map ref 5C3*

Units 1
Sleeps 1-4
PER UNIT PER WEEK
£265.00 - £450.00

Townend Cottage

Contact: Mrs Margaret Begg, Owner, Townend Farmhouse, High Lane, Beadlam, Nawton, York YO62 7SY **T:** (01439) 770103 **E:** margaret.begg@ukgateway.net
W: www.townendcottage.co.uk

A very warm, comfortable, oak beamed stone cottage. Off main road 3 miles from charming market town of Helmsley. Ideal for walking/touring moors, coast and York. Cosy log fire. Special offers available for low season short breaks. Minimum stay 2 nights £120, 3 nights £180. **Open:** All year **Nearest Shop:** 3 miles **Nearest Pub:** 0.25 miles

Site: P Leisure: Property: Children: Unit:

HORTON IN RIBBLESDALE, North Yorkshire   Map ref 5B3

Units 1
Sleeps 1-5
PER UNIT PER WEEK
£360.00 - £460.00

Blind Beck Holiday Cottage

Contact: Heather Huddleston, Blind Beck Holiday Cottage, Blindbeck, Horton-in-Ribblesdale, Nr. Settle BD24 0HT **T:** (01729) 860396 **E:** h.huddleston@daelnet.co.uk
W: www.blindbeck.co.uk **£ BOOK ONLINE**

Blind Beck is a 17th century cottage situated in the centre of the 3 peaks and offers a very home to home feeling with oak beams and magnificant country screenery. The Settle to Carlisle railway runs near the cottage and the station is only a 6 minutes walk away. The Picturesque towns of Settle, Malham and Hawes are only a short drive away, as are Ingleton White Scar Caves and Waterfalls.
Open: All year **Nearest Shop:** 1 mile **Nearest Pub:** 0.5 miles

Site: ✿ P **Property:** 🖥 🖵 **Children:** 🛏 🛏 🚶 **Unit:** 🖥 💻 🖵 📺 🔌 BBQ

HUTTON-LE-HOLE, North Yorkshire   Map ref 5C3

Units 1
Sleeps 1-5
PER UNIT PER WEEK
£270.00 - £578.00

Primrose Hill Farmhouse

Contact: Nigel Custance, Booking Enquiries, Primrose Hill Farm, Hutton-le-Hole, North Yorkshire YO62 6UA **T:** (01751) 417752 / 07929 188661
E: nigel.custance@btinternet.com **W:** primrosehillfarmhouse.com **£ BOOK ONLINE**

Delightful cottage style farmhouse set in picturesque village overlooking the beck. From your parking and enclosed garden at the rear, enjoy the owner's fields with their sheep and horses. Great place to relax, walk, bike, visit the Moors & coast. Sleeps 5 in two bedrooms with Kingsize beds. Farmhouse kitchen with dishwasher, washing machine, tumble drier, cooker and microwave. Freesat TV & Wi-Fi. **Open:** All year **Nearest Shop:** 3 miles
Nearest Pub: 0.5 miles

Site: ✿ P **Payment:** € **Leisure:** 🚵 🎣 🏹 ↻ **Property:** 🐾 🏠 🖥 🖵 **Children:** 🛏 🛏 🚶 **Unit:** 🖥 🖵 💻 🖵 🔌
📺 🔌 DVD ♨

INGLEBY GREENHOW, North Yorkshire   Map ref 5C3

Units 6
Sleeps 2-6

PER UNIT PER WEEK
£343.00 - £887.00

SPECIAL PROMOTIONS
Special winter breaks 4 nights for the price of 3.

5% discount on bookings confirmed before Christmas.

5% discount on second and subsequent weeks of bookings in the same summer season.

Ingleby Manor

Contact: Christine Bianco, Ingleby Manor, Ingleby Greenhow, Great Ayton TS9 6RB
T: (01642) 722170 **E:** christine@inglebymanor.co.uk
W: www.inglebymanor.co.uk

Ingleby Manor, once the home of a Courtier of Henry VIII, is an important 16th century Grade II* Listed building in 50 acres of beautiful formal gardens and woodland, with a trout stream in a peaceful hidden valley in the North York Moors National Park.

Spacious apartments and cottages individually designed with appropriate furnishings, log fires and full central heating, fully equipped kitchens with dishwasher, clothes washer and dryer, etc. Ingleby Manor has been awarded 5 Star Gold Award from VisitEngland for 'Exceptional quality of accommodation and customer service'.

Open: All year
Nearest Shop: 3 miles
Nearest Pub: 0.5 miles

Units: 4 apartments in the Manor House itself, 3 ground floor and suitable for accompanied disabled guests. 2 separate cottages sleep 4 each.

Site: ✿ P **Payment:** 💳 € **Leisure:** 🚵 🎣 ↻ **Property:** ⫽ 🐾 🖥 🖵 **Children:** 🛏 🛏 🚶
Unit: 🖥 🖵 💻 🖵 📺 DVD ♨ BBQ ☎

f

KIRKBYMOORSIDE, *North Yorkshire* Map ref 5C3

Cowldyke Farm

Contact: Mrs Janet Benton, Owner, Salton Road, Great Edstone, Kirkbymoorside, York, North Yorkshire YO62 6PE **T:** (01751) 431242 **E:** janetbenton@btconnect.com
W: www.cowldyke-farm.co.uk

Units 6
Sleeps 2-6
PER UNIT PER WEEK
£220.00 - £560.00

Our family cottages sleeping 4 or more, are all rated 4 star and are very spacious. All are tastefully decorated, spotlessly clean, cosy, and warm. Three cottages have the added attraction of an open fire or a log burning stove in addition to the central heating. There is plenty to see and do on the farm. Down by the river is a good place for a bit of wildlife spotting. Bring your fly fishing rod.
Open: All Year **Nearest Shop:** 4 miles **Nearest Pub:** 4 miles

Site: ✿ P **Leisure:** ♪ **Property:** ▣ ▥ **Children:** ➴ **Unit:** ▯ ▮ ▭ ▤ ⚒ TV DVD ⊘ BBQ

KIRKBYMOORSIDE, *North Yorkshire* Map ref 5C3

Surprise View Cottage, Field Barn Cottage & Lowna Farmhouse

Contact: Mrs Ruth Wass, Surprise View Cottages, Sinnington Lodge, Sinnington, York YO62 6RB **T:** (01751) 431345 **E:** info@surpriseviewcottages.co.uk
W: www.surpriseviewcottages.co.uk **£ BOOK ONLINE**

Units 3
Sleeps 1-8

PER UNIT PER WEEK
£310.00 - £1260.00

SPECIAL PROMOTIONS
Short breaks available all year round in the farmhouse except for school holidays, 3 day breaks in the smaller cottages November, December, January & February.

Lowna Farmhouse and 2 Barn conversions; historic location, originally old mill and tannery, giving panoramic views over moorland edge and immediate access to field and woodland walks. Warm, roomy accommodation with quality furnishings and fittings. A wealth of beams and original stone and brick features. 'Comfort' is the key word. Tranquillity is assured at Surprise View Cottages; in the heart of the countryside yet central for touring, walking, cycling. Whether it's history, scenery, wildlife, pub life or farm activities - you'll find it here!

Open: All year
Nearest Shop: 3 miles
Nearest Pub: 1 mile

Units: Three cottages, two smaller units sleeping 4, large farmhouse sleeping up to 8

Site: ✿ P **Leisure:** ⚴ ♪ ↱ ↻ ✈ **Property:** ⊼ ⌷ ▣ ▥ **Children:** ➴ ⌸ ♨
Unit: ▯ ▮ ▭ ▤ ⚒ TV Ⓒ DVD ⊘ BBQ ✆

Need more information?

Visit our websites for detailed information, up-to-date availability and to book your accommodation online. Includes over 20,000 places to stay, all of them star rated.
www.visitor-guides.co.uk

LASTINGHAM, *North Yorkshire*   *Map ref 5C3*

Units 1
Sleeps 1-5

PER UNIT PER WEEK
£300.00 - £500.00

SPECIAL PROMOTIONS
Please phone us or
visit our website.

Old Reading Room

Contact: Jane Wood, Propriotor, Lastingham Grange, Lastingham, North Yorkshire
YO62 6TH **T:** (01751) 417345 **F:** 01751 417358 **E:** reservations@lastinghamgrange.com
W: www.lastinghamgrange.com **£ BOOK ONLINE**

A three bedroom holiday cottage located in the historic village of Lastingham, a peaceful backwater in the heart of the North York Moors National Park. Lastingham is a perfect centre for the Moors and the Dales, ruined abbeys and castles, the ancient city of York and the coast, with its smugglers' coves and its long sandy Beaches, a mere twenty or so miles away.

The Cottage has a ground floor sitting room, dining room and kitchen then on the first floor, two double bedrooms and one single bedroom and bathroom with bath and walk in shower. Linen and towels are provided.

Open: All year
Nearest Shop: 5 miles
Nearest Pub: 0.10 miles

Units: Ground floor sitting room, dining room and kitchen. First floor, three bedrooms (2 double, 1 single) and bathroom with bath and walk in shower.

Site: P Payment: 🏦 **Leisure:** 🎣 ∪ **Property:** 📶 📱 🖫 **Children:** 🐾 🏛 🧍 **Unit:** 🗄 📷 🖬 🗜 TV DVD 📞

LEYBURN, *North Yorkshire*   *Map ref 5B3*

Units 1
Sleeps 4
PER UNIT PER WEEK
£350.00 - £520.00

Colling Well Cottage

Contact: Maria Ramskill, Owner, Colling Well House, Hunton, Lower Wensleydale,
North Yorkshire DL8 1QG **T:** (01677) 450742 **E:** collingwell@hotmail.com
W: www.collingwell.co.uk

A single level stone cottage located in the owner's delightful garden and convenient for village amenities. A comfortable home from home, with two en suite bedrooms and quality furnishings. Hunton is a pretty village situated in Lower Wensleydale. Village facilities include a pub with a restaurant, a shop / Post Office and a village green with play area. An ideal base for touring the Dales.
Open: All year **Nearest Shop:** 0.25 miles **Nearest Pub:** 0.25 miles

Site: ❀ **P Leisure:** ▶ **Property:** 📶 🖫 **Children:** 🐾 **Unit:** 🗄 📷 🗜 TV DVD **BBQ**

LITTLE BARUGH, *North Yorkshire*   *Map ref 5C3*

Units 5
Sleeps 4-10
PER UNIT PER WEEK
£285.00 - £950.00

Stainers Farm Cottages

Contact: Jackie Smith, Stainers Farm Cottages, Stainers Farm, Little Barugh YO17 6UY
T: (01653) 668224 / 07879 636979 **E:** info@stainersfarm.co.uk
W: www.stainersfarm.co.uk **£ BOOK ONLINE**

Renovated country cottages with individual character and charm in a peaceful rural setting with wonderful views of open countryside. 1 pet allowed by arrangement, friendly cottage, Wi-Fi available.
Open: All year **Nearest Shop:** 5 miles
Nearest Pub: 1.5 miles

Site: ❀ **Property:** 📶 📱 🖫 **Children:** 🐾 🏛 🧍 **Unit:** 🗄 🗄 📷 TV DVD 🎣 **BBQ**

MALTON, *North Yorkshire* *Map ref 5D3*

Home Farm Holiday Cottages

Contact: Mrs Rachel Prest, Owner, The Old Fold, Railway Street, Slingsby, York YO62 4AL
T: (01653) 628277 / 07803 186941 **E:** rachelprest@yahoo.co.uk
W: www.yorkshire-holiday-cottage.co.uk

Attractive single storey, ground floor, stone barn conversions in a lovely village setting. The spacious cottages are furnished and equipped to a very high standard with the inclusion of antique and mellow pine and co ordinating fabrics and furnishings. Ideally situated for moors, coast and York. Three miles from Castle Howard.
Open: All Year **Nearest Shop:** 400m **Nearest Pub:** 100m

Units	2
Sleeps	4-6

PER UNIT PER WEEK
£335.00 - £620.00

Site: ❈ P Property: 🖥 📱 💻 Children: 🎠 🛏 🧍 Unit: 🔌 🗄 📺 🧺 🍳 📺 📀 ✎ 📞

MALTON, *North Yorkshire* *Map ref 5D3*

Walnut Garth

Contact: Cas Radford, Proprietor, Walnut Garth, c/o Havendale, High Street, Swinton, Malton YO17 6SL **T:** (01653) 691293 / 07766 208348 **F:** 01653 691293
E: cas@walnutgarth.co.uk **W:** www.walnutgarth.co.uk **£ BOOK ONLINE**

Units	1
Sleeps	1-4

PER UNIT PER WEEK
£225.00 - £445.00

SPECIAL PROMOTIONS
£25 discount for stays of 2 weeks or longer.

Tastefully decorated, two-bedroom cottage furnished to a high standard with all modern conveniences. Set in owner's grounds at edge of Swinton village, yet only 2 miles from market town of Malton with excellent selection of local amenities and attractions. Easy access to York, coast and Moors. Gym on site. £25 discount for stays of 2 weeks or longer. Christmas cake, pudding & 'Winter Warmer' for Christmas weeks.

Open: All year
Nearest Shop: 0.25 miles
Nearest Pub: 0.25 miles

Units: All rooms are on the ground floor - floor plan available on website for further information.

Site: ❈ P Leisure: 🏌 ⛳ Property: 🐕 🖥 📱 💻 Children: 🎠 🛏 🧍 Unit: 🔌 🗄 📺 🧺 🍳 📺 🎧 📀 BBQ 📞

NORTHALLERTON, *North Yorkshire* *Map ref 5C3*

The Byre

Contact: Mary Crowe, Hill View Farm, Bullamoor, Northallerton, North Yorkshire DL6 3QW
T: (01609) 776072 **E:** stuart@stuartcrowe.wanadoo.co.uk

Single storey conversion comprising through lounge dining kitchen, 2 bedrooms 1 double, 1 twin, bathroom, entrance lobby with additional WC. Central heating, welcome starter pack provided. Ideal location for Dales. Moors, coast and York. 1.5 miles from Northallerton in an elevated position with spectacular views. Owner maintained. **Open:** January- November
Nearest Shop: 1 mile **Nearest Pub:** 600 metres

Units	1
Sleeps	1-4

PER UNIT PER WEEK
£295.00 - £425.00

Site: ❈ P Leisure: 🏌 Property: 📱 💻 Children: 🎠 🧍 Unit: 🔌 🗄 📺 🧺 🍳 📺 📀

NUNTHORPE, North Yorkshire   Map ref 4C1

Blackthorn Gate

Contact: Mrs Rita Corrigan, Blackthorn Gate, Eastfields Farm, Nunthorpe, Nr Stokesley, North Yorkshire TS7 0PB **T:** (01642) 324496 **E:** info@blackthorngate.co.uk
W: www.blackthorngate.co.uk **£ BOOK ONLINE**

| Units | 4 |
| Sleeps | 1-5 |

PER UNIT PER WEEK
£360.00 - £898.00

SPECIAL PROMOTIONS
Weekend and midweek breaks available. Friday to Monday or Monday to Friday.

Four Swedish designed two bedroomed log Lodges set in 230 acres of beautiful open farmland with stunning views of Roseberry Topping. A tranquil haven for your holiday, perfect for spotting wildlife and bird watching. Private on site fishing with 3 fully stocked ponds. Games Room with table tennis, bar football and pool table. Ideally situated for touring and walking in North Yorkshire and the Tees Valley. Larger Lodges wheelchair friendly with downstairs bathroom with wet room style shower.

Open: All year
Nearest Shop: 2 miles
Nearest Pub: 1.5 miles

Units: Living/dining room, fully fitted kitchen, master en suite, separate bathroom with sauna. Each Lodge has a bbq, veranda with garden furniture.

Site: ✿ P **Payment:** 🖃 € **Leisure:** ♪ ▸ ♒ ♣ **Property:** 🐕 🚃 🔲 🗐 **Children:** 🐎 🛏 🏃
Unit: 🗋 🗒 🔲 🗝 TV DVD BBQ

PATELEY BRIDGE, North Yorkshire   Map ref 5C3

Helme Pasture Lodges & Cottages

Contact: Mrs Rosemary Helme, Helme Pasture Lodges & Cottages, Hartwith Bank, Summerbridge, Harrogate HG3 4DR **T:** (01423) 780279 **E:** info@helmepasture.co.uk
W: www.helmepasture.co.uk

| Units | 4 |
| Sleeps | 2-10 |

PER UNIT PER WEEK
£195.00 - £792.00

Enjoy a comfortable stay in one of our genuine Scandinavian lodges or converted cottage. Situated in natural tranquil woodland. David Bellamy & Friends of the A.O.N.B. awards. Endless country walks. Markets, villages, abbeys and castles. Visit York, Harrogate, Skipton and Ripon. Warm welcome. **Open:** All year
Nearest Shop: 0.30 miles **Nearest Pub:** 0.30 miles

Site: ✿ P **Payment:** 🖃 € **Leisure:** ♪ ▸ ♒ **Property:** 🐕 🔲 🗐 **Children:** 🐎 **Unit:** 🗋 🗒 🔲 🗝 TV DVD BBQ ☎

PICKERING, North Yorkshire   Map ref 5D3

SELF CATERING ★★★★

Gold AWARD

Units   3
Sleeps   2-8

PER UNIT PER WEEK
£320.00 - £1120.00

SPECIAL PROMOTIONS
Short breaks available in Low and Mid-Season.

For our latest offers and up to date availability and prices, please visit our website or phone us.

Ashfield Cottages

Contact: Carol & Simon Fisk, Owners, Ashfield Cottages, Lockton, Pickering, North Yorkshire YO18 7PZ **T:** (01751) 460218 **E:** info@ashfieldcottages.co.uk
W: www.ashfieldcottages.co.uk

Situated in the National Park village of Lockton and close to Dalby Forest, the cottages offer you the opportunity to take that "get away from it all holiday". They have been awarded a 4 Star Gold rating by Visit England for quality of accommodation and customer service. The cottages are spacious, comfortable and well equipped, they have south facing gardens, private parking and Wi-Fi / Internet access, also gas central heating, electricity and linen are included in the price.

Located in the perfect location to stay, while enjoying all that this area has to offer. You can go walking on heather covered moors, mountain biking in Dalby Forest, travel on the North York Moors Steam Railway, enjoy a day at the seaside resorts of Whitby or Scarborough, or visit the ancient City of York, then come back and relax in your comfortable country cottage.

Open: All year
Nearest Shop: 5 miles
Nearest Pub: 1 mile

Units: Cottage One - sleeps 4 to 5 guests.
Cottage Two – sleeps 7 to 8 guests.
Cottage Three – sleeps 3 guests.

Site: ✿ P **Leisure:** ▶ ∪ **Property:** 🖵 🖳 **Children:** 🛏 🏠 ≮ **Unit:** 🗄 🖥 🖵 🖨 🖐 📺 📀

PICKERING, North Yorkshire   Map ref 5D3

SELF CATERING ★★★★

Gold AWARD

Units   1
Sleeps   2-5

PER UNIT PER WEEK
£325.00 - £625.00

SPECIAL PROMOTIONS
Weekend and mid week short breaks available November to February.

Kale Pot Cottage

Contact: Diane & Mike Steele, Kale Pot Cottage, Kale Pot Hole, Newtondale, Pickering YO18 8HU **T:** (01751) 476654 **E:** enquiries@northyorkmoorscottage.co.uk
W: northyorkmoorscottage.co.uk **£ BOOK ONLINE**

Comfortable, spacious, individual cottage situated in our paddock in beautiful Newtondale. A converted 18th century barn, the cottage is well equipped and completely restored. Stunning views of forest and the North York Moors. An ideal base for walking and mountain biking or just relaxing, with the North York Moors steam railway nearby. We are remote, but the market town of Pickering is just 10 miles away, Whitby and the coast 15 miles and historic York 35 miles. Owners living nearby.

Open: All year
Nearest Shop: 10 miles
Nearest Pub: 3 miles

Units: Kitchen, lounge and dining areas upstairs to take advantage of the views, double bedroom en suite, twin room with space for third bed, has its own wetroom.

Site: ✿ P **Payment:** € **Leisure:** 🎣 ♪ ∪ **Property:** 🐾 🖵 🖳 **Children:** 🛏 🏠 ≮
Unit: 🗄 🖥 🖵 🖨 🖐 📺 🎬 📀 ⌀ BBQ 📞

PICKERING, North Yorkshire Map ref 5D3

Units 2
Sleeps 2-3
PER UNIT PER WEEK
£270.00 - £370.00

Old Forge Cottages

Contact: Judy French, Proprietor, The Old Forge, Wilton, Pickering, North Yorkshire YO18 7JY **T:** (01751) 477399 **E:** theoldforge1@aol.com
W: www.forgecottages.co.uk

Welcoming, cosy cottages for two. Bathroom downstairs, folding bed available. Well-equipped, with own patio and barbeque area. Private parking. Near Pickering Steam Railway, Dalby Forest, Yorkshire Moors and Eden Camp. Fishing. Cyclists and walkers are welcome. Secure storage for bikes and equipment. Thornton-le-Dale 1 mile. Excellent local public transport. Please contact us for seasonal offers. **Open:** All year **Nearest Shop:** 1 mile **Nearest Pub:** 1 mile

Site: P **Leisure:** **Property:** **Children:** **Unit:** BBQ

REETH, North Yorkshire Map ref 5B3

Units 1
Sleeps 1-4
PER UNIT PER WEEK
£435.00 - £605.00

2 Nurse Cherry's Cottage

Contact: Mrs Vivian Velangi, Owner, The Orchard, 55 Denehall Drive, Bishop Auckland, Co. Durham DL14 6UF **T:** (01388) 450640 **E:** v.velangi@yahoo.com
W: www.cottageinreeth.com

Our beautiful 5 star Gold Award Stone Cottage lies in the heart of the picturesque village of Reeth, Swaledale. Well placed for all amenities, walks from the door. Cosy Cottage, home from home. Fully equipped. 2 bedrooms, 2 bathrooms, one is en suite. Private parking. Beautiful spacious garden which is fully enclosed.
Open: All year. **Nearest Shop:** 2 min walk
Nearest Pub: 2 min walk

Site: P **Payment:** € **Leisure:** **Property:** **Children:** **Unit:**

RICHMOND, North Yorkshire Map ref 5C3

Units 1
Sleeps 4
PER UNIT PER WEEK
£200.00 - £400.00

Croft Cottage

Contact: Shirley, Vermont Grove, Sydenham, Royal Leamington Spa, Warwickshire CV31 1SE **T:** (01926) 428784 / 07939 861453 **E:** shirlscottage@hotmail.com
W: www.yorkshirecottage.org.uk

Stone-built cottage, central heating, parking. Entrance porch, beamed lounge/dining room, kitchen, 2 bedrooms, 1 double, 1 twin. Bathroom with shower over bath. Patio area with garden furniture. Within easy reach of Richmond's Market square and surrounding Dales and coast.
Open: All Year **Nearest Shop:** 0.5 Miles **Nearest Pub:** 0.5 Miles

Site: P **Property:** **Unit:**

Book your accommodation online

Visit our websites for detailed information, up-to-date availability and to book your accommodation online. Includes over 20,000 places to stay, all of them star rated.

www.visitor-guides.co.uk

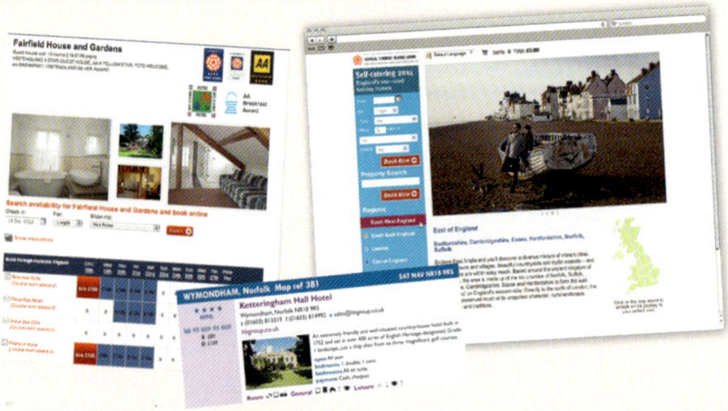

RICHMOND, North Yorkshire   Map ref 5C3

Units   18
Sleeps   2-6

PER UNIT PER WEEK
£525.00 - £1712.00

SPECIAL PROMOTIONS
Offers only available at
www.naturalretreats.com

Natural Retreats - Yorkshire Dales

Contact: Aislabeck Plantation, Hurgill Road, Richmond, North Yorkshire DL10 4SG
T: (01625) 416 430 **E:** info@naturalretreats.com
W: www.naturalretreats.com **£ BOOK ONLINE**

An ideal location for family holidays and just a stroll away from the quaint town of Richmond, Natural Retreats offer award-winning three bedroom lodges nestled into the rich green hills of the Yorkshire Dales, offering unbeatable views of the Swale Valley. Highlights include floor to ceiling windows, luxurious interiors and furnishings and wood burning stoves. Every guest also receives a complimentary welcome hamper containing delicious local produce such as bread, cheese and wine.

Open: All Year
Nearest Shop: 1.5 miles
Nearest Pub: 1.5 miles

Units: Open plan, three bedroom, ground floor residences, some have en suites for every bedroom, others family bathroom.

Site: P Payment: ⊞ **Leisure:** ♪ ▶ **Property:** ⫽ ⊨ ▭ ▤ ▨ **Children:** ⇆ ⊞ ⚤
Unit: ▯ ▱ ▭ ▨ ⚲ ◉ ⟳ ⫽

RIPON, North Yorkshire   Map ref 5C3

Units   1
Sleeps   1-2

PER UNIT PER WEEK
£395.00 - £525.00

SPECIAL PROMOTIONS
Off peak short breaks
Mon-Fri and Fri-Mon.

The Old Telephone Exchange

Contact: Vanessa Parry, Owner, Moor Road, Bishop Monkton, Ripon, North Yorkshire HG3 3QF **T:** (01937) 832040 / 07717 170965 **E:** vanessaparry444@btinternet.com
W: www.holidayatcottages-in-yorkshire.co.uk

The Old Telephone Exchange nestles on the outskirts of the pretty village of Bishop Monkton and is easily accessible for both the cathedral city of Ripon and the spa town of Harrogate. The cottage has lovely countryside views and benefits from under floor central heating and is double glazed throughout. Lounge with corner sofa, log burning stove, mini hi-fi, colour TV with DVD and video, sky+ package, telephone (for local calls) and broadband internet access. High specification kitchen with granite work surfaces and Smeg appliances.

Open: All year
Nearest Shop: 0.75 miles
Nearest Pub: 0.75 miles

Units: En suite master bedroom with four poster effect king sized bed, dressed in rich Laura Ashley fabrics and complete with colour TV/DVD.

Site: ❀ **P Property:** ⊨ ▭ ▤ ▨ **Unit:** ▯ ▱ ▭ ▨ ⚲ ⊞ ◉ ⟳ ⫽ BBQ ☎

Yorkshire - North Yorkshire

ROSEDALE ABBEY, North Yorkshire Map ref 5C3

Rosedale Abbey Holiday Cottages
Contact: Rosedale Abbey Caravan Park, Pickering, North Yorkshire YO18 8SA
T: (01723) 584311 **E:** info@flowerofmay.com
W: www.flowerofmay.com **£ BOOK ONLINE**

Units 5
Sleeps 2-4

PER UNIT PER WEEK
£250.00 - £524.00

The cottages and apartment are immaculately presented, beautifully furnished and equipped to a very high standard. In a peaceful village setting nestling in the North York Moors National Park. Ideal walking country within easy reach of Yorkshire's Heritage Coast. Many guests comment that they cannot wait to return to our cosy, comfortable cottages.

Open: All year
Nearest Shop: 0.05 miles
Nearest Pub: 0.10 miles

Site: P Payment: Property: Children: Unit:

SCARBOROUGH, North Yorkshire Map ref 5D3

The Sands Sea Front Apartments
Contact: Reservations Team, Escape 2 The Sands Ltd, The Sands, Scarborough, N Yorkshire YO12 7TN **T:** (01723) 364714 **F:** 01723 352364 **E:** enquiries@escape2thesands.com
W: www.escape2thesands.com **£ BOOK ONLINE**

Units 61
Sleeps 2-6

PER UNIT PER WEEK
£500.00 - £2500.00

Stylish and contemporary, these 5-star luxury apartments have a magnificent location on Scarborough's North Bay, on Yorkshire's rugged and beautiful East Coast. The Sands award-winning apartments and have been given a 5-star Gold rating by VisitBritain. All apartments have modern 5-star furnishings, flat-screen TVs, DVD players and designer kitchens. Internet access and car parking are available. **Open:** All year **Nearest Shop:** 0.10 miles **Nearest Pub:** 1 mile

Site: P Payment: Leisure: Property: Children: Unit:

SCARBOROUGH, *North Yorkshire* *Map ref 5D3*

Units 3
Sleeps 1-5

PER UNIT PER WEEK
£320.00 - £740.00

White Acre & White Gable

Contact: David Squire, Manager, JG Squire Ltd, 15 Victoria Park, Scarborough, North Yorkshire YO12 7TS **T:** (01723) 374220 **E:** david@scarborough.co
W: www.scarborough.co **£ BOOK ONLINE**

Large, self-contained flats in the heart of the holiday area. Close to the beach and most holiday attractions. Own off street parking.
White Acre is well situated in the heart of the holiday area, near to the beach and Peasholm Park. The property stands alongside decorative gardens and enjoys lovely views of the Peasholm area. White Gable is quietly situated in one of the most desirable districts of Scarborough, directly opposite the golf course at Scalby Mills, close to the Sea-Life centre, sea-front promenade, beach, miniature railway and the open air theatre. White Gable has Wi-Fi.

Open: All year
Nearest Shop: 200m & 600m
Nearest Pub: 200m

Units: Each flat has own entrance; two bedrooms with flat-screen TV; lounge with 42 inch Plasma HD TV; Fitted Kitchen; Bathroom. No extras.

Site: P Property: 🔲 🔲 **Children:** 🐴 🛏 ⚲ **Unit:** 🔲 🔲 🔲 🔲 🔲 TV 🔲

SETTLE, *North Yorkshire* *Map ref 5B3*

Units 1
Sleeps 1-7

PER UNIT PER WEEK
£175.00 - £475.00

SPECIAL PROMOTIONS
Minimum stay 3 nights.

Bent House Farm Cottage

Contact: Jacky Frankland, Owner, Frankland Farm Cottages, Swainsteads Farm, Rathmell, Settle, North Yorkshire BD24 0JX **T:** (01729) 822865 / 07971 325000 **F:** 01729 824803
E: info@benthousefarm.co.uk **W:** www.benthousefarm.co.uk

Detached Farmhouse with large conservatory, 2 sitting rooms, kitchen diner, 4 bedrooms, 2 bathrooms and games room. Private parking and gardens. Free Wi-Fi. Fully equipped, centrally heated. Sleeps 7. Spectacular views, quietly located between the Yorkshire Dales and Ribble Valley. Excellent walking and cycling.

Open: All year
Nearest Shop: 6 miles
Nearest Pub: 2 miles

Units: Set on a working sheep farm, access from the road via a limestone track.

Site: ❀ **P Payment:** 💷 **Leisure:** 🎵 ✎ **Property:** 🐾 🔲 🔲 🔲 **Unit:** 🔲 🔲 🔲 🔲 🔲 TV 🔲

SKIPTON, North Yorkshire Map ref 4B1

enjoyEngland.com ★★★★ SELF CATERING

Units 1
Sleeps 14
PER UNIT PER WEEK
£750.00 - £1200.00

Craven House

Contact: Joanne Rushton, Owner, 56 Keighley Road, Skipton BD23 2NB
T: (01756) 794657 / 07960 864916 **E:** info@craven-house.co.uk
W: www.craven-house.co.uk

Victorian terraced house with 7 bedrooms (3 en suite), 3 house bathrooms, kitchen with Aga cooker and basement games area. Pets welcome by arrangement. Outdoor activities, leisure facilities and cinema close by. Christmas period £2000 a week.
Open: All year **Nearest Shop:** 50 metres **Nearest Pub:** 50 metres

Site: **Leisure:** **Property:** **Children:** **Unit:** BBQ

STAITHES, North Yorkshire Map ref 5C3

enjoyEngland.com ★★★ SELF CATERING

Units 1
Sleeps 1-5
PER UNIT PER WEEK
£320.00 - £630.00

SPECIAL PROMOTIONS
Short breaks on request - mainly in Low Season or at short notice.

Pennysteel Cottage

Contact: Ms Chris Wade, Waterfront Cottages, 2 Mere Cottages, Star Row, North Dalton, Driffield, East Yorkshire YO25 9UX **T:** (01377) 219901 / 07801 124264 **F:** 01377 217754
E: chris.wade@adastra-music.co.uk **W:** www.waterfrontcottages.co.uk **£ BOOK ONLINE**

Old fisherman's cottage with original character and features, including beamed ceilings and wood panelled walls. All rooms and terrace overlooking the attractive harbour of Staithes and its lifeboat station. Sit and relax with the comfort of a log burning stove and watch the ships go past. Perfect for those with a romantic love of the past. Located off the main High Street in a quiet corner, just a couple of minutes from the beach, pubs, restaurant and shops. Ideal for walking (on the Cleveland Way long distance footpath) and the coast. Close to Whitby, Heartbeat Country, and the Moors.

Open: All year
Nearest Shop: 0.10 miles
Nearest Pub: 0.10 miles

Units: Kitchen, living and dining room on ground floor. Double bedroom, single bedroom and toilet on first floor. Twin attic room, shower and bathroom on second floor.

PETS! WELCOME

Site: **Payment:** **Leisure:** **Property:** **Children:**
Unit: BBQ

THIRSK, North Yorkshire Map ref 5C3

enjoyEngland.com ★★★ SELF CATERING

Units 1
Sleeps 2-10
PER UNIT PER WEEK
£250.00 - £490.00

80 St James Green

Contact: Joanna Todd, Owner, 79 St James Green, Thirsk, North Yorkshire YO7 1AJ
T: (01845) 523522 **E:** enquiries@80stjamesgreen.co.uk
W: www.80stjamesgreen.co.uk

Cosy well equipped cottage in a quiet area of town overlooking St James Green, only a few minutes walk from the Market Place with plenty of shops, pubs and restaurants. An ideal base for exploring the Yorkshire Dales, Coast and is only a half hour drive from the historic city of York. **Open:** All Year **Nearest Shop:** 0.2 miles
Nearest Pub: 20 yards

Property: **Children:** **Unit:**

THIRSK, North Yorkshire   Map ref 5C3

★★★★ SELF CATERING

Cedar Lodge and Carlton Court

Contact: Mrs Ann Robson, Proprietor, White Horse Holiday Cottages, Ings Lane, Carlton Husthwaite, Thirsk, North Yorkshire YO7 2BP **T:** (01845) 501581 / 07974 751332 **E:** tim-robson@btconnect.com **W:** www.white-horsecottages.co.uk **£ BOOK ONLINE**

Units   2
Sleeps   2-7

PER UNIT PER WEEK
£373.00 - £757.00

Both Cedar Lodge and Carlton Court are situated on the edge of The North Yorkshire Moors and have panoramic views of The Vale of York. Both sleep 4-7 and have large quiet patios with private parking. They provide warm, cosy home from home comforts with oil central heating. Easy access for walking, cycling and exploring local attractions. **Open:** All Year **Nearest Shop:** 5 miles **Nearest Pub:** 0.25 miles

Site: ✿ P **Property:** 🏠 📺 **Children:** 🐾 🛏 ☂ **Unit:** 📺 📶 💻 📺 🍳 TV 📀

WHITBY, North Yorkshire   Map ref 5D3

★★★★ SELF CATERING

Croft Farm Holiday Cottages

Contact: Emma Carpenter, Owner, Croft Farm, Ruswarp, Whitby, North Yorkshire YO21 1NY **T:** (01947) 825853 **E:** emma@croftfarm.com **W:** www.croftfarm.com

Units   3
Sleeps   1-16

PER UNIT PER WEEK
£390.00 - £620.00

These superb cottages in the village of Ruswarp near Whitby are furnished to a very high standard with private parking and a friendly welcome. Short breaks are available and pets by arrangement. **Open:** Open all year. **Nearest Shop:** 50m **Nearest Pub:** 150m

Site: P **Property:** 🐾 📺 📺 **Unit:** 📺 📺 📶 📀

WHITBY, North Yorkshire   Map ref 5D3

★★★★★ SELF CATERING   **Gold AWARD**

Forest Lodge Farm

Contact: Peter & Kate Stannard, Owners, Forest Lodge Cottages, Castleton, Whitby, North Yorkshire YO21 2DZ **T:** (01287) 660024 / 07980 159071 **E:** pandkstannard@aol.com **W:** www.forestlodgecottages.co.uk **£ BOOK ONLINE**

Units   3
Sleeps   2-18

PER UNIT PER WEEK
£450.00 - £1300.00

SPECIAL PROMOTIONS
Friday to Monday and Monday to Friday breaks available. For other breaks please contact us. All 3 cottages can be booked together to sleep 18 plus infants.

In the North York Moors National Park, Forest Lodge is an organic farm with three luxury 5* Gold Award, Grade 2 Listed cottages around a flagged courtyard. Each cottage has its own garden/sitting area with table/chairs/BBQ and is surrounded by our meadows and open moorland with footpaths and bridleway from the farm. There is also a 2 acre field with slide/swings/play area with goalpost and badminton net and plentiful car parking on site. Beautiful sandy beaches are a short drive away at Whitby, Robin Hoods Bay, Runswick Bay and Saltburn. NYM Railway steam trains run from Whitby to Pickering.

Open: All year
Nearest Shop: 0.75 miles
Nearest Pub: 0.75 miles

Units: Dale House (8) 4 double, 2 and shower ground floor. North Range (6) 3 double, 1 ground floor. Coltus (4) 2 double, 1 en suite. All with underfloor heating.

Site: ✿ P **Payment:** 💷 **Leisure:** ▶ **Property:** 📺 📺 📺 **Children:** 🐾 🛏 ☂
Unit: 📺 📶 💻 📺 🍳 TV 🎬 📀 🧺 BBQ

WHITBY, North Yorkshire   Map ref 5D3

Lemon Cottage

Contact: Andy Martin, Park Manager, Northcliffe & Seaview Holiday Parks, Bottoms Lane,
High Hawsker, Whitby YO22 4LL **T:** (01947) 880477 **F:** (01947) 880972
E: enquiries@northcliffe-seaview.com **W:** www.northcliffe-seaview.com **£ BOOK ONLINE**

Units   1
Sleeps   1-4
PER UNIT PER WEEK
£395.00 - £725.00

Lemon Cottage is a Gold Award 4 Star holiday cottage situated on
our 5 Star Seaview Holiday Park. Sleeping 4 with 2 en suite
bedrooms, a stunning interior and private sun terrace. Ground floor
accommodation. Fabulous location with easy access to the
beautiful Heritage Coast & Cinder Cycle Path. 3 night weekend
breaks from £240 & 4 night mid week breaks from £270. **Open:** 1st
March - 7th November **Nearest Shop:** 500m **Nearest Pub:** 800m

Site: P Payment: Leisure: Property: Children: Unit:

WHITBY, North Yorkshire   Map ref 5D3

Lupine Cottage

Contact: Elaine Horton, Owner, 5b Well Close Square, Whitby, North Yorkshire YO21 3AP
T: 07980 054414 **E:** bookings@lupinecottage.co.uk
W: www.lupinecottage.co.uk

Units   1
Sleeps   4-6
PER UNIT PER WEEK
£240.00 - £440.00

Centrally located maisonette (over 3 floors), close to all amenities.
Freesat TV, DVD, broadband/wifi, fully equiped kitchen, large
shower, harbour view from top room, airbrushed wolf paintings on
walls. Central Heating. 2 Double bedrooms and a room with a
double futon. Linen discount available if you prefer to bring your
own linen (duvet and pillows provided) 3 night breaks or weekly
bookings available. **Open:** All Year **Nearest Shop:** 100 yds
Nearest Pub: 20 yds

Property: Children: Unit:

YORK, North Yorkshire   Map ref 4C1

44 Postern Close

Contact: Mrs Christine Turner, Booking Enquiries, 44 Postern Close, Meadowcroft,
Millfield, Willingham, Cambridge CB24 5HD **T:** (01954) 201218 / 07840 989915
E: c.turner1@hotmail.com **W:** www.yorkholidayflat.co.uk

Units   1
Sleeps   1-2
PER UNIT PER WEEK
£320.00 - £445.00

One double-bedroomed apartment, within the prestigious Bishops
Wharf Riverside development. Five minutes walking distance from
city centre. Sitting/dining room, kitchen, bathroom, small balcony
and parking space. No smoking. **Open:** All year
Nearest Shop: 5 mins walk **Nearest Pub:** 2 mins walk

Site: P Payment: Leisure: Property: Unit:

YORK, North Yorkshire   Map ref 4C1

The Blue Rooms

Contact: Ms Kirsty Reid, The Blue Rooms, 4 Franklins Yard, Fossgate, York YO1 9TN
T: (01904) 673990 **F:** 01904 658147 **E:** info@thebluebicycle.com
W: www.thebluebicycle.com **£ BOOK ONLINE**

Units 6
Sleeps 1-4
PER UNIT PER WEEK
£875.00 - £1400.00

Beautifully decorated apartments, some with wood beam ceilings, four poster beds and views over the River Foss. Guests will be welcomed on arrival with a complimentary bottle of champagne and fruit basket. Guests also receive a breakfast platter for each morning of their stay which they prepare at their leisure in the fully fitted kitchen in each apartment. Each apartment also includes a fridge full of complimentary mixers, fruits juices, soft drinks, beers and milk. **Open:** All year **Nearest Shop:** 0.10 miles **Nearest Pub:** 0.10 miles

Site: **P** Payment: Leisure: Property: Children: Unit:

YORK, North Yorkshire   Map ref 4C1

The Dutch House

Contact: Mrs Colette Rogers, 16 Hempland Avene, Stockton Lane, York YO31 1DE
T: (01904) 654251 **E:** coletterogers@rogersliving.com
W: www.thedutchhouse.co.uk **£ BOOK ONLINE**

Units 1
Sleeps 1-4
PER UNIT PER WEEK
£800.00 - £1050.00

The Dutch House is a listed building believed to be York's oldest brick-built house dating from 1648, also one of York's finest historical private residences, which has been sympathetically renovated. Book 7 nights or more at The Dutch House, relax and enjoy a bottle of Champagne on your arrival. **Open:** All year **Nearest Shop:** 100 metres **Nearest Pub:** 100 metres

Site: **P** Payment: Property: Children: Unit:

YORK, North Yorkshire   Map ref 4C1

Knowle House Apartments

Contact: Mr Greg Harrand, Proprietor, Knowle House Apartments, 5 Bootham Terrace, York YO30 7DH **T:** (01904) 637404 **F:** 01904 639774 **E:** greg@hedleyhouse.com
W: www.hedleyhouse.com **£ BOOK ONLINE**

Units 6
Sleeps 1-4
PER UNIT PER WEEK
£325.00 - £575.00

City-centre apartments carefully maintained and recently updated next to the owners' hotel. Superbly located to explore York and the surrounding countryside. Garden Sauna, jacuzzi and decked barbecue area. Off-street car parking. DVD players and DVD library. Laundry and cleaning service available. Close to bus and rail stations. **Open:** All year **Nearest Shop:** 0.02 miles **Nearest Pub:** 0.05 miles

Site: **P** Payment: Leisure: Property: Children: Unit: BBQ

YORK, North Yorkshire   Map ref 4C1

Manor Farm Cottage

Contact: Liz Stephenson, Owner, Manor Farm, Goodmanham, York YO43 3JA
T: (01430) 873510 / 07779 246214 **F:** 01430 873510 **E:** info@manorfarm-cottages.co.uk
W: www.manorfarm-cottages.co.uk **£ BOOK ONLINE**

Units 1
Sleeps 1-4
PER UNIT PER WEEK
£325.00 - £415.00

Deep in the heart of rural Yorkshire, Manor Farm Cottage is a beautiful retreat overlooking the stunning Yorkshire Wolds. The single storey cottage has adjacent parking with level access. **Open:** All year **Nearest Shop:** 1 mile **Nearest Pub:** 0.20 miles

Site: **P** Property: Children: Unit: BBQ

YORK, North Yorkshire   Map ref 4C1

Merricote Cottages

Contact: Mr Michael Streak, Booking Enquiries, Merricote Cottages, Malton Road, Stockton-on-Forest YO32 9TL **T:** (01904) 400256 **F:** 01904 400846
E: enquiries@merricote-holiday-cottages.co.uk **W:** www.merricote-holiday-cottages.co.uk

Units   8
Sleeps   2-8

PER UNIT PER WEEK
£150.00 - £1500.00

Merricote is situated in 8 acres of rural Yorkshire, 4 miles from York City centre, providing a great place to relax and explore the surrounding area. **Open:** All year **Nearest Shop:** 2 miles **Nearest Pub:** 1 mile

Site: ✿ **P** **Payment:** 🔲 **Leisure:** 🏊 ♪ ⏵ ∪ **Property:** 🐾 📺 🗐 🗐 **Children:** 🛏 🍴 🚼 **Unit:** 🔲 🗐 TV ᴰⱽᴰ BBQ

YORK, North Yorkshire   Map ref 4C1

Minster's Reach Apartments

Contact: Jill Aspin, Minster's Reach, High Newbiggin Street, York YO31 7RD
T: 07793 942003 **E:** jill@yorkcityholidaylets.co.uk
W: www.yorkcityholidaylets.co.uk **£ BOOK ONLINE**

Units   4
Sleeps   5

PER UNIT PER WEEK
£400.00 - £800.00

SPECIAL PROMOTIONS
We offer weekly stays and short weekend or midweek breaks.

We are very flexible, so please get in touch and we can arrange your stay!

Regular special offers can be found on our website.

Minster's Reach is our collection of beautifully luxurious, 4 Star Gold holiday apartments, centrally located in York within our private walled courtyard. They provide a private, relaxing setting for your visit to York - everything you need for a home from home experience, and all in reach of York Minster.

Choose between our ground floor apartments with their private garden areas, or our first floor loft style apartments. Each apartment has been decorated to a high standard, with modern fittings and furniture throughout. Situated in the midst of everything the Historical City of York has to offer.

Open: All year
Nearest Shop: Less than 50 metres
Nearest Pub: Less than 50 metres

Units: All apartments within a private courtyard. Two are 1 bedroomed (sleeps 4), and two have 2 bedrooms (sleeps 5), all have modern bathrooms and kitchens. The ground floor apartments have private garden areas.

Site: ✿ **Payment:** 🔲 **Property:** ∥ 📺 🗐 🗐 **Children:** 🛏 🍴 🚼 **Unit:** 🗐 🗐 🔲 🗐 TV ᴰⱽᴰ BBQ 📞

YORK, North Yorkshire   Map ref 4C1

The Riverside York

Contact: Patrick Lavers, 8/8a Peckitt Street, York YO1 9SF **T:** (01904) 623008 / 07734 554755 **F:** 01904 656588 **E:** relax@riverside-york.co.uk
W: www.riverside-york.co.uk **£ BOOK ONLINE**

Units   2
Sleeps   2-8

PER UNIT PER WEEK
£590.00 - £1390.00

Situated in the heart of historic York, our beautiful 5-star Victorian riverside townhouse and apartment offers the perfect luxury self-catering base. The Riverside House offers three double bedrooms and spacious living with Digital Freeview, DVD, Wii console and free parking. The Riverside Apartment has one large kingsize bedroom, with generous ground floor living space, bathroom and kitchen. **Open:** All year **Nearest Shop:** 300 yards **Nearest Pub:** 150 yards

Site: P **Payment:** 🔲 **Property:** ∥ 📺 🗐 🗐 **Children:** 🛏 🍴 🚼 **Unit:** 🗐 🗐 🔲 🗐 🗐 TV ᴰⱽᴰ

YORK, North Yorkshire   Map ref 4C1

| Units | 3 |
| Sleeps | 1-4 |

PER UNIT PER WEEK
£630.00 - £980.00

SPECIAL PROMOTIONS
Discounts are given on stays over three nights.

Suite Stays

Contact: Mrs Lyndie Dilaveris-Koromilias, Suite 5, 35 Fossgate YO1 9TF **T:** 0208 123 2662
E: frontdesk@suitestays.co.uk
W: www.suitestays.co.uk

SuiteStays offers three apartments with 4*Gold Award rating in the heart of York. Suite 5 and Suite 10 are in a Grade II listed building on the fabulous foodie street of Fossgate, minutes from the bustling central square. Cherry Hill Suite is within a residential development on the banks of the River Ouse. While each Suite has its own character, all offer spacious, tastefully decorated and well-equipped luxury accommodation for the discerning visitor. Free parking is available on site or at a nearby location. Free WiFi is also provided.

Open: Open all year
Nearest Shop: 50 metres
Nearest Pub: 50 metres

Units: Suite 5 (1-4 persons) Shower room. Suite 10 (1-4 persons) Family bathroom and en suite. Cherry Hill Suite (1-2 persons) Shower room.

Site: P Property: ⫻ ▱ ▢ ▣ **Children:** ⛷ **Unit:** ▢ ▢ ▣ ▢ ⚲ TV DVD

YORK, North Yorkshire   Map ref 4C1

| Units | 16 |
| Sleeps | 2-7 |

PER UNIT PER WEEK
£260.00 - £895.00

York Lakeside Lodges

Contact: Mr Neil Manasir, Booking Enquiries, York Lakeside Lodges, Moor Lane, York YO24 2QU **T:** (01904) 702346 / 07831 885824 **E:** neil@yorklakesidelodges.co.uk
W: www.yorklakesidelodges.co.uk

Lodges and cottages around a large fishing lake, in parkland yet two miles from the city centre with Tesco and a coach service to city centre just over the road. **Open:** All year **Nearest Shop:** 0.10 miles **Nearest Pub:** 0.60 miles

Site: ✿ **P Leisure:** ♪ ∪ **Property:** ⊸ ▱ ▣ **Children:** ⛷ ▦ ⚲ **Unit:** ▣ ▢ TV ⓒ BBQ ☎

PENISTONE, South Yorkshire   Map ref 4B1

| Units | 2 |
| Sleeps | 1-8 |

Moor Royd House

Contact: Janet Hird, Booking Enquiries, Moor Royd House, Manchester Road, Millhouse Green, Sheffield S36 9FG **T:** (01226) 763353 **F:** 01226 763353
E: info@moorroydhouse.co.uk **W:** moorroydhouse.co.uk

'The Other Side' and 'The Old Farmhouse' are at Moor Royd House, as is the guest suite which can take two more people. Peak District National Park only one mile away. **Open:** All year **Nearest Shop:** 1 mile **Nearest Pub:** 1 mile

Site: ✿ **P Leisure:** ⚘ ♪ ∪ **Property:** ⊸ ▱ ▢ ▣ **Children:** ⛷ ▦ ⚲ **Unit:** ▢ ▢ ▣ ▢ ⚲ TV ⓒ DVD BBQ ☎

BRADFORD, West Yorkshire   Map ref 4B1

Hewenden Mill Cottages

Contact: Janet Emanuel, Owner, Cullingworth Road, Cullingworth, Bradford, West Yorkshire BD13 5BP **T:** (01535) 274259 **E:** hewendenmill@btconnect.com
W: www.hewendenmillcottages.co.uk **£ BOOK ONLINE**

Units   9
Sleeps   2-7
PER UNIT PER WEEK
£370.00 - £750.00

Ideally placed in the heart of heritage rich Bronte Country, nestled deep within a tranquil and secluded valley, our 18th century cotton mill complex has been lovingly converted into 4/5 star self catering apartments, houses and cottages. Surrounded by ancient woodlands, vast mill ponds and glorious gardens - a perfect place to relax and unwind. Short breaks and last minute discounts available. **Open:** All year **Nearest Shop:** 1 mile **Nearest Pub:** 1 mile

Site: ❀ P **Payment:** ⊡ **Leisure:** ♪ ▶ ∪ ⚘ **Property:** ▭ 🗎 🗐 **Children:** ⛺ 🎠 ⚹ **Unit:** 🗇 🗄

HEBDEN BRIDGE, West Yorkshire   Map ref 4B1

Chalet at Cairnacre

Contact: Mrs Ruth Price, Chalet at Cairnacre, Midgehole, Hebden Bridge, West Yorkshire HX7 7AL **T:** (01422) 842861 **E:** chalet@price.org.uk

Units   1
Sleeps   1-2
PER UNIT PER WEEK
£190.00 - £230.00

Set in a woodland garden in the magnificent Hardcastle Crags valley. Comfortable self-catering chalet, accessed by steps with handrails. One bedroom that sleeps 2; living room, galley kitchen, drying facilities and shower room. This popular walking and cycling area with woodland, moorland, canal and river trails saw Le Grand Tour this year. 2 miles from Hebden Bridge, 8 miles from Haworth. **Open:** All year subject to availability. **Nearest Shop:** 2 miles **Nearest Pub:** 50 Yards

Site: ❀ P **Property:** ▭ 🗐 **Unit:** 🗇 🗄 🗐 🗑 📺 ⓥ BBQ

LEEDS, West Yorkshire   Map ref 4B1

Harman Suites 1 & 2 Self Catering Apartments

Contact: Mr Kulwinder Singh & Mrs Harjinder Kaur, Owner / Booking Enquiries, Harman Suites, 48 St Martins Avenue, Leeds, West Yorkshire LS7 3LG **T:** (01132) 955886 / 07974 350799 / 0791 244 5558 **F:** 01132 622734 **E:** info@harmansuite.co.uk
W: www.harmansuite.co.uk **£ BOOK ONLINE**

Units   2
Sleeps   1-5

PER UNIT PER WEEK
£249.00 - £449.00

SPECIAL PROMOTIONS
£90 per suite for 2 nights minimum stay for weekend breaks (Friday to Sunday) subject to availability.

Harman Suites are 3 Star, high quality, fully equipped, self-contained, elegantly and tastefully furnished en suite ground floor apartment/studio flats. These are compact and comfortable, situated in peaceful and secure surroundings and close to public transport, shops, banks, supermarkets and restaurants. Harman Suites are also the perfect base for those visiting Leeds Universities, Hospitals; Leeds Arena and City Centre. Harman means pleasing everyone and welcoming all. You are wholeheartedly welcome to one of the best and highly commended self-catering apartments in Leeds. We assure you the best service at the best price.

Open: All year
Nearest Shop: 0.2 miles
Nearest Pub: 0.3 miles

Units: Wi-Fi internet and all the Sky Sports and Movie Channels are available. Both Suites provide King/Double-size beds, en suite and open plan/fitted kitchens.

Site: ❀ P **Payment:** ⊡ € **Property:** ▭ 🗐 **Children:** ⛺ 🎠 **Unit:** 🗇 🗄 🗐 🗑 📺 ⓓ ⓥ ☎

MELTHAM, West Yorkshire   Map ref 4B1

Millmoor Cottage

Contact: Paul White, Booking Enquiries, Millmoor Cottage, 5 Sefton Lane, Meltham, Holmfirth HD9 5JX **T:** (01484) 308995 **E:** p.g.white@ntlworld.com

Units	1
Sleeps	1-4

PER UNIT PER WEEK
£270.00 - £540.00

Grade II listed 17th century weavers cottage renovated and furnished to a high standard with stone mullions and oak beams. Situated near the village centre with all services but edge of the Peak District with superb walks and scenery. Two bedrooms, one king size and one twin and off street parking. Open fire with fuel provided, up to two pets welcome. Special offer breaks, 3 nights min stay. **Open:** All year **Nearest Shop:** 0.10 miles **Nearest Pub:** 0.10 miles

Site: ❀ P Leisure: ♿ ☋ Property: ☈ ▣ ▣ Children: ⛱ ⊞ ☂ Unit: ▣ ▣ ▣ TV ◉ DVD ◊

TODMORDEN, West Yorkshire   Map ref 4B1

Lower Birks Farm

Contact: Ray Cooper, Owner, Grey Stone Lane, Todmorden, West Yorkshire OL14 8RN **T:** (01706) 814316 / 07813 139526 **E:** ray@lowerbirksfarm.co.uk **W:** www.lowerbirksfarm.co.uk

Units	1
Sleeps	2

PER UNIT PER WEEK
£300.00 - £350.00

An attractive property in a quiet and scenic rural location. Well appointed and enjoying extensive views across the Upper Calder Valley. Located in Todmorden in the heart of the Pennines and 3 miles from Hebden Bridge. **Open:** All year **Nearest Shop:** 2 miles **Nearest Pub:** 2 miles

Site: ❀ P Property: ▣ ▣ Unit: ▣ ▣ ▣ ▣ ◉ DVD BBQ

Don't Miss...

Blackpool Illuminations

Sept-Nov, Blackpool
www.blackpool-illuminations.net
This world famous display lights up Blackpool's promenade with over 1 million glittering lights that will make you oooh and aaah in wonder. Head for the big switch on or buy tickets for the Festival Weekend.

Chester Zoo

Cheshire CH2 1EU
(01244) 380280
www.chesterzoo.org
The UK's number one zoo with over 11000 animals and 400 different species, including some of the most exotic and endangered species on the planet.

Jodrell Bank Discovery Centre

Macclesfield, Cheshire SK11 9DL
(01477) 571766
www.jodrellbank.net
A great day out for all the family, explore the wonders of the universe and learn about the workings of the giant Lovell Telescope.

Muncaster Castle

Ravenglass, Cumbria CA18 1RQ
(01229) 717614
www.muncaster.co.uk
Medieval Muncaster Castle is a treasure trove of paintings, silver, embroideries and more. With acres of Grade 2 woodland gardens, famous for rhododendrons and breathtaking views of the Lake District.

Tate Liverpool

Merseyside L3 4BB
(0151) 702 7400
www.tate.org.uk/liverpool
Tate Liverpool presents displays and international exhibitions of modern and contemporary art in beautiful light filled galleries and is free to visit except for special exhibitions.

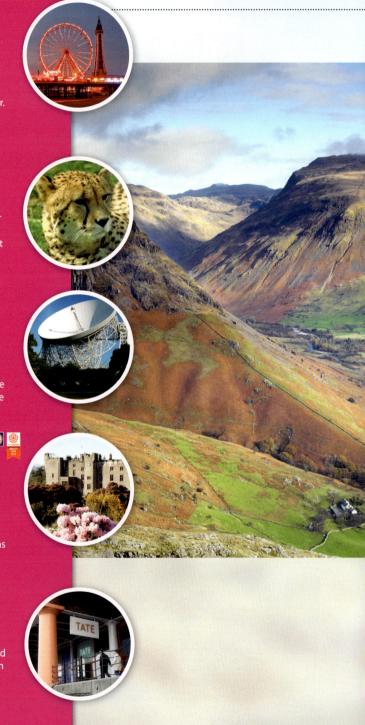

North West

Cheshire, Cumbria, Lancashire,
Greater Manchester, Merseyside

Cumbria

Lancashire

Greater Manchester

Merseyside

Cheshire

The breathtaking scenery of the Lake District dominates the North West, but urban attractions such as cosmopolitan Manchester and Liverpool, with its grand architecture and cultural credentials, have much to recommend them. Further afield, you can explore the Roman and Medieval heritage of Chester, discover Lancashire's wealth of historic houses and gardens, or make a date for one of the huge variety of events that take place in this region throughout the year.

Explore – North West

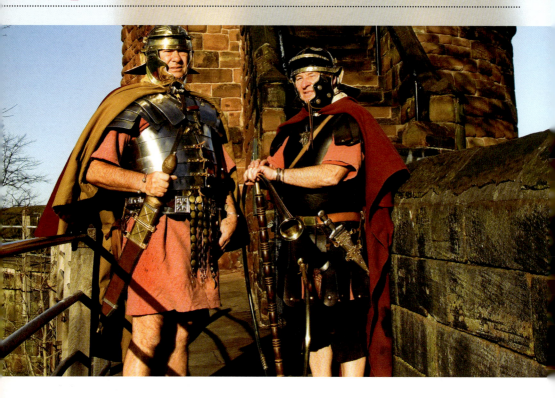

Cheshire

The charms of the old walled city of Chester and the picturesque villages that dot Cheshire's countryside contrast sharply with the industrial towns of Runcorn and Warrington. Iron age forts, Roman ruins, Medieval churches, Tudor cottages and elegant Georgian and Victorian stately homes are among the many attractive sights of the county. South Cheshire, like Cumbria to the north, has long been the home of the wealthy from Manchester and Liverpool and boasts a huge selection of of excellent eateries. It also has peaceful, pretty countryside, and is within easy reach of the wilder terrain of the Peak District and North Wales.

Hotspot: Walk the city walls, step inside the magnificent gothic Cathedral, take a cruise along the River Dee or browse the picturesque medieval shopping streets of Eastgate and Watergate - Chester has over 2000 years of Roman and Medieval history to show you, as well as some seriously good shopping and eating on offer too!

Hotspot: Explore the breathtaking beauty of England's largest lake with a cruise on Lake Windermere for the most scenic views of the Lakeland fells.

Cumbria

In this lovely corner of England, there is beauty in breathtaking variety. The area is loved by many who come back time and again to its inspirational magic, brilliant blue lakes and craggy mountain tops. The central Lake District with its mountains, lakes and woods is so well known that there is a tendency to forget that the rest of Cumbria contains some of the most varied and attractive landscape in Britain. In the east of the county, the peaceful Eden Valley is sheltered by the towering hills of the Pennines, with charming little red sandstone villages and reminders of the Roman occupation everywhere. Alston, with its cobbled streets is the highest town in England, and has been used for numerous TV location sets.

Cumbria's long coastline is full of variety with rocky cliffs, sea birds, sandy estuaries, miles of sun-trap sand dunes and friendly harbours. In Autumn the deciduous woodlands and bracken coloured hillsides glow with colour. In Winter, the snow covered mountain tops dazzle magnificently against blue skies. In Spring, you can discover the delights of the magical, constantly changing light and the joy of finding carpets of wild flowers.

The Lake District is an outdoor enthusiasts paradise offering everything from walking and climbing to orienteering, potholing, cycling, riding, golf, sailing, sailboarding, canoeing, fishing and waterskiing. A great way to take in the beauty of this unique area is to plan your own personal route on foot, or cycle one of the many formal trails such as the Cumbria Cycle Way. The Cumbrian climate is ideal for gardens and the area is famous for the rhododendrons and azaleas which grow here in abundance. If you fancy a break from the great outdoors there is a wealth of historic houses, from small cottages where famous writers have lived to stately homes, that have seen centuries of gracious living and architectural importance.

Hotspot: Cholmondeley Castle Garden in Cheshire is among the most romantically beautiful gardens in the country. Visitors can enjoy the tranquil Temple Water Garden, Ruin Water Garden, memorial mosaic, Rose garden & many mixed borders. www.cholmondeleycastle.com

Lancashire

Lancashire's Forest of Bowland is an area of outstanding natural beauty with wild crags, superb walks, streams, valleys and fells. Blackpool on the coast has been the playground of the North West for many years and still draws millions of holiday makers every year, attracted to its seven miles of beach, illuminations, Pleasure Beach Amusement Park and golf. Morecambe, Southport, Lytham St Annes and Fleetwood also offer wide beaches, golf and bracing walks. Lancaster, a city since Roman times, has fine museums, a castle and an imitation of the Taj Mahal, the Ashton Memorial.

Manchester

Manchester's prosperity can be traced back to the 14th century when Flemish weavers arrived to transform a market town into a thriving boom city at the forefront of the Industrial Revolution. Now known as The Capital of the North, the city is rich in culture with plenty of galleries, museums, libraries and theatres. The City Art Gallery displays its famous pre-Raphaelite collection while the Halle Orchestra regularly fills the Bridgewater Hall. At Granada Studios you can still tour the set of Coronation Street and you can find quality shopping locations and sporting (particularly football) traditions. Cosmopolitan Manchester makes a great place to stay for a spot of retail therapy too!

Hotspot: Set in a stunning waterside location at the heart of the redeveloped Salford Quays in Greater Manchester, The Lowry is an architectural gem that brings together a wide variety of performing and visual arts, including the works of LS Lowry and contemporary exhibitions. www.thelowry.com

Merseyside

Liverpool was an important city long before The Beatles emerged from their Cavern in the Swinging Sixties. It grew from a village into a prosperous port, where emigrants sailed for the New World and immigrants arrived from Ireland. Today the ocean going liners are fewer, but the revitalised dock complex ensures that the city is as vibrant as ever. Liverpool's waterfront regeneration flagship is the Albert Dock Village, which includes the Maritime Museum and Tate Gallery Liverpool. The city has two modern cathedrals, a symphony orchestra, plenty of museums and Britain's oldest repertory theatre The Playhouse. In recent years, Liverpool has seen the opening of an extensive range of cafés, restaurants and accommodation to suit all tastes and budgets.

Hotspot: Discover objects rescued from the Titanic among the treasures at the Merseyside Maritime Museum, one of the venues that make up the National Museums Liverpool, an eclectic group of free museums and galleries.
www.liverpoolmuseums.org.uk

Indulge – North West

Treat yourself to delicious sandwiches, scones, cakes, a nice chilled glass of Champagne and breathtaking views at the **White Star Grand Hall**, 30 James Street, Liverpool. Formerly the White Star Line's first-class lounge, the superb architecture recreates the splendour of a more glamorous era. www.rmstitanichotel.co.uk

One for the boys? Experience the world's greatest sport at the **National Football Museum** in Manchester. Whether you're a diehard football fan, planning a visit with your family or on a weekend break to the great city of Manchester, visit the world's biggest and best football museum. www.nationalfootballmuseum.com

Indulge in some seriously foodie fun at the 10th Anniversary of the **World's Original Marmalade Awards & Festival** at historic Dalemain Mansion & Gardens, in the Lake District. With a range of events including of course, delicious marmalade tasting. Saturday 28th Feb-Sun 1st Mar 2015. www.dalemainmarmaladeawards.co.uk

Enjoy a sophisticated feast at Simon Radley's chic, award-winning **Restaurant at the Chester Grosvenor** which has retained its Michelin star since 1990 and holds 4 AA Rosettes. (01244) 324024 www.chestergrosvenor.com

Take a trip on a steam-hauled dining train with the **East Lancashire Railway** and step into a world of vintage glamour and sophistication. Excellent food and a relaxed and friendly atmosphere in plush surroundings capture the essence of bygone days. www.eastlancsrailway.org.uk

Visit – North West

 Attractions with this sign participate in the Visitor Attraction Quality Assurance Scheme.

Cheshire

©Val Corbett

Arley Hall & Gardens
Northwich, Cheshire CW9 6NA
(01565) 777353
www.arleyhallandgardens.com
Arley Hall's gardens are a wonderful example of the idea that the best gardens are living works of art.

Catalyst Science Discovery Centre
Widnes, Cheshire WA8 0DF
(0151) 420 1121
www.catalyst.org.uk
Interactive science centre whose aim is to make science exciting and accessible to people of all ages and abilities.

Chester Cathedral
Cheshire CH1 2HU
(01244) 324756
www.chestercathedral.com
A must-see for Chester, a beautiful cathedral with a fascinating history.

Go Ape! Hire Wire Forest Adventure - Delamere
Northwich, Cheshire CW8 2JD
(0845) 643 9215
www.goape.co.uk
Take to the trees and experience an exhilarating course of rope bridges, tarzan swings and zip slides, all set high above the forest floor.

Grosvenor Park Open Air Theatre
July-August, Grosvenor Park, Chester, Cheshire
www.grosvenorparkopenairtheatre.co.uk
The greatest open air theatre outside of London returns for a summer of exciting performances.

Hare Hill Gardens
Macclesfield, Cheshire SK10 4QB
(01625) 584412
www.nationaltrust.org.uk/harehill
A small but perfectly formed and tranquil woodland garden.

National Waterways Museum
Ellesmere Port, Cheshire CH65 4FW
(0151) 335 5017
www.canalrivertrust.org.uk
Unlock the wonders of our waterways.

RHS Flower Show Tatton Park
July, Tatton Park, Knutsford, Cheshire
www.rhs.org.uk
A fantastic display of flora and fauna and all things garden related in stunning Cheshire countryside.

Cumbria

Coniston Water Festival
July, Coniston Water, Lake District, Cumbria
www.conistonwaterfestival.org.uk
*Features fun activities and events focused on the
Coniston lake and the unique aspects of water-
related culture and sport.*

Grizedale Forest Visitor Centre
Hawkshead, Cumbria LA22 0QJ
(01229) 860010
www.forestry.gov.uk/northwestengland
*Grizedale Forest offers a range of activities for all
ages through the year, from mountain biking to
relaxing walks, Go-Ape to the sculpture trails.*

Holker Hall & Gardens
Grange-over-Sands, Cumbria LA11 7PL
(01539) 558328
www.holker.co.uk
*Home to Lord and Lady Cavendish, Victorian wing,
glorious gardens, parkland and woodlands.*

Museum of Lakeland Life
Kendal, Cumbria LA9 5AL
(01539) 722464
www.lakelandmuseum.org.uk
*This award-winning museum takes you and your
family back through time to tell the story of the Lake
District and its inhabitants.*

Penrith Castle
Cumbria CA11 7HX
(01912) 691200
www.english-heritage.org.uk/daysout/properties/
penrith-castle/
*The mainly 15th Century remains of a castle begun
by Bishop Strickland of Carlisle and developed by the
Nevilles and Richard III.*

Ravenglass & Eskdale Railway
Cumbria CA18 1SW
(01229) 717171
www.ravenglass-railway.co.uk
*Heritage steam engines haul open-top and cosy
covered carriages from the Lake District coastal
village of Ravenglass to the foot of England's highest
mountains.*

South Lakes Safari Zoo
Dalton-in-Furness, Cumbria LA15 8JR
(01229) 466086
www.southlakessafarizoo.com
*The ultimate interactive animal experience. Get close
to wildlife at Cumbria's top tourist attraction.*

Ullswater Steamers
Cumbria CA11 0US
(01768) 482229
www.ullswater-steamers.co.uk
*The 'Steamers' create the perfect opportunity to
combine a cruise with some of the most famous and
spectacular walks in the lake District.*

Windermere Lake Cruises, Lakeside
Newby Bridge, Cumbria LA12 8AS
(01539) 443360
www.windermere-lakecruises.co.uk
*Steamers and launches sail daily between Ambleside,
Bowness and Lakeside.*

Great North Swim
June, Windermere, Cumbria
www.greatswim.org
*Europe's biggest open water
swim series comes to the
Lake District.*

The World of Beatrix Potter
Bowness, Cumbria LA23 3BX
(01539) 488444
www.hop-skip-jump.com
*A magical indoor attraction that brings to life all 23
Beatrix Potter's Peter Rabbit tales.*

Lancashire

Blackpool Dance Festival
May, Blackpool, Lancashire
www.blackpooldancefestival.com
The world's first and foremost festival of dancing.

Blackpool Pleasure Beach
Blackpool, Lancashire FY4 1EZ
(0871) 222 1234
www.blackpoolpleasurebeach.com
The UK's most ride intensive theme park and home to the legendary Big One and Valhalla.

Clitheroe Food Festival
August, Clitheroe, Lancashire
www.clitheroefoodfestival.com
Celebrating the very finest Lancashire food and drink produces. Includes chef demos, tastings and cookery workshops.

Farmer Ted's Farm Park
Ormskirk, Lancashire L39 7HW
(0151) 526 0002
www.farmerteds.com
An interactive children's activity park, sited on a working farm within the beautiful Lancashire countryside.

Garstang Walking Festival
May, Garstang, Lancashire
www.visitlancashire.com
A celebration of springtime in the stunning countryside of Garstang and the surrounding area. Guided walks and activities for all the family.

Lytham Proms Festival
August, Lytham & St Annes, Lancashire
www.visitlancashire.com
Summer proms spectacular with shows from leading performers.

Sandcastle Waterpark
Blackpool, Lancashire FY4 1BB
(01253) 343602
www.sandcastle-waterpark.co.uk
The UK's Largest Indoor Waterpark and with 18 slides and attractions.

Ribchester Roman Museum
Preston, Lancashire PR3 3XS
(01254) 878261
www.ribchesterromanmuseum.org
Lancashire's only specialist Roman museum, located on the North bank of the beautiful River Ribble.

Wyre Estuary Country Park
Thornton Lancashire FY5 5LR
(01253) 857890
www.wyre.gov.uk
The award winning Wyre Estuary Country Park offers year-round activities and events for all the family including ranger-led walks, environmentally themed activities and annual events like the Family Sculpture Day.

Manchester

East Lancashire Railway
Bury, Greater Manchester BL9 0EY
(0161) 764 7790
www.eastlancsrailway.org.uk
The beautifully restored East Lancashire Railway takes you on a captivating journey to discover the region's rich transport heritage.

Greater Manchester Marathon in Trafford
April, Trafford, Manchester
www.greatermanchestermarathon.com
The UK's flattest, fastest and friendliest Marathon with a superfast course, great entertainment, outstanding crowd support and glorious finish at Manchester United Football Club.

Manchester Art Gallery
Greater Manchester M2 3JL
(0161) 235 8888
www.manchestergalleries.org
Houses one of the country's finest art collections in spectacular Victorian and Contemporary surroundings. Also changing exhibitions and a programme of events and a host of free family friendly resources.

Manchester Histories Festival
March, Various city centre locations
www.manchesterhistoriesfestival.org.uk
The ten-day MHF celebrates the heritage and history of Manchester across numerous city centre venues. The festival offers a fantastic opportunity to explore and learn this great city and is a great event for old and young alike.

Whitworth Art Gallery
Manchester M15 6ER
(0161) 275 7450
www.manchester.ac.uk/whitworth
The Whitworth Art Gallery is home to an internationally-famous collection of British watercolours, textiles and wallpapers.

Manchester Museum
Greater Manchester M13 9PL
(0161) 275 2648
www.manchester.ac.uk/museum
Found on Oxford Road, on The University of Manchester campus (in a very impressive gothic-style building). Highlights include Stan the T.rex, mummies, live animals such as frogs and snakes, object handling and a varied programme of events.

Manchester United Museum & Tour Centre
Greater Manchester M16 0RA
(0161) 868 8000
www.manutd.com
The official museum and tour offers every football fan a unique insight into Manchester United Football Club and a fantastic day out.

People's History Museum
Greater Manchester M3 3ER
(0161) 838 9190
www.phm.org.uk
National centre for the collection, conservation, interpretation and study of material relating to the history of working people in Britain.

Ramsbottom Chocolate Festival
April, Ramsbottom, Greater Manchester
www. ramsbottomchocolatefestival.com
Alongside the two-day chocolate market expect interactive workshops and activities for adults/ children, alfresco dining, chocolate real ale tour, music, competitions, Giant Easter Egg display, and much more.

Saddleworth and District Whit Friday Brass Band Contest
June, Oldham, Greater Manchester
www.whitfriday.brassbands.saddleworth.org
Well over a hundred brass bands compete in contests at venues scattered around the moorland villages and towns on the western edge of the Pennines. All of the contests are open-air, many in delightful surroundings.

Merseyside

Beatles Story

Liverpool, Merseyside L3 4AD
(0151) 709 1963
www.beatlesstory.com
*Located within Liverpool's historic Albert Dock,
the Beatles Story is a unique visitor attraction that
transports you on an enlightening and atmospheric
journey into the life, times, culture and music of the
Beatles.*

Birkenhead Festival of Transport
September, Birkenhead, Merseyside
www.bheadtransportfest.com
*Featuring classic cars, steam engines and other
modes of vintage transport.*

Croxteth Hall & Country Park
Liverpool, Merseyside L12 0HB
(0151) 233 6910
www.liverpoolcityhalls.co.uk/croxteth-hall/
*Stately home with 500 acres estate including visitor
farm, Victorian walled garden and seasonal events.*

The Gallery Liverpool
Merseyside L8 5RE
(0151) 709 2442
www.thegalleryliverpool.co.uk
*Set in the heart of Liverpool's Independent Cultural
District, the gallery occupies the entire upper floor of
the industrial premises of John O'Keeffe and Son Ltd.*

Grand National
April, Aintree, Merseyside
www.aintree.co.uk
*The most famous horse race over jumps takes place
over the challenging Aintree fences.*

Knowsley Safari Park
Merseyside L34 4AN
(0151) 430 9009
www. knowsleysafariexperience.
co.uk
*Enjoy a 5 mile safari through 450
acres of historic parkland.*

Liverpool Football Club
Merseyside L4 0TH
(0151) 260 6677
www.liverpoolfc.com
*Meet an LFC Legend; get your photograph with one
of our many trophies or indulge yourself in one of our
award winning Experience Days.*

Liverpool Sound City
May, Bramley Moore Dock, Liverpool
www.liverpoolsoundcity.co.uk
*An unrivalled 3-day festival of incredible live music
and arts that includes a groundbreaking 2-day music
and digital industry conference.*

Speke Hall, Gardens & Estate
Liverpool, Merseyside L24 1XD
(0151) 427 7231
www.nationaltrust.org.uk/main/w-spekehall
*One of the most famous half timbered houses in
Britain, dating from the 15th century.*

Walker Art Gallery
Liverpool, Merseyside L3 8EL
(0151) 478 4199
  www.walkerartgallery.org.uk
  *Home to outstanding works by Rubens,
  Rembrandt, Poussin, Gainsborough and Hogarth,
  the Walker Art Gallery is one of the finest art
  galleries in Europe*

Wirral Folk on the Coast Festival
June, Wirral, Merseyside
www.wirralfolkonthecoast.com
*All-on-one-site friendly festival at Whitby Sports &
Social Club, with fine music real ale and good food
being served plus many more visitor attractions.*

World Museum Liverpool
Merseyside L3 8EN
(0151) 478 4393
www.liverpoolmuseums.org.uk/wml
*One of Britain's finest museums, with extensive
collections from the Amazonian Rain Forest to the
mysteries of outer space.*

Tourist Information Centres

When you arrive at your destination, visit the Tourist Information Centre for quality assured help with accommodation and information about local attractions and events, or email your request before you go.

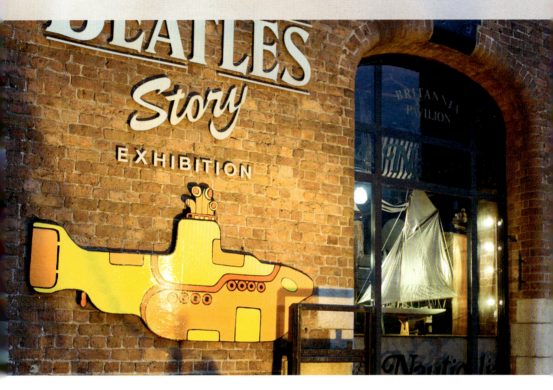

Accrington	Town Hall	01254 380293	information@leisureinhyndburn.co.uk
Alston Moor	Town Hall	01434 382244	alston.tic@eden.gov.uk
Altrincham	20 Stamford New Road	0161 912 5931	tourist.information@trafford.gov.uk
Ambleside	Central Buildings	015394 32582	tic@thehubofambleside.com
Appleby-In-Westmorland	Moot Hall	017683 51177	tic@applebytown.org.uk
Barnoldswick	Post Office Buildings	01282 666704 / 661661	tourist.info@pendle.gov.uk
Barrow-In-Furness	Forum 28	01229 876543	touristinfo@barrowbc.gov.uk
Blackburn	Blackburn Market	01254 688040	visit@blackburn.gov.uk
Blackpool	Festival House, The People's Promenade	01253 478222	tic@blackpool.gov.uk
Bolton	Central Library Foyer	01204 334321 / 334271	tourist.info@bolton.gov.uk
Bowness	Glebe Road	015394 42895	bownesstic@lakedistrict.gov.uk
Brampton	Moot Hall	016977 3433/ 01228 625600	bramptontic@gmail.co.uk
Broughton-In-Furness	Town Hall	01229 716115	broughtontic@btconnect.com
Burnley	Regeneration and Planning Policy	01282 477210	tic@burnley.gov.uk
Bury	The Fusilier Museum	0161 253 5111	touristinformation@bury.gov.uk
Carlisle	Old Town Hall	01228 625600	tourism@carlisle.gov.uk
Chester (Town Hall)	Town Hall	0845 647 7868	welcome@chestervic.co.uk
Cleethorpes	Victoria Square	01253 853378	cleveleystic@wyrebc.gov.uk
Clitheroe	Platform Gallery & VIC	01200 425566	tourism@ribblevalley.gov.uk
Cockermouth	4 Old Kings Arms Lane	01900 822634	cockermouthtouristinformationcentre@btconnect.com

Congleton	Town Hall	01260 271095	congletontic@cheshireeast.gov.uk
Coniston	Ruskin Avenue	015394 41533	mail@conistontic.org
Discover Pendle	Boundary Mill Stores	01282 856186	discoverpendle@pendle.gov.uk
Egremont	12 Main Street	01946 820693	lowescourt@btconnect.com
Ellesmere Port	McArthur Glen Outlet Village	0151 356 5562	enquiries@cheshiredesigneroutlet.com
Garstang	1 Cherestanc Square	01995 602125	garstangtic@wyrebc.gov.uk
Glennridding Ullswater	Bekside Car Park	017684 82414	ullswatertic@lakedistrict.gov.uk
Grange-Over-Sands	Victoria Hall	015395 34026	council@grangeoversands.net
Kendal	25 Stramongate	01539 735891	info@kendaltic.co.uk
Keswick	Moot Hall	017687 72645	keswicktic@lakedistrict.gov.uk
Kirkby Stephen	Market Square	017683 71199	visit@uecp.org.uk
Lancaster	The Storey	01524 582394	lancastervic@lancaster.gov.uk
Liverpool Albert Dock	Anchor Courtyard	0151 233 2008	jackie.crawford@liverpool.gov.uk
Liverpool John Lennon Airport	Information Desk	0151 907 1058	information@liverpoolairport.com
Lytham St Annes	c/o Town Hall	01253 725610	touristinformation@fylde.gov.uk
Macclesfield	Town Hall	01625 378123 / 378062	karen.connon@cheshireeast.gov.uk
Manchester	45-50 Piccadilly Plaza	0871 222 8223	touristinformation@visitmanchester.com
Maryport	The Wave Centre	01900 811450	info@thewavemaryport.co.uk
Millom	Millom Council Centre	01946 598914	millomtic@copelandbc.gov.uk
Morecambe	Old Station Buildings	01524 582808	morecambevic@lancaster.gov.uk
Nantwich	Civic Hall	01270 537359	nantwichtic@cheshireeast.gov.uk
Northwich	Information Centre	01606 288828	infocentrenorthwich@cheshirewestandchester.gov.uk
Oldham	Oldham Library	0161 770 3064	tourist@oldham.gov.uk
Pendle Heritage Centre	Park Hill	01282 677150	pendleheritagecentre@htnw.co.uk
Penrith	Middlegate	01768 867466	pen.tic@eden.gov.uk
Preston	The Guildhall	01772 253731	tourism@preston.gov.uk
Rheged	Redhills	01768 860015	tic@rheged.com
Rochdale	Touchstones	01706 924928	tic@link4life.org
Rossendale	Rawtenstall Queens Square	01706 227911	rawtenstall.library@lancashire.gov.uk
Saddleworth	Saddleworth Museum	01457 870336	saddleworthtic@oldham.gov.uk
Salford	The Lowry, Pier 8	0161 848 8601	tic@salford.gov.uk
Sedbergh	72 Main Street	015396 20125	tic@sedbergh.org.uk
Silloth-On-Solway	Solway Coast Discovery Centre	016973 31944	sillothtic@allerdale.gov.uk
Southport	112 Lord Street	01704 533333	info@visitsouthport.com
Stockport	Staircase House	0161 474 4444	tourist.information@stockport.gov.uk
Ulverston	Coronation Hall	01229 587120 / 587140	ulverstontic@southlakeland.gov.uk
Windermere	Victoria Street	015394 46499	info@ticwindermere.co.uk

Regional Contacts and Information

For more information on accommodation, attractions, activities, events and holidays in North West England, contact one of the following regional or local tourism organisations. Their websites have a wealth of information and many produce free publications to help you get the most out of your visit.

Visit Chester
www.visitchester.com

Cumbria Tourism
T (01539) 822 222
E info@cumbriatourism.org
www.golakes.co.uk

Visit Lancashire
T (01257) 226600 (Brochure request)
E info@visitlancashire.com
www.visitlancashire.com

Visit Manchester
T 0871 222 8223
E touristinformation@visitmanchester.com
www.visitmanchester.com

Visit Liverpool
T (0151) 233 2008 (information enquiries)
T 0844 870 0123 (accommodation booking)
E info@visitliverpool.com (accommodation enquiries)
E liverpoolvisitorcentre@liverpool.gov.uk (information enquiries)
www.visitliverpool.com

Stay – North West

Entries appear alphabetically by town name in each county. A key to symbols appears on page 7

CHESTER, Cheshire Map ref 4A2

4* Gold Wharton Lock Canalside Balcony Apartment

Contact: Mrs Sandra Jeffrey, Owner / Manager, 4* Gold Wharton Lock Balcony Apartment, Chester City Centre, Cheshire CH2 3DH **T:** (01258) 817 816 / 07454 379933
E: rentals@stayinchester.com **W:** www.stayinchester.com **£ BOOK ONLINE**

Units 1
Sleeps 1-4
PER UNIT PER WEEK
£450.00 - £630.00

Luxury canalside apartment, private lounge balcony overlooking lock gates, peaceful location, short walk to city centre. Hypnos beds, granite kitchen, lounge with 'Living Art' fire, kingsize bedroom, twin bedroom, two bathrooms, free allocated parking and free Wi-Fi. Romantic breaks, family holidays, business trips. 2/3 night weekends from £310, 4 night midweeks from £310, weeks from £450. **Open:** All year **Nearest Shop:** 0.25 miles
Nearest Pub: 0.2 miles

Site: ✿ **P Payment:** 💳 **Leisure:** 🚲 ♪ ▶ ∪ **Property:** ⋔ 📺 📖 🖥 **Children:** ⌂ **Unit:** ▯ 🗄 💻 🔌 📺 📀

CONGLETON, Cheshire Map ref 4B2

Broomfield Barns

Contact: Mrs Anita Lockett, Landlady, Broomfield Barns, Broomfield House, Trap Road, Congleton, Cheshire CW12 2LT **T:** (01260) 224581/266 **E:** creativespace@clonter.com / info@broomfieldbarns.co.uk **W:** www.broomfieldbarns.co.uk

Units 1
Sleeps 2-6
PER UNIT PER WEEK
£655.00 - £750.00

Broomfield Barn provides self-catering accommodation for two to six people. 3 bedrooms, 1 double, 1 triple and 1 single. Located in the heart of the Cheshire countryside with easy access to the Derbyshire hills, lovely gardens, Stately Homes, award winning country pubs and nearby Clonter Theatre.
Open: All year **Nearest Shop:** 5 miles **Nearest Pub:** 0.5 miles

Site: ✿ **P Leisure:** 🚲 ♪ ▶ 🔍 **Property:** 📖 🖥 **Children:** ⌂ **Unit:** ▯ 📖 🔌 📺 ◿

MACCLESFIELD, Cheshire Map ref 4B2

Cheshire Hunt Holiday Cottages

Contact: Mrs Anne Gregory, Owner, Cheshire Hunt Holiday Cottages, Hedge Row, Off Spuley Lane, Rainow Macclesfield, Cheshire SK10 5DA **T:** (01625) 572034 / 07506 825480 **E:** enquiries@cheshirehuntholidaycottages.co.uk
W: www.cheshirehuntholidaycottages.co.uk

Units 2
Sleeps 2-11
PER UNIT PER WEEK
£595.00 - £890.00

Situated on a small track which winds through a valley, each cottage has its own unique character and both enjoy wonderful views over open countryside but are within walking distance of the local village and amenities. Both cottages have separate facilities and share the use of a games room. There is also the flexibility of hiring both properties for extended family holidays and weddings.
Open: All year **Nearest Shop:** 1 mile **Nearest Pub:** 0.5 miles

Site: ✿ **P Leisure:** 🚲 🔍 **Property:** ⋔ 📺 📖 🖥 **Children:** ⌂ 🛏 🚸 **Unit:** ▯ 🗄 💻 🔌 📺 📀 ◿

The Official Tourist Board Guide to **Self Catering 2015**

EXPLORE
two heritage visitor attractions in the
LAKE DISTRICT

Explore Ullswater onboard the 'Steamers', that link to some of the most famous and spectacular walking routes in the National Park or climb aboard La'al Ratty and take a journey from the coast to the mountains. Visit one and get 50% off the other*

*on full fare day tickets only

01229 717171 ravenglass-railway.co.uk   017684 82229 ullswater-steamers.co.uk

ALLONBY, Cumbria   Map ref 5A2

Units   3
Sleeps   2-15

PER UNIT PER WEEK
£375.00 - £1400.00

SPECIAL PROMOTIONS
Short break prices available on request.

Crookhurst Farm Cottages
Contact: Brenda Wilson, Bowscale Farm, Allonby CA15 6RB **T:** 07773 047591
E: brenda@crookhurst.com
W: www.crookhurst.com **£ BOOK ONLINE**

Crookhurst Farm & Cottages is set in lovely open countryside and situated half a mile to Allonby, on the Solway coast. Spacious 5 bedroomed House suitable for limited mobility with wheelchair access. Private garden and ample parking. Sleeps 12 plus cots, adjoining cottages sleeping 2-3.

Bowscale View is nestled within beautiful valleys and fields, a half mile from Allonby and the beach. This is Dog friendly. Spacious, luxury self-catering accommodations suitable for those looking for a rural, tranquil and peaceful getaway, surrounded by beautiful scenery. Suitable for limited mobility with wheelchair access.

Open: All year
Nearest Shop: 0.5 miles
Nearest Pub: 0.5 miles

Units: Weekly prices available on website. Open over Christmas and New Year. Wi-Fi Available.

Site: ❀ P Leisure: ♪ ▶ ∪ ☂ Property: 🐾 ▣ ▣ Children: ☂ 🛏 ☂ Unit: ▣ ▣ ▣ ▣ ▣ TV ▣ ▣ ☎

North West - Cumbria

AMBLESIDE, Cumbria   Map ref 5A3

The Lakelands

Contact: Janine Wagstaff, Site Coordinator, Lower Gale, Ambleside, Cumbria LA22 0BD
T: (015394) 33777 **E:** admin@resort-solutions.co.uk
W: www.the-lakelands.com

Sleeps   2-8

PER UNIT PER WEEK
£260.00 - £1050.00

Comfortable self-catering apartments and a separate four bedroomed house, all with access to a leisure centre on the site. We are situated in a unique position overlooking the popular town of Ambleside. The Lakelands offers superb, unspoilt views of the town, Lakeland countryside and the fells beyond - and enjoys easy access to the many delights of the area.

Popular Ambleside offers an excellent selection of shops, restaurants and friendly inns. While walkers are spoilt for choice with a number of pathways directly accessed from the town.

Open: All year

Units: Designed and furnished to a high standard, one- and two-bedroom apartments and a separate four bedroomed house, all self contained and fully-equipped.

Site: ✿ P Payment: 🔲 Leisure: ☌ Property: 🚗 🗄 🔲 Children: 🏇 🛏 ⚓ Unit: 🗄 🔲 🔧 📺 📀

BORROWDALE, Cumbria   Map ref 5A3

Over Brandelhow

Contact: Kath Manners, T manners & Sons Ltd, 2 Dovecote hill,
South Church Enterprise Park, Bishop Auckland, Co. Durham DL14 6XW **T:** 07711 592156
E: peter@overbrandelhow.com **W:** www.overbrandelhow.com

Units   1
Sleeps   6
PER UNIT PER WEEK
£500.00 - £975.00

The views down the Borrowdale valley from the cottage must be some of the best in the area. The location is so peaceful and has great walks from the doorstep. The sitting room has a wood-burning stove. **Open:** All year **Nearest Shop:** 4 miles **Nearest Pub:** 1 mile

Site: ✿ P Property: 🐾 🚗 🗄 Children: 🏇 🛏 ⚓ Unit: 🗄 🔲 🔧 📺 📀 ♨

BOWNESS-ON-WINDERMERE, *Cumbria* Map ref 5A3

SELF CATERING ★★★★

Units 46
Sleeps 2-6

PER UNIT PER WEEK
£460.00 - £1180.00

SPECIAL PROMOTIONS
Short breaks are available throughout the year starting from £240 for minimum 2 nights in a sleep 4.

Burnside Park

Contact: Lisa Holden, Resort Manager, Hapimag Resorts & Residences UK Ltd, The Lodge, Burnside Park, Kendal Road, Bowness-on-Windermere LA23 3EW
T: (01539) 446624 **F:** 01539 447754 **E:** bowness@hapimag.com
W: www.burnsidepark.co.uk **£ BOOK ONLINE**

Luxury self catering apartments 300m from Lake Windermere and Bowness centre. Sleeping 2-6 guests.Your stay here includes use of the leisure facilities at Parklands Country Club (Burnside Hotel). Complimentary Wi-Fi. Our apartments are let on a weekly basis Saturday to Saturday, short breaks available on a minimum 2 night stay.

Open: All year
Nearest Shop: 0.5 miles
Nearest Pub: 0.5 miles

Site: ✿ P **Payment:** 💷 **Leisure:** 🎣 ♨ ☂ **Property:** 🐕 🛏 ▢ ▦ 🔲 **Children:** 🐎 🛏 🚼
Unit: ▢ ▣ 🔲 📺 ◉ 📀 📞

BROUGHTON-IN-FURNESS, *Cumbria* Map ref 5A3

★★★-★★★★ **SELF CATERING**
Gold AWARD

Units 6
Sleeps 1-6

PER UNIT PER WEEK
£230.00 - £650.00

SPECIAL PROMOTIONS
Short breaks available all year round. Please email for further details.

Thornthwaite

Contact: Mrs Jean Jackson, Thornthwaite, Woodland, Broughton in Furness, Cumbria LA20 6DF **T:** (01229) 716340 **E:** info@lakedistrictcottages.co.uk
W: www.lakedistrictcottages.co.uk **£ BOOK ONLINE**

Situated in the unspoilt Woodland Valley, there are five cottages and a luxury Log Cabin with stunning views of the Lakeland fells. Ideally situated for walking, cycling or just relaxing, with many walks from your cottage, we even have our own private fishing lake. Guests can enjoy going badger watching at dusk, watch the fox cubs playing or catch a glimpse of the barn owls out hunting. Within easy reach of the main attractions. However if you need to get away from it all and relax in a friendly atmosphere, our farm is perfect.

Open: All year
Nearest Shop: 3 miles
Nearest Pub: 3 miles

Site: ✿ P **Leisure:** 🎣 ▸ ♨ **Property:** 🐕 🛏 🔲 **Children:** 🐎 🛏 🚼 **Unit:** ▢ ▣ 🔲 📺 ◉ 📀 ⌀ BBQ

CARLISLE, Cumbria   Map ref 5A2

Brackenhill Tower & Jacobean Cottage

Contact: Mrs Jan Ritchie, Manageress, Brackenhill Estates, Brackenhill, Longtown, Carlisle, Cumbria CA6 5TU **T:** (01461) 800285 / 07779 138 694
E: enquiries@brackenhilltower.co.uk **W:** www.brackenhilltower.co.uk **£ BOOK ONLINE**

Units 2
Sleeps 2-16
PER UNIT PER WEEK
£780.00 - £3600.00

A 16thC castle with wow factor! Stated luxury and comfort in a real historic landmark of character and authentic clan Graham Reiver stronghold. **Nearest Shop:** Longtown **Nearest Pub:** Longtown

Site: ✿ **P Payment:** 🔳 **Property:** 📺 📶 **Children:** 🍼 🛏 🚶 **Unit:** 🍴 🍴 📺 📶 🍳 TV 📀 BBQ 📞

COCKERMOUTH, Cumbria   Map ref 5A2

Garden Cottage

Contact: Colin Wornham, Dower Cottage, Pardshaw Hall, Cockermouth, Cumbria CA13 0SP **T:** (01900) 823531 **E:** wornham2@aol.com
W: www.pardshawcottage.co.uk

Units 1
Sleeps 1-2
PER UNIT PER WEEK
£130.00 - £280.00

A very comfortable, quiet and well-equipped cottage set in the tiny hamlet of Pardshaw Hall. It overlooks the small scenic hill of Pardshaw Crag from where visitors can view the western Lake District and Solway coasts. Nearest lake - Loweswater (3 miles) and the nearest town is Cockermouth (3 miles). Arrivals from 15:00. **Open:** All year **Nearest Shop:** 2.5 miles **Nearest Pub:** 0.75 miles

Site: ✿ **P Property:** 📺 🍴 📶 **Unit:** 📺 🍳 TV 📀

COCKERMOUTH, Cumbria   Map ref 5A2

Linskeldfield holiday cottages

Contact: Marion and Pauline, Owners, Linskeldfield Farm, Isel, Cockermouth, Cumbria CA13 9SR **T:** (01900) 822136 / 07740 307069 **E:** info@linskeldfield.co.uk
W: www.linskeldfield.co.uk

Units 4
Sleeps 2-6
PER UNIT PER WEEK
£211.00 - £640.00

[f]

Our beautiful cottages are based on our working farm set in open countryside with panaramic views of Skiddaw and our local fells. 5 miles from the picturesque town of Cockermouth and situated perfectly for exploring the Western Lakes and Fells. Sleeping from 2 to 6 people or up to 16 as a whole with excellent quality fixtures and fittings. Fresh home made bread and our own eggs await your arrival. **Open:** All year **Nearest Shop:** 5 miles **Nearest Pub:** 5 miles

Site: ✿ **P Leisure:** ♿ 🎣 ↟ 🔍 **Property:** 🐕 📺 🍴 📶 **Children:** 🍼 🛏 🚶 **Unit:** 🍴 🍴 📺 📶 🍳 TV 📀 BBQ 📞

CONISTON, Cumbria   Map ref 5A3

Shelt Gill

Contact: Rosalind Dean, Shelt Gill, c/o 9 The Fairway, Sheffield S10 4LX **T:** (08450) 093998
E: holiday@sheltgill.co.uk
W: www.sheltgill.co.uk **£ BOOK ONLINE**

Units 1
Sleeps 4-5
PER UNIT PER WEEK
£290.00 - £590.00

[f]

Shelt Gill is a medieval cruck cottage that has been modernised and extended to make a comfortable, fully equipped and attractive holiday home. There is a view of Lake Coniston from the timbered living room, a stream in the garden and easy access to hill walks. The pubs and shops in Coniston Village are not far away. **Open:** All year **Nearest Shop:** 1 mile **Nearest Pub:** 0.10 miles

Site: ✿ **P Payment:** € **Leisure:** ☉ **Property:** 🐕 **Children:** 🍼 🛏 🚶 **Unit:** 🍴 📺 🍳 TV 📀

GRANGE-OVER-SANDS, *Cumbria* Map ref 5A3

3★-4★ SELF CATERING

Units	3
Sleeps	2-4

PER UNIT PER WEEK
£299.00 - £435.00

SPECIAL PROMOTIONS
For short breaks of 3 or 4 nights, discounted last minute vacancies and other special offers, either search website and book online, or phone us on our low cost to call number 033 033 00033. Thanks.

Wycombe Holiday Flats

Contact: Geoff & Auriel Benson, Owners, Wycombe Holiday Flats, 22 The Esplanade, Grange-over-Sands, Cumbria LA11 7HH **T:** (0800) 321 3179 / 033 033 00033
E: mail@wycombeholidayflats.com **W:** www.wycombeholidayflats.com **£ BOOK ONLINE**

Each spacious apartment has 1 or 2 bedroom options accommodating 2 - 4 persons. King-size four poster and French sleigh beds or baronial twin bed styles ensure a memorable and restful stay. All have private sitting rooms with magnificent open views. Own kitchen/laundry/ironing facilities. Free Wi-Fi.

A short walk to Grange shops, cafes, boutiques and leisure amenities. Exciting opportunity to enjoy a meal at UK's Top Restaurant (Good Food Guide) (4km). There are also many other good eating places in South Lakeland. Ideal tourist base for Lakes, Dales and historic places. Train passengers met.

Open: All year
Nearest Shop: 0.10 miles
Nearest Pub: 0.10 miles

Units: 3 apartments, each with large lounge/diner with panoramic views, 1 or 2 bedrooms, fully tiled shower-bathroom (underfloor heating) and fitted kitchen.

Site: ❀ **P Payment:** 💳 € **Leisure:** ↱ ∪ **Property:** 🐾 🛏 📶 **Children:** 👶
Unit: 📷 🗄 📺 📻 🔍 📺 🎧 📀 📞

HIGH LORTON, *Cumbria* Map ref 5A3

★★★★★ SELF CATERING

Units	1
Sleeps	2

PER UNIT PER WEEK
£400.00 - £500.00

Holemire Barn

Contact: Mrs Angela Fearfield, Holemire Barn, c/o Holemire House, High Lorton, Cockermouth CA13 9TX **T:** (01900) 85225 **E:** enquiries@lakelandbarn.co.uk
W: www.lakelandbarn.co.uk **£ BOOK ONLINE**

Traditional Lakeland barn with exposed beams, converted to high quality accommodation. Close to Keswick. Warm, light and sunny. In superb walking country. Ospreys nesting close by. Red squirrels in garden. **Open:** All year **Nearest Shop:** 0.25 miles
Nearest Pub: 0.25 miles

Site: ❀ **P Leisure:** 🚴 ⚓ ↱ ∪ **Property:** 📶 🛏 **Unit:** 📷 📺 📻 🔍 📺 🎧 📀

KENDAL, *Cumbria* Map ref 5B3

★★★★ SELF CATERING

Units	4
Sleeps	2-18

PER UNIT PER WEEK
£265.00 - £490.00

Shaw End Mansion

Contact: Mr & Mrs Edward & Karlyn Robinson, Shaw End Holidays, Haveriggs Farm, Whinfell, Kendal LA8 9EF **T:** (01539) 824220 **F:** 01539 824220 **E:** info@shawend.co.uk
W: www.shawend.co.uk **£ BOOK ONLINE**

Shaw End Mansion is set on 200-acres of farm and woodland in a beautiful location. Shaw End - a restored Georgian house - contains spacious and elegant apartments with fantastic views and walks from the doorstep. Why not rent the whole house, which is ideal for weddings and parties. **Open:** All year **Nearest Shop:** 3 miles
Nearest Pub: 3 miles

Site: ❀ **P Payment:** 💳 **Leisure:** ⚓ ∪ **Property:** 🛏 📶 🛏 **Children:** 👶 🏏 ⚲ **Unit:** 📷 🗄 📺 📻 🔍 📺 🎧 📀 ♨

KENDAL, *Cumbria* Map ref 5B3

★★★★ SELF CATERING

Gold AWARD

Swallow Barn

Contact: Dave Whitcombe, c/o 39 Gladstone Place, Aberdeen AB10 6UX **T:** 07786 275954
E: david.n.whitcombe@btinternet.com
W: www.swallowbarncumbria.weebly.com

Units   1
Sleeps   2-8
PER UNIT PER WEEK
£410.00 - £895.00

Rural setting with stunning views of the Langdale Fells and the Kent Estuary. Ideally located between the Lake District and Yorkshire Dales. Easy access in either direction. Accommodation features a large living room with log burning stove, gallery, original beams and high standard facilities. Sleeps 8+cot. Discounts and short breaks are available. One well behaved pet by arrangement.
Open: All year **Nearest Shop:** 1 mile **Nearest Pub:** 1 mile

Site: ✿ P **Property:** ∥ 🐾 ▭ 🖥 🖵 **Children:** 🎠 🛏 🧒 **Unit:** 🗔 🗒 🖭 🖥 🗲 ⓔ 📀 🧺 BBQ 📞

KESWICK, *Cumbria* Map ref 5A3

Brewery Lane Holiday Cottages

Contact: The Heads, Keswick, Cumbria CA12 5ER **T:** (017687) 72750
E: info@brewery-lane.co.uk
W: www.brewery-lane.co.uk **£ BOOK ONLINE**

Units   4
Sleeps   2-4
PER UNIT PER WEEK
£330.00 - £650.00

Superior, centrally situated, comfortable cottages with either 2 double bedrooms or 1 double and 1 twin bedroom. Private parking in enclosed landscaped courtyard area. Keswick town centre's shops, pubs and restaurants are within easy walking distance as is Derwentwater and The Theatre by the Lake. All cottages are well equipped and owner maintained to a high standard. Quality Cumbria Assessed. **Open:** All Year

Site: ✿ P **Property:** ▭ 🖵 **Children:** 🎠 🛏 🧒 **Unit:** 🗔 🗒 🖭 TV 📀

KESWICK, *Cumbria* Map ref 5A3

★★★★ SELF CATERING

Peter House Cottages

Contact: Valerie & Cerita Trafford, Owners, Peter House Farm, Bassenthwaite, Keswick, Cumbria CA12 4QX **T:** (01768) 776018 / 07743 898729 **E:** info@peterhousecottages.co.uk
W: www.peterhousecottages.co.uk **£ BOOK ONLINE**

Units   2
Sleeps   2-5

PER UNIT PER WEEK
£380.00 - £495.00

SPECIAL PROMOTIONS
Short breaks available. Minimum stay 3 nights. Please contact for information.

Peterhouse cottage and Pembroke cottage are situated on a lakeland hill farm with wonderful scenery. Situated in a peaceful location at the foot of Skiddaw, with Dash Falls, Ullock Pike and Binsey literally on the doorstep.

Close by is the village of Bassenthwaite and the market town of Keswick. The cottages are spacious, comfortable and well equipped and are an ideal base for either walking, cycling or relaxing. Private off road parking.

Open: March - December
Nearest Shop: 2 mile
Nearest Pub: 2 mile

Units: Both cottages have two bedrooms sleeping 5 and 4, electric hob/ovens, microwave, kettle, toaster, fridge/freezer. Linen, towels & heating inclusive. Electric showers over bath, toilet & wash basin. TV/DVD player and electric storage heating.

Site: ✿ P **Leisure:** ▸ **Property:** 🐾 🖥 🖵 **Children:** 🎠 🛏 🧒 **Unit:** 🗔 🖭 🖥 🗲 TV 📀 🧺

KESWICK, Cumbria   Map ref 5A3

SELF CATERING ★★★★

Gold AWARD

Units 1
Sleeps 8
PER UNIT PER WEEK
£750.00 - £1995.00

San Ging Keswick

Contact: Helen Ball, Manager, Gratitude, Grange, Keswick CA12 5UQ **T:** 017687 77448 / 07720 034494 **E:** helen@sangingkeswick.co.uk
W: www.sangingkeswick.co.uk

San Ging is a modern split level house built into the hillside just above Keswick town centre with stunning views towards Bassenthwaite lake. The house provides comfortable accommodation for up to 8 people and is ideally suited to groups and families. With easy access to all parts of the Lake District it makes a good base for many outdoor activities and other attractions. See website for details. **Open:** All year
Nearest Shop: 1 mile **Nearest Pub:** 1mile

Site: ✿ **P** **Property:** 🖥 📻 🖵 **Children:** 🛏 🏠 🧍 **Unit:** 🖵 🖵 🖵 🖵 🍴 tv 🎧 dvd 🖊 BBQ 📞

LAMPLUGH, Cumbria   Map ref 5A3

SELF CATERING ★★★★

Units 1
Sleeps 1-4
PER UNIT PER WEEK
£300.00 - £385.00

2 Folly

Contact: Mrs Alison Wilson, Felldyke Cottage Holidays, c/o Dockray Nook, Lamplugh, Workington, Cumbria CA14 4SH **T:** (01946) 861151 / 07766 548259 **F:** 01946 862367
E: dockraynook@btinternet.com **W:** www.felldykecottageholidays.co.uk

19th century middle cottage, owner maintained. Situated in small hamlet at the base of the Western Fells. Fully central heated. Panoramic views. Good walking from cottage, near Ennerdale and Loweswater lakes. **Open:** All year **Nearest Shop:** 2.5 miles
Nearest Pub: 2 miles

Site: ✿ **P** **Leisure:** 🎵 **Property:** 🐕 🖵 **Children:** 🛏 🏠 🧍 **Unit:** 🖵 🖵 🍴 tv 🎧 dvd 🖊 BBQ 📞

LONGSLEDDALE, Cumbria   Map ref 5B3

SELF CATERING ★★★

Units 1
Sleeps 1-2
PER UNIT PER WEEK
£160.00 - £300.00

The Coach House

Contact: Jenny Farmer, The Coach House, c/o Capplebarrow House, Kendal, Longsleddale, Cumbria LA8 9BB **T:** (01539) 823686 **E:** jenyfarmer@aol.com
W: www.capplebarrowcoachhouse.co.uk **£ BOOK ONLINE**

Stone-built, converted coach house with ground-floor shower room, bedroom and open staircase to first-floor kitchen and lounge. Excellent views. Located in peaceful, picturesque valley. Log burner and super-king bed. Pets welcome. **Open:** All year
Nearest Shop: 6 miles **Nearest Pub:** 7 miles

Site: ✿ **P** **Property:** 🐕 🖥 📻 🖵 **Children:** 🛏 🏠 🧍 **Unit:** 🖵 tv 🎧 dvd 🖊 BBQ

LUPTON, Cumbria   Map ref 5B3

SELF CATERING ★★★★

Units 1
Sleeps 2-6
PER UNIT PER WEEK
£320.00 - £675.00

Hornsbarrow Farmhouse

Contact: Gill Gibbs, Owner, Hornsbarrow New End, Lupton, Nr Kirkby Lonsdale, Via Carnforth LA6 2PS **T:** (015395) 67618 **E:** info@hornsbarrow.co.uk
W: www.hornsbarrow.co.uk **£ BOOK ONLINE**

Hornsbarrow Farmhouse dates from 1681 and is ideally located for visiting both the Lake District and the Yorkshire Dales. It retains period features and furniture but has modern facilities and views of open countryside from all the rooms. The picturesque and historic market town of Kirkby Lonsdale is just 3 miles away; it has a variety of places to eat as well as many local independent shops.
Open: February half term to New Year **Nearest Shop:** 3 miles
Nearest Pub: 1 mile

Site: ✿ **P** **Leisure:** ⚑ **Property:** 🐕 🖥 🖵 **Unit:** 🖵 🖵 🖵 🍴 🎧 dvd 🖊

PENRITH, Cumbria   Map ref 5B2

Holme Lea

Contact: Alan Price, Owner, 27 Church Close, Buxton, Norwich NR10 5ER
T: (01603) 279713 **E:** jprice@albatross.co.uk
W: www.cumbriaselfcater.co.uk

Units 1
Sleeps 4
PER UNIT PER WEEK
£190.00 - £400.00

Village bungalow. Lounge/dining room, sun lounge, two twin bedded bedrooms. Bath with shower over, Re-fitted kitchen, Pets welcome. Enclosed garden. Parking for two cars. Near to shop. Linen provided. **Open:** All year **Nearest Shop:** 40 yards **Nearest Pub:** 0.5 miles

Site: ❀ P Children: 🛝 Unit: 📺 📀 BBQ 📞

PENRITH, Cumbria   Map ref 5B2

Tirril Farm Cottages

Contact: Mr David Owens and Trish Little, Proprietors, Tirril View, Tirril, Penrith, Cumbria CA10 2JE **T:** (01768) 864767 **E:** enquiries@tirrilfarmcottages.co.uk
W: www.tirrilfarmcottages.co.uk

Units 4
Sleeps 2-5
PER UNIT PER WEEK
£215.00 - £580.00

Opened in 2001, Tirril Farm Cottages are situated in the charming village of Tirril near Lake Ullswater and on the fringe of the Lake District. Tasteful barn conversions sleeping 2-5 people offering 4 Star accommodation in a quiet courtyard setting. Outstanding views over the fells and easy access to low level footpaths in and around the village add to the overall appeal. A warm welcome awaits you from the resident proprietors. **Open:** All year **Nearest Shop:** 100 metres **Nearest Pub:** 100 metres

Site: ❀ P Leisure: ▶ Property: 🖥 Children: 🛝 ♿ Unit: 📺 📀

ST. BEES, Cumbria   Map ref 5A3

Springbank Farm Lodges

Contact: Carole Woodman, Joint Owner, Springbank Farm, High Walton, St Bees, Cumbria CA22 2TY **T:** (01946) 822375 / 07880 597109 **F:** 01946 822375
E: stevewoodman@talk21.com **W:** www.springbanklodges.co.uk **£ BOOK ONLINE**

Units 2
Sleeps 4-5
PER UNIT PER WEEK
£300.00 - £600.00

Luxury 2 bedroomed log cabins in tranquil farm setting with spectacular open views. Spacious accommodation, fully fitted kitchen, main bedroom en suite plus family wet room. Criffell sleeps 4 and Manx sleeps up to 2 adults and 3 children. Wheelchair friendly with ample parking. On farm experience yet close to amenities. Farm walks, rare breeds and wildlife. Close to beach and Western Lakes. **Open:** All Year **Nearest Shop:** 1 mile **Nearest Pub:** 1 mile

Site: ❀ P Payment: 💷 Leisure: ▶ Property: 🖥 Children: 🛝 ♿ Unit: BBQ

TIRRIL, *Cumbria* Map ref 5B2

Broad Ing Cottage

Contact: Mrs Carol Kay, Broad Ing Cottage, c/o 36 Masham Close, Harrogate HG2 8QG
T: (01423) 881886 **E:** gjkay.tr6@ntlworld.com
W: www.broadingcottage.co.uk **£ BOOK ONLINE**

| Units | 1 |
| Sleeps | 2-6 |

PER UNIT PER WEEK
£385.00 - £750.00

SPECIAL PROMOTIONS
Peak holiday period - June, July & August, Christmas & New Year and school half terms - no short breaks allowed unless agreed with the owners. Out of season, minimum short breaks are 2 nights minimum.

Broad Ing Cottage is situated on the edge of the village of Tirril, which nestles on the fringe of the Lake District National Park close to Ullswater and Penrith. The cottage is equipped to a very high standard warranting a Visit Britain 4* rating. All the rooms are on one level and overlook the pleasant rear garden or open fields.

The rear garden is very private and peaceful and catches the sun from early morning to late afternoon - perfect for al-fresco dining - appealing to families and couples alike.There is a comprehensive range of garden furniture to aid your relaxation.

Open: All year
Nearest Shop: 0.25 miles
Nearest Pub: 0.25 miles

Units: All rooms are on one level. 2 double and 1 twin bedroom. Large lounge. Large kitchen diner. House bathroom with separate shower cubicle. Shower room.

Site: ✿ P Leisure: 🎿 ♪ ▶ ∪ Property: 🖥 📶 Children: 🐾 🛏 🚶 Unit: 🗄 🗄 📺 🖥 🍵 TV ◉ DVD ∅ BBQ

TROUTBECK, *Cumbria* Map ref 5A3

Troutbeck Inn Holiday Cottages

Contact: Rowan Mahon, Booking Enquiries, Troutbeck Inn & Holiday Cottages, Troutbeck, Penrith CA11 0SJ **T:** (01768) 483635 **E:** info@troutbeckinn.co.uk
W: www.thetroutbeckinn.co.uk **£ BOOK ONLINE**

| Units | 3 |
| Sleeps | 2-4 |

PER UNIT PER WEEK
£285.00 - £545.00

Our cottages were converted from stone barns and are very spacious. The one bedroom cottage has a king size sleigh bed and the two bedroom cottages offer wonderful fell views. **Open:** All year **Nearest Shop:** 6 miles

Site: P Payment: 💳 Property: 🐴 🖥 📶 Children: 🐾 Unit: 📺 TV ◉ DVD

WASDALE, *Cumbria* Map ref 5A3

Bleng Barn

Contact: Thomas & Isabelle Ostle, Owner, Bleng Farms, Bleng Barn Cottage, Mill House Farm, Wellington, Gosforth CA20 1BH **T:** (01946) 725671 / 07775 512918
F: 01946 725671 **E:** info@blengfarms.co.uk **W:** www.blengfarms.co.uk **£ BOOK ONLINE**

| Units | 1 |
| Sleeps | 1-8 |

PER UNIT PER WEEK
£280.00 - £693.00

This newly converted rural property, is on a large working farm and has many traditional features and modern conveniences. Providing a base for leisurely breaks or activity holidays, well situated for walking & climbing, especially Scawfell. We are between the sea and the Lake District fells, close to two 18 and one 9 hole golf course. Larger groups can be catered for by arrangement.
Open: All year **Nearest Shop:** 1 mile **Nearest Pub:** 0.60 miles

WALKERS CYCLISTS / WALKERS CYCLISTS Site: ✿ P Payment: € Leisure: ♪ ▶ Property: 🐴 🖥 📶 Children: 🐾 🛏 🚶 Unit: 🗄 🗄 📺 🍵 TV ◉ DVD BBQ

WIGTON, Cumbria   Map ref 5A2

Foxgloves

Contact: Mrs Janice Kerr, Foxgloves, Greenrigg Farm, Westward, Wigton, Cumbria CA7 8AH **T:** (01697) 342676 **E:** kerr_greenrigg@hotmail.com
W: www.foxgloves.moonfruit.com

| Units | 1 |
| Sleeps | 1-8 |

PER UNIT PER WEEK
£295.00 - £625.00

SPECIAL PROMOTIONS
Please contact for short breaks information.

Spacious, extremely well-equipped, comfortable cottage with Aga, offering a high standard of accommodation. Superlative setting and views. Large, safe garden. Guests are welcome to explore the farm and fields where a variety of wildlife can be seen. Within easy reach of Lake District, Scottish Borders and Roman Wall. Children and Pets very welcome.

Open: All year
Nearest Shop: 1 mile
Nearest Pub: 1 mile

Site: ✿ P Leisure: ⛷ ♪ ► ∪ Property: ♞ ▣ ▣ Children: ⛺ ♨ ☂ Unit: ▢ ▤ ▣ ▨ ⚲ 📺 ⓓ 💿 ◿ BBQ

WINDERMERE, Cumbria   Map ref 5A3

Graythwaite Cottages

Contact: Graythwaite, Newby Bridge, Ulverston, Nr Windermere, Cumbria LA12 8BQ
T: 015395 31351 **E:** cottages@graythwaite.com
W: www.graythwaite.com

| Units | 20 |
| Sleeps | 2-10 |

PER UNIT PER WEEK
£497.00 - £2537.00

Thirteen cottages and barn conversion are located within a secluded courtyard. The original Victorian farmstead of the estate was skillfully converted in the early 1990's. **Open:** All Year

Site: ✿ P Leisure: ♪ ♦ Property: ♞ ▣ ▣ ▣ Children: ⛺ ♨ ☂ Unit: ▢ ▤ ▣ ▨ ⚲ ⓓ 💿 ◿ BBQ

WINDERMERE, Cumbria   Map ref 5A3

Hill of Oaks Park

Contact: Newby Bridge Road, Windermere, Cumbria LA12 8NR **T:** (015395) 31578
E: enquiries@hillofoaks.co.uk
W: www.hillofoaks.co.uk **£ BOOK ONLINE**

| Units | 2 |
| Sleeps | 2-4 |

PER UNIT PER WEEK
£325.00 - £595.00

This five star award winning Park has a selection of self catering properties available for weekly rental. Located on over a kilometre of Windermere shoreline, the Parks excellent facilities include private jetties and moorings, fabulous lake views from each property, on site shop, woodland walks, children's play area and electric car Twizy hire. Free Wi-Fi for self catering holidays.
Open: March to Mid November **Nearest Shop:** On Site
Nearest Pub: 2 miles

Site: P Payment: 💷 Leisure: ♪ ► Property: ▣ ▣ ▣ Children: ⛺ ☂ Unit: ▢ ▤ ▣ ⚲ 📺 💿

BLACKPOOL, Lancashire   Map ref 4A1

Units 10
Sleeps 2-6

PER UNIT PER WEEK
£150.00 - £450.00

Lynton Apartments

Contact: Iggy or Koko, Lynton Apartments, 227 Promenade, Blackpool FY1 5DL
T: (01253) 624 296 **E:** info@lyntonapartments.co.uk
W: www.lyntonapartments.co.uk

Lynton Apartments offer spacious, self-catering holiday flats at the heart of the Promenade located halfway between Blackpool Tower and the Pleasure Beach with stunning sea views, fully equipped kitchens & private bathrooms. Our units are refurbished annually to very high standards & have flat screen colour TV's with Freeview in all lounges & free Wi-Fi throughout the building. **Open:** All year
Nearest Shop: 0.10 miles **Nearest Pub:** 0.10 miles

Payment: 🔲 **Property:** 🔲 🔲 **Children:** 🔲 🔲 🔲 **Unit:** 🔲 🔲 🔲

CARNFORTH, Lancashire   Map ref 5B3

Units 4
Sleeps 4-6

PER UNIT PER WEEK
£280.00 - £620.00

SPECIAL PROMOTIONS
70% of the weekly booking charge; minimum charge of 3 nights.

Brackenthwaite Cottages

Contact: Matthew or Susan Clarke, Brackenthwaite Farm, Yealand Redmayne, Near Carnforth, Lancashire LA5 9TE **T:** (015395) 63276 **E:** info@brackenthwaite.com
W: www.brackenthwaite.com

Relax comfortably in one of our four cottages based in Arnside/Silverdale Area of Outsanding Beauty. You can walk our nature trail or through nearby nature reserves in the AONB. There are lots of lovely activities close-by such as bird watching at Leighton Moss RSPB reserve, golf in Silverdale and water sports at Carnforth. The area is a haven for walkers and cyclists. Nature lovers will find a wealth of flora and forna, especially at the nearby Gaitbarrows National Nature Reserve and Trowbarrow Local Nature Reserve. The Lakes, coast and Dales are all easily accessible by either the A6 or M6. www.facebook.com/brackenthwaite

Open: All Year
Nearest Shop: 3 miles
Nearest Pub: 2.5 miles

Units: We have four holiday cottages, two that sleep up to six and two that sleep up to four. One is 4 star graded and the other three are 3 star graded.

Site: ✿ P **Payment:** 🔲 **Leisure:** ▶ **Property:** 🐾 🔲 🔲 🔲 **Children:** 🔲 🔲 🔲
Unit: 🔲 🔲 🔲 🔲 🔲 🔲 🔲 BBQ

CARNFORTH, Lancashire   Map ref 5B3

Units 1
Sleeps 5
PER UNIT PER WEEK
£150.00 - £395.00

Deroy Cottage

Contact: Mr Colin Cross, The Heights, Hawk Street, Carnforth, Lancashire LA5 9LA
T: (01524) 733196 **E:** colin@cross00.orangehome.co.uk
W: www.colincross.co.uk

At The Heights we offer excellent self-catering accommodation with use of a summerhouse and BBQ and magnificent views over Morecambe Bay to the Lakeland fells. We are ideally situated for Lancaster Canal, Ingleton Waterfalls and Arnside. **Open:** All year
Nearest Shop: 100 yards **Nearest Pub:** 100 yards

Site: ✿ P **Property:** 🐾 🔲 **Children:** 🔲 🔲 🔲 **Unit:** 🔲 🔲 🔲 🔲 🔲 BBQ

CARNFORTH, Lancashire   Map ref 5B3

Units 1
Sleeps 2-4

PER UNIT PER WEEK
£290.00 - £550.00

Hill View Cottage
Contact: Joanne Murray, Owner, Main Street, Burton- in- Kendal, Carnforth, Lancashire LA6 1NA **T:** 07725 327128 **E:** hillviewholidays@hotmail.co.uk
W: www.hillview-cottage-holidays-cumbria.co.uk

Hill View is a beautiful garden fronted 18th Century stone cottage ideally placed in the Cumbrian village of Burton- in- Kendal Tastefully renovated and refurbished to high standards with exposed stonework and beamed ceilings. Relax home from home in front of the wood burning stove and enjoy the peace.
Open: All year **Nearest Shop:** 5 metres **Nearest Pub:** 50 metres

Site: **Property:** **Children:** **Unit:**

CARNFORTH, Lancashire   Map ref 5B3

Units 124
Sleeps 1-6

PER UNIT PER WEEK
£419.00 - £1267.00

SPECIAL PROMOTIONS
Enjoy two nights or more with complimentary champagne and chocolates on arrival, please call for latest pricing.

Pine Lake Resort
Contact: Dock Acres, Carnforth, Lancashire LA6 1JZ **T:** (0800) 358 6991
E: EuHotels@diamondresorts.com
W: www.DiamondResortsandHotels.com **£ BOOK ONLINE**

These unique Scandinavian-style Lodges lie in a tranquil location by Pine Lake near Carnforth. Guests can enjoy water skiing, sailing and canoeing and there is also an indoor swimming pool, fitness centre and spa. The on site restaurant provides a varied menu including children's options and evening entertainment is available in the bar area.

Each 2 bedroom lodge or studio comes with a fully equipped kitchen and some have lake views. Complimentary toiletries, a flat-screen TV and a DVD player are all included, Wi-Fi can be purchased as extra.

Open: All year
Nearest Shop: 1 Mile
Nearest Pub: On Site

Units: A choice of Studios and two bedroom apartments available. All apartments boast a modern bathroom, kitchen and Television with DVD player.

Site: P **Payment:** **Leisure:** **Property:** **Children:** **Unit:**

CLITHEROE, Lancashire   Map ref 4A1

Units 1
Sleeps 4
PER UNIT PER WEEK
£300.00 - £570.00

Cobden View
Contact: John and Margaret Wright, Co-owners, Cobden Farm, Sabden, Clitheroe, Lancashire BB7 9ED **T:** (01282) 776285 / 07989 401595 **E:** enquiries@cobdenview.co.uk
W: www.cobdenview.co.uk

Enjoy the spectacular Pendle Hill countryside by staying in Cobden View, a 4-star, sleep four, Forest of Bowland self catering holiday cottage. Set on our Sabden Valley hillside working farm, the cottage is cosy yet spacious with stunning views. Cyclists, walkers and families welcome. Dogs welcome. **Open:** All year, including Christmas & New Year. **Nearest Shop:** 1 mile **Nearest Pub:** 1 mile

Site: P **Leisure:** **Property:** **Children:** **Unit:** BBQ

LANCASTER, Lancashire Map ref 5A3

Cleveleymere 5* Luxury Lakeside Lodges

Contact: Roger Burnside, Owner, Cleveleymere, Cleveley Bank Lane, Scorton, Lancashire PR3 1BY **T:** (01524) 793644 / 07711 055544 **E:** sales@cleveleymere.com **W:** www.cleveleymere.com

Units 8
Sleeps 1-40

Imagine your perfect holiday - A 5* lakeside lodge, a private lake, your own boat, picnicking on an island, a spot of fishing or clay-pigeon shooting perhaps, canoeing and a lazy bike ride late into the evening, ending with a BBQ in the woods. The Lake at Cleveleymere is a totally unique nature reserve. We provide free bikes, pedalos, kayaks, crazy golf and a trampoline. Please contact for prices. **Open:** All year **Nearest Shop:** 3 mins **Nearest Pub:** 5 mins

Site: ✿ **P Payment:** 💷 **Leisure:** 🚲 🎵 ▶ 🔍 **Property:** 🐾 📺 💻 **Children:** 🧸 🎱 🧍 **Unit:** 📼 📀 📺 🔌

LANCASTER, Lancashire Map ref 5A3

The Glassworks Apartments

Contact: Peter Hearne, Director, The Glassworks Apartments, 7-11 Chapel Street, Lancaster, Lancashire LA1 1NZ **T:** (01524) 840240 **E:** stay@theglassworksapartments.co.uk **W:** www.theglassworksapartments.co.uk **£ BOOK ONLINE**

Units 4
Sleeps 1-4
PER UNIT PER WEEK
£420.00 - £525.00

Fully serviced Apartments offering high style and comfort in the heart of historic Lancaster. These fine Georgian buildings were originally built in the mid 18th Century as opulent town houses for Lancaster's wealthy Merchant class. Sensitively restored and newly redeveloped, they once more offer luxurious self-catering living accommodation for those with discerning tastes. Apartments can be booked from 1 week to 3 months. **Open:** All year **Nearest Shop:** 50 metres **Nearest Pub:** 100 metres

Payment: 💷 **Property:** ⁄ 📺 📀 💻 **Unit:** 📺 📀 🔌 📺

Need more information?

Visit our websites for detailed information, up-to-date availability and to book your accommodation online. Includes over 20,000 places to stay, all of them star rated.

www.visitor-guides.co.uk

2015 Official Tourist Board Guides

LANCASTER, Lancashire   Map ref 5A3

Units   60
Sleeps   1-6

PER UNIT PER WEEK
£280.00 - £1267.00

SPECIAL PROMOTIONS
Enjoy two nights or more with complimentary champagne and chocolates on arrival, please call for latest pricing.

Thurnham Hall

Contact: Thurnham, Nr Lancaster, Lancashire LA2 0DT **T:** (0800) 358 6991
E: EuHotels@diamondresorts.com
W: www.DiamondResortsandHotels.com **£ BOOK ONLINE**

With an elegant Jacobean Great Hall, this resort a features a leisure centre and traditional restaurant. Thurnham Hall is a 12th-century country estate, set in nearly 30 acres of grounds in scenic Lancashire. The stylish, self-catering accommodation is set in either the historic main house or in modern courtyard buildings. All apartments and studios have a satellite TV and a private bathroom.

The leisure centre at Thurnham Hall has a large indoor swimming pool and a state-of-the-art fitness suite. Guests can relax in the sauna and spa bath, or enjoy treatments in the beauty salon.

Open: All year
Nearest Shop: 2 miles
Nearest Pub: 2 miles

Units: A choice of Studio, one and two bedroom apartments available. All apartments boast a full kitchen, modern bathroom and Television with DVD player.

Site: ✿ P Payment: 💷 Leisure: ♪ ▶ ✎ Property: 🖥 ⛶ 🍴 Children: ⛹ 🛏 ⚲ Unit: 🗄 🍽 🖥 🔌 📺 📀 📞

ORMSKIRK, Lancashire   Map ref 4A1

Units   4
Sleeps   1-6
PER UNIT PER WEEK
£310.00 - £595.00

Martin Lane Farm Holiday Cottages

Contact: Mrs Elaine Stubbs, Owner, Martin Lane Farm Holiday Cottages, 5 Martin Lane, Burscough, Ormskirk, Lancashire L40 8JH **T:** (01704) 893527 / 07803 049128
E: cottages@btinternet.com **W:** martinlanefarm-holidaycottages.co.uk **£ BOOK ONLINE**

Four beautiful, award-winning country cottages, one fully accessible for guests with disabilities. Nestling in the peaceful, arable farmland of West Lancashire, a haven of rest and tranquility. For those who don't want a 'quiet life' we are just 4 miles from Southport's seaside attractions and the quaint market town of Ormskirk. Martin Mere Wildfowl Trust and Rufford Old Hall, just 2 miles away. **Open:** All year **Nearest Shop:** 4 miles **Nearest Pub:** 0.25 miles

Site: ✿ P Payment: 💷 € Leisure: ♿ ♪ ▶ ♻ Property: 🖥 ⛶ 🍴 Children: ⛹ 🛏 ⚲ Unit: 🗄 ⛶ 🍽 🔌 ♻ 📺 📷 📀 BBQ

POULTON-LE-FYLDE, Lancashire   Map ref 4A1

Units   4
Sleeps   2-20
PER UNIT PER WEEK
£225.00 - £560.00

Hardhorn Breaks

Contact: Nicholas Pawson, Owner, High Bank Farm, Fairfield Road, Poulton-le-fylde, Lancashire FY6 8DN **T:** (01253) 890422 / 07563 723058 **E:** blackpoolnick@btinternet.com
W: www.highbank-farm.com

A complex of 4 recently converted cottages, in the pretty village of Hardhorn, near Poulton-le-Fylde, with Blackpool a short drive away. We are also ideally located for convenient access to a whole host of trip destinations, from the natural splendour of the Lake District and Yorkshire Dales to the urban metropolis of Manchester and several traditional North West textile towns all within easy reach. **Open:** All year **Nearest Shop:** 0.5 miles **Nearest Pub:** 0.5 miles

Site: ✿ P Payment: 💷 Property: 🐾 🖥 ⛶ 🍴 Children: ⛹ 🛏 ⚲ Unit: 🗄 🍽 ⛶ 🔌 ♻ 📺 📀 BBQ

PRESTON, Lancashire   Map ref 4A1

Crabtree Narrowboat Hire

Contact: Robert Foulkes, Owner, Crabtree Farm, Hagg Lane, St Michael's On Wyre, Preston, Lancashire PR3 0UJ **T:** (01995) 671 712 / 07572 664949
E: info@crabtreenarrowboathire.com **W:** www.crabtreenarrowboathire.com

Units   3
Sleeps   2-6
PER UNIT PER WEEK
£700.00 - £1200.00

Crabtree Narrowboat Hire is a friendly, family run narrowboat hire company based on the beautiful, lock-free Lancaster Canal. Looking for a holiday with a difference or do you just want to unwind and take life at a more tranquil pace? Your boating holiday with Crabtree Narrowboat Hire offers you a different perspective on life and the world around you. **Open:** March to October
Nearest Shop: 25 Yards **Nearest Pub:** 1 Mile

Site: **P** Payment: ... Property: ... Children: ... Unit: ...

PRESTON, Lancashire   Map ref 4A1

Gardeners Cottage at Growing With Nature

Contact: Alan and Debra Schofield, Owners, Bradshaw Lane Nursery, Pilling, Preston, Lancashire PR3 6AX **T:** (01253) 790046 / 07971 968560 **F:** 01253 790046
E: alan@gwnhome.demon.co.uk **W:** www.growing-with-nature.co.uk **£ BOOK ONLINE**

Units   1
Sleeps   4-6
PER UNIT PER WEEK
£350.00 - £500.00

A quirky Eco cottage near Pilling 10 miles from Lancaster, Preston and Blackpool standing in 1/2 acre of private garden full of wildlife on an organic small holding. Sleeps six, one double, one twin and a double bed settee downstairs. Features a rain shower, spa bath and oak tree staircase. The cottage is within easy reach of the Fylde Coast, Lancaster Canal Lake District and Forest of Bowland.
Open: April-September **Nearest Shop:** 1 mile **Nearest Pub:** 1 mile

Site: ... **P** Payment: ... Property: ... Children: ... Unit: ... BBQ

TEWITFIELD, Lancashire   Map ref 5B3

Sleeps   1-7

PER UNIT PER WEEK
£245.00 - £725.00

SPECIAL PROMOTIONS
1 night break (£75.00 -
£125.00), Weekend
breaks (£150.00-
£325.00), special
promotions all year
round please ring/
email for details.

Tewitfield Marina
Contact: Shirley Dennison, Bookings Office, 2 Lapwing House, Tewitfield Marina,
Chapel Lane, Carnforth LA6 1GP **T:** (01524) 782092 **F:** 01524 782461
E: info@tewitfieldmarina.co.uk **W:** www.tewitfieldmarina.co.uk **£ BOOK ONLINE**

Tewitfield Marina offers a home from home environment in its luxury 1, 2, 3 and 4 bedroom self-catering holiday homes. All properties are furnished to the highest standard with linen/towels on arrival, majority have a balcony view. Kitchens are fully equipped, inc washing machine, dishwasher, fridge freezer, microwave & oven. TV's in lounge and bedroom area. Free parking and play area. Pub and Restaurant on site.

Open: All year
Nearest Shop: Less than 1 mile
Nearest Pub: On site

Site: ❀ P Payment: 💳 Leisure: ♿ ♪ ▶ ∪ Property: 🐾 🛏 📺 🍴 Children: 🎠 🛏 🎒
Unit: 🍳 🗄 📺 📷 ⚒ 📺 🎧 📀

WADDINGTON, Lancashire   Map ref 4A1

Units   1
Sleeps   1-4
PER UNIT PER WEEK
£335.00

Blackbird Cottage
Contact: Ms Joanne Bywood, Blackbird Cottage, Waddington BB7 3HP **T:** (00352) 498014
E: blackbird.cottage@yahoo.co.uk
W: www.blackbirdcottage.weebly.com **£ BOOK ONLINE**

Providing comfortable, centrally-heated accommodation for up to 4 people, Blackbird Cottage has one double bedroom, one bedroom with bunkbeds, fully fitted kitchen and comfortable living room with TV and DVD player. **Open:** All year **Nearest Shop:** 0.01 miles **Nearest Pub:** 0.01 miles

Payment: € Property: ∥ 🐾 🛏 🍴 Children: 🎠 Unit: 🍳 📺 📷 ⚒ 📺 📀

WORSTON, Lancashire   Map ref 4A1

Units   3
Sleeps   1-6
PER UNIT PER WEEK
£280.00 - £580.00

Angram Green Holiday Cottages
Contact: John Haworth, Angram Green Holiday Cottages, Angram Green Cottage,
Worston, Clitheroe, Lancashire BB7 1QB **T:** (01200) 441455 / 07782 215984
E: info@angramgreen.co.uk **W:** www.angramgreen.co.uk

Farm-based cottages in rural Lancashire. Stunning views across open countryside. Ideal base for walkers and cyclists. One double bedroom, one pair of child-size bunks in smaller units. Two double bedrooms and one twin room in the larger unit. Also dishwasher and washing machine in larger unit. Pets in Pendleside only. Restaurant and bar within walking distance. **Open:** All year
Nearest Shop: 2 miles **Nearest Pub:** 0.5 miles

Site: ❀ P Leisure: ♪ ▶ Property: 🐾 🍴 Children: 🎠 🛏 🎒 Unit: 📺 ⚒ 📺 🎧 📀

SOUTHPORT, Merseyside Map ref 4A1

Sandy Brook Farm

Contact: Mrs W Core, Sandy Brook Farm, 52 Wyke Cop Road, Scarisbrick, Southport
PR8 5LR **T:** (01704) 880337 / 07719 468712 **E:** sandybrookfarm@gmail.com
W: www.sandybrookfarm.co.uk **£ BOOK ONLINE**

Units   5
Sleeps   2-6

PER UNIT PER WEEK
£205.00 - £395.00

SPECIAL PROMOTIONS
Last minute short
breaks available.
Please ring for details.

Our converted barn stands in peaceful countryside, offering five superbly equipped and
traditionally furnished self-catering holiday apartments. The comfortable apartments sleep 2/4/6
and 'The Dairy' is equipped for disabled guests. The seaside town of Southport is 3.5 miles and the
historic town of Ormskirk is 5 miles away.

Open: All year
Nearest Shop: 2 miles
Nearest Pub: 1 mile

Units: Fully equipped apartments, with one or
two bedrooms and sofa beds in the lounge.
Sleeps 2/4/6.

Site: ❀ P Leisure: ♪ ► ☋ Property: 🖵 📻 🍽 Children: 🍼 🛏 🚶 Unit: 📺 📻 📺

WIRRAL, Merseyside Map ref 4A2

Port Sunlight Holiday Cottages

Contact: Housing Officer, Port Sunlight Village Trust, c/o 23 King George's Drive,
Port Sunlight, Wirral CH62 5DX **T:** (0151) 644 4805
E: accommodation@portsunlightvillage.com **W:** www.portsunlightvillage.com

Units   3
Sleeps   1-6
PER UNIT PER WEEK
£650.00 - £795.00

Port Sunlight Village Trust are proud to present for hire, three
outstanding Grade II Listed holiday cottages. One 5 star and two 4
star accredited by Visit England Quality Assured, a guarantee of
quality fittings and furnishings. Come and enjoy this 19th century
village with 21st century home comforts. **Open:** All year
Nearest Shop: 0.5 miles **Nearest Pub:** 0.5 miles

Site: ❀ P Payment: 💳 Leisure: ♪ ► ☋ Property: 🖵 🍽 Children: 🍼 🛏 🚶 Unit: 📺 📻 📺 📀
BBQ

Sign up for our newsletter

Visit our website to sign up for
our e-newsletter and receive
regular information on events,
articles, exclusive competitions
and new publications.

www.visitor-guides.co.uk

Don't Miss...

Alnwick Castle
Northumberland NE66 1NQ
(01665) 511100
www.alnwickcastle.com
Alnwick Castle's remarkable past is filled with drama, intrigue, tragedy and romance, as well as a host of fascinating people including gunpowder plotters, kingmakers and England's most famous medieval knight: Harry Hotspur. Today, it is a significant visitor attraction with lavish State Rooms and superb art collections, as well as engaging activities and events for all ages, and all set in beautiful landscape by Northumberland-born 'Capability' Brown. Potter fans will recognise Alnwick as Hogwarts from the Harry Potter films - don't miss Potter-inspired magic shows and broomstick training!

BALTIC Centre for Contemporary Art
Gateshead, Tyne and Wear NE8 3BA
(01914) 781810
www.balticmill.com
Housed in a landmark industrial building on the south bank of the River Tyne in Gateshead, BALTIC is a major international centre for contemporary art and is the biggest gallery of its kind in the world. It presents a dynamic, diverse and international programme of contemporary visual art, ranging from blockbuster exhibitions to innovative new work and projects created by artists working within the local community.

Beamish Museum
County Durham DH9 0RG
(01913) 704000
www.beamish.org.uk
Beamish - The Living Museum of the North, is a world-famous open air museum vividly recreating life in the North East in the early 1800's and 1900's. It tells the story of the people of North East England during the Georgian, Victorian, and Edwardian periods through a costumed cast, engaging exhibits and an exciting programme of events including The Great North Festival of Transport, a Georgian Fair, The Great North Festival of Agriculture.

Durham Cathedral
County Durham DH1 3EH
(0191) 3864266
www.durhamcathedral.co.uk
Durham Cathedral is perhaps the finest example of Norman church architecture in England or even Europe. It is a World Heritage Site and houses the tombs of St Cuthbert and The Venerable Bede.

Lindisfarne Priory
Holy Island
Northumberland TD15 2RX
(01289) 389200
www.english-heritage.org.uk/lindisfarnepriory
Lying just a few miles off the beautiful Northumberland coast, Holy Island contains a wealth of history and is home to one of the region's most revered treasures, Lindisfarne Priory. The epicentre of Christianity in Anglo Saxon times and once the home of St Oswald, it was the birthplace of the Lindisfarne Gospels, one of the world's most precious books and remains a place of pilgrimage today. Take in panoramic views of the Northumbrian coast, unpack a picnic in the priory grounds, and take a break from the hustle and bustle of life. NB: watch the tides as the causeway is only open at low tide.

North East

County Durham, Northumberland, Tees Valley, Tyne & Wear

Northumberland

Tyne & Wear

County Durham

Tees Valley

The North East contains two Areas of Outstanding Natural Beauty, a National Park, Hadrian's Wall, the dynamic city of Newcastle, and County Durham, with its fine cathedral and castle. This region is awash with dramatic hills, sweeping valleys, vast expanses of dune-fringed beaches and ragged cliffs with spectacular views. Littered with dramatic castles, ruins and historic houses, there are plenty of exciting family attractions and walking routes galore.

Explore – North East

County Durham & Tees Valley

Durham Cathedral, the greatest Norman building in England, was once a prison and soars grandly above the Medieval city and surrounding plain. Famed for its location as much as for its architecture, it is the burial place of both St Cuthbert, a great northern saint, and the Venerable Bede, author of the first English history.

The Vale of Durham is packed full of award-winning attractions including Locomotion: The National Railway Museum at Shildon and Beamish – The Living Museum of the North, the country's largest open air museum. Auckland Castle was the palace of Durham's unique Prince Bishops for more than 900 years. Part of the North Pennines Area of Outstanding Natural Beauty, the Durham Dales including Teesdale and Weardale, is a beautiful landscape of hills, moors, valleys and rivers, with numerous picturesque villages and market towns.

Comprising miles of stunning coastline and acres of ancient woodland, Tees Valley covers the lower, flatter area of the valley of the River Tees. This unique part of the UK, split between County Durham and Yorkshire, has nearly a hundred visitor attractions, including Preston Hall and Saltholme Nature Reserve, which can both be found in Stockton-on-Tees.

The Durham Heritage Coast, from Sunderland to Hartlepool, is one of the finest in England. The coastal path that runs along much of its length takes you on a spectacular journey of natural, historical and geological interest, with dramatic views along the shore and out over the North Sea. The historic port city of Hartlepool has award-winning attractions, a fantastic marina, beaches and countryside.

Hotspot: Durham University is home to The Oriental Museum, housing a unique collection of Chinese, Indian & Egyptian Art, and the Botanic Garden is also well worth a visit while you are there.

Step back in time 2,000 years along Hadrian's Wall, explore the hills, forests and waterfalls of the National Parks, and discover historic castles, splendid churches and quaint towns. Visitors can trace man's occupation of the region from prehistoric times through rock carvings, ancient hill forts, Saxon churches, Norman priories, medieval castles, and a wealth of industrial archaeology.

Newcastle & Tyne And Wear

Newcastle-upon-Tyne, once a shipbuilding centre, is a rejuvenated city of proud civic tradition with fine restaurants, theatres, and one of the liveliest arts scenes outside London. As well as the landmark Baltic, there's the Laing Art Gallery, the Great North Museum and The Sage concert venue. The Theatre Royal is the third home of the Royal Shakespeare Company and a venue for major touring companies. The Metro Centre in neighbouring Gateshead attracts shoppers from all over the country with more than 300 outlets and 11 cinema screens.

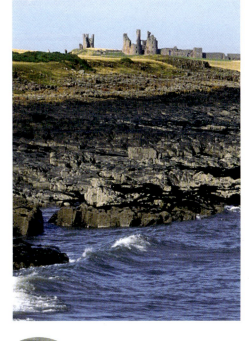

Northumberland

Northumbria, to use its ancient name, is an undiscovered holiday paradise where the scenery is wild and beautiful, the beaches golden and unspoiled, and the natives friendly. The region is edged by the North Sea, four national parks and the vast Border Forest Park. Its eastern sea boundary makes a stunning coastline, stretching 100 miles from Staithes on the Cleveland boundary, to Berwick-on-Tweed, England's most northerly town, frequently fought over and with the finest preserved example of Elizabethan town walls in the country. In between you'll find as many holiday opportunities as changes of scenery.

Housesteads Roman Fort at Haydon Bridge is the most complete example of a British Roman fort. It features magnificent ruins and stunning views of the countryside surrounding Hadrian's Wall.

The region has a rich maritime heritage too. Ruined coastal fortifications such as Dunstanburgh and fairy-tale Lindisfarne are relics of a turbulent era. Agriculture is also one of the region's most important industries. Take a trip on the Heatherslaw Light Railway, a narrow gauge line operating from Etal Village to Heatherslaw Mill, a restored waterdriven corn mill and agricultural museum near the delightful model village of Ford.

Indulge in a leisurely sightseeing trip along the **River Wear at Durham**. A one hour cruise includes sepctacular views of historic Durham City, Cathedral, Castle and bridges with full commentary including history, natural history and geography. www.princebishoprc.co.uk or call (0191) 386 9525 for sailing times and prices.

Don't miss **The Rugby World Cup 2015** which will see three matches played at **St James' Park** in Newcastle. South Africa vs Scotland, New Zealand vs Tonga and Samoa vs Scotland all take place in early October and are sure to be spectacular sporting events. www.rugbyworldcup.com

Enjoy an elegant lunch or tempting tea at the fabulous **Earl Grey Tearooms**, Howick – home of Earl Grey for whom the tea was invented. Situated in the old ballroom of the hall, it serves a variety of teas, home made and local produce, snacks and light lunches exclusively for visitors to the garden and makes a great place for a rest while exploring the arboretum and stunning gardens. See www.howickhallgardens.org for opening times.

It's hard not to get caught up in the quirky atmosphere of **Barter Books** at the Victorian Alnwick Railway Station. This rambling, atmospheric secondhand bookshop has open fires, armchairs, a simple cafe and best of all, model trains, and is noted for its use of a barter system, whereby customers can exchange their books for credit against future purchases. It is one of the largest second-hand bookstores in Europe and an unmissable diversion if you're in this neck of the woods. www.barterbooks.co.uk or call (01665) 604888 for opening times.

For a romantic dinner for two or a great night out with friends, dine in style at **Alnwick Garden's Treehouse Restaurant**, one of the most magical and unique restaurants to be found anywhere. Set high up in the treetops, with a roaring fire in the centre of the room and trees growing through the floor, this stunning restaurant serves local fish and seafood, meats from Northumberland's farmlands and other mouthwatering local and regional specialities. Call (01665) 511852 for reservations.

Attractions with this sign participate in the Visitor Attraction Quality Assurance Scheme.

County Durham & Tees Valley

Adventure Valley
Durham, County Durham DH1 5SG
(01913) 868291
www.adventurevalley.co.uk
Adventure Valley, split into six Play Zones (with three under cover), you'll find the very best in family fun come rain or shine.

Billingham International Folklore Festival
August, Billingham, County Durham
www.billinghamfestival.co.uk
A festival of traditional and contemporary world dance, music and arts.

Bishop Auckland Food Festival
April, Bishop Auckland, County Durham
www.bishopaucklandfoodfestival.co.uk
Be inspired by cookery demonstrations and entertained by performers.

The Bowes Museum
Barnard Castle, County Durham DL12 8NP
(01833) 690606
www.thebowesmuseum.org.uk
The Bowes Museum houses a collection of outstanding European fine and decorative arts and offers an acclaimed exhibition programme, alongside special events and children's activities.

DLI Museum and Durham Art Gallery
Durham, County Durham DH1 5TU
(01913) 842214
www.dlidurham.org.uk
Telling the 200-year story of Durham's famous regiment. Art Gallery has changing exhibition programme.

Durham Book Festival
October/November, Durham, County Durham
www.durhambookfestival.com
With writers covering everything from politics to poetry, and fiction to feminism, there's something for everyone at the Durham Book Festival. See website for dates and full programme.

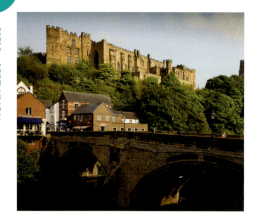

Durham Castle
County Durham DH1 3RW
(01913) 343800
www.durhamcastle.com
*Durham Castle is part of the Durham City World
Heritage Site and has enjoyed a long history of
continuous use. Along with Durham Cathedral, it
is among the greatest monuments of the Norman
Conquest of Britain and is now home to students of
University College, Durham. Entrance is by guided
tour only, please telephone opening and tour times.*

Durham Folk Party
July, Durham, County Durham
www.communigate.co.uk/ne/durhamfolkparty
*It is a celebration of folk song, music and dance
which began in 1990 after the demise of the
excellent Durham City Folk Festival and has
developed into an important part of the music year
of the city.*

Hall Hill Farm
Durham, County Durham DH7 0TA
(01388) 731333
www.hallhillfarm.co.uk
*Award-winning farm attraction set in attractive
countryside, see and touch the animals at
close quarters.*

Hamsterley Forest
Bishop Auckland, County Durham DL13 3NL
(01388) 488312
www.forestry.gov.uk/northeastengland
*A 5,000 acre mixed woodland open to the public
all year.*

Hartlepool Art Gallery
Hartlepool, Tees Valley TS24 7EQ
(01429) 869706
www.hartlepool.gov.uk/info/100009/leisure_and_
culture/1506/hartlepool_art_gallery/1/3
*Former church building also includes the TIC and a
bell tower viewing platform looking over Hartlepool.*

Hartlepool's Maritime Experience
Tees Valley TS24 0XZ
(01429) 860077
www.hartlepoolsmaritimeexperience.com
An authentic reconstruction of an 18th century seaport.

Head of Steam
Tees Valley DL3 6ST
(01325) 460532
www.darlington.gov.uk/Culture/headofsteam/
welcome.htm
*Restored 1842 station housing a collection of
exhibits relating to railways in the North East of
England, including Stephenson's Locomotion, call for
details of events.*

High Force Waterfall
Middleton-in-Teesdale, County Durham DL12 0XH
(01833) 640209
www.rabycastle.com/high_force.htm
The most majestic of the waterfalls on the River Tees.

HMS Trincomalee
Hartlepool, Tees Valley TS24 0XZ
(01429) 223193
www.hms-trincomalee.co.uk
*HMS Trincomalee, built in 1817, is one of the oldest
ship afloat in Europe. Come aboard for a unique
experience of Navy life two centuries ago.*

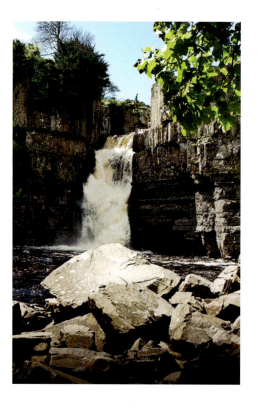

Killhope, The North of England
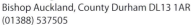
Lead Mining Museum
Bishop Auckland, County Durham DL13 1AR
(01388) 537505
www.killhope.org.uk
Fully restored Victorian lead mine and the most complete lead mining site in Great Britain.

Locomotion: The National Railway Museum at Shildon

Shildon, County Durham DL4 1PQ
(01388) 777999
www.nrm.org.uk/locomotion
The first National Museum in the North East. Free admission. View over 60 vehicles, children's play area and interactive displays.

mima

Middlesbrough, Tees Valley TS1 2AZ
(01642) 726720
www.visitmima.com
mima, Middlesbrough Institute of Modern Art, is a £14.2m landmark gallery in the heart of Middlesbrough. mima showcases an international programme of fine art and applied art from the 1900s to the present day.

Preston Hall Museum and Park
Stockton-on-Tees, Tees Valley TS18 3RH
(01642) 527375
www.prestonparkmuseum.co.uk
A Georgian country house set in beautiful parkland overlooking the River Tees. A Museum of social history with a recreated Victorian street and working craftsmen.

Hotspot: *Hartlepool Museum, situated beside Hartlepool Historic Quay, includes local historical exhibits, PSS Wingfield Castle and the original lighthouse light. (01429) 860077*
www.hartlepoolsmaritimeexperience.com

Raby Castle

Staindrop, County Durham DL2 3AH
(01833) 660202
www.rabycastle.com
Home of Lord Barnard's family since 1626, includes a 200 acre deer park, gardens, carriage collection, adventure playground, shop and tearoom.

Saltburn Smugglers Heritage Centre
Saltburn-by-the-Sea, Tees Valley TS12 1HF
(01287) 625252
www.redcar-cleveland.gov.uk/museums
Step back into Saltburn's past and experience the authentic sights, sounds and smells.

Saltholme Wildlife Reserve

Middlesbrough, Tees Valley TS2 1TU
(01642) 546625
www.rspb.org.uk/reserves/guide/s/saltholme
An amazing wildlife experience in the Tees Valley.

Newcastle & Tyne And Wear

Arbeia Roman Fort and Museum
South Shields, Tyne and Wear NE33 2BB
(01914) 561369
www.twmuseums.org.uk/arbeia
Arbeia is the best reconstruction of a Roman fort in Britain and offers visitors a unique insight into the every day life of the Roman army, from the soldier in his barrack room to the commander in his luxurious house.

Centre for Life
Newcastle-upon-Tyne, Tyne and Wear NE1 4EP
(01912) 438210
www.life.org.uk
The Centre for Life is an award-winning science centre where imaginative exhibitions, interactive displays and special events promote greater understanding of science and provoke curiosity in the world around us.

Discovery Museum
Newcastle-upon-Tyne, Tyne and Wear NE1 4JA
(01912) 326789
www.twmuseums.org.uk/discovery
A wide variety of experiences for all the family to enjoy.

Hotspot: *Enjoy an ever-changing programme of exhibitions, live glass blowing, and banqueting and a stunning restaurant at the National Glass Museum, overlooking the River Wear.* (01915) 155555 www.nationalglasscentre.com

Evolution Festival
May, Newcastle, Tyne and Wear
www.evolutionfestival.co.uk
The North East's premier music event, taking place over a Bank Holiday.

Great North Museum: Hancock
Newcastle-upon-Tyne, Tyne and Wear NE2 4PT
(01912) 226765
www.twmuseums.org.uk/great-north-museum
See major new displays showing the wonder of the animal and plant kingdoms, spectacular objects from the Ancient Greeks and a planetarium and a life-size T-Rex.

Hatton Gallery
Newcastle-upon-Tyne, Tyne and Wear NE1 7RU
(01912) 226059
www.twmuseums.org.uk/hatton
Temporary exhibitions of contemporary and historical art. Permanent display of Kurt Schwitters' Merzbarn.

Laing Art Gallery
Newcastle-upon-Tyne, Tyne and Wear NE1 8AG
(01912) 327734
www.twmuseums.org.uk/laing
The Laing Art Gallery is home to an important collection of 18th and 19th century painting, which is shown alongside temporary exhibitions of historic and contemporary art.

Newcastle Theatre Royal
Newcastle upon Tyne NE1 6BR
(0844) 811 2121
www.theatreroyal.co.uk
The Theatre Royal is a Grade I listed building situated on historic Grey Street in Newcastle-upon-Tyne. It hosts a variety of shows, including ballet, contemporary dance, drama, musicals and opera in a restored 1901 Frank Matcham Edwardian interior.

Segedunum Roman Fort, Baths & Museum
Wallsend, Tyne and Wear NE28 6HR
(01912) 369347
www.twmuseums.org.uk/segedunum
Segedunum Roman Fort is the gateway to Hadrian's Wall. Explore the excavated fort site, visit reconstructions of a Roman bath house, learn about the history of the area in the museum and enjoy the view from the 35 metre viewing tower.

Tyneside Cinema
Newcastle upon Tyne, Tyne and Wear NE1 6QG
(0845) 217 9909
www.tynesidecinema.co.uk
Showing the best films in beautiful art deco surroundings, Tyneside Cinema's programme ranges from mainstream to arthouse and world cinema. As the last surviving Newsreel theatre still operating full-time in the UK, this Grade II-listed building is a must-visit piece of lovingly restored heritage.

WWT Washington Wetland Centre
Washington, Tyne and Wear NE38 8LE
(01914) 165454
www.wwt.org.uk/visit/washington
45 hectares of wetland, woodland and wildlife reserve. Home to wildfowl, insects and flora with lake-side hides, wild bird feeding station, waterside cafe, picnic areas, sustainable garden, playground and events calendar.

Northumberland

Alnwick Beer Festival
September, Alnwick, Northumberland
www.alnwickbeerfestival.co.uk
If you enjoy real ale, or simply want to enjoy a fantastic social event, then make sure you pay this festival a visit.

The Alnwick Garden
Alnwick, Northumberland NE66 1YU
01665 511350
www.alnwickgarden.com
An exciting, contemporary design with beautiful and unique gardens, features and structures, brought to life with water and including the intriguing Poison Garden which holds dangerous plants and their stories. Fantastic eating, drinking, shopping and a range of events throughout the year.

Bailiffgate Museum
Alnwick, Northumberland NE66 1LX
(01665) 605847
www.bailiffgatemuseum.co.uk
Bailiffgate Museum brings to life the people and places of North Northumberland in exciting interactive style.

Bamburgh Castle
Northumberland NE69 7DF
(01668) 214515
www.bamburghcastle.com
A spectacular castle with fantastic coastal views. The stunning Kings Hall and Keep house collections of armour, artwork, porcelain and furniture.

Chillingham Castle
Northumberland, NE66 5NJ
01668 215359
www.chillingham-castle.com
A remarkable Medieval fortress with Tudor additions, torture chamber, shop, dungeon, tearoom, woodland walks, furnished rooms and topiary garden.

Cragside House, Gardens & Estate
Morpeth, Northumberland NE65 7PX
01669 620333
www.nationaltrust.org.uk/cragside/
Built on a rocky crag high above Debdon Burn, the house is crammed with ingenious gadgets and was the first in the world to be lit electrically. The gardens are breathtaking with 5 lakes, one of Europe's largest rock gardens, and over 7 million trees and shrubs.

Haydon Bridge Beer Festival
July, Haydon Bridge, Northumberland
www.haydonbeerfestival.co.uk
Annual celebration of the finest real ales and wines.

Hexham Abbey Festival
September-October, Hexham, Northumberland
www.hexhamabbey.org.uk
An exciting array of events to capture the imagination, bringing the very best world-class musicians and artists to Hexham.

Hexham Old Gaol
Northumberland NE46 3NH
(01434) 652349
www.hexhamoldgaol.org.uk
Tour the Old Gaol, 1330AD, by glass lift. Meet the gaoler, see a Reiver raid and try on costumes.

Kielder Castle Forest Park Centre
Northumberland NE48 1ER
(01434) 250209
www.forestry.gov.uk/northeastengland
Features include forest shop, information centre, tearoom and exhibitions. Bike hire available.

Lindisfarne Castle
(01289) 389244
www.nationaltrust.org.uk/lindisfarne-castle/
A picture perfect castle that rises from the sheer rock face at the tip of Holy Island off the Northumberland coast. It was built to defend a harbour sheltering English ships during skirmishes with Scotland and revamped by celebrated architect Edward Lutyens in 1901, today it remains relatively unchanged. Lindisfarne Castle.

RNLI Grace Darling Museum
Bamburgh, Northumberland NE69 7AE
(01668) 214910
www.rnli.org.uk/gracedarling
A museum dedicated to Grace Darling and her family, as well as all those who Save Lives at Sea.

Warkworth Castle
Warkworth, Northumberland NE65 0UJ
(01665) 711423
www.english-heritage.org.uk/warkworthcastle
Set in a quaint Northumberland town, this hill-top fortress and hermitage offers a fantastic family day out.

Tourist Information Centres

When you arrive at your destination, visit the Tourist Information Centre for quality assured help with accommodation and information about local attractions and events, or email your request before you go.

Alnwick	2 The Shambles	01670 622152/ 01670 622151	alnwick.tic@northumberland.gov.uk
Amble	Queen Street Car Park	01665 712313	amble.tic@northumberland.gov.uk
Bellingham	Station Yard	01434 220616	bellinghamtic@btconnect.com
Berwick-upon-Tweed	106 Marygate	01670 622155/ 625568	berwick.tic@northumberland.gov.uk
Bishop Auckland	Town Hall	03000 269524	bishopauckland.touristinfo@durham.gov.uk
Corbridge	Hill Street	01434 632815	corbridge.tic@northumberland.gov.uk
Craster	Craster Car Park	01665 576007	craster.tic@northumberland.gov.uk
Darlington	Central Library	01325 462034	crown.street.library@darlington.gov.uk
Durham Visitor Contact Centre	1st Floor	03000 262626	visitor@thisisdurham.com
Gateshead	Central Library	0191 433 8420	libraries@gateshead.gov.uk
Guisborough	Priory Grounds	01287 633801	guisborough_tic@redcar-cleveland.gov.uk
Haltwhistle	Westgate	01434 322002	haltwhistle.tic@northumberland.gov.uk
Hartlepool	Hartlepool Art Gallery	01429 869706	hpooltic@hartlepool.gov.uk
Hexham	Wentworth Car Park	01434 652220	hexham.tic@northumberland.gov.uk
Middlesbrough	Middlesbrough Info.	01642 729900	tic@middlesbrough.gov.uk
Middleton-in-Teesdale	10 Market Place	01833 641001	tic@middletonplus.myzen.co.uk
Morpeth	The Chantry	01670 623455	morpeth.tic@northumberland.gov.uk
Newcastle-upon-Tyne	Newcastle Gateshead	0191 277 8000	visitorinfo@ngi.org.uk
North Shields	Unit 18	0191 2005895	ticns@northtyneside.gov.uk
Once Brewed	National Park Centre	01434 344396	tic.oncebrewed@nnpa.org.uk
Otterburn	Otterburn Mill	01830 521002	tic@otterburnmill.co.uk
Saltburn by Sea	Saltburn Library	01287 622422/ 623584	saltburn_library@redcar-cleveland.gov.uk
Seahouses	Seafield Car Park	01665 720884/ 01670 625593	seahouses.tic@northumberland.gov.uk
South shields	Haven Point	0191 424 7788	tourism@southtyneside.gov.uk
Stockton-on-Tees	High Street	01642 528130	visitorinformation@stockton.gov.uk
Whitley Bay	York Road	0191 6435395	susan.clark@northtyneside.gov.uk
Wooler	The Cheviot Centre	01668 282123	wooler.tic@northumberland.gov.uk

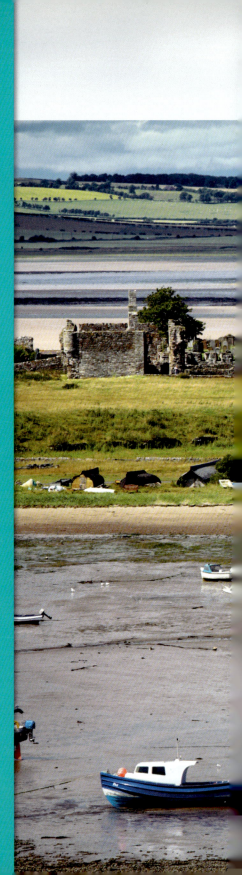

Regional Contacts and Information

For more information on accommodation, attractions, activities, events and holidays in North East England, contact one of the regional or local tourism organisations. Their websites have a wealth of information and many produce free publications to help you get the most out of your visit.

www.visitnortheastengland.com

www.thisisdurham.com
www.newcastlegateshead.com
www.visitnorthumberland.com
www.visithadrianswall.co.uk
www.visitnorthtyneside.com
www.visitsouthtyneside.co.uk
www.seeitdoitsunderland.co.uk

Stay – North East

Entries appear alphabetically by town name in each county. A key to symbols appears on page 7

BARNARD CASTLE, Co Durham   Map ref 5B3

★★★
SELF CATERING

Units   1
Sleeps   2-6

PER UNIT PER WEEK
£195.00 - £475.00

Country Cottage
Contact: Robin Burman, Newbiggin in Teesdale, Middleton in Teesdale, Barnard Castle, Middleside DL12 0UQ **T:** (01618) 607123 / 07946 462986 **E:** rb@hlfberry.com
W: www.bellcottagenewbiggin.co.uk

A 200-year-old cottage, in quiet and peaceful rural location. Superb views and walking from doorstep, surrounded by farm. Car parking on grass verge adjacent to quiet lane leading to property. Comfortable, nicely decorated and well fitted throughout.
Open: All year **Nearest Shop:** 1.5 miles **Nearest Pub:** 1.5 miles

Site: P Property: 🅿 **Children:** **Unit:** 📺 📀

BARNARD CASTLE, Co Durham   Map ref 5B3

★★★★
SELF CATERING   Gold AWARD

Units   2
Sleeps   2-6

PER UNIT PER WEEK
£230.00 - £400.00

SPECIAL PROMOTIONS
Short breaks available throughout the year. Three night breaks in The Stone Byre £160-£235; Curlew Cottage £135-£180: combined cottages £295-415.

Hauxwell Grange Cottages
(The Stone Byre & Curlew Cottage)
Contact: Mrs Val Pearson, Proprietor, Hauxwell Grange Cottages, Hauxwell Grange, Marwood, Barnard Castle, County Durham DL12 8QU **T:** (01833) 695022 / 07887 366801
F: 01833 695022 **E:** hauxwellvmp@supaworld.com
W: www.hauxwellgrangecottages.co.uk

Sparklingly clean, well equipped, very comfortable stone cottages, set in the glorious open countryside of unspoilt Teesdale. Both cottages are cosy and warm with multifuel stoves. A tranquil retreat only two miles from the historic market town of Barnard Castle. Perfect for walking and cycling and ideally situated for exploring the Durham Dales and Yorkshire Dales. Linen and towels provided. Welcome basket. Brochure available.

Open: All year
Nearest Shop: 2 miles
Nearest Pub: 1.5 miles

Units: The Stone Byre has double and twin bedrooms (+cot) and a bathroom. Curlew Cottage, all at ground level, has one twin bedroom and a large shower room.

Site: P Leisure: Property: Children: Unit: BBQ

BISHOP AUCKLAND, Co Durham   Map ref 5C2

★★★★
SELF CATERING

Units   1
Sleeps   2

PER UNIT PER WEEK
£260.00 - £275.00

New Cottage
Contact: Margaret Partridge, Owner, Hollymoor Farm, Cockfield DL13 5HF
T: (01388) 718567 **E:** margandpatpartridge@tiscali.co.uk
W: www.hollymoorfarm.co.uk

New Cottage is on a working farm in County Durham, on the borders of the beautiful Durham Dales, Teesdale and Weardale. With its elevated position it is surrounded by beautiful views. The panoramic views from the lounge are a never-ending source of delight - they are stunning. The sunsets are truly magnificent.
Open: All Year **Nearest Shop:** 1 Mile **Nearest Pub:** 1 Mile

Site: P Property: Unit: BBQ

BISHOP AUCKLAND, Co Durham   Map ref 5C2

Units   1
Sleeps   7
PER UNIT PER WEEK
£281.00 - £513.00

Whitfield House Cottage

Contact: 21 Front Street, Wolsingham, Bishop Auckland DL13 3DF **T:** (01388) 527466
W: www.whitfieldhousecottage.co.uk

Spacious accommodation in part of an attractive Queen Anne period house. Near the centre of this small former market town which is situated in Weardale, one of the North Pennine Dales. Contact us by phone for 2015 booking details. **Open:** All year **Nearest Shop:** 5 mins walk **Nearest Pub:** 100 yards

CORNRIGGS, Co Durham   Map ref 5B2

Units   2
Sleeps   2-6
PER UNIT PER WEEK
£399.00 - £495.00

Cornriggs Cottages

Contact: Mrs Janet Elliott, Low Cornriggs Farm, Cowshill in Weardale, Bishop Auckland, Durham DL13 1AQ **T:** (01388) 537600 / 07760 766794 **E:** cornriggsfarm@btconnect.com
W: www.cornriggsfarm.co.uk **£ BOOK ONLINE**

Both luxury cottages have, spectacular views. Easy access to Durham, Beamish and The Lakes. Three large accessible bedrooms, two WC's with shower and bathroom. Dining kitchen very well equipped, large lounge with fire and big comfy sofas, Satellite TV & Garden. Working farm with Hereford cattle and beautiful wild flower meadows/birds. Breakfast is available. Near to the village of Cowshill **Open:** All year **Nearest Shop:** 1.5 miles **Nearest Pub:** 1 mile

DURHAM, Co Durham   Map ref 5C2

Units   1
Sleeps   6
PER UNIT PER WEEK
£250.00 - £400.00

Albert Cottage

Contact: Paul Harle, 18 South Road, Tofthill, Durham DL14 0HZ **T:** (01388) 777427 / 07939 127806 **E:** paul.harle@btopenworld.com
W: www.durhamholidayhome.com

Situated close to Hamsterley Forest, Durham & Bishop Auckland it gives comfortable accommodation for the holiday maker or people working in the area. **Open:** All Year **Nearest Shop:** 150 metres **Nearest Pub:** 100 metres

DURHAM, Co Durham   Map ref 5C2

Units   2
Sleeps   1-5
PER UNIT PER WEEK
£720.00 - £1400.00

Durham Riverside Apartments

Contact: Christopher Headley, Director, Flat 5 St Andrews Court, Durham City, Durham DH1 3AH **T:** 07809 601955 **E:** info@durham-riverside-apartment.com
W: www.durham-riverside-apartment.com **£ BOOK ONLINE**

Two luxury apartments within a newly converted historic building located in the heart of Durham City. Each apartment features French doors opening onto a large deck overlooking the river Wear and Elvet Bridge. The location offers an atmosphere of serenity where you can relax for an afternoon with a book and enjoy the views from the decking. **Open:** All year **Nearest Shop:** 10 metres **Nearest Pub:** 15 metres

LANCHESTER, Co Durham   Map ref 5C2

Browney Cottage & Browney Close

Contact: Mrs Ann Darlington, Proprietor, Browney Cottage & Browney Close, Hall Hill Farm, Lanchester, Durham DH7 0TA **T:** (01207) 521476 / 07980 011124
F: 01388 731996 **E:** ann@hallhillfarm.co.uk **W:** www.hallhillfarm.co.uk

Units   2
Sleeps   1-4
PER UNIT PER WEEK
£225.00 - £480.00

Browney Cottages are charming traditional cottages, both sleep 4 people with a double and a twin bedroom and upstairs bathroom with bath and shower. Downstairs the cottages have a large family kitchen and living room. The cottages are near the village of Lanchester which dates back to Roman times with several pubs and restaurants, and are ideally situated for Durham, Beamish and Hadrians Wall. **Open:** All year **Nearest Shop:** 2.5 miles **Nearest Pub:** 1.5 miles

Site: ✿ **P Property:** 🗐 🗐 **Children:** 🛝 🛏 🧍 **Unit:** 🗐 📺 🗐 🗐 📺 🗐

MIDDLETON-IN-TEESDALE, Co Durham   Map ref 5B3

Firethorn Cottage

Contact: Mrs Clare Long, Firethorn Cottage, 53 Union Street, Fairview, Cheltenham, Gloucestershire GL52 2JN **T:** (01242) 700308 / 07780 951162
E: Firethorncottage@hotmail.co.uk

Units   1
Sleeps   2
PER UNIT PER WEEK
£150.00 - £250.00

A delightful Grade II listed, detached stone-built lead miner's cottage. One up/one down with flagstone floor, lounge diner, open fire, traditional rag rugs and beamed ceiling. Modern bathroom upstairs with bath and shower over and heated towel rail. Double bedroom with storage. Outside a small cottage garden with views. Night storage heaters throughout. Superb walking and fishing close by. **Open:** All year **Nearest Shop:** 200 yards **Nearest Pub:** 300 yards

Site: ✿ **Property:** 🐕 🗐 **Unit:** 📺 🗐 📺 🗐 ⌀

MIDDLETON-IN-TEESDALE, Co Durham   Map ref 5B3

Snaisgill Farm Cottage

Contact: Mrs Susan Parmley, Proprietor, Snaisgill Farm Cottage, Snaisgill Road, Middleton-in-Teesdale DL12 0RP **T:** (01833) 640343

Units   1
Sleeps   2-4
PER UNIT PER WEEK
£195.00 - £315.00

Cosy cottage adjoining owners farmhouse. Very quiet with beautiful views. One mile from Middleton-in-Teesdale. Come and enjoy the silence. **Open:** All year **Nearest Shop:** 1 mile **Nearest Pub:** 1 mile

Site: ✿ **P Leisure:** ∪ **Property:** 🐕 🗐 🗐 **Children:** 🛝4 **Unit:** 📺 🗐 📺 🗐 ⌀

ALLENDALE, Northumberland   Map ref 5B2

Fell View Cottage

Contact: Mr & Mrs Colin & Carole Verne-Jones, Fell View Cottage, 69 Buckinghamshire Road, Belmont, Durham DH1 2BE **T:** (0191) 3869045
E: info@fellviewcottage.co.uk **W:** www.fellviewcottage.co.uk **£ BOOK ONLINE**

Units   1
Sleeps   1-7
PER UNIT PER WEEK
£495.00 - £790.00

Rebuilt barn, now detached, three-bedroom stone cottage in designated Area of Outstanding Natural Beauty with wonderful unrestricted views of the Allendale Valley and beyond. Built to the highest possible standards of a traditional Northumberland cottage, it has a large master bedroom with a king-size bed, two further twin bedrooms and Wi-Fi. **Open:** All year **Nearest Shop:** 1.5 miles **Nearest Pub:** 1.5 miles

🟦 WALKERS 🟩 CYCLISTS
🟦 WALKERS 🟩 CYCLISTS
Site: ✿ **P Payment:** 💷 € **Leisure:** ♿ ♪ ⸾ ∪ **Property:** ∥ 🐎 🖳 🗐 🗐 **Children:** 🛝 🛏 🧍
Unit: 🗐 🗐 📺 🗐 🗐 📺 🗐 ⌀ BBQ

Quality Self Catering Cottages throughout Northumbria & the Borders

Northumbria Byways

www.northumbria-byways.com **016977 46777**
enquiries@northumbria-byways.com **016977 46888**

ALLENHEADS, Northumberland   Map ref 5B2

SELF CATERING ★★★★

Units   1
Sleeps   1-4

PER UNIT PER WEEK
£240.00 - £450.00

SPECIAL PROMOTIONS
Weekend, short breaks and special offers available.

Molecatcher's Cottage

Contact: Miss Sarah Marriner, Bookings Administrator, Springboard Sunderland Trust, Springboard, 184 Roker Ave, Sunderland, Tyne and Wear SR6 0BS **T:** (01915) 640291
F: 01915 142429 **E:** smarriner@springboard-ne.org **W:** www.molecatcherscottage.co.uk

Mole Catchers is a cosy cottage with a contemporary twist in the heart of the secret North Pennines, in the village of Allenheads. Beamed throughout, the cottage has one double and one twin bedroom, a living room with wood burning stove a charming modern kitchen and bathroom and a walled garden. The cottage provides a fantastic base to explore the surrounding countryside. Weekend, short breaks and special offers available, please see our website for details.

Open: All year
Nearest Shop: 6 miles
Nearest Pub: 0.5 miles

Site: ✿ P **Leisure:** 🐾 ♪ ▶ ∪ **Property:** 🖥 🗑 **Children:** 🍼 **Unit:** 🗄 🖥 📺 📀 🍳 BBQ

ALNWICK, Northumberland   Map ref 5C1

SELF CATERING ★★★★

Units   1
Sleeps   7

PER UNIT PER WEEK
£275.00 - £650.00

3 Jubilee Court

Contact: Mrs Jenny Robinson, Owner, 8 Howick Street, Alnwick NE66 1UY
T: (01665) 605153 **E:** wwr@globalnet.co.uk

Number 3 Jubilee Court is a warm, comfortable 3 storey town house set in a quiet location but close to the centre of Alnwick. The master bedroom with en suite is on the top floor, along with a single bedroom and fully fitted family bathroom. On the first floor there is a double bedroom with tri-bunk bed and a large living room which includes a sofa bed. The large diner on the ground floor has a well equipped kitchen and dining area. There is a also a downstairs cloakroom. There is allocated parking for 1 car in the courtyard. We regret we do not consider the house suitable for pets. **Open:** All year **Nearest Shop:** 100 yds **Nearest Pub:** 20 yds

Site: P **Payment:** € **Leisure:** ♪ ▶ **Property:** 🖥 🗑 **Children:** 🍼 🎠 🚼 **Unit:** 🗄 🖥 📺 🗑 🍳 📺 📀

ALNWICK, Northumberland   Map ref 5C1

27 Pottergate

Contact: Mr Richard Evans, 3 Longdyke Steading, Shilbottle, Alnwick, Northumberland NE66 2HQ **T:** (01665) 581188 / 07878 756732 **E:** enquiries@alnwickpottergate.co.uk
W: www.alnwickpottergate.co.uk

Units   1
Sleeps   1-6

PER UNIT PER WEEK
£600.00 - £900.00

Architect designed four bedroom town house just round the corner from Alnwick Castle and short walk to Alnwick Garden. Surrounded by lovely countryside Alnwick is three miles from the coast.
Open: All year **Nearest Shop:** 0.10 miles **Nearest Pub:** 0.10 miles

Site: ❀ P **Payment:** € **Leisure:** ⟁ ♪ ▶ ∪ **Property:** ⋈ 🗐 🖳 **Children:** 🏕 🎠 ⅋ **Unit:** 🗍 🖩 🖵 🕮 TV 📀

ALNWICK, Northumberland   Map ref 5C1

Harehope Estate

Contact: Ms Alison Wrangham, East Lilburn Farmhouse, Alnwick NE66 4ED
T: (01668) 217329 **F:** 01688 217346 **E:** aliwrangham@btconnect.com
W: www.harehope.com **£ BOOK ONLINE**

Units   2
Sleeps   4

PER UNIT PER WEEK
£300.00 - £500.00

SPECIAL PROMOTIONS
Please see website or contact for up to date offers.

Wonderful walking on the doorstep of two idyllic cottages. Beautiful views of the Cheviot hills and half an hour's drive to many wonderful beaches. The Harehope Estate welcomes dogs and horses. We have outside kennels and stables with grazing.

Open: All year
Nearest Shop: 4 miles
Nearest Pub: 4 miles

Site: ❀ P **Leisure:** ⟁ ♪ ∪ **Property:** 🐾 🖳 **Children:** 🏕 🎠 ⅋ **Unit:** 🗍 🖩 🖵 TV 📀 ✎ ☏

BAMBURGH, Northumberland   Map ref 5C1

Outchester & Ross Farm Cottages

Contact: John and Heather Sutherland, Outchester & Ross Farm Cottages, The Farmhouse, Ross, Belford, Northumberland NE70 7EN **T:** (01668) 213336 **E:** stay@rosscottages.co.uk
W: www.rosscottages.co.uk **£ BOOK ONLINE**

Units	17
Sleeps	2-6

PER UNIT PER WEEK
£300.00 - £1020.00

SPECIAL PROMOTIONS
Special offers from time to time. Discounts for under occupancy. Please look on the website.

Enjoy a peaceful break in spacious, warm cottages in lovely Northumbrian coastal locations near Holy Island and Farne Islands. Close to cycle and walking routes. Unspoilt countryside, romantic castles and secluded sandy beaches. Our well equipped 4 and 5* cottages sleep 2 – 6, with own garden and parking. Or enjoy a romantic break in our 5 star Ducket, an 18th century tower with 21st century facilities. Star gazing telescopes are available.

Open: All year
Nearest Shop: 3 miles
Nearest Pub: 3 miles

Site: ❋ **P** **Payment:** 💷 **Leisure:** 🚲 ⛵ ∪ **Property:** 📺 🔲 🗄 **Children:** 🐴 🛏 ⛹
Unit: 🗄 🖥 💻 🔲 🖨 📺 ◎ 📀 ☎

BAMBURGH, Northumberland   Map ref 5C1

Point Cottages

Contact: Mrs Elizabeth Sanderson, Point Cottages, 30 The Oval, Benton, Newcastle-upon-Tyne NE12 9PP **T:** (01912) 662800 **F:** 01912 151630 **E:** info@bamburgh-cottages.co.uk
W: www.bamburgh-cottages.co.uk **£ BOOK ONLINE**

Units	5
Sleeps	2-6

PER UNIT PER WEEK
£295.00 - £1250.00

SPECIAL PROMOTIONS
3 night winter breaks from £190. Please contact for details.

A cluster of one, two and three bedroom cottages in a superb location next to a beautiful links golf course at the edge of historic Bamburgh overlooking magnificent sandy beaches. Large shared garden. Views to Farne Islands, Lindisfarne & Bamburgh Castle. Ten car parking spaces, two per cottage. Guest comments: really cosy - beautiful - comfortable - peaceful - very enjoyable - great beds - will return.

Open: All year
Nearest Shop: 1 mile
Nearest Pub: 1 mile

Units: All ground floor except Aiden. Cuthbert/ Bede interconnectable (10 person), shared laundry at rear of cottages. £1 coin metre only pay for the electricity you use.

Site: ❋ **P** **Leisure:** 🚲 ⛵ ∪ **Property:** 🐕 🔲 🗄 **Children:** 🐴 🛏 ⛹ **Unit:** 🔲 📺 📀

BAMBURGH, Northumberland   Map ref 5C1

Units   1
Sleeps   1-4

PER UNIT PER WEEK
£550.00 - £980.00

Seal Waters

Contact: Mr Peter Carr-Seaman, Owners, Seal Waters, Aydon South Farm, Corbridge
NE45 5PL **T:** (01434) 632839 **F:** 01434 632849 **E:** info@sealwaters.com
W: www.sealwaters.com **£ BOOK ONLINE**

An outstanding location with spectacular views overlooking Budle
Bay and Holy Island. The beach is just a short "hop" through the
dunes and there is a lovely walk from the cottage to Bamburgh and
the Castle. The golf course is close by and Budle Bay is also a very
popular spot for bird watching. Good safe parking outside the door.
Many guests say that the cottage has the 'wow' factor. **Open:** All
year **Nearest Shop:** 2 miles **Nearest Pub:** 2 miles

Site: ✿ P Leisure: ♪ ┃ Property: 🐕 🖥 🖳 Children: 🛏 🏠 🎎 Unit: 🗄 🗄 🖥 🗄 📶 TV 📀 🎧 ☎

BELLINGHAM, Northumberland   Map ref 5B2

Units   4
Sleeps   1-5

PER UNIT PER WEEK
£160.00 - £490.00

SPECIAL PROMOTIONS
Please see website for
current special offers.

Riverdale Court

Contact: Simon Irving, Manager, Riverdale Hall Hotel, Bellingham, Hexham,
Northumberland NE48 2JT **T:** (01434) 220254 **E:** reservations@riverdalehallhotel.co.uk
W: www.riverdalehallhotel.co.uk

Set in the grounds of the Riverdale Hall Hotel, Riverdale Court consists of four self-catering
apartments with splendid river views and ample parking. The two first-floor apartments, Blakey and
Graham, have balconies. The ground-floor apartments, Abrahams and Milburn have patio areas. All
overlooking the cricket field, the North Tyne River and bridge and Dunterley Fell (Pennine Way).
Guests enjoy free use of pool, sauna and amenities. Fishing, golf, cricket, walking and mountain
biking all near by. Please see website for further details.

Open: All year.
Nearest Shop: 1 Mile.
Nearest Pub: 1 Mile.

Units: The Abrahams, Blakey and Graham all
have two bedrooms. The Milburn has one large
bedroom. All apartments have open plan
lounges and a kitchen with dishwasher.

Site: ✿ P Payment: 💷 Leisure: 🚲 ♪ ┃ ♻ 🏌 Property: 🏊 🐕 🖥 🖳 Children: 🛏 🏠 🎎
Unit: 🗄 🗄 🖥 🗄 📶 TV 📀 📀 ☎

BERWICK-UPON-TWEED, Northumberland   Map ref 5B1

Units   1
Sleeps   1-5

PER UNIT PER WEEK
£175.00 - £375.00

Broadstone Cottage - Norham

Contact: Mr Edward Chantler, Broadstone Farm, Grafty Green, Maidstone ME17 2AT
T: (01622) 850207 **E:** davidchantler@btconnect.com

Village cottage. Ideal centre for touring, walking and fishing
holidays. 20 minutes to beach. Shops and pubs nearby. Full central
heating. Bathroom with shower. One double, one twin. **Open:** All
year **Nearest Shop:** 0.05 miles **Nearest Pub:** 0.05 miles

Site: ✿ P Property: 🐕 🖳 Children: 🛏 🏠 Unit: 🗄 🖥 🗄 📶 TV

BERWICK-UPON-TWEED, Northumberland Map ref 5B1

Units 1
Sleeps 1-5
PER UNIT PER WEEK
£295.00 - £595.00

Marlborough Cottage

Contact: Mr Peter Adamson, Proprietor, Marlborough House, 133 Main Street, Spittal, Berwick-upon-Tweed TD15 1RP **T:** (01289) 305293 / 07443 953857
E: marlboroughcottage@live.co.uk **W:** www.marlboroughcottage.info

Superior two-bedroomed cottage, stunning seafront location, fully equipped kitchen, shower-room, ramped access, all on one level, off-road parking. **Open:** All year **Nearest Shop:** 0.25 miles **Nearest Pub:** 0.25 miles

Site: ❁ P Leisure: ♿ ♪ ▶ ♻ Property: ▭ ▯ ▱ Children: ⅋ Unit: ▯ ▯ ▭ ▯ ▯ TV ◉ DVD

BERWICK-UPON-TWEED, Northumberland Map ref 5B1

Units 1
Sleeps 6
PER UNIT PER WEEK
£375.00 - £575.00

Seaview Cottage

Contact: Brenda Crowcroft, Owner, Berwick Cottage Holidays, Cow Road, Spittal, Berwick-upon-Tweed TD15 2QS **T:** (01289) 304175 **E:** b.crowcroft@talk21.com
W: www.berwickcottageholidays.co.uk

Charming, stone built cottage, sleeps six in comfort. Wood-burner, patio garden, stunning sea views and easy access A1 Newcastle and Edinburgh. Access to lovely beaches. **Open:** All year **Nearest Shop:** 1 mile **Nearest Pub:** 1 mile

Site: ❁ P Leisure: ♪ ▶ Property: ▯ ▱ Children: ⅋ ▥ ⚲ Unit: ▯ ▯ ▭ ▯ ▯ TV DVD ◢ BBQ

CORBRIDGE, Northumberland Map ref 5B2

Units 1
Sleeps 1-5
PER UNIT PER WEEK
£350.00 - £460.00

April Cottage

Contact: Mrs Kate Dean, 21 Woodland Close, Chelford, Macclesfield SK11 9BZ
T: (01625) 861718 **E:** peterandkatedean@btinternet.com

19th century cottage, centre village with garden. Situated near Hadrian's Wall and Roman camps. Within easy reach Northumbrian castles and Kielder Forest. Good shops, food outlets, near historic Newcastle with bridges, Sage and Baltic. **Open:** All year **Nearest Shop:** 0.10 miles **Nearest Pub:** 0.10 miles

Site: ❁ Leisure: ♪ Property: ▭ ▯ ▱ Children: ⅋ ▥ Unit: ▯ ▯ ▭ ▯ ▯ TV DVD BBQ ☎

CRASTER, Northumberland Map ref 5C1

Units 1
Sleeps 1-8
PER UNIT PER WEEK
£650.00 - £1840.00

Craster Tower Penthouse Apartment

Contact: Mrs Fiona Craster, Craster Tower Penthouse Apartment, Craster Tower, Alnwick, Northumberland NE66 3SS **T:** (01665) 576674 **E:** stay@crastertower.co.uk
W: www.crastertower.co.uk **£ BOOK ONLINE**

Spacious comfortable apartment encompassing the whole top floor of historic Craster Tower, beside picturesque fishing village producing world famous kippers. Elegantly furnished, with spectacular sea views. Ideal for beaches, walkers, golfers and history lovers. Comprehensively equipped kitchen, comfortable sitting room with flat screen TV, log burner and Wi-Fi, 18th century drawing room and tennis. **Open:** All year including Christmas and New Year **Nearest Shop:** 0.10 miles **Nearest Pub:** 0.5 miles

Site: ❁ P Payment: £☰ € Leisure: ♿ ♪ ▶ ♻ ⚲ Property: ⚲ ▭ ▯ ▱ Children: ⅋ ▥ ⚲ Unit: ▯ ▯ ▭
▯ ▯ TV ◉ DVD ◢ BBQ ☎

FALSTONE, Northumberland   Map ref 5B2

Station Cottage

Contact: Mrs June Banks, Owner, Station Cottage, Station House, Hexham NE48 1AB
T: (01434) 240311

Old Station waiting room has recently been converted into a small but very comfortable cottage with beautiful views across valley. **Open:** All year **Nearest Shop:** 0.25 miles **Nearest Pub:** 0.25 miles

Units   1
Sleeps   1-2
PER UNIT PER WEEK
£300.00 - £350.00

Site: ❋ **Leisure:** ♪ ♞ ◕ **Property:** ◱ **Unit:** ▯ ▭ ▤ TV ◉ ⑩

HALTWHISTLE, Northumberland   Map ref 5B2

Lambley Farm Cottages

Contact: Lambley Farm Cottages, Lambley CA8 7LQ **T:** 07967 274286
E: stay@lambleycottages.co.uk
W: lambleycottages.co.uk **£ BOOK ONLINE**

This cluster of barn conversions are set within 90 acres. Close to the South Tyne River. Outside space is not in short supply here, as our guests are welcome to explore all of the 100-acre Lambley Country Estate. From the cottages, there are spectacular views along the salmon-rich River South Tyne and down the valley towards Lambley Viaduct. Sauna facilities now available and indoor games room. **Open:** All year **Nearest Shop:** 4 miles **Nearest Pub:** 1.5 miles

Units   5
Sleeps   3-28
PER UNIT PER WEEK
£299.00 - £845.00

Site: ❋ P **Payment:** ▣ € **Leisure:** ♿ ♪ ▸ ∪ ◕ **Property:** ⊷ ▭ ▤ ▣ **Children:** ⛲ ▥ ⅄ **Unit:** ▯ ▤ ▭ ▤ TV ⑩ BBQ

HEXHAM, Northumberland   Map ref 5B2

Braemar

Contact: Mrs Cynthia Bradley, Owner, Edenholme, John Martin Street, Haydon Bridge, Northumberland NE47 6AA **T:** (01434) 684622 / 07949 369222
E: edenholme@btinternet.com **W:** www.edenholme.co.uk **£ BOOK ONLINE**

Delightful two-bedroomed bungalow with large garden to front and back. Sleeping 4/5 it is located in a small village with shops, pub and restaurant 100yds away. Ideal location for visiting Hadrian's Wall, Northumberland, Kielder Water, Metro Centre, Durham, Carlisle, Lakes and Scotland. **Open:** All year **Nearest Shop:** 100 Yards **Nearest Pub:** 100 Yards

Units   1
Sleeps   5
PER UNIT PER WEEK
£220.00 - £415.00

Site: ❋ P **Leisure:** ♪ ▸ **Property:** ⊷ ▤ ▣ **Children:** ⛲ ▥ ⅄ **Unit:** ▯ ▭ ▤ ◔ TV ⑩ ⑩ BBQ

HEXHAM, Northumberland   Map ref 5B2

High Dalton Cottage

Contact: Mrs Judy Stobbs, Owners, High Dalton Cottage, High Dalton Farm, Hexham, Northumberland NE46 2LB **T:** (01434) 673320 **E:** stobbsjudy@aol.com

Nestled within 270 acres of wild and beautiful countryside the cottage has oak flooring, exposed beams, wood burning stove and a bistro balcony! On a working farm with two burns to fish and play in. Short journey to Newcastle and Metrocentre. Hadrians wall, racecourse and golf nearby. **Open:** All year **Nearest Shop:** 4.5 miles **Nearest Pub:** 2 miles

Units   1
Sleeps   1-6
PER UNIT PER WEEK
£400.00 - £690.00

Site: ❋ P **Leisure:** ♿ ♪ ▸ ∪ **Property:** ⁄⁄ ▤ ▣ **Children:** ⛲ ▥ ⅄ **Unit:** ▯ ▤ ▭ ▤ ◔ TV ⑩ ⑩ ⁄ BBQ

HOLY ISLAND, Northumberland   Map ref 5C1

Units   3
Sleeps   1-8

PER UNIT PER WEEK
£356.00 - £886.00

SPECIAL PROMOTIONS
Short breaks usually
out of season.

Farne View House & 2 Cottages

Contact: Mr George Farr, Farne View House and Holiday Cottages, Pallinsburn House, Cornhill-on-Tweed, Northumberland TD12 4SG **T:** (01890) 820233 / 820579
F: 01890 820233 **E:** george.farr@virgin.net **W:** www.holyislanaccommodation.co.uk

18th century house sleeps 7/8 (two s/k double rooms, 1 with en suite shower, 1 single room has 3-4 single beds plus family bathroom on top floor and toilet on ground floor). Two cotts, sleeping 4 in each, (FCC: 1 x double, one s/k zip-and-link, FVC: 2 x s/k zip-and-link). Cotts have bathroom on second floor (toilet, hand basin, bath and separate shower unit.)
Woodburner in Farne Court Cottage. Views of castle and coast (not Farne Court Cottage). Electric storage heating inclusive – all three properties. Private courtyard garden. Parking. One pet by arrangement. No pets Farne View Cottage.

Open: All year
Nearest Shop: 0.10 miles
Nearest Pub: 0.10 miles

Units: FVH: singles room sleeps 3 plus 1 using a 'z' bed if required. FCC: 1 x double & 1 x s/k zip-and-link. FVC: 2 x s/k zip-and-link beds.

Site: ❀ **P** **Leisure:** ♪ ▶ ∪ **Property:** 🐾 🏭 **Children:** 🛏 🍴 ♿ **Unit:** 🗄 🖥 🛁 🍳 📺 📀 ⬤

LOW NEWTON-BY-THE-SEA, Northumberland   Map ref 5C1

Units   1
Sleeps   6
PER UNIT PER WEEK
£450.00 - £650.00

4 Coastguard Cottages

Contact: Ms Susan Jarratt, **T:** (01242) 517772 **E:** susanmjarratt@hotmail.com

Our warm and comfortable three-bedroom holiday cottage is well equipped for six people and overlooks the sea and Dunstanburgh Castle. The long sandy beach is less than 200 yards from the garden gate. Sorry, no pets. **Open:** All year **Nearest Shop:** 2 miles
Nearest Pub: 300 yds

Site: ❀ **P** **Leisure:** ♪ ▶ **Property:** 🏭 **Children:** 🛏 **Unit:** 🗄 🗄 🖥 🛁 🍳 📺 📀 ⬤

MORPETH, Northumberland   Map ref 5C2

Units   1
Sleeps   2
PER UNIT PER WEEK
£200.00 - £300.00

Cartwheel Cottage

Contact: Sarah Chisholm, Proprietor, Westerheugh Farm, Longhorsley, Morpeth, Northumberland NE65 8RH **T:** (01665) 570661 **E:** sarah@cartwheelcottage.com
W: www.cartwheelcottage.com **£ BOOK ONLINE**

Semi-detached farm cottage, sleeps 2. Can be made up as a double or a twin room. Situated on traditional working farm. Well situated for all attractions, the coast, hill walking, National Trust properties, Cragside and Wallington. **Open:** All year except December and January. **Nearest Shop:** 4 miles **Nearest Pub:** 4 miles

f

Site: **P** **Property:** 🖥 🗄 🏭 **Children:** 🛏 🍴 ♿ **Unit:** 🗄 🖥 🛁 🍳 📺 📀 **BBQ**

NEWTON-BY-THE-SEA, Northumberland   Map ref 5C1

Link House Farm Holiday Cottages

Contact: Mrs Kathleen Thompson, Owner, Link House Farm, Newton-by-the-Sea, Alnwick, Northumberland NE66 3ED **T:** (01665) 576820 **E:** stay@linkhousefarm.co.uk
W: www.linkhousefarm.com

Units   13
Sleeps   2-8
PER UNIT PER WEEK
£165.00 - £1600.00

Northumbrian Luxury coastal cottages, located on our farm between the fishing villages of Craster & Beadnell. Each property is completely self contained and equipped to a high standard with their own garden area and seating. Also, a large adventure play ground and football area. Ideal for families, couples, walkers, cyclists and bird watchers or for those who deserve and crave a peaceful holiday on our beautiful picturesque coastline. No pets.
Open: All Year **Nearest Shop:** 2.5 Miles **Nearest Pub:** 0.5 Miles

Site: P **Payment:** ▭ **Leisure:** ♪ ▶ ♻ **Property:** ▯ ▯ **Children:** ⚲ **Unit:** ▬ ▢ TV DVD

NEWTON-BY-THE-SEA, Northumberland   Map ref 5C1

Sea Winds

Contact: Mrs Jo Leiper, Sea Winds, Bygate, Black Heddon, Newcastle-upon-Tyne NE20 0JJ
T: (01661) 881506 / 07720 051201 **E:** stay@seawinds-lownewton.co.uk
W: www.seawinds-lownewton.co.uk

Units   1
Sleeps   2-6
PER UNIT PER WEEK
£375.00 - £750.00

Situated within the picturesque village of Low Newton-by-the-Sea, this former fisherman's cottage is just 200m from a beautiful sandy beach which is part of Northumberland's Heritage Coast. High-quality and offering many home comforts make it an exceptional family base to discover the secrets of the surrounding area.
Open: All year **Nearest Shop:** 3 miles **Nearest Pub:** 0.25 miles

Site: ✿ P **Leisure:** ♣ **Property:** ⚞ ▯ ▯ **Children:** ⚲ ▦ ⚡ **Unit:** ▯ ▯ ▬ ▯ ▯ TV ◉ DVD ◿ BBQ ☎

PONTELAND, Northumberland   Map ref 5C2

The Old Tack Room

Contact: Clare Stephenson, Owner, Eland Green Farm Holiday Cottages, Eland Green Farm, Ponteland, Newcastle upon Tyne, Northumberland NE20 9UR
T: (01661) 822188 / 07786 537424 **F:** 01661 822188 **E:** elandgreen@msn.com
W: www.elandfarm.co.uk

Units   2
Sleeps   1-12
PER UNIT PER WEEK
£315.00 - £540.00

Just 9 miles North West of Newcastle and set in the idyllic surrounding of 200 acres of grass farm, Eland Green Farm provides self-catering holiday homes to escape the hustle and bustle of the big city. Undercover parking at door. Large garden with use of hard tennis court (open April - October). Sorry no smokers/dogs. Towels £6 per person extra. Free Wi-Fi. Ideal for business / holidays.
Open: All year **Nearest Shop:** 0.5 miles **Nearest Pub:** 0.5 miles

[f]

Site: ✿ P **Payment:** € **Leisure:** ▶ ♣ ⚲ **Property:** ▭ ▯ ▯ **Children:** ⚲ ▦ ⚡ **Unit:** ▯ ▬ ▯ ▯ TV DVD BBQ

SEAHOUSES, Northumberland *Map ref 5C1*

1, 2 & 3 The Old Bakery

Contact: Susan Parker, Owner, No's 1, 2 & 3 The Old Bakery, Crown Street, Seahouses, Northumberland NE68 7TQ **T:** (01484) 665633 / 07833 357974
W: www.oldbakeryseahouses.co.uk

Units	3
Sleeps	2

PER UNIT PER WEEK
£255.00 - £430.00

SPECIAL PROMOTIONS
Short break information available upon request.

Numbers 1, 2 & 3 The Old Bakery are 3 separate one double-bedroomed properties converted from the old bakery in Seahouses. Each cottage is individually and tastefully furnished and offers excellent accommodation with private parking for a couple wishing to be based on the Northumbria Coast. The harbour and village amenities are a few minutes walk away, with another 10 minute walk to the beach. The Bakery is a member of Seahouses Ocean Club.

Open: All year
Nearest Shop: 3 minute walk
Nearest Pub: 4 minute walk

Units: 3 x 1 double-bedroomed cottages with bath & over bath shower, lounge, kitchen/diner and private parking.

Site: P Payment: € **Leisure:** ▶ ∪ **Property:** 📺 📖 🎱 🍴 **Unit:** 📱 🖥 🍴 🎱 📺 📀

WOOLER, Northumberland *Map ref 5B1*

Conifer Cottage

Contact: Dickie or Jane Jeffreys, Owners, Kimmerston Riding Centre, Wooler NE71 6JH
T: (01668) 216283 / 07765 262422 **E:** jane@kimmerston.com
W: www.kimmerston.com

Units	1
Sleeps	1-6

PER UNIT PER WEEK
£300.00 - £450.00

Situated on a farm / riding centre beside a quiet country road in the beautiful countryside of Northumberland, the cottage has a breath-taking view across to the Cheviot Hills with a large enclosed garden. Visitors are always amazed by the scenic beauty, tranquillity, quiet roads and ancient tradition of Northumberland. Walking, cycling, gliding, golf, fishing and great riding all nearby.
Open: All year **Nearest Shop:** 1.5 miles **Nearest Pub:** 2 miles

Site: ❀ **P Payment:** € **Leisure:** 🚴 ♪ ▶ ∪ **Property:** 🐾 🖥 **Children:** 🍼 🛏 🪑 **Unit:** 📱 🖥 🍴 🎱 📺 📀 🍳 BBQ

HARTLEPOOL, Tees Valley *Map ref 5C2*

Waters Edge

Contact: Mrs Rosalie Reeder, Owner, 107 Lutterworth Rd, Aylestone, Leicester LE2 8PL
T: 07966 793067 **E:** reeder.rosalie720@gmail.com

Units	1
Sleeps	2-5

A luxury front line 2 bedroom, 2 bathroom, 2nd floor apartment with spectacular views across Hartlepool Marina. Modern accommodation providing a fabulous location to enjoy Hartlepool's facilities. Located on the quiet side of the marina, 5 minutes walk to numerous Quayside bars and restaurants. Please contact Rosalie Reeder for availability and tariff. **Open:** All year **Nearest Shop:** 200 yards **Nearest Pub:** 25 yards

Site: P Leisure: 🚴 ♪ ▶ 🎣 🎿 **Property:** 📺 📖 🖥 **Children:** 🍼 **Unit:** 📱 🍴 🖥 🎱 📺 📀

NEWCASTLE UPON TYNE, Tyne and Wear   Map ref 5C2

Units   1
Sleeps   1-4
PER UNIT PER WEEK
£280.00 - £350.00

135 Audley Road Self Catering Flat

Contact: Miss Linda Wright, 137 Audley Road, South Gosforth, Newcastle-upon-Tyne NE3 1QH **T:** (0191) 2856374 / 07733 617784 **E:** lkw@audleyroad.co.uk
W: www.audleyroad.co.uk

Self-contained flat, accommodates four people, close to shops and Metro, with easy access to city centre. All amenities. Short lets accepted, price for this on enquiry. Approximately 2.5 miles from city centre and 6.5 miles from Newcastle Airport. Ideal as a base to visit the North East for leisure or work-related trips. **Open:** All year **Nearest Shop:** 0.20 miles **Nearest Pub:** 0.20 miles

Property: ▢ ▢ ▢   **Children:** ▢ ▢   **Unit:** ▢ ▢ ▢ ▢ ▢ ▢ ▢

SOUTH SHIELDS, Tyne And Wear   Map ref 5C2

Units   1
Sleeps   1-4
PER UNIT PER WEEK
£325.00 - £525.00

Embla

Contact: Jon & Sue,   **T:** (08442) 327805   **E:** embla@fastmail.co.uk
W: www.selfcateringapartmentnortheast.co.uk

A unique 2 bedroom luxury apartment, free Wi-Fi. Just a few metres from the parks & beaches of South Shields. Perfect for anyone wanting to relax, walk, enjoy culture, shopping, history etc. We are unique in that there is no one below and no one above, so guests don't have to suffer noise from people below or above them. Private covered parking. Beautifully decorated throughout to a very high standard, ideal for anyone who demands comfort and modern surroundings. Strictly no smoking & no pets. **Open:** All year **Nearest Shop:** 500 metres **Nearest Pub:** 500 metres

Site: ▢ P   **Payment:** ▢   **Leisure:** ▢ ▢ ▢   **Property:** ▢ ▢   **Unit:** ▢ ▢ ▢ ▢ ▢ ▢ ▢

The Official Tourist Board Guide to **Self Catering 2015**

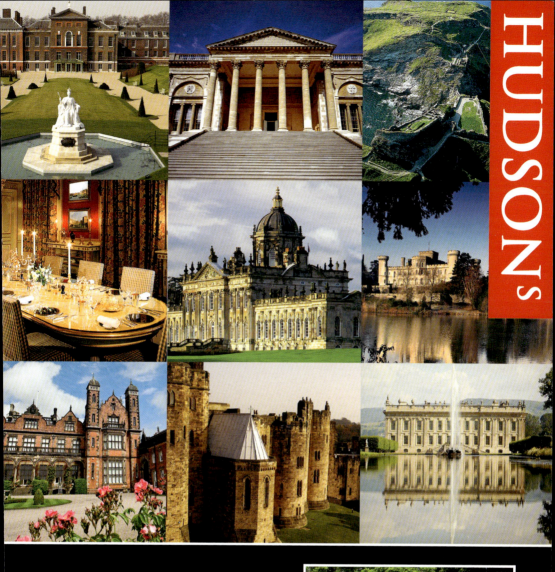
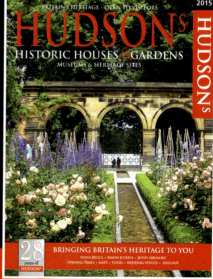

Map 1

Location
Maps

Every place name featured in the regional accommodation sections of this guide has a map reference to help you locate it on the maps which follow. For example, to find Colchester, Essex, which has 'Map ref 3B2', turn to Map 3 and refer to grid square B2.

All place names appearing in the regional sections are shown with orange circles on the maps. This enables you to find other places in your chosen area which may have suitable accommodation – the place index (at the back of this guide) gives page numbers.

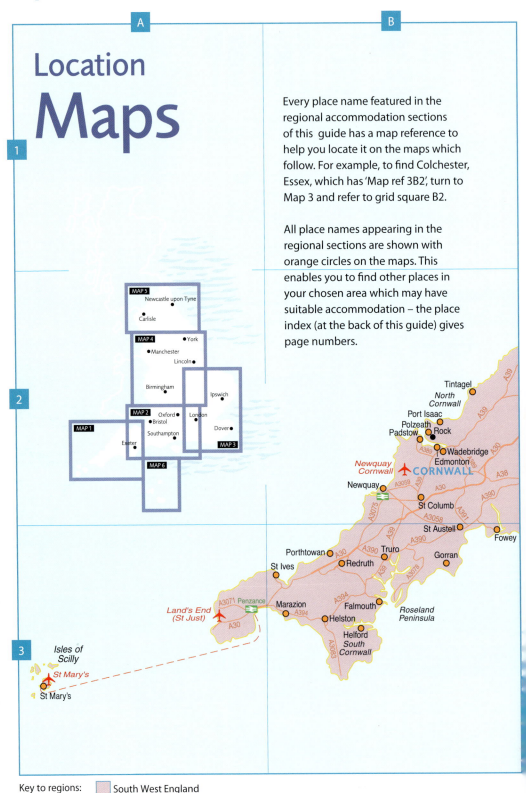

Key to regions: South West England

Map 1

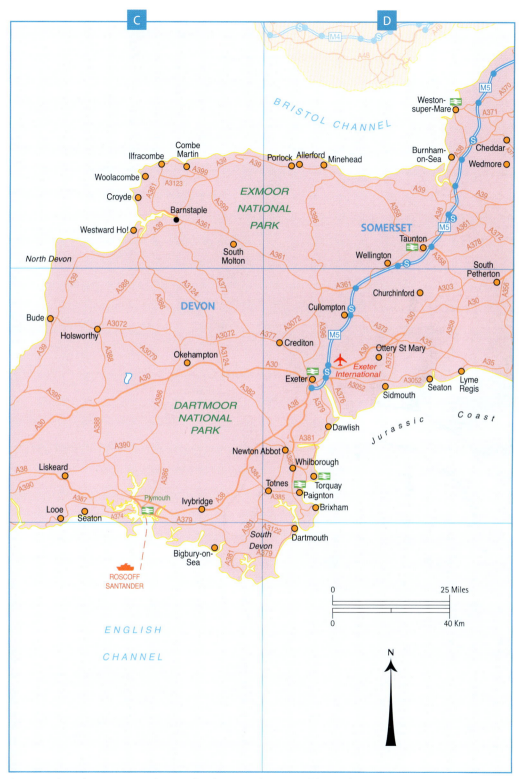

Orange circles indicate accommodation within the regional sections of this guide

Map 2

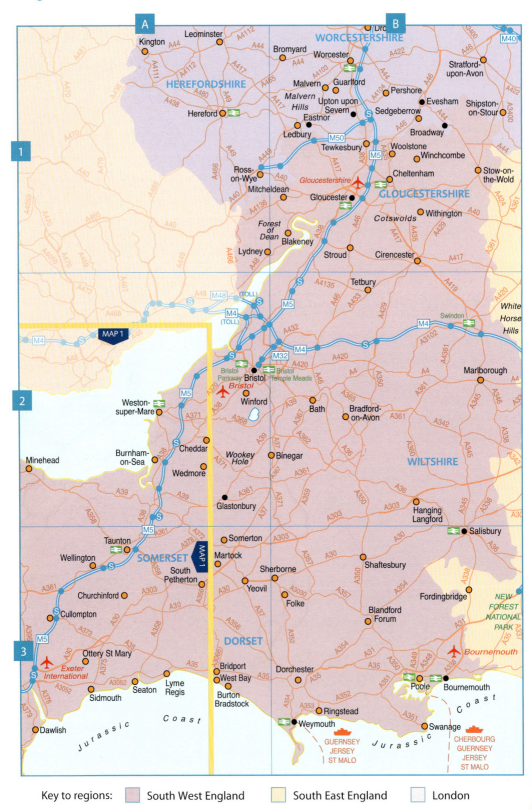

Key to regions: South West England   South East England   London

Map 2

East of England   East Midlands   Heart of England

Orange circles indicate accommodation within the regional sections of this guide

Map 3

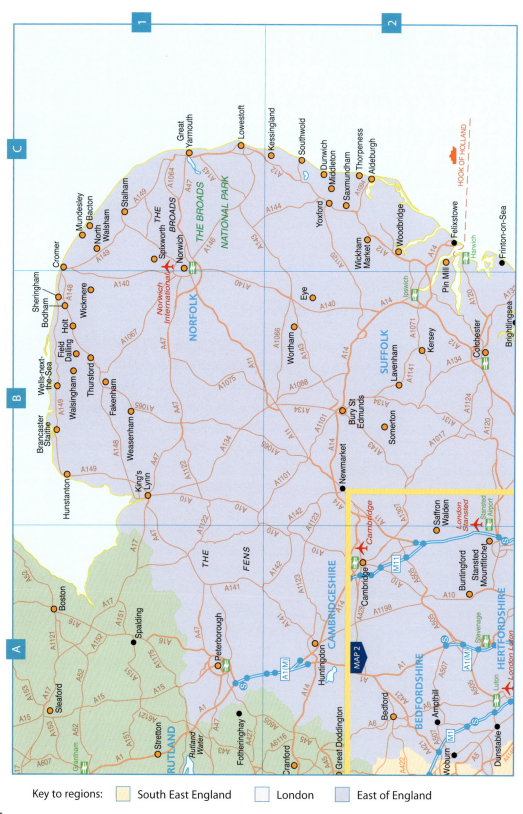

Key to regions: South East England   London   East of England

Map 3

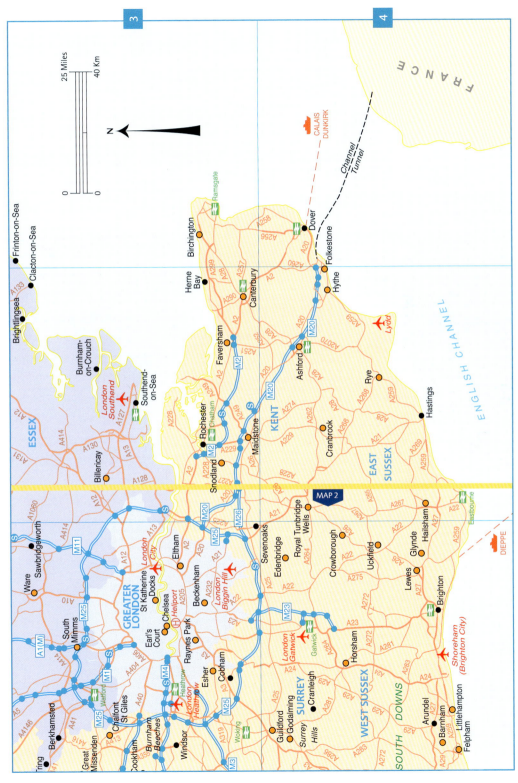

East Midlands

Orange circles indicate accommodation within the regional sections of this guide

Map 4

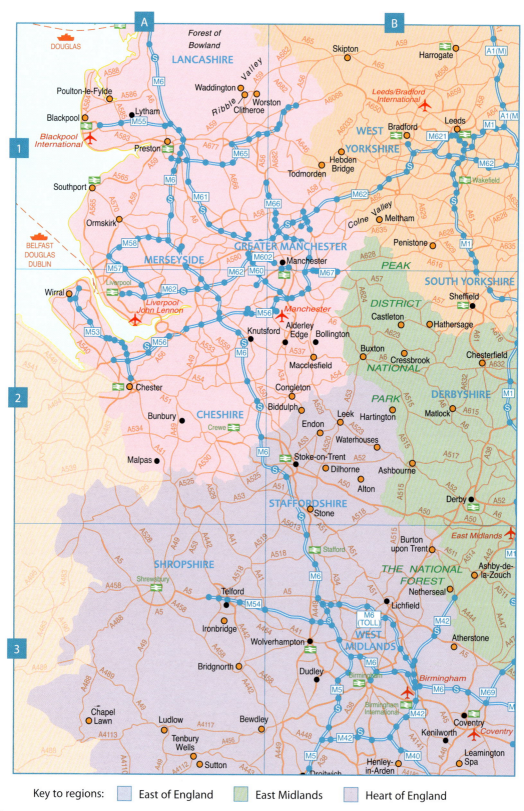

Key to regions: ☐ East of England   ☐ East Midlands   ☐ Heart of England

Map 4

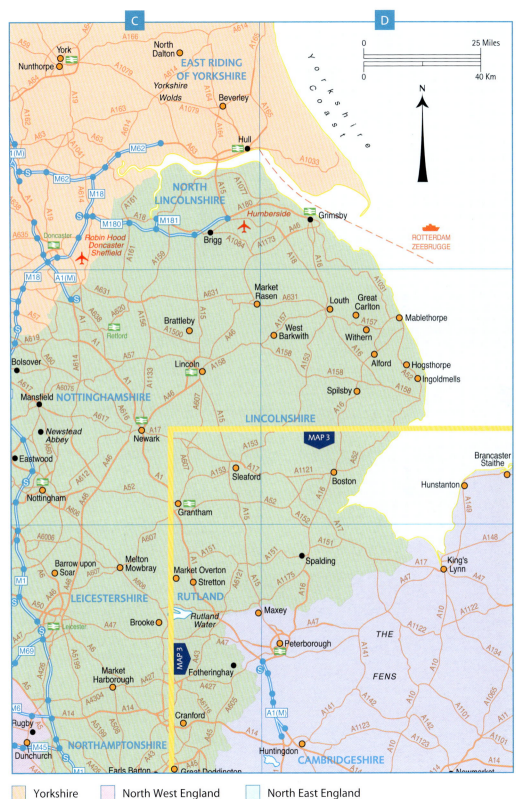

Yorkshire   North West England   North East England

Orange circles indicate accommodation within the regional sections of this guide

349

Map 5

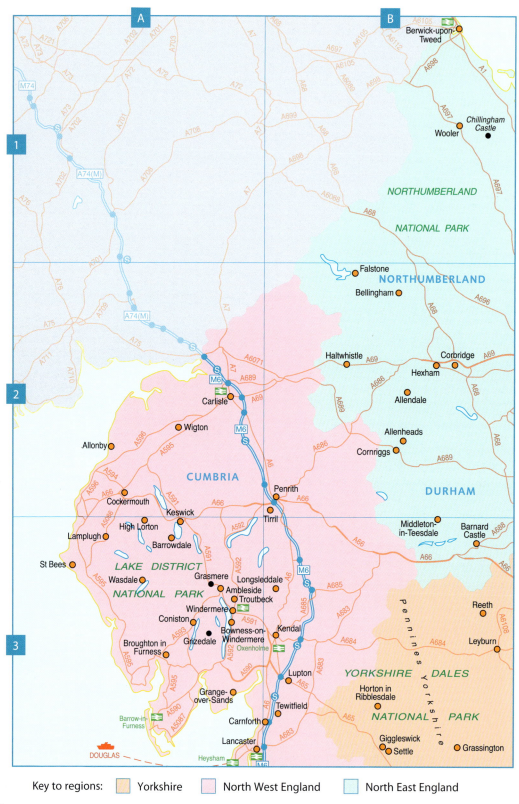

A   B

1

2

3

Berwick-upon-Tweed

Wooler
Chillingham Castle

NORTHUMBERLAND

NATIONAL PARK

Falstone
Bellingham

NORTHUMBERLAND

Haltwhistle
Corbridge
Hexham
Allendale

Allenheads
Cornriggs

DURHAM

Carlisle

Wigton

Allonby

CUMBRIA

Penrith

Tirril

Cockermouth
Keswick
High Lorton
Lamplugh
Barrowdale

St Bees

Middleton-in-Teesdale
Barnard Castle

LAKE DISTRICT

Wasdale
Grasmere
Longsleddale
Ambleside
Troutbeck

NATIONAL PARK

Coniston
Windermere
Bowness-on-Windermere
Grizedale
Kendal

Oxenholme

Reeth

P e n n i n e s   Y o r k s h i r e

Leyburn

Broughton in Furness

Lupton

YORKSHIRE   DALES

Grange-over-Sands

Horton in Ribblesdale

Tewitfield

NATIONAL PARK

Barrow-in-Furness

Carnforth

Lancaster

Giggleswick
Settle
Grassington

DOUGLAS

Heysham

Key to regions: Yorkshire   North West England   North East England

350

Map 5

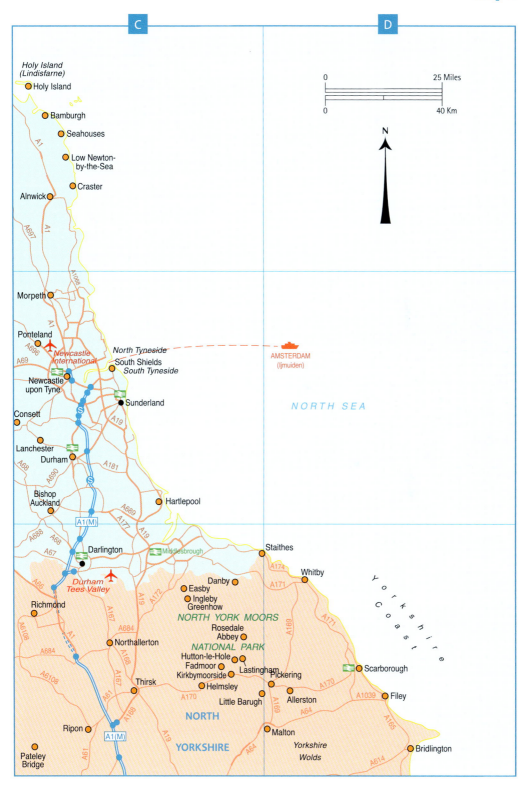

C

D

Holy Island
(Lindisfarne)
- Holy Island
- Bamburgh
- Seahouses
- Low Newton-
  by-the-Sea
- Craster
Alnwick

A1
A697
A1

Morpeth

A1

Ponteland
A696
Newcastle
International
A69
Newcastle
upon Tyne
A1068

North Tyneside
South Shields
South Tyneside

AMSTERDAM
(Ijmuiden)

NORTH SEA

Consett

Lanchester
Durham
A68
A690
A181
A19

Sunderland

Bishop
Auckland

A1(M)
A689
A177
A19

Hartlepool

A688   A68

A67

Darlington

Middlesbrough

Staithes

A174

Whitby

A171

Durham
Tees Valley

A66

Richmond

A6108
A684

Danby
Easby
Ingleby
Greenhow

NORTH YORK MOORS

Rosedale
Abbey

NATIONAL PARK

Hutton-le-Hole
Fadmoor
Kirkbymoorside
Lastingham

Pickering

A170

Scarborough

A1039   Filey

Northallerton

A167
A172
A19
A168

A684

A6108

Thirsk

A167

Helmsley

Little Barugh

A170

Allerston

A169
A64

A64

Yorkshire
Coast

A171

A169

A165

Ripon

A1(M)
A61
A19

NORTH

YORKSHIRE

Malton

Yorkshire
Wolds

Pateley
Bridge

A61

A64

A614

Bridlington

0 ————————— 25 Miles
0 ————————— 40 Km

N

Orange circles indicate accommodation within the regional sections of this guide

Map 6

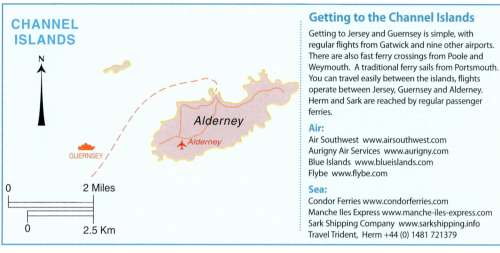

Getting to the Channel Islands

Getting to Jersey and Guernsey is simple, with regular flights from Gatwick and nine other airports. There are also fast ferry crossings from Poole and Weymouth. A traditional ferry sails from Portsmouth. You can travel easily between the islands, flights operate between Jersey, Guernsey and Alderney. Herm and Sark are reached by regular passenger ferries.

Air:
Air Southwest www.airsouthwest.com
Aurigny Air Services www.aurigny.com
Blue Islands www.blueislands.com
Flybe www.flybe.com

Sea:
Condor Ferries www.condorferries.com
Manche Iles Express www.manche-iles-express.com
Sark Shipping Company www.sarkshipping.info
Travel Trident, Herm +44 (0) 1481 721379

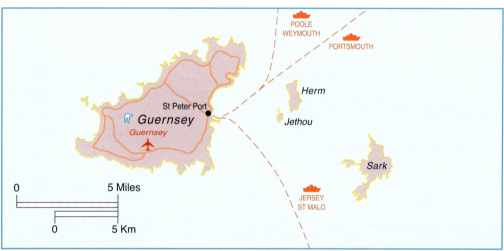

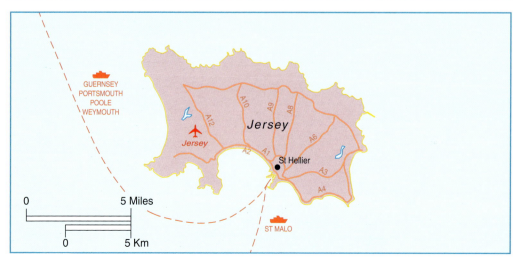

Key to regions: Channel Islands

Orange circles indicate accommodation within the regional sections of this guide

Map 7
London

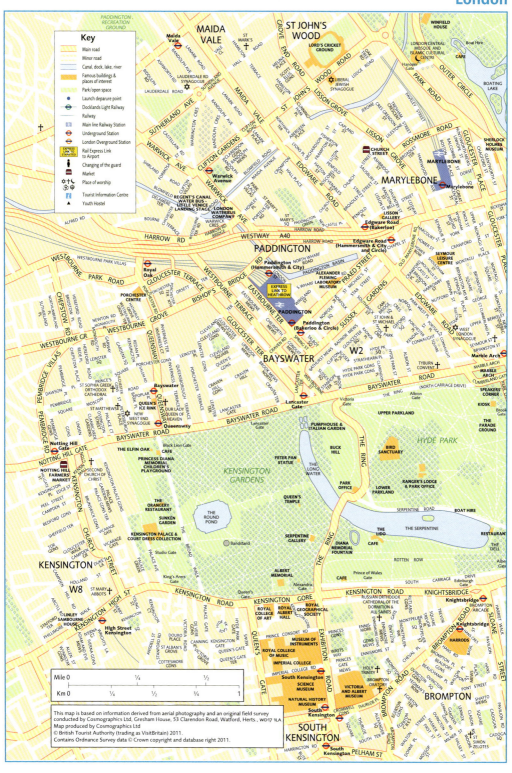

Key

- Main road
- Minor road
- Canal, dock, lake, river
- Famous buildings & places of interest
- Park/open space
- Launch departure point
- Docklands Light Railway
- Railway
- Main line Railway Station
- Underground Station
- London Overground Station
- Rail Express Link to Airport
- Changing of the guard
- Market
- Place of worship
- Tourist Information Centre
- Youth Hostel

This map is based on information derived from aerial photography and an original field survey conducted by Cosmographics Ltd, Gresham House, 53 Clarendon Road, Watford, Herts., WD17 1LA.
Map produced by Cosmographics Ltd
© British Tourist Authority (trading as VisitBritain) 2011.
Contains Ordnance Survey data © Crown copyright and database right 2011.

Map 8
London

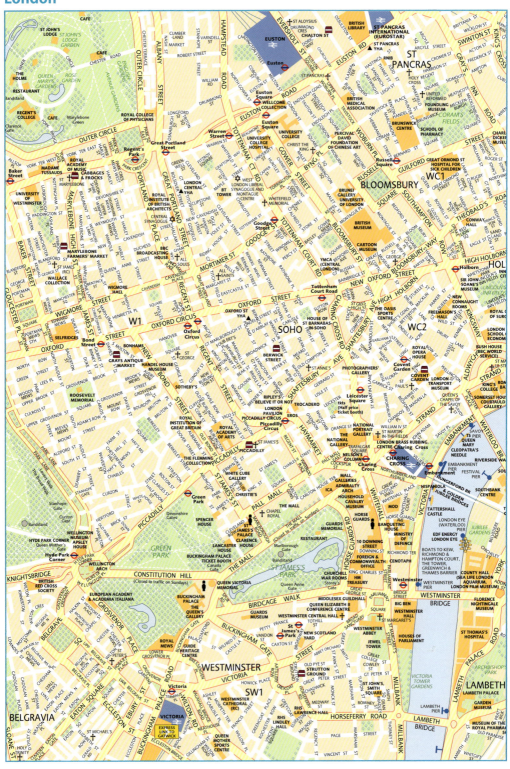

Map 8
London

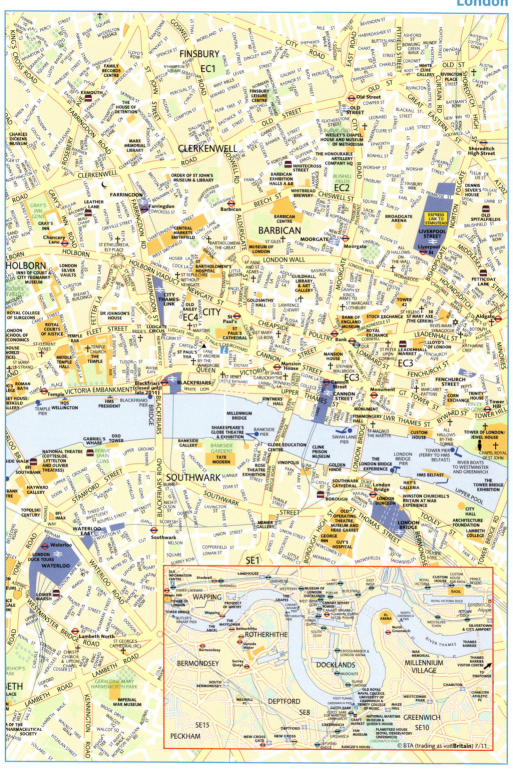

Motorway Service Area Assessment Scheme

Something we all use and take for granted but how good are they?

The star ratings cover over 250 different aspects of each operation, including cleanliness, the quality and range of catering and also the quality of the physical aspects, as well as the service. It does not cover prices or value for money.

OPERATOR: EXTRA

Baldock	★★★★
Beaconsfield	★★★★
Blackburn	★★★★
Cambridge	★★★
Cullompton	★★★
Peterborough	★★★★

OPERATOR: MOTO

Birch E	★★★
Birch W	★★★
Bridgwater	★★★
Burton in Kendal	★★★
Cherwell Valley	★★★★★
Chieveley	★★★
Doncaster N	★★★★
Donington Park	★★★★
Exeter	★★★
Ferrybridge	★★★
Frankley N	★★★
Frankley S	★★★
Heston E	★★★
Heston W	★★★
Hilton Park N	★★★
Hilton Park S	★★★
Knutsford N	★★★
Knutsford S	★★★
Lancaster N	★★★
Lancaster S	★★
Leigh Delamere E	★★★★
Leigh Delamere W	★★★★
Medway	★★★
Pease Pottage	★★★
Reading E	★★★★
Reading W	★★★
Severn View	★★
Southwaite N	★★★
Southwaite S	★★★

Stafford N	★★★★
Tamworth	★★★
Thurrock	★★★★
Toddington N	★★★★
Toddington S	★★★
Trowell N	★★★
Trowell S	★★★
Washington N	★★★
Washington S	★★★★
Wetherby	★★★★
Winchester N	★★★★
Winchester S	★★★
Woolley Edge N	★★★★
Woolley Edge S	★★★★

OPERATOR: ROADCHEF

Chester	★★
Clacket Lane E	★★★
Clacket Lane W	★★
Durham	★★★
Killington Lake	★★★
Maidstone	★★★
Northampton N	★★★
Northampton S	★★★
Norton Canes	★★★★
Rownhams N	★★
Rownhams S	★★★
Sandbach N	★★
Sandbach S	★★★
Sedgemoor S	★★
Stafford S	★★★
Strensham N	★★★★
Strensham S	★★★
Taunton Deane N	★★
Taunton Deane S	★★★
Tibshelf N	★★★
Tibshelf S	★★★
Watford Gap N	★★★
Watford Gap S	★★

OPERATOR: WELCOME BREAK

Birchanger Green	★★★★
Burtonwood	★★★
Charnock Richard W	★★★
Charnock Richard E	★★★
Corley E	★★★
Corley W	★★★
Fleet N	★★★★
Fleet S	★★★
Gordano	★★★★
Hartshead Moor E	★★★
Hartshead Moor W	★★★
Hopwood Park	★★★★
Keele N	★★★
Keele S	★★★
Leicester Forest East N	★★★
Leicester Forest East S	★★★
London Gateway	★★★★
Membury E	★★★
Membury W	★★★★
Michaelwood N	★★★
Michaelwood S	★★★
Newport Pagnell S	★★★
Newport Pagnell N	★★★
Oxford	★★★★
Sedgemoor N	★★★
South Mimms	★★★★
Telford	★★★
Warwick N	★★★
Warwick S	★★★★
Woodall N	★★
Woodall S	★★★

WESTMORLAND

Tebay N	★★★★
Tebay S	★★★★★

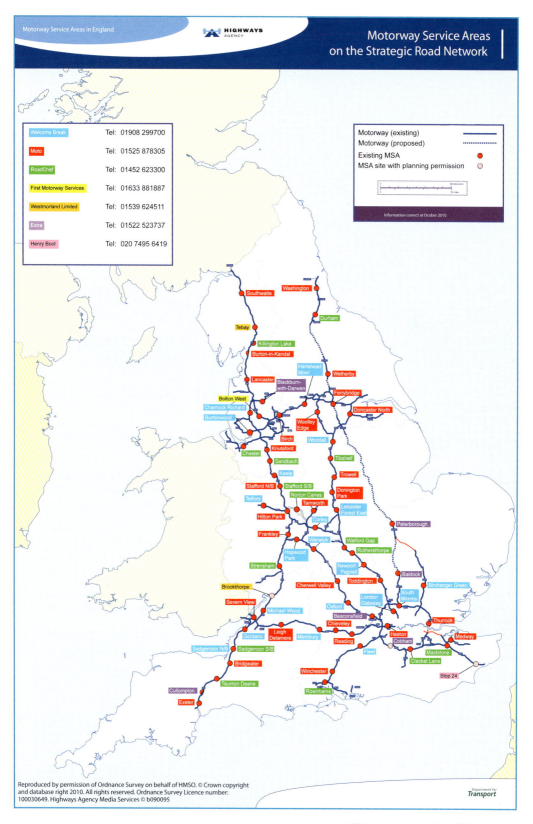

Motorway Service Areas in England

Motorway Service Areas on the Strategic Road Network

HIGHWAYS AGENCY

Welcome Break	Tel: 01908 299700
Moto	Tel: 01525 878305
RoadChef	Tel: 01452 623300
First Motorway Services	Tel: 01633 881887
Westmorland Limited	Tel: 01539 624511
Extra	Tel: 01522 523737
Henry Boot	Tel: 020 7495 6419

Motorway (existing)
Motorway (proposed)
Existing MSA
MSA site with planning permission

Information correct at October 2010

Southwaite
Washington
Durham
Tebay
Killington Lake
Burton-in-Kendal
Hartshead Moor
Wetherby
Lancaster
Blackburn-with-Darwen
Ferrybridge
Bolton West
Charnock Richard
Burtonwood
Woolley Edge
Doncaster North
Birch
Woodall
Chester
Knutsford
Sandbach
Keele
Tibshelf
Trowell
Stafford N/B
Stafford S/B
Donington Park
Telford
Norton Canes
Tamworth
Leicester Forest East
Hilton Park
Corley
Peterborough
Frankley
Warwick
Watford Gap
Rothersthorpe
Hopwood Park
Strensham
Newport Pagnell
Baldock
Cherwell Valley
Toddington
Birchanger Green
Brookthorpe
South Mimms
Severn View
London Gateway
Michael Wood
Oxford
Beaconsfield
Thurrock
Gordano
Leigh Delamere
Membury
Chieveley
Heston
Cobham
Medway
Reading
Maidstone
Sedgemoor N/B
Sedgemoor S/B
Fleet
Clacket Lane
Bridgwater
Winchester
Stop 24
Cullompton
Taunton Deane
Rownhams
Exeter

Department for Transport

Self-catering agencies

All of the self-catering agencies listed below offer a selection of cottages and holiday homes over particular geographical areas. Many of the agencies only promote properties that are assessed annually by VisitEngland, however some only promote a percentage of properties that have a star rating. To avoid disappointment, you are advised to check if your desired accommodation has a VisitEngland star rating before booking. Agencies that promote the highest percentage of quality assessed accommodation at the time of publishing feature at the top of the list.

Cottages4you
0345 268 1243
www.cottages4you.co.uk
Accommodation throughout the country.

Welcome Cottages
0845 268 0819
www.welcomecottages.com
Properties across the UK.

English Country Cottages
0845 268 0788
www.english-country-cottages.co.uk
Hand-picked holiday cottages in England.

Cumbrian Cottages
01228 599 960
www.cumbrian-cottages.co.uk
enquiries@cumbrian-cottages.co.uk
A large Collection of holiday properties in Cumbria and the Lake District.

Norfolk Country Cottages
01263 715 779
www.norfolkcottages.co.uk
info@norfolkcottages.co.uk
Over 450 properties in the county of Norfolk.

Coast & Country Cottages
01548 843 773
www.coastandcountry.co.uk
Properties in Salcombe, Dartmouth and South Devon.

Lakelovers
01539 488 855
www.lakelovers.co.uk
enquiries@lakelovers.co.uk
Collection of individual properties in Cumbria.

Ingrid Flute's Yorkshire Holiday Cottages
01947 600 700
www.yorkshireholidaycottages.co.uk
info@yorkshireholidaycottages.co.uk
Holiday homes across Yorkshire.

Marsdens Devon Cottages
01271 813 777
www.marsdens.co.uk
devon@marsdens.co.uk
Over 380 holiday cottages throughout North Devon and Exmoor.

Suffolk Secrets
01502 722 717
www.suffolk-secrets.co.uk
holidays@suffolk-secrets.co.uk
Family-owned, with over 350 properties across Suffolk.

Dream Cottages
01305 789 000
www.dream-cottages.co.uk
admin@dream-cottages.co.uk
Providing cottages across Dorset, Devon, and Somerset.

Freedom Holiday Homes
01580 720 770
www.freedomholidayhomes.co.uk
info@freedomholidayhomes.co.uk
Over 250 cottages throughout Kent and Sussex.

Dorset Coastal Cottages
0800 980 4070
www.dorsetcoastalcottages.com
hols@dorsetcoastalcottages.com
Self catering on the Dorset coast.

Harbour Holidays, Padstow
01841 533 402
www.padstow-self-catering.co.uk
contact@harbourholidays.co.uk
A wide range of self-catering accommodation in Padstow, Cornwall.

Carbis Bay Holidays
0800 012 2241
www.carbisbayholidays.co.uk
enquiries@carbisbayholidays.co.uk
Self-catering accommodation in Carbis Bay and St Ives, Cornwall.

Marsdens Cornish Cottages
01503 289 289
www.cornish-cottages.co.uk
cornwall@marsdens.co.uk
Self-catering accommodation throughout Cornwall.

Lakeland Cottage Company
01539 538 180
www.lakeland-cottage-company.co.uk
info@lakeland-cottage-company.co.uk
A large range of cottages in the Lake District.

Birds Norfolk Holiday Homes
01485 534 267
www.norfolkholidayhomes-birds.co.uk
shohol@birdsnorfolkholidayhomes.co.uk
Self-catering accommodation along the North West Norfolk Coast.

Quay Holidays
01202 683 333
www.quayholidays.co.uk
stay@quayholidays.co.uk
Self-catering accommodation in, and around, Poole.

Keswick Cottages
01768 780 088
www.keswickcottages.co.uk
info@keswickcottages.co.uk
Cottages in and around Keswick, the Lake District.

Linstone Chine Holiday Services
01983 755 933
www.linstone-chine.co.uk
enquiries@linstone-chine.co.uk
Offering accommodation on the isle of Wight.

Cornish Horizons Holiday Cottages
01841 533 331
www.cornishhorizons.co.uk
cottages@cornishhorizons.co.uk
Providing a large portfolio of properties in North Cornwall

Island Cottage Holidays
01929 481 555
www.islandcottageholidays.com
mail@islandcottageholidays.com
Providing a wide collection of cottages on the Isle of Wight.

Roseland Holiday Cottages
01872 580 480
www.roselandholidaycottages.co.uk
enquiries@
roselandholidaycottages.co.uk
A selection of cottages in St Mawes and Portscatho, Cornwall.

The Coppermines & Coniston Lake Cottages
01539 441 765
www.coppermines.co.uk
info@coppermines.co.uk
A wide range of cottages set in the Lake District.

Estuary & Rock Holidays
01208 863 399
www.rockholidays.co.uk
info@rockholidays.co.uk
A collection of accommodation in Cornwall.

Milkbere Holiday Cottages
01297 20729
www.milkberehols.com
info@milkberehols.com
Accommodation in Devon and Dorset.

Dorset Cottage Holidays
01929 481 547
www.dhcottages.co.uk
enquiries@dhcottages.co.uk
A collection of cottages and apartments in Dorset.

Porthleven Harbour Cottages
01326 563 198
www.cornishhideaways.co.uk
info@cornishhideaways.com
Self-catering holiday accommodation in the Porthleven and Rinsey area of West Cornwall.

Askrigg Cottage Holidays
01969 650 022
www.askrigg.com
stay@ askrigg.com
Holiday cottages in the Yorkshire Dales National Park.

Whitby Holiday Cottages
01947 603 010
www.whitby-cottages.net
enquiries@whitby-cottages.net
Offering a large collection of cottages in Yorkshire.

The Cornish Collection Ltd
01503 262 736
www.cornishcollection.co.uk
enquiries@cornishcollection.co.uk
A selection of properties in Looe and across South-East Cornwall.

Portscatho Holidays
01326 270 900
www.portscathoholidays.co.uk
info@portscathoholidays.co.uk
Offering accommodation in the Roseland Peninsula, including St Mawes and Portscatho in South Cornwall

Holiday Homes and Cottages SW
01803 299 677
www.swcottages.co.uk
iain@swcottages.co.uk.
Holiday cottages and apartments across Devon and Cornwall.

Coquet Cottages
01665 710 700
www.coquetcottages.co.uk
info@coquetcottages.co.uk
Self-catering holiday accommodation based in Northumberland.

Bath Holiday Rentals
01225 482 225
www.bathholidayrentals.com
alexa@bathholidayrentals.com
Self-catering apartments and cottages in and around Bath.

Country Hideaways
01969 663 559
www.countryhideaways.co.uk
info@countryhideaways.co.uk
*Cottages and apartments
throughout the Yorkshire
Dales.*

Wight Locations
01983 617 322
www.wightlocations.co.uk
enquiries@wightlocations.co.uk
*Holiday Cottages on the Isle
of Wight.*

Home from Home Holidays
01983 532 385
www.homefromhomeiow.co.uk
hfromh@crldirect.co.uk
*A selection of self-catering
properties on the Isle of Wight.*

Scilly Self Catering
01720 422 082
www.scillyselfcatering.com
*Self-catering accommodation on
the Isles of Scilly.*

Lakeland Cottage Holidays
01768 776 065
www.lakelandcottages.co.uk
info@ lakelandcottages.co.uk
*Self-catering holiday
accommodation in the Lake District.*

Harrogate Holidays
01423 523 333
www.harrogateholidays.co.uk
bookings@harrogateholidays.co.uk
*Self-catering in the Yorkshire
town of Harrogate and across
North Yorkshire.*

Holiday Cottages Cornwall
01525 402 204
www.holidaycottagescornwall.com
*Cottages and apartments in the
coastal resorts of South Cornwall.*

Stay Northumbria
01665 721 380
www.staynorthumbria.co.uk
info@staynorthumbria.co.uk
*Self-catering holiday cottages in
Northumberland.*

Acanthus Holidays
01502 724 033
www.southwold-holidays.co.uk
websales@southwold-holidays.co.uk
*Self-catering properties along
Suffolk's heritage coastline.*

The Good Life Cottage Company
01539 437 417
www.thegoodlifecottageco.co.uk
stay@thegoodlifecottageco.co.uk
*Holiday cottages in the heart of the
Lake District.*

Lyme Coast Holidays
01297 791 792
www.lymecoastholidays.co.uk
info@lymecoastholidays.co.uk
*Self-catering cottages in Devon
and Dorset.*

The following agencies have been accredited by VisitEngland following an annual assessment of their policies and procedures. Individual accommodation that these agencies promote may not be part of the VisitEngland Quality Assessment Scheme. However, if the agency is part of the VisitEngland Quality Accredited Agency Scheme the agency should have their own programme of inspections in place, ensuring the accommodation they promote is rated to a comparable standard.

Accommodate London
020 7351 4849
www.accommodatelondon.com
Joanna@tennislondon.co.uk
*Accommodation based in
central London.*

Aspects Holidays
01736 754 242
www.aspects-holidays.co.uk
hello@aspects-holidays.co.uk
*In West Cornwall, St Ives and
Carbis Bay.*

Best of Brighton and Sussex Cottages
01273 308 779
www.bestofbrighton.co.uk
enquiries@bestofbrighton.co.uk
*Covering coastal Sussex from
Worthing to Eastbourne, as well as
Brighton and Hove.*

Blue Chip Holidays
0333 3317 152
www.bluechipholidays.co.uk
info@bluechipholidays.co.uk
*Accommodation available in
Cornwall, Devon, Dorset, the Isle of
Wight, and Yorkshire.*

Cadgwith Cove Cottages
01326 290 162
www.cadgwithcovecottages.co.uk
Covecottages@aol.com
*Self-catering in Cadgwith Cove and
surrounds on the Lizard peninsula in
coastal Cornwall.*

Classic Cottages
01326 555 555
www.classic.co.uk
enquiries@classic.co.uk
info@cornishrivieraholidays.co.uk
*Self-catering accommodation in the
South West.*

Coast & Country Cottages
01548 843 773
www.coastandcountry.co.uk
salcombe@coastandcountry.co.uk
*Properties in Salcombe, Dartmouth
and South Devon.*

Cornish Cottage Holidays
01326 573 808
www.cornishcottageholidays.co.uk
enquiries@
cornishcottageholidays.co.uk
Holiday cottages in Cornwall.

Cornish Horizons Holiday Cottages
01841 533 331
www.cornishhorizons.co.uk
cottages@cornishhorizons.co.uk
*Holiday cottages throughout
Cornwall*

Cornish Riviera Holidays
01736 797 891
www.cornishrivieraholidays.co.uk
info@cornishrivieraholidays.co.uk
St Ives fisherman's cottages and harbour side flats on the North Cornwall coast.

The Cornish Traditional Cottage Company
01208 821 666
www.corncott.com
bookings@corncott.com
Coastal and countryside self-catering holiday cottages in Cornwall.

Cottages4you
0345 268 1243
www.cottages4you.co.uk
Accommodation throughout the country.

Dorset Coastal Cottages
0800 980 4070
www.dorsetcoastalcottages.com
hols@dorsetcoastalcottages.com
Self-catering on the Dorset coast.

English Country Cottages
0845 268 0788
www.english-country-cottages.co.uk
Hand-picked holiday cottages in England.

Freedom Holiday Homes
01580 720 770
www.freedomholidayhomes.co.uk
info@freedomholidayhomes.co.uk
Over 250 cottages in Kent and Sussex.

Holiday Cottages
01237 459 999
www.holidaycottages.co.uk
bookings@holidaycottages.co.uk
Over 2,000 holiday cottages in popular destinations across the UK.

John Bray Cornish Holidays
01208 863 206
www.johnbraycornishholidays.co.uk
lettings@johnbray.co.uk
Cornish holiday cottages in Rock, Daymer Bay, Polzeath and Port Isaac.

Lakelovers
01539 488 855
www.lakelovers.co.uk
enquiries@lakelovers.co.uk
Properties to suit every occasion throughout the southern and central Lake District.

Lyme Bay Holidays
01297 443 363
www.lymebayholidays.co.uk
email@lymebayholidays.co.uk
Holiday homes in Lyme Regis and the surrounding coast and countryside areas.

Marsdens Cornish Cottages
01503 289 289
www.cornish-cottages.co.uk
cornwall@marsdens.co.uk
Self-catering accommodation throughout Cornwall.

Marsdens Devon Cottages
01271 813 777
www.marsdens.co.uk
devon@marsdens.co.uk
Over 380 cottages throughout North Devon and Exmoor.

Miles & Son
01929 423 333
www.milesandson.co.uk
holidays@milesandson.co.uk
Self-catering accommdation in Swanage and the surrounding villages on the Isle of Purbeck.

Milkbere Holiday Cottages
01297 20729
www.milkberehols.com
info@milkberehols.com
Accommodation in Devon and Dorset.

New Forest Cottages
01590 679 655
www.newforestcottages.co.uk
Self-catering holiday cottages in the New Forest area.

Norfolk Country Cottages
01263 715 779
www.norfolkcottages.co.uk
info@norfolkcottages.co.uk
Over 450 properties in Norfolk.

Rumsey Holiday Homes
01202 707 357
www.rhh.org
info@rhh.org
Central south coast houses, flats and bungalows in the Poole, Bournemouth and South Dorset area.

Salcombe & Dartmouth Holiday Homes
01548 843 485
www.salcombe.com
shh@salcombe.org
Properties within Salcombe and rural farm ares in the South Hams.

Suffolk Secrets
01502 722 717
www.suffolk-secrets.co.uk
holidays@suffolk-secrets.co.uk
Family owned with over 350 properties across Suffolk.

Toad Hall Cottages
01548 202 020
www.toadhallcottages.co.uk
thc@toadhallcottages.co.uk
Rural and waterside cottages in the South West.

Welcome Cottages
0845 268 0819
www.welcomecottages.com
Properties across the UK.

Whitby Holiday Cottages
01947 603 010
www.whitby-cottages.net
enquiries@whitby-cottages.net
Offering a large collection of cottages in Yorkshire.

There are hundreds of "Green" places to stay and visit in England from small bed and breakfasts to large visitor attractions and activity holiday providers. Businesses displaying this logo have undergone a rigorous verification process to ensure that they are sustainable (green) and that a qualified assessor has visited the premises.

We have indicated the accommodation which has achieved a Green award... look out for the 🌱 symbol in the entry.

Advice and information

Making a booking

When enquiring about accommodation, make sure you check prices, the quality rating and other important details. You will also need to state your requirements clearly and precisely, for example:

- Arrival and departure dates, with acceptable alternatives if appropriate;
- The accommodation you need;
- The number of people in your party and the ages of any children;
- Special requirements, such as ground-floor bathroom, garden, cot.

Confirmation

Misunderstandings can easily happen over the telephone, so do request a written confirmation, together with details of any terms and conditions that apply to your booking.

Deposits

When you book your self-catering holiday, the proprietor will normally ask you to pay a deposit immediately, and then to pay the full balance before your holiday date.

The reason for asking you to pay in advance is to safeguard the proprietor in case you decide to cancel at a late stage, or simply do not turn up. He or she may have turned down other bookings on the strength of yours, and may find it hard to re-let if you cancel.

Cancellations

Legal contract

When you accept accommodation that is offered to you, by telephone or in writing, you enter into a legally binding contract with the proprietor. This means that if you cancel your booking, fail to take up the accommodation or leave early, you will probably forfeit your deposit and may expect to be charged the balance at the end of the period booked if the place cannot be re-let. You should be advised at the time of the booking of what charges would be made in the event of cancelling the accommodation or leaving early, which is usually written into the property's terms and conditions. If this is not mentioned, you should ask the proprietor for any cancellation terms that apply before booking your accommodation to ensure any disputes are avoided. Where you have already paid the full amount before cancelling, the proprietor is likely to retain the money. However if the accommodation is re-let, the proprietor will make a refund to you which normally excludes the amount of the deposit.

Remember, if you book by telephone and are asked for your credit card number, you should check whether the proprietor intends to charge your credit card account, should you later cancel your reservation. A proprietor should not be able to charge your credit card account with a cancellation fee without your consent unless you agreed to this at the time of your booking. However, to avoid later disputes, we suggest you check whether this is the intention before providing your details.

Travelling with pets

Dogs, cats, ferrets and some other pets can be brought into the UK from certain countries without having to undertake six months' quarantine on arrival, provided they meet the requirements of the Pet Travel Scheme (PETS).

For full details, visit the PETS website at
w www.gov.uk/take-pet-abroad
or contact the PETS Helpline
t +44 (0)370 241 1710
e pettravel@ahvla.gsi.gov.uk
Ask for fact sheets which cover dogs and cats, ferrets or domestic rabbits and rodents.

There are no requirements for pets travelling directly between the UK and the Channel Islands. Pets entering Jersey or Guernsey from other countries need to be Pet Travel Scheme compliant and have a valid EU Pet Passport. For more information see www.jersey.com or www.visitguernsey.com.

Insurance

There are so many reasons why you might have to cancel your holiday, which is why we strongly advise people to take out a cancellation insurance policy. In fact, many self-catering agencies now advise their customers to take out a policy when they book their holiday.

Arrival time

If you know you will be arriving late in the evening, it is a good idea to say so when you book. If you are delayed on your way, a telephone call to say that you will be late is often appreciated.

It is particularly important to liaise with the proprietor about key collection as he or she may not be on site.

The proprietor/management is required to undertake the following:

Prior to booking
- To describe accurately in any advertisement, brochure, or other printed or electronic media, the facilities and services provided;
- To make clear to guests in print, electronic media and on the telephone exactly what is included in all prices quoted for accommodation, including taxes and any other surcharges. Details of charges for additional services/facilities should also be made clear, for example breakfast, leisure etc;
- To provide information on the suitability of the premises for guests of various ages, particularly for the elderly and the very young;
- To allow guests to view the accommodation prior to booking if requested.

At the time of booking
- To clearly describe the cancellation policy to guests i.e. by telephone, fax, internet/email as well as in any printed information given to guests;
- To adhere to and not to exceed prices quoted at the time of booking for accommodation and other services;
- To make clear to guests if the accommodation offered is in an unconnected annexe or similar, and to indicate the location of such accommodation and any difference in comfort and/or amenities from accommodation at the property.

On arrival
- To welcome all guests courteously and without discrimination in relation to gender, sexual orientation, disability, race, religion or belief.

During the stay
- To maintain standards of guest care, cleanliness, and service appropriate to the type of establishment;
- To deal promptly and courteously with all enquiries, requests, bookings and correspondence from guests;
- To ensure complaints received are investigated promptly and courteously to an outcome that is communicated to the guest.

On departure
- To give each guest, on request, details of payments due and a receipt, if required/requested.

General
- To give due consideration to the requirements of guests with special needs, and make suitable provision where applicable;
- To ensure the accommodation, when advertised as open, is prepared for the arrival of guests at all times;
- To advise guests, at any time prior to their stay, of any changes made to their booking;
- To have a complaints handling procedure in place to deal promptly and fairly with all guest complaints;
- To hold current public liability insurance and to comply with all relevant statuory obligations including legislation applicable to fire, health and safety, planning and food safety;
- To allow, on request, VisitEngland representatives reasonable access to the establishment, to confirm that the Code of Conduct is being observed or in order to investigate any complaint of a serious nature;

Comments and complaints

Information

Other than rating information, the proprietors themselves supply descriptions of their properties and other information for the entries in this book. They have all signed a declaration to confirm that their information accurately describes their accommodation business. The publishers cannot guarantee the accuracy of information in this guide, and accept no responsibility for any error or misrepresentation. All liability for loss, disappointment, negligence or other damage caused by reliance on the information contained in this guide, or in the event of bankruptcy or liquidation or cessation of trade of any company, individual or firm mentioned, is hereby excluded. We strongly recommend that you carefully check prices and other details before you book your accommodation.

Quality signage

All establishments displaying a quality sign have to hold current membership of VisitEngland's Quality Assessment Scheme.

When an establishment is sold, the new owner has to re-apply and be re-assessed. In certain circumstances the rating may be carried forward before the property is re-assessed.

Problems

Of course, we hope you will not have cause for complaint, but problems do occur from time to time. If you are dissatisfied with anything, make your complaint to the management immediately. Then the management can take action by investigating the matter in attempts to put things right. The longer you leave a complaint, the harder it is to deal with it effectively.

In certain circumstances, the national tourist board may look into your complaint. However, they have no statutory control over establishments or their methods of operating and cannot become involved in legal or contractual matters such as financial compensation.

If you do have problems that have not been resolved by the proprietor and which you would like to bring to their attention, please write to:
Quality in Tourism, 1320 Montpellier Court, Pioneer Way, Gloucester Business Park, Gloucester, Gloucestershire GL3 4AH

About the accommodation entries

Entries

All accommodation featured in this guide has been assessed or has applied for assessment under a quality assessment scheme.

Start your search for a place to stay by looking in the 'Where to Stay' sections of this guide, where proprietors have paid to have their establishment featured in either a standard entry (includes photograph, description, facilities and prices) or an enhanced entry (photograph(s) and extended details).

Locations

Places to stay are listed by town, city or village. If a property is located in a small village, you may find it listed under a nearby town (providing it is within a seven-mile radius).

Within each region, counties run in alphabetical order. Place names are listed alphabetically within each county, and include interesting county information and a map reference.

Complete addresses for rental properties are not given and the town(s) listed may be a distance from the actual property. Please check the precise location before booking.

Map references

These refer to the colour location maps at the back of the guide. The first figure shown is the map number, the following letter and figure indicate the grid reference on the map. Only place names that have a standard or enhanced entry feature appear on the maps. Some standard or enhanced entries were included in the scheme after the guide went to press, therefore they do not appear on the maps.

Telephone numbers

Booking telephone numbers are listed below the contact address for each entry. Area codes are shown in brackets.

Prices

The prices printed are to be used as a guide only; they were supplied to us by proprietors in summer 2014.

Remember, changes may occur after the guide goes to press, therefore we strongly advise you to check prices before booking your accommodation.

Prices are shown in pounds sterling, including VAT where applicable, and are per unit per week. Prices often vary throughout the year and may be significantly lower outside of peak periods. You can get details of other bargain packages that may be available from the establishments themselves, regional tourism organisations or your local Tourist Information Centre (TIC). Your local travel agent may also have information and can help you make your booking.

Some establishments do not accept pets at all. Pets are welcome by arrangement where you see this symbol ☍. The quarantine laws have changed and now dogs, cats and ferrets are able to come into Britain and the Channel Islands from over 50 countries. For details of the Pet Travel Scheme (PETS) please turn to page 365.

Payments accepted

The types of payment accepted by an establishment are listed in the payment accepted section. If you plan to pay by card, check that the establishment will accept the particular type of card you own before booking. Some proprietors will charge you a higher rate if you pay by credit card rather than cash or cheque. The difference is to cover the charges paid by the proprietor to the credit card company.

When you book by telephone, you may be asked for your credit card number as confirmation. Remember, the proprietor may then charge your credit card account if you cancel your booking. See details of this under Cancellations on page 364.

Opening period

If an entry does not indicate an opening period, please check directly with the proprietor.

Symbols

The at-a-glance symbols included at the end of each entry show many of the services and facilities available at each property. You will find the key to these symbols on page 7.

Smoking

In the UK and the Channel Islands, it is illegal to smoke in enclosed public spaces and places of work. Smoking may be allowed in self-contained short-term rental accommodation, such as holiday cottages, flats or caravans, if the owner chooses to allow it.

If you wish to smoke, we advise you to check the proprietor's smoking policy before you book.

Pets

Many places accept guests with dogs, but we advise that you check this with the proprietor before booking, remembering to ask if there are any extra charges or rules about exactly where your pet is allowed. The acceptance of dogs is not always extended to cats and it is strongly advised that cat owners contact the property well in advance of their stay.

Awaiting confirmation of rating

At the time of going to press some properties featured in this guide had not yet been assessed therefore their rating for this year could not be included. The term 'Rating Applied For' indicates this throughout your guide.

Getting around

Travelling in London

London transport

Each London Underground line has its own unique colour, so you can easily follow them on the Underground map. Most lines run through central London, and many serve parts of Greater London. Buses are a quick, convenient way to travel around London, providing plenty of sightseeing opportunities along the way. There are over 6,500 buses in London operating 700 routes every day. You will need to buy a ticket or Travel Pass before you board the bus.

London's National Rail system stretches all over London. Many lines start at the main London railway stations (Paddington, Victoria, Waterloo, Kings Cross) with links to the tube. Trains mainly serve areas outside central London, and travel overground.

Children usually travel free, or at reduced fare, on all public transport in London.

Oyster cards

Oyster cards can be used to pay fares on all London Underground, buses, Docklands Light Railway and trams, however are generally not valid for National Rail services in London.

Oyster cards are very easy to use, you just touch the card on sensors at stations or on buses and you are charged the lowest fare available for your journey. You buy credit for your journey and when it runs out you simply top up with more.

Oyster cards are available to adults only. Children below the age of 11 can accompany adults free of charge. Children between the ages of 11 and 15 can travel free on buses and trams and at child rate on Tube, DLR and London Overground services, provided they have an 11-15 Zip Oyster photocard. You can purchase an Oyster card for a fee of £5, which is refundable on its return, at any underground station, one of 3,000 Oyster points around London displaying the London Underground sign (usually shops), or from www.visitbritainshop.com, or www.oyster.tfl.gov.uk/oyster

London congestion charge

The congestion charge is £11.50 daily charge to drive in central London at certain times. Check if the congestion charge is included in the cost of your car before booking. If your car's pick up point is in the congestion-charging zone, the company may pay the charge for the first day of your hire.

Low Emission Zone

The Low Emission Zone is an area covering most of Greater London, within which the most polluting diesel-engine vehicles are required to meet specific emissions standards. If your vehicle does not, you will be required to pay a daily charge.

Vehicles affected by the Low Emission Zone are older diesel-engine lorries, buses, coaches, large vans, minibuses and other heavy vehicles such as motor caravans and motorised horse boxes. This also includes vehicles registered outside of Great Britain. Cars and motorcycles are not affected by this scheme. For more information visit www.tfl.gov.uk

Rail and train travel

Britain's rail network covers all main cities and smaller regional towns. Trains on the network are operated by a few large companies running routes from London to stations all over Britain. Therefore smaller companies that run routes in regional areas. You can find up-to-the-minute information about routes, fares and train times on the National Rail Enquiries website (www.nationalrail.co.uk). For detailed information about routes and services, refer to the train operators' websites (see page 377).

Railway passes

BritRail offer a wide selection of passes and tickets giving you the freedom to travel on all National Rail services. Passes can also include sleeper services, city and attraction passes and boat tours. Passes can usually be purchased from travel agents outside Britain or by visiting the BritRail website www.britrail.net.

Bus and coach travel

Public buses

Every city and town in Britain has a local bus service. These services are privatised and managed by separate companies. The largest bus companies in Britain are First (www.firstgroup.com/ukbus), Stagecoach (www.stagecoachbus.com) and Arriva (www.arrivabus.co.uk), and run buses in most UK towns. Outside London, buses usually travel to and from the town centre or to the busiest part of town. Most towns have a bus station, where you'll be able to find maps and information about routes. Bus route information may also be posted at bus stops.

Tickets and fares

The cost of a bus ticket normally depends on how far you're travelling. Return fares may be available on some buses, but you would usually need to buy a 'single' ticket for each individual journey.

You can also buy your ticket when boarding a bus by telling the driver where you are going. One-day and weekly travel cards are available in some towns, and these can be purchased from either the driver or from an information centre at the bus station. Tickets are valid for each separate journey rather than for a period of time, so if you get off the bus you'll need to buy a new ticket when getting on another.

Domestic flights

Flying is a time-saving alternative to road or rail when it comes to travelling around Britain. Domestic flights are fast and frequent and there are 33 airports across Britain that operate domestic routes. You will find airports marked on the maps at the front of this guide.

Domestic flight advice

Photo ID is required to travel on domestic flights. However it is advisable to bring your passport as not all airlines will accept other forms of photo identification. Please be aware of the high security measures at all airports in Britain which include include restrictions on items that may be carried in hand luggage. It is important that you check the restrictions in place with your airline prior to travel, as these can vary over time and don't forget to allow adequate time for check-in and boarding on arrival.

Cycling

Cycling is a great way to see some of England's iconic scenery and there are many networks of cycling routes available across England. The National Cycle Network offers over 10,000 miles of walking and cycling routes details for connecting towns and villages, countryside and coast across England. For more information and view these routes see page 373 or visit Sustrans at www.sustrans.co.uk.

Think green

If you'd rather leave your car behind and travel by 'green transport' to some of the attractions highlighted in this guide you'll be helping to reduce congestion and pollution as well as supporting conservation charities in their commitment to green travel.

The National Trust encourages visits made by non-car travellers and it offers admission discounts or a voucher for the tea room at a selection of its properties if you arrive on foot, cycle or public transport (you may need to produce a valid bus or train ticket if travelling by public transport.).

More information about The National Trust's work to encourage car-free days out can be found at www.nationaltrust.org.uk. (Refer to the section entitled 'Information for Visitors').

If you have
access needs...

Guests with hearing, visual or mobility needs can feel confident about booking accommodation that participates in the National Accessible Scheme (NAS).

Look out for the NAS symbols which are included throughout the accommodation directory. Using the NAS could help make the difference between a good holiday and a perfect one!

For more information on the NAS and tips & ideas on holiday travel in England, go to: www.visitengland.com/accessforall

Here are just some of the most popular long distance routes on the 12,000 mile Sustrans National Cycle Network. To see the Network in it's entirety and to find routes near you, visit **www.sustrans.org.uk**

Sustrans is the UK's leading sustainable transport charity working on practical projects to enable people to choose to travel in ways which benefit their health and the environment.

68 National Cycle Network Route Number

Long Distance Routes

1. Coast & Castles Cycle Route
2. Pennine Cycleway - North Pennines
3. Hadrian's Cycleway
4. Sea to Sea
5. Pennine Cycleway - South Pennines & the Dales
6. Derby to York
7. Hull to Fakenham
8. East of England
9. South Midlands Cycle Route
10. Thames Valley Cycle Route
11. Garden of England
12. Downs & Weald Cycle Route
13. Devon Coast to Coast
14. The Cornish Way
15. The West Country Way
16. The Severn & Thames

Map reproduced from Ordnance Survey material with the permission of Ordnance Survey on behalf of the Controller of Her Majesty's Stationery Office © Crown copyright. Unauthorised reproduction infringes Crown copyright and may lead to prosecution or civil proceedings. Licence number 100020852 (2009)

By car and by train

Distance chart

The distances between towns on the chart below are given to the nearest mile, and are measured along routes based on the quickest travelling time, making maximum use of motorways or dual-carriageway roads. The chart is based upon information supplied by the Automobile Association.

To calculate the distance in kilometres multiply the mileage by 1.6
For example: Brighton to Dover
82 miles x 1.6 =131.2 kilometres

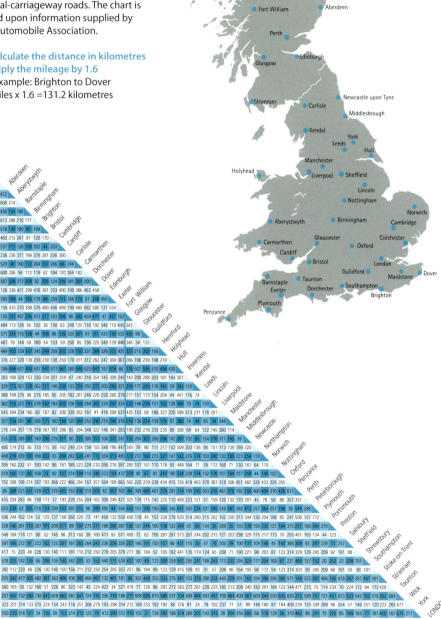

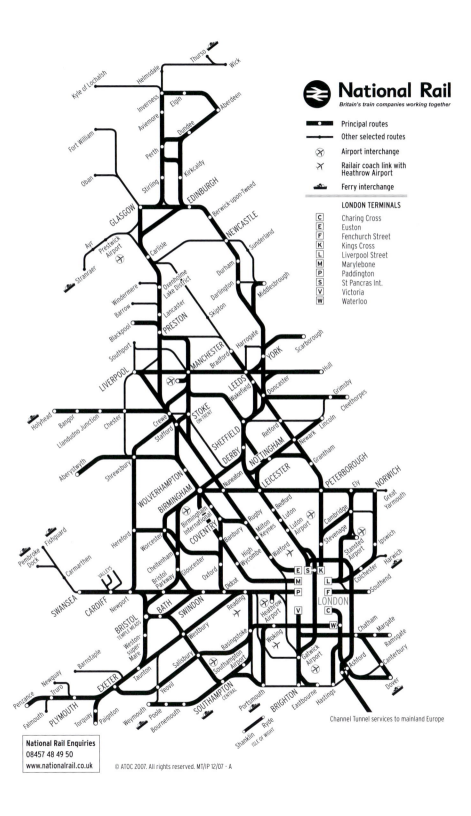

National Rail
Britain's train companies working together

Principal routes	
Other selected routes	
✈	Airport interchange
✈	Railair coach link with Heathrow Airport
⛴	Ferry interchange

LONDON TERMINALS

C	Charing Cross
E	Euston
F	Fenchurch Street
K	Kings Cross
L	Liverpool Street
M	Marylebone
P	Paddington
S	St Pancras Int.
V	Victoria
W	Waterloo

Channel Tunnel services to mainland Europe

Travel information

General travel information

Streetmap	www.streetmap.co.uk	
Transport for London	www.tfl.gov.uk	0843 222 1234
Travel Services	www.departures-arrivals.com	
Traveline	www.traveline.info	0871 200 2233

Bus & coach

Megabus	www.megabus.com	0900 160 0900
National Express	www.nationalexpress.com	08717 818 178
WA Shearings	www.shearings.com	0844 824 6351

Car & car hire

AA	www.theaa.com	0800 085 2721
Green Flag	www.greenflag.com	0845 246 1557
RAC	www.rac.co.uk	0844 308 9177
Alamo	www.alamo.co.uk	0871 384 1086*
Avis	www.avis.co.uk	0844 581 0147*
Budget	www.budget.co.uk	0844 544 3407*
Easycar	www.easycar.com	
Enterprise	www.enterprise.com	0800 800 227*
Hertz	www.hertz.co.uk	0870 844 8844*
Holiday Autos	www.holidayautos.co.uk	0871 472 5229
National	www.nationalcar.co.uk	0871 384 1140
Thrifty	www.thrifty.co.uk	01494 751500

Air

Air Southwest	www.airsouthwest.com	0870 043 4553
Blue Islands (Channel Islands)	www.blueislands.com	08456 20 2122
BMI	www.flybmi.com	0844 848 4888
BMI Baby	www.bmibaby.com	0905 828 2828*
British Airways	www.ba.com	0844 493 0787
British International (Isles of Scilly to Penzance)	www.islesofscillyhelicopter.com	01736 363871*
CityJet	www.cityjet.com	0871 663 3777
Eastern Airways	www.easternairways.com	08703 669100
Easyjet	www.easyjet.com	0843 104 5000
Flybe	www.flybe.com	0871 700 2000*
Jet2.com	www.jet2.com	0871 226 1737*
Manx2	www.manx2.com	0871 200 0440*
Ryanair	www.ryanair.com	0871 246 0000
Skybus (Isles of Scilly)	www.islesofscilly-travel.co.uk	0845 710 5555
Thomsonfly	www.thomsonfly.com	0871 231 4787

Train

National Rail Enquiries	www.nationalrail.co.uk	0845 748 4950
The Trainline	www.trainline.co.uk	0871 244 1545
UK train operating companies	www.rail.co.uk	
Arriva Trains	www.arriva.co.uk	0191 520 4000
c2c	www.c2c-online.co.uk	0845 601 4873
Chiltern Railways	www.chilternrailways.co.uk	0845 600 5165
CrossCountry	www.crosscountrytrains.co.uk	0844 811 0124
East Midlands Trains	www.eastmidlandstrains.co.uk	0845 712 5678
Eurostar	www.eurostar.com	08432 186 186*
First Capital Connect	www.firstcapitalconnect.co.uk	0845 026 4700
First Great Western	www.firstgreatwestern.co.uk	0845 700 0125
Gatwick Express	www.gatwickexpress.com	0845 850 1530
Heathrow Connect	www.heathrowconnect.com	0845 678 6975
Heathrow Express	www.heathrowexpress.com	0845 600 1515
Hull Trains	www.hulltrains.co.uk	0845 071 0222
Island Line	www.islandlinetrains.co.uk	0845 600 0650
London Midlands	www.londonmidland.com	0121 634 2040
Merseyrail	www.merseyrail.org	0151 702 2071
National Express East Anglia	www.nationalexpresseastanglia.com	0845 600 7245
National Express East Coast	www.nationalexpresseastcoast.com	0845 722 5333
Northern Rail	www.northernrail.org	0845 000 0125
ScotRail	www.scotrail.co.uk	0845 601 5929
South Eastern Trains	www.southeasternrailway.co.uk	0845 000 2222
South West Trains	www.southwesttrains.co.uk	0845 600 0650
Southern	www.southernrailway.com	0845 127 2920
Stansted Express	www.stanstedexpress.com	0845 600 7245
Translink	www.translink.co.uk	(028) 9066 6630
Transpennine Express	www.tpexpress.co.uk	0845 600 1671
Virgin Trains	www.virgintrains.co.uk	08450 008 000*

Ferry

Ferry Information	www.discoverferries.com	0207 436 2449
Condor Ferries	www.condorferries.co.uk	0845 609 1024*
Steam Packet Company	www.steam-packet.com	08722 992 992*
Isles of Scilly Travel	www.islesofscilly-travel.co.uk	0845 710 5555
Red Funnel	www.redfunnel.co.uk	0844 844 9988
Wight Link	www.wightlink.co.uk	0871 376 1000

Phone numbers listed are for general enquiries unless otherwise stated.
* Booking line only

National Accessible Scheme index

Establishments with a detailed entry in this guide who participate in the National Accessible Scheme are listed below. At the front of the guide you can find information about the scheme. Establishments are listed alphabetically by place name.

🦽 Mobility level 1

Bacton, East of England	**Primrose Cottage ★★★**	162
Bamburgh, North East	**Outchester & Ross Farm Cottages ★★★★ - ★★★★★ Gold**	333
Bath, South West	**Greyfield Farm Cottages ★★★★ - ★★★★★ Gold**	82
Canterbury, South East	**Broome Park Golf and Country Club ★★★★**	116
Dilhorne,	**Little Summerhill Cottages ★★★★**	235
Falmouth, South West	**Mylor Harbourside Holidays ★★★★**	46
Hartington,	**Old House Farm Cottages ★★★★**	199
Hogsthorpe,	**Helsey House Holiday Cottages ★★★★**	204
Ledbury,	**Old Kennels Farm ★★★ - ★★★★**	229
Lydney, South West	**2 Danby Cottages ★★★★**	78
Malton,	**Walnut Garth ★★★★ Gold**	267
Minehead, South West	**Woodcombe Lodges & Cottages ★★★★**	85
Newquay, South West	**The Park ★★★★ - ★★★★★ Gold**	50
Padstow, South West	**Yellow Sands Cottages ★★★ - ★★★★ Gold**	52
Porthtowan, South West	**Rosehill Lodges ★★★★ Gold**	53
Ross-on-Wye,	**Flanesford Priory ★★★ - ★★★★★**	229
St. Bees,	**Springbank Farm Lodges ★★★★**	304

🦽 Mobility level 2

Bacton, East of England	**Primrose Cottage ★★★**	162
Fowey, South West	**South Torfrey Farm Ltd ★★★★ - ★★★★★**	46
Hartington, East Midlands	**Old House Farm Cottages ★★★★**	199
Lydney, South West	**2 Danby Cottages ★★★★**	78
Minehead, South West	**Woodcombe Lodges & Cottages ★★★★**	85
Newquay, South West	**The Park ★★★★ - ★★★★★ Gold**	50
Pateley Bridge, Yorkshire	**Helme Pasture Lodges & Cottages ★★★★**	268
Southport, North West	**Sandy Brook Farm ★★★**	3137

♿ Mobility level 3 Independent

Haltwhistle, North East	**Lambley Farm Cottages ★ ★ ★ ★**	336
Ormskirk, North West	**Martin Lane Farm Holiday Cottages ★ ★ ★ ★ - ★ ★ ★ ★ ★**	310

♿ Mobility level 3 Assisted

Cornriggs, North East	**Cornriggs Cottages ★ ★ ★ ★ ★**	329
Spixworth, East of England	**Spixworth Hall Cottages ★ ★ ★ ★**	172

Hearing impairment level 1

Cornriggs, North East	**Cornriggs Cottages ★ ★ ★ ★ ★**	329
St. Bees, North West	**Springbank Farm Lodges ★ ★ ★ ★**	304

Visual impairment level 1

Canterbury, South East	**Broome Park Golf and Country Club ★ ★ ★ ★**	116
St. Bees, North West	**Springbank Farm Lodges ★ ★ ★ ★**	304

Gold Award winners

Establishments with a detailed entry in this guide that have achieved recognition of exceptional quality are listed below. Establishment are listed alphabetically by place name.

South West

Bath, **Greyfield Farm Cottages** ★★★★ - ★★★★★	82
Bath, **Nailey Cottages** ★★★★	82
Bigbury-on-Sea,	
Apartment 5, Burgh Island Causeway ★★★★★	60
Blakeney, **Oatfield Country Cottages** ★★★★	76
Bradford-on-Avon, **Bridge Cottage** ★★★★	89
Bude, **Tamar Valley Cottages** ★★★★	42
Bude, **Whalesborough Cottages** ★★★★★	43
Bude, **Wooldown Holiday Cottages** ★★★★ - ★★★★★	44
Cheltenham, **Church Court Cottage**s ★★★★★	76
Cirencester, **The Stables** ★★★★★	77
Cullompton, **Wayside House** ★★★★★	61
Gorran, **Owls Roost** ★★★★	47
Helston, **Lizard Peninsula Holiday Cottages** ★★★★	47
Holsworthy, **Woodford Bridge Country Club** ★★★	64
Liskeard, **Rivermead Farm** ★★★★	48
Martock, **Anne's Place** ★★★	85
Mitcheldean, **Holme House Barn** ★★★★	78
Newquay, **Headland Cottages** ★★★★★	49
Newquay, **The Park** ★★★★ - ★★★★★	50
Okehampton, **Peartree Cottage** ★★★★	65
Padstow, **Honeysuckle Cottage** ★★★	50
Padstow, **Sunday & School Cottages** ★★★★	51
Padstow, **Yellow Sands Cottages** ★★★ - ★★★★	52
Port Isaac, **Green Door Cottages Port Gaverne** ★★★★	53
Porthtowan, **Rosehill Lodges** ★★★★★	53
Redruth, **Trengove Farm Cottages** ★★★★ - ★★★★★	54
Ringstead, **Upton Grange Holiday Cottages** ★★★★	74
Seaton, **Mount Brioni Holiday Apartments** ★★★ - ★★★★	5
South Molton, **Drewstone Farm** ★★★★	67
St. Austell, **Natural Retreats - Trewhiddle** ★★★★★	55
St. Columb, **Cornish Holiday Lodges** ★★★ - ★★★★	55
St. Ives, **The Apartment, Porthminster Beach** ★★★★	56
St. Mary's, **Dunmallard - Lower Flat** ★★★	59
Stow-on-the-Wold, **Broad Oak Cottages** ★★★★★	78
Stroud, **Barncastle** ★★★★★	79
Tetbury, **The Tythe House and Barn Complex** ★★★★★	79
Totnes, **Aish Cross Holiday Cottages** ★★★★★	68
Truro, **The Valley** ★★★★★	57
Wadebridge, **St Moritz Self Catering** ★★★★★	58
Wedmore, **Pear Tree Cottages** ★★★★	87
Wellington, **The Cottage Beyond** ★★★★★	87
Wellington, **Tone Dale House** ★★★★★	88

Westward Ho!, **Seascape** ★★★★★	69
Whilborough, **Long Barn Luxury Holiday Cottages** ★★★★	69
Yeovil, **Mrs Bests Holiday Cottage** ★★★★	89

South East

Alresford, **Cheriton Wood Studio** ★★★★	109
Bicester, **Grange Farm Country Cottages** ★★★★	121
Chichester, **Honer Cottage** ★★★	125
Chichester, **Laneside** ★★★★	125
Chipping Norton,	
Heath Farm Holiday Cottages ★★★★ - ★★★★★	121
Crowborough, **Hodges** ★★★★★	126
Edenbridge, **Medley Court - Hever Castle** ★★★★★	117
Fordingbridge, **Burgate Manor Farm Holidays** ★★★★	110
Glynde, **Caburn Cottages** ★★	127
Godalming, **Prestwick Self Catering** ★★★★	123
Hailsham, **Little Marshfoot** ★★★★	127
Pitt, **South Winchester Lodges** ★★★★★	111
Portsmouth and Southsea,	
Admiralty Apartments ★★★★ - ★★★★★	112
Uckfield, **Sunnymead Farm Cottages** ★★★★	129
Whitwell, **Nettlecombe Farm**	
Holiday Cottages & Fishing Lakes ★★★★	114

East of England

Billericay, **The Pump House Apartment** ★★★★★	159
Bodham, **Rookery Farm Norfolk** ★★ - ★★★★	162
Bury St. Edmunds, **Lackford Lakes Barns** ★★★★	177
Cromer, **Cromer Country Club** ★★★ - ★★★★	164
Cromer,	
The Poplars Caravan & Chalet Park ★★★ - ★★★★	164
Eye, **Log Cabin Holidays** ★★★★	178
Fakenham, **2 Westgate Barns** ★★★★	165
Fakenham, **Brazenhall Barn & Lodge** ★★★★★	165
Field Dalling, **Hard Farm Barns** ★★★★	166
King's Lynn, **Rainbow Cottage** ★★★	169
North Walsham, **Courtyard Barns** ★★★★	170
Saxmundham, **Buff's Old Barn** ★★★★	180
Weasenham, **Lavender Lodge** ★★★★	173
Wickmere, **Church Farm Barns** ★★★ - ★★★★	175

East Midlands

Alford, **Woodthorpe Hall Country Cottages** ★★★★	202
Buxton, **Pyegreave Cottage** ★★★★	198
Castleton, **Riding House Farm Cottages** ★★★★★	198

Walkers and cyclists welcome

Look out for quality-assessed accommodation displaying the Walkers Welcome and Cyclists Welcome signs.

Participants in these schemes actively encourage and support walking and cycling. In addition to special meal arrangements and helpful information, they'll provide a water supply to wash off the mud, an area for drying wet clothing and footwear, maps and books to look up cycling and walking routes and even an emergency puncture-repair kit! Bikes can also be locked up securely undercover.

The standards for these schemes have been developed in partnership with the tourist boards in Northern Ireland, Scotland and Wales, so wherever you're travelling in the UK you'll receive the same welcome.

Walkers Welcome & Cyclists Welcome

Establishments participating in the Walkers Welcome and Cyclists Welcome schemes provide special facilities and actively encourage these recreations. Accommodation with a detailed entry in this guide is listed below. Place names are listed alphabetically.

▶ 🚲 Walkers Welcome & Cyclists Welcome

Allendale, North East	**Fell View Cottage ★ ★ ★ ★**	330
Allonby, North West	**Crookhurst Farm Cottages ★ ★ ★ ★**	297
Ashby-de-la-Zouch, East Midlands	**Forest Lodge ★ ★ ★ ★**	201
Atherstone, Heart of England	**Hipsley Farm Cottages ★ ★ ★ ★**	237
Barnard Castle, North East	**Hauxwell Grange Cottages**	
	(The Stone Byre & Curlew Cottage) ★ ★ ★ ★ Gold	328
Bewdley, Heart of England	**Fern Cottage ★ ★ ★ ★**	239
Bishop Auckland, North East	**Whitfield House Cottage ★ ★ ★**	329
Bodham, East of England	**Rookery Farm Norfolk ★ ★ - ★ ★ ★ ★ Gold**	162
Bradford, Yorkshire	**Hewenden Mill Cottages ★ ★ ★ ★ - ★ ★ ★ ★ ★**	280
Brooke, East Midlands	**America Lodge ★ ★ ★**	210
Buxton, East Midlands	**Pyegreave Cottage ★ ★ ★ ★ Gold**	198
Castleton, East Midlands	**Riding House Farm Cottages ★ ★ ★ ★ ★ Gold**	198
Chapel Lawn, Heart of England	**The Squire Farm Holiday Cottages ★ ★ ★ ★**	230
Chesterfield, East Midlands	**Pottery Flat Chesterfield ★ ★ ★ Gold**	198
Clitheroe, North West	**Cobden View ★ ★ ★ ★**	308
Dawlish, South West	**Cofton Country Holidays ★ ★ ★ ★**	62
Fakenham, East of England	**Pollywiggle Cottage ★ ★ ★ ★**	166
Fareham, South East	**Cowes View Coastguard Cottage ★ ★ ★ ★**	109
Farnham, South East	**Bentley Green Farm ★ ★ ★ ★ ★**	123
Field Dalling, East of England	**Hard Farm Barns ★ ★ ★ ★ Gold**	166
Fordingbridge, South East	**Burgate Manor Farm Holidays ★ ★ ★ ★ Gold**	110
Giggleswick, Yorkshire	**Ivy Cottage (Giggleswick) Limited ★ ★ ★ ★**	261
Great Yarmouth, East of England	**Clippesby Hall Holiday Park**	167
Hailsham, South East	**Little Marshfoot ★ ★ ★ ★ Gold**	127
Hebden Bridge, Yorkshire	**Chalet at Cairnacre ★ ★**	280
Helford, South West	**Mudgeon Vean Farm Holiday Cottages ★ ★ ★ - ★ ★ ★ ★**	47
Helston, South West	**Lizard Peninsula Holiday Cottages ★ ★ ★ ★ Gold**	47
Hereford, Heart of England	**Monkhall Cottages ★ ★ ★ ★ ★ Gold**	228
Horsham, South East	**Ghyll Cottage ★ ★ ★ ★**	127
Kersey, East of England	**Wheelwrights Cottage ★ ★ ★ ★ ★**	178
Louth, East Midlands	**Church Cottage ★ ★ ★ ★ Gold**	205
Louth, East Midlands	**Louth Barn ★ ★ ★ ★ Gold**	205
Ludlow, Heart of England	**Glebe Barn ★ ★ ★ ★ Gold**	23
Ludlow, Heart of England	**Sutton Court Farm Cottages ★ ★ ★ - ★ ★ ★ ★**	233
Ludlow, Heart of England	**The Silver Pear Apartments ★ ★ ★ ★ Gold**	233

Lyme Regis, South West	Cecilia's Cottage ★★★★★	73
Market Harborough, East Midlands	Foxton Locks Lodges ★★★★ - ★★★★★ Gold	202
Mitcheldean, South West	Holme House Barn ★★★★ Gold	78
Netherseal, East Midlands	Sealbrook Farm ★★★★	200
Newquay, South West	The Park ★★★★ - ★★★★★ Gold	5
North Dalton, Yorkshire	Old Cobbler's Cottage ★★★	259
Nunthorpe, Yorkshire	Blackthorn Gate ★★★★ Gold	268
Okehampton, South West	Peartree Cottage ★★★★ Gold	65
Oxford, South East	Oxford Country Cottages ★★★★	122
Pickering, Yorkshire	Ashfield Cottages ★★★★ Gold	269
Pickering, Yorkshire	Kale Pot Cottage ★★★★ Gold	269
Ringstead, South West	Upton Grange Holiday Cottages ★★★★ Gold	74
Saxmundham, East of England	Saxmundham Cottages ★★★★	181
Seahouses, North East	1, 2 & 3 The Old Bakery ★★★	339
Settle, Yorkshire	Bent House Farm Cottage ★★★★	273
Snodland, South East	Sandhole Barn ★★★★	120
Spixworth, East of England	Spixworth Hall Cottages ★★★★	172
St. Bees, North West	Springbank Farm Lodges ★★★★	304
Stretton, East Midlands	Stretton Lakes ★★★★ - ★★★★★ Gold	210
Tewkesbury, South West	9 Mill Bank ★★	79
Totnes, South West	Aish Cross Holiday Cottages ★★★★ Gold	68
Wadebridge, South West	St Moritz Self Catering ★★★★ Gold	58
Wasdale, North West	Bleng Barn ★★★★	305
Waterhouses, Heart of England	Greenside Cottages ★★★ - ★★★★	236
Wellington, South West	Tone Dale House ★★★★ Gold	88
Whitby, Yorkshire	Forest Lodge Farm ★★★★ Gold	275
Worston, North West	Angram Green Holiday Cottages ★★★★	312

Walkers Welcome

Bath, South West	Nailey Cottages ★★★★ Gold	82
Corbridge, North East	April Cottage ★★★★	335
Fakenham, East of England	Brazenhall Barn & Lodge ★★★★★ Gold	165
Guarlford, Heart of England	Rhydd Barn ★★★★ Gold	240
Henley-in-Arden, Heart of England	The Cottage Kyte Green ★★★★	237
Hexham, North East	Braemar ★★★★	336
Malvern, Heart of England	Apartment 3 Highlea ★★★	240
Morpeth, North East	Cartwheel Cottage ★★★	337
Pershore, Heart of England	Garth Cottage ★★★★	241
Ross-on-Wye, Heart of England	Flanesford Priory ★★★ - ★★★★★	229
St. Columb, South West	Cornish Holiday Lodges ★★★ - ★★★★ Gold	55
Wedmore, South West	Pear Tree Cottages ★★★★ Gold	87
York, Yorkshire	Minster's Reach Apartments ★★★★ Gold	278

Welcome Pets!

Want to travel with your faithful companion? Look out for accommodation displaying the **Welcome Pets!** sign. Participants in this scheme go out of their way to meet the needs of guests bringing dogs, cats and/or small birds. In addition to providing water and food bowls, torches or nightlights, spare leads and pet washing facilities, they'll buy in food on request, and offer toys, treats and bedding. They'll also have information on pet-friendly attractions, pubs, restaurants and recreation. Of course, not everyone is able to offer suitable facilities for every pet, so do check if there are any restrictions on type, size and number of animals when you book.

Look out for the following symbol in the entry.

Families and Pets Welcome

Establishments participating in the Families Welcome or Welcome Pets! schemes provide special facilities and actively encourage families or guests with pets. Accommodation with a detailed entry in this guide is listed below. Place names are listed alphabetically.

Families and Pets Welcome

Allonby, North West	Crookhurst Farm Cottages ★★★★	297
Ashby-de-la-Zouch, East Midlands	Forest Lodge ★★★★	201
Beverley, Yorkshire	Heron Lakes ★★★★ Gold	258
Blakeney, South West	Oatfield Country Cottages ★★★★ Gold	76
Bodham, East of England	Rookery Farm Norfolk ★★ - ★★★★ Gold	162
Brooke, East Midlands	America Lodge ★★★	210
Clitheroe, North West	Cobden View ★★★★	308
Fakenham, East of England	Brazenhall Barn & Lodge ★★★★★ Gold	165
Fordingbridge, South East	Burgate Manor Farm Holidays ★★★★ Gold	110
Hartington, East Midlands	Old House Farm Cottages ★★★★	199
Henley-in-Arden, Heart of England	The Cottage Kyte Green ★★★★	237
Louth, East Midlands	Church Cottage ★★★★ Gold	205
Macclesfield, North West	Cheshire Hunt Holiday Cottages ★★★★	296
Mitcheldean, South West	Holme House Barn ★★★★ Gold	78
Newquay, South West	The Park ★★★★ - ★★★★★ Gold	50
Nunthorpe, Yorkshire	Blackthorn Gate ★★★★ Gold	268
Okehampton, South West	Peartree Cottage ★★★★ Gold	65
Oxford, South East	Oxford Country Cottages ★★★★	122
Shanklin, South East	Luccombe Villa Holiday Apartments ★★★★	113

🏠 Families Welcome

Bath, South West	**68 Ashgrove ★ ★ ★**	82
Bewdley, Heart of England	**Fern Cottage ★ ★ ★ ★**	239
Binegar, South West	**Spindle Cottage ★ ★ ★ ★**	83
Carlisle, North West	**Brackenhill Tower & Jacobean Cottage ★ ★ ★ ★ - ★ ★ ★ ★ ★ Gold**	300
Chesterfield, East Midlands	**Pottery Flat Chesterfield ★ ★ ★ Gold**	198
Easby, Yorkshire	**Abbey House ★ ★ ★ ★ Gold**	260
Edenbridge, South East	**Medley Court - Hever Castle ★ ★ ★ ★ Gold**	117
Fakenham, East of England	**2 Westgate Barns ★ ★ ★ Gold**	165
Fakenham, East of England	**Pollywiggle Cottage ★ ★ ★ ★**	166
Helston, South West	**Lizard Peninsula Holiday Cottages ★ ★ ★ Gold**	47
Hereford, Heart of England	**Monkhall Cottages ★ ★ ★ ★ Gold**	228
Horsham, South East	**Ghyll Cottage ★ ★ ★ ★**	127
London SW20, London	**Thalia Holiday Home ★ ★ ★ ★**	143
Louth, East Midlands	**Louth Barn ★ ★ ★ Gold**	205
Ludlow, Heart of England	**The Silver Pear Apartments ★ ★ ★ ★ Gold**	233
Netherseal, East Midlands	**Sealbrook Farm ★ ★ ★ ★**	200
Pin Mill, East of England	**Alma Cottage ★ ★**	180
Scarborough, Yorkshire	**The Sands Sea Front Apartments ★ ★ ★ ★ Gold**	272
Sedgeberrow, Heart of England	**Hall Farm Cottages ★ ★ ★ ★**	241
Spixworth, East of England	**Spixworth Hall Cottages ★ ★ ★ ★**	172
St. Austell, South West	**The Old Inn, Pentewan ★ ★ ★**	55
St. Columb, South West	**Cornish Holiday Lodges ★ ★ ★ - ★ ★ ★ ★ Gold**	55
Stretton, East Midlands	**Stretton Lakes ★ ★ ★ ★ - ★ ★ ★ ★ ★ Gold**	210
Stroud, South West	**Barncastle ★ ★ ★ ★ Gold**	79
Wadebridge, South West	**St Moritz Self Catering ★ ★ ★ ★ Gold**	58
Whilborough, South West	**Long Barn Luxury Holiday Cottages ★ ★ ★ Gold**	69
Whitby, Yorkshire	**Forest Lodge Farm ★ ★ ★ ★ Gold**	275
York, Yorkshire	**Minster's Reach Apartments ★ ★ ★ Gold**	278

🐾 Pets Welcome

Bishop Auckland, North East	**Whitfield House Cottage ★ ★ ★**	329
Field Dalling, East of England	**Hard Farm Barns ★ ★ ★ ★ Gold**	166
Ludlow, Heart of England	**Ashford Farm Cottages ★ ★ ★ ★ - ★ ★ ★ ★ ★ Gold**	231
North Dalton, Yorkshire	**Old Cobbler's Cottage ★ ★ ★**	259
Pateley Bridge, Yorkshire	**Helme Pasture Lodges & Cottages ★ ★ ★ ★**	268
Poole, South West	**Harbour Holidays ★ ★**	74
Saxmundham, East of England	**Saxmundham Cottages ★ ★ ★ ★**	181
Settle, Yorkshire	**Bent House Farm Cottage ★ ★ ★ ★**	273
Staithes, Yorkshire	**Pennysteel Cottage ★ ★ ★**	274
Totnes, South West	**Swift Cottage ★ ★ ★ ★**	69
Worcester, Heart of England	**Hop Pickers Rural Retreats ★ ★ ★ ★ Gold**	243

Swimming Pools index

If you're looking for accommodation with swimming facilities use this index to see at a glance detailed accommodation entries that match your requirement. Establishments are listed alphabetically by place name.

🏊 Indoor pool

Abingdon-on-Thames, South East	**Kingfisher Barn Holiday Cottages ★★★★**	120
Allonby, North West	**Crookhurst Farm Cottages ★★★★**	297
Ambleside, North West	**The Lakelands ★★★★**	298
Bellingham, North East	**Riverdale Court ★★★**	334
Bigbury-on-Sea, South West	**Apartment 5, Burgh Island Causeway ★★★★★ Gold**	60
Bowness-on-Windermere, North West	**Burnside Park ★★★★**	299
Bude, South West	**Coombe View ★★★★**	42
Bude, South West	**Whalesborough Cottages ★★★★★ Gold**	43
Bude, South West	**Woodland Lodge Holidays ★★★★**	43
Burnham-on-Sea, South West	**Pear Tree Cottage ★★★★**	83
Burton Upon Trent, Heart of England	**Wychnor Park Country Club ★★★ - ★★★★ Gold**	235
Bury St. Edmunds, East of England	**Culford Farm Cottages ★★★★ - ★★★★★**	177
Canterbury, South East	**Broome Park Golf and Country Club ★★★★**	116
Carnforth, North West	**Pine Lake Resort ★★★★**	308
Colchester, East of England	**Stoke by Nayland Country Lodges**	160
Combe Martin, South West	**Wheel Farm Cottages ★★★ - ★★★★**	60
Cromer, East of England	**Cromer Country Club ★★★ - ★★★★ Gold**	164
Cullompton, South West	**Wayside House ★★★★★ Gold**	61
Dawlish, South West	**Cofton Country Holidays ★★★★**	62
Dorchester, South West	**Luccombe Farm & Country Holidays ★★★★**	72
Fakenham, East of England	**Moor Farm Stable Cottages ★★★ - ★★★★**	165
Falmouth, South West	**Budock Vean Cottages ★★★★**	45
Falstone, North East	**Station Cottage ★★★★**	336
Filey, Yorkshire	**Kev's Cottage ★★★**	261
Folke, South West	**Folke Manor Farm Cottages ★★★★**	73
Fowey, South West	**South Torfrey Farm Ltd ★★★★ - ★★★★★**	46
Hartlepool, North East	**Waters Edge ★★★★**	339
Holsworthy, South West	**Woodford Bridge Country Club ★★★★ Gold**	64
Lancaster, North West	**Thurnham Hall ★★★★**	310
Newquay, South West	**Headland Cottages ★★★★★ Gold**	49
Newquay, South West	**The Park ★★★★ - ★★★★★ Gold**	50
Southwold, East of England	**Highsteppers at Blythview ★★★★**	183
St. Columb, South West	**Cornish Holiday Lodges ★★★ - ★★★★ Gold**	55
Sutton, Heart of England	**Long Cover Cottage & The Coach House ★★★★ Gold**	242
Taunton, South West	**Millgrove House ★★★★★**	87

Outdoor pool

Index by property name

Accommodation with a detailed entry in this guide is listed below.

Index by place name

The following places all have detailed accommodation entries in this guide. If the place where you wish to stay is not shown the location maps (starting on page 342) will help you to find somewhere to stay in the area.

M — Page

N — Page

O — Page

P — Page

R — Page

S — Page

K — Page

L — Page

Index to display advertisers

Published by: Hudson's Media Ltd
35 Thorpe Road, Peterborough, PE3 6AG
Tel: 01733 296910 Fax: 01733 209292

On behalf of: VisitBritain, Sanctuary Buildings, 20 Great Smith Street, London SW1P 3BT

Editor: Deborah Coulter
Editorial Contributor: Neil Pope
Production team: Deborah Coulter, Rhiannon McCluskey, Rebecca Owen-Fisher

Creative: Jamieson Eley
Advertising team: Ben Piper, Matthew Pinfold, Seanan McGrory, James O'Rawe
Email: VEguides@hudsons-media.co.uk Tel: 01733 296913
Production System: NVG – leaders in Tourism Technology. www.nvg.net
Printer: Stephens & George, Merthyr Tydfil
Retail Sales: Compass – Tel: 020 8996 5764